Japan's International Relations

This comprehensive and user-friendly textbook provides a single-volume resource for all those studying Japan's international relations. The book offers a clear and concise introduction to the most important aspects of Japan's role in the globalized economy of the twenty-first century.

Japan's International Relations:

- examines the historical context of Japan's emergence on to the world stage
- looks at Japan's international relations in terms of the core issues of politics, economics and security
- provides detailed accounts of Japan's key relationships with the US, East Asia, the EU and global institutions
- explores the effects of contemporary events such as the Asian financial crisis and the launch of the euro
- is extensively illustrated throughout with statistics, maps, photographs, chapter summaries and suggestions for further reading.

This book is essential reading for those studying Japanese politics and the international relations of the Asia Pacific, as well as US and European foreign policy.

Glenn D. Hook is Professor of Japanese Studies in the School of East Asian Studies, University of Sheffield. **Julie Gilson** is Lecturer in the Department of Politics and International Studies, University of Birmingham. **Christopher W. Hughes** is Senior Research Fellow in the ESRC Centre for the Study of Globalization and Regionalization, University of Warwick. **Hugo Dobson** is Lecturer in the School of East Asian Studies, University of Sheffield.

Sheffield Centre for Japanese Studies/Routledge Series
Series Editor: Glenn D. Hook
Professor of Japanese Studies, University of Sheffield

This series, published by Routledge in association with the Centre for Japanese Studies at the University of Sheffield, both makes available original research on a wide range of subjects dealing with Japan and provides introductory overviews of key topics in Japanese Studies.

The Internationalization of Japan
Edited by Glenn D. Hook and Michael Weiner

Race and Migration in Imperial Japan
Michael Weiner

Japan and the Pacific Free Trade Area
Pekka Korhonen

Greater China and Japan
Prospects for an Economic Partnership?
Robert Taylor

The Steel Industry in Japan
A Comparison with the UK
Hasegawa Harukiyo

Race, Resistance and the Ainu of Japan
Richard Siddle

Japan's Minorities
The Illusion of Homogeneity
Edited by Michael Weiner

Japanese Business Management
Restructuring for Low Growth and Globalization
Edited by Hasegawa Harukiyo and Glenn D. Hook

Japan and Asia Pacific Integration
Pacific Romances 1968–1996
Pekka Korhonen

Japan's Economic Power and Security
Japan and North Korea
Christopher W. Hughes

Japan's International Relations
Politics, Economics and Security
Glenn D. Hook, Julie Gilson, Christopher W. Hughes and Hugo Dobson

Japan's Contested Constitution
Documents and Analysis
Edited by Glenn D. Hook and Gavan McCormack

Japanese Education Reform
Nakasone's Legacy
Christopher P. Hood

The Political Economy of Japanese Globalization
Glenn D. Hook and Hasegawa Harukiyo

Japan's International Relations

■ Politics, economics and security

Glenn D. Hook, Julie Gilson, Christopher W. Hughes and Hugo Dobson

London and New York

First published 2001
by Routledge
11 New Fetter Lane, London EC4P 4EE

Simultaneously published in the USA and Canada
by Routledge
29 West 35th Street, New York, NY 10001

Routledge is an imprint of the Taylor & Francis Group

Typeset in Century Old Style by Bookcraft Ltd, Stroud, Gloucestershire
Printed and bound in Great Britain by
T.J. International Ltd, Padstow, Cornwall

British Library Cataloguing in Publication Data
A catalogue record for this book is available from the British Library

Library of Congress Cataloging in Publication Data
Japan's international relations: politics, economics and security/Glenn D. Hook … [et al.]
p. cm.
"Simultaneously published in the USA and Canada" – T.p. verso.
Includes bibliographical references and index.
1. Japan–Foreign relations–1989–
I. Hook, Glenn D.
JZ1745 .J37 2000
327.52–dc21 00-069000

ISBN 0–415–24097–2 (hbk)
ISBN 0–415–24098–0 (pbk)

Yoraba taiju no kage

To Eleanor, who contributed more than she yet knows

Contents

Illustrations

Figures

Plates

Tables

Glossary

Japanese

amakudari	Descent from heaven or 'parachuting from on high'.
beiatsu	American pressure.
chō	Agencies
chōsakai	Special Advisory Committee
Daitōa Kyōeiken	Greater East Asia Co-prosperity Sphere.
datsua nyūō	Abandonment of Asia, and joining with the West.
dōbun dōshu	Same Chinese writing characters, same race.
55 nen (seiji) taisei	1955 political system.
fukoku kyōhei	Rich country, strong army.
Heisei	The Heisei era began with the ascension to the throne of the new emperor in 1989. As the recession started in the same year, the term 'Heisei recession' is often used in Japan.
gaiatsu	Foreign pressure.
gakubatsu	University cliques or factions.
gyaku kōsu	'Reverse course'.
habatsu	Factions.
hakkō ichiu	Eight corners of the world under one roof.
ittō koku	First class country
jinmyaku	Human networks.
juche	Self-reliance.
kagemusha	Literally, 'shadow warrior'.
kakehashi	Bridging role.
Keidanren	Federation of Economic Organizations.
keiretsu	Large conglomerates, often linking a variety of different sectors.
Keizai Dōyūkai	Japan Committee for Economic Development.

keizaishugi	Economism.
kisha kurabu	Press club.
kōdo seichō	High-speed economic growth.
kojin gaikō	Personal diplomacy.
kokusai kokka	International state.
manga	Comic or satiric pictures, cartoons, strips and magazines.
nawabari	(Inter-)jurisdictional dispute or sphere of influence.
nemawashi	'Wrapping around the roots' or laying the groundwork.
Nichibei	US–Japan, *nichi* and *bei* representing the Japanese characters for Japan and the US respectively.
Nihonjinzuma	Japanese-born spouses of North Korean citizens resident in North Korea.
Nihon Shōkō Kaigi Shō	Japan Chamber of Commerce.
Nikkei	*Nihon Keizai Shimbun* (newspaper).
Nikkeiren	Japan Federation of Employers' Associations.
nishigawa no ichiin	Member of the Western camp.
Nisshō	Japan Chamber of Commerce and Industry.
Nōgyō Kyōdō Kumiai	National Association of Agricultural Cooperatives, or *Nōkyō*.
oitsuke oikose	Catch up and overtake (the West).
omiyage gaikō	Gift-bearing diplomacy.
omoiyari yosan	Sympathy budget as financial support for the deployment of US troops in Japan.
omote	Surface or explicit.
racchi jiken	Alleged abductions by North Korea of Japanese citizens.
renkei	Policy of linkage between improvements in Japan–North Korea relations and North Korea–South Korea relations.
ringisho	gain sanction for decision by use of a seal.
sakoku	Policy of national isolation.
seikei bunri	Separation of politics and economics.
seitōkan gaikō	Party-to-party diplomacy.
shigen gaikō	Resource diplomacy.
shingikai	Special advisory committees.
shō	Ministries.
shūhen	Periphery (surrounding Japan).
sōgō shōsha	General trading companies.
sonnō jōi	Revere the emperor and expel the barbarians.
Sōrifu	Prime Minister's Office.
Taikō	Charter or outline.

tennō gaikō	Emperor diplomacy.
tokubetsu hōjin	Quasi-governmental special corporations.
ura	Back or implicit.
wakon kansai	Japanese spirit combined with Chinese learning.
wakon yōsai	Japanese spirit combined with Western learning.
watashiyaku	Bridging role.
'yoraba taiju no kage'	'stay under the wing of the big power' (Hiroshi 1975: 552, authors' translation).
yōseishugi	Allocation of ODA on principle of request.
zaibatsu	Pre-war industrial conglomerates.
zaikai	Big business.
zenhōi gaikō	Omnidirectional diplomacy.
zoku	'Policy tribes'.

Non-Japanese

'big bang'	Range of measures taken to liberalize and deregulate the Japanese financial system.
bubble economy	A period from 1985 to 1990 when companies and individuals borrowed money and bought shares based upon the over-inflated value of their existing land and shares.
chaebol	Large industrial conglomerates in South Korea.
Council presidency	Each member state of the EU holds the presidency for six months at a time.
Delegation	European Commission representatives based in capital cities outside the EU.
Diet	Japanese parliament, comprising the two elected chambers of the (upper) House of Councillors and (lower) House of Representatives.
EU	European Union (Austria, Belgium, Denmark, Finland, France, Germany, Greece, Ireland, Italy, Luxemburg, The Netherlands, Portugal, Spain, Sweden, the United Kingdom).
EU Council of Ministers	Organ of the national governments of the EU member states.
euro	Single European currency, launched in January 1999.
euro-zone	Countries of the EU which have joined the single currency.
European Commission	Executive of the EU, which recommends policy and administers EU activities based on its founding treaty.

European Parliament	EU's parliament, which comprises elected MEPs (members of the European Parliament).
Fifteen Years' War (1931–45)	A perspective on Japan's involvement in the 'Pacific War' war as commencing with the invasion of China in 1931, with the Pacific War of 1941–5 simply being a part of this longer war.
Fukuda Doctrine	Announced by Prime Minister Fukuda Takeo in August 1977, and stating that Japan will not become a military big power; will build mutual confidence and trust based on 'heart-to-heart' understanding; and will forge an equal relationship with ASEAN, as well as build mutual understanding with Indo-China.
G5	Group of Five industrialized countries: Japan, the US, (West) Germany, the UK, France.
G7	Group of Seven industrialized countries, comprising the G5 plus Italy and Canada.
G8	Group of Eight industrialized countries, comprising the G7 plus Russia.
G24	Group of Twenty-Four. Created in January 1972 with the purpose of promoting the interests of developing countries in Africa, Asia and Latin America within the IMF and World Bank. Members are: Algeria; Argentina; Brazil; Colombia; Democratic Republic of the Congo; Egypt; Ethiopia; Gabon; Ghana; Guatemala; India; Iran; Ivory Coast; Lebanon; Mexico; Nigeria; Pakistan; Peru; Philippines; Serbia and Montenegro; Sri Lanka; Syria; Trinidad and Tobago; Venezuela.
Guidelines	Guidelines for US–Japan Defence Cooperation 1978; revised 1999.
juche	North Korean political philosophy of self-reliance.
1955 system	Political dominance of the Liberal-Democratic Party as the governing party which lasted from 1955 to 1993.
Nixon shocks (1971)	Jettisoning of the gold standard (the move to floating exchange rates) and the introduction of an import surcharge.
Occupation	Occupation of Japan, August 1945–March 1952, by the Allied powers. The Occupation was dominated by the US.
oil shock	The first oil shock, which occurred following the Arab–Israeli War of October 1973, resulted from Arab states using the 'oil weapon' against the

	West by raising the price of Persian Gulf crude oil. Another 'oil shock' occurred in 1979 following the decision by Iran, which produced approximately 17 per cent of OPEC exports, to stop supplies of oil.
peace treaty	San Francisco peace treaty signed by Japan in September 1951.
Plaza Accord	1985 agreement among the G5 at the Plaza Hotel, New York, agreeing the devaluation of the dollar, and hence the rise in value of the yen.
reverse course	Change around 1948 in US Occupation policy from placing priority on the demilitarization and democratization of Japan to making Japan a bastion against communism in the Far East.
Revisionist school	Used here to refer to observers such as Chalmers Johnson and Karel van Wolferen who in the 1980s pointed to the 'exceptionalism' of Japan and the failure of Western social sciences to understand it.
security treaty	The US–Japan security treaty, signed in September 1951, put in force in April 1952 and revised in June 1960. It remains in force today.
SEM	Single European Market of the member states of the EU, completed in 1992 and allowing for the free passage of goods, people and services between these countries.
Tiananmen Square incident	Chinese pro-democracy protest of June 1989 in Beijing which was brutally put down by the government and army.
Troika	European Union system, whereby the country holding the presidency works alongside the previous and next holders, in order to retain consistency.
Yoshida Doctrine	Doctrine placing high priority on Japan's economic growth and position in the world and low spending and priority on the military.

Abbreviations

AAB	Asian Affairs Bureau
AARJ	Association to Aid Refugees, Japan
ABM	Anti-Ballistic Missile
ACSA	Acquisition and Cross-Servicing Agreement
ADB	Asian Development Bank
AMF	Asian Monetary Fund
ANZUS	Australia, New Zealand, the US
APEC	Asia Pacific Economic Cooperation (forum)
ARF	ASEAN Regional Forum
ASDF	Air Self-Defence Force
ASEAN	Association of Southeast Asian Nations
ASEAN-PMC	ASEAN Post-Ministerial Conference
ASEAN + 3	ASEAN, South Korea, China and Japan
ASEAN-10	Indonesia, Malaysia, the Philippines, Singapore, Thailand, Brunei, Vietnam, Laos, Cambodia and Burma
ASEM	Asia-Europe Meeting
Benelux	Belgium, The Netherlands and Luxemburg
BMD	Ballistic Missile Defence
BOJ	Bank of Japan
CARs	Central Asian Republics
CCP	Chinese Communist Party
CFE	Conventional Armed Forces in Europe
CFSP	Common foreign and security policy
CGP	Clean Government Party
CIA	Central Intelligence Agency
CSCAP	Council for Security Cooperation in the Asia-Pacific
CSCE	Conference on Security and Cooperation in Europe
CSIS	Center for Strategic and International Studies
CTBT	Comprehensive Test Ban Treaty
DAC	(OECD) Development Assistance Committee
DM	Deutschmark
DPJ	Democratic Party of Japan

DPRK	Democratic People's Republic of Korea (North Korea)
DSP	Democratic Socialist Party
EAEC	East Asian Economic Caucus
EASR	East Asian Strategic Review
EBRD	European Bank for Reconstruction and Development
EC	European Community
ECSC	European Coal and Steel Community
EDC	European Defence Community
EEC	European Economic Community
EFTA	European Free Trade Association
EOAB	European and Oceania Affairs Bureau
EU	European Union
FDI	foreign direct investment
FRG	Federal Republic of Germany
FSX	Fighter Experience
GATT	General Agreement on Tariffs and Trade
GCHQ	General Command Headquarters
GDP	gross domestic product
GDR	German Democratic Republic
GNP	gross national product
GSDF	Ground Self-Defence Force
G7	Group of Seven industrialized countries
G24	Intergovernmental Group of Twenty-Four on International Monetary Affairs
IAEA	International Atomic Energy Agency
IBRD	International Bank for Reconstruction and Development
ICBM	Inter-Continental Ballistic Missile
ICJ	International Court of Justice
IDA	International Development Association
IFC	International Finance Corporation
IISS	International Institute for Strategic Studies
IMF	International Monetary Fund
INF	Intermediate-Range Nuclear Forces
IPE	international political economy
IPPNW	International Physicians for the Prevention of Nuclear War
IR	international relations
ISEAS	Institute of Southeast Asian Studies
ISIS	Institutes of Strategic and International Studies
ITB	International Trade Bureau
JAMA	Japanese Automobile Manufacturers' Association
JCIE	Japan Center for International Exchange
JCP	Japan Communist Party
JDA	Japan Defence Agency
JETRO	Japan External Trade Organization
JICA	Japan International Cooperation Agency
JNP	Japan New Party

JSP	Japan Socialist Party
KCIA	Korean Central Intelligence Agency
KEDO	Korean Peninsula Energy Development Organization
KMT	Kuo Min Tang
KWP	Korean Workers' Party
LDP	Liberal-Democratic Party
LP	Liberal Party
LWR	light water reactors
MAFF	Ministry of Agriculture, Forestry and Fisheries
MEDSEA	Ministerial Conference for Economic Development in Southeast Asia
MFN	most-favoured nation (status)
MITI	Ministry of International Trade and Industry
MOF	Ministry of Finance
MOFA	Ministry of Foreign Affairs
MSDF	Maritime Self-Defence Force
MTCR	Missile Technology Control Regime
NAAB	North American Affairs Bureau
NAFTA	North American Free Trade Agreement
NAM	non-aligned movement
NATO	North Atlantic Treaty Organization
NDPO	National Defence Programme Outline
NFP	New Frontier Party
NGOs	non-governmental organizations
NHK	*Nihon Hōsō Kyōkai*
NIEs	newly industrialized economies
NPR	National Police Reserve
NPT	Nuclear Non-Proliferation Treaty
NTT	Nippon Telegraph and Telecommunications
ODA	Official Development Assistance
OECD	Organization for Economic Cooperation and Development
OECF	Overseas Economic Cooperation Fund
ONUMOZ	United Nations Operation in Mozambique
OPEC	Organization of Petroleum Exporting Countries
OSCE	Organization for Security and Cooperation in Europe
PARC	Policy Affairs Research Council
PECC	Pacific Economic Cooperation Conference
PFP	Partnership for Peace
PHARE	Poland, Hungary Aid for Reconstruction
PIDG	Peace Issues Discussion Group
PKO	peacekeeping operations
PLA	People's Liberation Army
PLO	Palestine Liberation Organization
PMC	Post-Ministerial Conference (of ASEAN)
PMO	Prime Minister's Office or *Sōrifu*
PRC	People's Republic of China

RIMPAC	Rim of the Pacific
ROC	Republic of China
ROK	Republic of Korea (South Korea)
SALT	Strategic Arms Limitation Talks
SCAP	Supreme Command for the Allied Powers
SDF	Self-Defence Forces
SDI	Strategic Defence Initiative
SDPJ	Social Democratic Party of Japan
SEATO	Southeast Asia Treaty Organization
SEM	Single European Market
SII	Structural Impediments Initiative
SLBM	Submarine-Launched Ballistic Missile
SLOC	sea lines of communication
SMMT	(European) Society of Motor Manufacturers and Traders
START	Strategic Arms Reduction Treaty
TC	Trilateral Commission
TEU	Treaty on European Union (or 'Maastricht Treaty')
TICAD-I	First Tokyo International Conference on African Development
TICAD-II	Second Tokyo International Conference on African Development
TMD	Theatre Missile Defence
TNCs	transnational corporations
UK	United Kingdom
UN	United Nations
UNDOF	United Nations Disengagement Observer Force
UNESCAP	United Nations Economic and Social Commission for Asia and the Pacific
UNESCO	United Nations Educational, Scientific and Cultural Organization
UNFICYP	United Nations Peacekeeping Force in Cyprus
UNGA	United Nations General Assembly
UNHCR	United Nations High Commission for Refugees
UNHQ	United Nations Headquarters
UNICEF	United Nations Children's Fund
UNMIK	United Nations Mission in Kosovo
UNOSOM	United Nations Operation in Somalia
UNPKO	United Nations peacekeeping operations
UNSC	United Nations Security Council
UNTAC	United Nations Transitional Authority in Cambodia
UNTAG	United Nations Transition Assistance Group
UNU	United Nations University
US	United States
USAAF	United States of America Air Force
USSR	Union of Soviet Socialist Republics
USTR	United States trade representative
VERs	voluntary export restraints
WB	World Bank
WEU	Western European Union

WHO	World Health Organization
WMD	weapons of mass destruction
WTO	World Trade Organization
ZOPFAN	Zone of Peace, Freedom and Neutrality

A note on the text

It is the convention in Japanese for the family name to precede the given name. This convention is followed here, except in the bibliography, where the order is as used in English. Long vowels are indicated by macrons, except when referring to authors and works published in English and to the names of the cities of Kobe, Kyoto, Osaka and Tokyo. Thus, a work written in Japanese by an author named Satō appears in the text and in the Japanese bibliography as Satō, but if it is written in English it appears in the text and in the English bibliography as Sato.

Insofar as the names of political parties are concerned, the convention adopted here is to refer to the *Jiyū Minshutō* as the Liberal-Democratic Party or LDP, the *Kōmeitō* as the Kōmei Party and the *Shakai Minshutō* as the Social Democratic Party of Japan or SDPJ. For reference, it should be noted that, since November 1998, when the *Shintō Heiwa* and the *Kōmeitō* joined forces, the party has been known as *Shin Kōmeitō* (New Kōmei Party). The SDPJ was known before 1991 in English as the Japan Socialist Party (JSP), a translation of *Nihon Shakaitō*. That year it changed its name in English to Social Democratic Party of Japan, but did not change its Japanese name from *Nihon Shakaitō* to *Shakai Minshutō* (Social Democratic Party) until 1996.

The names and functions of most Japanese government ministries changed on 6 January 2001. The Ministry of Posts and Telecommunications, the Ministry of Home Affairs, and the Management and Coordination Agency became the Ministry of Public Management, Home Affairs, Posts and Telecommunications. The Ministry of Education and the Science and Technology Agency combined to become the Ministry of Education, Culture, Sports, Science and Technology. The Ministry of Health and Welfare and the Ministry of Labour combined to become the Ministry of Health, Labour and Welfare. The Ministry of International Trade and Industry became the Ministry of Economy, Trade and Industry. The Ministry of Transport, the Ministry of Construction, the Hokkaidō Development Agency and the National Land Agency became the Ministry of Land, Infrastructure and Transport. The Prime Minister's Office, the Economic Planning Agency and the Okinawa Development Agency combined to become the Cabinet Office. The Environment Agency became the Ministry of Environment, and took over some of the functions of the Ministry of Health and Welfare and the Ministry of International Trade and Industry. The Ministry of Justice, the Ministry of Foreign Affairs, the Ministry of Finance, the Ministry of Agriculture, Forestry and Fisheries, the Defence Agency and the National Public Safety Commission remained the same.

Acknowledgements

This book is the product of intensive work during 1999 and early 2000. It draws on our experience living and researching in Japan and in teaching about Japan's international relations at four British universities, Birmingham, Kent, Sheffield and Warwick. Along the way, we all have incurred many debts of gratitude in Japan, the United Kingdom and further afield. We would first like to thank those involved directly in the production of this book, through commenting on the proposal, draft chapters, or both. These include Reinhard Drifte, Ellis Kraus, Takahashi Susumu and several anonymous referees. For general encouragement and inspiration, we are particularly indebted to Sakamoto Yoshikazu and Arthur Stockwin. The International Center for Comparative Law and Politics, Graduate School of Law and Politics, the University of Tokyo has been our home away from home. We are grateful to Wada Keiko for her warm welcome. The Graduate School of East Asian Studies at Sheffield and the Centre for the Study of Globalisation and Regionalisation at Warwick hosted our meetings. Richard Higgott deserves special thanks for not only making us welcome at Warwick, but for providing such an appropriately named venue for discussing Japan's regionalization and globalization. We thank Kimura Makoto of JETRO's London office for materials, Takeda Hiroko for assistance in the preparation of the tables, and Mark Aldred for the expert reproduction of the maps. We are also grateful to Simon Gilson for spending time away from his own research to help on the bibliography, abbreviations and glossary, and Kenko Hook for gastronomic nourishment. We would like to thank the copyright holders for permission to reproduce photographs and illustrations; the relevant credits are given below each illustration. Finally, for financial support in completing this project, we are all extremely grateful to the Chubu Electric Power Company and the Toshiba International Foundation, and Glenn Hook to the Japan Foundation Endowment Committee and the British Academy.

Preface

Japan can be explained. It needs to be explained because it matters. That it matters accounts for the wide range of information available in English on Japan's international relations. Nevertheless, the authors of this book believe that further efforts still need to be made in order to explain Japan's place in the world. This is because, even though readers in the three regions of North America, Europe, East Asia and elsewhere share at least a general understanding of Japan's global and regional role in the world, they often view the specific political, economic and security dimensions of the activities that it carries out in these three core regions and in global institutions as anomalous, if not abnormal. Part of the reason for this is that most, if not all, books on Japan's international relations simply deal with a truncated version of them. In comparison with the approach taken in *Japan's International Relations*, which deals with the 'what', 'why' and 'how' of Japan's international relations in these three dimensions of politics, economics and security as well as in the four core sites of Japan's international activity, the United States (US), Europe, East Asia and global institutions, the majority of other single- and co-authored works tend to examine them with reference to only one dimension, one issue or one region, or produce no unified conclusions to guide the reader towards a fundamental and holistic understanding of Japan's international relations. Thus, they may deal with the 'what', providing rich detail on Japan's international relations without theoretical input; or the 'why', as in a detailed study of a specific foreign policy-making process without any reference to the actual impact of Japan's economic role and presence in the world; or the 'how', offering insights into the function of Official Development Assistance (ODA) as a means to instrumentalize political relations in East Asia without touching on Japan's presence and role in other parts of the world.

The overarching purpose of *Japan's International Relations* is to change this situation by demonstrating that, through the rigorous application of social scientific tools of analysis, Japan's international relations can be explained as normal in a comprehensive and theoretically-informed way. Here lies the motivation for writing this book: to explain in a single volume the complex web of these relations especially to advanced undergraduate and postgraduate students, as well as to practitioners, policy-makers and other readers around the world. In order to carry out this task, the chapters examine the 'what', in terms of trying to establish what has been and is Japan's pattern of behaviour and role in the international system; the 'why', in terms of explaining why Japan opts to behave in the way it does; and the 'how', in terms of the means, methods and effectiveness of how Japan pursues its international role. In this way, *Japan's International Relations* offers the reader a description, an analysis and an explanation of Japan's international relations in these three dimensions and four sites of activity, drawing on both Japanese- and English-language research.

This coverage is both broadly encompassing and narrowly limited. It is encompassing as it argues that Japan's place in the world can be comprehended best by taking into account all three dimensions at the regional and global levels, and then, by drawing all of this material together, to provide a holistic explanation. It is limited in the sense that, despite the importance of dealing fully with Japan's international relations, its geographical focus is on the world's three core regions and their most important constituent states, whereas only minimal attention is paid to Japan's dealings with other states and emergent regional groupings in Eastern Europe, South Asia, the Middle East, Africa, and Latin America. This spatial and dimensional focus has been adopted as these are the international relations of Japan that matter most to the Japanese state and its people as well as to the world.

In order to provide the answers to the 'what', 'why' and 'how' of Japan's international relations, this volume draws upon the best in the dominant traditions of international relations (IR) and international political economy (IPE) by taking into account the international activities of both the Japanese state and its people. It does so by examining the role and interests of the state as the key, but not the only, actor in Japan's international relations, and complements the study of the state by examining non-state actors. It also supplements the study of state interests with an analysis of norms, or the ideas, beliefs and principles held by policy-makers and other political actors about how the world should be, which shape their conception of interests. Most important, it combines the study of the international behaviour of the Japanese state and non-state actors in the context of internationally embedded norms with the study of these actors in the context of domestically embedded norms and the policy-making process. This eclectic, yet comprehensive, approach has been adopted in order to analyse more fully the type of inter-national relations the Japanese state and its people have pursued in the Cold War and post-Cold War periods, even though their behaviour may not appear 'normal' in terms of the way their interests and norms have been instrumentalized and conceived. In other words, *Japan's International Relations* aims to explain how Japan's international relations have been instrumentalized through the actions and behaviour of both state and non-state actors in the political, economic and security dimensions in the three core regions and in global institutions. This task will be accomplished by drawing on important insights from IR and IPE scholarship.

The book's other main purpose is to carry out this task by regarding Japan's international relations as normal. The difficulty of successfully completing this task is twofold: first, in answering the 'what', 'why' and 'how' of Japan's international relations, cognizance must be taken of the complex and dynamic relationship between the structure of the international system, the embedded norms of international society, the embedded norms of domestic society, and the Japanese state and its people's attempts to realize their perceived interests within these historically-contingent conditions. The second difficulty is to explain Japan's international relations as normal in a world where the dominant Western journalistic and scholarly discourses view them, in extreme cases, as 'abnormal', or at least anomalous or aberrant. Whereas, on the one hand, any claims to originality or theoretical innovation, especially in a book written with advanced undergraduate and postgraduate students in mind, might smack of hubris, on the other hand, by treating Japan's international relations as normal, this book seeks to offer insights which are lacking in other less innovative and comprehensive works. In a sense, the present work posits an eclectic social science approach to Japan's international relations by elucidating the contested nature of these issues from the outset. It does so by examining the norms that shape the interests of the state, and brings within its purview non-state actors such as transnational corporations (TNCs), non-governmental organizations (NGOs) and social movements.

The book has been designed with a number of different audiences in mind. First, it has been designed for use on courses about Japan's international relations, political economy or politics and society. Its comprehensive treatment of Japan's relations with Europe and global institutions, as well as the United States and East Asia, cannot be found elsewhere. Thus, the book as a whole could act as the core text in a course on Japan's international relations as well as the core text for the international relations part of a course dealing with Japan's domestic and foreign policy. In this case, *Japan's International Relations* will prove an ideal companion volume to J. A. A. Stockwin's *Governing Japan*, which focuses on domestic politics.

Second, it can provide a Japanese dimension to a range of other university courses. For instance, a course on the international relations of North America, East Asia, Europe or global institutions could refer students to these separate parts of the book, each of which has been written as a self-contained whole. The parts of the book on Japan's role in the four key sites of its international relations could also be used for a course examining different countries' relations with the United States, East Asia, Europe and global institutions. Similarly, the separate chapters on politics, economics and security in the four core sites would be ideal for a course focusing specifically on Japan's international relations in these separate dimensions. Finally, Part I of the book should prove invaluable for general courses on IR and IPE theory.

Third, the book has been designed as essential reading for researchers, teachers, practitioners and policy-makers who need a comprehensive, up-to-date and easy-to-use book on the international relations of Japan. In particular, the detailed table of contents, chronology, appendices, list of websites and comprehensive tables of statistics on Japanese trade, foreign direct investment (FDI) and other essential data, which are available on the worldwide web at www.japansinternationalrelations.com, mean *Japan's International Relations* will remain an indispensable and reliable reference work for many years to come.

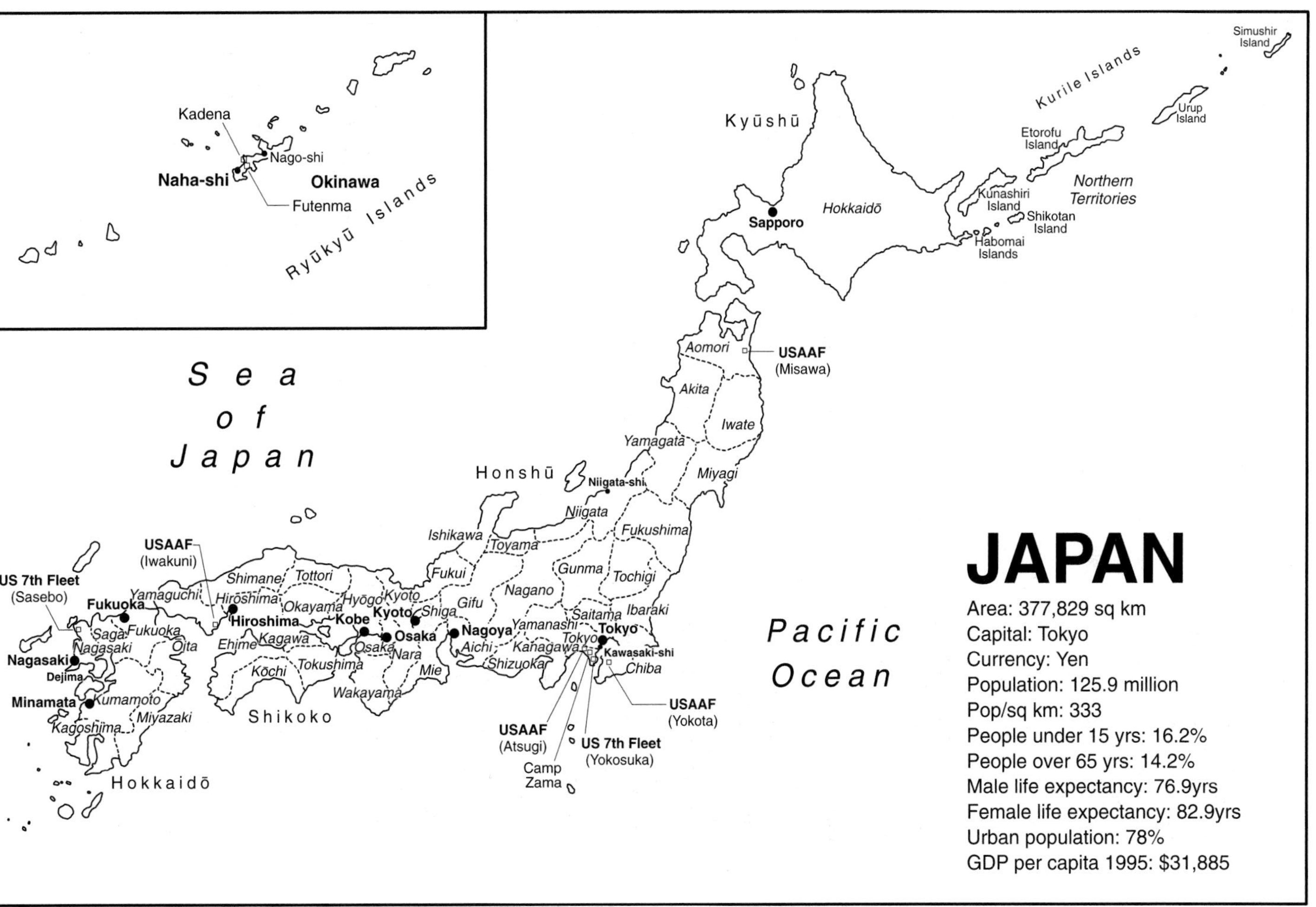

Map 1 Japan's administrative districts, US bases in Japan and basic statistics on Japan

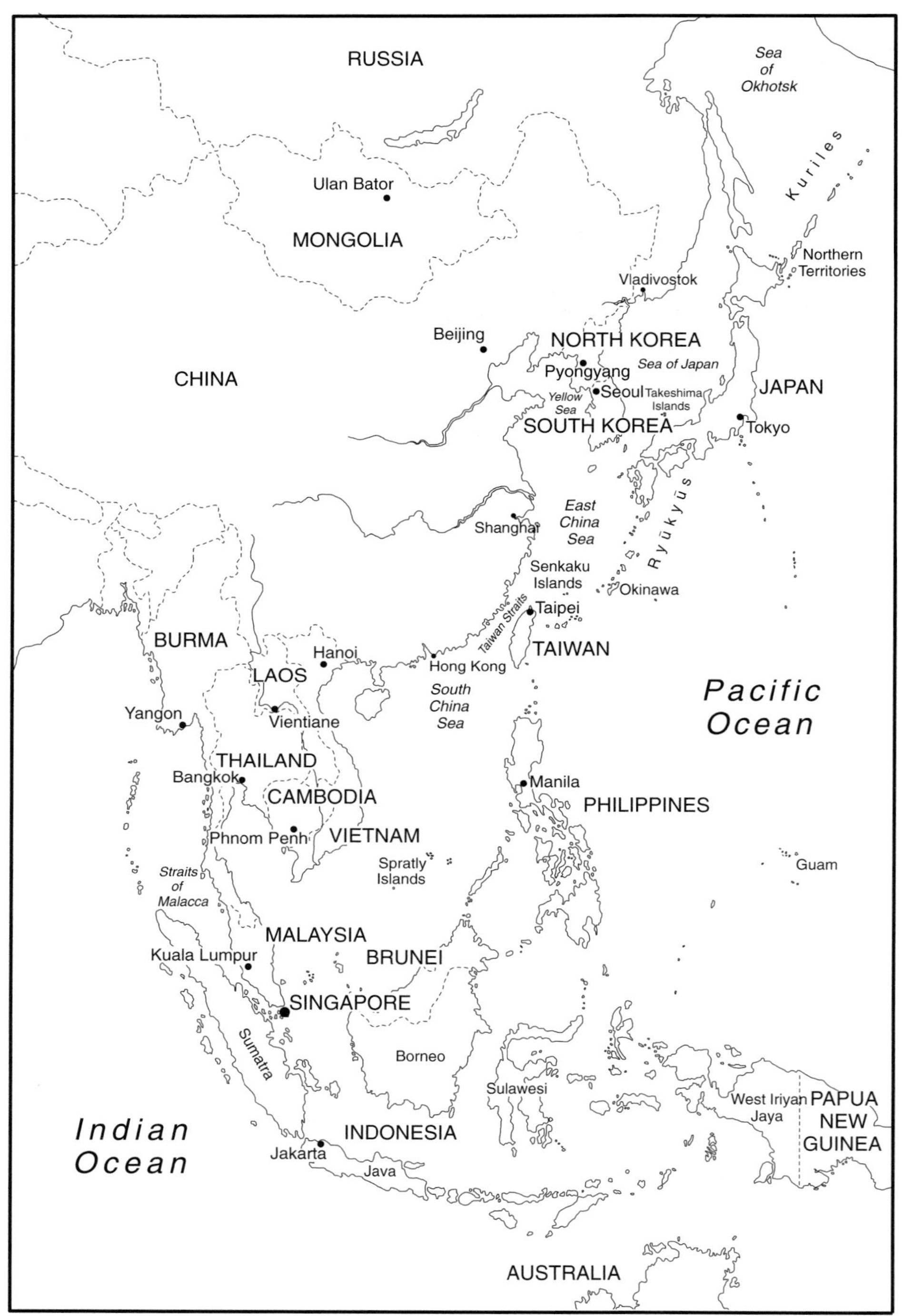

Map 2 Japan and East Asia

Part I

JAPAN'S INTERNATIONAL RELATIONS

WHAT, WHY AND HOW

Chapter 1

The significance of Japan's international relations

1.1 Debates on Japan's international relations

1.1.i Metaphors of change

Japan seems to be unique among the major industrialized powers in terms of the extent to which its international relations in the post-World War II era (hereafter, post-war era) have been subject to a range of contending interpretations. An examination of the titles of journalistic books and academic tomes, a search through newspaper clippings or a surf on the Internet confirms the complexity of the discourses associated with Japan. This rise to international prominence of an East Asian latecomer has evinced, and continues to evince, metaphors and polemics of change, challenge and contradiction. From the 1960s onwards, the metaphor was that of the 'rising sun'. This implied Japan's ascent to great power status in the economic, political, and possibly even the security dimension following its economic rehabilitation and re-emergence onto the world stage. In 1962, two years before the government proudly took up its seat in the Organization for Economic Cooperation and Development (OECD), a move which signified its entry into the club of major industrialized powers, *The Economist* tantalizingly invited its readers to 'Consider Japan' and its startling economic advances (*The Economist*, 1 September 1962, 8 September 1962). By 1971, Japan had earned the epithet of an emerging 'superstate' (Kahn 1971); by 1976, it had grown to the stature of East Asia's new economic 'giant' (Patrick and Rosovsky 1976); and, by 1979, Japan's achievement of rapid economic growth, seemingly bereft of the social dislocation which had blighted this process in the other major industrialized powers, was to lead Harvard academic Ezra Vogel to warn the American people that Japan was likely to overtake the US to become the world's 'No. 1' (Vogel 1979). Japan's meteoric economic ascendance was declared a 'miracle' in 1982 (Johnson 1986); in 1986, Vogel even went so far as to declare that the 'American Century' and age of *Pax Americana* could be replaced in the next century by an era of *Pax Nipponica* (Vogel 1986); and, by the 1990s, Japan was talked of routinely as an economic 'superpower' (Horsley and Buckley 1990; Garby and Brown Bullock 1994).

1.1.ii Metaphors of challenge

These metaphors and polemics of change were inevitably accompanied by a cacophony of criticism which drew attention to the complex nature of the economic challenge posed by Japan. Vogel and other students of the 'Japanese way' of management, industrial policy and economic development viewed Japan's rise in a positive light: on the one hand, it would galvanize US businesses to upgrade their competitiveness and prompt the government to take measures to eradicate the social costs of growth; on the other, it would provide the US with a new partner to share the burden of maintaining the global order. As far as other observers are concerned, Japan's new international position was seen more darkly as a negative challenge: this time, its economic prowess appeared as a deliberate strategy of mercantilist 'free riding' on the back of the established economic, political and

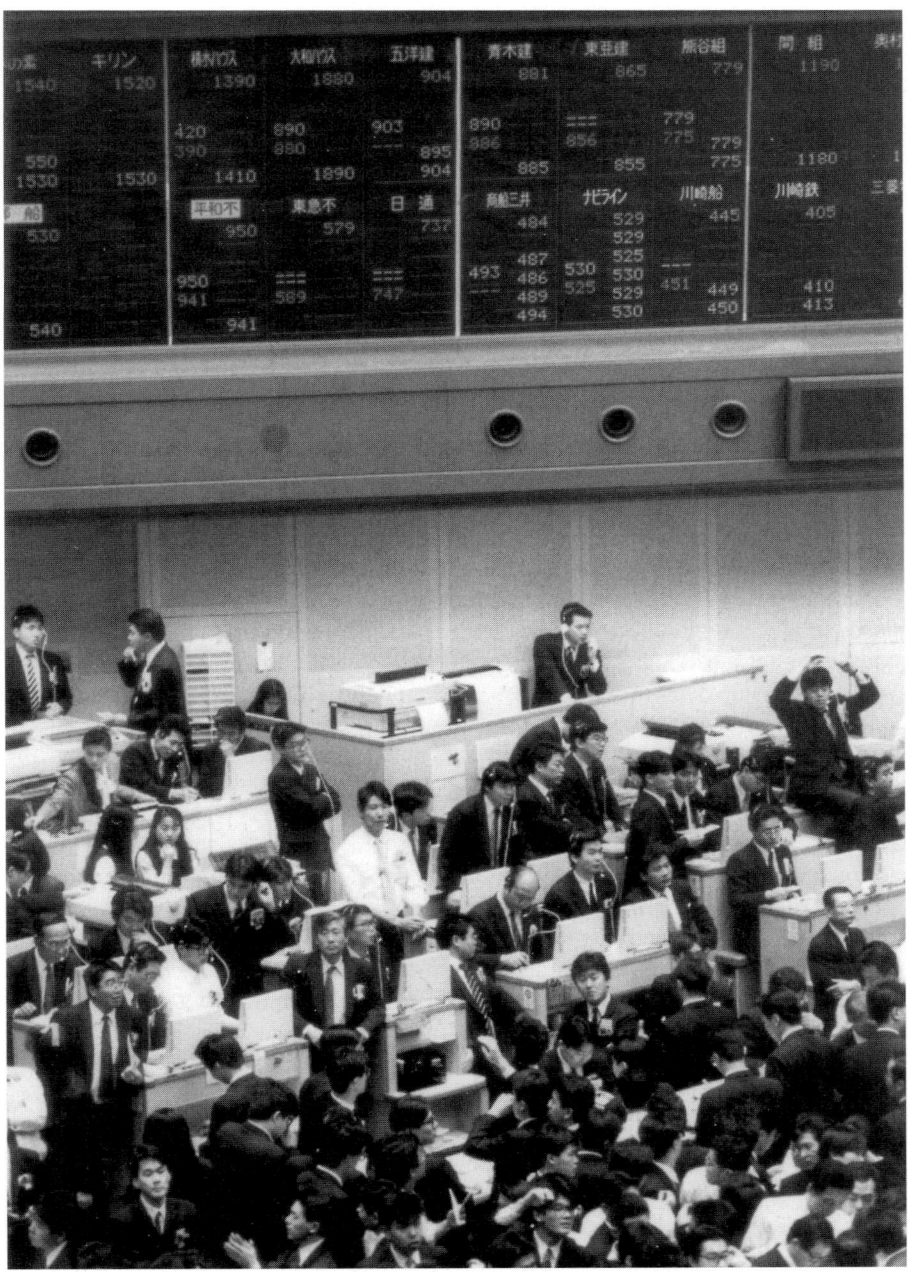

Plate 1.1 Business as usual? The Tokyo Stock Exchange appears calm soon after the bubble economy burst in February 1990. However, worse was to come, with financial crashes and a prolonged recession lasting throughout the 'lost decade' of the 1990s.

Source: Courtesy of Mainichi Shimbunsha

security order maintained by the other major industrialized powers, especially the US (Prestowitz 1988). In other cases, the Japanese state and its transnational corporations (TNCs) were viewed as essentially devoid of any clear policy direction as international actors. From this perspective, the new superpower had no aim in the international sphere save the short-sighted and reckless pursuit of market share and the systematic crushing of economic rivals (van Wolferen 1990). In this way, members of the so-called Revisionist school such as Karel van Wolferen viewed Japan as having climbed to prominence, and perhaps even pre-eminence, on the backs of the other major industrialized powers. At the same time, however, Japan was seen to be courting disaster for itself and other states by undermining, through its lack of reciprocity in trade and refusal to accept international responsibilities commensurate with its economic power, the liberal order upon which the world was perceived to depend for its prosperity. Thus, Japan, at best, evoked images of an economic juggernaut, driverless and careering out of control; at worst, it appeared as a peril and a parasitic threat to the international order. Nevertheless, whatever the specifics, the 'Japan problem' rose to international salience during the 1980s (van Wolferen 1986/7).

Such vitriolic criticism of Japan's international stance peaked during the Gulf crisis and war (1990–1, hereafter, Gulf War). At this time, even though its economic prowess appeared to have reached its zenith and it was talked of as a possible new hegemonic power, its leaders and people proved unable to fashion a consensus on Japan's global security and military role. Since the end of the Gulf War in 1991, however, as the Japanese state and its people continue to grope for an appropriate international role, the economic slowdown and the relative waning of its economic power, heralded by the collapse of the 'bubble economy' and the onset of the Heisei recession in 1989, have served to provoke a new series of metaphors associated with Japan's decline.

Consequently, a panoply of journalists and academics, having discovered serious flaws in Japan's political economy, now desperately sought to breathe new life into the tired 'sun' metaphor by announcing that the Japanese sun inevitably 'also sets' and is 'divided' (Emmott 1989; Callon 1997); that Japan is 'anything but number one' (Woronoff 1991); that its economic miracle, and the related miracle that it spurred in East Asia, is over (Katz 1998); or even that, when examined by economist Paul Krugman, Japan is 'head[ing] for the edge' (*Financial Times*, 20 January 1999). Again, accompanying these metaphors of change is a series of perceived challenges for international society. Although certain commentators regard Japan's sudden fall as bringing just desserts for its apparently overweening economic pride, and some even heave a sigh of relief that the Japanese economic tsunami, or tidal wave, no longer seems to pose a threat to Western industries, Japanese economic instability is now seen to challenge the macro-economic stability of the entire world. The crisis in the Japanese banking system and widespread economic recession mean that the recent 'setting' sun is viewed by some to be just as problematic for the international order as its earlier 'rising' counterpart.

1.1.iii Metaphors of contradiction

Turning next to Japan's role in international politics and security, colourful metaphors, this time of contrast and cunning, are frequently encountered. To start with, the metaphor of the economic giant is usually contrasted to that of the political pygmy. With the pygmy in the world of power politics conjuring up the image of size, Japan appears as somehow dysfunctional, disproportionately large in terms of its economic, but small in terms of its political, power in the world. Not only does Japan not possess nuclear weapons, but the Preamble and Article 9 of the so-called 'Peace' Constitution, which was promulgated in November 1946 and has remained in force without change from May 1947, means that it possesses only the tri-service 'Self-Defence Forces' (SDF). These are composed of the Ground Self-Defence Force (GSDF), Maritime Self-Defence Force (MSDF) and Air Self-Defence Force (ASDF), not 'military forces' in the form of an army, navy and air force. The existence of the Preamble and Article 9, which in part states that, 'land, sea, and air forces, as well as other war potential, will never be maintained' (Appendix 1.1), as well as the tri-service SDF, thus means that respective Japanese governments have been forced to interpret Article 9 as allowing forces for self-defence. This accounts for the euphemistic naming of Japan's military forces. Whereas this article was once praised as a prescient piece of legislation in the world's gradual move towards disarmament and non-violent means of solving human problems, it is now treated as a naïve encumbrance preventing Japanese military forces from taking part in collective defence and from playing a full role in promoting security in the region and in the world. Thus, Japan appears not as a paid-up member of international society, but as a cunning free rider, deriving the benefits whilst paying few of the costs of maintaining the security of the global and regional orders. In this way, the Japanese state and its people, like no other, have been stamped with a number of extreme and opposing labels to describe the character of their international relations over a time span of no more than a few decades. Only Japan, it seems, can move – in the space of even less than a decade – from being trumpeted as a potential superpower to being derided as an international weakling; from being an economic juggernaut to being an economic write-off.

It is tempting to regard such extreme views as belonging to the members of those motley groups who jump on the bandwagon of Japan-'apologist' and -'bashing' sentiments. Nevertheless, whether Japan-watchers seek to 'apologize' for, 'bash', or adopt a more balanced approach to investigate the nature of Japan's international relations, as the present volume seeks to do, the vehemence of the debate and its propensity to swing to extremes cannot be doubted. Even those observers of the late 1990s and early twenty-first century who have dropped the sport of 'Japan-bashing' in favour of 'Japan-passing' – that is, passing over Japan in favour of China in their analysis of the crucial actors in the international system, as Japan's economic superpower status is alleged to be on the decline – may once again be tempted to rejoin the debate on excoriating or defending Japan's international relations. Indeed, it appears that even those critics who seek to ignore the presence of Japan are really only again berating it for its perceived shortcomings in contributing to international stability. In this sense, the critics also implicitly recognize Japan's vital position in the political, economic and security dimensions of the regional and international orders. This is because they are forced to accept, either implicitly or explicitly, that Japan matters greatly in the international system and affects the lives and livelihoods of not just academics and journalists who write about it, but, far more important, a vast range of peoples and other international actors across the world (Williams 1994: 3). Despite its clear significance, however, past efforts to construct a comprehensive understanding of Japan's international relations and their implications for the rest of the world have been frustrated. The reason for this is complex, but in essence derives from the fact that Japan's international behaviour exhibits a number of characteristics, or even seeming paradoxes, which contrast sharply to those of the other major industrialized powers. As a result, attempts to conveniently categorize Japan in line with traditional interpretations of international relations remain frustrated.

1.2 Why Japan matters: economics, politics and security

1.2.i Economics

Japan's embarkation upon the process of modernization in the Meiji era (1868–1912) brought with it the national goals of catching up with the West in the military and economic dimensions of power – as embodied in the slogan of the time, *fukoku kyōhei* ('rich country, strong army'). Before the Pacific War (1941–5), Japan had made great strides towards the achievement of these twin military and economic objectives. The experience of the atomic bombings of Hiroshima (6 August 1945) and Nagasaki (9 August 1945), followed by the surrender and defeat of 15 August 1945, however, effectively eliminated any post-war ambition to match the other major industrialized powers militarily. Nevertheless, the economic catch-up and overtaking (*oitsuke oikose*) of the West have remained key national goals in the post-war era. In this situation, the Japanese state, its corporations and its people have been forced to channel their energies into attempts to recover from wartime devastation.

Deprived of any international status likely to accrue from the possession of military power, the Japanese people took immense pride instead in their ability to rebuild the national economy. In the process, Japan outstripped the gross national product (GNP) of the other major industrialized powers and OECD members. The 'income-doubling' policies implemented in the early 1960s by Prime Minister Ikeda Hayato's administration, which promoted high-speed economic growth (*kōdo seichō*), gave concrete shape to the norm of 'economism' (*keizaishugi*). As a result, since 1945 the principal image of Japan's international relations has been linked firmly to the pursuit of economic interests. Conversely, this has meant that political and security interests have been less salient. Whether it is images of Japanese success, as illustrated by the flood of Japanese automobiles rolling off container ships in European and American ports in the 1970s and 1980s, or images

Plate 1.2 Financial and emotional breakdown. In November 1997, Yamaichi Securities, Japan's fourth largest brokerage, collapsed with debts of ¥3 trillion. President Nozawa Shōhei wept as he apologized for this high-profile failure.
Source: Courtesy of Mainichi Shimbunsha

of Japanese failure, as symbolized by the tearful faces of senior executives in a major security company apologizing for humiliating bankruptcies in the late 1990s, the most familiar and evocative images remain overwhelmingly economic.

Indeed, Japan instantly conjures up telephone-number-like statistics of economic prowess and sheer size. After the US, it possesses the second largest national economy in the world. With a GNP of US$4.6 trillion in 1996, accounting for 16 per cent of world's total (Asahi Shimbunsha 1999: 80), Japan is clearly an economic giant. Other statistics paint a similar picture: in 1998 Japan's exports and imports amounted to US$388 billion and US$281 billion respectively, occupying 7 per cent and 5 per cent of world totals, and ranking it as the third largest trader in the world after the US and Germany (Table 1; JETRO 1999a: 7–8). In the realm of finance, Japan's external net assets exceed ¥125 trillion and it has been the largest creditor since 1985 (Asahi Shimbunsha 1999: 113). Japan's foreign exchange reserves at US$217 billion in 1996 are the world's largest (Asahi Shimbunsha 1999: 113). Japan in 1996 was the fifth largest source of foreign direct investment (FDI) (US$55 billion) and has been the world's number-one investor in 1990 (US$51 billion) (Table 2; JETRO 1999b: 2). Japan also disburses the world's largest amount of Official Development Assistance (ODA), totalling US$9.4 billion in 1997 (MOFA 1998b: 101).

In contrast, the size of Japan's national debt has been growing in the wake of the bursting of the 'bubble economy'. The government's general deficit has widened to more than 8 per cent of the gross domestic product (GDP). According to the International Monetary Fund (IMF), Japan's gross public debt amounted to 128 per cent of GDP at the end of 1999, an enormous 69 per cent increase compared to the 1990 figure. This now makes the Japanese government the biggest borrower among the major industrialized powers. The IMF forecasts that, by 2004, government debt will have risen to as high as 150 per cent of GDP. The problem of Japan's opaque accounting has led some to argue that, even now, Japan has reached this figure (all figures from *The Economist,* 22 January 2000).

Beyond these broad headline statistics, Japan's economic presence is felt materially also through the products and activities of its TNCs and other business enterprises. Since Japan's economic renaissance in the early 1960s, its products have come to dominate rapidly and successively markets in shipbuilding, steel, chemicals, consumer electronics and automobiles. The words 'Made in Japan', stamped on the Honda Accord, the Toyota Lexus, the Sony Walkman as well as the Panasonic Camcorder, are now consumer bywords for quality and innovation. In contrast, an earlier post-war generation viewed the label as synonymous with shoddy, cheap toys and trinkets. Now, Japanese TNCs, such as Honda, Toyota, Mitsubishi, Nissan and Sony, have become household names and stand at the forefront of global business. They are in many cases the 'face' of Japan's overseas economic activities and the physical manifestation of its global power and reach (Emmott 1991).

Finally, Japan's rise to economic superpower status has been given substance through its gradually-enhanced presence in global economic institutions. Its rehabilitation started with the US's sponsorship of its entry into the three pillars of the Cold War political economy: the IMF and World Bank (WB, originally established as the International Bank for Reconstruction and Development (IBRD), which remains one of four autonomous branches of the World Bank) in August 1952; and the General Agreement on Tariffs and Trade (GATT), effective from September 1955. Ever since, the Japanese government has worked assiduously to increase both its economic and its political power within these multilateral institutions through the expansion of its financial contribution and attendant voting shares. By 1992, Japan was the second largest financial contributor to the IMF and the WB, and had secured, after the US, the second largest share of votes in both institutions, at 6.41 per cent and 7.89 per cent respectively (Yasutomo 1995: 121).

1.2.ii Politics

Japan's international presence traditionally has been less salient in the political dimension. Its ability to pursue a fully-independent foreign policy and to demonstrate decisive international political leadership along the lines of the other major industrialized powers has been seriously circumscribed since defeat in World War

II. Wartime memories in East Asia and elsewhere have left Japanese policy-makers wary of making attempts to reassert global or regional leadership. This 'legitimacy deficit' (Rapkin 1990: 195) has been compounded by Japan's apparent lack of any universalistic values which can be exported to other countries. In contrast to Western states, such as Great Britain (also referred to as the United Kingdom or UK) and the US, which have sought at varying times to purvey, albeit in support of their own national interests, the political values of liberalism, democracy and human rights, Japan has often been seen to lack a readily identifiable or forceful political and international ideology. Certainly, the people's anti-nuclearism has at times inspired political movements to protest against nuclear weapons in other parts of the world as well as in Japan. Nevertheless, whilst broadly and quietly supportive of liberal and democratic values, the Japanese government has not actively deployed political ideology in the service of its international relations, and has lacked the political appetite and capacity to assert a clearly-identifiable leadership role on the world's political stage.

Whilst Japan's political prowess has failed in general to match its power in the field of economics, policy-makers do appear to have worked consistently and gradually during the post-war era to restore the political dimension of Japan's international relations. Its economic weight, moreover, has brought it inevitably a degree of political power in global institutions. Japan stands as the only East Asian country with membership of the exclusive club of the G7, and at times has shown itself capable of playing an increasingly confident role at summits, as demonstrated most memorably at the Williamsburg summit in 1983. At the time, Prime Minister Nakasone Yasuhiro (1982–7) elbowed himself and Japan to the front ranks of the attendant G7 leaders. As the second largest contributor, Japan has also enhanced its presence in the United Nations (UN), providing a 20 per cent contribution in 1999, rising to 20.6 per cent in 2000. This represents a jump from 16.8 per cent in 1997 and 1998. The expectation is that Japan's increased contribution to the UN budget might eventually lead it to join the other exclusive club of permanent members of the United Nations Security Council (UNSC) (Asai 1995).

Moreover, although Japan may have been reluctant to articulate a distinctive political ideology since the start of the post-war era, it has begun to acquire some of the trappings of non-military or what has been called 'soft' political power (Nye 1990; Drifte 1998). Such power is seen to derive from the diffusion of Japan's economic products throughout the world, which is accompanied by a degree of acceptance of Japanese culture and knowledge frameworks. These influence the norms and value judgements of the recipients, which in turn influence their economic, political and security decisions and policies (Strange 1988: 120). Still, even today, the style of Japanese diplomacy in global institutions and in respect of the recipients of Japanese economic products remains low-key. This can be seen in the government's concentration on consensus-building and financial support in global institutions. This makes the exact extent of Japan's global political power hard to aggregate and to compare on the same basis as the other major industrialized powers. Nevertheless, its acquisition of a major stake in these institutions suggests that, at the start of the twenty-first century, Japan could be poised for a more assertive political leadership role in the world.

1.2.iii Security

Japan's security role has been the least salient of the three dimensions of its international relations in the post-war era. The prosecution of an imperialist war against East Asia, the Greater East Asia War or Fifteen Years' War (1931–45) means that many, on both the mass and elite levels in the region, recoil at the idea of Japan ever again assuming major responsibilities in this dimension. The historical legacies of the Fifteen Years' War, the atomic bombings of Hiroshima and Nagasaki and the prohibitions imposed upon the exercise of armed force by Article 9 of the Constitution serve to constrain the state's use of the military as a legitimate instrument of state policy (Hook 1996a). This effectively deprived Japan of all credibility as a major security actor in the Cold War period. Its principal ideological contribution to security came instead from its fusion of the experience of the war and the atomic bombings into anti-nuclear and anti-military sentiments, together with the spread of anti-nuclearism around the world as a result of the actions taken by the Japanese people as well as the state. However, the constraints placed upon Japan's military contribution to international security in this period were counterbalanced to some extent by its elucidation of comprehensive conceptions of security (Chapman *et al.* 1983) and a contribution to global security based upon the extension of economic power and cooperation.

The Japanese state and its people, then, harbour a view of security which is much broader than the military, or guns-bombs-and-tanks, approach found in most of the other major industrialized powers (Katzenstein 1996a: 121–4). Nevertheless, since the coming into force in 1952 of the Security Treaty between the United States and Japan (revised in 1960 as the Treaty of Mutual Cooperation and Security between the United States and Japan) (Appendices 1.3 and 1.4), it also has maintained an alliance with the US, the world's most powerful military actor (see Chapter 6). Moreover, since the establishment of the SDF proper in 1954, Japan has maintained its own independent military capabilities.

The function of the US–Japan security treaty expanded incrementally in the 1980s and 1990s. It has come to imply that, irrespective of Japan's own security needs, the bilateral alliance performs both a regional and an international security function in line with the enhancement of the US's own military power projection capability. Likewise, the size and role of the SDF have increased incrementally. In terms of size, Japan now maintains the fourth largest defence budget in the world in raw dollar terms, projected at US$41 billion in 1999 (Table 3), and technologically-sophisticated military forces comparable in manpower and firepower to those of the UK. The euphemistically-dubbed Ground Self-Defence Force, Maritime Self-Defence Force and Air Self-Defence Force numbered 240,000 personnel in 1997, and jointly deployed over 1,000 main battle tanks, 510 aircraft, and 160 surface ships and submarines (International Institute for Strategic Studies 1999: 191–3).

On the popular, and even for many on the elite level, however, the possession of nuclear weapons and the development of an independent nuclear deterrent have not been regarded as essential for Japanese security. In terms of role, the Gulf War shattered the 'taboo' on the overseas despatch of the SDF, allowing MSDF minesweepers to embark on operations in the Persian Gulf after the cessation of hostilities. This shortly afterwards led to the passage through the Japanese Diet (bicameral parliament) in June 1992 of the Peacekeeping Operations Bill, which has since enabled the SDF to undertake UN peacekeeping operations (PKO) in Cambodia (1992–3), Mozambique (1993–5), Rwanda (1994), the Golan Heights (1996 to present) (Leitenberg 1996) and East Timor (1999 to present). It can be seen, therefore, that Japan possesses considerable military resources which provide it with the potential to be a major actor in the security dimension and complement its already significant global economic and growing political presence.

1.2.iv A tri-dimensional perspective

These three dimensions of economics, politics and security present a picture of the relative weight of Japan in the world. This picture is reflected in the dominant metaphors used to refer to Japan's international relations, as seen above. Nevertheless, whilst these metaphors serve an important heuristic purpose in highlighting certain salient features of its international relations, at the same time they tend to downplay, if not obfuscate, the political and security role of Japan in favour of the economic. As the chapters in this book will demonstrate, however, Japan is not a uni-dimensional actor, a mercantilist state with only economic interests, but a full actor in the political and security dimensions of international relations as well. Therefore, in order to challenge the preconceived notion of Japan as solely an economic power, the parts of this book dealing with Japan and the US, East Asia, Europe and global institutions will adopt a tri-dimensional perspective dealing respectively with the political, economic and security dimensions of Japan's international relations, even though the common tendency is to treat economics first.

1.3 Why Japan matters: regional and global perspectives

1.3.i United States

The significance of Japan's tri-dimensional relations can be identified similarly on the regional level. Economically, Japan's presence in North America is most conspicuous with regard to its bilateral trade and investment relations with the US. During the 'reverse course' (*gyaku kōsu*) period (starting *circa* 1948) of the Occupation (1945–52), US policy-makers sought to determine the direction Japan would chart in the wake of defeat. The goal was to make it a bulwark against communism, with strong economic, political and security ties with the US. The US government promoted bilateral economic relations and economic reconstruction in Japan by opening its markets to Japanese exports, albeit with a view of the defeated country emerging as no more than a second-rate economic power.

Clearly, Japan's economic development would have been entirely different had not the US played a central role as an absorber of Japanese exports. Yet this has led over the years to a massive trade surplus for Japan, totalling in 1998 US$51 billion (Table 1). As a result of FDI, moreover, Japanese TNCs are now part of the American landscape. Whilst this sort of growing economic interdependency between Japan and the US has given rise to what has been termed the *Nichibei* economy (Gilpin 1987: 336–9) (*nichi* and *bei* representing the Japanese characters for Japan and the US respectively), at the same time trade and FDI have generated periodically a range of economic conflicts and antagonistic sentiments on both sides. This is illustrated by the negative American reaction to Matsushita's purchase of the Rockefeller Center and Sony's purchase of Universal Studios. It is also epitomized by the actions of members of the US Congress in smashing some of these 'Made in Japan' products (see plate 5.1 p. 107).

In contrast to the economic relationship, which witnessed Japan move beyond a second-rate economic power to become a major challenger to the US in a range of industries and products, the political relationship seems more in line with the original expectations of the victor and vanquished. At times, the government's relations with the US have served to constrain Japan's political and diplomatic independence, but in other instances foreign pressure (*gaiatsu*) or, more accurately, American pressure (*beiatsu*), has worked to expand Japan's political contribution to global and regional orders.

Security, the final dimension of the relationship, lies at the heart of the other two. The signing of the US–Japan security treaty, along with the Treaty of Peace with the Allied Powers (commonly referred to as the San Francisco peace treaty), in September 1951 (in force from April 1952) provided the US with the right to use bases in Japan. These documents formalized Japan's integration into the Cold War order on the US side. They also ensured the need for close bilateral political and economic cooperation, and opened the way for the defeated country's political and economic rehabilitation in the wider world. Above all else, security issues have been fraught with many of the same difficulties as the other two dimensions of the bilateral relationship. Japan's incorporation into the US's conventional and nuclear strategies in East Asia and beyond has long been viewed anxiously by public opinion, the opposition parties and even some elements of the governing Liberal-Democratic Party (LDP). The fear is that, as a result of Japan's obligations under the security treaty, pre-war militarism might recrudesce and the stationing of US troops in Okinawa and elsewhere might lead to entanglement in a war of the US's making.

1.3.ii East Asia

Japan's regional economic, political and security presence is also strongly manifest in East Asia: defined here as including the People's Republic of China (hereafter referred to as China or PRC), the Republic of China (hereafter referred to as ROC or Taiwan), the Republic of Korea (ROK, hereafter referred to as South Korea), the Democratic People's Republic of Korea (DPRK, hereafter referred to as North

Korea) and the ASEAN-10 (the Association of Southeast Asian Nations: Indonesia, Malaysia, the Philippines, Singapore, Thailand, Brunei, Vietnam, Laos, Cambodia and Burma (Myanmar)).

Economically, Japan dominates East Asia, owing to its position as the largest provider of ODA. Indeed, until the late 1970s, when Japan began to offer ODA to countries outside East Asia in line with US strategic interests, so-called 'aid to US aid' (Pharr 1993: 251), East Asia was the almost exclusive focus. Such ODA has been complemented by FDI to the region, the development of trade links, and the creation of extended production networks through the activities of Japanese TNCs. These link the economies of the region together internally, between other East Asian countries, as well as externally to Japan. The economic significance of the relationship is illustrated by the size of Japanese ODA, investment and trade. In 1997, for instance, approximately 29.4 per cent of Japan's total ODA was concentrated in East Asia and the rest of Asia (MOFA 1998b), 20.6 per cent of its total world FDI in East Asia (Table 2), and approximately 38 per cent of its total world trade in this region (Table 1).

In terms of political relations, the legacies of World War II and the Cold War have hindered Japan from building the same degree of interdependency with East Asia as in the economic dimension. Japan is still distrusted by many East Asian states and involved in territorial and resource disputes with China and South Korea over the Senkaku (Diaoyu in Chinese) and Takeshima (Tok-do in Korean) islands respectively. At the same time, however, Japan can be said to have constructed carefully a set of special political relationships with the ASEAN states. This has been achieved through the conduct of regional summitry in the Japan–ASEAN Forum, the gradual upgrading of its diplomatic relations with South Korea, the attempt to improve relations with North Korea, and its engagement with China.

Continued fears of Japanese militarism mean that Japan's military contribution to East Asian security remains indirect – namely, it contributes through the US–Japan alliance. Its main direct contribution to East Asian security in the post-war era has been made through the provision of economic aid to the region, which is designed to build political and security stability. Military security remains, then, the missing link for Japan if it is to create a comprehensive set of international relations in the region. Yet even here Japan can be seen to be making progress, as is illustrated by the launch of the ASEAN Regional Forum (ARF) in 1994. This was the first government-level multilateral body in the region in the post-Cold War period to discuss security matters. Progress can also be seen in the growth of bilateral security exchanges between Japan and South Korea. Thus, it would seem that at the start of the new millennium Japan has returned to a central, and possibly dominant, position within the East Asia region as a political, economic and security player and organizer.

1.3.iii Europe

In contrast to the situation with the US and East Asia, Japan's relations with Europe have elicited little attention from either political or academic observers for most of the post-war era. Europe as understood here refers primarily to the fifteen member states of the European Union (EU) (namely, in order of accession, Belgium, France, Germany, Italy, Luxemburg, The Netherlands, Denmark, Ireland, the UK, Greece, Portugal, Spain, Austria, Finland and Sweden) and to the countries of Central and Eastern Europe that have applied for EU membership and which comprise Bulgaria, the Czech Republic, Estonia, Hungary, Latvia, Lithuania, Poland, Romania, Slovakia and Slovenia. The ending of the Cold War in 1989, as symbolized by the tearing down of the Berlin Wall and the following break-up of the Union of Soviet Socialist Republics (USSR), has created the possibility for former members of the Soviet bloc in Eastern Europe to be considered for EU membership.

On the mass level, the people of both Japan and Europe share only rare opportunities to learn about each other. As far as many Europeans are concerned, this archipelago in the 'Far East' represents a global economic threat or challenge, whereas for others, especially in the UK, Japan offers the chance of employment as one after another of its TNCs sets up manufacturing plants there. At the other side of the world, many Japanese seem to view the machinations of the EU as a complete mystery, such that 'Europe' still appears as a composite of separate countries. In spite of their apparent mutual neglect, however, the 1980s, 1990s and the start of the twenty-first century have witnessed growing signs of engagement between the Japanese government and businesses and their European counterparts.

However, the 'Europe' with which Japan interacts varies across time and issue areas. This is one of the reasons why this aspect of Japan's international relations remains difficult to analyse. It is clear, nevertheless, that the arrival of the Single European Market (SEM) in 1992 and the advent of the euro in 1999 have made Europe a key economic partner as well as a rival for the Japanese. It is this economic dimension of Japan's international relations that has been most developed in bilateral Japan–EU relations to date. The same is true of Japan's relations with peripheral Europe, a region that has grown in importance for Japan as its relations with the EU have developed. Indeed, prior to 1992, fears surfaced within Japan's government and business circles that the EU would develop into a 'Fortress Europe' from whose economic benefits Japan would be excluded.

Political relations between Japan and Europe are less well developed. Nevertheless, in this dimension, also, new areas of cooperation have begun to be identified between government, business and non-governmental organizations (NGO). These include concern for the environment, attempts to counter drugs trafficking and cooperation within the Korean Peninsula Energy Development Organization (KEDO). In addition, Japan and many European countries share concerns over the future of Russia and other areas of the former USSR, as well as a mutual interest in ensuring the US's continued security presence in Europe. Such issues are addressed at the various levels of engagement which now sustain political relations between the two sides.

As with Japan and East Asia, the least-developed dimension of EU–Japan relations is security. This situation is unsurprising, given the continued importance of the role of the US–Japan security treaty in Japan's regional security policy, and the central role of the North Atlantic Treaty Organization (NATO) on the European continent. Nevertheless, the Japanese have started to engage in a broader discussion of security with Europe as a result of the establishment of multilateral fora (such as the ARF and KEDO) in the post-Cold War period. What is more, questions of regional security have been extended to involve mutual concerns in both East Asia and Europe. For instance, in Europe Japan takes an active interest in Bosnia and has pledged financial contributions to the United Nations High Commission for Refugees (UNHCR) towards the resolution of the continuing crisis in Kosovo. In East Asia, the EU is now a significant member of the KEDO process. Growing security concerns within both East Asia and Europe have prompted policy-makers on both sides to work together to bind the US to political and security commitments in these two regions.

1.3.iv Global institutions

Since the 1980s, and especially following the end of the Cold War, Japan has begun both to play a more proactive role in the major global institutions and to exert a growing degree of power within them. Of the numerous multilateral institutions in which Japan plays a role, the UN, the WB, IMF, GATT and the World Trade Organ-ization (WTO) are regarded as most important by policy-makers in expanding Japan's global role.

Unlike during the Cold War period, this multilateral stance affords the Japanese state and its people the opportunity to shape the policies of institutions which are set to play a more prominent role in the management of global human, security and economic issues in the new millennium. This recent trend in Japanese policy constitutes part of a more sustained appeal to the internationalism of the post-World War I period. Indeed, it can now be asserted that these global institutions matter to Japan and Japan's presence in these institutions matters to the other member states. For example, in the UN – the successor to the pre-war League of Nations – Japanese personnel over recent years have come increasingly to occupy positions of responsibility. Along with Brazil, moreover, Japan has become one of the two most regularly re-elected non-permanent members of the UNSC. Furthermore, Japan has demonstrated its continuing economic power through the annual payment of contributions to both the regular UN budget and the peacekeeping budget. As elsewhere, the security dimension of Japan's relations with the UN, peacekeeping operations, remains controversial.

Within global economic institutions, as with IMF and GATT, Japan has moved from a position of initial reactivity conditioned by its rehabilitation into the established international order to one of greater proactive behaviour. In terms of the exercise of economic power, Japan makes its presence felt through its increasing financial contributions and voting rights. In addition, Japan has attempted to promote its own model of economic development, as seen in its support for the publication of *The East Asian Miracle: Economic Growth and Public Policy* (World Bank 1993).

Finally, in G7 summitry Japan has played three overlapping roles. First, it has aligned itself as a member of the Western camp (*nishigawa no ichiin*). Second, it has shouldered the responsibilities of an international state (*kokusai kokka*), as illustrated by the efforts made in hosting the rotating summit process. The 2000 meeting of the G7/8, for instance, was held in Okinawa. Third, Japan, as the only non-Western member of the summit process, has sought to represent East Asian interests.

1.3.v Balancing regional and global perspectives

In the same way as metaphors of Japan's international relations lead to the highlighting of the economic more than the political or security dimensions of these relations, focusing on the site of Japan's international activities tends to lead to an overemphasis on Japan's relationship with the US. Although this relationship does remain predominant, the transformation in the structure of the international system engendered by the end of the Cold War has provided the Japanese state and its people with new opportunities to develop fuller relations with East Asia, Europe and global institutions in all three dimensions of their international activities. The relative weight of Japan in these four sites of activities differs with the dimension in question, but the general tendency is towards an increase in the salience of relations with East Asia, Europe and global institutions. As the US still remains predominant, however, this book will deal with relations in the following order: Japan–US, Japan–East Asia, Japan–Europe and Japan–global institutions.

1.4 Paradigmatic paradoxes?

1.4.i Japan's role: what, why and how

The overall impression gained from the above account is of a Japan that matters in terms of its presence and capacity in the three dimensions of economics, politics and security at the regional and global levels. It suggests, too, a Japan poised in many instances to assume pre-eminence in world affairs alongside the other major industrialized powers. Despite the wide-ranging and inescapable evidence of its importance, however, a sense remains in which Japan's intent as an international actor and the implications of its presence for the rest of the world remain opaque.

Indeed, even the most perceptive of Japan-watchers, whether drawn from the academic, media or policy-making communities, is faced with two difficulties in seeking to interpret Japan's international relations through the orthodox lenses of international relations (IR) theory and international political economy (IPE) theory. First, Japan has not assumed a position of international importance commensurate with the sheer mass of its power resources; second, it does not conform to the typical pattern of international behaviour seen among the other major industrialized powers. Indeed, Japan's international relations seem to display instead a number of apparent paradoxes which jar uncomfortably with the orthodox paradigms of these disciplines. They emerge in the following terms: the type of role played by Japan in the international system; the way in which it uses the power resources available to fulfil these roles; and the degree to which the state and other international actors formulate and possess a coherent international strategy.

For instance, the evidence of Japan's prowess in the economic dimension is abundant and places it ahead of most of the other major industrialized powers, but scant evidence can be found of overt attempts to establish global economic institutions and lead the way in the provision of international 'public goods' – that is, shouldering international burden in order to maintain the established order (see Chapter 2) – as would be mandated by the orthodox realist and liberal schools of IR. In the dimension of politics, Japan holds membership of the G7 and strives to attain a permanent seat on the UNSC. Although Japan set out to acquire such high-profile trappings of global and regional influence, however, the story of its participation in past international summits hardly demonstrates a concerted effort to raise a voice equal to those of the other major industrialized powers. In fact, the Japanese leader who has taken a seat on such occasions has usually been something of the odd man out, tongue-tied if not completely speechless. In the area of security, as well, Japanese policy appears hard to fathom if measured against the established criteria of the other major industrialized powers and IR theory.

As an illustration, Japanese and foreign commentators of the realist school, as described in Chapter 2, suggest that Japan's rise to economic superpower status can be expected to be accompanied by the acquisition of comparable military power, including even nuclear weapons. Similarly, they see that, faced with a great enough threat, Japan would swiftly seek once again to dominate East Asia, and perhaps even the world, through armed force. From this perspective, the presence of US forces in Japan is seen as essential in order to act as the 'cap in the bottle' of Japanese militarism. However, any reader of a foreign or Japanese newspaper at the time of the 1990–1 Gulf War would have been patently struck by Japan's determined resistance to the expansion of its military role. This demonstrates that, even if Japan is pushed hard to increase its role, the military is not easily deployed without an internal political crisis. In short, it is not inevitable that Japan will devote its power resources to the build-up of its military capabilities, modelling itself in the image of a military superpower, or using armed force in pursuit of its national interest. Put simply, the realist school's focus on the material power of the state and the relentless logic of the structure of the international system do not explain the behaviour of Japan internationally.

Added to the uncertainties raised about what type of role Japan plays and is likely to play in the international system and how the state and its people have sought to use their power resources to achieve their international ends, questions are raised for IR, IPE and other disciplines in respect of the manner in which and why Japan opts for the role it does. Witness the way in which Japan is portrayed as lacking a policy-making process where leaders can readily pursue a set of dynamic international relations along the lines of the other major industrialized powers. The immobilism of the foreign policy-making system has often been cited (Stockwin 1988), with the implication that, whatever the merits of the system for the Japanese, policy can only be implemented after much domestic foot-dragging, unprofitable infighting and a yawning gap opening up between the expectations of the other major industrialized powers and Japan's response. Japanese foreign policy also has been described as highly 'reactive' (Calder 1988a), suggesting this time that, in contrast to the typical 'proactive' model and stance of the other major industrialized powers, the Japanese state and its people simply react to, rather than shape, international events. Finally, other commentators have gone so far as to suggest that Japan lacks totally the ability to produce a coherent foreign policy at all, marking it apart from the rest of the major industrialized powers. It is thus branded as akin to a 'headless chicken' (van Wolferen 1990: 39) in the international system.

1.4.ii Japan's international relations as normal

All such characterizations of the Japanese policy-making process tend towards a view of Japan as anomalous, if not abnormal. The same is true of the state's international role and the types of power it uses to support it. In other words, Japan defies the conventional stereotypes of the behaviour of the major industrialized powers or earlier great powers found in IR and IPE theory. Indeed, at first glance, Japan's role in the world seems to defy all identification and characterization based on our 'normal' perceptions of the conduct and study of international relations. To wit: the image of the US's role in the world is easily evoked by the cliché of the 'world's policeman', the UK's as 'punching above its weight', France's as maintaining a 'Gaullist' distance from entanglement with the US, and Germany's as the leader of the 'European Project'. In the case of Japan, however, no clear image of its role or strategy seems to exist.

To start with, Japan hardly seems interested in policing the world, let alone its own region; given its economic size, it would appear to punch below its weight in international affairs; it maintains close adherence to and collaboration with the US; and it does not appear openly to lead any regionalist project. Consequently, in the case of Japan, a set of international relations that obviously matters enormously to the world in the dimensions of economics, politics and security has already been identified, but this does not fit readily into the existing models and preconceptions of international relations theory.

The fundamental argument of this volume is that, despite the proclivity of a range of observers to view the Japanese state and its people as somehow anomalous with sufficient methodological rigour Japan can be explained by the analytical tools of the social sciences. Finding a way through the apparent paradoxes and inconsistencies of Japan's international relations and presenting a coherent analysis is a task which lends itself to controversy, but it is the central goal of this book.

1.5 Summary

Chapter 1 has highlighted some of the key features of the dominant debates on Japan's international relations and elucidated the reasons why these relations matter in the political, economic and security dimensions at the regional and global levels. It has demonstrated that, as in the metaphorical movement in the images of Japan over the post-war era, opinions have tended to swing to extremes in seeking to characterize the international relations of the Japanese state and its people.

The significance of these relations, however, is in no doubt. From a global perspective, they are characterized by the rise of Japan to superpower economic status, but without a concomitant rise in its political and security role. It has no seat at the high table of the UNSC, nor is it a member of the nuclear club. From a regional perspective, the international relations of Japan are characterized by close economic ties with the three core regions of the global political economy: the US, East Asia and Europe, but again, the political and security roles of Japan are less clear cut. Japan remains a junior partner in political relations with the US, has only recently developed meaningful political links with Europe, and continues to struggle to mend political fences with East Asia. In terms of security, the alliance with the US remains the cornerstone of Japan's security interests, but its role is constrained by opinion at home as well as in East Asia. It has some emerging security links with Europe and East Asia, but again not at the level that might be expected in IR theory.

Nevertheless, these apparent paradoxes are no more than that: apparent. As Chapter 2 will demonstrate, even though the international relations of the Japanese state and its people are regarded as anomalous, aberrant or abnormal, the application of the eclectic yet comprehensive theoretical approach used in this volume can explain them as the normal behaviour of international actors obliged to pursue their interests in the context of the complex and dynamic relationship amongst the structure of the international system, domestic agents and the embedded norms of international and domestic societies.

Chapter 2

Explaining Japan's international relations

2.1 Methodology

As Chapter 1 has shown, the international relations of the Japanese state and its people appear paradoxical. All commentators are forced to acknowledge the significance of Japan's international presence across the three dimensions of politics, economics and security, and regionally and globally with regard to the US, East Asia, Europe and global institutions. Nevertheless, Japan is seen to defy many of the conventional media and academic categorizations of the way that states behave in the international system. Japan's pattern of behaviour, exact role and agenda, and policies and strategies in the international system remain puzzling to many when compared to the other major industrialized powers. The reasons and motivations for Japan's pattern of behaviour and choice of roles are also subject to intense controversy. Finally, Japan's mode of interaction and selection of policy tools in the international system, and especially its predilection for economic over military forms of power, are seen to differ markedly from the other major industrialized powers, with the possible exception of Germany (Maull 1990–1; Berger 1998). For these reasons, a major debate has unfolded about whether or not Japan is a truly effective player in the international system.

In short, therefore, for many observers, both academic and non-academic alike, key questions about Japan's international relations remain unanswered. These are related to the 'what', in terms of trying to establish what has been and is Japan's pattern of behaviour and role in the international system; the 'why', in terms of trying to explain why Japan opts to behave in the way it does; and the 'how', in terms of the means, methods and effectiveness of how Japan pursues its international role. Indeed, as Chapter 1 has demonstrated, the lack of apparently ready answers to these questions to date has even encouraged certain academics and policy-makers to regard Japan as abnormal.

As the Preface and Chapter 1 have also indicated, however, the objective of this volume is to answer these questions as to the 'what', 'why' and 'how' of Japan's international relations, and to dispel the myth of Japan as enigmatic, inexplicable or abnormal. The consequent aim of this chapter is to provide a conceptual and methodological framework to assist in the overall task of explaining Japan's international relations. The methodology of Chapter 2 is premised upon the belief that Japan can be explained if sufficient intellectual rigour is applied, combined with an eclectic, but integrated and holistic, historical and theoretical approach. Hence, the chapter and methodological framework is divided into three interrelated parts, each of which concentrates upon beginning to analyse the 'what', 'why' and 'how' of Japan's international relations. This structure is then deployed in subsequent parts and chapters of the book in order to provide analytical focus and explanation to the discussions dealing with Japan in the three core regions and in global institutions as well as across the three dimensions of politics, economics and security.

Specifically, section 2.2 of this chapter begins by explaining the 'what' of Japan's international relations by offering a historical overview of Japan's interaction with the outside world from the period of the Chinese world order to the post-Cold War period. This section can be read usefully as a straight historical account of Japan's international relations. It is indispensable in order to orient the reader to the development of Japan's political, economic and security relations with each of the three core regions and to place in historical context many of the contemporary and future problems that Japan faces. Just as important, however, the aim of the section is to highlight the patterns of structural change in the international system over these periods and the dominant pattern of Japan's response to them. Hence, the section will initiate the argument, later returned to in subsequent sections, that the Japanese state and its people have certainly experimented with, undertaken and reprised a number of different international roles during the various phases of Japan's history. At the same time, however, Japan has followed these roles in each historical phase and context with a consistent and calculating strategy, and thus is no different from the other major industrialized powers and has exhibited the same type of behaviour in pursuit of its perceived interests as these powers.

Sections 2.3 and 2.4 begin next to move deeper into the analysis of Japan's international relations, and to deal with the second of the volume's principal questions, by seeking to explain the reasons 'why' Japan has followed the pattern of behaviour in the international system outlined in the historical overview. These sections employ a combination of IR and IPE theory to demonstrate that Japan's international relations have been determined by the interaction of changes in the structure of the international system and the response of domestic policy-making agents informed by a range of domestic and international norms.

Sections 2.5 and 2.6 then turn to providing a methodological and conceptual framework for understanding the third of the questions, namely 'how' Japan and its people have managed to pursue and instrumentalize their international relations. Section 2.5 looks in particular at the way Japan has responded to international events and changes in the structure of the international system. Section 2.6 then proceeds to analyse the forms of power and mode of instrumentalization Japanese policy-making agents have employed in pursuing the perceived interests of the Japanese state and its people.

2.2 Historical overview: from the Chinese world order to the post-Cold War world

2.2.i Chinese world order

The first historical phase of Japan's interaction with the outside world occurred during the 'Chinese world order' (Fairbank 1968), which embraced continental China, the Korean Peninsula, and parts of Northeast, Central and Southeast Asia from the establishment of the T'ang dynasty (AD 618–906) through to the mid-nineteenth century. China, as the most powerful civilization of the day, and literally, as in the Chinese characters for its name, the 'middle kingdom', created a structure of hierarchical suzerainty. It located the Chinese empire at the centre of the world and was accompanied by a degree of integration on the economic, political and security dimensions of international relations among the various East Asian tributary kingdoms. In the economic dimension, the tributary system enhanced trade in raw materials, manufactured goods, medicinal herbs and works of art; whilst in the political and security dimensions, the kingdoms of East Asia were tied to the suzerain in terms of their duty to pledge political allegiance at the imperial court and to perform military service in overseas expeditions. This centripetal world order was bound loosely together by the shared norms of Buddhism and Confucianism. In essence, therefore, Chinese hegemony allowed for the establishment in East Asia of complete and congruent world and regional systems, characterized by a measure of economic, political and security interdependence, and a shared identity.

Japan was incorporated into this Sino-centric order. Its position as an island kingdom meant that, at times, it could remain indifferent towards the continental powers. Despite that, successive Japanese ruling dynasties were forced to acknowledge the reality of China's superior civilization and were drawn towards the economic, political and security benefits accruing from association with the middle kingdom. In the economic dimension, the Japanese people maintained vibrant trading across the East China, Yellow and Japan seas (Hamashita 1997). Japanese rulers were interested in the political and security dimensions of relations with China because these brought them access to the advanced administrative skills and weaponry (*wakon kansai*, Japanese spirit combined with Chinese learning) necessary to unify their homeland and bolster their country's power. By the mid-eighth century Japan's administration had been remodelled along Chinese lines, and the country's submission to China's political and military suzerainty was marked by its despatch of naval forces to support the Chinese empire's position in Korea in the mid-seventh century. Japan's import of Buddhism from China via Korea in the mid-sixth century had already completed its ideological integration into the Sino-centric order, and in this period the Japanese state and its people rarely questioned the assumption that 'East Asia was coeval with the civilised world' (Welfield 1988: 2).

Nevertheless, this is not to say that the Japanese were unaware of the problems of political and security alignment with China and entanglement with continental Asia. The attempted Mongol invasions of Japan in 1274 and 1281 were sufficient demonstration of the dangers of military attack from dominant powers in China and the Korean Peninsula. Moreover, on occasions Japanese rulers sought to challenge the Chinese regional and world orders, either by attempts to usurp the middle kingdom's political and military position, or by a defiant withdrawal and isolation from them. Japanese relations with East Asia were remarkably pacific in most of this period, but during the rule of Toyotomi Hideyoshi (1537–98) the leaders of Japan made their own, albeit ultimately unsuccessful, bid for regional and consequently world hegemony by launching invasions of Korea in 1592 and 1597. These were intended to open the way for the conquest of China. In turn, the combination of Japan's military failures in East Asia, the threatened intrusion of the European powers following their discovery of Japan in the same period, and the completion by Tokugawa Ieyasu (1543–1616) of the internal unification of

Japan with the establishment in 1603 of the Edo Bakufu, or Tokugawa Shogunate, was sufficient to persuade Japan's rulers that the country should retreat into isolation from the world and the destabilizing influence of external forces. Thereafter followed the period of isolation, or *sakoku*. This was hardly total, however, as the Dutch and Chinese were allowed to trade out of Dejima island, Nagasaki harbour and the Koreans out of Tsushima.

2.2.ii Imperial world order

The country's relative isolation from the Sino-centric order lasted close to two hundred years. It was then dragged into a new imperial world order by the early-starters of Europe and the United States. The arrival of superior Western industrial, technological and military power in the mid-nineteenth century brought with it the imposition upon East Asia of a hierarchical structure of territorial states and empires. The early-starters sought to acquire East Asian colonies, whether in the Philippines, Indonesia or elsewhere. Their imperial ambitions contributed to the dismemberment of China, the result of which was to fracture the unity of the Chinese and East Asia world and regional orders. In their place, East Asia was carved up into a series of economic, political and military systems which were linked externally to the imperial powers.

As was mentioned above, the initial reaction of Japan's rulers to the encroachment of the Western powers was isolation and resistance to incorporation into the emerging imperialist world order, as encapsulated in the slogan *sonnō jōi* ('revere the emperor and expel the barbarians'). However, the forced entrance of the 'Black Ships' of Commander William Perry of the US into Edo Bay (now Tokyo Bay) in 1853 and the display of irresistible Western military might soon convinced Japanese policy-makers of the inevitability of their opening to the outside world and the need to modernize their country along Western lines. Once again, and in a fashion similar to that in the era of the Chinese world order, Japanese leaders perceived clearly the need to import and 'catch up' with the superior administrative and military technology of an external civilization in order to unify their country internally and to augment their national power (Samuels 1996). The assimilation of Western technology into Japan whilst maintaining Japanese spirit (*wakon yōsai*, Japanese spirit combined with Western learning) was designed to enable the leadership to fashion a modern state with the economic, political and military might necessary to stave off China's fate of gradual dismemberment and colonization. By the end of the nineteenth century, Japan had undergone rapid industrialization and built up naval and land forces powerful enough to gain victory in the Sino-Japanese War of 1894–5. The signing of the Anglo-Japanese alliance in 1902 confirmed Japan's rapid ascent to great power status and a repeat of the earlier pattern of international behaviour seen during the era of the Chinese world order, namely, of seeking alignment with the leading global power of the day.

Further evidence of Japan's burgeoning international presence can be found in its victory against a 'white power' in the Russo-Japanese War of 1904–5. This stunned the West, unlike the defeat of 'yellow' China. The reconfiguration of the international order in East Asia represented by the advance of the West and the Japanese response produced two intertwined, but ultimately divergent, reactions among the policy-making agents of the Meiji era. On the one hand, they remained cognizant of the fact that, even after the collapse of the Chinese world order, their country continued to form part of an East Asian regional order geographically, racially and culturally. Thus, as expressed in sentiments such as pan-Asianism, Japan as the first modern state in the region was seen to shoulder a special responsibility to take the lead in protecting East Asia from the ravages of Western imperialism. On the other hand, however, this vision of Japan's role in the region was counteracted by an awareness that, in order to survive and prosper in a world dominated by the early-starter, imperial powers, Japan required the physical, economic and military resources to rival those of the West. Thus, the Meiji leaders copied that imperialist pattern of behaviour and steadily acquired colonies of their own, albeit closer to home in East Asia, unlike the early-starter imperialists. The outcome was that, in opposition to the identity of Japan as an Asian state, another viewpoint arose which stressed Japan's new-found position and interests among the Western powers. Such sentiments were typified in the Meiji era by the political thinker Fukuzawa Yukichi (1835–1901), who espoused the future course for modern Japan to charter: *datsua nyūō* (abandonment of Asia, and joining with Europe). The Western and imperialist impulse proved to be dominant, and led to Japan's acquisition of Taiwan in 1895 following the first Sino-Japanese War of 1894–5, and the annexation of Korea in 1910.

Still, even though Japan managed by the early twentieth century to rescind the unequal treaties imposed by the Western powers (which gave the latter special privileges), to secure independence and to metamorphose into a fully-fledged imperial power, none of these guaranteed it equality of treatment in the international order of the day. Despite Japan's participation on the Allied side in World War I (1914–18), for instance, it received unfavourable treatment at the Paris Peace Conference (1919). This was reinforced by the major industrialized powers' rejection of its proposal for the insertion in the newly-founded League of Nations of a clause on the racial equality of nations (Shimazu 1998). We thus find that, although the pattern of international relations pursued by the Japanese state and its people had been modelled on the early-starter imperialists, this new entrant to the high table of the advanced West was not welcomed, despite possessing all of the capabilities of a major economic, political and military power. As a result, Japanese policy-makers viewed international institutions and the other major industrialized powers as biased against them. The Washington Naval Treaty of 1922, for instance, disadvantaged Japan in comparison to Great Britain and the US. What is more, the Japanese empire's attempts at expansion following its 1931 invasion of Manchuria were censured by the European powers in the League of Nations.

Although the imperial government dabbled in participation in international institutions and the creation of a world order underpinned by international cooperation in the 1920s and 1930s, its increasingly ultra-nationalist leaders came to see only one route to continued expansion and to prevent Japan's perceived suffocation at the hands of the early-starters, namely, to forge an alliance with the then rising, or more accurately resurgent, power of the day, Nazi Germany. The conclu-

Plate 2.1 Defeat. On 2 September 1945, Foreign Minister Shigemitsu Mamoru signed the instrument of surrender aboard the USS *Missouri* in Tokyo Bay bringing an end to Japan's military attempt at regional dominance in East Asia.

Source: Courtesy of Mainichi Shimbunsha

sion of the Tripartite Pact in September 1940 enabled Japan to ally with the fascist powers of Germany and Italy, and set it on the path to assault the US at Pearl Harbor in December 1941 and to challenge head-on the international and regional orders in East Asia and beyond. The rapid conquest of US, British and Dutch colonial possessions in Southeast Asia in 1941–2, followed by the proclamation of the Greater East Asia Co-prosperity Sphere (*Daitōa Kyōeiken*), enabled Japan to construct under its own imperial auspices a new regional order centred upon itself. The militarists in this way replaced China's 'land under one heaven' in East Asia with Japan's own design of 'eight corners of the world under one roof' (*hakkō ichiu*) – that is, the whole world's unification under the emperor of Japan. With the turn of the war to the Allies' advantage, however, Japan's regional order in East Asia was swept away in 1945 by defeat in the Pacific War and the cataclysm of the atomic bombings of Hiroshima and Nagasaki.

2.2.iii Cold War order

The end of World War II and the emergence of Cold War tensions from 1945 onwards produced yet another radical transformation of the international and regional orders. The Cold War order was characterized essentially by bipolar confrontation between the US and the USSR, and their respective economic, political and security alliance systems. The intensity of bipolar confrontation varied considerably throughout the Cold War period, but occasionally spilled over into 'hot wars' in East Asia, as with US fighting in the Korean War in the 1950s and the Vietnam War in the 1960s and early 1970s. The Cold War can be regarded as being made up of the 'first' Cold War, running until the early 1970s when the US began to seek withdrawal from Vietnam, *rapprochement* with China, and détente with the USSR; and the 'second' Cold War, starting in the late 1970s following the USSR's invasion of Afghanistan in December 1979.

Japan's total defeat and exhaustion in the Pacific War, followed by the Allied Occupation of Japan (1945–52), which at first sought through General Douglas MacArthur, the commander of the Supreme Command for the Allied Powers (SCAP), to expunge Japan's material and psychological capacity to wage offensive war (Schaller 1985), meant that Japan was once again reduced to the status of a minor power. The USSR's involvement in the war against Japan for the short period 9–15 August, at the end of which Japan surrendered, and the US's need for military bases in East Asia, meant that Japan not only lost its former colonies, but also suffered the occupation by Soviet troops of islands off the north of the Japanese archipelago, the so-called 'Northern Territories' made up of Etorofu, Kunashiri, Shikotan and the Habomais group of islands (see Chapter 4), and, as part of the peace settlement, agreed to the US's administrative control of Okinawa in the south (see Chapter 6). In this situation, Japanese policy-making agents faced the same question as in the past of how to survive in an international hierarchy populated by bigger, and now nuclear, powers. As will be outlined in Chapter 4 dealing with Japan's political relations with the US, in order to end the Occupation and restore national independence, Japanese policy-makers chose, after much internal debate, the path of dependence upon and alignment with the US. Unarmed neutrality and non-alignment were hotly debated and promoted as viable alternative options by sections of Japan's policy-making agents, the political opposition, intellectuals and political movements, as will be seen in Chapter 3. However, key policy-makers reverted eventually to their traditional pattern of international relations by relying upon the hegemonic power of the day, the US. This national strategy was embodied in the so-called 'Yoshida Doctrine', laid down by Yoshida Shigeru (twice prime minister: 1946–7 and 1948–54). The doctrine determined that the basic pattern of Japan's international relations in the immediate post-war years would be to concentrate upon the task of national rebuilding, whilst seeking economic, political and security guarantees from the US.

The predominance of the Yoshida Doctrine meant Japan's near total integration into the US half of the bipolar divide during the early Cold War years. Economically, Japan belonged to the US and capitalist camps owing to its reliance upon the US export market – a dependence given an initial boost by the supply of war material to the US during the Korean War of 1951–3 (Stubbs 1994) – and upon the US's ability to open up to Japanese manufacturers the key markets and raw material supplies of Southeast Asia. However, the reverse side of the US sponsorship of Japan's economic position in the capitalist world and in key economic frameworks, such as GATT, was its relative economic isolation from the newly-established communist economies of East Asia. The political integration of Japan into the US camp was initiated following the outbreak of the Korean War and the so-called 'reverse course' policy, and then confirmed with the signing of the Treaty of Peace with Japan at San Francisco in September 1951.

The San Francisco peace treaty constituted only a partial peace because the communist powers refused to sign it, so highlighting Tokyo's alignment with the capitalist half of the world. As referred to earlier and will be dealt with in greater detail in Part II, especially in Chapter 6, Japan's military incorporation into the US camp was cemented by the signing in September 1951 of the US–Japan security treaty simultaneously with the San Francisco peace treaty. The consequence was that Japan became an integral part of US conventional and nuclear strategy in East Asia. Its role in providing military bases for the US under the security treaty placed it in the front line of the US's military containment policy with regard to communism on the East Asian continent.

The development of Japan's post-war domestic policy and international relations took place, therefore, within the protected, and at times restrictive, framework, or 'greenhouse' (Hellman 1988), of US hegemony. Nevertheless, this is not to go so far as to say that, in cases where their national interests conflicted with this overarching US framework, Japanese policy-makers failed to assert an independent course of action. As in the pre-Meiji period, Japan's leaders sought to ensure that their alignment with the hegemonic power of the day did not mean excessive entanglement with continental politics. This can be seen, for instance, in firm Japanese resistance to direct involvement in the US's wars in Korea and Vietnam (Havens 1987; Shiraishi 1990). Under President Richard Nixon's Guam (or Nixon) Doctrine of July 1969, Japan took on a greater defensive role, as will be touched on in Chapter 6. This was a response to the doctrine, which sought to increase the South Vietnamese role in the war with the communist North, to avoid entanglement in future ground wars in Asia and to pressure allies to accept greater responsibility for regional defence. Despite the overarching confrontation between the East and West, moreover, Japanese policy-making agents were quite prepared to exploit any diplomatic room afforded by the US alliance system in order to pursue improved economic relations with China, as in the process of the separation of politics and economics (*seikei bunri*) (Johnson 1995: 235–63), as will be seen in Chapter 10. What is more, Japanese policy-makers became less consistent in following US foreign policy goals as the strength of US global hegemony began to wane and multipolarity in the international system started to wax in the early 1970s.

The declining economic power of the US can be seen in President Nixon's twin decisions, or 'shocks', of August 1971. The first was the decision to devalue the dollar by abandoning its convertibility to gold and moving shortly thereafter to floating exchange rates. Further reflecting the US's declining power, the president also imposed an import surcharge. These actions in the economic dimension signified the erosion of the international post-war economic order (Gill and Law 1988: 173). The second decision was in the political dimension, which symbolized the breakdown in the political order of bipolar confrontation between the West and monolithic communism: the Nixon administration broke the mould of post-war US policy by seeking *rapprochement* with communist China. In this way, the early 1970s were the prelude to a more fluid international system and a thawing in Cold War tensions, in which Japanese policy-making agents sought to promote the interests of the Japanese state and its people, even in the face of US pressure to pursue a different policy line.

Thus, following the first 'oil shock' in October 1973, Japan's dependence on oil imports from the Middle East meant that it refused to tow the US's policy line of attempting to organize a consumers' cartel to counteract the increased bargaining power of the Organization of Petroleum Exporting Countries (OPEC). Instead, Japan launched an independent and vigorous campaign of resource diplomacy (*shigen gaikō*) as a way to re-establish its access to these vital energy supplies (Ozaki 1985). To many, the Japanese challenge appeared to arise from its mercantilist and free-riding trading policies, which had allegedly eroded US economic power and generated severe bilateral trade friction in the late 1960s and 1970s, with disputes over Japanese textile and automobile exports. Whatever the motivation, this illustrates clearly the willingness of Japanese policy-making agents to go so far as to challenge the foundations of American leadership, if the interests of the Japanese state and its people can only be pursued in this way. This strengthening of relations with other parts of the world beside the US in the early 1970s was termed omnidirectional diplomacy (*zenhōi gaikō*).

Nevertheless, despite the fact that Japan's adherence to the overarching US hegemonic framework was seen to loosen in the 1970s and the rationale for bilateral cooperation came to be questioned with increasing frequency, the fundamental pattern of international relations remained the Yoshida Doctrine and alignment with the US (Edström 1999: 178). Japan continued to rely on the US market and the US-inspired liberal trading system, US sponsorship in international political institutions and US military might for security. The result was that, even though successive Japanese administrations worked steadily for the improvement of bilateral relations with the countries of Europe and East Asia, and occasionally pursued regionalist and multilateral concepts such as the 1980 Pacific Basin Cooperation under the administration of Prime Minister Ōhira Masayoshi (1978–80) (Nagatomi 1988; Korhonen 1994), the prime focus of their diplomatic efforts was to maintain healthy bilateral relations with the US. This policy was strengthened by the onset of the second Cold War following the USSR's invasion of Afghanistan in December 1979 and the perceived necessity under the administrations of President Ronald Reagan of the US (1980–8) and Prime Minister Nakasone Yasuhiro (1982–7) for enhanced cooperation between the US and Japan to counter Soviet military activity in East Asia.

2.2.iv Post-Cold War period

The fall of the Berlin Wall in 1989 and the ensuing collapse of the Soviet bloc ushered in yet another fundamental transformation in the structure of the international system with significant implications for the international relations of Japan – many of which are yet to be revealed. Following the US's seemingly resounding victory in the 1990–1 Gulf War, many observers expected that the US, as the world's sole remaining economic and military superpower, would proceed to establish a new unipolar and hegemonic global order. However, whilst the US certainly remains by far the most powerful state in the international system, other observers have noted challenges to US unipolar dominance by the rise of other major single-state actors, such as Germany and Japan (Maull 1990–1).

The present post-Cold War world can perhaps be most accurately characterized as an era of transition, with neither the US nor any other state taking on the mantle of global hegemon. As such, no widely-accepted interpretation of the newly-emerging order is readily available, although a near consensus does exist on the ending of the previous global Cold War order. In the context of this volume's focus on the political, economic and security dimensions of international relations, the Cold War's ending can be understood as the drawing to a close of the major confrontation in these three dimensions between the capitalist and communist worlds. The ending of the political confrontation implies the end of the confrontation between two different modes of organizing political life, democracy based on the popular ballot, and a less representative form of political organization based on the predominant role of the communist party. The ending of the economic confrontation can be seen in the way the capitalist free-market economy has swept over the globe, with the planned centralized economy discredited, if not totally extinct. Finally, the military confrontation based on the nuclear arms build-up between the US and the USSR has been replaced by arms reduction if not complete nuclear disarmament. Of course, remnants of the Cold War international order still remain in these three dimensions, as with the survival of the North Korean regime and the military confrontation on the Korean Peninsula, as well as the challenges India and Pakistan posed by their 1998 nuclear weapons tests. Still, no one doubts that deep-rooted changes are now under way in the structure of the international system.

What are the most salient features of the emerging order? Despite the valuable insights that different attempts to come to grips with the emerging global and regional orders have offered, as illustrated by talk of the 'end of history' (Fukuyama 1992) and the 'clash of civilizations' (Huntington 1993), this book argues that the interlinked forces of regionalization and globalization represent the quintessential feature of the newly-emerging order.

2.2.iv.a Regionalization

The process of regionalization – defined here as a dynamic process leading to the formation of units of social interaction with at least some degree of geographical proximity and interdependence in the economic, political, or security dimensions – has contributed forcefully to the strengthening or emergence in the post-Cold War world of three core regions in the global political economy. The regions of Europe, North America and East Asia are intersecting in complex ways, yet remain distinct (Gamble and Payne 1996). They are emerging as both 'hard' and 'soft' regions, depending on their degree of institutionalization.

In the case of Europe, regionalization is being promoted as part of a regionalist project led by key European states. This is the earliest regionalist project and has acted as a stimulus for the creation of regional groupings in the other two core regions. It is characterized by a highly-developed level of institutional governance, as seen in the numerous bodies of the EU, among relatively homogeneous states. In the case of North America, the dominant political economy, the US, is playing a lead role in promoting two separate regionalist projects involving both developed and developing economies: the Asia Pacific Economic Cooperation (APEC) forum and the North American Free Trade Agreement (NAFTA). Both APEC and NAFTA embody the globalist project pursued by the US of spreading the norms of neo-liberal, free-market economics and liberal democracy. A certain amount of institutionalization is taking place in these two groupings, as seen in the annual meetings of the APEC forum and the regularized meetings of policy-makers in the NAFTA process. In the case of East Asia, state-led regionalist projects, such as the Association of Southeast Asian Nations (ASEAN), have been in existence since the 1960s, but the most important regionalist development in the post-Cold War world is the role Japanese transnational corporations (TNCs) have been playing in the regionalization of the East Asian economies. This is the least institutionalized and 'softest' region, being characterized by minimal concentration on institution-building and less formal governance. It can be seen in the case of the East Asian Economic Caucus (EAEC), which has failed to establish a clear institutional framework and functions as part of the APEC as well as a grouping in the Asia-Europe Meeting (ASEM and the ASEAN +3 meetings) (Gilson 1999; Hook 1999a).

These regions, and the regionialist sentiments which drive their normative as well as institutional creation, are not necessarily formed directly in opposition to the US. In the post-Cold War world, the US appears more clearly as a dominant rather than as a hegemonic global power. In this environment, as the regionalist groupings engender their own dynamics, they cannot be easily dominated by a single power. This complicates the US's exercise of its unilateral influence, as regionalism offers these states a framework for economic, political and, as in the case of the EU, potential security interaction and cooperation.

2.2.iv.b Globalization

The term 'globalization' has become a popular buzzword. Whilst its meaning often remains vague, it can be defined here as a set of dynamic processes leading to the lowering of borders to all forms of interaction, which challenges the way people communicate, interact and do business with one another around the globe. It signals the fact that one state can no longer be isolated from others, and it heralds the interlinking of human relationships across space and time (Malcolm 1998: 18). Observers of the phenomena attached to globalization view its progress from a wide range of perspectives. It can be seen, for instance, as a global insurance policy by which the US garners support for its own ideological project. It can also be viewed as the simultaneous interaction of different policy-making agents through multiple channels of engagement (Jones 1995). It can further be regarded as the expansion of all forms of knowledge, spread through the phenomenal growth in communications and information technologies, with the result that local and national roots become weakened and 'local' issue-areas are discussed at global level (Robertson 1992: 8; Thrift 1994: 367; Schaeffer 1997: 2). These trends may lead at one extreme to a 'borderless world' (Ohmae 1990), or at the other to the fragmentation of contemporary global political, economic and security relations.

Globalization challenges the role of the state. For instance, by eliminating divisions between time and space and thereby destabilizing former identities, globalization renders outmoded accepted notions of the state (Giddens 1991). Activities now take place instantaneously through rewritten notions of space and time: the Internet facilitates split-second action and e-engagements bypass the level of the state to bring sub-state actors into direct contact with their counterparts across the world. At the same time, transnational representatives accrue global knowledge to overcome state impediments. Non-governmental actors themselves have expanded in number as people seek to construct institutions to govern rules in their daily lives in the face of exposure to global economic and political forces.

For all that, the sound of warning voices against viewing globalization as a 'unidirectional process' (Albrow 1996: 94), or seeing the state as anything but the principal site of political authority and the locus around which multilateral structures converge (Weiss 1998: 169), must be noted. These contending views of globalization illustrate its still indefinable status and suggest that, whilst globalization is not a 'myth' (Ruigrok and van Tulder 1995: 169), even as a concept lacking clarity it cannot be ignored. It needs to be taken into account in terms of an inexorable force of technological progress and intensifying communication across national boundaries. It also cannot be ignored in terms of identifying new sites of resistance (Gills 1997), as seen at the demonstrations surrounding the WTO meeting in Seattle in 1999. In this way, globalization does and will continue to affect the ability of a state to act in the international system, and may over time come to challenge the very notions upon which the constitution of that state is founded. Whatever effects are engendered by globalization, as will be seen in Chapter 24, the phenomena associated with it must be taken seriously by the Japanese state and its people.

2.2.iv.c Regionalization, globalization and Japan

The final outcome of the intersection of the forces of globalization and regionalization remains unknown, but their impact upon Japan can already be noted. The basic reaction of Japanese policy-making agents and other political actors to the transformation in the structure of the international system has been to follow their traditional pattern of international relations by maintaining strong bilateral support for the dominant power of the day, the US. For Japan, the US remains the principal provider of economic, political and security public goods (Islam 1993: 326–31). In this sense, Japan in the post-Cold War world continues to act as a supporter of the US, as in the Cold War period (Inoguchi 1988). At the same time, however, as will be demonstrated throughout this book, the US oft-times enables Japanese policy-makers to forge ahead with new policies in response to changes in the structure of the international system.

In this way, the Japanese state and its people have exploited the freedom afforded by the end of the Cold War order to open up new multilateral relations with Europe and East Asia and to adopt a more pronounced role in global institutions (Yasutomo 1995; Dobson 1998; Gilson 2000a). For instance, Japan has taken steps increasingly to play a major part in multilateral fora, such as ASEM (Gilson 1999) and the ARF (Hughes 1996; Hook 1998). This participation in regionalist projects has been accompanied by the role that Japanese corporations have played through their FDI policies in breaking down barriers to economic interaction and the embedding of globalization processes.

Japan's role in reshaping the global and regional orders has inevitably brought predictions, most of which are undoubtedly premature, of Japan emerging as a new hegemon to challenge or even supplant the US. Chapter 1 noted that Japan has been labelled 'number one'. Other observers have viewed Japan's economic might as a means not just to substitute Japanese for US hegemony, but also to redefine great power status completely (Williams 1994). Hence, talk of whether Japan can fulfil the role of a 'global civilian power', which relies mainly on the 'soft power' of economics rather than the 'hard power' of the military to achieves its international security objectives, grew in salience in the 1990s (Maull 1990–1; Funabashi 1991–2; Drifte 1998; Gilson 1999; Hughes 1999).

2.2.v Dominant historical patterns of Japan's international relations

The above historical overview reveals a wide range of patterns in the conduct, or the 'what', of Japan's international relations. At one extreme end of the spectrum of international behaviour, Japan has shown a propensity to withdraw into international isolation altogether, as during the Edo period (also called Tokugawa period, 1603–1867). At the other end of the spectrum, Japan has been seen to have sought global hegemony, as at the turn of the twentieth century when it was talked about as a possible global economic, and, consequently, political and security hegemon. On a more intermediate level, although often viewed in the past as a stepping-stone towards global hegemony, Japan has displayed a pattern of international behaviour seemingly designed to achieve the integration of and dominance over an East Asian region, as during Toyotomi's rule, in the Pacific War and in the contemporary period. On a similar level, Japan has also experimented with a pattern of external relations based upon international cooperation and global institutions, and sought to remodel the global political economy in trilateral cooperation with the EU and US. Nevertheless, the dominant pattern of the Japanese state and its people's international behaviour has undoubtedly been their gravitation towards and support for the major power of the day, whether this is the middle kingdom of China, imperialist Great Britain, revanchist Germany or the hegemonic US.

Japan has clearly pursued various patterns of international behaviour over considerable spans of time and during different historical epochs. The ability to discern these different strands of international behaviour is clearly significant: it indicates that, even though the dominant preference of Japanese policy-making agents has been to depend upon the hegemon of the day, they have been aware of, and experimented with, other options in charting a course in the world for the Japanese state and its people. These have included Japan's bids for its own unilateral hegemony, East Asian region-building, and attempts at trilateral cooperation and multilateral cooperation in global institutions. Indeed, in exactly the same way as other states, Japan has carefully constructed its international strategy in the past by choosing from the various options available to it, which suggests that it is necessary to consider the influence of these options when examining Japan's contemporary relations with the US, East Asia, Europe and global institutions. In sum, the historical overview presented above provides invaluable information about the development of the international structure in which Japan operates and the various problems that it faces in its dealings with each of the core regions and global institutions. At the same time, it contributes the perspective and understanding that Japan has always been and continues to be a calculating international actor aware of the various international options at its disposal, and one which chooses to adhere to the major power of the day and usually not to exercise to the full its other international options based upon a range of motivations and careful calculations.

2.3 Determinants of Japan's international relations: structure, agency and norms

2.3.i Theoretical approach

Having outlined in the last section what has been the dominant pattern of Japan's international relations historically and into the contemporary period, this next section now shifts focus to provide a theoretical framework in order to analyse the essential factors and motivations which account for why Japan has pursued these particular patterns of behaviour. In addition, the same body of theory will also be used in this section 3 to explain how Japan has instrumentalized its international relations.

As noted in Chapter 1 and at the beginning of this chapter, in many ways the Japanese state and its people do not fit conveniently into the standard categories found in the fields of IR and IPE and present a series of apparent paradoxes. Nevertheless, simply because Japan causes difficulties for these disciplines does not mean that they must be abandoned as the prime theoretical tools for the study of Japan's international relations. Quite the contrary: the aim of this book is rather to build upon IR and IPE theory in order to provide information of relevance not just to students of Japan's international relations, but also to specialists in the media and policy-making fields.

The apparent paradoxes noted above nevertheless still do indicate that, in order to constitute such an understanding of Japan's international relations, the tight paradigmatic frameworks of IR and IPE at least must be jettisoned. In their stead, an eclectic approach is called for which draws upon the collective insights and strengths of four traditions in the study of international relations, whilst at the same time striving to overcome their individual shortcomings and weaknesses: namely, a blending of realism and liberalism (in their classic and newer forms), constructivist approaches and policy-making studies.

The insights from realism, liberalism and constructivist approaches, when mixed in the right measure, offer jointly, more than singly, a deeper understanding of the historical, material and normative forces which account for the external and structural factors shaping a state's international behaviour. An understanding of domestic policy-making agents and other political actors in international relations is in turn assisted by policy-making studies and constructivist approaches. These different traditions in the study of IR provide the tools required to examine the mechanics of the Japanese policy-making process and to analyse the norms at the base of Japan's response to the structure of the international system.

Broadly framed, realists and neo-realists pay overwhelming attention to the material forces of a state and the structure of the international system in seeking to explain its behaviour (Waltz 1979; Keohane 1986a). The state's pursuit of an immutable national interest, through power political means, including the use of military force if necessary, is at the heart of the realist's approach to international relations. If one image dominates in the realist literature, it is that of an international system made up of unitary actors, as in the billiard ball metaphor, even if more sophisticated versions of realism paint a more complex picture of a state's domestic policy process influencing international behaviour (Carr 1946).

In contrast, liberals and neo-liberals widen the scope of their enquiry in order to take into account the role of non-state and private actors, such as TNCs, NGOs and other groups in domestic society (Nye 1988). Whereas realists consider military might and war as the final arbiters in international life, the liberals draw attention to the interconnectedness and interdependence created as a result of peaceful international activities, such as business and trade. Like the realists, however, liberals view actors in the international system as basically rational in their pursuit of interests and profits.

For their part, constructivist approaches demonstrate how policy-making agents and other political actors are socialized through mutual interaction into patterns of behaviour, which shape their definition of interests and rationality (Wendt 1994; Onuf 1985). Such socialization leads to different understandings and definitions of interests and rationality. In this way, actors are socialized into a specific set of expectations, norms and identities which serve to constrain and provide opportunities for them to define how they will behave internationally. Thus, no one rationality, which in some way defines an immutable national interest as implied by realists, is seen to exist.

Finally, policy-making studies highlight how the state is a composite of actors and pressures, not a unitary actor (Rosenau 1980; Clarke and White 1989; Macridis 1992). In this sense, the policy of the state is the outcome of domestic political processes, where domestic policy-making agents and other political actors, such as interest groups and pressure groups, seek to achieve their own perceived individual and national interests by influencing the policy-making process. Thus, foreign policy and the understanding as well as the deciding of national interests are the outcome of domestic competition, reflecting domestic priorities and interests, not the product of an abstract national interest determined by the structure of the international system and pursued by national actors.

In addition, IPE draws attention to the consensual and coercive nature of hegemony, the military and economic dimensions of power, and the opportunities and constraints embedded in the structure of the international system (Strange 1988; Cox 1996). This approach is useful for identifying the actual means by which Japan has instrumentalized and carried out its international relations, as in the idea of 'relational power' and 'structural power', that is, respectively, 'the power of A to get B to do something that they would not otherwise do' and the power 'to change the range of choices open to others' (Strange 1988: 24–5). This is because, given the state's pre-war history and domestic society's aversion to the exercise of armed force, Japanese policy-making agents often pursue the interests of the Japanese state and its people by relying upon economic rather than military means. Thus, the ascent of Japan economically is seen to provide a degree of 'structural power' to policy-making agents. The result of this 'structural power' has been that, over the longer term, Japan's extension of regional and global power has come to exhibit the potential to counteract or even undermine the global dominance of the US.

In this way, insights from these diverse theoretical traditions provide the basis for an integrated and comprehensive theoretical approach. This approach provides the tools to answer the 'why' and 'how' of Japan's international relations: that is, the structure and agency accounting for the dominant pattern of Japan's international relations, and the means by which these relations are instrumentalized.

2.3.ii International structures

The basic theoretical approach employed in this volume in order to explain the 'why' of Japan's international relations involves a classic combination of structure and agency. 'Structure' is defined as the external environment in which a state and its people are enmeshed and interact. It consists of other states, global institutions, regional frameworks and organizations, TNCs, NGOs and other political actors.

The structure of the international system is clearly of paramount importance in determining the international relations of a state and its people. It is historically contingent – that is, it is capable of undergoing both gradual and sudden change over time – as can be seen in the shift from bipolarity to multipolarity and back again, as illustrated in the move from bipolarity to multipolarity in the early 1970s and the return to bipolarity at the end of the decade. The transformation in the structure of the international system in turn places different levels of constraint upon a state and its people as well as offering them a new range of opportunities to pursue their international relations.

As noted above in the section on the 'what' of Japan's international relations, Japan's position as a late-starter has meant that it has been forced to interact with an international system shaped largely by the other major industrialized powers. Thus, its pattern of behaviour has been influenced heavily by the structure of the international system, particularly the bilateral relationship with the US. This relationship imposed considerable constraints on the international relations of Japan during the Cold War period. At times, the Japanese state and its people have found the international structure to be overly restrictive and have sought to challenge it by launching their own bid for regional or global hegemony. At other times, they have sought to turn their backs altogether on the restrictions imposed by the structure of the international system and have chosen relative isolation from the world. More usually, however, the Japanese state and its people have chosen to work within the perceived 'realities' of the structure of the international framework by aligning themselves bilaterally with the major powers of the day which have taken the leading role in determining the structure of the international system, a point which will be returned to throughout this book.

The importance of structure in determining the dominant pattern of Japan's international relations also means that, as for other states, fluctuation, change or transformation in the structure of the international system can serve to induce major changes in its international behaviour as well. Hence, as will be seen in the separate chapters dealing with Japan's relations with the US, East Asia, Europe and global institutions, the weakening of the bipolar structure of the international system in the early 1970s and the move to multipolarity lifted some of the constraints placed upon Japan's freedom of diplomatic manoeuvre. This offered a range of new opportunities, as illustrated by the government's move to improve political and economic relations with China and the European Community (EC).

Moreover, it is clear that the dynamic and changing structure of the international system does not just passively place different levels of constraint upon the Japanese state and its people but also offers them a range of opportunities to pursue their international relations. Over and above that, it can impinge actively upon the policy-making process within Japan itself. This is because the bilateral relationship with the US in the post-war era has subjected Japan to a large degree of external pressure, which can make for both initiative as well as inertia in the policy-making process in the political, economic and security dimensions of international relations (Calder 1988a; Vogel 1997).

2.3.iii Domestic agency

To note that the structure of the international system is crucial to any understanding of Japan's international relations is nevertheless not to imply a ready acceptance of the realist or neo-realist position that it is the only or overriding factor which shapes the international relations of a state. The argument of this volume throughout is that Japan as well as other states should not be seen as hermetically-sealed units which are pushed around helplessly by the vagaries of the international system and which ultimately have no control over shaping their own destiny. Instead, Japan's response to, and degree of acquiescence in, the limitations of the structure of the international system is determined by interactions between domestic policy-making agents and a range of other political actors. These actors possess their own perceptions of individual and national interests which may both conform to and conflict with the pressures arising from the structure of the international system. This means that Japanese policy-making agents and other political actors, whilst often aware of the overarching constraints imposed by the international structure, seek to secure their own interests both in conformity and in tension with it. What is more, when necessary, they act in the same way as do policy-makers in the other major industrialized powers in being quite prepared to find ways to circumvent, probe and even challenge the obstacles imposed upon the conduct of their international relations by the structure of the international system.

Just as international structure should be seen, not as a passive, but as an active and dynamic force in shaping the pattern of Japan's international relations, domestic actors also should be seen not as passive and compliant in the face of the structure of the international system, but as working to fashion active policy responses to the constraints and opportunities that it offers. In addition to viewing the policy-making process as an amalgam of a range of policy-making agents and political actors operating within an international structure, it needs to be seen as an amalgam of their different perceptions of interests, too. In other words, Japan's international relations should be viewed as the product of a dialectical, or two-way, relationship between international structure and domestic agency, which determines the actions of the latter in response to the former in the context of interest perceptions.

Accordingly, the following sections aim to open up the Japanese state, to debunk the myth of it as a unitary actor, and to examine domestic agency and the internal policy-making process in Japan. The next sections will then examine the identities of the principal policy actors, the normative and ideational factors which condition their perceived interests, and the processes and outcomes of interaction between them. It is in this way that Japan's response to the international structure and ultimately the dominant pattern of its international relations in the contemporary period can be explained.

2.3.iii.a Policy-making models

The best-known post-war model of Japanese policy-making stresses the elitist nature and high degree of interdependence between its principal actors, identified as the central bureaucracy, big business (*zaikai*)and the governing party, the Liberal-Democratic Party (LDP). Often referred to as the tripartite elite model of policy-making, it echoes the classic study of C. Wright Mills on the American power elite (Mills 1956). A range of accounts of the policy-making process in Japan have not denied competition between the bureaucracy, big business and ruling politicians, but have stressed more their shared human networks and tendency towards collaboration in order to exclude other actors from political influence (Fukui 1972). In this way, the elites have been seen to form an interlocking directorate, or alternatively an 'iron triangle' (Nester 1990), capable of governing Japan's rapid economic development, albeit with the acknowledgement that these elites are subject to infighting and factionalism within themselves as well as between each other.

This tripartite policy-making model is often seen to be dominated by one participant over the others. An early study offered evidence of the overriding importance of the central bureaucracy in the policy-making process, given SCAP's decision to adopt indirect military rule in Japan. This left the bureaucracy basically intact as the Allied Forces needed to rely on it for the implementation of policy (Oka 1958). Indeed, the bureaucracy, with its access to policy-making expertise in the political, economic and security dimensions, has been seen by a range of commentators as the dominant player (Pempel 1979; Johnson 1986). Others have contended that big business has been able to use its financial influence to shape the policy agendas of both the bureaucrats and the politicians (Yanaga 1968; Samuels 1987; Calder 1993); whilst still others have asserted that the LDP's growing policy knowledge, through bodies such as the Policy Affairs Research Council (PARC) (Satō and Matsuzaki 1984; Inoguchi and Iwai 1987; Pempel 1987; Masumi 1995: 253) and its general control over the political system (Ramseyer and McCall Rosenbluth 1993), has enabled LDP politicians to dominate the policy-making process.

It is arguable that, viewed from the perspective of the post-war era as a whole, what these attempts to highlight the dominance of one elite over the other really demonstrate is the increasingly pluralistic nature of policy-making in Japan (Muramatsu and Krauss 1987). This is because, even whilst policy-making tends to remain highly elitist in nature, a host of other political actors do have an input into the final policy outcome depending on the time frame and the specific issue involved (Calder 1997; Calder 1988b). The growing diversity of Japanese society as a whole, and the rise in salience of a range of new political, economic and security issues, mean that it is necessary to consider the policy-making input not just of the tripartite elite, but also of the opposition parties and wider domestic society. This suggests that, where possible, a pluralistic and 'polyarchical' (Milner 1998) model of policy-making in Japan should be adopted.

2.3.iii.b Tripartite elite model

2.3.iii.b.i CENTRAL BUREAUCRACY

The various ministries (*shō*) and agencies (*chō*) of the central bureaucracy located in or close to the Kasumigaseki area of Tokyo have traditionally exercised a strong and often leading influence over foreign policy-making and hence the state's international relations. The central bureaucracy takes general responsibility for undertaking foreign policy initiatives in the dimensions of politics, economics and security; the conduct of negotiations in bilateral and multilateral settings; and the drafting of legislation and treaties related to foreign affairs.

The influence of the central bureaucracy is based largely upon the talent, skill and accumulated policy expertise of its personnel. The 'best and brightest' are highly educated and are drawn from the top universities in Japan, with the University of Tokyo, and in particular its Faculty of Law, typically providing around 80 per cent of Ministry of Foreign Affairs (MOFA) and 90 per cent of Ministry of Finance (MOF) officials (Koh 1989: 67–123; van Wolferen 1990: 111;

Zhao 1993: 124; Johnson 1995: 149; Hartcher 1999: 12–14). Competition to enter the elite ministries is fierce, and successful career stream recruits share a sense of *esprit de corps* and dedication to the service of the state. Indeed, few observers would deny that Japan's bureaucrats have demonstrated remarkable technical competence in guiding their country's political, economic and security relations throughout the post-war era.

In addition to technocratic expertise, the influence of the bureaucrats over the policy-making process has been reinforced by the human networks (*jinmyaku*) that exist both between themselves and *vis-à-vis* other policy-making agents. As already noted, the high numbers of graduates entering the bureaucracy from a limited number of academic institutions tend to create university cliques or factions (*gakubatsu*) within and between ministries. At times, these extend to other graduates from the same institutions in the LDP, big business and wider domestic society. For instance, in the mid-1980s around one-quarter of Diet members and the presidents of 401 out of the top 1,454 largest firms in Japan were graduates of the University of Tokyo (van Wolferen 1990: 111).

Furthermore, the central ministries have succeeded to some extent in actively 'colonizing' the LDP, as approximately one-quarter of party members in both the House of Representatives and the House of Councillors are former bureaucrats (Stockwin 1999: 96). The central bureaucracy, and in particular the economic ministries, have exercised also a degree of influence over big business through the practice of *amakudari* (literally: descent from heaven or 'parachuting from on high'). *Amakudari* involves the placing of retired officials on the boards of companies or quasi-governmental special corporations (*tokubetsu hōjin*), especially in order both to provide a financially lucrative post for the ex-official and to ensure closer relations between the bureaucracy and private sector (Schaede 1995). These ex-bureaucrats have functioned at various times to heighten the influence of the central bureaucracy over the policy-making process.

Thus, the central bureaucracy possesses considerable potential influence over the foreign policy-making process and other policy-making agents, but at the same time the extent of this influence is counteracted by the conflicts of interest which often occur within and between the ministries themselves. As the following sections reveal, the central bureaucracy is not a monolithic actor. What is more, the influence of the principal ministries and agencies themselves is undercut by *nawabari*, or inter-jurisdictional, disputes; limits upon human and financial resources; and competition from other political actors.

2.3.iii.b.i.a Ministry of Foreign Affairs

The ministry chiefly responsible for the day-to-day running of Japanese diplomatic policy is MOFA. Most important, its remit includes the creation and implementation of overall foreign political, economic and security policy; information gathering; and the protection of Japanese nationals overseas (Kusano 1993: 62–3). MOFA employs 5,169 personnel (Tōyō Keizai Shimbunsha 1999: 502) and is divided into nine bureaux: five functional (Foreign Policy; Economic Affairs; Economic Cooperation; Treaties; Intelligence and Analysis) and five regional affairs

(North American; Asian; European and Oceania; Latin American and Caribbean; Middle Eastern and African). The Economic Cooperation Bureau plays a leading role in facilitating the projection of Japan's economic power owing to its general control over the acceptance of requests for and distribution of grant ODA (Orr 1990: 39–44; Kusano 1993: 189). It also plays a role in consulting with other ministries and agencies about the disbursal of Japan's more extensive loan ODA.

The Economic Cooperation Bureau in particular and MOFA more generally have been more concerned than the other involved ministries with formulating an overt political and security strategy for aid distribution (Yasutomo 1986; Inada 1990: 113). This explains the key role they played in producing Japan's 1993 ODA Charter (Rix 1993a). As well as having responsibility for Japan's economic diplomacy, MOFA is responsible for the management of cultural diplomacy through its funding of the Japan Foundation, which plays a crucial role in promoting Japanese culture in the three core regions of the global political economy and elsewhere in the world, and in determining the central features of Japanese security policy.

The most powerful of the bureaux is the North American Affairs Bureau (NAAB). The reason is straightforward: the NAAB supervises the pivotal bilateral relationship with the US. This bureau has been staffed generally by the super-elite of MOFA. These high-flyers often spend time at a US ivy-league institution, or at UK universities and elsewhere, as part of their training. This no doubt helps to explain why MOFA is penetrated by bilateralism (Asai 1989). Many of the elite receive English-language and IR training at graduate schools in the US. The top echelons are groomed for the senior vice-ministerial and ambassadorial positions. The NAAB is devoted to the preservation of the alliance with the US and has given the pro-US and pro-bilateral tilt to MOFA's general policy stance – encapsulated in the occasional media description of MOFA as the 'Kasumigaseki branch consulate of the US embassy in Japan'.

Arguably, the second most powerful bureau is the Asian Affairs Bureau (AAB). It clashes frequently with the NAAB, reflecting Japan's dual and occasionally conflictual interests with regard to the US and East Asia. The AAB, whilst constantly aware of the importance of maintaining healthy bilateral ties with the US as the fundamental priority of Japan's foreign policy, has also sought to promote with caution its interests and ties with East Asia. In particular, the China 'faction' (Mendl 1995: 35) of the AAB's China and Mongolia Division has become increasingly influential as Japan's bilateral relations with China have developed in the post-war era, and the Southeast Asia Divisions have forged a special relationship with ASEAN (Funabashi 1995: 319). The rising influence of the AAB is also demonstrated by the fact that a growing number of its 'Asianist' specialists have reached senior positions within MOFA. For instance, Kuriyama Takakazu, the ex-ambassador to Malaysia, was appointed as vice-minister of MOFA and then ambassador to the US (Calder 1997: 9–10).

The European and Oceania Affairs Bureau (EOAB) and the Economic Affairs Bureau have been the principal coordinators of Japan–Europe political and economic relations. The EOAB's First and Second West Europe Divisions cover political relations with the EU and its member states, but the weaker political links of Japan as a whole with Europe mean that the EOAB is also weaker politically within MOFA, compared to the NAAB and the AAB (Gilson 2000a).

Prime responsibility for relations with the UN rests with the Foreign Policy Bureau, which has sought to promote Japan's participation in PKO and ultimately to secure a permanent seat on the UNSC. In doing so, although wary like the other bureaux of straining the bilateral relationship with the US, the Foreign Policy Bureau has been prepared to take a policy line more vocal and independent of Japan's ally (Gaikō Fōramu 1994).

MOFA functions in many ways as the coordinator of Japan's international relations and as the state's window upon the world. However, its ability to direct and manipulate Japanese foreign policy is constrained by its own internal organizational limitations and the influence it exerts over the other ministries and actors. Despite the vast expansion in Japan's overseas economic and political activities in recent years, MOFA remains understaffed and underfunded compared to the diplomatic services of many other states, with roughly one-half and one-third of the personnel of the UK Foreign and Commonwealth Office and the US Department of State respectively. As a consequence, MOFA is unable to oversee the implementation of many ODA programmes and is notoriously weak in gathering information relating to political and security matters (Chapman *et al.* 1983: 88–9). Factionalism within the different bureaux further hinders effective policy formation, and the adherence to bilateral links with the US means that certain sections of MOFA lack experience of operating in multilateral fora (Funabashi 1995: 321).

Finally, MOFA has no strong political constituency within Japan itself to allow it to push forward its policy agenda. This is illustrated by the ministry's poor representation in the Diet: in 1992, for instance, only three members of the more powerful House of Representatives had MOFA backgrounds (Calder 1997: 9), although the number had increased to six a few years later (Seisaku Jihōsha 1999: 7–9). The result of the ministry's institutional make-up and bilateral outlook is complex, but in general even the top echelons are hesitant to exercise leadership on controversial issues or to act in contravention of perceived US interests. This adds to the tendency of the Japanese state to eschew high-risk policy initiatives in favour of low-key diplomacy.

2.3.iii.b.i.b Ministry of Finance

The Ministry of Finance (MOF) is involved in shaping Japan's foreign policy owing to its role in international monetary and financial matters. Its influence versus that of the other ministries and agencies in the policy-making process rests on its control over their budgets (Fingleton 1995). This can be seen in the case of the budget for grant and loan ODA, and its considerable *amakudari* representation in private sector corporations. It has greater representation in the Diet than MOFA, with 27 ex-officials in the House of Representatives in 1992 (Calder 1997: 9), and 21 a few years later (Seisaku Jihōsha 1999: 7–9). Although at the end of the 1990s MOF's influence was seen to be threatened by a series of domestic corruption scandals, the calls made for root-and-branch reform and the fundamental break-up of this over-mighty ministry remain to be implemented (Eda 1999; Ogino 1998).

MOF has been seen traditionally as most interested in the protection of the domestic banking industry and fiscal rectitude. Its main focus in the past has thus been on ensuring the survival of Japanese banks and the elimination of financial waste. Within the vast ministry, the understaffed International Finance Bureau (155 employees out of a total of 22,394) is the only administrative arm of MOF devoted to international finance – this being despite Japan's position as the largest provider of ODA and the largest creditor in the world.

Nevertheless, as Japan's integration into the international financial system and the pressures arising from the globalization of finance have increased since the breakdown of the Bretton Woods arrangement in the early 1970s, MOF has been forced to deal with a range of global and regional financial issues. The International Trade Bureau (ITB) is thus responsible for the supervision of the international activities of Japanese banks; international exchange rate management; relations with global financial institutions such as the IMF, the WB, the G7 and the OECD; and bail-out packages for debtor countries. As in the case of MOFA, officials often receive training in the US, as with Sakakibara Eisuke, a fluent English-speaker who earned his PhD at the University of Michigan. Until the summer of 1999 he was the vice-minister of international affairs and was thereafter put forward, albeit unsuccessfully, as the Japanese nominee to fill the post of managing director of the IMF.

In East Asia, the ITB and MOF have had a major input in policy decisions over yen loans to China and to other states in the region, working, for instance, to persuade the G7 in 1990 to accept Japan's resumption of bilateral aid to China following the June 1989 Tiananmen Square incident. MOF also has been a powerful force in formulating the developmental policy of the multilateral Asian Development Bank (ADB). The ADB, which receives a large proportion of its funds from Japan, hosts on secondment a number of staff from MOF, usually including the bank's governor. For instance, the present governor, Chino Tadao, the former vice-minister for international finance, was seconded from MOF in 1999. In addition, as seen in Chapter 10, MOF has taken a leading role, alongside MOFA and the Ministry of International Trade and Industry (MITI), in devising financial rescue packages for a number of states in East Asia following the outbreak of currency crises starting in July 1997.

MOF, like all the other ministries, is aware of the US's central role in the international financial system. Consequently, it has often willingly cooperated with the US Treasury in bilateral, regional and global development bank fora in order to stabilize the global economy. In other instances, however, the ministry has been prepared to challenge quietly the US's global and regional financial leadership. Its involvement with the ADB, for instance, is said to have produced an 'Asian Mafia' inside the International Finance Bureau. This group of officials, drawing on the experience of East Asia's and Japan's own 'economic miracles', has become attached since the early 1990s to regional and international developmental strategies which emphasize the role of state guidance and staged liberalization in the promotion of private sector industries, in support of an 'East Asian model' of development. It thus contradicts in many respects the rapid financial and trade liberalization programmes favoured by the US and other proponents of the orthodox neo-liberal agenda in the WB and the IMF.

As a result, MOF has joined MITI in becoming a strong advocate of the developmental state model. It has also worked in combination with other Japanese government ministries to promote this concept within the World Bank by funding the 1993 *East Asian Miracle* report mentioned in Chapter 1. This report attributed much of East Asian economic dynamism to cooperation between the state and private sectors (Yasutomo 1995: 72–102; Wade 1996; World Bank 1993). As Chapter 10 will demonstrate, the developmental state model has come under attack since the onset of the 1997 currency and wider economic crises in East Asia. Despite this, MOF's continuing attachment to the model helps to explain its apparent readiness to contest US and IMF leadership in tackling the financial and wider economic crises in the region, first by proposing a regional Asian Monetary Fund (AMF) in 1997, and then by the announcement of the 'New Miyazawa Initiative' in 1998.

2.3.iii.b.i.c Ministry of International Trade and Industry

MITI's function is to promote Japan's overseas trade and commercial interests. It therefore performs an important role in international trade negotiations, development policy and the distribution of ODA. Its personnel numbered 9,046 in 1998 (Tōyō Keizai Shimbunsha 1999: 611). The ministry is divided into seven bureaux as well as possessing a number of special corporations such as the Japan External Trade Organization (JETRO) – an organization with considerable information-gathering capabilities. The ITB holds the chief responsibility for administering Japan's multilateral economic relations with the WTO, the OECD, the G7, the EU, ASEM, APEC and ASEAN. It also deals with bilateral economic relations with all of Japan's trading partners, including the US and China. The Economic Cooperation Department of the ITB assists in the formulation of Japan's ODA policy. In contrast to MOFA, the Economic Cooperation Department stresses as its priority the commercial and developmental aspects of Japan's ODA policy, especially in East Asia.

MITI has always been cognizant of the importance of the US market and the US-dominated global trading system for Japan's general economic well-being. It thus has sought wherever possible to work within and uphold this framework, as well as to preserve smooth economic relations with the US. At the same time, however, MITI's awareness of the economic opportunities for Japan in East Asia, Europe and other regions means that this ministry, in particular, recently has been prepared to pursue them even if such action threatens and sometimes causes friction with the US. This is related to the generational change within MITI (Schoppa 1999). Indeed, the various bureaux within MITI are far less US-oriented than those of MOFA. Hence, MITI was a supporter of improved relations with China for commercial reasons long before MOFA. It also favoured the continuation of economic relations with communist Vietnam, despite the US's embargo on trade after the Vietnam War (Orr 1990: 37).

In contrast to MOFA, MITI's position in the policy-making process is buttressed by a significant domestic political constituency. This is evidenced in the way business interests often ally themselves with MITI over international economic issues. It can also be seen in the large number of MITI officials who move by *amakudari* into the private business sector. Finally, the representation of MITI in the Diet is relatively high, as illustrated by the thirteen seats held by its ex-officials in the House of Representatives in 1992 (Calder 1997: 9), with eleven a few years later (Seisaku Jihōsha 1999: 7–9). Thus, even though fluctuations do occur in the number of Diet seats secured by bureaucrats from the top ministries, the pecking order remains MOF, MITI and MOFA.

2.3.iii.b.i.d Other ministries and agencies

MOFA, MOF and MITI are the principal ministries involved in determining foreign policy, but the continuing globalization and regionalization of the Japanese political economy, along with the impact of these processes on domestic society, mean a role for other ministries and agencies in the policy-making process. For instance, the Ministry of Agriculture, Forestry and Fisheries (MAFF) has taken a protectionist stance in textile negotiations with China in the 1960s and trade liberalization with APEC in the 1990s. It also has had an input into MOFA's negotiation of fishing rights with South Korea and China.

The Ministry of Posts and Telecommunications has clashed with the Ministry of Education over control of Japan's information industry; and the latter also became embroiled indirectly in the textbook controversy with China and South Korea in the 1980s, as illustrated in Chapter 9. Frequent clashes have also emerged between MITI and the Ministry of Posts and Telecommunications. Similarly, the Ministry of Home Affairs has clashed with the Ministry of Labour over how to respond to the inflow of migrant workers into Japan (Sellek 2000).

Two other parts of the central bureaucracy which have played and continue to play an important role in the foreign policy-making process are the Japan Defence Agency (JDA) and the Prime Minister's Office (PMO or *Sōrifu*). First, the JDA is responsible for the implementation of Japan's defence policy and in 1999 managed the fourth largest military budget in the world, despite the different way of calculating Japan's defence spending, as with the exclusion of pension payments to members of the pre-war military (for details, see Hummel 1996). Despite this, the JDA has not been able to exercise the substantial power in the policy-making process this might imply. This is because other bureaucratic actors, especially MOFA and the PMO, tend to dominate in policy-making on security. The position of the JDA in the policy-making process relates to the ambiguous position of the SDF: in order to avoid the possible revival of Japanese militarism and to ensure full civilian control over the military, the SDF have been placed under the direct command of the prime minister who, along with other ministers of state, must be a civilian in accordance with Article 66 of the Japanese Constitution (Appendix 2.1). Therefore, in contrast to the other major industrialized powers, the JDA has been denied full ministerial status and placed within the administrative structure of the PMO. Its almost 'pariah'-like status is illustrated by the fact that, unlike the key ministries, which are in Kasumigaseki, the JDA has been exiled to the Roppongi area of Tokyo, although a rebuilding programme is now underway. Responsibility for overall security and defence planning has been allocated to MOFA in place of the JDA (Chapman *et al.* 1983: 39–40).

What is more, the JDA has been effectively colonized by the other ministries. Its vice-minister, for instance, generally has been drawn from MITI or MOF. However, in recent years, as Japan's security role has expanded, the JDA has raised its policy profile and begun to push, although as yet unsuccessfully, for ministerial status. Along the way, it has become engaged closely with MOFA in bilateral security planning with the US Department of Defense and Department of State (Funabashi 1997: 111–16). It also has participated in cooperative security dialogue with East Asian states, both bilaterally and multilaterally, through the ARF (Hughes 1996). Nevertheless, despite the JDA's and the SDF's exploration of bilateral and multilateral security dialogue with East Asia, the history and continuing strength of Japan's security links with the US have ensured that both remain stalwarts in support of the bilateral military alliance.

Second, the Prime Minister's Office functions to adjust the conflicting interests of the central bureaucracy and to produce a unified Japanese policy stance. However, the executive leadership of the PMO and the prime minister himself are undermined by a dual weakness: first, a shortage of staff (totalling only eleven, compared to around seventy for the 10 Downing Street office of the UK prime minister, Tony Blair); and second, the fact that most of these staff are drawn from the main ministries (Hayao 1993: 157–83).

To combat these weaknesses, Nakasone Yasuhiro introduced an independent Cabinet Councillors' Office on External Affairs and a Cabinet Security Affairs Office in 1986. It was hoped this would improve the coordination of foreign and security policy between the Cabinet and ministries. However, as the membership of the Cabinet Councillors' Office on External Affairs consisted of officials on loan from the main ministries, inter-ministerial disputes were not resolved but merely carried over into this body and effective policy-making hindered (Kusano 1993: 75–7). Added to these institutional shortcomings, the fact that the premiership changes in Japan with such relative rapidity – with twenty-five different prime ministers between 1945 and 1999 in Japan, compared to eleven in the same period in the UK – does not assist continuity in executive leadership in Japan's international relations (Stockwin 1998).

Despite these institutional weaknesses, however, the prime minister of the day still occasionally retains a crucial and decisive role in the shaping of foreign policy. Domestically, prime ministers have made use of *ad hoc* study groups, composed of private sector experts drawn from the business, academic and wider communities in order to activate debate between policy-making agents and other political actors on key issues (Drifte 1990: 17). For example, Ōhira Masayoshi commissioned a number of study groups which devised the concepts of Comprehensive National Security and Pacific Basin cooperation. Again, Hosokawa Morihiro (1993–4) introduced a Prime Minister's Advisory Group on Defence which initiated MOFA's and the JDA's revision of the National Defence Programme Outline in 1996. Internationally, the proliferation of summits has provided prime ministers, such as Nakasone, with an opportunity to grandstand their diplomatic skills,

Plate 2.2 Whose round? LDP statesmen and kingmakers Miyazawa Kiichi, Takeshita Noboru, Nakasone Yasuhiro and Abe Shintarō play drinking and political games at Nakasone's mountain retreat in October 1987. This scene represents the close-knit nature of the 1955 political system. Two weeks later, Takeshita succeeded Nakasone as prime minister.

Source: Courtesy of Mainichi Shimbunsha

heighten their international and domestic political standing, and pledge Japan to undertake some bold new international policy initiatives (Saito 1990).

Crucially, prime ministers have usually enjoyed sufficient reserves of moral authority to carry the governing party, bureaucracy and domestic society with them in order to achieve at least one major foreign policy goal, although their interest in foreign policy-making was often outweighed by the incentives of the electoral system (revised in 1994) to pay attention to constituency services and interests, as touched on below. Thus, Hatoyama Ichirō (1954–6) was able to effect the normalization of relations with the USSR in 1956; Kishi Nobusuke (1957–60) the revision of the US–Japan security treaty in 1960; Satō Eisaku (1964–72) the return of Okinawa to Japan in 1972; Tanaka Kakuei (1972–4) the normalization of relations with China in 1972; Fukuda Takeo (1976–8) the 1976 Fukuda Doctrine and improved relations with ASEAN; Suzuki Zenkō (1980–2) the patrolling of the sea lines of communication; Nakasone Yasuhiro (1982–7) the formal breaking of the 1 per cent of GNP ceiling on defence spending, the agreement on the exchange of defence-related technology with the US, and the strengthening of relations with South Korea; Takeshita Noboru (1987–9) the settlement of the bilateral construction dispute with the US; Miyazawa Kiichi (1991–3) the passage of the PKO Bill in 1992; Hashimoto Ryūtarō (1996–8) the reconfirmation of the US–Japan security treaty, initialization of the revision of the 1978 Guidelines for US–Japan Defence Cooperation (hereafter, 1978 Guidelines) and improvement in Russo-Japanese relations; and Obuchi Keizō (1998–2000) the passage of the revised Guidelines formulated in September 1997 through the Japanese Diet in spring 1999 (hereafter, 1999 Guidelines).

2.3.iii.c Liberal-Democratic Party and the transition in the party system

The LDP has traditionally been the subject of much public and academic derision insofar as foreign policy-making is concerned. This derives from the party's apparent deference to the central bureaucracy, lack of policy vision in the international sphere and greater interest in constituency politics than in Japan's place in the world. In this last regard, until electoral reform in 1994, election to the Diet involved politicians in a high degree of personalized politics. Electoral reform introduced new disclosure rules on campaign financing and the move away from multi-member constituencies to a dual system of first-past-the-post single-member constituencies and proportional representation (Stockwin 1999: 126–9). This has gone some way to combating the former tendency, engendered by personalized politics, for politicians to avoid taking a stance on international issues in favour of low-key policy statements and a focus on the particular interests of the voters at the grassroots level (Curtis 1988).

Nevertheless, as a member of the tripartite elite, the party has since its formation in 1955 exercised a crucial role in determining the course of Japan's international relations. Political parties, in particular the LDP, are able to shape Japan's foreign policy agenda owing to their increasing policy-making expertise *vis-à-vis* the central bureaucracy; their role in adjusting the interests of the various elite state and non-state actors; and their democratic mandate as elected representatives. This allows them to project onto the policy-making process the interests of pressure groups and wider domestic society as a whole. What is more, the members of the Diet possess the ultimate sanction over the state's foreign policy as they control the passage in the Diet of defence, ODA and ministerial budgets, as well as legislation relating to foreign political, economic and security matters. As will be seen in Chapter 9, the political parties and their individual members also serve at times as active intermediaries between the Japanese state and its people and the external international structure, as they take on a role in conducting personal diplomacy (*kojin gaikō*) and party-to-party diplomacy (*seitōkan gaikō*) with influential policy-making agents in other states.

The LDP has been without doubt the dominant political party in the post-war era and a key player in the foreign policy-making process. Following its formation in 1955 as a result of the merger of the conservative Liberal and Democratic parties, the LDP's dominance rested upon its absolute majorities in both the House of Representatives and the House of Councillors, and its working links with the central bureaucracy and the business community. This '1955 political system' (*55 nen [seiji] taisei*) ensured LDP one-party governance in Japan and the relative marginalization of the Social Democratic Party of Japan (as mentioned in the Note on the text, the SDPJ was known in English as the Japan

Socialist Party (JSP) before 1991); the Japan Communist Party (JCP), *Kōmeitō* (Kōmei Party or Clean Government Party, hereafter, Kōmei Party, formed originally in 1964) and other political parties. It is also known as the 'one-and-a-half party system', an expression coined in order to capture the dominance in the Diet of the LDP and the weakness of the main opposition party, the SDPJ, throughout most of the post-war era.

The 1955 system began to break down in 1989 when the LDP lost its majority in the elections for the upper house, the House of Councillors, and then collapsed altogether as a consequence of the breakaway of splinter parties from the LDP and the formation of new parties in 1992–4 (for details, see Kitaoka 1995; Nihon Seijigakkai 1996; Stockwin 1999: 132–61). These included the Japan New Party (JNP, or *Nihon Shintō* formed in 1992) and the New Frontier Party (NFP, or *Shinshintō* formed in 1994). The LDP lost power following the 1993 general election, when the party split and a large number of elected LDP members bolted from the party, enough to form new parties. In this way, although the party lost only three seats compared with its strength before the election, the loss of its majority in the lower and more powerful House of Representatives accelerated the transition in the party system. LDP one-party governance was replaced for a brief period by an anti-LDP coalition under the prime ministership of the JNP leader, Hosokawa Morihiro, which included the SDPJ, the NFP and other conservative and left-of-centre parties. Nevertheless, the LDP soon regained political power by forming a coalition with its erstwhile political enemy, the SDPJ, and even installed the leader of the party, Murayama Tomiichi, as prime minister (1994–6). Then, having clawed back its majority in the House of Representatives following the 1996 general election and the return to the fold of a number of individual Diet members, the LDP was able to form a single-party government between 1996 and 1998 under the leadership of Hashimoto Ryūtarō.

In the meantime, the opposition parties regrouped, with the SDPJ declining in political strength and losing its position as the main opposition party, moderate former NFP members and SDPJ splinter groups merging to form the centrist and new main opposition Democratic Party of Japan (DPJ, formed in 1996 and reconstituted in 1998), and the remainder of the NFP and other smaller conservative parties reconstituting themselves as the Liberal Party (LP, formed in 1998) under the leadership of the ex-LDP secretary-general, Ozawa Ichirō. The LDP has maintained its majority in the House of Representatives, but its defeat in the House of Councillors' elections in 1998 forced it to enter into a coalition government with the LP and later the Kōmei Party (see below) in order to gain a working majority in the Diet. The consequences for Japan's foreign policy of the breakdown of the 1955 system and the rise of new political parties will be explored throughout this and the later section on other political parties. At this point it is sufficient to note that since 1955 – and even allowing for the brief interruption in LDP government between 1993 and 1994 – the LDP has remained the main party in power and the overall dominant political party in determining Japan's international relations.

The LDP is a 'catch-all', diverse political party, which is reflected in its make-up and the party's complex and shifting range of views on Japan's international relations. The overall conservative, pro-bilateral orientation of the party has nevertheless meant that, throughout the Cold War and post-Cold War periods, the great constant of the party's foreign policy stance has been support for bilateral alignment with the US. This has remained the fundamental basis and framework for Japan's political, economic and security relations with the world bar none. For, as will be explained in detail in later parts of this book, the most influential body of opinion within the LDP has coalesced around a foreign policy of being prepared to work in line with US interests in order to improve Japan's relations with East Asia, Europe and global institutions. Within this context, the LDP has laboured hard throughout both the Cold War and post-Cold War periods to preserve domestic support for the security alliance and wider relationship with the US. During the Cold War, for instance, this meant that the LDP often advocated support by the Japanese government for US client states in East Asia, such as the provision of ODA to South Korea and South Vietnam, and usually voted in accordance with US pressure on issues such as the Korean Peninsula and the representation of communist China in the UN (Dobson 1998: 261). In the post-Cold War period, for instance, the party has invited into a coalition the LP (1999–2000), which has advocated a much more proactive line on Japan's military cooperation with the US.

Indeed, the differing backgrounds of the party's membership also mean that alternative bodies of opinion have arisen periodically which have doubted Japan's interests in these regions, institutions and dimensions to the exclusion of others. These forces have sometimes challenged the official LDP line, even whilst being conscious of the need to avoid the image of the LDP's open dissension from US policy, which would risk harming the overall US–Japan bilateral relationship. The most notable example of this type of counter opinion was the debate that raged in the LDP over the normalization of relations with China during the first half of the Cold War period. This debate is discussed in Chapter 9, but essentially revolved around a strong current of opinion in the LDP which argued that, even within the framework of US containment policy in East Asia, Japan needed to exploit all possible avenues in order to improve relations with its giant communist neighbour, overcome the legacy of imperialism and the Cold War, and, most importantly, regain access to traditional markets in mainland China. The decision was not an easy one, however: the LDP split between, on one side, study groups of LDP members in favour of improved relations with communist China, and, on the other, study groups which formed a 'Taiwan lobby'. LDP 'policy tribes' (*zoku*) – consisting of party members with a specific interest in a policy issue or region, and often with policy-making experience at the ministerial level – in this way sought to influence the formation of LDP policy (Inoguchi and Iwai 1987). They play a similar role in areas such as trade liberalization and defence. Moreover, the LDP, although watchful of a positive or negative reaction from the US, has increasingly pushed Japan's independent national interests by supporting research into Japan's participation in military PKO and MOFA's quest for a permanent seat on the UNSC, as will be seen in Chapter 19.

The LDP's differing internal policy stances towards various foreign policy issues have been manifested and mediated through individual power-brokers in the LDP; official party policy institutions; factions (*habatsu*), split along lines of loyalty to particular powerful LDP leaders or split by particular issues; study groups; and the above-mentioned *zoku* or 'policy tribes'. Whereas the relationship with the US has remained fairly constant in the sense that the key policy-making agents have maintained a strong attachment to the US–Japan bilateral relationship, certain influential LDP politicians and faction leaders have been able to effect changes in Japan's international relations with East Asia, Europe and elsewhere over the short and long terms.

In the case of East Asia, for example, Tanaka Kakuei, after campaigning for the LDP party presidency and position of prime minister on the issue, was able to push for rapid normalization of relations with China in 1972. Other figures, such as the ex-prime ministers Takeshita Noboru and Nakasone Yasuhiro, have been involved over a number of years in patiently building up support within the LDP for Japan's links with China and South Korea by a process of forging ties with the political elites of these states. In the case of Europe, Prime Minister Ikeda proposed the establishment of trilateral relations between Japan, the US and Europe. More recently, the former prime minister Hata Tsutomu (1994–) has been an active Europhile who headed the Japan–EU Inter-Parliamentary Delegation. In the case of global institutions, politician Ozawa Ichirō, leader of the LP, and MOFA bureaucrat Owada Hisashi, permanent representative of Japan to the UN (1994–8), have both promoted a more salient role for Japan in the work of the UN. Ozawa, in particular, has sought to promote Japan's peacekeeping in the UN, regardless of constitutional constraints, by appealing to the UN Charter and as part of his attempt to make Japan into a 'normal state' (Ozawa 1994).

The LDP internal institution which has taken chief responsibility for articulating the party's official policy line has been PARC's foreign affairs division. This has researched and produced reports, often in conjunction with policy advice from the central bureaucracy, concerning political, economic and security issues such as relations with East Asia and the future of the US–Japan relationship (Nakajima 1999: 100). Indeed, in early 1996 PARC took a proactive lead into research for the revision of the 1978 Guidelines. This later became the basis of the Japan–US Joint Declaration on Security (Appendix 6.1) in April of the same year, to initiate the central bureaucracy's own research into the revision of the 1978 Guidelines, and to lead eventually to the strengthening of the US–Japan alliance, as will be examined in Chapter 6.

The often ferocious intra-party debates between factions and study groups have also had a vital input in deciding the LDP's official foreign policy line. Individual party members have promoted their foreign policy interests as well, by forging temporary political alliances on certain issues with other political parties or by calling on personal links with the leaders of parties. At various times cross-party groups have been active in seeking to influence the foreign policy-making process, as in the case of the Dietmen's Leagues for the Promotion of Japan–North Korea Friendship, Japan–China Friendship, and Comprehensive Security; and the Japan–EU Inter-Parliamentary Delegation; all of which have attempted to improve Japan's foreign relations by exchanges at the political party level.

The differing stances and allegiances of LDP members mean, therefore, that party policy on various aspects of Japan's international relations is subject to a range of conflicts. At times these conflicts remain unresolved and can produce stalemate and fence-sitting. This helps to account for the often immobilist, Janus-faced and apparently abnormal nature of Japan's international relations, as was touched on in Chapter 1. At other times, the conflicts can be settled and a dramatic change in Japan's policy produced by the victory of one faction over another, occasioned by careful internal negotiations, external pressure or a major change in the structure of the international system. Regardless of whether these internal policy debates produce dynamism or immobilism, however, the point is that they demonstrate the importance of domestic agency in determining Japan's international relations. For even though the LDP as the main conservative party and guardian of the bilateral relationship with the US has in the final outcome usually chosen to place paramount importance on Japan–US relations in comparison to relations with other regions or global institutions, another salient feature of Japanese foreign policy cannot be denied. That is, the Japanese state and its people have shown a propensity to test and exploit any flexibility in the structural limits imposed upon them by the US in order to inch towards fuller engagement with even those states and institutions at apparent loggerheads with US interests.

2.3.iii.d Business community

Japan's private sector business community, which consists of large TNCs and business conglomerates and associations, completes the third side of the 'iron triangle' model of policy-making in Japan. Small and medium-sized enterprises, and business cooperatives, are also part of the wider business community. Business interests exercise influence over the foreign policy-making process and the general pattern of Japan's international relations because of their close financial and human network connections with the LDP and other political parties; the natural constituency and links that they form with the economic ministries of MITI and MOF; and the role that they can play as international actors in their own right, either independently or in cooperation with Japanese government policies, by serving on government committees and as a result of their extensive trading and investment links in the US, East Asia, Europe and other parts of the globe.

The basic interest of the Japanese business community is clearly to advance profitable private sector links with the US, Europe, East Asia and elsewhere, but as with the central bureaucracy and the LDP, the business community should not be viewed as a unitary actor. The views of the *zaikai* are represented by the four business federations: Federation of Economic Organizations (*Keidanren*); Japan Council for Economic Development (*Keizai Dōyūkai*); Japan Chamber of Commerce (*Nihon Shōkō Kaigi Shō*); and Japan Federation of Employers' Associations (*Nikkeiren*). The *Keidanren* is the largest federation, with 800 of Japan's largest corporations and 110 industry-wide groups as members (Calder 1997: 180). It has taken a lead in promoting Japanese FDI abroad and the liberalization of the Japanese economy. Throughout much of the post-war era and until it officially announced a halt in 1993, the *Keidanren* also provided massive funding to the LDP as a means to gain indirect influence on policy. More directly, members of the *Keidanren* and other business associations often take up places on the government's special advisory committees (*shingikai* and *chōsakai*). These offer a direct way to articulate business interests and to try to influence international economic and other policies (Schwartz 1998). Ranged against the big business organizations are associations, such as the National Association of Agricultural Cooperatives (*Nōgyō Kyōdō Kumiai* or *Nōkyō*) (for details, see Pempel 1998), which have allied with MAFF in order to slow down the pace of agricultural trade liberalization in the international bodies of APEC and the WTO.

The business community is active internationally in a number of ways. Japanese businesses, especially the general trading companies (*sōgō shōsha*), enjoy extensive information-gathering abilities on economic and political conditions in various regions, which are believed to exceed those of MOFA and even JETRO. Business intelligence is also backed by extensive personal links with the political and economic elites of states such as Indonesia (Nishihara 1976), and transnational business interests in the Trilateral Commission (Gill 1990). In addition, Japanese firms have built up strong lobbying capacities in the developed democracies of Europe and the US, with up to 120 agents actively petitioning in the US Congress alone (Choate 1990: 250–6). The competition between states to attract Japanese FDI also means that private business enterprises can exercise power over national governments and bargain for the best investment conditions. Hence, it has become commonplace for statesmen from the three core regions when visiting Japan to call first on the heads of major corporations such as Sony and Toyota, before then going on to pay their respects to Japanese government leaders.

The overseas activities of Japanese TNCs and other business corporations have at times been seen to have complemented and assisted the Japanese government's foreign policy objectives. For instance, East Asia has clearly been attractive to many Japanese businesses in the post-war era because of its raw materials and energy resources, and increasingly since the 1970s as a low-cost production and re-export platform as well as a growing market for consumer goods. Hence, business corporations have often been in the vanguard of efforts to engage Japan more fully in the region, and have supported the Japanese government's efforts. Big, medium and small enterprises alike have used their close links with the LDP and bureaucracy to push for the improvement of economic and political relations with nearly all of the states of the region, including those which during the Cold War were on the opposite side of the bilateral divide, such as China and North Vietnam. Indeed, during the Cold War many businesses exploited their position as private sector actors in order to circumvent the structure of political and economic isolation imposed by the US upon the Japanese state's relations with the region, and thus cooperated actively in the government's policy of *seikei bunri*, to provide a dynamic input into Japan's relations with East Asia.

Still, even though the business community has at various times and in various regions demonstrated a propensity to cooperate with Japanese government policy, the increasing globalization and regionalization of Japanese business and the mobility of capital means that the government has only a limited capacity for controlling the activities of corporations and cannot coerce them into cooperation. The Japanese government can in fact only create the political and economic conditions, through the distribution of ODA and working to stabilize diplomatic relations and similar activity, which serve to encourage Japanese firms to trade and invest with other states. Thus, as Chapter 9 will demonstrate, the lack of business interest in North Korea has added to the factors which have rendered immobile Japan's engagement policy towards this state.

2.3.iii.e Other political parties

As noted above, the 1955 political system normally precluded the other political parties, whether on the left or the right of the political spectrum, from exerting a level of influence on Japan's foreign policy similar to that of the LDP. Nevertheless, even during the Cold War period, these other parties were at times able to exercise some influence upon the pattern of Japan's international relations owing to their role in both impeding and facilitating the policy of the LDP and central bureaucracy. Moreover, since the end of the Cold War and the collapse of the 1955 system, along with the LDP's concurrent need to enlist the support of other political parties in coalition governments, the role of these parties has arguably been enhanced. Certainly, the end of the 1955 system has created a more fluid situation for shaping Japan's international relations.

2.3.iii.e.i SOCIAL DEMOCRATIC PARTY OF JAPAN

In contrast to the LDP, which generally sought to work within the structural limitations imposed by the bilateral relationship with the US, the SDPJ, the main opposition party during the Cold War period, worked to loosen and indeed reject the limitations imposed by the US and the LDP upon the pattern of Japan's international relations. The SDPJ has clearly shared with certain sections of the LDP an interest in promoting Japan's economic relations, and the improvement of ties with all the regions of the world. In comparison with some of the LDP's more outspoken supporters of Japan's colonial policies in East Asia, however, the party has been concerned to try to 'right the wrongs' of the past, especially in respect of the ex-colonies in East Asia. This can be seen, for instance, in the party's support for greater recompense for the damage these colonies suffered during the years of Japanese occupation, as illustrated in the recent case of the SDPJ's efforts to ensure that the voices of Korean and other 'comfort women' (women used as sexual slaves by the Japanese military during the war) were able to influence the Diet policy-making discussions on compensation for their suffering.

Most important, the anti-militarist stance taken by the SDPJ during the Cold War meant that, until the 1994 advent of the Murayama administration, the official party line was to reject the LDP's and MOFA's support for the constitutionality of the SDF and the US–Japan security treaty. The SDPJ thus resisted US containment policy through opposition to the deployment of US troops in Japan, as was mentioned earlier and will be examined in detail in Chapters 3 and 6; it also opposed the Japanese government's decision, described in more detail in Part II and Part III, on a range of international issues. This is illustrated by the party's opposition to a 'partial peace', the LDP's official policy stance of one-sided support for Taiwan over China until 1972, and for South Korea over North Korea

Plate 2.3 Reviewing the troops after reviewing policy. Despite traditional attachment to the anti-militarist norm, the SDPJ shifted to more centrist positions in the 1990s. The review of the Self-Defence Forces in October 1995 by the socialist prime minister, Murayama Tomiichi, can be seen as a culmination of this process.

Source: Courtesy of Mainichi Shimbunsha

throughout the Cold War and beyond. The SDPJ regarded the Japanese government's and the LDP's policy as a confirmation of national divisions in the region, and, consequently, also opposed the government's support for the US war effort in the 1960s and early 1970s in a divided Vietnam. Instead, the SDPJ advocated that Japan should rely on a UN-centred security policy and be prepared to engage in multilateral political and security dialogue in East Asia and beyond. This is illustrated by the party's participation in a joint 1978 proposal with the Australian and New Zealand socialist parties for a nuclear-free zone in the Asia Pacific (Kawakami 1994: 48) and the party's constant support for the creation of an economic zone of cooperation in the Sea of Japan, which is seen to enhance general interdependence and stability between Japan and its East Asian neighbours.

Nevertheless, even as the SDPJ opposed official LDP policy in East Asia and other regions, party members still saw grounds for bipartisan cooperation on certain issues, including the improvement of political relations between Japan and North Korea, as will be described in Chapter 9. Furthermore, with the end of the Cold War and the SDPJ's entry into a coalition government with the LDP, which as mentioned above was accompanied by the party's first official acceptance of the constitutionality of the SDF and the US–Japan security treaty, cooperative relations between the LDP and SDPJ have been strengthened on issues such as

Japan's participation in non-military UNPKO and the search for a permanent UNSC seat. Still, the main impact of the SDPJ's decision to enter into coalition governments with the LDP has been actually to facilitate the loosening of some of the domestic political restraints upon the Japanese government's and the LDP's hold on the foreign policy-making process. This is because, even though, as will be discussed in Chapter 6, the party has continued to oppose staunchly the extension of Japan's bilateral military cooperation with the US in East Asia and globally, the principal effect of the SDPJ's declining political strength and breaching of its own anti-militaristic taboos has been to weaken the anti-militaristic norm in Japan and to open the way for the concomitant strengthening of the US–Japan alliance and Japan's independent, bilateral and multilateral security role in East Asia and UNPKO.

2.3.iii.e.ii KŌMEI PARTY

The Kōmei Party (*Kōmeitō*) is the political arm of *Sōka Gakkai*, a conservative lay Buddhist religious organization (White 1970). In its various reincarnations the party has wavered between opposition to, and cautious cooperation with, the LDP in both the Cold War and post-Cold War periods. During the period of political flux following the collapse of LDP government in 1993, the party merged with the NFP when it was formed in December 1994 (see section 2.3.iii.c). The NFP collapsed in December 1997 and the Kōmei Diet members re-emerged as the New Party Peace (*Shintō Heiwa*). In November 1998 the New Kōmei Party was created by the amalgamation of the New Party Peace and the Kōmei Party.

The LDP has often been alarmed at the rise of the Kōmei Party as a highly-organized and competitive conservative party, and attacked it for its religious associations. As at the time of normalization of relations with China, however, leaders of both parties have been prepared to cooperate in realizing a shared foreign policy goal. Since October 1999, moreover, the LDP has been prepared to work with both it and the LP in a coalition government. In the dimension of security and relations with the US, the Kōmei Party has over the years moved closer to the official LDP policy line, as seen in its gradual acceptance of the constitutionality of the SDF and the US–Japan security treaty. It also has offered support for attempts to strengthen the alliance with the US in the post-Cold War period. Nevertheless, differences on security also remain as the party, constrained by the anti-military stance of many of its supporters, has traditionally stressed a UN-centred security policy and participation in PKO on a non-military basis.

2.3.iii.e.iii LIBERAL PARTY

Further on the right of the political spectrum, the LP has emerged as the second main conservative party. The LP's main impact in shaping Japan's international relations has been in the dimension of security. Like the LDP, the LP advocates the maintenance of a strong US–Japan alliance. Indeed, one of the party's motivations for entering the coalition government with the LDP in January 1999 was to ensure the passage of legislation on the revised Guidelines. At the same time, however, the LP also goes beyond LDP policy in the realm of security, as seen in its call for the government to change its interpretation of the Japanese Constitution to allow Japan to exercise the right of collective self-defence and for the SDF to participate fully in military UNPKO across the globe (Ozawa 1999; Hook and McCormack 2001). The LP's radical proposals look unlikely to alter immediately the LDP's and government's cautious security policy stance. Nevertheless, as will be seen in the later section on norms, the LP's leader, Ozawa Ichirō, has undoubtedly played a crucial role in creating the conditions for a domestic political debate which favours a more proactive military role for Japan, both bilaterally within the framework of the US–Japan alliance, and more independently within the framework of the UN.

2.3.iii.e.iv DEMOCRATIC PARTY OF JAPAN

On the left of the political centre, the DPJ has emerged as the successor to the SDPJ. The DPJ's mix of ex-SDPJ and NFP members means that, because of divergent views, formulating a unified policy stance on many international issues has been fraught with difficulty. In the dimension of US–Japan relations and security, for instance, the DPJ favours the maintenance of the bilateral relationship, but is more willing than the LDP to consider the eventual scaling-down of the presence of US bases in Japan, and emphasizes more strongly the importance of multilateral security frameworks in East Asia. It is thus critical of the LP's stance on the Constitution (Hatoyama 1999). The DPJ also matches the LDP in seeking a permanent UNSC seat, but generally remains more cautious on participation in military PKO, stressing Japan's constitutional limitations, and instead lays emphasis on the importance of Japan's non-military contribution to international stability through the use of ODA. In the same fashion as the other parties, the DPJ seeks to promote better relations with all the states of East Asia and Europe.

2.3.iii.e.v JAPAN COMMUNIST PARTY

In contrast to the SDPJ, the JCP has remained implacably opposed to the LDP and government policy in most regions and dimensions throughout the Cold War and post-Cold War periods. The JCP has criticized the US–Japan alliance as an extension of US imperialism in East Asia and globally, and calls instead for Japan to adopt a policy of neutralism and to promote equally ties with all the states of the world (Bōei Handobokku 1999: 694–5). The result of the JCP's refusal up until the present day to cooperate with the government and the party's reluctance to enter into coalitions with other opposition parties at the national level has been to limit severely its input in the foreign policy-making process, other than acting as one of the political forces which exercises indirect veto pressure. However, at times the JCP has at least served as a conduit for information between Japan and certain communist states, and its influence may increase in the coming years as its electoral support has undergone a small resurgence since the 1996 general election. Indeed, at the cusp of the twenty-first century, it is beginning to show signs of being prepared to work with the other opposition parties in an anti-LDP alliance.

2.3.iii.f Domestic society

Beyond these policy-making agents is a range of other political actors in wider domestic society. Although these actors are not normally regarded as direct contributors to the foreign policy-making process in orthodox realist approaches to IR, depending on the issue and time frame adopted, all of them can be seen to exert to some extent at least both general and specific influences on Japan's international relations. These include the mass media, think-tanks, the academic community, sub-state political authorities, pressure groups, NGOs, social movements and public opinion. Although full justice cannot be done to each of these as political actors, either below or in the following chapters, the end of the Cold War, together with the globalization and regionalization of Japan's international relations in the political, economic and security dimensions, has provided increasing opportunities for such non-state actors to exert an influence on Japan's international relations.

2.3.iii.f.i MASS MEDIA

The mass media have a potentially enormous role in shaping the agenda of Japan's international relations owing to the saturation of Japanese society with newspapers and television stations (Feldman 1993; Pharr and Krauss 1996). The daily circulation of Japan's national newspapers (*Yomiuri Shimbun*, 14.3 million; *Asahi Shimbun*, 12.9 million; *Mainichi Shimbun*, 6 million; *Nihon Keizai Shimbun (Nikkei)*, 4.6 million; *Sankei Shimbun*, 2.9 million) (McCargo 1996: 252) far surpasses that of other developed states (*New York Times*, 1 million; *The Times* (London), 500,000; *France Soir*, 500,000); and each of these newspapers is usually linked to a *keiretsu* network of television stations and publishing houses. The Japanese media have occasionally exercised their power in the past by raising public awareness on issues such as the 1960 security treaty revision (discussed in Part II) and the 1990–1 Gulf War (discussed in Part V); bringing down major LDP politicians, or at least making them uncomfortable, through digging up and covering bribery and other scandals (Farley 1996).

The stance they take is seen by some observers to result from a degree of political bias, with the *Asahi* and *Mainichi* generally aligned with opposition forces, and the *Yomiuri*, *Nikkei* and *Sankei* taking a more pro-conservative line. Furthermore, the structure of the international system has also occasionally impinged on the Japanese media in order to influence the domestic discourse on Japan's international relations. As Chapter 9 will demonstrate, the Chinese government has frequently attempted to manipulate the media and public opinion in Japan, using 'people's diplomacy', to effect a change in the government's policy towards China. However, the overall influence of the media on the policy-making process is reduced by the press club (*kisha kurabu*) system. This system ensures that journalists are attached to, and can obtain only heavily-managed news information from, a particular government department, political party or private sector business institution.

2.3.iii.f.ii THINK-TANKS

A range of think-tanks and policy institutions does exist, although many of them lack a truly independent policy stance as they are linked to either the government establishment or major business enterprises. As a result of burgeoning think-tank activity, the year 1970 is usually regarded as 'the first year of Japanese think-tanks' (*shinku tanku gannen*) (Noda 1995: 384). This suggests their late arrival on the scene in Japan in comparison with the other major industrialized powers, although their existence was not unknown before the 1970s. As far as the ministries are concerned, MOFA has created the Japan Institute for International Affairs, and MOF the Japan Centre for International Finance. The Institute for International Policy Studies draws researchers from the ministries, academia and the private sector, and has generated debate in particular on security policy, although, again, the institute's policy orientation is strongly influenced by its association with the ex-prime minister, Nakasone Yasuhiro. Private sector research institutes include the Nomura and Mitsubishi institutes. These think-tanks have raised the sophistication of the debate on Japan's international relations, but continue to suffer from their focus on the dissemination of information to their corporate sponsors rather than to wider international and domestic audiences (Ueno 1998). It should also be noted that, as part of its strategy to ensure a continuing influence on the policy-making process, irrespective of the party in power, the *Keidanren* in April 1997 inaugurated its own research institute, the Twenty-First Century Policy Institute (*Nijūisseiki Seisaku Kenkyūjo*).

2.3.iii.f.iii ACADEMIC COMMUNITY

Members of the academic community seek to influence the policy-making process through their role as policy experts and intellectual leaders. Some act as government supporters or advisers, as in the invitation of professors from top universities to sit on the government's special advisory committees and to provide briefings for political and bureaucratic policy-makers. For others, however, the preferred option has been to remain at a distance from such official positions in the government and to remain active in the wider policy debates, or to act more generally as government opponent and critic. In the field of international relations, for instance, the roles of leading intellectual figures such as Kōsaka Masataka of Kyoto University and Sakamoto Yoshikazu of Tokyo University were crucial to the policy debates on Japanese security policy in the 1960s and 1970s. The former favoured achieving Japan's peace and security through the maintenance of the US–Japan security treaty (Kōsaka 1963); the latter, in contrast, sought to achieve them through rescinding the treaty and forging a new security arrangement with the UN (Sakamoto 1959). Whereas Kōsaka played his role close to the government, as evidenced by his participation in government advisory panels such as the Comprehensive Security Study Group, Sakamoto played his role more at arm's length, through the media and social movements. With the pluralization of media sources, along with changes in Japanese society, a younger generation of academic leaders is now unable to exert the same level of influence on the foreign policy-making process and on domestic society as did these intellectual titans, but the academic community continues to play a significant role in influencing the pattern of Japan's international relations. This can be seen, for instance, in the role played by Professor Yamazawa Ippei of Hitotsubashi University as one of the eminent persons involved in the APEC process (Funabashi 1995).

2.3.iii.f.iv SUB-STATE POLITICAL AUTHORITIES

The role of sub-state political authorities – that is, cities, prefectures and other local governments – in Japan's international relations has a long tradition dating back to the 1950s, when city and prefectural assemblies passed resolutions at odds with the central government's policy of supporting the US's global and regional security strategies. This can be seen, for instance, in the wave of resolutions passed in opposition to the US's March 1954 hydrogen bomb test at Bikini atoll, Marshall Islands, which led to the exposure of Japanese fishermen to radiation, despite being aboard a vessel outside of the restricted testing area (A-Bomb Committee 1979: 575–6). It is also evident in the actions taken by a number of local authorities to curtail the government's cooperation with US fighting in the Vietnam War. Examples include the deployment of local ordinances to prevent public roads from being used by US military vehicles. Similarly, protests against the entry of US warships bearing nuclear weapons have been made by port towns around Japan, as in the city of Kobe's declaration of a nuclear-free port (Ishiyama 1985). Finally, it has emerged concretely in the efforts by prefectural governments from especially the 1980s onwards to develop their own foreign policy. This can be seen, for instance, in the case of Kanagawa prefectural government's promotion of 'people-to-people diplomacy' (Nihon Toshi Sentā 1995; Nagasu and Sakamoto 1983).

At the same time, sub-state political authorities in recent years have been playing an active role in promoting the creation of economic zones of cooperation with other sub-national parts of East Asia, breaking down the boundaries of the state. This is illustrated by the case of the city and prefecture of Fukuoka, which are attempting to promote the creation of the Yellow Sea Zone in cooperation with sub-national parts of China and the Korean Peninsula (Kokusai Higashi Ajia Kenkyū Senta 1995). Another example is that of the city and prefecture of Niigata, which are attempting to promote the Japan Sea Zone in cooperation with sub-national parts of the Russian Far East, the Korean Peninsula and China (Hook 1999b). Despite the role these authorities are playing, however, they remain constrained in their international activities by a variety of factors, not least the power of the central government to control their flow of financial and other resources.

2.3.iii.f.v PRESSURE GROUPS, NON-GOVERNMENTAL ORGANIZATIONS, SOCIAL MOVEMENTS AND PUBLIC OPINION

Pressure groups, NGOs, social movements and public opinion seek to influence Japan's international relations, specifically as well as generally. Examples of pressure groups include farmers trying to prevent the importation of foreign rice and trade unions seeking to improve the lot of migrant workers. As far as NGOs are concerned, a range of diverse groups is active in Japan (Menju and Aoki 1996), as illustrated by Greenpeace working to stop Japan's drift-net fishing and the Japan International Volunteer Centre offering help to Indo-Chinese refugees. Furthermore, social movements have taken action and continue to take action on issues of immediate concern: for example, groups of citizens have taken to the streets in opposition to the government's closer military cooperation with the US. Finally, public opinion, which in poll after poll during the Cold War period demonstrated a reluctance to support the overseas despatch of the SDF, provides the backdrop against which policy-making agents implement policy. All of these represent different channels for domestic society to exert political pressure on the government's response to specific as well as general international issues.

In some instances, the pressure groups and NGOs have been involved in promoting totally different policies, as with the fishing industry and Greenpeace, with the former supporting and the latter opposing drift-net fishing. In others, they work together in promoting a common goal, as with the NGO Network on Indonesia, which seeks to facilitate cooperation between NGOs interested in promoting the country's sustainable economic development. In still others, these actors respond to an international crisis, as in the case of the response to the Rwanda refugee crisis of 1994, when NGOs such as the Africa Education Fund took direct action to aid the refugees (Tanaka Hiroto 1997: 260–6). Whatever the case, these actors will try to influence the policy-making process through a wide range of tactics, such as financial contributions to political parties, personal contacts, appeals in the media and grassroots education, although their success in exerting any influence on Japan's international relations is dependent on the timescale and nature of the issue addressed.

As far as social movements are concerned, a wide range of movements has sought to influence Japan's policy-making process and international relations through extra-parliamentary and, occasionally, extra-legal, means. These movements have occurred along the range of the political spectrum, from the far right to the far left, but movements on the left have been dominant. They have been particularly active in responding to issues of normative salience in domestic society, as seen in protests against the US–Japan security treaty, movements to protect Article 9 of the Japanese Constitution, and grassroots action against the export of polluting industries to Southeast Asia. Whilst some of these protests only attract several hundred participants, at times, as in the widespread opposition to the revision of the security treaty in 1960, as will be discussed in Chapter 6, several hundred thousand take part. Most significant have been those movements aimed at spreading the anti-nuclear message of Hiroshima and Nagasaki, as witnessed in the mass movements to promote nuclear disarmament (Fujiwara 1992; Itō 1985). Illustrative of the scale of popular protests were the rallies attended by hundreds of thousands in support of the UN Special Session on Disarmament in 1982, as will be seen in Chapter 19. These social movements have played a major role in helping to maintain anti-militarist norms under threat from conservative political forces, but, as in other societies, they tend to undergo periods of high activity followed by dormancy.

Finally, public opinion is regularly canvassed by the mass media and government and published as polls in newspapers, magazines and books. Newspapers such as the *Asahi* and the *Yomiuri* publish the results of surveys on a range of international issues, as seen at the time of the 1990–1 Gulf War (Hook 1996a: 100–28). The Prime Minister's Office conducts interviews on aspects of Japan's foreign and defence policies, as seen in the monthly magazine *Yoron Chōsa*, which regularly produces data on Japanese diplomacy and the SDF. In the case of diplomacy, for instance, members of the public have been asked among other things about their attitude towards taking up a seat on the UNSC, ODA and the type of role Japan should play in international society. Similarly, *Nihon Hōsō Kyōkai* (NHK, the public broadcaster) carries out polls relating to various aspects of international affairs, which are reproduced widely in newspapers, magazines and books as well as broadcast on television and radio. In NHK's *Gendai Nihonjin no Ishiki Kōzō* (1991) (The Attitudinal Structure of Modern-Day Japanese), for instance, can be found surveys on the public's attitude towards nationalism and the increasing salience of an international perspective at the mass level (Nihon Hōsō Kyōkai 1991: 97–108, 136–46). Whatever the source of the information, public opinion can be said to form the general background against which policy-making agents reach decisions on pursuing the Japanese state and its people's perceived interests internationally. Thus, it exerts an influence on Japan's international relations, albeit indirectly more than directly.

2.3.iv Norms

Whilst the above has concentrated on the role of policy-making agents and other political actors in the policy-making process, this section examines the norms which shape the behaviour of these actors. Norms create new interests and categories of action, and order and govern the behaviour of actors (Katzenstein 1996a: 18; Katzenstein 1996b). These norms exert an important influence upon a state's behaviour, certainly far more than allowed for in the orthodox neo-realist and neo-liberal approaches to international relations, which acknowledge the power of norms only as being dependent upon a state's material capabilities and functionalism. Norms are dynamic and capable of appearing, disappearing, being abused or becoming moribund. Often they are promoted by individual or institutional norm entrepreneurs who seek to imbue their ideas with legitimacy and to internalize them within organizations and national and international society at large (Finnemore and Sikkink 1998). The practices which drive them also create norms for behaviour (Risse-Kappen 1995). In the case of policy-making agents, for instance, the 'interaction contexts' within which they seek to formulate foreign policy can influence the nature and extent of the collective action they seek to promote, as well as the definition and identity of the policy-makers themselves (Wendt 1994: 389).

2.3.iv.a Internationally embedded norms

Although a growing and evolving literature on norm creation now exists, the concern of this volume is to emphasize how Japanese state and non-state actors adopt (and adapt) their behaviour in accordance with norms which are embedded in structures, both internationally and domestically. The internationally embedded norms which will play a salient role in the four main parts of this volume that follow are: bilateralism, Asianism, trilateralism and internationalism.

2.3.iv.a.i BILATERALISM

The norm of bilateralism, embedded through the US–Japan security treaty system, builds up a powerful consensual constituency in Japan for behaving in a bilateral fashion. This implies that Japan's foreign policy ought to be conducted on a bilateral basis, and that Japan should behave in the international system within the remit of the bilateral alliance and rarely in opposition to it. This is the dominant norm that has guided the Japanese state and its people's role in the world since 1945. Prime Minister Yoshida Shigeru played the role of norm entrepreneur in promoting bilateralism in the late 1940s and early 1950s. Although the Yoshida Doctrine has served as a guiding principle for many subsequent prime ministers, more recently it has been called into question as a result of the end of the Cold War.

2.3.iv.a.ii ASIANISM

Asianism, which encourages Japan to develop its East Asian identity, can be seen in the traditional intermediary role Japan has played as a bridge (*kakehashi* or *watashiyaku*) between East Asia and the West. With the end of the Cold War and the growth of regional security and economic frameworks, however, state-sponsored regional projects in East Asia have encouraged certain political actors in Japan to push forward with a policy of leaving the West and entering East Asia. This reverses the Meiji-period policy of *datsua nyūō*, described earlier. In the contemporary period, a norm entrepreneur for Asianism has been the former LDP Diet member, present incumbent of the governorship of Tokyo (1999 to date) and self-confessed nationalist, Ishihara Shintarō. His role can be seen, for instance, in the book he jointly authored with Prime Minister Mahathir Mohamad of Malaysia, where he called for a Japan and an Asia that can say 'no' to US influence in East Asia (Mahathir and Ishihara 1994).

2.3.iv.a.iii TRILATERALISM

At the beginning of the twenty-first century, trilateralism is still an emerging and not an embedded norm. In the wake of the ending of the Cold War, it came to be premised upon evidence of a growing three-pillar system of economic interaction amongst Japan, the US and Europe. This 'new trilateralism' differs from its older form in the US-led Trilateral Commission (TC) because it serves both to counterbalance US regional and global interests as well as to support the US within the framework of multilateral institutions. In January 1999,

Prime Minister Obuchi acted as a norm entrepreneur when he promoted the idea of a three-pronged currency system based on the dollar, the euro and the yen. Since the 1990s, trilateralism has slowly begun to be applied to non-economic dialogues.

2.3.iv.a.iv INTERNATIONALISM

The norm of internationalism is the expression of cooperation with and support for the ideals of international society constructed by the early-starters of the West. These ideals stress the idea of a 'normal' state, or, in other words, a fully-rounded and orthodox state which makes full use of its material capabilities, both military and economic, to provide international public goods and uphold the multilateral global institutions discussed in Part V of this volume. The examples of both participation in UNPKO and prompt payment of budgetary contributions to these institutions are embedded as 'normal' and appropriately internationalist behaviour. As will be seen in Chapter 18, however, Japan's response to the 1990–1 Gulf War provoked a flurry of criticisms of so-called 'free-riding' and 'chequebook' diplomacy from international society, particularly the United States. These criticisms were turned to practical account by the norm entrepreneur, Ozawa Ichirō, who has sought to imbue these ideas of internationalism and normality with legitimacy and to embed them as a norm within Japanese domestic society. His ultimate goal has been to encourage the Japanese state and its people to greater activity at the multilateral level and thereby make Japan a 'normal state' (Ozawa 1994). This interpretation of internationalism is in tension with the domestically embedded norm of anti-militarism discussed next.

2.3.iv.b Domestically embedded norms

In addition to these internationally embedded and emerging norms, a number of domestically embedded norms can be identified as exerting a powerful influence on the perceptions and interests of policy-making agents and other political actors and their responses to external pressures and the structure of the international system. Three are central to an understanding of Japan's international behaviour: anti-militarism, developmentalism and economism.

2.3.iv.b.i ANTI-MILITARISM

The norm of anti-militarism grew out of the way the Japanese people's experience of World War II and the traumatic effects of the atomic bombings of Hiroshima and Nagasaki have been embedded in political discourse (Hook 1986). Whilst this norm might not constrain individual policy-makers to the same degree, as with Prime Minister Nakasone Yasuhiro's determination to build up Japan's military capabilities in the early 1980s, the acceptance of the norm on the popular level acts as a powerful constraint on the government's use of military force as a legitimate instrument of state policy (Hook 1996a). This acceptance is manifest in public opinion surveys and the activities of social movements, as seen, for instance, at the time of the 1960 revision of the US–Japan security treaty (see Chapter 6). The result has been that, despite considerable pressure on Japan from structural factors, such as *beiatsu,* to assume greater military responsibilities in East Asia, the Japanese government has only re-armed incrementally and resisted the acquisition of the type of military power that usually accompanies economic superpower status. Leaders of the SDPJ, such as Ishibashi Masashi during the 1980s, have acted as norm entrepreneurs in promoting policies giving voice to the anti-militarist norm (Ishibashi 1980).

2.3.iv.b.ii DEVELOPMENTALISM

The norm of developmentalism, which grew out of Japan's historical struggle as a latecomer to catch up, especially economically, with the major industrialized powers of the West, permeates the very fabric of Japanese society. It therefore forms the backdrop for many of the policies in the political and economic dimensions of Japan's international relations and is at the heart of Japan's export of economic prescriptions for the development of East Asia. The goal is to catch up both in terms of the crude measures of economic success, as in per capita GNP, as well as in terms of international political influence, as with the ambition to gain a seat on the UNSC. Paying single-minded attention to catching up with, if not overtaking, the other major industrialized powers infuses many of the policies adopted by respective Japanese governments. Meiji leaders such as Iwakura Tomomi epitomize the developmentalist norm entrepreneur.

2.3.iv.b.iii ECONOMISM

The norm of economism, which in the post-war era combines creatively the two other norms of anti-militarism and developmentalism, has served as the guiding beacon for post-war governments, especially LDP governments from the 1960s. On the one hand, economism, which prioritizes economic activity and imputes it with positive value, embodies a rejection of the militarism of the pre-war period and a confirmation of the anti-militarism of the post-war era; on the other hand, economism undergirds post-war developmentalism, as it is through an 'economics-first' policy that developmentalism has been given substance. The advent of the Cabinet of the entrepreneur of this norm, Prime Minister Ikeda Hayato, saw the government specifically prioritize economism in the policy-making process.

These domestically embedded norms have dictated that, as far as the overall international position of Japan is concerned, it has for the last fifty-five years pursued the non-military, chiefly economic, foreign policy of a trading nation (Rosecrance 1986). What this means is that, as the internationally embedded norms outlined above have tended to shape a more proactive, 'normal' role for Japan, as defined by the normative structure of the international system, domestic norms have been in constant tension with them. Thus, economism, like the other two domestically embedded norms, and in competition or in harmony with internationally embedded norms, has contributed to the characterization of Japan as an 'abnormal' state. At the same time, however, the norm has informed the range and type of international activity and the deployment of power in the political, economic and security dimensions of Japan's international relations.

2.4 Reactivity and proactivity

The above suggests that the international activity of the Japanese state and its people, just as in any other state, can be explained by reference to the interplay of pluralistic policy-making agents and other political actors, informed and constrained by domestic interests and norms. These actors are bound within the constraints and opportunities of a historically-contingent order in both domestic and international settings.

2.4.i Reactivity and immobilism

Chapter 1 has shown how, for many observers, Japan appears anomalous, if not abnormal, in terms of its international behaviour. A key reason for this perception is the tendency for Japan to adopt a reactive stance in dealing with international affairs. Certainly, like any other state, Japan reacts to the occurrence of international events and changes in the structure of the international system. This can be seen, for instance, in the Japanese reaction to the Gulf War (an international event) and the normalization of relations with China (a change in structure). The characterization of Japan as a reactive state, however, suggests not simply a response to international events and changes, but rather a lack of leadership in seeking to shape their outcome. This is the quintessence of the characterization of Japan as a reactive state (Calder 1988a). The reasons for this are complex, but relate at the international level to the status of Japan as a latecomer to the international system set in place by the early-starters of the West. In other words, the constraints and opportunities created by the norms and structures of the international system make Japan appear reactive and immobilist to a range of both foreign and domestic observers.

Japan as a latecomer has sought to catch up with the early-starters of the West by modelling its behaviour on theirs. This pattern of behaviour is illustrated by the decision of Japanese policy-making agents to follow the West in acquiring colonies in the late nineteenth and early twentieth centuries. At the time of Japan's annexation of Korea in 1910, for instance, the internationally embedded legal and normative framework of behaviour accepted the possession of colonies. Thus, in seeking to become a big power, Japan set out on the same path as the Western early-starters, acquiring an empire with colonies of its own. In the post-1945 nuclear world, however, Japan has not followed the same path as the other big powers, the US, France and the UK, as seen in the anti-nuclear policies adopted by the Japanese state and the anti-nuclear actions of the Japanese people. More generally, whereas the use of the military as a legitimate instrument of state power has remained largely consistent with both international and domestic norms, with the exception of Germany (Berger 1998), in Japan the use of this policy option is controversial and likely to create a political crisis. Nevertheless, it is as normal for policy-makers to be constrained in Japan over the use of the military as it is in Ireland for them to be constrained over introducing a policy to legalize abortion or in the US over legislation to rescind a citizen's right to bear arms. As domestic issues, however, the last two do not engender the same sort of international pressure Japan faces in resisting the use of the military as an instrument of state policy in order to respond to an international crisis, as in the case of the 1990–1 Gulf War (see Chapter 18).

In terms of the constraints and opportunities created by the policy-making process, the increasingly pluralistic nature of policy-making in Japan means that certain foreign policy issues are characterized by a struggle for influence among a wide range of policy-making agents and other political actors, with the result that the policy outcome can become highly immobile and reactive, or even fails to appear entirely (Calder 1988a; Stockwin 1988). ODA policy at times is a case in point, whereby each of the different actors and their different interests and norms seek to exert influence: MOFA seeking a political usage for ODA; MITI concerned about the commercial and trade benefits; MOF anxious to control the budgetary costs; the LDP keen to allocate ODA to friendly states and use it to buy political favours with big business; the business community intent on securing a slice of the ODA contracts for themselves; the media critical of ODA misuse and wastage; NGOs seeking to spread international standards of ODA distribution in Japan; and the general public mindful of the use of their tax contributions. The consequence is that ODA and other foreign policy measures in Japan have developed slowly and somewhat inflexibly in the post-war era. What makes for Japanese reactivity, then, is not only the nature of the policy-making process, but the extent to which the policy in question is at odds with or consistent with domestically embedded norms. That is what helps to account for the controversy of the policy.

2.4.ii Proactivity

Yet it would be quite wrong to view Japanese policy-making as perennially subject to immobilism, for, although this at times does characterize the policy-making process, at others immobilist log-jams can be and have been broken. The relatively rapid and decisive policy-making taking place in Japan clearly depends on the level of controversy and immediacy of the issue. In certain cases, what are akin to standard operating procedures and established guidelines of interaction between predetermined groups of policy actors can produce a quick policy outcome. As will be discussed in Chapter 9, for instance, by the time of Prime Minister Tanaka Kakuei's rise to power, policy-making agents and other political actors involved in the policy-making process to normalize relations with China were able to move forward quickly. In other instances, even though the range of actors is larger, the issue may be of such paramount national importance that even antagonistic actors are quite prepared to compromise on their differences and work closely on a policy issue. The Japanese government's response to the 1973 oil shock illustrates how it responded with almost lightning-fast speed by Japanese standards, with the quick despatch to the Middle East of a diplomatic mission in a successful attempt to secure Japan's exemption from the oil embargo on the other major industrialized powers, the pledging of new economic aid for the region, and even the willingness to defy the US's policy of non-cooperation with OPEC and the organization of a consumer's cartel.

2.4.iii Normal reactivity and proactivity of the Japanese state

Quintessentially, therefore, immobilism, on the one hand, and rapid policy initiatives in crisis situations, on the other, represent the two extremes of Japanese foreign policy-making. It is nevertheless probably fair to say that most foreign policy-making in Japan, as elsewhere, lies somewhere in between these two extremes. Still, whilst a definite overall tendency towards immobilism and reactivity does exist, there is an active attempt cautiously to push forward Japan's international relations and create sufficient consensus between policy-making agents and other political actors to avoid tipping altogether towards immobilism. The subsequent chapters will argue that, despite these two extremes, the final outcome of the foreign policy-making process can best be understood as a range of consistently low-risk and low-profile international initiatives, leading to the characterization of Japanese diplomacy as 'quiet'. This choice of quiet diplomacy reflects Japan's behaviour as a normal state, with normal modes and means of deploying different forms of power, given the structure of the international system, the policy-making agents and other political actors involved, and the domestic and international norms which inform their behaviour.

2.5 Normal modes of instrumentalization

More specifically, the reasons for the choice of 'quiet diplomacy' in this book relate to 'how' Japanese policy-making agents pursue the interests of the Japanese state and its people. These modes of instrumentalization are the normal way for Japan to conduct its international affairs along the temporal dimension, by formal, informal and proxy channels and on different levels of activity. In other words, as with the policy-makers of the other major industrialized powers, Japanese policy-making agents and other political actors instrumentalize Japan's international relations by means of a range of power resources in terms of a specific temporal dimension, channel for instrumentalization and level of activity.

2.5.i Crisis and long-term policy-making

The characterization of Japan as a reactive state reflects a focus on the performance of Japanese policy-making agents in deploying power in a crisis. Whilst in no way wishing to suggest that they have always responded effectively to crises, the difficulty faced by the policy-makers of any country in facing a crisis cannot be denied. This can be seen, for instance, in the inability of the US president to bring a swift end to the Iranian hostage crisis in 1979–80, when the Iranian government held American citizens in retaliation for the US support of the ousted shah of Iran.

For the most part, however, policy-making processes are much longer term. From this perspective, the ability of Japanese policy-makers to pursue the interests of the Japanese state and its people within a longer time frame is patently evident. Thus, the longer-term developmentalist goal of the Meiji leaders, for Japan to become a major industrialized power, has been realized and the Japanese people now enjoy peace and a high standard of living. In this way, although Japan may in a crisis appear reactive, over the longer term policy-makers can be seen to have successfully achieved two key goals of all of the major industrialized powers: peace and prosperity. Perhaps more than for the leaders of the other major industrialized powers, in Japan the time frame adopted for the realization of these goals is measured in the longer rather than the shorter term. In other words, Japanese policy-making agents adopt a long-term perspective on diplomacy and the pursuit of state interests.

The incrementalist approach taken by Japanese policy-makers in dealing with defence and security issues illustrates this trend. A case in point is the skilful way these agents have been able to balance internal and external pressures in the controversy over the build-up of Japan's military strength. Although Japanese policy-making agents have been averse to taking bold decisions on defence, given the domestically embedded norm of anti-militarism, over the longer term the SDF have become an ultra-modern fighting force. This incremental build-up in their military hardware under pressure from the US, however, has been balanced by the imposition of constraints on the way the SDF can be deployed by policy-makers. As will be discussed in Chapter 6, despite Prime Minister Nakasone Yasuhiro's 1986 decision to abandon the ban on spending more than 1 per cent of GNP on the military in the 1987 budget, the following years did not witness a dramatic increase in military spending. In this way, the policy-making process on defence has been to push incrementally any build-up, taking careful account of both internal and external pressures.

2.5.ii Formal, informal and proxy channels

The formal and informal channels used by Japanese policy-making agents, as represented by the Japanese terms *omote* (surface or explicit) and *ura* (back or implicit), are two of the three key modes for laying the groundwork in order to deploy Japanese power. The third is the proxy channel. As with other states in the international system, Japanese policy-makers enjoy a range of formal channels for interacting and communicating with policy-makers in other states, whether this be in bilateral settings, as illustrated by a summit meeting between the Japanese prime minister and the US president or British prime minister, or multilateral settings, as in participating in the ARF or G7. This formal process of interaction is the *omote* channel. As quiet diplomats, however, Japanese policy-making agents prefer, perhaps more than those of the other major industrialized powers, to work behind the scenes in order to lay the groundwork for the pursuit of their norms and interests in an international setting. This informal process of interaction involves the *ura* and proxy channels. They are often characterized by the Japanese domes-

Plate 2.4 Mickey Mouse meets the emperor. Thirty years after the historic first meeting between the Shōwa emperor and General Douglas MacArthur, the emperor visited Disneyland in October 1975. An early example of the emperor's role as a cultural and diplomatic ambassador for Japan.
Source: Courtesy of Mainichi Shimbunsha

tic practice of *nemawashi* ('wrapping around the roots') or laying the groundwork. The *ura* channel can be seen, for instance, in the informal visits to China and North Korea by LDP and SDPJ politicians in order to promote a specific policy of the Japanese government. The proxy channel can be seen to operate in behind-the-scenes negotiations with the policy-makers of other states. This strategy means that Japanese policy-making agents do not always take international credit for their initiatives. Thus, the announcement of an international initiative – even if actually developed by Japan – may be put forward by another power, as in the case of Australia's announcement of APEC (see Chapter 4). It can also be seen in the government's use of domestic proxies to promote the state's interests, as in emperor diplomacy (*tennō gaikō*) to build up international goodwill, and NGO 'human face' diplomacy, to build up outside understanding of Japan's ODA policy in East Asia and elsewhere.

2.5.iii Sources of quiet diplomacy

Chapter 1 has portrayed the commonly-accepted view that Japan lacks a readily-identifiable international role comparable to the other major industrialized powers. This chapter has demonstrated how Japan can be understood as a low-profile actor pursuing quiet diplomacy on the international stage. The methods employed to conduct this type of quiet diplomacy have a variety of sources.

The history of Japan's conduct of foreign relations over the years suggests the importance of domestic sources in explaining the tendency for policy-making agents to pursue the interests of the Japanese state and its people in the way they do. Consensus-building, which requires widespread consultation through *nemawashi, ringisho* (gain sanction for decision by use of a seal) and other techniques, can hinder rapid policy-making. The preference for the obfuscation of power capabilities, ever since the Japanese Shōguns seized real power from the emperor but allowed established institutions to provide a cloak of legitimacy for their rule, can lead to puzzlement as to the exact location of power in the policy-making process. The role of the *kagemusha* (literally, 'shadow warrior', meaning the true leader who remains in the shadow) makes the task even more complex. This helps to explain why policy-making agents appear uncomfortable with making open efforts at leadership in the international system, and become involved in international *nemawashi* and carrying out negotiations not bound by the strictly legal interpretation of international affairs. As touched on above, the real preference of Japanese policy-makers appears to be for patient and delicate manoeuvring behind the scenes in order to deploy Japanese power and exert influence.

2.5.iv Cultural determinism?

This is not to suggest a culturally-deterministic explanation of the international relations of Japan based on the way policy-making agents and other political actors behave in domestic society. Rather, these patterns of behaviour are governed by both internal and external factors. The international dimension suggests why the Japanese state, faced with the dual problems in the post-war era arising from external factors – latent hostility on the part of the ex-colonies of East Asia and the constraints on diplomatic action imposed by the bilateral attachment to the US – often had to undertake a form of highly cautious 'tip-toe' diplomacy (Ampiah 1997) in international fora. This can be seen, for instance, in the case of the Japanese role in the non-aligned movement (NAM), where it sought to pursue the very circumscribed aims of rehabilitating Japan's international image in East Asia, albeit without disturbing the interests of its superpower sponsor.

Clearly, this is one more area where Japan fails to conform to the usual stereotype of the great power. Japanese leadership and presence in the world does not conform with the criteria of other powers, such as the US, as few traces of the same sorts of overt military power and leadership emerge in the case of Japan. Nevertheless, by suspending the usual conceptions of leadership and looking at areas of consensus-building, facilitating, patient diplomacy and agenda-setting, then Japan's 'leadership from behind' (Rix 1993b) or, more provocatively, leadership by 'stealth' (Drifte 1998), or, as preferred here, quiet diplomacy, can be said to be in evidence on three different levels of activity.

2.5.v Unilateral, bilateral and multilateral levels

Thus, the formal, informal and proxy channels used to lay the groundwork for the deployment of Japanese power are deployed on the unilateral, bilateral and multilateral levels. The structure of the international system, the policy-making agents and other actors involved, and the norms which shape their behaviour, determine the specific level for the deployment of Japanese power. Especially when compared with the US, which demonstrates a predilection to pursue its interests on the unilateral rather than on all three levels, Japanese policy-making agents skilfully pursue the norms and interests of the Japanese state and its people by exploiting opportunities on all of these three levels, depending upon the policy issue at stake. Thus, Japan acts unilaterally, as will be seen in Chapter 4 on 'resource diplomacy'; bilaterally, as will be detailed in Chapter 6 on the US–Japan security treaty; and multilaterally, as will be examined in Chapter 19 on financial contributions to the UN. Japanese policy-making agents often work skilfully on all of these levels simultaneously, depending on the issue being addressed. As will be evidenced throughout the subsequent chapters of this book, with the ending of the Cold War, multilateral engagement as a supplement to bilateralism, albeit not a replacement thereof, has risen in salience. In this way, Japanese policy-makers play a role on all three levels as the optimal strategy for pursuing the interests and norms of the Japanese state and its people.

2.6 Instrumentalizing policy

This book's choice of the term 'quiet diplomacy' is intended to capture the normal modes and methods of instrumentalizing policy employed by policy-making agents in Japan. These agents and other political actors pursue the perceived interests of the Japanese state and its people through a range of power options available to them. The deployment of power is a question of different forms of power and the instruments employed to channel them – all of which are again conditioned by international and domestic norms.

In Japan's case, despite an international order where military power is accepted, within certain limits, as a legitimate instrument of state policy, the domestically embedded norm of anti-militarism has constrained the behaviour of the Japanese state in seeking to deploy military power. As a result, Japan's presence in the world has been shaped by the use of economic rather than military power. Military power is not neglected altogether, of course: for, as already noted, Japan relies on the US for security in East Asia and continues to expand incrementally its own independent military capabilities within the context of its bilateral security relationship. Still, the form of power which Japan has most frequently deployed in order to pursue the interests of the state and its people and to make its own presence felt regionally and globally has been, without doubt, economic.

Economic power has been manifest on the state level by the Japanese government's extension of ODA, both bilaterally and multilaterally, and on the private level through the FDI and financial activities of Japanese TNCs and other actors. This conceptualization of the importance of economic power is echoed in the idea of Japan as a 'global civilian power', as touched on earlier in this chapter; or, more precisely, a state which does not eliminate totally the use of the military as a mode of power for solving international problems, but which tends, nevertheless, to place a premium on the pursuit of economic, technological and development assistance (Okawara 1993; Shikata 1995).

2.6.i Primacy of economic power

The usage and effects of Japan's economic power are twofold. First, the state, in conjunction with Japanese-based TNCs, often deploys economic power as both a 'carrot' and a 'stick' to induce cooperative behaviour from other actors in the international system. The stick is sometimes used to impose potential, or actual, economic costs upon states identified as threats to Japanese security. The introduction of the 1992 ODA Charter (*ODA Taikō*) is a case in point (Soderberg 1996). Henceforth, Japan has given a more overt political edge to its ODA policy by taking into consideration whether or not recipient countries are involved in the development of weapons of mass destruction (WMD), on the one hand, and progress towards democracy, on the other. The result, to some, may not indicate strict adherence to the Charter, as touched on below, but the government did suspend briefly grant aid to China in 1995 in the wake of renewed nuclear tests, and quickly moved to stop assistance to India and Pakistan following their own nuclear tests in 1998. The government also has deployed the stick of economic power to withhold food aid and energy assistance via the Korean Peninsula Energy Development Organization (KEDO) to North Korea in protest at its ballistic missile tests of August 1998 (see Chapter 9).

Despite these examples, the general preference of Japanese policy-making agents has been to continue to extend economic assistance and cooperation even to states identified as a security risk, or to states seen as far from democratic in their political make-up. In part, this can be explained by the state's support for the commercial interests of Japanese TNCs seeking to benefit from a share of aid contracts in the recipient states, but it also can be explained more forcefully by reference to the state's longer-term policy goals of deploying economic power, as outlined in section 2.6 above. These are that engagement with a range of political regimes by the maintenance of ODA programmes encourages economic exchange and interdependence on the state and private sector levels, which over the longer term can serve to moderate the political and security behaviour of other states and actors in the international system, in the interests of the peace and prosperity of the Japanese state and its people.

As mentioned earlier, the Japanese state has long shown a propensity to allow home-grown TNCs to conduct business with authoritarian regimes in East Asia. It has more often than not also eschewed establishing a direct link between political ideology and economic exchange. This can be seen, for instance, in the policy of *seikei bunri* over the short term, in the hope that, over the long term, the separation of politics and economics will lead to a convergence of political and economic interests. Consequently, Japan has continued to engage economically so-called 'pariah' states, such as Burma, and to work to achieve economic interdependence with China, even as fears of the latter's military might grow in the early twenty-first century.

Certainly, the efficacy of deploying economic power often has been called into question, not least at the time of the 1990–1 Gulf War, when Japan was seen to have failed to contribute to international stability by refusing to provide a direct military contribution to the Allied war efforts. Indeed, despite Japan's provision of US$13 billion to the US-led coalition, Kuwait offered no official thanks, suggesting how deeply embedded the acceptance of the use of force is in the normative structure of the international system. Yet even though Japan's economic power clearly does not always convert into immediate gains or a principled reputation, it does work almost imperceptibly and quietly towards bolstering Japan's international position.

Thus, the growth of the *Nichibei* economy has not only added to the US's hold over Japan; it has simultaneously worked to lock the two political economies into a near unshakeable relationship of interdependence. Whether consciously manipulated or not, as will be outlined in Chapter 5, this economic relationship delivers to Japanese policy-makers a degree of political and security leverage over the US leviathan. Likewise, as will be seen in Chapter 9, Japan's extension of economic cooperation to China fosters interdependence, which may serve to moderate the rivalry and security behaviour of both states over the longer term. Moreover, although not a central concern of this volume, accompanying this growth of interdependence in political economy has come a degree of 'soft' cultural power, as manifest in the popularity of *manga* comic books and Japanese pop music to the youth of East Asia and elsewhere (Shiraishi S. 1997). It can also be seen in MOFA's promotion of 'cultural diplomacy' through the activities of the Japan Foundation (Drifte 1998: 150–67). In this way, Japan can begin to shape the norms and policies of other states.

What this suggests, then, is that the Japanese state and its people seek to deploy power through non-violent means as a way to promote their interests on a range of temporal dimensions, through formal, informal and proxy channels, on different international levels, depending on the issues, norms and interests at stake.

2.7 Summary

This chapter has provided an overview of the eclectic approach adopted in this book in order to explain Japan's international relations. It draws on a number of different traditions in the study of IR and IPE as a way to facilitate an understanding of a state and its people which, as was shown in Chapter 1, have often been regarded as anomalous, if not abnormal, in orthodox studies of Japan's international relations. By drawing attention in this way to insights from realism, especially the need to take account of the structure of the international system; liberalism, especially the need to look at actors other than the state; policy-making studies, especially the need to examine the range of actors involved in the policy-making process; and constructivist approaches, especially the need to pay attention to both domestically and internationally embedded norms, *Japan's International Relations* offers a more sophisticated explanation of the international relations of the Japanese state and its people than can be found in many other works: for rather than the apparent paradox outlined in Chapter 1, this book will show quite clearly that Japan's international relations in the post-war era are a product of the very international and domestic factors outlined in this chapter.

Whilst in this volume reference to the outcome of the foreign policy-making process is in terms of Japan's 'quiet diplomacy', whatever term is adopted reflects with varying degrees of accuracy the behaviour of the Japanese state in the world, and the way the Japanese people have supported, acquiesced in or opposed it. Nevertheless, even though quiet diplomacy can be identified as the leadership style of Japan in the post-war era, it represents only one aspect of its international relations. The remainder of the book will explain in turn the dominant pattern of Japan's international relations in the three core regions and in global institutions. Thus, the next part moves to focus on Japan–US relations.

Part II

JAPAN–UNITED STATES RELATIONS

Chapter 3

Introduction

3.1 Changing places?

On 15 October 1995, the *New York Times* published a scoop on how the Central Intelligence Agency (CIA) had been tapping the phone of the then minister of international trade and industry and future prime minister of Japan, Hashimoto Ryūtarō. The aim was to gather sensitive information on the strategy of the Ministry of International Trade and Industry (MITI) for the forthcoming automobile negotiations between Japan and the US. These spying activities no doubt could be expected to assist the administration of President Bill Clinton (1993–2001) to reduce its US$60-odd billion annual trade deficit with Japan. Forty-five years earlier, in February 1949, the famous Detroit banker, Joseph Dodge, arrived at the headquarters in Tokyo of General Douglas MacArthur, commander of the Supreme Command for the Allied Powers (SCAP), on a mission to kick-start the Japanese economy. His aims were to bring rampant inflation under control, balance the budget and adopt other measures to help the defeated country to recover economically. The post-Occupation years started out with Dodge stating that, 'Japan can be independent politically but dependent economically' (LaFeber 1997: 323).

The success of the Japanese economy over the decades since Dodge's visit to Tokyo indicates that, at least in the eyes of the CIA, Japan now poses a threat and is no longer dependent economically on the US. Indeed, the fear seems to be that the two are changing places: that the US may become economically dependent upon Japan. The question of Japan's political independence, however, is less clear cut. In this sense, these two vignettes of a radical change in the place of Japan and the US in the global political economy really call for a closer examination of the continuity as well as the change, the interdependence as well as the dependence or independence, of these two Pacific powers. As Chapter 2 has demonstrated, maintaining a bilateral relationship with the current most powerful state in the world has been the *sine qua non* of Japan's international relations throughout most of its history, but determining the dominant pattern of its relations with the most powerful state of the last fifty-five years, the US, requires further elaboration. By drawing on the approach introduced in Chapter 2 in terms of the 'what', 'why' and 'how' of the Japanese state and its people's international relations, Part II of this volume will provide answers to these questions in the political, economic and security dimensions during the post-war era.

3.2 Approach

The approach adopted will be first to provide in this Introduction an overview of the relationship within the context of the ending of the Pacific War in 1945 and the transformation in the structure of the international, regional and domestic orders. It will demonstrate not only the importance of the US to Japan, a defeated country seeking to recover from the terrible damage caused by the war, but also the importance of Japan to the US. Indeed, the advent of two antagonist nuclear superpowers, with the US as the leader of the capitalist West in the emerging Cold War confrontation with the communist East, profoundly affected the transformation of these orders. This section will highlight a number of issues of crucial importance for understanding the more detailed analysis of Japan's international relations in the dimensions of politics, economics and security, which will be covered respectively in Chapters 4, 5 and 6. The aim of these chapters will be to identify the dominant pattern of the bilateral relationship in these three dimensions. In the process, norms and agency as well as structures will be of central concern.

3.3 Historical overview

3.3.i Changing international structures

The ending of the imperial world order and the rise to post-war hegemony of the US in place of Great Britain was achieved in the process of meeting the challenge posed to that order by three latecomers to the international system: the Axis powers of Germany, Italy and Japan. From the late nineteenth century onwards, Japan had emulated the early-starters of the West, employing means similar to those used by these states in order to achieve its own imperial and colonial ambitions. Given the status of Japan as a late-starter, however, these ambitions could only be realized near to the Japanese homeland in East Asia; the European powers, in contrast, had colonized far from home in Africa, Asia and elsewhere earlier in the century. By the early 1930s, the world was heading towards a confrontation between the Allied and Axis powers. During World War II, the challenge to the world and regional orders mounted by the Axis powers through military power, as represented most vividly in East Asia by the Japanese attack on Pearl Harbor in December 1941, was met in kind by the Allied powers, leading ultimately to the failure of the challenge by the Axis powers. The military struggle between the Axis and Allied powers during the course of the war led to the development and deployment of various new means of violence, most notably the atomic weapons used against Japan, which came to shape the structure of the emerging post-war orders.

The US atomic bombings of Hiroshima and Nagasaki in August 1945 and the emperor's radio announcement of Japan's willingness to 'bear the unbearable' brought to an end the Japanese attack on the established world and regional orders. The use of atomic bombs against Japan at the very end of the war, despite the availability of other means to resolve the conflict (Miles 1985), has led scholars to argue that, far from them being deployed to end the Pacific War, these new instruments of war were in fact used by the US as the first blow in the emerging Cold War confrontation with the USSR (Alperovitz 1995). What this interpretation suggests is that, whether in terms of the transition in the structure of the international system from an imperial order to an emerging bipolar Cold War order, or the transition in the structure of the regional order through the defeat of Japan and the start of decolonization, as will be discussed in Part III of this book, the US's use of nuclear weapons and its Occupation of Japan fundamentally changed the structure and norms of the international, regional and domestic orders as well as the relationship between the victor and vanquished in the ensuing years.

Henceforth, the international and regional orders would be dominated by considerations of nuclear power and the confrontation with communism. When the USSR successfully detonated its own nuclear device in August 1949, the international and regional orders moved rapidly towards nuclear bipolarity. It was unclear at the time, of course, whether or not these awesome weapons would be used again in order to establish a unipolar global or regional order through the use of force, but both the US and the USSR sought to build up their stockpiles in anticipation of this possibility, thereby consolidating the bipolar nuclear order. It was an order based on confrontation between two different political, economic and social systems, with the two nuclear superpowers – the US and the USSR – at its centre, consolidating an alliance system in the West and East in order to strengthen their respective global and regional positions.

In East Asia, the end of Japan's imperial ambitions and the overwhelming power of the US in comparison with the war-torn economies of Europe, not to mention those of the USSR and China, provided the US hegemon with the opportunity to restructure the international and regional orders in line with the needs of the new, nuclear era. The political and economic needs of East Asia, as seen in the political struggle between the East and the West and the alternatives of communism and capitalism, went hand in hand with a need to prepare to meet any threat arising from communism, by the use of nuclear weapons if necessary. At a time before the advent of intercontinental ballistic missiles, this included the primary task of securing a staunch regional ally able to provide the military bases for the stationing of US troops. Without these bases, US policy-making agents could not easily meet the threat from communism, either by nuclear or by conventional means. Japan became that bulwark against communism in East Asia, as symbolized by Prime Minister Yoshida Shigeru's signing of the security treaty, along with the San Francisco peace treaty, in September 1951.

As will be seen in Chapter 4 and Chapter 9, the nature of the peace settlement left a number of territorial issues unresolved. This is the case with the Sino-Japanese dispute over sovereignty of the Senkaku Islands and the dispute with the USSR over sovereignty of the 'Northern Territories'. The former dispute arose out of the US's decision to return the administrative authority to the Senkaku Islands, along with Okinawa as part of the Ryūkyū Islands, in May 1972. The latter, in contrast, came about as a result of the USSR's occupation of the islands at the end of the war, as was touched on in Chapter 2. In this way, the cost of Yoshida's acceptance of the US-sponsored peace treaty was to leave an outstanding legacy of territorial disputes which remain unsettled at the beginning of the twenty-first century.

3.3.ii Changing domestic order

From the perspective of the ending of the Pacific War and the emerging structures of the international and regional orders, therefore, the US Occupation of Japan can be seen as a means to restructure the domestic order so as to realize two quite different goals. First, the immediate, war-inspired goal of ensuring that Japan never again became a threat to the international and regional orders established by the early-starters. In order to achieve this goal, the US set in motion a radical transformation of Japan's domestic political economy, pushed forward under the slogans of demilitarization and democratization. At its heart, the US policy sought to deracinate the pernicious roots of militarism from domestic society and to plant in their place the seeds of anti-militarism and democracy.

In this way, SCAP quickly sought to restructure the political, economic and social systems of Japan. Politically, the measures taken included the setting-up of a bicameral house of elected political representatives, thereby abolishing the hereditary upper house, the House of Peers, and the extension of the franchise to include all citizens aged 20 and over. This reform enabled women to become voters for the first time. Measures were also taken to preclude the re-emergence of militarism as well, as seen in the ban on war potential, the possession of military forces and the holding of a Cabinet post by military personnel. These were given legal force through Article 9 and Article 66 of the 1947 Constitution (Appendices 1.1 and 2.1). Although voices had been raised in China, Australia and the US in support of prosecuting the emperor, with a poll in the summer of 1945 showing that 70 per cent of US pollees favoured his execution or life imprisonment (Nakamura 1992: 78), SCAP's chief goal, of ensuring the security of the Occupation and the democratization of Japan, meant that the emperor was rehabilitated and became the 'symbol of the State' in the new Constitution (Article 1). Clearly, the US's goal was not to introduce republican-style democracy to Japan.

In the economic dimension, Japanese industrial power was weakened by the break-up of the *zaibatsu* (pre-war industrial conglomerates) which were at the heart of the war effort. A land reform was implemented in the countryside in order to destroy the feudal system of land tenure. Social, educational and other reforms were carried out, as in the purging of militarist teachers and the revision of school textbooks, used to indoctrinate youth into the militarist ethos. A range of other reforms was set in motion as a result of the policies introduced by SCAP in order to prevent Japan's re-emergence as a threat to the international and regional orders (Dower 1999).

Nevertheless, this immediate goal had by around 1948 been replaced by the second, more important and longer-term goal of making Japan a bastion against communism in East Asia. In this way, the intensification of bipolar confrontation outside Japan led to the start of this 'reverse course' inside Japan: demilitarization and democratization now took second place to anti-communism (Dower 1979, 1989). This illustrates the close relationship between the Cold War abroad and the Cold War at home, as the transformation in the structure of the international and regional orders reinforced the role of the US's anti-communist policy in restructuring the domestic order.

Thus, instead of pressing forcefully ahead with the reforms meant to ensure the demilitarization and democratization of Japan, SCAP and the US government began to place greater weight on integrating it into the Western camp, politically, economically and militarily. The short-lived coalition Cabinet (1947–8), headed by

Katayama Tetsu of the Japan Socialist Party (now the Social Democratic Party of Japan or SDPJ), was in part a victim of these changed circumstances. The outbreak of the Korean War in June 1950 created even greater pressures in this direction, as seen with the pressure on Japan to rearm, with Japan emerging centrally and over the longer term as the main bulwark against communism in East Asia (Kan 1992). In this way, the change in the structure of the international and regional orders served to reinforce the ideological bifurcation of the world into two camps: communist and capitalist.

Prime Minister Yoshida opted for military alignment with the US as the perceived optimal strategy to achieve the national goals of peace and prosperity. His strategy soon led to economic development domestically and political rehabilitation internationally, at least within the Western camp. The result of his choice of reliance on the US to achieve these national goals, however, was to divide Japan internally as the world and the region were divided externally. His reproduction of the Cold War structure within Japan can be seen in terms of the division of the state, as a result of Okinawa's severance from the mainland, placing it outside the scope of the new Constitution; and in terms of domestic society, as a result of the split between the supporters and opponents of the political choice made by Prime Minister Yoshida and the ensuing stand-off between conservative and socialist political forces.

Clearly, given the emerging military confrontation with communism, the US's paramount concern was to maintain some form of control over Okinawa, which it had conquered in the last stages of World War II. The reason is related closely to US military strategy, as will be discussed more fully in Chapter 6: bases on Okinawa, along with those on the mainland, provided the means to prosecute both conventional and nuclear wars in East Asia. Whilst this demonstrates the willingness of the conservative political elite in Tokyo to sacrifice Okinawa and its people on the altar of the post-war settlement, Article I of the 1951 security treaty, which permitted the use of US forces 'to put down large-scale internal riots and disturbances in Japan' (Appendix 1.3), implied they could even be used to prevent the election of an anti-American government in mainland Japan. As will be discussed in Chapter 6, the elimination of this clause was a goal pursued by Prime Minister Kishi Nobusuke when the treaty came up for renewal in 1960.

3.3.iii Changing domestic society

Thus, the nature of the post-war settlement and the reproduction of the international Cold War domestically thrust the security treaty into the centre stage of Japan–US relations. In terms of norms, this can be seen in the tension between bilateralism and anti-militarism. On the one hand, the government promoted the norm of bilateralism, which was at the heart of the Yoshida Doctrine; on the other, the opposition parties, social movements and progressive intellectuals promoted the norm of anti-militarism, which was at the heart of the alternative regional and global roles these and other actors envisaged for Japan in the nuclear era.

This points to how, even during the Occupation, domestic actors did not simply remain passive, reacting with a nod of the head to Yoshida's choice of a truncated peace treaty, a security treaty with the US and integration into the Western camp. Rather, against the background of the experience of the war and the atomic bombings, along with the ideals of demilitarization and democratization, especially as given legal voice in the 1947 Constitution, a flurry of alternative identities and strategies was put forward by a range of political actors set on influencing the international relations of the new Japan. Intellectual elites, radical labour unions and social movements struggled to prevent a recrudescence of the nightmare of war and militarism. They set out to chart a new course for Japan, based on the norm of anti-militarism; in no way were they the imposition of new ideas and ideals by an alien, occupying army. They were an attempt, rather, to forge a new identity and role for Japan in the region and the world based upon the norm of anti-militarism, which influenced at least to some extent Prime Minister Yoshida himself, as seen in the discussion of the Yoshida Doctrine in Chapter 2.

The active role played by political actors in domestic society is illustrated by the Peace Issues Discussion Group (PIDG), a gathering of prominent progressive intellectuals, which found widespread support among the opposition political parties, particularly the SDPJ, and on the mass level (Hook 1996a: 26–44; Igarashi 1985). Instead of accepting as ineluctable the need to bow to the constraints imposed by the structure of the international and regional systems and to join one side or the other in the bifurcated Cold War order, the PIDG offered an alternative identity and strategy for Japan based on anti-militarism. If this had been implemented, Japan would have been the precursor of the non-aligned movement, as the option chosen was peaceful coexistence with all states and 'unarmed neutrality' or, more precisely, unarmed non-alignment. The group proved to be an important fountainhead of ideas for the SDPJ's policy of championing the cause of peaceful coexistence with all countries and the signing of an all-embracing peace treaty (unlike the truncated version signed by Yoshida), unarmed neutrality and opposition to a bilateral security treaty and foreign bases on Japanese soil. These 'principles of peace' were reinforced by a call on the government not to move forward with remilitarization.

The efforts the socialists made to realize these goals during the Cold War period served to nurture forcefully the anti-militaristic norm in domestic society and to provide an alternative political vision to that of the conservative political elite. Instead of proposing a policy which implied being locked into a subordinate position as a junior partner in the US-dominated Western camp, or opting for a policy of allying with the USSR, which implied the same junior position in the Eastern camp, the socialists pushed the idea of Japan becoming an independent 'peace state'. This idea was given concrete shape in the form of the party's policy of peaceful coexistence and unarmed neutrality. In this sense, the norm of anti-militarism, as noted in Chapter 2, can be seen to have roots running back to these early post-war years and the integration of the wartime experience, the atomic bombings and the Constitution into an anti-nuclear and anti-militaristic discourse and identity giving voice to an alternative role for Japan in the nuclear era. Crucially, the role envisaged for Japan was of a 'peace state' deploying non-violent means in order to realize the peace and prosperity of the Japanese state and its people.

3.4 Summary

The above historical overview has set the scene for the following three chapters, especially in terms of the way the structure of the international and regional orders as well as the norms of bilateralism and anti-militarism have influenced Japan's international relations with the US. It has shown how the structure of the international system can influence the structure of domestic society as well as the policy chosen by the government. At the same time, however, it has suggested how agency plays a role in determining that policy choice in the context of international and domestic norms. It has further demonstrated how the roots of the norms of bilateralism and anti-militarism can be traced back to the Occupation period. Finally, it has highlighted how, even in a period of physical occupation by foreign forces, policy-making agents in the government and political actors in domestic society sought to influence Japan's international relations.

Chapter 4

Japan–United States political relations

Plate 4.1 Victor and vanquished. The famous photograph of the Shōwa emperor and General Douglas MacArthur's first meeting on 27 September 1945 depicts the mismatch of US and Japanese physical and material power.

Source: US Army Signal Corps Photograph/MacArthur Memorial Archives, Norfolk, Virginia, US

4.1 Overview

Part I and Chapter 3 above have pointed to the bilateral relationship with the US as the master key for unlocking the door to understanding the dominant pattern of Japan's international relations in the post-war era. As the hegemon in the early Cold War and the dominant, if not hegemonic, power in the later Cold War and early post-Cold War years, the US has been able to shape generally the structure of the international system and embed US-sponsored norms in international society. It has done so more than any other state in the system by building on the legacy of the other early-starters as well as by meeting forcefully the challenges posed to the international and East Asian orders by a range of actors throughout these years, most notably those from the communist states.

At the same time, as a result of the policies it pursued in relation to Japan, particularly during the Occupation, the US has been able to shape specifically the course Japan has charted in the post-war world. As was touched on in Chapter 3, whilst at the outset of the Occupation the US government sought to eradicate militarism from domestic society and to embed anti-militarism and democracy, it soon turned instead to prioritizing Japan's integration into the emerging bipolar Cold War confrontation as a front-line state in the fight against communism.

Thus, the defeat by the Allies and the pivotal role the US Occupation forces played in 'remaking' the body politic and domestic society 1945–52 (Schonberger 1989), along with the overwhelming political, economic and military power of the US in the post-war international system, have meant that Japan's relationship with the big power of the post-war world has been and remains its most important. Of course, Japanese policy-making agents have not always followed the US's lead, as will be seen below and in the following two chapters. In spite of that, the dominant pattern of Japan's international relations has been to place highest priority on maintaining a strong and healthy bilateral relationship with the US, although the nature of that relationship has changed, as was intimated in Chapter 3.

4.2 Changes in the structure of the international system

As was seen in Chapters 2 and 3, the intensification of the Cold War in the late 1940s and early 1950s profoundly influenced the nature of the post-war settlement and the future direction of Japan's international relations. As could be expected, with the consolidation of the bipolar structure of the international system during the Occupation and early post-Occupation years, Japan's international relations remained tightly linked to the US. Moreover, under the Yoshida Doctrine, close political ties were being forged between the political elite of both countries, with some of the Japanese elite, including Kishi Nobusuke (1957–60), having been arrested and imprisoned during the Occupation as 'Class A' war crimes suspects. This ensured the survival and later rehabilitation of a range of policy-making agents and other political actors linked closely with the wartime militarist regime. As Kishi later stated: 'The development of the Cold War saved my life ... It was the US–Soviet discord that led to my release from prison' (cited in Hara 1987: 30). The anti-communism of these Japanese policy-making agents meant that, backed by strong antipathy towards the USSR within domestic society, they offered firm support for bilateralism and resistance to the normalization of relations with the USSR.

Even so, the reduction of international tensions and the gentle weakening of bipolarity in the mid-1950s provided an opportunity for domestic political actors to improve relations across the bipolar divide. This opportunity arose following a number of historic changes, such as the Korean War Armistice and the death of the leader of the USSR, Joseph Stalin, in 1953, the launch of the non-aligned movement (NAM) and the four powers' agreement on the neutralization of Austria in 1954, and USSR leader Nikita Khrushchev's denunciation of Stalin at the Twentieth Party Congress in 1956. More generally, fear of nuclear war and at least a partial, if not total, acceptance of the anti-militarist norm even by conservative politicians meant that some policy-making agents within the governing party were willing to take advantage of the thaw in East–West relations in order to promote closer ties with the USSR. Whatever the pragmatic support for the nuclear alliance by Japanese leaders may have been, few were willing to swallow the ideologically powerful 'red-or-dead' logic of US nuclear strategy.

4.2.i Normalization of relations with the Union of Soviet Socialist Republics

Bilateralism did not mean passive acceptance by all in the mainstream conservative political parties of Japan's diplomatic isolation from the East. Indeed, with the final fall from power of Prime Minister Yoshida in December 1954 and the start of the '1955 system', political space emerged for the new prime minister, Hatoyama Ichirō (1955–6), to challenge the dominance of bilateralism. He did so by pushing forward with the normalization of relations with the USSR. The policy-making process on normalization was dominated by the Hatoyama and other mainstream factions of the LDP. Hardly any influence was exerted by the bureaucracy, and only the fishing industry was able to make any policy input from outside the tripartite elite (Hellman 1969). This helps to explain the role of domestic agency in Japan's normalization of relations in December 1956.

At the same time, however, the failure of the prime minister to settle the conflict with the USSR over sovereignty of the Northern Territories and sign a peace treaty cannot be explained by reference solely to these actors. Rather, antagonism towards the USSR on the part of the anti-mainstream factions, and more widely within society, needs also to be taken into account (Stephan 1974; Mendl 1990; Wada 1999). In this sense, widespread anti-communism and the role of the supporters of bilateralism within the governing party and MOFA, along with other domestic pressures, helped to destroy any chance of a final settlement, including a treaty of peace.

Nevertheless, this outcome did not stem simply from the sort of immobilist tendencies in the policy-making process, as was discussed in Chapter 2. More importantly, it resulted from the continuing power of the US to constrain the international behaviour of the Japanese government. Clearly, the change in the international environment in the mid-1950s had provided the opportunity for Hatoyama to push forward with normalization at the time he did, but he did not sign a peace treaty, an outstanding issue which even today remains a thorn in the side of Japan's relations with Russia. Crucial here was pressure exerted on Japan by the US, a concrete manifestation of the way bilateralism constrained Hatoyama's foreign policy. For even though the possibility of achieving a settlement on two of the disputed islands was within reach, *beiatsu* ruled out this option. One specific example of the type of concrete pressure exerted was the threat made by top US official John Foster Dulles to continue the occupation of Okinawa in the event that Japan signed the peace treaty (Nakamura 1985). With the US at the time still occupying Okinawa, the Senkaku Islands and other southern islands as the administrative authority, the end to the political division of Japan in the north of the archipelago that the signing of the peace treaty with the USSR implied would leave only the division in the south as the war's territorial legacy. In the context of the Cold War bipolar confrontation, the possibility of the US being characterized as the single remaining divider of the Japanese state and its people would have provided an intolerable level of political capital to the USSR as well as to political forces in Japan and around the world opposed to 'US imperialism'.

4.2.ii Japan's response to the Vietnam War

As will be discussed in Chapter 6, in the late 1950s the government was faced with mass protests over the June 1960 revision of the US–Japan security treaty. Such mass action by students, trade unions and ordinary citizens affirmed the continuing strength of anti-militarism and the attraction of the policy of unarmed neutrality in domestic society. The strength of the opposition was such that, shortly after the renewal, Kishi was forced to step down. Despite this setback for the LDP, the renewal of the treaty reaffirmed Japan's position as a key ally of the US in the Cold War confrontation in East Asia (Muroyama 1992: 187–208).

Kishi was replaced as leader of the LDP and thus as prime minister of Japan by Ikeda Hayato (1960–4), a former bureaucrat from the Yoshida school. The politics of economic growth he pursued, as symbolized by his administration's goal of doubling the workers' income, embedded the norm of economism. Rather than tackle the opposition head-on over the security treaty, the new government moved the sensitive issue of war and peace from the centre stage of politics. Still, Ikeda's foreign policy remained tied firmly to the US. Its essence is captured succinctly by one Japanese analyst who commented that Ikeda had 'no foreign policy except to follow America's lead' (cited in Havens 1987: 20). Whilst in the early 1960s this meant only the minimum support necessary for the US's policy in Vietnam and the gradual depoliticization of the US–Japan relationship as far as domestic society was concerned, the US's intensified bombing of the North and the escalation of the Vietnam War from the mid-1960s onwards provided Ikeda's successor, the staunchly anti-communist Satō Eisaku (1964–72), with the opportunity to demonstrate his anti-communism by offering full public support for the US war in Vietnam. In comparison with Ikeda, therefore, Satō was faced with a far greater challenge in balancing US and domestic pressures on his foreign and security policy.

The US pressure on the Satō government to play a more active role in support of the war in Vietnam was opposed by large segments of domestic society, as evidenced by the growth of the anti-Vietnam War movement. Popular opposition arose out of a fear that Japan could become entangled in a war of the US's making as well as a result of the norm of anti-militarism and Asianism, as will be discussed in Chapter 9. Accordingly, the political support offered by the Satō administration, as seen in his government's backing of South Vietnam against North Vietnam, was not matched by the same level of military support. Whilst bases in Okinawa were used by US bombers bound for Vietnam, thus suggesting Satō's indirect support for the US war effort, no Japanese troops joined directly in the war, unlike other US allies such as Australia and South Korea.

This illustrates the power of the anti-militarist norm to constrain policy. It was manifest concretely on the mass level in a widespread anti-Vietnam War movement, as symbolized by the group called *Beheiren* (Citizens' League for Peace in Vietnam). The political power of the movement was such that, although it was unable to prevent Japan's indirect support of the war, the holding of mass rallies, building of cross-national opposition to the war, aiding of draft resisters and other anti-war activities proved a major constraint on the level of cooperation the Japanese government was able to offer the US. Accordingly, in determining policy on Vietnam and the Vietnam War, Japanese policy-making agents were faced with *beiatsu* and obligations under the US–Japan security treaty, on the one hand, and domestic opposition and support for the anti-militarist norm, on the other. Their task was thus to balance these external and internal pressures. Overall, however, political relations between Japan and the US drew closer during the Satō years. This is suggested by the prime minister's 1969 speech at the National Press Club in Washington where, in the context of the impending decision on extending or scrapping the security treaty (see Chapter 6), he declared that a 'new order will be created by Japan and the United States' in the Asia Pacific (cited in Havens 1987: 199). Henceforth, Japan could be expected to play a greater role in support of US strategy in the region.

4.2.iii Normalization of relations with China

Despite the 'hot war' in Vietnam, the US was by the early 1970s rethinking its strategy towards the other main antagonist in the Cold War confrontation, China. As will be discussed in Chapter 9, the communist victory in 1949 and the US's support for Taiwan instead of China ensured that any attempt to normalize Sino-Japanese relations would undermine the Cold War order established by the US. By the early 1970s, however, the gradual weakening of the US as a hegemonic power, which resulted from the costs of the Vietnam War in particular, together with rising doubts about the political wisdom of pursuing a uniform anti-communist policy in the administration of President Richard Nixon (1969–74), called into question the continuing need to isolate the Chinese communist regime.

Accordingly, against a background of rising tensions between China and the USSR, President Nixon took the initiative to recognize the People's Republic of China (PRC) by making an official visit to China in February 1972, following National Security Advisor Henry Kissinger's secret mission to Beijing in July 1971. In the February 1972 Shanghai communiqué agreed between the two sides President Nixon accepted the PRC's principle of the existence of 'one China' and that Taiwan was an integral part of China, as will be discussed in Chapter 9. This action signalled the move of the international system away from bipolarity towards multipolarity, as the premise of a unified communist 'bloc' was shattered by this decision. It was like a bolt from the blue for Japanese policy-makers, as no-one had been informed of this momentous change in US policy. During the 1950s, Ambassador Asakai Kōichirō had fretted over such a possibility when he was serving in Washington. His concern was so great that, as history was to prove, it was 'Asakai's nightmare' come true. As for the prime minister, he felt completely betrayed by the two architects of this change of policy, Nixon and Kissinger. Despite his faithful support of the US, not even he had been informed. As a tearful Satō blurted: '"I have done everything" the Americans "have asked" ... but "they have let me down"' (Schaller 1997: 225, 229). As pointed out above, however, the prime minister had not done quite everything, as popular opposition had prevented him from cooperating fully in the US war in Vietnam. Nevertheless, the extent to which Satō supported the norm of bilateralism is well illustrated by this remark.

As was mentioned in Chapter 2, President Nixon's July 1971 shock announcement of the US decision to recognize the PRC, along with the August 1971 Nixon shocks – the jettisoning of the gold standard (the move to floating exchange rates) and the introduction of an import surcharge – brought about a fundamental restructuring of the Cold War international order. The impending collapse of the post-war, Bretton Woods system signalled the declining power of the US, the start of a relaxation of Cold War tensions, as well as the increasing pace of internationalization, especially in financial and other markets. Clearly, the change in the structure of the international system symbolized by the Nixon shocks provided the opportunity for Satō to push forward with the normalization of Sino-Japanese relations. The reason he did not do so is complex. In essence, however, it is because a change in US policy was a necessary, but not by itself a sufficient, condition for the China decision to be made. As will be discussed in detail in Chapter 9, normalization had to await the rise to the premiership of a new prime minister, Tanaka Kakuei.

4.2.iv Opportunities of multipolarity

The emerging multipolar structure of the international system provided Prime Minister Tanaka with the opportunity to carve out a more independent foreign policy for Japan. This is illustrated by the Tanaka government's response to the start of the first oil crisis in October 1973, when the policies adopted by the Organization of Petroleum Exporting Countries (OPEC) brought about a quadrupling of world oil prices. The oil crisis brings into sharp relief how resource-poor Japan can resist the constraint of bilateralism in cases of a foreign policy-making process representing a strongly consensual norm, for example developmentalism and economism, which can be instrumentalized in order to realize a key national goal without challenging the anti-militarist norm.

At the time of the October 1973 Fourth Middle East War, the Japanese government's commitment to bilateralism, as seen in the support it offered for the US's Middle East policy, provoked strong criticism in the region. The oil crisis resulting from the war led to a hasty change in Japanese policy. The decision by

Tanaka to adopt a policy at odds with the US, which was putting political pressure on alliance partners to oppose OPEC, demonstrates Japan's proactive foreign policy. In other words, in the context of the structural change in the international system as represented by the Nixon shocks, Japanese leaders could exercise a greater degree of independence than before. For resource-poor Japan, the threat to cheap oil supplies, arising from OPEC's new rights to set crude oil prices and determine the quantity of crude oil produced, made policy-making agents painfully aware of the economy's resource vulnerability, particularly as Japan's oil reserves were less than two months' worth at the time. Keeping the economic trajectory moving towards the goal of catching up with the West was prioritized by Tanaka, who sought to ensure the continual flow of oil in line with the norms of developmentalism and economism, rather than bow to *beiatsu*, in line with resource diplomacy (*shigen gaikō*).

Tanaka's decision to prioritize energy policy should be seen in the context of the grander Japanese project of realizing the norm of developmentalism by maintaining high economic growth to catch up with the West. In a concrete way, the increase in oil prices put this project at risk, whereas, for the US, with oil at home and the gigantic oil majors flying the US flag abroad, the same risk in countering OPEC's policy did not exist. The Tanaka administration's emerging pro-Arab policy can be seen in the instrumentalization of policy through the provision of Official Development Assistance (ODA) to the Arab world, including loans, technical cooperation and the financing of oil refineries (Arase 1995: 74–6). It can be seen, too, in the government's decision to break further away from US policy in hosting an August 1975 visit by the leader of the Palestine Liberation Organization (PLO), Yasser Arafat. This led to the opening of a PLO office in Tokyo in February 1977, despite Japan's earlier abstentions in the UN on the PLO's right to self-determination (see Chapter 19).

In this way, despite characterizations of the Japanese policy-making process as immobilist, as was discussed in Chapter 2, it can be seen that the threat to the national economy was considered serious enough at the time of the first oil crisis to galvanize key policy-making agents into rapidly implementing a new policy at odds with the US. Clearly, Japanese policy-makers considered the risk of turning off the oil taps to be greater than the damage to US–Japan relations resulting from adopting a pro-Arab stance. When interests diverge, therefore, Japan can adopt and has adopted unilateral policies independent of the US and out of character with its dominant pattern of international relations.

4.2.v Opportunities and constraints of renewed bipolarity

Nevertheless, as was clear in the foreign policy pursued by Fukuda Takeo as prime minister (1976–8), Japan's diplomatic activities remained 'premised on relations with the United States' (Edström 1999: 96). What is more, the outbreak of the second Cold War and the strengthening of the bipolar structure of the international system in the late 1970s served to tighten Japan's relations with the US, and more broadly the Western camp. In the late 1970s, although reluctant to endorse harsh US sanctions, the government followed the US political line in opposing the USSR's invasion of Afghanistan (1979). It also offered support to the US during the Iranian hostage crisis (1979–80) and followed the US in boycotting the Olympic games held in Moscow (1980). In addition, the government deployed economic power in a way to support broader US strategic objectives. This can be seen, for instance, in the political use of ODA in line with US strategic interests in the wider world, as was touched on in Chapter 2. It is illustrated by the significant increase in aid to Pakistan and Turkey following the USSR's invasion of Afghanistan as part of an emerging strategy of supporting front-line states in accordance with the interests of the Western allies (Yasutomo 1995: 9).

With the election of the more openly nationalistic LDP leader, Nakasone Yasuhiro, to power (1982–7), three of the leading G7 states, the US under President Ronald Reagan (1981–9), the UK under Prime Minister Margaret Thatcher (1979–90) and Japan under Prime Minister Nakasone, were ideological bedfellows set on cutting back the state at home and countering the USSR's expansion abroad, both politically and militarily. Politically, the Nakasone administration backed the US and generally sought to play a more prominent role on the world stage. From this perspective, the second Cold War can be seen to have led to renewed constraints on Japan's international relations. From another perspective, however, the changed circumstances offered political leaders such as Nakasone the opportunity to reinvigorate bilateralism in the struggle against the domestically embedded norm of anti-militarism, which constrained the international role Japan could play.

This is symbolized by the above conservative triumvirate and, more particularly, the close bilateral relationship between Reagan and Nakasone (the so-called 'Ron–Yasu' relationship deriving from their given names of Ronald and Yasuhiro). It emerged as part of Nakasone's political project to make Japan an 'international state'. Already, Japan had achieved this goal in the economic dimension, and it would strive under Nakasone to do so also in the political and security dimensions. Politically, the prime minister sought to realize two aims, one domestic and one international. Domestically, he took measures to erode support for the Constitution and other post-war institutions which had given succour to anti-militarism by calling for the 'settlement of the post-war accounts'. Internationally, he became literally the first post-war prime minister to stride onto the world stage in an attempt to represent Japan as a big political power.

Although Nakasone did not neglect East Asia – his first visit as prime minister was to South Korea, rather than to the US – his main goal was to play an international political role alongside the other conservative leaders of the G7, especially President Reagan. More telling is the fact that, following the four trips to the US for bilateral consultations made by Satō in his eight years in office, Nakasone made three in his shorter five-year term (January 1983, January 1985 and April 1986: Appendix 4.1). Paradoxically, in seeking to play a major political role on the world stage, Nakasone's nationalism, for which he was renowned at home, was overshadowed by the bilateralism at the heart of the post-war US–Japan relationship.

This period is important to our discussion of US–Japan political relations, as Nakasone's rejection of cross-party consensus politics, which had been established in Japan during the 1960s and 1970s, created a schism among Japan's conservative political elite (Watanabe 1993). The schism emerged between those LDP politicians who, with an eye to the change in the structure of the international system, sought a more prominent role for Japan in the world as a political big power; and those who, content with the *status quo*, continued to support the norms of anti-militarism, developmentalism and economism, particularly the last two. As Nakasone's goal of making Japan a global political power went hand in hand with his commitment to the US–Japan bilateral relationship, he was more receptive to the idea of building up the military than the *status quo* conservatives, who gave greater weight to the norms embedded in domestic society. In this sense, the constraint imposed on Nakasone in playing a role as the representative of a global political big power, possibly backed by the active use of military force, stemmed not only from the norms embedded in domestic society, but also from the reaction of East Asians who had suffered under Japanese imperialism (see Part III). The debate that emerged during the Nakasone era has remained central to the question of Japan's political place in the world in the post-Cold War era, as illustrated by Liberal Party leader Ozawa Ichirō's political project to make Japan a 'normal state', as was mentioned in Chapter 2. In this sense, Nakasone was Ozawa's precursor.

4.2.vi Opportunities and constraints of the post-Cold War period

The ending of the Cold War radically transformed the structure of the international system. In the new international environment, Japanese policy-makers have been presented with a range of opportunities to reformulate political relations with the US and, more widely, the world. At the same time, however, the legacy of Cold War structures and the power of bilateralism continue to impose constraints and provide opportunities for Japanese policy-making agents to promote Japan's international relations. The reason is that, although the essentially bipolar structure of the international system ended with the Cold War, this nevertheless did not lead to the end of the bilateralism at the heart of the US–Japan relationship.

As has been mentioned in Chapter 3 and above, a major outstanding issue of the post-war settlement for Japan has been and remains the resolution of the sovereignty dispute with Russia over the Northern Territories. During the Cold War, Japanese policy-makers and other political actors considered that a major impediment to its resolution was the effect this might have upon the borders between the East and the West in Europe. In other words, the settlement of a territorial issue between the East and the West in one part of the world (East Asia) might have repercussions in another (Europe), which could lead to the unravelling of the borders set in place as part of the Cold War divide. In this sense, the end of the Cold War, which meant the end of the East–West territorial divide in Europe, offered an opportunity for Japanese policy-makers to resolve the territorial issue; the Berlin Wall, after all, now lay in ruins. However, as many of these policy-making agents remained committed to bilateralism, particularly in MOFA, they were unable to push forward immediately with a resolution of their own territorial dispute with Russia.

Despite the change of borders in Europe, therefore, no new policy initiative was at first taken to solve the problem of the Northern Territories. As one former diplomat mused in 1992: 'I think that probably in the whole wide world only Japan's Liberal-Democratic Party administration stills clings to the idea of the Soviet threat' (Asai 1992: 180). Quite clearly, with this mindset, the ability of MOFA officials to solve the territorial conflict was severely constrained. Thus, although progress was made on the political level shortly after the end of the Cold War, as illustrated by the October 1993 summit meeting between the leader of Japan's first coalition government, Prime Minister Hosokawa Morihiro, and President Boris Yeltsin, a significant change in thinking did not take place within MOFA until several years later. This occurred after the return to Tokyo in August 1996 of the Russian ambassador, Tōgō Kazuhiko, and other personnel changes within the ministry. As a result, 'new thinking' was introduced in order to break the deadlock on MOFA's policy of not separating politics and economics in any dealings with Russia (Wada 1999: 362–3).

With the end of the bipolar structure of the international system, moreover, the US became a unipolar power, at least militarily. As seen at the time of the 1990–1 Gulf War, however, the legitimacy of the US's deployment of military power needed to be bolstered by condemnation by the UN of President Saddam Hussein's August 1990 invasion of Kuwait. When in January 1991 the US-led multinational forces moved against Iraq, Japan came under intense US pressure to make both a human and a financial contribution to the war effort.

As will be elaborated in Chapter 18, bilateral political pressure from the US, although successful in prompting the government to make a financial contribution of US$13 billion, failed to break the ban on making a direct military contribution of military personnel and *matériel*. In other words, despite the transformation in the structure of the international system that the ending of the Cold War implied, the domestically embedded norm of anti-militarism and the Japanese preference for instrumentalizing policy through economic means continued to hold sway. At the same time, however, at the mass and even political elite level, awareness of the financial and other contributions the government made to the Gulf War remained almost totally lacking in the US.

The collapse of the international Cold War structures at the turn of the 1990s contributed significantly to the demise of the domestic Cold War structure in Japan, as was seen in Chapter 2. Whilst the advent of coalition governments and the rapid rise and fall of premiers reflect the changes at home, as most of these new leaders lacked foreign policy-making experience, MOFA has sought to take the upper hand in Japan's political relations with the US. Nevertheless, the Diet's decision to push ahead with legislation on sending Japanese troops abroad, on the one hand, and the meeting between Prime Minister Hosokawa and President Bill Clinton in February 1994, on the other, demonstrate the changes underway in the new era. These changes are illustrated in the former case by Japanese participation in UNPKO, which eroded the norm of anti-militarism, and in the latter case by Hosokawa's loud 'no' to the Clinton administration's pressure to accept quantifiable objective criteria in seeking a resolution to the bilateral trade dispute, which eroded bilateralism (see Chapter 5). Whilst the former led the socialists to filibuster all night against the undermining of the anti-militarist norm, Hosokawa created a palpitation, if not a seizure, of the political heart of the bilateral relationship by uttering the taboo 'no' to the US.

The LDP's return to power from 1996 onwards has demonstrated how the ending of the Cold War not only provided new opportunities for Japan to chart a more independent course internationally, but also confirmed the health of bilateralism. As it stands, the most salient feature of the post-Cold War relationship now emerging is not the end of bilateralism, which remains the dominant pattern of Japan's international relations, but rather the strengthening of the other norms introduced in Chapter 2: namely, Asianism, as will be discussed in Part III; trilateralism, as will be discussed in Part IV; and internationalism, as will be discussed in Part V. In this sense, the power of the US to constrain Japanese international behaviour, whilst remaining strong, can be said to have weakened. As a result, Japanese policy-making agents can be expected to play an increasingly important role in a range of international activities, which may over time provide a new generation of leaders with an opportunity to outgrow the bilateral dependency of the Cold War period.

In the post-Cold War world, therefore, bilateralism has been supplemented by a range of new political relations in a multilateral context. As will be seen in Part V, throughout most of the post-war era Japan has been involved in a range of multilateral global institutions. With the end of the Cold War, the government has not only strengthened its role at the global level, but also boosted actively its participation in multilateral regional and subregional fora. In the realm of security, for instance, the ASEAN Regional Forum (ARF) has emerged as a new site for dialogue, as will be seen in Chapter 11, but the main regional site insofar as multilateral political relations are concerned is the Asia Pacific Economic Cooperation (APEC) forum. This initiative was put forward in 1989 by the Australian prime minister, Bob Hawke, although Japanese policy-making agents played a crucial part in the development of the APEC idea.

As the title of the forum testifies, the main focus of APEC is economics, but APEC is important politically, too, as it is emerging as the main regional vehicle through which the US is promoting its globalist project of spreading the neo-liberal, free-market economy. This can be seen, for instance, in US political pressure on Japan not to support the 1991 proposal by the Malaysian prime minister, Mahathir Mohamad, to establish the subregional forum, the East Asian Economic Caucus (EAEC) (Hook 1999a). In prioritizing APEC over EAEC at that time, the Japanese government confirmed the continuing dominance of bilateralism, despite the growing strength of Asianism, as will be addressed in Chapter 10.

4.3 Domestic society

During the Cold War and post-Cold War periods the changes in the structure of the international system constrained as well as presented opportunities for Japanese policy-making agents to pursue the interests of the Japanese state and its people. In domestic society, the government's central policy of close political relations with the US has engendered both opposition and support. Over the long term, however, support for the US–Japan relationship and the norm of bilateralism has grown, as is illustrated by the cases of the academic community and public opinion.

4.3.i Americanization of the academic community

As was discussed in Chapter 3, the Peace Issues Discussion Group (PIDG) was the fountainhead for the policy of unarmed neutrality adopted by the SDPJ. The members of this group symbolized the intellectual elite of Japan in the late 1940s and early 1950s, and were in that sense representative of the academic community's response to the government's policy of pursuing the peace and security of the Japanese state and its people through maintaining close political relations with the US. After the renewal of the security treaty in 1960, however, the policies growing out of the LDP's and MOFA's support for bilateralism were increasingly legitimized by a panoply of international relations specialists who had been trained in the realist academic tradition in ivy-league US universities. Fellowships under the Fulbright programme, the Japanese Ministry of Education, and financing by other public and philanthropic bodies supported their studies. From this time onwards, the realist school began to mount a challenge to the dominant international relations scholarship growing out of the PIDG tradition, as in the cases of Sakamoto Yoshikazu and Seki Hiroharu, both of Tokyo University. Scholars such as Kōsaka Masataka of Kyoto University and Nagai Yonosuke of Tokyo University of Technology played a pivotal role in providing the intellectual legitimation for the policy choices made by the LDP government, particularly in respect of the US–Japan security treaty. Whereas intellectuals in the PIDG tradition were part of 'the other Japan', seeking to establish Japan's identity and role as a 'peace state', many of the realist scholars who returned from the US became part of 'bilateral Japan', providing intellectual sustenance for the government's policy of bilateralism and close political relations with the US.

4.3.ii Public opinion

Similarly, at the mass level, support for close relations with the US has increased over the years. At the time of the signing of the peace and security treaties, support for the socialist option of unarmed neutralism was strong, suggesting that an alternative to close political relations with the US enjoyed popular backing. Even after the outbreak of the Korean War, for instance, a September 1950 poll by the *Asahi Shimbun* showed that 22 per cent of the pollees favoured neutrality as the policy Japan should pursue. This support remained high a decade later, at the time of the revision of the treaty. This is illustrated by a January 1960 poll, when as many as 35 per cent of those surveyed chose neutrality, and 24 per cent chose dependence on the UN, as the best way to protect Japanese security (multiple answers permitted). The pronouncements of leading intellectuals and other political actors, along with changes in the structure of the international system, are no doubt factors leading to the growth in support for the US over the years. In poll after poll, it has emerged as popular, except for a short period during the Vietnam War. In a 1997 poll, for instance, 75 per cent of the pollees were favourably disposed towards the US, about the same as the 73 per cent registered a decade earlier (Naikaku Sōri Daijin Kōhōshitsu 1997).

The benefits to the Japanese state and its people of close cooperation with the big power in the post-war world are clearly visible in terms of Japan's political rehabilitation, not to mention its economic success, in the last fifty-five years. It is only occasionally, as symbolized by mass protests against the rape by US military personnel of an Okinawan schoolgirl in September 1995 as well as the protests against US bases and the 1996 reaffirmation of the security treaty (see Chapter 6), that the costs of this choice are likely to impinge upon domestic society and mass support.

Needless to say in Japan, as in other democracies, the voters make a choice politically in supporting or opposing the government, even if international relations may not be the most important determinant of their political preference. Whatever the specifics of Japan's international relations, Japanese citizens, as political actors, ultimately have supported, opposed or acquiesced in the policies pursued by respective Japanese governments throughout the post-war era. As is clear from the above polls, support for the bilateral relationship with the US is widespread on the popular level.

4.4 Summary

The above discussion of political relations between Japan and the US has sought to trace the evolution of political ties between these two Pacific powers by drawing attention to different aspects of the approach put forward in Chapter 2. The chapter has sought to answer the 'what', 'why' and 'how' of Japan's political relations with the US by examining a number of foreign policy decisions within the context of changes in the structure of the international system and domestic society. The normalization of relations with the two communist big powers, the response to the Gulf War, and the move to Asianism, trilateralism and internationalism in the post-Cold War period, stand out in importance for clarifying the nature of the US–Japan political relationship. In essence, this chapter has elucidated the continuing importance of bilateralism as the dominant pattern of Japan's international relations. It has at the same time taken care to highlight the ability of Japanese policy-making agents and other actors to take advantage of the opportunities presented by changes in the structure of the international system in order to promote the interests and goals of the Japanese state and its people. With the end of the Cold War, this is now being carried out increasingly within a range of new fora, as will be discussed in Parts III, IV and V of this volume. This does not, however, represent the end of bilateralism, but rather the emergence of a supplemental strategy to bilateralism through the strengthening of other international relations. In this, the influence of domestic society cannot be ignored.

Chapter 5

Japan–United States economic relations

5.1 Overview

As outlined in Part I, the global economic ascent of Japan from the 1950s to the 1980s and the subsequent downturn in the economy in the 1990s and at the beginning of the twenty-first century have taken place in the context of international structures set in place by the early-starters of the West. Within the structural constraints thereby imposed, the Japanese state and its people have sought to catch up with the advanced Western economies, giving substance to the norms of developmentalism and economism. In this process, the economy has relied heavily on the export of manufactured goods to the world market, especially the most advanced consumer market, the US. Over time, these exports have moved from imitation goods at the lower end of the technology spectrum to sophisticated goods at the higher. This is not the economic role US policy-making agents had envisaged for Japan after the end of the Occupation. Then, Japan's future was seen to be as a second-tier economy, not a leading economy capable of challenging America's industrial and technological might (Cumings 1984). Yet Japan has emerged as a challenger in sector after sector of the US economy. As a consequence, the two now compete in many of the same high-technology, high-value-added areas. This has caused a range of trade and other economic conflicts. Here the norm of developmentalism at the heart of Japan's export-led strategy has often been perceived to generate tension with the norms of free-market capitalism at the heart of the US's strategy.

As has been demonstrated in the previous chapter, bilateralism is at the heart of the political relationship, but how the rise of Japan economically has affected the bilateral economic relationship still needs to be elaborated.

5.2 Trade relations

The pattern of Japan's trade relations with the world is characterized by a heavy reliance on the US market for the export of finished products. From the time Japan entered the high growth period in the 1950s, the overall pattern of trade has been for around one-quarter to one-third of total exports to be absorbed by the US market. Over time, the specifics have differed in terms of the items exported, with textiles representative of the 1960s, colour televisions the 1970s, automobiles the 1980s and semi-conductors the 1990s. Export dependence on the US was 27 per cent in 1960, 31 per cent in 1970, 24 per cent in 1980, 32 per cent in 1990 and 31 per cent in 1998 (Table 1). The highest ratio was 39 per cent in 1986. The importance of exports to the US is even greater in particular sectors of the economy, for which the United States is the main absorber market. Exports to the US have formed a large percentage of total Japanese world exports in the automobile and electronics industries, accounting for 56 per cent of total Japanese automobile exports in both 1975 and 1985, and climbing from 36 per cent of total Japanese electronics exports in 1975 to 43 per cent in 1985 (Tsūshō Sangyōshō 1976: 227–9, 678–80; 1986: 118–20, 530–1). As section 5.3 below makes clear, the rise in

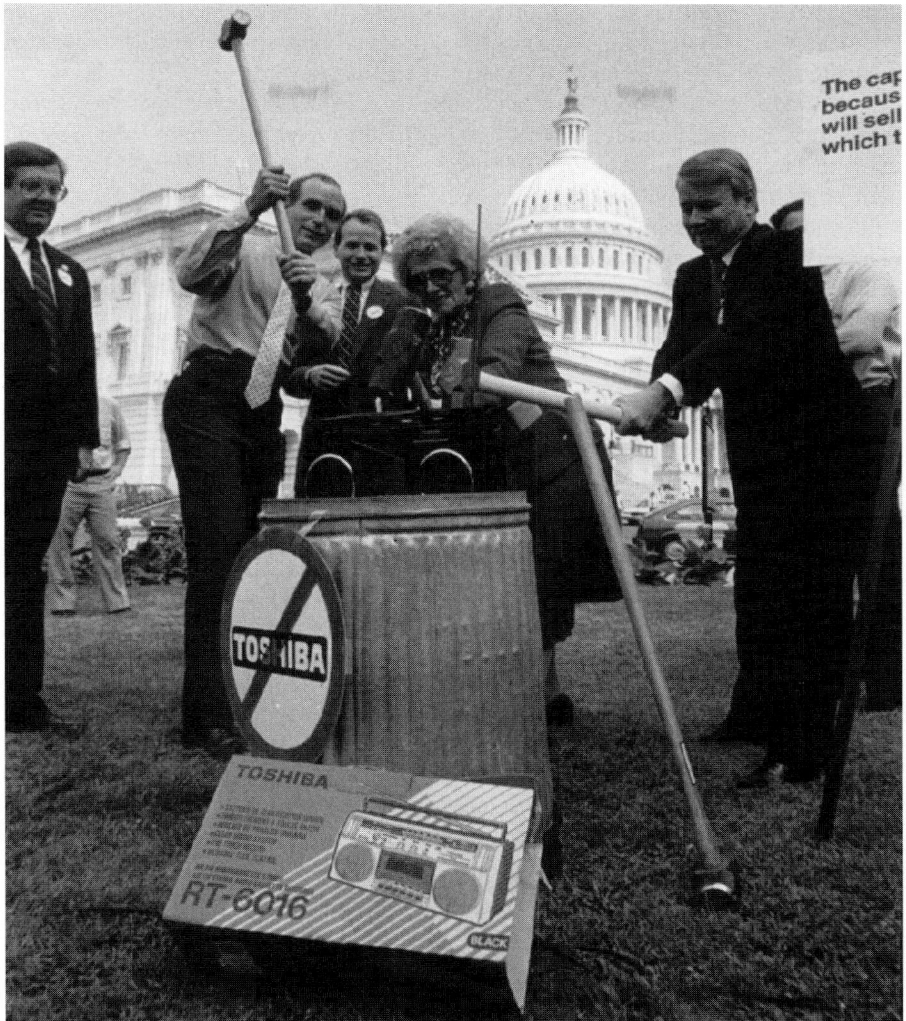

Plate 5.1 Congressmen take a sledgehammer to Toshiba. On 1 July 1987 congressmen vented their anger at Toshiba for supplying advanced dual-use technology to the Soviet Union.

Source: Courtesy of Associated Press

the value of the yen following the 1985 Plaza Accord (Table 4) spurred leading Japanese auto and electronic goods makers to move production facilities offshore by investing in new plants in the US. This led to a consequent downturn in the percentage of these exports to the US market in the late 1980s, the start of exports to other regions and the beginning of a small amount of reverse imports to Japan. Even in 1998, however, 29 per cent of Japan's total exports to the US are accounted for by automobiles (37 per cent of Japan's worldwide exports of automobiles), and 20 per cent by electronics (26 per cent of Japan's worldwide exports of electronics) (JETRO 1999a: 424–7).

As far as imports from the US are concerned, for the last forty years or so the trend has been generally downwards, with an overall decline from around one-third to one-fifth of the total imported. Imports from the US made up 34 per cent of the total in 1960, 29 per cent in 1970, 17 per cent in 1980, 22 per cent in 1990 and 24 per cent in 1998 (Table 1). The highest ratio was 44 per cent in 1950 (Table 1). These imports have been concentrated in certain high-technology sectors, such as aircraft and defence equipment, but many of them are more representative of the relationship between an advanced and a developing economy, as in Japan's import of US citrus fruit, soya beans and other agricultural products. For instance, in 1998, 27 per cent of Japan's imports from the US consisted of agricultural products and raw materials, whereas close to 100 per cent of the US's imports from Japan consisted of manufactured goods (JETRO 1999a: 424–7). This stark imbalance in the pattern of trade between the two most important national economies in the world, with high-value exports from Japan to the US but many low-value-added exports from the US to Japan, has contributed to one of the major sources of economic conflict between the two countries: Japan's trade surplus, the most salient manifestation of the 'Japan problem' referred to in Part I.

The trade surplus was originally on the US side, as expected by policy-makers during the Occupation. Still, the rapid economic recovery and spectacular economic growth experienced by Japan during the 1950s and early 1960s meant that, by 1965, the trend was reversed and Japan for the first time moved into surplus (Table 1). Japan's trade balance with the US has continued in the black ever since. Although the amount has risen and fallen, the total has reached at times historically enormous proportions, at around US$40–50 billion during the 1980s and 1990s: US$39 billion in 1985, US$38 billion in 1990, US$45 billion in 1995 and US$51 billion in 1998 (Table 1). Japan's trade surplus with the US surplus reached its highest peak at a staggering US$55 billion in 1994.

Whilst economists of various intellectual persuasions have offered a range of cogent reasons for the causes of the deficit, as far as President Bill Clinton's administration (1993–2001) was concerned, it stemmed from the imbalance between imports and exports arising from Japan's unfair trading practices. With over two-thirds of the US general public and opinion leaders pointing to unfair trading practices as the root cause of the imbalance in a 1994 opinion survey, the perception of these 'unfair' practices as the cause of the US deficit can be said to be widely accepted in US society (Haraguchi 1995: 65). This led the Clinton and previous administrations to call for restrictions on the flow of Japanese exports to the US as well as to exert pressure for the further opening, liberalization and deregulation of the Japanese economy. In this way, the trade surplus has contributed to the politicization of economic relations between these two Pacific powers, with the US president and Japanese prime minister themselves often playing a central role in seeking to resolve the trade conflicts which have emerged over the years. This involvement of policy-makers at the highest levels suggests the political importance of trade in the overall relationship between Japan and the US.

5.2.i Trade conflicts

Whilst the trade conflicts between Japan and the US symbolize for many the economic ascent of Japan and the economic decline of the US, the success of Japanese exports to the US market ultimately stems from US demand. Not only have Japanese automobiles, audio-visual equipment, computers and other products proved popular with US consumers, but high-technology products such as semi-conductors have also become an essential part of many of the US's most sophisticated weapons systems, as highlighted at the time of the 1990–1 Gulf War. The reverse side of Japan's success, however, is often the failure of US business in the very same sector of the economy. As a result, a panoply of industrial lobbies have used their political muscle to influence economic fundamentals by calling on various US administrations to cut the flow of Japanese exports to the US market or boost the flow of US imports to Japan.

Each stage in the development of the bilateral economic relationship has been represented by a particular dispute involving Japanese manufacturers. In the 1960s, for instance, US textile manufacturers sought political support in order to curtail Japanese exports to the home market. Thus it was that, at their behest, President Richard Nixon exerted pressure on Prime Minister Satō Eisaku to impose restraints on Japanese textile exports to the US (Destler *et al.* 1979). Such export restrictions, often dressed up in the euphemistic garb of voluntary export restraints (VERs), were in the 1970s and the early 1980s also applied to colour televisions, machine tools, automobiles and other exports. The response by Japanese manufacturers, particularly in the 1980s, was to circumvent these restrictions by setting up production facilities in the US and export 'launch platforms' in East Asia, as will be elaborated in Chapter 10. Despite the downturn in the economy, Japanese manufacturers during the 1990s and early twenty-first century continued to invest in the US at the same time as the Clinton administration continued to pursue numerical trade targets rather than impose VERs.

From the middle of the 1980s onwards, the US government increasingly exerted pressure on Japan to open the home market to US products and to make structural changes in the domestic political economy. Such pressure has been brought to bear through a range of bilateral channels, such as the Bush administration's call for negotiations under the Structural Impediments Initiative (SII) of September 1989 to June 1990 and the US–Japan Framework Talks on Bilateral Trade announced at a bilateral summit in July 1993, which finally reached a conclusion in June 1995. In contrast to the VERs used against Japanese exporters, these are market-access approaches. As such, they aim to bring about changes in the very nature of the Japanese economy. In the former case, the US employed the SII as a way to address issues such as the distribution system, domestic and overseas price differentials, cross-holding of company shares, land use, enforcement of the anti-monopoly law and the balance between domestic savings and investments. As far as Japan's approach to the SII is concerned, the structural issues to be dealt with on the US side were seen to be the balance between investments and savings, corporate investment behaviour, export controls, research and development, qualitative improvement in the labour force and improvement in corporate strategy.

Rather than these talks focusing on the structural changes highlighted for discussion by both sides, however, the emphasis shifted to focus almost exclusively on bringing about changes in the Japanese economy. This points to how, despite its economic ascendance, Japan remains weak in making actual political use of its economic power. The US continues to take advantage of this political weakness by shaping the agenda of bilateral economic negotiations for its own ends. The results can be seen, for instance, in the revision of the law relating to large retail stores, which has allowed large US retailers such as the toy giant, Toys 'R 'Us, to set up supermarket-type outlets in Japan. As the changes brought about by US pressure were frequently difficult to realize, the SII was welcomed by domestic forces seeking to promote the liberalization and deregulation of the economy, although others criticized it as interference in Japan's domestic affairs (Ito 1993: 411). In either case, although these types of investments undermine the business of the 'mom and pop' small stores, the reforms brought about have clearly been in the interests of Japanese consumers, who have benefited from the liberalization and deregulation of the economy set in motion by external pressure. Like their counterparts as far back as the Occupation (Dower 1999), then, Japanese policy-makers today are still willing and able to instrumentalize policy by the use of *beiatsu*, as illustrated by these negotiations. In other words, US pressure has acted as a vehicle to promote reform in the face of entrenched domestic opposition.

In the US–Japan Framework Talks on Bilateral Trade, the aim of promoting the liberalization and deregulation of the Japanese economy was pursued by the Clinton administration through a results-oriented approach to market access, whereby specific numerical targets were set in certain key sectors of the economy. In view of the belief that it was impossible to change the Japanese system as such, these talks dealt with a wide range of issues such as government procurement, intellectual property rights, insurance, medical equipment, plate glass and, as will be examined below, semi-conductors, automobiles and auto-parts. The setting of numerical targets engendered a large degree of resistance across the Japanese political spectrum, even at the highest level. In the February 1994 meeting between President Clinton and Prime Minister Hosokawa Morihiro, for instance, the parties failed to come to an agreement on government procurement. Later in 1994 the two sides did reach a settlement on insurance and plate glass as well as government procurement; however, in the face of the US introduction into the negotiations of possible retaliatory measures, Japanese policy-makers broke off negotiations on automobiles and auto-parts. The end result, which will be returned to below, illustrates how Japan has come to instrumentalize its international relations through multilateral as well as bilateral frameworks.

The retaliatory measures threatened by the US can be taken unilaterally as a result of a number of protectionist laws which have been passed by the US Congress – for instance, the August 1988 Omnibus Trade and Competitiveness Act and the Clinton administration's revival in March 1994 of the lapsed Super 301 provision of that Act, which was signed into law in 1988. These measures allow the automatic investigation of foreign trade practices and the threat as well as the retaliatory implementation of trade sanctions by the president. Thus, despite the emergence of Japan as an economic challenger, the US government has been able both to restrict Japanese exports and to exert pressure on Japanese policy-making agents to boost US imports as a result of the continuing strength of US political and military power in shaping the overall nature of the bilateral economic relationship.

5.2.i.a Automobiles

As the vignette at the beginning of Chapter 3 illustrated, the trade conflict in automobiles highlights a significant change in the nature of the economic relationship between Japan and the US. The trade in automobiles is of particular concern to the US government as up to two-thirds of Japan's trade surplus is said to result from the auto-related trade (Nihon Keizai Shimbun 1995: 2). Conflict over automobiles has been a recurring theme in trade relations going back to 1979, when the leader of the United Auto Workers called on US consumers to boycott Japanese cars, but the most recent instance, alluded to earlier, flared in the 1990s. This conflict was at first being dealt with as part of the negotiations taking place in the US–Japan Framework Talks on Bilateral Trade. The dispute revolved around the Clinton administration's attempt to gain a larger share of the Japanese automobile and auto-parts market by agreeing numerical targets. The Japanese government was determined to resist the imposition of a US-contrived numerical solution to the conflict through an appeal to multilateralist institutions.

As on other occasions, the US threatened to impose tariffs through the provisions of the Omnibus Trade and Competitiveness Act of 1988. In response, the Japanese government appealed to the principle of free trade and the WTO's principle of multilateral engagement. What is most significant about the Japanese response at this time, however, is that despite the Clinton administration's threat to impose a 100 per cent tariff on luxury Japanese cars bound for the US market, the Japanese government continued to resist US pressure. In the end, the Clinton administration abandoned the goal of establishing a numerical target and a settlement was reached. As one commentator put it:

> Never before had the United States threatened a trading partner with such punitive sanctions in such a high-profile case involving such an important industry. Never before had Japan so resolutely resisted such foreign trade pressure. Most important, the auto dispute marked the end of an era. No longer could the United States threaten sanctions and assume Japan would capitulate.
>
> (Stokes 1996: 284)

Despite the continuing power of bilateralism, then, the government in this way appealed to multilateralist and global institutions as a way of deploy its power *vis-à-vis* the US.

5.2.i.b Semi-conductors

Similarly, the changing nature of the bilateral economic relationship is symbolized by the semi-conductor dispute, which illustrates the US–Japan trade conflict in the high-technology sector of the economy. The dispute goes back to the action brought in June 1985 through the office of the US Trade Representative (USTR) by the US Semi-conductor Industry Association against Japanese producers under provision 301 of the 1974 Omnibus Trade Act. This led to the signing of the first US–Japan Semi-conductor Accord in September 1986. The main aim of this and various other agreements reached between the two sides has been to expand foreign (most important, US) access to the Japanese market as well as to forestall any dumping of Japanese semi-conductors overseas. These agreements have enabled the US government to bring actions against Japan. As a result of Japanese manufacturers not abiding by the 1986 agreement, for instance, the US government in March 1987 introduced retaliatory measures against Japan by imposing a 100 per cent tariff on personal computers, colour televisions and power tools. As is clear from the nature of this penalty, the US government targeted Japanese finished goods, not semi-conductors *per se*. This is because US users of semi-conductors are dependent upon supplies from Japan. Here the interests of Japanese and US businesses can be seen to coincide as well as to be in competition.

Meanwhile, under continuing US pressure, the Japanese government sought to expand foreign access to the home market in semi-conductors. By pushing for numerical targets, US producers aimed to gain a 20 per cent share of the Japanese market by the end of 1992. MITI exerted pressure on Japanese buyers to ensure that this numerical target was reached (Tsuchiya 1995), suggesting again how *beiatsu* can be used by domestic policy-making agents to promote their own goals. Despite this success, the dispute flared up again in the summer of 1996, when it was resolved by the two sides making a new agreement. The most significant aspect of this agreement is the setting-up of a multilateral forum for dealing with future disputes in this sector. This move from a bilateral to a multilateral forum no doubt reflects the US's decreasing concern over the threat posed by Japanese semi-conductor makers, but also sharply illustrates the difficulty for the Japanese government in exercising the latent power created by the changing nature of the bilateral economic relationship.

Clearly, as a result of the crucial role semi-conductors play in missiles and other defence equipment, their source of supply has been of concern to the US government. Reliance on Japanese producers for this supply could make the US vulnerable in terms of national security – a clear recognition of the potential for Japan to deploy its power *vis-à-vis* the US through the high-technology sector. The former LDP nationalist politician and incumbent governor of Tokyo, Ishihara Shintarō, has in his writings called on the Japanese government to exercise this sort of power (Ishihara and Morita 1989). Even at the time of the US's heavy reliance on Japanese suppliers, however, this form of power seems to have remained latent, not manifest. Indeed, the various semi-conductor agreements have led to the interpenetration of the US and Japanese markets, rather than Japan's use of the high-technology sector as a means to deploy economic power *vis-à-vis* the US.

In this sense, the twenty-first century is likely to see the further development of shared interests between Japan and the US as well as competition.

The semi-conductor and auto-related trade disputes are typical of the change in the way trade conflicts were dealt with in the 1990s. In the case of the semi-conductors and in bilateral negotiations through the SII and US–Japan Framework Talks, it is clear that the US side is now more willing to accept that certain trade issues should be dealt with before multilateral bodies. Similarly, a dispute between Eastman Kodak and Fuji Photo Film, which was settled in Fuji's favour in April 1998, was brought before the WTO. It can be expected that, over time, such multilateral mechanisms will continue to be used alongside the bilateral fora the two countries have established for resolving trade disputes. As Japan remains in the weaker position in bilateral fora, appeals to move to multilateral fora provide a new opportunity for Japanese policy-making agents to resist US pressure. In this sense, a multilateral approach for dealing with trade disputes suggests that, far from Japan being able to exercise economic power over the US directly, multilateral fora may in the future be used increasingly to depoliticize bilateral trade issues.

5.3 Investment relations

The rise of Japan to international prominence in the high-technology and high-value-added sectors of the economy has created the trade surpluses that, together with the high domestic savings rate, have brought about Japan's presence as a major investor in the US and other economies. Over the years, the US has been the main target of Japanese FDI, with around 24 per cent of total global investments directed towards the US between 1951 and 1964, rising to 32 per cent by 1980, and then reaching a level of around 40 per cent or more from 1985 onwards (Table 2). The proportion of Japanese investment in the US reached its peak in 1989, when it made up over 48 per cent of the world total. Since then the proportion of total Japanese FDI devoted to the US has declined. However, at 39 per cent in 1997, the amount remains far ahead of the second placed destination, East Asia, with 21 per cent, and next placed EU, with 20 per cent (Table 2). Overall, in 1997 Japan was the sixth most important investor in the US, but the largest investor over the cumulative period of 1991 to 1997 (JETRO 1999b: 93).

Looking back, Japan started to become a major investor in the US economy following the Nixon shocks of 1971. The yen has risen almost ever since until 1998: from the peg of 360 yen to the dollar set in 1949 it moved to 308 yen in 1971 and 210 yen in 1978. Following the Plaza Accord of 1985, when the value of the yen was pushed higher through an agreement to weaken the dollar by the G5 (Group of Five), the 150 yen barrier was broken in 1987. The 100-yen barrier then went in 1994. The late 1990s did not see the yen return to its all-time high of 80 yen to the dollar set in 1995 (Table 4). Whatever the range in terms of value, however, the continuing dominance of the dollar as both a store of value and as a means of carrying out international trade means that Japanese policy-makers are limited in the degree to which they can deploy Japanese power through the yen.

5.3.i Manufacturing investment

Japanese manufacturers have traditionally maintained a strong preference for production at home, given the efficiency of the workforce and their ability to maintain high-quality production output. The main reasons for the surge in overseas manufacturing FDI have thus been external not internal: the rise in the value of the yen and the need to circumvent the US's protectionist measures aimed at curtailing Japanese imports. Whilst investments in the US have involved a wide range of companies, the investments in the automobile and electronic sectors are illustrative of the way Japanese manufacturers have sought to circumvent the VERs imposed on Japanese imports. In particular, as the rise in the yen against the dollar has made investments in the US cheap in comparison with investment at home, which would burden exporters with the cost of producing goods in yen for export to the US, the automotive, electronic and other manufacturers have set up plants to produce the goods for the US market in the US itself.

This move overseas can be seen in the electronics industry by Sony's investment in a Californian plant in 1972, followed by the entry into the US of other brand-name producers such as Matsushita, Mitsubishi, Toshiba and Sharp. The electronics giants all built production facilities in order to maintain their market share in the face of protectionist measures, such as the May 1977 Orderly Market Agreement restricting the export of Japanese colour televisions to the US market. Similarly, the automobile and transport machinery industry in general established production facilities in the US from the late 1970s onwards, with Honda in 1978, Nissan in 1980 and Toyota in 1984. The auto giants were also influenced by the threat and eventual introduction of the first VER on Japanese automobiles in May 1981. In this way, the move to the US by electronic and transport machinery manufacturers in the 1970s and early 1980s was prompted by both the rise in the yen and the US's resort to protectionist measures against Japanese exports.

The boom in Japanese investment in the US, especially after the September 1985 Plaza Accord, was part of the wider globalization of Japanese business. As was mentioned in Chapter 1, during the 1980s Japanese corporations hit the headlines for their high-profile acquisitions rather than their investments in the electronic and automobile industries. Their purchase of real-estate landmarks such as the Rockefeller Center in New York and well-known film studios such as Universal Studios and Columbia Pictures was given heavy coverage by the US media. The changed position of Japanese corporations in the post-bubble 1990s and early twenty-first century is illustrated by the fact that neither the Rockefeller Center nor Universal Studios is now in Japanese hands. It hardly would have been expected from the hyperbole of the time.

Nevertheless, the continuing importance of the US market to Japanese manufacturers is confirmed by the new investments made by the automobile industry in the 1990s. Indeed, FDI in the transport machinery sector of the US economy accounted for over one-half of Japanese investments between 1991 and 1997 (JETRO 1999b: 98–9). At the same time, however, the worsening global market conditions in semi-conductors, along with the high yen, have forced some restructuring in the industry. In 1998, for instance, Hitachi halted production of semi-conductor memory at its Texas plant and merged the computer design and production plant in California with the loss of 500 jobs. Again in 1998, other chip makers (Mitsubishi, Nippon Electric Company [NEC] and Fujitsu) announced restructuring leading to a withdrawal from markets, workers being laid off, the merger of plants and other measures (JETRO 1999b: 101). The situation in the late 1990s was thus clearly different from at the time of the semi-conductor dispute of the mid-1990s. From this perspective, US fears of 'Japan Incorporated' being able to deploy its economic power through such types of investments can be seen to be a reaction more to the declining power of the US than to the rising power of Japan.

These manufacturing and other investments in the US have created a situation where Japanese companies have become an integral part of the economic landscape. This means that, far from Japan being a distant producer of finished goods for the US market, it now provides employment opportunities in the states where the plants have been built. Indeed, a large number of US citizens now work in the automobile, electronics and other industries started by Japanese manufacturers. The result of these investments has been to spur US manufacturers to introduce Japanese management and production techniques such as the just-in-time production system, to try to maintain international competitiveness. This transfer of Japanese management techniques and their localization has led to the adoption of new skills and approaches by US industry and employees (Abo 1998).

At the same time, as producers for the US market in the US, Japanese manufacturers have been required to interact with US society. This is significantly different from being a producer in Japan for the US export market. As can be seen in the case of Honda, moreover, manufacturing investments have often implied the creation of self-reliant companies, which carry out research, development, design and production. In other words, these companies do not simply represent the establishment of a Japanese subsidiary of the parent company abroad. Over the years, Honda has moved from being a producer of Japanese cars for the US market to become, by 1996, an 'American firm' producing for the US and, with exports back to Japan as well as to Europe and South America, the world market (Suzuki 1998). In this way, the Japanese manufacturing presence in the US has created a two-way interaction between Japanese companies and US society, with both being influenced as a result.

5.3.ii Finance

The surplus of Japanese capital has been employed for investment in a range of financial instruments as well as in the manufacturing sector. Under US pressure the 1980s saw various measures implemented in order to bring about financial deregulation in Japan. The Reagan administration's demands for reform of the Japanese financial system at the beginning of the 1980s and the agreement to set up the Yen–Dollar Committee in November 1983 are illustrative of the US success in this regard. Many of the reforms implemented served to open Japanese financial markets to US and other foreign players. This is evidenced in the case of the Yen–Dollar Agreement of November 1985, for instance, which opened membership of the Tokyo Stock Exchange to foreign firms. In contrast, other measures facilitated the move overseas of Japanese capital, as in the December 1979 revision of the Foreign Exchange Law. The same can be said about the June 1984 decision to remove restrictions on currency conversion, thereby allowing, in principle, speculative currency trading. Such measures created the environment for Japanese banks and security houses to become active players in US financial markets. The role Japan played in this regard was important in funding the budget deficit in the US, which was caused in part by the build-up of the US military under Reagan. Of course, capital outflows have been pushed by a range of factors, such as differentials in interest rates, particularly in the early 1980s, but US pressure to open markets was closely tied to the needs of US administrations to generate external funds.

The dramatic rise in the value of the yen following the Plaza Accord and the change in interest rates in the run-up to the collapse of the US stock market in late 1987 had an important impact on capital outflows from Japan. Before the burst of the Japanese bubble, the 1980s saw a growing awareness of Japan as a potential challenger in overseas financial markets, as Japanese financial houses became major players in the US treasury bond and other markets. By mid-1986, for instance, Japanese investors made bids for between 20 and 40 per cent of all new US treasury issues (Malcolm 1998: 196). Following the banks, Japanese pension funds became major purchasers of long-term treasury bills in the 1980s. This move into international waters was not without its costs, however: it is reported that, as a result of the fall in the dollar's value against the yen and the rise in US interest rates, between September 1986 and April 1987 Japanese pension funds suffered losses of nearly US$20 billion. This led pension funds and other institutional investors to move out of treasury instruments and into the US stock market, with stock market investments by Japanese players surpassing treasury bill investments for the first time in March 1987 (Gomi 1999: 154).

In these years, the Japanese appetite for treasury issues and other financial instruments engendered concern in the US over the growing financial power of Japan. It was feared that, as a result of the leverage their actions created, Japanese policy-makers would be able to exercise power through their hold on US financial instruments. Despite the decline in US economic power these borrowing needs indicated, however, Japanese investments were difficult for policy-makers actually to exercise as relational power, although the crucial role of Japanese finance for the US did offer a degree of structural power (see Chapter 2). As seen particularly at the time of the close ties between the US and Japan symbolized by the 'Ron–Yasu' relationship, however, the choices made by Japan were usually congruent with those of the US, leaving little need to make use of any structural power gained as a result of increased financial leverage. What is more, as a consequence of political bilateralism and the government's continuing reliance on the security treaty, a strong sense of vulnerability *vis-à-vis* the US, rather than a determination to exert power over the US, dominated thinking. In any event, policy-making agents were not often in a position directly to influence financial transfers based on market-driven decisions by Japanese institutional investors. Even though the names of Japanese banks and security houses may have dominated the financial headlines, therefore, this does not translate into their exercise of power on behalf of the Japanese state. This is not completely to deny the government the ability to deploy power through financial means in order to instrumentalize Japan's international relations, but rather to suggest that, given the overriding importance of bilateralism, any attempt to deploy this power was constrained by fears of damaging the overall US–Japan relationship.

For all that, in the 1990s and the early twenty-first century the bursting of the Japanese bubble and the almost decade-long economic downturn have served to calm US fears of Japan deploying its financial might in order to instrumentalize its relations with the US. Moreover, the East Asian financial and economic crises, which will be discussed in Chapter 10, have created a new motivation for the movement of capital to the US. This can be seen in the introduction in November 1996 of Prime Minister Hashimoto Ryūtarō's 'big bang' financial deregulation package and the passage by the Diet of the package's major laws in June 1998. In essence, the 'big bang' is a range of measures taken in order to liberalize and deregulate the Japanese financial system as well as open it up to the forces of globalization. These moves were welcomed by Japanese investors, who were now able to look out to the world for investment opportunities. This was an especially welcome change for private investors as the domestic interest rate, near zero from the middle of 1995, was actually reduced to zero in March 1999. The liberalization of the Foreign Exchange Law in April 1998 enabled individual Japanese citizens as well as the banks, pension funds and other institutional investors to invest in the US. They, too, have thus become investors in US stocks, bonds and other financial instruments.

Against the background of the post-bubble trauma, however, the late 1990s and early twenty-first century also have seen a large amount of funds flow out of the yen and into the dollar in order to prevent the default of Japanese financial institutions (Gomi 1999: 73–4). These flows helped to drive the yen down to 146 yen to the dollar in June 1998, its lowest level against the greenback for eight years. In other words, rather than these flows representing the overwhelming strength of Japanese financial power, they symbolize its weakness. Clearly, therefore, the rise of Japanese economic power has not yet engendered a fundamental restructuring of the global political economy, which remains firmly anchored to the US dollar as the currency of last resort.

5.4 Japan, the United States and regional projects

With the change in US trade policy in the 1980s, as represented by the abandonment of non-discriminatory trading practices and the promotion of regional frameworks, Japan's economic relations with the US took on a new regional as well as bilateral dimension. As seen in the January 1994 launch of the North American Free Trade Agreement (NAFTA), embracing the US, Canada and Mexico, as well as the growing US commitment to take a leadership role in APEC following the Seattle meeting of November 1993, US policy-making agents are now involved fully in two regional groupings. The key difference, of course, is that Japan remains an outsider as far as NAFTA is concerned, but is a key member of the APEC forum. It has therefore been crucial for Japanese manufacturers to respond to NAFTA in order to ensure the continuing competitiveness of their products in the North American market.

5.4.i North American Free Trade Agreement

NAFTA aims to eliminate both tariff and non-tariff barriers between the three economies and to promote trade, investment and the further liberalization and deregulation of Mexico. After some initial misgivings, the Japanese government welcomed the advent of NAFTA, although policy-makers continued to express concern over the direction the new grouping might take. For instance, any measures likely to harm third-party (read Japanese) interests were opposed, as in the development of a discriminatory regional trading bloc – a reflection of the growing importance of multilateral approaches as a means to promote Japanese interests (Takenaka 1994: 113). As NAFTA allows the three members autonomy in terms of their relations with non-members, Japanese manufacturers have sought to ensure that their products remain competitive in the US and wider North American market by moving production facilities to Mexico. The lower cost of production, especially in terms of labour costs, has been as much an incentive for Japanese manufacturers to relocate production facilities as for those of the US. Both aim to build cheap production bases to serve the NAFTA market. Clearly, a 'launch platform' in Mexico allows Japanese companies to follow their US counterparts in taking advantage of the NAFTA trading arrangements in order to remain competitive.

A number of Japanese manufacturers have responded to NAFTA by moving their production facilities from East Asia to Mexico, for example Toshiba, which moved the production of television parts from Singapore. Other industries have adopted a similar strategy: the toy maker Bandai, for instance, decided to move toy production aimed at exports to the US market from China to Mexico. Similarly, the lifting of tariffs on intra-NAFTA trade has led manufacturers to move production facilities across the border. Toshiba, Matsushita and Hitachi have all consolidated the assembly of colour televisions in Mexico, as the lifting of tariffs on the movement of brown tubes allowed the economical supply of production lines in Mexico with tubes produced in Canada and the US (Takii 1996: 117).

The attraction of Mexico can also be seen in the decision of Japanese auto-part makers to launch new operations there. In addition, NAFTA's call for an increase in the local content ratio from 50 per cent to 62.5 per cent by 2002 stimulated greater investment by Japanese manufacturers in North America: the auto-giant Toyota decided to build a new engine assembly line in the US in 2000. The only Japanese manufacturers likely to suffer as a result of NAFTA are those lacking the resources to establish new production facilities in Mexico, such as Japanese textile manufacturers in East Asia (Fukushima 1995: 34). In this respect, globalization and regionalization are fragmentary in their impact on Japanese manufacturers.

5.4.ii Asia Pacific Economic Cooperation

In contrast to the position regarding NAFTA, Japan and the US are both members of APEC. APEC has emerged gradually since its inaugural meeting in Canberra in November 1989 as the key multilateral forum for dealing with economic issues on a regional basis. Although the initiative to establish APEC in fact came from MITI, the formal proposal was made by Prime Minister Bob Hawke of Australia (Funabashi 1995). As will be dealt with in Part III of this book, the sensitivity of East Asian governments to the possibility that Japan might play a leading role in a regional grouping, thereby reviving memories of the pre-war strategy of establishing imperial domination through the Greater East Asia Co-prosperity Sphere, meant that Japanese policy-makers did *not* seek to play that leading role in APEC in the early years. Similarly, until the 1993 APEC meeting in Seattle, when President Clinton pushed for leadership in APEC, US policy-making agents had not sought actively to promote APEC. Thereafter, however, the Clinton administration used APEC as a vehicle to promote the liberal free-trade and investment regime as well as the liberal model of economic development, as it had used NAFTA. The US's role in APEC emerged as a crucial determinant of the overall direction APEC has taken in the intervening years.

From the outset, MITI called for the US's participation in APEC, thereby ensuring that the Pacific region was not divided along the East Asian fault line. Since then, the Japanese government has in general adopted policies supportive of the US's proactive role in APEC, with growing support in some quarters for Japan to play a larger role in the East Asian Economic Caucus (EAEC). Even though they are competitors in exploiting market opportunities in developing East Asia, as industrially-developed economies both the US and Japan benefit from the liberalization of trade and investment in the wider Asia-Pacific region. In this respect, Japanese policy-making agents proved particularly effective at the November 1995 meeting of APEC in Osaka when, as the hosts, they drew up a detailed programme for implementing further liberalization measures. In the Osaka Action Agenda adopted at the time, for instance, the members of APEC agreed a wide range of measures aimed at ensuring that the agreements reached at the 1994 Bogor meeting to create an open region for free and open trade and investment by 2010 for the industrialized economies and 2020 for the industrializing economies were realized. The Agenda called for the implementation of measures to reduce tariffs, expand trade, harmonize telecommunications and transport, promote investment in energy, and other liberalization measures. As the APEC Business Advisory Council warned in 1999, however, the barriers to trade and investment remain strong, particularly in view of the need to stimulate heavier investment to help the recovery of the East Asian economies hit by the 1997 East Asian economic crises (*Financial Times*, 25 August 1999).

Despite the shared interests of Japan and the US in the above regard, US attempts to push forward liberalization in certain sectors of the economy reveal the underlying difference between the two countries in terms of interests and norms. This can be seen in agriculture. As a result of the domestic political pressure exerted by the agricultural lobby in Japan, Japanese policy-makers have at times resisted the US's agenda of promoting liberalization in this sector of the economy. This means that, as with the resistance of industrializing economies to opening their home markets to the full breeze of international competition, Japan has shared interests with its East Asian neighbours rather than the US. This can be seen, for instance, in the concern Prime Minister Murayama Tomiichi expressed to President Suharto of Indonesia at the 1994 APEC meeting in Bogor about the liberalization of agricultural products (Funabashi 1995: 283). Similarly, at the 1998 APEC meeting in Kuala Lumpur, Japan baulked at US demands to open the marine and forestry sectors of the economy (Hughes 2000). In this way, Japanese policy-making agents have resisted, at least to some extent, US political pressure to open the primary sector of the economy through the APEC process by mounting common cause with their East Asian neighbours, thereby giving voice to the East Asianist norm.

5.5 Clash of developmental and liberal economic norms

The shared interests of Japan and its East Asian neighbours go further than agriculture. As will be outlined in Chapter 10, the Japanese developmental model has proved particularly attractive to certain East Asian developing economies, suggesting the potential for a clash of developmentalist and liberal norms in the APEC process. As noted above, although major trade conflicts with the US have surfaced since the late 1960s and even before, the US response has shifted over time from VERs to attempts fundamentally to transform the very nature of the Japanese economy. This type of response became especially salient under the Bush administration's SII, when the call to make changes in the structural features of the Japanese economy was in essence a call to make changes in areas the US regarded as 'abnormal'. In other words, through changes in the structural features of the Japanese economy, US policy-makers can be seen ultimately to have sought to transform the norms of developmentalism and economism at the heart of the Japanese model of development. Whether directly or indirectly, this goal was promoted by the Revisionist school's characterization of Japan as the 'problem', as touched on in Chapter 1.

Similarly, the Clinton administration's call to expand trade and investment between the two economies, based on a results-oriented approach, harboured implications for the perception of 'free' and 'fair' trade. As far as the Clinton government was concerned, the international competitiveness of Japanese high-technology industries stemmed in part from the tight relationship between government and business and the closed nature of the Japanese domestic market. In calling for 'fair trade' rather than 'free trade', therefore, US policy-making agents in effect sought to institutionalize further liberal norms in the economic relationship between the two Pacific powers. By this call for 'fair' trade the US implied that, as a consequence of the model of development and policies pursued, Japanese trading practices are inherently 'unfair'. It followed that, just as Japanese high-technology companies have access to the US market, US companies should also have access to the Japanese market. As this lack of US access is seen to stem from the norms and practices inherent in the Japanese model of capitalism, the Clinton administration sought to create a level playing-field by proposing measurable targets for US companies in the Japanese market, as in the case of semi-conductors, with the threat of sanctions if specific sectors of the economy lacked reciprocity. In this way, the Clinton administration demonstrated concretely how Japan continues to remain vulnerable to US pressure.

Certainly, the perceived failure of Japan to abide by trade and other agreements with the US was part of the background for the Clinton administration's demand for a results-oriented approach to trade relations. For instance, it is reported that, at their February 1994 summit, Clinton informed Hosokawa that 'in the past Japan had failed to fulfil the objectives of over thirty US–Japan agreements' (Haraguchi 1995: 69). From the perspective of MOFA, however, the efforts made by Japan to meet US demands had already borne fruit. As one official stated:

> Procurement measures by NTT [Nippon Telegraph and Telephone] were agreed in 1980 and were revised several times thereafter. Based on this the procurement value for foreign products and services had in the thirteen-year period to 1993 increased by sixty-four fold. The import of medical equipment from the US had increased between 1985 and 1992 … 3.7 fold. Timber imports from the US have increased 4.1 fold. In the year after the introduction of government procurement measures the share of foreign products and services in the computer sector increased from 7.5 per cent to 15.5 per cent.
>
> (Haraguchi 1995: 69)

As this confirms, in working in such a way to meet US demands, Japanese policy-making agents are in fact confirming the continuing power of the US to influence both the nature and the perception of the bilateral economic relationship.

5.6 Summary

The economic relationship between Japan and the US has been transformed over the last fifty-five years. In the early post-Occupation years Japan was a second-tier economy; now, despite the economic downturn, it remains a challenger to the US in the high-technology and high-value-added sectors of the economy. An examination of the trade and investment relations between the two countries has revealed a picture of a large Japanese presence in the US, but one which has not necessarily produced for policy-making agents the means to deploy Japan's economic and financial power in the instrumentalization of Japan's international relations. The conflict over trade has demonstrated the continuing dominance of the US in bilateral negotiations, although the automobile negotiations, when the prime minister said a firm 'no', together with the new US willingness to settle disputes in a multilateral framework, symbolize the potential for change in the relationship. Still, bilateral negotiations have been central in the US's attempt to bring about a fundamental shift in the nature of the Japanese political economy. Whilst Japan is gradually moving in the direction of further liberalization and deregulation, domestic political forces, such as the agricultural sector, continue to resist full acceptance of the liberal economic norm. What makes Japan vulnerable to US pressures, however, is not simply the continuing reliance on the US market for exports, nor the bilateralism at the heart of the political relationship, but also the pivotal role of the US–Japan security treaty to the security of Japan. This is the focus of Chapter 6.

Chapter 6

Japan–United States security relations

6.1 Overview

Chapter 2 outlined how the coming into force in April 1952 of the US–Japan security treaty, along with the San Francisco peace treaty, tied Japan firmly into the Western camp in the early Cold War period. The security relations that developed between these two Pacific powers, which have centred on the security treaty system, have significantly shaped the nature of the overall relationship between Japan and the US. This is because dependence on the US nuclear and conventional alliance has made Japan highly vulnerable to US pressure in the political and economic as well as the security dimension of the relationship, especially given the norm of bilateralism.

At the same time, however, the anti-militarist norm has served to constrain the government in deploying the military to pursue state objectives. Indeed, Japanese policy-making agents at various times have taken advantage of this domestic resistance to the further embedding of bilateral military links as a means to oppose US pressure to play a more active security role. Whether in terms of Japan as a bastion against communism during the 1950s, supporting the war in Vietnam during the 1960s and early 1970s, offering closer military cooperation in the late 1970s and early 1980s or introducing legislation for logistical and other support of US forces in the late 1990s, bilateral security relations have been forged out of the tension between the pressures brought to bear on the Japanese government by the US and by domestic political forces.

6.2 Interpreting the security treaty

For the past fifty years the security treaty has remained at the heart of the bilateral relationship. Whilst under the original 1951 treaty US forces assumed no obligation to defend Japan, despite their deployment in and around the archipelago, since its revision in June 1960 the US government has been granted the use of bases and other facilities 'for the purpose of contributing to the security of Japan and the maintenance of international peace and security in the Far East' (Article VI: Appendix 1.4). As patently stated by Under-secretary of State U. Alexis Johnson in 1970, however, the latter purpose was far more important than the former: 'we have no forces, either ground or air, in Japan that are directly related to direct conventional defense of Japan' (cited in Havens 1987: 184). The 1960 treaty was agreed for ten years, with either party thereafter being able to serve one year's notice to terminate it. As neither of the parties has opted to do so, this treaty remains in force today as amended and renewed forty years ago. So pivotal has the treaty been in determining the post-war course charted by Japan that it, not the Japanese Constitution, can be said to be at the heart of the Japanese security role in the world.

As with the Constitution, the security treaty's role in maintaining Japan's peace and security has been subject to a range of interpretations. Depending on the time, the approach taken or the motivation of the policy-making agents and other political actors making the pronouncements, the treaty has been trumpeted as a means to 'keep Japan down'; viewed as a conduit to pressure Japan to build the military up; praised as the guarantor of peace and security; or lambasted as a magnet likely to drag the Japanese state and its people into a war of US making.

More specifically, the idea of the security treaty as a means to keep Japan down is captured powerfully by the metaphor of US troops as the 'cap in the bottle', which was used by the then commander of the US Marine Corps in Okinawa, Lieutenant-General Henry Stackpole (*Daily Yomiuri*, 20 March 1990). This expression evinces the image of the US military presence in Japan acting to prevent the militarist genie from escaping from the post-war anti-militarist bottle. On the contrary, others argue that, given Article 9 of the Constitution and the deeply-embedded nature of the anti-militarist norm, far from limiting Japan's military growth, the treaty has instead acted as a conduit for *beiatsu* to be exerted on the government to build up its military forces. Indeed, the government is obliged to do so under Article III of the revised 1960 security treaty. For some, the extension of nuclear deterrence to Japan and the presence of US forces in and about the archipelago has guaranteed its peace and security for the last half century, especially at the height of the Cold War, when Japan faced the communist threat. For others, however, the threat of nuclear war, rather than the threat of communism, has been viewed as presenting the greatest danger to the peace and security of a highly-urbanized, fragile country like Japan. From this perspective, the security treaty has contributed not to security but to the Cold War's nuclear arms race, has embroiled Japan indirectly in the Vietnam War, and in other ways has eroded the Japanese state and its people's peace and security. In any case, the argument runs, the US would be unlikely to use nuclear weapons in order to protect Japan as this would entail a possible retaliatory nuclear attack on the US itself.

Whatever interpretation is adopted, however, the role of the treaty in linking Japan firmly to US security interests and norms cannot be denied. The norm of bilateralism and the interests at the heart of the US–Japan relationship have been, for the most part, shared by large sections of the key political and bureaucratic policy-making agents in Japan. Consequently, the paramount importance these leaders have attached to the security treaty has left them vulnerable to US pressure to boost defence spending, purchase US weapons, carry out new military roles, and in other ways cooperate with US military strategy and objectives in the region and the globe. The power of the US to exploit this vulnerability has been salient especially at times of political or economic conflict. This is the quintessence of Japan's vulnerability in the face of *beiatsu*.

Nevertheless, the dominant pattern of Japan–US security relations cannot be understood fully without taking into account Japanese domestic society and the role of other political actors. For here the anti-militarist norm has acted as a countervailing pressure on the security policy adopted by the Japanese government. In certain instances, the norm has clashed sharply with the government's policy, which is often pursued under pressure from the US. In others, the government has responded to domestic demand by promoting policies supportive of anti-militarism, thereby more carefully balancing external and internal pressures. This complex interplay between domestic agency and international structural forces can be seen by tracing in outline form the way the treaty, whilst remaining at the core of Japanese security policy, has not prevented policy-making agents from supplementing it, as and when Japan's own security interests require.

6.3 Cold War period

6.3.i International setting and domestic agency

The security relations between Japan and the US have developed in the context of the structure of the international system and the bilateralism at the heart of the US–Japan relationship. As mentioned in Part I, this structure imposes constraints on, as well as offers opportunities for, a range of domestic policy-making agents and other political actors to play a role in shaping security policy. In doing so, the change in the structure of the international system is a crucial explanatory variable for understanding the way in which the bilateral security relationship developed during the Cold War period.

Broadly speaking, the international system moved from a bipolar structure in the 1950s and 1960s, to a multipolar structure during the 1970s, and then returned to a looser bipolar structure after the outbreak of the second Cold War in the late 1970s. In responding to these changes in the context of the bilateral relationship, the transition in the US's own role needs to be taken into account. In essence, the US's position as the hegemon in the international system, which was secure in the 1950s and early 1960s, was weakened thereafter as a result of the economic rise of Japan and (West) Germany. Whilst a debate has raged in the international relations literature on the degree to which US hegemony has indeed declined (Strange 1987), the ascent of these two defeated powers to economic prominence during the 1970s did induce a fundamental change in the structure of the international system. From the perspective of US–Japan relations, Japan's rise to economic superpower status and the inability of the US to shoulder alone the full burden of maintaining a military presence in East Asia led successive US administrations and the Congress to exert immense pressure on the Japanese government to boost defence spending and play a greater military role in the region.

What should be highlighted for an understanding of the dominant pattern of the bilateral relationship is the dual role played by US pressure. On the one hand, the US sought to promote its own interests by exerting pressure on Japan. On the other hand, however, domestic policy-making agents, such as the LDP, MOFA and the JDA also used US pressure to promote their own interests and agenda. In the 1980s, for instance, such domestic policy-making agents employed pressure from the US as a means to push forward with security policies giving a greater military role to the SDF. Yet *beiatsu* still needed to be balanced against the pressures emerging as a consequence of the anti-militarist norm embedded in domestic society.

The attempts by successive LDP governments to balance these competing international and domestic pressures are a hallmark of Japanese foreign policy-making during the Cold War period. At certain times, as a result of the security agenda pushed by a powerful policy-making agent, such as the prime minister, *beiatsu,* rather than the domestic anti-militarist norm, gained in salience; at other times, it was the reverse. In either case, one common feature of Japanese administrations during the Cold War and, indeed, post-Cold War period has been their agreement to cooperate with US security policy at the most fundamental level. In short, whether or not Japan should provide military facilities for the exclusive use of US forces in the preparation for and possible fighting of both nuclear and conventional wars has not been questioned.

6.3.ii Balancing internal and external pressures

The dominant pattern of Japan's security relations during the Cold War period can be seen in the policies pursued by different administrations in the context of the competing pressures emerging from the US and from Japanese domestic society.

6.3.ii.a Kishi administration

Until the advent of the Kishi Nobusuke administration (1957–60) the security policy adopted after the end of the Occupation by Yoshida Shigeru (1948–54) and his two successors, Hatoyama Ichirō (1954–6) and Ishibashi Tanzan (1956–7), did not directly challenge the anti-militarist norm in domestic society. The Yoshida Doctrine of close cooperation with the US, even though it limited the build-up of Japanese military forces, remained the order of the day. As a result, although the lower House of Representatives passed legislation to establish the SDF and the JDA in May 1954, the political efficacy of the anti-militarist norm in domestic society and the political weight of the SDPJ in the upper House of Councillors ensured that, when the JDA Establishment Law and the SDF Law came into effect in July 1954, constraints were imposed on the SDF from the start. As was seen in Chapter 1, the euphemistic name adopted for Japan's military forces was the symbolic manifestation of this constraint. More concretely, a ban on the overseas despatch of troops was imposed when the legislation passed the upper House of Councillors in June 1954, despite government resistance.

As a member of the more nationalistic, anti-mainstream faction of the LDP, and an arch anti-communist, Kishi challenged head-on the norm of anti-militarism. This is evident, for instance, in the prime minister's declaration that nuclear weapons are not unconstitutional (Welfield 1988: 257–8). Kishi's position was that, despite their destructive power, nuclear weapons could be used for the defence of Japan. Therefore, as defensive weapons, atomic bombs are not unconstitutional. This constitutional interpretation did not lead to any change in Japanese security policy, although it did offend the anti-nuclear sensibilities of many in domestic society, especially the victims of the atomic bombings of Hiroshima and Nagasaki.

Plate 6.1 Mass protests. In May 1960 tens of thousands turned out to oppose the Kishi government's revision of the US–Japan security treaty.
Source: Courtesy of Mainichi Shimbunsha

It was Kishi's decision to railroad the revision of the security treaty through the legislative process in June 1960 that posed the most direct challenge to the anti-militarist norm in domestic society. For Kishi, the upcoming end to the security treaty's ten-year term provided the opportunity to negotiate a more equal treaty, whereas for the opposition it provided an opportunity to end the treaty and establish Japan as a 'peace state'. Kishi succeeded in making the treaty more equal by eliminating Article I, which, as was mentioned in Chapter 3, permitted the use of US forces 'to put down large-scale internal riots and disturbances in Japan'. The successful passage of the legislation to revise the treaty, however, was achieved only by the use of authoritarian tactics against the political Opposition in the Diet and the mass opposition outside the Diet. Both groups sought the treaty's elimination, not extension. Kishi's request to use the SDF in order to quell the demonstrators, though not put into force, suggests how close Japanese policy-making agents came to deploying the armed forces to silence their critics (Hara 1988: 425–8; Igarashi 1999: 166). In any event, the revision of the treaty polarized domestic society, as the demonstrations against the Kishi administration, which involved over 560,000 workers, students and other citizens turning out on 4 June 1960 and 580,000 on 15–16 June 1960, illustrate (for details, see Packard 1966).

As the issue of the revision of the security treaty cut to the very heart of the question of Japan's post-war identity, Kishi could not avail himself of *beiatsu* to promote his policy. In fact, the two sides were so concerned about the physical security of President Dwight Eisenhower (1953–61), who was scheduled to hold a summit meeting with Kishi in Tokyo, that his visit was cancelled. For the fundamental question of Japan's identity and security policy in the nuclear era was again at the heart of the controversy over the treaty. It pitted 'two Japans' against each other, as in the late 1940s. Thus, the Opposition in the Diet and protest groups outside the Diet argued that, rather than renewing the US–Japan security treaty, the government should realize Japan's identity as a 'peace state' by adopting a policy of unarmed neutrality and reliance on the United Nations (Sakamoto 1959). It was the norm of anti-militarism which galvanized mass action in support of this identity and policy.

Internationally, the government viewed the treaty as essential in order to guarantee Japanese security against the communist threat. It relied on the US nuclear and conventional deterrence in this regard. In his attempt to make the treaty more equal, Kishi also exchanged notes with the US secretary of state, Christian Herter, agreeing that the Japanese government would be consulted on major changes in US use of military facilities in Japan. In theory, 'prior consultation' between the two sides provides Japanese policy-makers with the right to say 'no' to the US's use of military facilities in Japan for purposes they oppose. The effectiveness of this agreement, however, has been called into question: on the one hand, no evidence exists of the US ever having sought prior consultation; and, on the other, given Japan's reliance on US deterrence, doubts have been raised about whether the government would in any event be able to say 'no' (Muroyama 1992: 200). As a result, widespread scepticism has been generated about the effectiveness of prior consultation, as will be seen below in the case of the 'introduction' of nuclear weapons.

At the same time, the actual geographical scope to be covered by the revised treaty highlighted the different interests of Japanese and US policy-making agents. In revising the treaty the Kishi administration was concerned to ensure that the US made a specific commitment to defend Japan, whereas US policy-makers viewed the use of bases in Japan as part of the US's global and regional strategy. As constitutional restrictions prevented Japan from taking part in a NATO-type collective defence arrangement with other US allies in East Asia, the US government sought to ensure that the scope of the treaty extended beyond the defence of Japan. Thus, in the same vein as the 1951 security treaty, which in Article I referred to 'international peace and security in the Far East', the revised 1960 treaty referred to the 'Far East' in both Article IV and Article VI. In Diet interpellations the government was pressured by the Opposition to define the geographical scope of the 'Far East'. Prime Minister Kishi stated the government's official position that, whilst the 'Far East' was not necessarily a clearly-designated geographical region, to which the treaty would be restricted, it broadly included the areas north of the Philippines and surrounding Japan, and the areas under the control of South Korea and Taiwan. As seen later in this chapter in the government's move away from a geographic to a situational understanding of the scope of the treaty, and as will be seen in Chapters 9 and 11 on the question of Taiwan and sovereignty over the Senkaku Islands, the actual scope of the 'Far East' has been of particular concern to China.

In domestic society, the tactics adopted by Kishi stoked fears of an erosion of democracy and a return to a pre-war domestic order within the constraints of the Cold War international order. The politics of the security treaty system, as seen in Kishi's tactics, together with the physical presence of US troops on Japanese soil, meant that many Japanese viewed themselves as victims of the Cold War division of the world. This was especially the case for the people of Okinawa, who were living in a militarized island outside the scope of the Japanese Constitution, as discussed later in this chapter. For those outside Japan, however, it was rather the Japanese who appeared as the beneficiaries of the Cold War, as Japan's post-war growth was stimulated by the outbreak of the 'hot war' on the Korean Peninsula. The policies pursued by Kishi's successor ensured that the economy continued to grow.

6.3.ii.b Ikeda administration

The Ikeda Hayato administration (1960–4) emerged with a 'soft' touch and consensus-oriented politics. As was stated in Chapter 4, rather than risk controversy over the security treaty, Ikeda sought to push issues of peace and war from centre stage. In place of the combative, turn-back-the-clock style of conservative politics practised by Kishi, the new prime minister eschewed controversy over security policy and instead sought to improve the material life of the people through his 'income-doubling' policy.

Despite the environmental and other costs paid by domestic society as a result of the policies pursued, Ikeda clearly sought to embrace the masses within the LDP's security policy by offering them material rewards. With this as the background, he pushed gently to strengthen the SDF. This can be seen, for instance, in his administration's revision of the laws establishing the JDA and SDF in June 1961, and its adoption of a new defence plan, which called for an expansion in the number of service personnel and the purchase of US Nike and Hawk surface-to-air missiles. As these weapons purchases illustrate, Ikeda was pursuing an income-doubling policy at the same time as he adopted policies supportive of bilateralism in line with constitutional restraints on weapons for defence.

6.3.ii.c Satō administration

The US's decision in 1965 to escalate the war in Vietnam by bombing the North meant that the Satō Eisaku administration (1964–72) was caught more sharply between domestic and US pressures. In the first place, Satō was strongly supportive of bilateralism. He therefore cooperated with the US in the Vietnam War, but this cooperation remained indirect, as in the provision of bases, not direct, as in the despatch of troops. In resisting US pressure to provide full-scale assistance in the war effort, the prime minister was able to make use of the strength of anti-militarism in domestic society.

At the same time as he cooperated with the US in Vietnam, however, Satō was forced to respond to pressure from domestic society to implement constraints on Japan's military role and US forces in Japan. A number of policies and principles were therefore put forward giving policy salience to the anti-militarist norm. In April 1967 his administration placed a ban on the export of arms to communist countries (already covered by Japan's membership of the Coordinating Committee on Export Control); countries currently involved in conflict; and countries bordering on involvement. In January 1968, moreover, it established as part of the government's four nuclear principles three non-nuclear principles pledging not to produce, possess or introduce nuclear weapons into Japan. Most significantly, as announced in the Satō–Nixon communiqué of November 1969, the prime minister succeeded in negotiating an agreement with President Nixon on the return of Okinawa to Japan. The islands were to be returned to Japan in 1972 *hondo nami*, in 'the same condition as the main islands' – that is, without US nuclear weapons. As a result, the US administration of Okinawa was brought to an end in May 1972. It was also in 1972 that Satō imposed a ban on the despatch of minesweepers. As will be seen in 6.4 below, however, even at the beginning of the twenty-first century Okinawa prefecture still remains heavily militarized as a result of its continued role in US regional and global strategy, far more than other parts of Japan.

The US fleet's port calls to Japan have been a particular point of contention owing to the problem of nuclear weapons. The inclusion of the three non-nuclear principles as part of the four nuclear principles Satō announced in January 1968 – adherence to the three non-nuclear principles; promotion of nuclear disarmament; reliance on nuclear deterrence in line with the US–Japan security treaty; priority on the peaceful use of nuclear energy – demonstrates explicitly that the non-nuclear principles were in no way meant to erode the central role of bilateralism and the security treaty system. Indeed, as confirmed in statements issued by high-ranking US military and government officials, the third of the three non-nuclear principles, not to permit the 'introduction' of nuclear weapons into Japan, was a dead letter from the start. Obviously, US naval vessels could hardly be expected to jettison their nuclear weapons before visiting Japanese ports (Hayes et al. 1986: 76, 98; Reischauer 1986: 299). In this sense, the return of Okinawa was more broadly related to the *quid pro quo* in the negotiations over textiles (see Chapter 5), Satō's support for the Vietnam War, and the general change in US regional and global strategy.

This change in strategy is represented by the July 1969 announcement of Nixon's Guam Doctrine, as was touched on Chapter 2. Against the background of declining US power, the most important aspect of the doctrine insofar as bilateral security relations are concerned was the US decision to cut back its regional security commitment and move the defence burden onto its allies. Whilst this did not mean any major reduction in US deployments in Japan, the change did mean mounting pressure on the Japanese government to boost defence spending in support of US goals in the region.

At the same time, on the same day that the Satō–Nixon communiqué was announced in November 1969, the prime minister made a speech at the National Press Club in Washington where he declared that Taiwan and South Korea were important to Japan's own security interests, as will be discussed in more detail in Chapter 11. China has naturally been sensitive to the question of Japan's possible involvement in the security of Taiwan, as will be discussed in Chapter 11. What with the Guam Doctrine, the winding-down of the Vietnam War, the impending return of Okinawa, and other changes in Japan and in the world, the large-scale popular protests against the automatic extension of the security treaty in 1970 did not exert the same degree of political impact as those at the time of the renewal of the treaty in 1960, which helped force Prime Minister Kishi from office (Welfield 1988: 281). Thus, as the treaty did not need to be revised, as in 1960, it was automatically extended.

In this way, during the Satō era a dual policy emerged of anti-militarism and economism, with widespread protests against the Vietnam War occurring at the same time as the masses enjoyed enhanced material well-being. With the wind-down of the Vietnam War in the early 1970s, however, anti-militarism became less salient, and cross-party consensus politics, as was mentioned in Chapter 4, sank roots in a more affluent society. Nevertheless, within this dual context, the Vietnam War did engender a growing realization in certain quarters of domestic society that, far from being a victim of the Cold War, Japan was rather an aggressor. From this perspective, it was precisely as a result of the security treaty's existence that Japan had taken on a supportive role in the Vietnam War. On the other hand, precisely as a result of the wind-down of the Vietnam War, economism and consensus politics became the order of the day. It was in this dual context that the Satō government moved ahead 'silently' with security politics.

6.3.ii.d Miki administration to Suzuki administration

The ending of the Vietnam War, détente and the transformation in the structure of the international system in the early 1970s provided new opportunities for Japanese policy-making agents to forge ahead with security policies in the context of both bilateralism and anti-militarism. In the emerging multipolar structure of the international system, the Japanese attachment to bilateralism remained, but greater salience was given to anti-militarism at the policy level. This is symbolized by the dualistic nature of the Miki Takeo administration (1974–6). As a 'dove' from the liberal wing of the LDP, Miki put forward a number of policies and principles supportive of the anti-militarist norm. This can be seen, for instance, in his February 1976 decision to strengthen the prohibition on arms exports by expanding the scope of the ban to all other countries and adding as a new dimension restrictions on the export of defence-related technology. It was also the Miki administration that, in November 1976, introduced a ceiling of 1 per cent of GNP on defence spending (Keddell 1993).

This ceiling symbolizes the strength of the anti-militarist norm, but also the government's need to push forward with building a consensus on the existence and size of the SDF. At the end of the 1960s Kubo Takuya, who was transferred from the National Police Agency to the position of Defence Bureau chief in the JDA, decided to take a 'twin-track' approach to this problem. Along the first track he pushed forward with the idea of a 'minimum defence' strategy – that is, a strategy to develop a military force structure premised on what would be needed by the SDF in order to repel aggression against Japan. It was a strategy that continued to rely on the US–Japan security treaty and did not attempt to build up the SDF in response to the force size of Japan's potential enemies. The other track he moved along was to placate the concerns of the political opposition and public over the development of a new defence strategy by limiting military spending to 1 per cent of GNP. When, in the Miki administration, Kubota was appointed vice-minister (administrative) in the JDA, he worked together closely with his immediate superior, the director-general, Sakata Michita, to implement this idea by actively taking the initiative to shape Japan's first post-war military doctrine (Kaminishi 1986: 148–9). This is evidenced in Sakata's pressure on the Cabinet to adopt in October 1976 the National Defence Programme Outline (NDPO) as well as in his introduction of the 1 per cent limit. This limit served as 'compensation' to the SDPJ for acceptance of the NDPO (Calder 1988b). Whereas the 1957 Basic Policy for National Defence did no more than state a number of general principles as the basis for Japan's defence policy, the NDPO enunciated an explicit role for the SDF in dealing with 'limited and small-scale aggression', backed up by US forces.

The NDPO emerged at a time of growing concern within the JDA, MOFA and the LDP over the possibility of US withdrawal from the region. It was in this sense a policy pursued not as a result of US pressure, but rather because of growing fear about abandonment. This fear of abandonment can be viewed as the reverse side of the coin to Japan's vulnerability to US pressure and the socialist's fear of entrapment in a US war. The risk of entrapment or abandonment is a perennial problem for a weaker alliance partner such as Japan (Green 1995: 3). Sakata's policy of actively promoting public acceptance of the SDF and of the value of the security treaty, even in a more peaceful world, marked a discernible shift in strategy. The government now quietly sought to build a consensus on the existence and use of the military as a legitimate instrument of state policy. From the late 1970s onwards, moreover, the greater threat perceived as a result of the outbreak of the second Cold War supported a concerted push to build up the military under the security treaty system. In this way, successive LDP administrations sought to ensure a continued US presence in Japan and East Asia.

More specifically, in the late 1970s and at the start of the 1980s the USSR embarked on a military build-up in the region. This is illustrated by the increase in USSR naval assets in the Pacific, as in the deployment of aircraft carriers; the strengthening of air assets in the Far East, as in the deployment of the highly accurate SS-20 mid-range (5,000 kilometres) nuclear missile and the Backfire strategic bomber; and the expansion of land forces on the Kurile Islands, part of the disputed Northern Territories. These actions provided legitimization for the administrations of Fukuda Takeo (1976–8), Ōhira Masayoshi (1978–80) and Suzuki Zenkō (1980–2) to support greater defence spending and a more salient military role for Japan. The continuing stalemate on sovereignty over the Northern Territories, along with the normalization of Sino-Japanese relations (see Chapter 9), meant Russo-Japanese Cold War relations entered a deep chill.

In this tense environment, closer military cooperation between Japan and the US forged ahead. This can be seen, for instance, in the Fukuda government's signing of the Guidelines for US–Japan Defence Cooperation (hereafter, Guidelines) in November 1978, as discussed later in this chapter. It is illustrated, too, by the closer ties between the military forces of both countries, as in the inauguration of combined exercises between the Japanese ASDF and the US air force in 1978, the start of participation by the MSDF in the biennial Rim of the Pacific (RIMPAC) naval exercise in 1980 with the US navy and other US allies, and the first participation by the GSDF in combined exercises with the US in 1980. In other words, by the late 1970s and at the start of the 1980s the Japanese military was emerging, albeit under mounting US pressure, as a military ally.

Nevertheless, in the political environment of the time, a direct challenge to the anti-militarist norm still could not be openly mounted in domestic society. This can be seen, for instance, in the political turmoil created when the Suzuki administration declared that Japan's bilateral security relationship with the US was an 'alliance'. As a result of openly declaring the military nature of the bilateral security relationship, the foreign minister was forced to pay the price by tendering his resignation (*Asahi Shimbun* 9 May 1981; Hook 1986: 34–7). As this example illustrates, an open challenge to the norm of anti-militarism entailed a high political cost.

Within this general normative context, from the April 1978 fiscal year onwards the government began to contribute financially to the stationing of US troops in Japan. As the term originally coined for these payments by the then director-general of the JDA, Kanemaru Shin, *omoiyari yosan* ('sympathy budget') suggests these financial outlays were not conceived under US pressure in the context of host nation support. Instead, as a Diet statement by Kanemaru in June 1978 indicates, this was an independent decision of the Japanese government in response to the rise in the value of the yen against the dollar: 'The US has no basis to raise this matter, but I decided that, for Japan to [make a budgetary item] under the high yen [*endaka*] will heighten the trust in the Japan–US relationship' (authors' translation; cited in Hahei Chekku Henshū Iinkai 1997: 12–13). In other words, the sums allocated were over and above any additional outlay in direct military spending on the SDF.

The budget was at the outset allocated towards the cost of employing Japanese workers on US military installations and for the construction of military and other facilities, including housing for US military personnel. However, not only were these sorts of payments neither discontinued nor reduced in the wake of the yen's weakening, they were rather extended to cover a range of other costs associated with the US presence in Japan. The euphemistic *omoiyari yosan* has now grown to around 10 per cent of Japan's annual defence budget (Bōeichōhen 1999: 406; see also Kitaoka 2000: 43). As the government's host nation support has in the process emerged as the most generous of any US ally, criticism of Japan as a 'free rider' – that is, that Japan has been able to take advantage of the US by not paying its own share of the defence burden in maintaining regional and global peace and security – can be said to obfuscate a quite different aspect of the security relationship (Hook 1996a: 58–64).

Nevertheless, as is illustrated by the Ōhira Masayoshi administration's introduction of 'comprehensive national security' (see Chapman *et al.* 1983), Japanese security policy continued to be formulated taking account of the anti-militarist norm. This policy is the clearest example so far of how Japan's attachment to bilateralism did not prevent it from promoting a strategy to supplement the US–Japan security treaty. In this sense, comprehensive security in no way implied the abandonment of bilateralism or the security treaty.

The policy emerged out of the recommendations of a private advisory group established by Prime Minister Ōhira: the Comprehensive Security Study Group (1980). It was chaired by Inoki Masamichi, a prominent realist scholar, then the president of the Defence Academy. Although the recommendations were not adopted formally as government policy, they were important in helping Ōhira to resist US pressure to shoulder more of the defence burden than politically tenable and to broaden the concept of security beyond military security. The oil crisis of October 1973 had shown Japanese policy-making agents that, when the concept was broadened to include economic and other aspects of security, the interests of Japan and the US need not coincide. It was thus in Japan's own interests to use these recommendations to highlight a broader sense of security than the military security at the centre of the US–Japan security treaty system.

6.3.ii.e Nakasone administration

The pace of Japan's military cooperation with the US quickened with the advent of the Nakasone Yasuhiro administration (1982–7). Like Prime Minister Kishi, Nakasone was a nationalist from the anti-mainstream faction of the LDP who favoured a stronger military and sought to challenge more directly the anti-militarist norm embedded in Japanese defence and security policies. His more proactive interest in defence followed the Suzuki Zenkō administration's May 1981 announcement to patrol the sea lines of communication (SLOC) up to 1,000 nautical miles from Japan. This and other measures implying a more active military role for the SDF were a concrete manifestation of the closer military cooperation developing between Japan and the US.

Trade and defence conflicts soured bilateral relations in the 1980s, as symbolized by the crisis in US–Japan defence cooperation in producing the FSX fighter plane (Green 1995: 86–107). This attempt at joint production of the FSX (fighter experimental) demonstrated Japan's continuing inability to develop advanced weapons without dependence on technology from the US. Nakasone backed the joint development and worked hard to reduce congressional anger at Japan's exploitation of US technology in the FSX project. At the same time, Japan's dual-use technology was of growing interest to US weapons manufacturers, and this added to pressure on Prime Minister Nakasone to work to return the alliance relationship to a solid footing.

As was touched on in Chapter 4, the triumvirate of Thatcher, Reagan and Nakasone mounted a challenge to the growing military power of the USSR. At home, Nakasone began by seeking to dismantle the constraints on the military's role as part of his call for the 'settlement of the post-war accounts'. Illustrative of the effect of this pronouncement on security policy is the government's weakening of the ban on the export of defence-related technology by making an exception of exports to the US under the Exchange of Technology Agreement between Japan and the United States of November 1983 (for details, see Drifte 1986: 95–100). This opened a route for US weapons manufacturers to gain access to technology such as homing devices for missiles (Drifte 1986: 80). In September 1986, Nakasone then agreed to participate in research on the Strategic Defence Initiative (SDI, so-called 'star wars') promoted by President Reagan. Lastly, Nakasone abolished the 1 per cent ceiling of GNP on defence spending in the 1987 fiscal budget, indicating a symbolic challenge to the anti-militarist norm (Table 3).

Although the following years did not witness the major additional defence spending feared by some of his critics, with 1.004 per cent of GNP in 1987, 1.013 per cent in 1988, 1.006 per cent in 1989 and 0.997 per cent in 1990 (Table 3), these moves did engender concerns in domestic society about the further erosion of Japan's identity as a 'peace state'. This was manifest concretely in the fear that, irrespective of the change in the external security environment, Nakasone's Japan was heading down the road to becoming a military big power. This was seen, for instance, in the growing percentage of the budget being devoted to military hardware rather than personnel and provisions, up 10 per cent in the decade to 1987, and the acquisition of a range of sophisticated weaponry, such as 41 P3C Orion anti-submarine patrol planes, eight E-2C Hawkeye early-warning planes and 94 F-15 Eagle air-to-air fighters during the early and mid-1980s (Hook 1988: 390). The gap between internal and external perceptions of Japan's military role was vividly illustrated when, on a trip to Washington, Nakasone declared he would make Japan into an 'unsinkable aircraft carrier'. When on his return to Tokyo he was questioned in Diet debates about his remark, however, he sought to deny the militarist implications of the metaphor (Hook 1986: 39–40). In this way, Nakasone significantly bolstered military links with the US and successfully challenged at the governmental level a number of the policies embodying the anti-militarist norm in domestic society.

6.4 Post-Cold War period

6.4.i Implications of the Cold War's ending

The ending of the global Cold War, as symbolized by the reduction of both USSR and US military forces, has led to a greater degree of military cooperation between Japan and the US. Today, however, in comparison with the Cold War years, Japanese policy-making agents do not face as much resistance on both the mass and the policy-making level to stronger bilateral security relations and a greater military role for the SDF.

The active role Japan now plays as an ally of the US has emerged gradually during the past decade. The ending of the Cold War, together with the outbreak of the 1990–1 Gulf War, at first stimulated widespread discussions on defence and security matters in domestic society. Various proposals, announced by politicians, newspapers, academics and others, sought to explore a range of possibilities in thinking about the security treaty, the Japanese Constitution and Japan's place in the world (Hook 1996a: 189–95; Ozawa 1999; Hatoyama 1999). Whether as a vehicle to legitimize the continued need for the security treaty in a changed international environment, or as a means to declare the time now ripe to implement policies embodying the norm of anti-militarism, the opening of a lively debate on defence and security matters at this time revived memories of similar debates in the late 1940s and late 1950s. Yet the result of this process was to reinforce the security relationship between Japan and the US, not to abandon it as called for by the SDPJ.

The reasons for this are complex, but cannot be understood without first taking into account the response to the outbreak of the 1990–1 Gulf War, which turned out to be a watershed in terms of Japanese security policy. During the Cold War the despatch of troops overseas engendered in domestic society the dual fear of becoming embroiled in a war of US making and of Japan's return to its military past. In other words, what at least some of the political and bureaucratic policy-making agents viewed as fulfilling Japan's obligations as an ally of the US or as a member of international society was viewed by many in the opposition parties, and on the mass level, as a threat to Article 9 of the Constitution. The Gulf War demonstrated to some that, far from the despatch of troops posing a threat to international peace, such action could help to restore it. By playing a role in this process Japan could thereby be perceived as fulfilling its obligation as a responsible member of international society in line with internationally embedded norms.

As will be seen in Chapter 19, the government's decision to offer mainly a financial contribution to the resolution of the Gulf War generated international criticism, not praise. Even with the despatch of minesweepers once the war had ended, moreover, Japan was not recognized as a major contributor to the war. Domestically, however, the despatch of the minesweepers was viewed by the hard-core supporters of the anti-militarist norm as an unwarranted threat. This is because, following the erosion of anti-militarist security policies under Nakasone, this action eliminated another anti-militarist principle: the 1972 ban on despatching minesweepers imposed by Prime Minister Satō. In this way, those political forces seeking to legitimize the SDF as an instrument of state policy could now cast the institutional face of the anti-militarist norm, the Constitution, against the norm of international cooperation, especially through the UN. Thenceforth, the government has been able to promote policies in terms of in what form, not whether, the SDF should be despatched overseas. This represents a dramatic change in the balance between domestic and international norms.

Second, as was seen in Chapter 2 and above, during the Cold War period the SDPJ had sought to promote a policy of 'unarmed neutrality', thereby linking an explicit policy option with the anti-militarist norm. In contrast, the LDP had pursued a policy of maintaining and, where appropriate, reinforcing security relations with the US. For years, the concrete actions taken by the socialists in line with the party platform of unarmed neutrality had acted as a brake on the militarization of US–Japan security relations under the LDP, at least to some extent. With the collapse of the international Cold War structures, however, came the collapse of the internal Cold War structures, too. Instead of confrontation between the conservatives and socialists, a realignment of political forces, leading to the advent of coalition governments, took place. As a result, the first socialist prime minister in nearly fifty years, Murayama Tomiichi (1994–6), was forced, as part of the compromise to enter and lead the coalition government, to abandon the two 'nos' at the centre of the socialists' security platform; that is, 'no' to the SDF and 'no' to the security treaty. With the acceptance of the two founding elements of the LDP's security policy, the brake the party had applied with varying degrees of pressure during the Cold War period finally had been eased, if not fully released. This radical change of policy and decline in the party's electoral fortunes served to erode the anti-militarist norm.

Third, with the end of the Cold War the two allies lost the purpose for which the security treaty was signed in the first place: the threat from communism, and especially Soviet communism. The new US thinking can be seen in the Department of Defense's 1992 *East Asian Strategic Initiative* (US Department of Defense 1992). Its call for a reduction in the deployment of US forces indicated to Japanese policy-making agents that President Bill Clinton's administration was responding to the transformation in the structure of the international system by cutting back on its regional commitment. Without a common enemy to unite Japan and the US, divisive issues moved to centre stage: economics, not security, became the order of the day. This can be seen during the first years of the Clinton administration, when the focus was overwhelmingly on the economy, not least the trade deficit with Japan.

By the mid-1990s, however, concern had emerged that, as a result of concentrating on divisive economic issues, the shared interests of the US and Japan in maintaining peace and security in East Asia were being jeopardized. With this in mind, Assistant Secretary of Defense for International Security Affairs, Joseph S. Nye, carried out a series of bilateral talks with Japanese defence and other officials in order to identify the scope of their shared interests in the changed international climate. Under Nye's supervision the Department of Defense in February 1995 issued a new review of strategy in East Asia entitled *United States Security Strategy for the East Asia-Pacific Region*, but usually dubbed the 'Nye Report'. This confirmed the US's commitment to the security treaty as the cornerstone of the government's policy as well as its determination to maintain, for at least the next twenty years, around 100,000 troops in East Asia (for a critique, see Johnson and Keehn 1995). It is in the wake of this renewed regional commitment that Japan's role in East Asian security has grown in significance, as discussed below concerning the revision of the 1978 Guidelines.

Fourth, despite the reluctance of certain policy-making agents to accept the end of the Cold War, as was illustrated in Chapter 4, the end of LDP governance and the rise to the premiership of Hosokawa Morihiro as the leader of the subsequent coalition government, led in February 1994 to the setting-up of a private advisory group, the Prime Minister's Advisory Group on Defence, to review defence and security policy in the context of the Cold War's ending. The recommendations of this group, finally issued during the Murayama administration, called for Japan to give priority to multilateral efforts to promote security, such as the SDF's participation in UNPKO; the strengthening of the functional operation of the security relationship with the US; and the improvement of information-gathering capabilities and the ability to respond to crises. These recommendations helped to shape the new NDPO announced in November 1995, which in the fiscal year 1996 replaced the 1976 NDPO (for details, see Bōei Handobokku 1997: 27–47), but the objection of the US meant that the government failed to push ahead with prioritizing multilateral security arrangements (Funabashi 1997: 231–8). This suggests a wider regional and more proactive role for the SDF than heretofore.

Fifth, as Part III will elucidate, the legacy of wartime actions meant that, during the Cold War, Japan's relations with East Asia were fraught with difficulty, especially in regard to Japan playing a role in regional security. Fear of a recrudescence of militarism, or even of a larger military role for Japan, strongly coloured the overall relationship during these years. However, with the end of the Cold War, together with the emergence of Japan as a member of the UNPKO in Cambodia and elsewhere (see Chapter 19), East Asian resistance to a regional security role for Japan became less uniform and salient. Whereas China and North Korea have continued to express concern about a Japanese military presence, policy-makers in Southeast Asia, and even in South Korea, are now much more supportive (see Chapter 11). The change in attitude is manifest concretely in the request made by the Cambodian government for Japan to take part in the PKO.

6.4.ii 'Reaffirmation' or 'redefinition' of the security treaty?

The treaty remains the basis of Japan's new security role. It is emerging in the context of the Japan–US Joint Declaration on Security: Alliance for the 21st Century (Appendix 6.1) (hereafter, Joint Declaration), which was signed by President Clinton and Prime Minister Hashimoto at a summit in Tokyo in 1996. The meeting originally had been scheduled for November 1995 prior to the meeting of the APEC forum in Osaka, during the term of the socialist prime minister Murayama Tomiichi, but did not in fact take place until the following April, officially because of the backlog of congressional business faced by the president. By postponing the visit, however, Clinton was able to hold the summit with Hashimoto several more months after the September 1995 mass protests against US bases in Okinawa, discussed below. The visit also followed shortly after China's test-firing of missiles to intimidate Taiwan in the run-up to the Taiwanese presidential election in March 1996. This served to heighten tension in the region and highlight the possible threat posed to Japanese security by its giant neighbour, China.

The controversy surrounding the Joint Declaration arises from the expanded scope of security cooperation it implies. It states that the two leaders

> reaffirmed that the Japan–US relationship, based on the Treaty of Mutual Cooperation and Security between Japan and the United States of America,

> remains the cornerstone for achieving common security objectives, and for maintaining a stable and prosperous environment for the Asia-Pacific region as we enter the twenty-first century ...
>
> (Japan–US Joint Declaration on Security: Alliance for the 21st Century: Appendix 6.1)

The revised treaty of 1960, however, refers to the 'Far East', not Asia Pacific. The change in geographic terminology has led to criticism that, as implied by the expressions 'Far East' and 'Asia Pacific', the scope of the security treaty has been extended beyond that of the 1960 treaty and the Satō–Nixon agreement of 1969. In other words, it has been redefined in terms of scope, not reaffirmed, as the Joint Declaration's mention of Asia Pacific a dozen times seems to imply.

Similarly, it refers to a number of other areas of importance in bolstering regional security relations, including the development of security dialogue and cooperation through the ASEAN Regional Forum. The following items have proved particularly controversial in Japan: the revision of the 1978 Guidelines for Japan–US Defence Cooperation; bilateral cooperation in coping with situations in 'areas surrounding Japan'; bilateral cooperation in Theatre Missile Defence (TMD); and the continuing scale of US military installations, especially in Okinawa.

6.4.iii Revised Guidelines for United States–Japan Defence Cooperation

As touched on above, the original Guidelines were agreed in November 1978 at a time when concrete military cooperation between Japan and the US was minimal. Whereas the 1978 Guidelines called for joint studies of operational issues in the three key areas of preventing aggression against Japan, dealing with attacks against Japan, and bilateral cooperation in case of conflict in the Far East, the revised Guidelines agreed after bilateral research involving MOFA, the Department of Defence and other ministries in September 1997 are much more wide-ranging in their implications (Tamura 1997). Significantly, in May 1999 legislation was passed by the Diet in order to facilitate military cooperation in line with the revised Guidelines, particularly in the area of logistics.

The 1999 Guidelines call on Japan to cooperate in responding to 'situations in areas surrounding Japan' in forty specific areas, such as relief work, dealing with refugees, and search and rescue; evacuation of non-combatants; activities to ensure the implementation of economic sanctions; offering the use of Japanese facilities to the US; logistical support in terms of supply and transportation; security of US military installations, communications and other areas; surveillance; and minesweeping. In order for Japan to be able to carry out these tasks as required under the revised Guidelines, the 1999 legislation was composed of three elements: the Law on Emergencies in Surrounding Areas, the revision of the Self-Defence Law, and the ratification of the revised US–Japan Acquisition and Cross-Servicing Agreement (for details, see Hōgaku Seminā Henshū Bu 1999; Hughes 1999: 193–201). Despite a last-minute revision of the Emergencies Law, the political cooperation between the LDP, Liberal Party and Kōmei Party ensured that the legislation was passed without difficulty, and indeed without full debate. As at the time of the 1960 security crisis, albeit without the same sort of mass demonstrations, the passage of the legislation again raised concerns in domestic society that the demands of the security treaty were eroding Japan's democratic process and constitutional principles, especially Article 9 of the Constitution.

6.4.iv 'Situations in areas surrounding Japan'

The reference to 'situations in areas surrounding Japan' (Article 5 of the revised Guidelines) has been a particular point of controversy, both in Japan and in the region. In the Joint Declaration the two leaders agreed on bilateral cooperation 'in dealing with situations that may emerge in the areas surrounding Japan'. In the revised Guidelines, however, reference is made in Article 5 to 'cooperation in situations in areas surrounding Japan'. Even within the government, the JDA has tended to view the range of activities to be geographically limited, whereas MOFA has tended to view the scope of activities as 'situational' (Asai 1997: 175). This points to the continuing influence of the norm of bilateralism in MOFA.

At the same time, MOFA has been particularly concerned about the reaction of China. Even if Russia and North Korea are targeted as part of the scope of activities, the question of the Japanese role in any crisis in the Taiwan Straits can soon call into question Japan's acceptance of the 'one China' policy (see Chapter 9). Whereas the Chinese government remained restrained in its response to the Joint Declaration, the revision of the Guidelines, together with concern about the resurgence of militarism in Japan, have led to pointed criticism of US–Japan military cooperation. The possibility of Japan cooperating with the US in any conflict over Taiwan will remain a thorn in the side of Sino-Japanese relations for the foreseeable future, as seen in the context of the scope of TMD dealt with below.

Thus, whereas MOFA has been trying to de-link the government's 'reaffirmation' of the security treaty and the revised Guidelines from the Taiwan question, China has focused precisely on this as an implication of their reaffirmation and revision. What is more, as political leaders such as LDP Cabinet Secretary, Kajiyama Seiroku, and the Liberal Party leader, Ozawa Ichirō, have stated that the Taiwan Straits do indeed fall within the scope of US–Japan bilateral cooperation, the interpretation adopted by China accords with some of Japan's leading politicians (Asai 1997: 152–3). From this perspective, the tortuous attempt to match the reality of Japan's existing military forces with the ban on 'land, sea, and air forces' in Article 9 of the Constitution is now being replayed in terms of the tortuous attempt to give concrete meaning to the expression 'areas surrounding Japan'.

The more far-reaching implication of the phrase is, of course, the implied redefinition, not reaffirmation, of the security treaty. It is for this reason that, given the Chinese criticism and the anti-militarist norms embedded in domestic society, the government has opted for a 'situational', not 'geographic', interpretation in Diet interpellations. Still, whether this will lead to any restriction on the actual role played by Japan in the context of reinforcing bilateral military cooperation remains to be seen.

6.4.v *Theatre Missile Defence*

The possibility of Japan cooperating with the US in the development of Theatre Missile Defence (TMD) has been mooted for some time. The genesis for Japanese involvement in TMD research can be found in the agreement made during the Nakasone era to cooperate in research on SDI (for details, see Yamashita *et al.* 1994). The two governments have carried out dialogue on possible collaboration in developing TMD since 1992, with the first administrative working party meeting held in December 1993. In August 1999, the two governments signed a memorandum of agreement, which commits each to further and to deepen joint collaboration on TMD technological research. The funds committed by the JDA for carrying out TMD research have already reached US$36 million, with the total cost of research predicted to run up to US$500 million. The outlay for deploying a TMD system would be in the region of US$16 billion.

In comparison with SDI, which sought to construct an all-embracing shield against incoming missiles, TMD is geographically limited to protecting Japan from missile attacks in Northeast Asia. It is for this reason called by the Japanese government Ballistic Missile Defence (BMD), rather than TMD, as the aim for Japan at least is national defence, not a regional shield. The different threat perceptions and evaluation of the potential for SDI to succeed meant that, for the most part, Japan's commitment to the Reagan project was lukewarm. The ending of the Cold War, along with the technical difficulties of implementation, led the US itself to abandon the project in 1993. In the case of TMD, too, discussions were not pursued with vigour by the Japanese side until after the North Korean test-firing of a suspect Taepodong-1 ballistic missile in August 1998, as will be dealt with in Chapters 9 and 11. The missile's flight over the archipelago and its landing in the sea off the coast of Japan sent shock-waves throughout the country. With at least parts of Japan already within range of North Korea's Scud C missiles and most of the rest within range of the North's 200 or so Nodong missiles, government critics suspect that the LDP and Liberal Party sought to exploit the 'Taepodong shock' in order to promote their security agenda (Handa 1999: 38). Certainly, the speed with which the memorandum was signed in the wake of the Taepodong crisis suggests a political motivation for the 'shock'.

Whatever the benefits of TMD to Japanese security, similar, if not greater, benefits will accrue to US forces deployed in Japan. Indeed, the history of the development of the TMD concept highlights a keen interest on the part of the US government in Japan's cooperation. In this sense, should the deployment of a functional TMD indeed go ahead later in the twenty-first century, the security interests of the Japanese state and its people will be tied even more closely to those of the US than they were in the Cold War period, as a result of the increased technological integration of US and Japanese defence. The extent to which these interests will continue to be shared in respect of the possible extension of TMD to Taiwan remains to be seen.

6.4.vi United States bases in mainland Japan

The US maintains military installations and deploys approximately 47,000 US military personnel in different parts of the Japanese archipelago. Although the US presence is concentrated in Okinawa, as discussed below, the main islands still host seven major military facilities (for details, see Bōei Handobokku 1999: 369–79). In the north of the main island of Honshū the US air force deploys over forty F-15 fighters at Misawa airbase. Close to Tokyo are four bases, Yokota, Camp Zama, Yokosuka and Atsugi. At Yokota, the air force deploys transportation and other military planes. This base also houses command headquarters for US forces as well as command headquarters for the fifth airborne division. Camp Zama is command headquarters for the army and is the main army base. Yokosuka serves as the command headquarters for the navy and acts as the home port for the aircraft carrier, the *Independence*, as well as the Seventh Fleet. Atsugi is home to the fifth aircraft carrier fighter squadron and to anti-submarine helicopters. To the south of Tokyo in Hiroshima prefecture, Iwakuni acts as a base for the marines. Finally, in the southern island of Kyūshū, minesweepers and rescue vessels are deployed at the naval base of Sasebo. The deployment and presence of US military personnel in this way are in accordance with the obligation of Japan under the security treaty.

Despite widespread support for the security treaty on the mass level, as illustrated by public opinion surveys showing approximately two-thirds in favour of its maintenance (Hook 1996a: 119–22), there is strong opposition to the concrete manifestation of the treaty: US bases and the deployment of military personnel. These have generated widespread opposition from local communities owing to political issues, such as the security treaty, as well as everyday life issues, such as the noise pollution generated by aircraft.

6.4.vii United States bases in Okinawa

As indicated above, it is Okinawa rather than the main islands which bears the greatest burden in fulfilling the obligation under the treaty to provide bases for the US. The truncating of the archipelago in the south by the severing of Okinawa from the main islands at the end of World War II means that, even after the 1972 reversion of Okinawa to Japanese sovereignty, the majority of US bases and military personnel remains located there. In this respect, nothing has changed in the last fifty-five years. The implications of the concentration of US forces on Okinawa can be seen from the fact that, although the prefecture occupies only 0.6 per cent of the archipelago's total land mass, approximately 25 per cent of all US facilities, a total of thirty-nine, are located in Okinawa. Nearly 20 per cent of the main island of Okinawa, and 10.7 per cent of the prefecture as a whole, is occupied by US military facilities. In six municipalities, moreover, the US occupies over 40 per cent of the land area, with US facilities taking up 82.8 per cent of Kadena town. Including family members, over 50,000 US personnel are deployed in Okinawa (Military Base Affairs Office 1999: 1).

Whatever interpretation is given to the utility of the treaty in terms of Japan's overall security, no doubt exists in the minds of the majority of Okinawans as to who has borne the brunt of the costs of US deployments. Over the years, the noise pollution from aircraft, the social pollution from bars and prostitution around the bases, crimes and military accidents, as well as the infringement of human rights, as illustrated by the rape of the schoolgirl discussed in Chapter 4, have left an indelible mark on the Okinawan psyche. For instance, a 1997 survey showed noise levels at Kadena airbase infringed Japan's environmental standards in 10 of 12 sites tested; since reversion in 1972, nearly 5,000 crimes, including murder, rape and robbery, have been committed by US military personnel, civilian employees or dependants; and 131 aircraft accidents, of which 37 have been crashes, have occurred (Military Base Affairs Office 1999: 3–7; also see Tōkai Daigakuhen 1997: 76–8).

At the same time, however, many Okinawans benefit from the existence of the bases. For some, work in US facilities provides a livelihood, albeit within the context of a 'base dependent' economy. The importance of the bases in this regard is illustrated by the May 1996 recruitment for work on US bases, when 6,196 Okinawans submitted an application (Tōkai Daigakuhen 1997: 77). In other cases, the land occupied by the US military is leased from private landowners. In contrast to the main Japanese islands, where 87 per cent of US bases are on national land, 33 per cent are located on private land in Okinawa prefecture. In central Okinawa, the ratio shoots up to 76 per cent. Many of these workers and landowners are 'beneficiaries' as a result of the salaries and rents they receive and are in general less inclined to oppose the US presence than other Okinawans. Their presence makes the politics of economism and anti-militarism in Okinawa much more complex than on the main islands.

Opposition to the quantity of US bases is, nevertheless, the dominant sentiment in Okinawa. Although various social movements opposed to the bases have emerged over the years, the September 1995 rape of a 12-year-old schoolgirl by three US servicemen, mentioned in Chapter 4 and above, galvanized this widespread feeling of opposition to US bases into a major protest movement leading to a rally in October 1995 with over 85,000 participants (Okinawa Taimususha 1997: 24). If such massive anti-base demonstrations had spread to the main Japanese islands, this would have jeopardized the closer military links being developed between Japan and the US from the mid-1990s onwards. The progressive governor at the time, Ōta Masahide, stirred up concern about the continuing US presence in the prefecture both at the central government level in Tokyo and in Washington by backing the popular call for a reduction in the US presence. Demonstrating the way political leaders of sub-national political authorities can work to challenge the security treaty and represent the norm of anti-militarism, Governor Ōta visited the US as many as seven times during his term in office (1990–8) in order to promote the anti-base cause. The political pressure generated by these protests, the governor's role and the fear of the protests in Okinawa weakening support for the security treaty throughout Japan led the Clinton administration to agree to a scaling-down of US facilities in Okinawa. Despite his success in this regard, however, the voters failed to return Ōta to office owing to the economic and other benefits promised by the rival candidate.

The most significant element of the agreement was the inclusion in the April 1996 Joint Declaration of a statement confirming their 'determination to carry out steps to consolidate, realign, and reduce US facilities'. In this respect, one of the main points of controversy has been Futenma airbase, which is the home base to about 100 helicopters and planes of the Marine Corps. The pressure to close Futenma base has been particularly strong as it is located in the midst of Futenma City. Needless to say, the presence of a US military base in a Japanese city has hindered urban development, the improvement of transport and communication facilities, and continues to endanger the health and welfare of Futenma's residents.

It should be noted in this context that, in 1974, the US government agreed to return Naha Port, the second largest military port in Okinawa, on the condition that an alternative was found. As this condition has still not been met over twenty-five years later, Naha Port remains in US hands. Similarly, the most controversial outcome of the present pressure to reduce the US presence has been the attempt to replace Futenma airbase with an offshore heliport, not simply to close the base. This transfer, rather than closure, of US facilities is one of the main targets of the anti-base movement. The central government has conducted preliminary surveys on the location of the new heliport near the city of Nago. Nevertheless, in the wake of a December 1997 referendum held by the citizens of the city, the planned project was rejected. Even though a new site has been chosen, the date for the completion of the heliport remains unclear. The difference in attitude between Okinawans and policy-making agents in Tokyo towards this US military presence is symbolized by the comments of then Chief Cabinet Secretary Kajiyama Seiroku, who stated at the time of the December 1997 referendum: 'The sound of helicopters is just like the singing of small insects' (Mashiki 1999: 26).

6.5 Summary

During the Cold War period Japan–US security relations developed in the context of successive LDP administrations being faced with both US and domestic political pressures. Although under certain political leaders, active promotion of a more militarized security policy can be identified, as during the Kishi and Nakasone administrations, the dominant pattern of security relations seems to be more acquiescence under US pressure than proactive support. Even though a number of anti-militarist policies were challenged successfully by Kishi, Nakasone and other leaders, Japan still maintains a ban on arms exports and only despatches the SDF abroad under constraints, as in UNPKO discussed in Chapter 19.

With the ending of the Cold War and the domestic political transformations set in motion as a result, however, the alliance relationship has tied the Japanese state and its people much more closely to a US war-fighting strategy. This follows a number of steps taken during the Cold War, such as the decisions to start combined exercises, patrol the sea lines of communication and export defence-related technology to the US. It takes shape as a consequence of the 'reaffirmation' of the security treaty and the revision of the Guidelines. The latter, in particular, has led to the passing of new legislation to enable Japan to cooperate with the US in actual war-fighting in still-to-be-defined 'areas surrounding Japan'.

Nevertheless, despite these changes and the release of the brake on the military previously applied by the SDPJ, domestic society remains strongly influenced by the anti-militarist norm, especially in Okinawa. Whilst this norm has been weakened, new governments in the twenty-first century still need to take it into consideration along with pressure from the US when determining Japanese security policy.

Chapter 7

Conclusion

7.1 The changing nature of Japan–United states relations

Chapter 3 presented a vignette of the CIA tapping the phone of MITI Minister Hashimoto Ryūtarō in the lead-up to the September 1995 bilateral automobile negotiations with the US. It was introduced as an illustration of how the relationship between Japan and the US has been transformed in the more than fifty years since Joseph Dodge made his visit to Tokyo in 1949 in order to kick-start the economy. As was noted in Chapter 3, the change in the bilateral relationship has been particularly marked in the economic dimension, with Japan's rise to economic superpower status enabling it to challenge the US in the automobile and a number of other key sectors of the economy. The degree of change in Japan's political and security relations with the US, however, remains more complex.

7.2 Continuing strength of bilateralism

The policies pursued by successive Japanese governments during the Cold War period demonstrate clearly that, far from policy-makers merely reacting to changes in the structure of the international system, at times they have proactively responded to these changes in line with the perceived interests of the Japanese state and its people. In the case of the normalization of Soviet–Japanese relations in the mid-1950s, for instance, the change in the structure of the international system and pressure from the US help to explain the change in policy towards the Northern Territories and the peace treaty made at the time. In the emerging post-Cold War period, the response to the 1990–1 Gulf War confirms the continuing importance of the anti-militarist norm in shaping policy. Whereas the former illustrates the power of the US to influence the direction of Japanese policy, the latter demonstrates how norms have served both to constrain and to empower policy-makers. Similarly, the Japanese response to the Gulf War confirms the continuing preference of policy-making agents for instrumentalizing international relations through economic power.

The policy-makers willing to lay less emphasis on the norm of bilateralism have tended to emerge from within the conservative political establishment, the LDP, rather than within the foreign policy bureaucracy. Overall, MOFA has been tied closely to the norm of bilateralism, whereas LDP policy-makers have been at times able to respond to wider national concerns as well as to more narrow concerns related to their own political fortune. Whether in the economy, in politics or in security, however, bilateralism has remained the dominant norm at the policy-making level. Indeed, the limited number of examples of Japanese policy-making agents making a determined effort to pursue interests which conflict with the norm of bilateralism suggests their continuing vulnerability in the face of US pressure.

One of the reasons for this, at least among the present older generation of policy-makers, is the start of Japan's rebirth under the tutelage of the US. In a sense, the nature of the Occupation and the peace settlement engendered a psychological dependence and vulnerability in their minds (Kamo 1994). This experience thus served to create a mindset conducive to support for bilateralism. The vulnerability of Japanese policy-making agents to *beiatsu* was particularly salient in the trade conflicts of the 1980s. In the automobile negotiations of the 1990s, of course, Japan was able to say 'no', yet the continuing dependence of Japan on the US market in the economic dimension, and on the security treaty in the security dimension, means that policy-making agents remain constrained in any attempt to challenge US power politically. This vulnerability has remained an overarching theme of the post-war power relationship between Japan and the US.

7.3 Salience of other norms

Nevertheless, the norms embedded in domestic society, especially anti-militarism, have offered policy-makers a way to conceive policy, despite US pressure. With the end of the Cold War, moreover, they have tended increasingly to supplement, if not challenge directly, bilateralism. The change in the structure of the international system and the willingness of the US to pursue multilateral as well as bilateral and unilateral initiatives have created new opportunities in this respect. For instance, at the same time as Japan has implemented the revised Guidelines, which reinforce bilateralism, it has given voice to supplemental strategies seeking to balance US–Japan bilateralism but not to erode it. In this sense, policies based on the norms of Asianism, trilateralism or internationalism, as will be discussed in Parts III, IV and V of this volume, should not be understood as a direct challenge to bilateralism, but rather as a manifestation of the opening of new political space in the context of Japan's continuing reliance on the security treaty.

In essence, Japan's political, economic and security relations with the US throughout the post-war era have been the result of a balance between the pressures from the bilateralism at the heart of the US–Japan relationship and the pressures from domestic society to maintain a high standard of living (economism) without becoming embroiled in a US war (anti-militarism). In line with the norms of economism and anti-militarism, domestic society has been willing to support the US, and in general the US–Japan security treaty. Yet this does not extend to acquiescing in the government's unfettered use of the military in line with US strategy. Some form of restraint on the SDF in the pursuit of state goals remains the preferred option of domestic society. This support for the treaty goes hand in hand with the uneven distribution of the costs of maintaining it. As was seen in Chapter 6, these costs have been borne disproportionately by those living in Okinawa.

7.4 Dominant pattern of Japan–United States relations

The dominant pattern of Japan's political, economic and security relations with the US to emerge is first and foremost the centrality of bilateralism in determining the course of action Japan has chartered in the international system. It suggests a number of other related features in the pattern of Japan–US relations. These are:

the need to take into account domestic actors, not just the structure of the international system; the ability of policy-making agents to respond to changes in the structure of the international system when important interests are at stake, despite immobilist tendencies; the necessity of paying attention to norms, with the norms of anti-militarism and economism in particular helping to shed light on the role of domestic society especially; and finally, the continuing preference of the state and its people for seeking non-military solutions to human problems by instrumentalizing their international relations through economic power.

Part III

JAPAN–EAST ASIA RELATIONS

Chapter 8

Introduction

8.1 Japan and the rejoining and remaking of East Asia: Association of Southeast Asian Nations + 3

On 14 December 1997, Prime Minister Hashimoto Ryūtarō of Japan, President Jiang Zemin of China and President Kim Young Sam of South Korea arrived in Kuala Lumpur, Malaysia, for a joint summit meeting with the leaders of the ASEAN-10. Called at the initiative of ASEAN prior to its own summit proper, this inaugural ASEAN + 3 meeting had been designed as a celebration of the thirtieth anniversary of the Southeast Asian organization's founding, but also as an informal opportunity to discuss mutual political, economic and security concerns. The degree of rivalry between Japan, China and South Korea, as well as rivalry between the ASEAN states themselves, and the problems engendered for interaction between all of them by the onset of the financial and economic crises in Southeast Asia in mid-1997, should not be underestimated. Nevertheless, this first exclusive gathering of all the major East Asian heads of state, and the first without the presence of a leader from the US, certainly indicated the increased recognition by all sides of convergent regional interests and the importance of region-based dialogue. This was especially true given the challenges of globalization as demonstrated by the burgeoning financial and economic crises from July 1997 onwards, which looked set to undermine the East Asian economic 'miracle' of the previous two decades. In addition, Japan's presence at the summit alongside China and South Korea indicated the increasing acceptance of it by the other East Asian states as a key partner, if not yet overt leader, in advancing regional and multilateral dialogue in the dimensions of politics, economics and security.

Thus, the holding of the ASEAN + 3 summit in 1997 and the subsequent agreement to institutionalize the meeting in future years (with meetings subsequently held in 1998, 1999 and 2000), along with the emergence since the early 1990s of other region-wide fora including the ASEAN Regional Forum (ARF), all represent significant steps forward in the delicate process of East Asian regional integration in the post-Cold War period, and highlight Japan's important role within this process. These developments are made even more extraordinary in the context of the highly-divergent nature of the East Asian political economy under the previous Cold War order, the impact of the failure of Japan's former regional ambitions which fostered the conditions for divergence in East Asia, and the consequent past tendency of the East Asian states to reject in varying degrees Japan's legitimacy as a regional political, economic and security actor. For, as the section on the historical pattern of Japan's international relations in Chapter 2 of this volume has made clear, Japan's previous attempts in the Meiji and early Shōwa eras to challenge the existing international order, and to create under its own imperial auspices greater regional cohesion in East Asia, produced the ultimately disastrous outcomes of the extension of Japanese colonial rule across most of Northeast and Southeast Asia, the onset of the Pacific War and Japan's total defeat in 1945 – the after-effects of which were to contribute to the increased fragmentation of East Asia as a regional unit and to Japan's frequent isolation from regional affairs.

Plate 8.1 Regional integration at last? The leaders of the ASEAN states and China, South Korea and Japan gather in Hanoi, Vietnam, from 15 to 16 December 1998 for the second ASEAN + 3 meeting, the first multilateral and all-East Asian body without the presence of the US.
Source: Courtesy of the Ministry of Foreign Affairs, Japan

8.2 Approach

Given the indications of a re-evaluation of Japan's standing within the region, and especially when set against the background of hostility and dislocation in the past, the purpose of this chapter is to examine the course and degree of Japan's remarkable political, economic and security reintegration into East Asia in the post-war era. Specifically, Chapters 9, 10 and 11 seek to elucidate the pattern of Japan's bilateral and multilateral relations with the states of East Asia over the last fifty-five years, and how far Japan has succeeded or failed in regaining a central position in the creation of an East Asia region in the midst of the challenges of the post-Cold War emerging global order. In addition, the chapters analyse the motives and actors behind Japan's building of relations with East Asia, and the capabilities and methods it has employed to achieve its interests in the region. Therefore, once again this section pursues the three major questions of this volume: the 'what', 'why' and 'how' of Japan's relations with each of the core regions of the world.

In order to answer these questions, the next sections of this chapter provide a brief historical framework for understanding Japan's approach towards East Asia. The sections adumbrate the extreme historical difficulties that Japan has faced in attempting to reintegrate, or even at first simply to re-ingratiate, itself with the states of the region. In particular, the sections outline the problems of the legacy of colonialism, national division, the Cold War and bipolarity, and the diversity and fragmentation of the region's political economies, which set in place by the mid-1950s a structure of international relations which has continued to hamper Japan's relations with the region ever since. This historical overview then leads into Chapters 9, 10 and 11 which deal with Japan's relations with East Asia in the dimensions of politics, economics and security, and the way in which Japan in both the past and the future has begun to reintegrate itself into the region. Each of these chapters outlines the patterns and issues of Japan's relations with East Asia through a historical narrative of the Cold War and post-Cold War periods, and also interweaves this with an analysis of the reaction of Japanese policy-makers to the external structure, in order to highlight the policy-making determinants and instrumentalization of Japan's extension of its presence in the region.

8.3 Historical overview 1945–56: the origins of structural barriers to Japan–East Asia interaction

The task of Japanese policy-making agents in seeking to reintegrate East Asia and to obtain a central place for Japan within it has been greatly complicated by Japan's historical involvement in the creation of four interrelated structural barriers to political, economic and security exchange in the region: colonialism, national division, bipolarization and the fragmentation of the regional political economy.

8.3.i Legacy of colonialism

As was noted in Chapter 2, the principal impulse of Japan's leaders in the pre-Pacific War period was to mould together an interdependent political, economic and security region in East Asia through the mechanism of imperialism and the Greater East Asia Co-prosperity Sphere. The origins and motivations of the Greater East Asia Co-prosperity Sphere were multifarious, comprising a mix of Japanese hunger for enhanced prestige and the resources of the region, but also a genuine element of pan-Asianist sentiment. Pan-Asianism argued that the expansion of Japanese imperialism in the region was necessary and legitimate in order to liberate East Asia from Western colonial rule, and to foster under Japanese guardianship East Asian solidarity and eventual independence (Beasley 1987: 245). However, increasingly after its proclamation in 1942, the Greater East Asia Co-prosperity Sphere came to be viewed within the region as a cynical exercise on Japan's part to disguise its intention to supplant Western colonial rule in East Asia with its own. Japanese colonial rule generated a good deal of suffering and anti-Japanese feeling not only in China and the Korean Peninsula, but also in the newly-acquired colonies of Southeast Asia, and especially in the Philippines, Singapore and Malaya. Japanese administrators in colonies and protectorates, such as Burma and Vietnam, were able to some extent to ameliorate Southeast Asian hostility by encouraging popular nationalist movements and holding out the prospect of independence (Mendl 1995: 113). Across most of the region, however, Japan's colonial rule has left a legacy of animosity and mistrust. This has served as a structural barrier to distance Japan from closer political, economic and security ties with the region in the post-war era.

8.3.ii National division

The rise and fall of Japan's imperial ambitions not only produced antipathy towards Japan in East Asia, but also produced the conditions for the fundamental reconstitution of the regional order in the dimensions of politics, economics and security. Japan's defeat of the Western powers at the beginning of the 1940s destroyed the myth of white colonial supremacy in the region, with the result that following Japan's surrender in 1945 the returning powers found it increasingly difficult to reimpose their mastery over their former colonies. In Southeast Asia, the colonial powers were eventually forced, often after armed struggles, to cede independence to the nationalist movements in the Philippines (1946), Malaya (1948), Burma (1948), Indonesia (1949) and Vietnam (1954). These nationalist movements had first fully emerged during the period of the Japanese Occupation, and brought about a transformation in the regional political order from one based on Western imperialism to one based on the emergence of newly independent states.

Similarly, in Northeast Asia, Japan's reckless expansion and then rapid defeat was also responsible for the dismantlement of colonialism, the rise of new states and for creating the conditions to reconstitute the entire regional political order. Following its surrender in August 1945, Japan was instantaneously stripped of its colonies in China, Taiwan, Korea and in the Pacific Islands. The political space opened up by Japan's withdrawal from the empire in East Asia was then filled by the rise of new nationalist regimes, both communist and anti-communist, and by the encroachment of the interests of the emerging global powers of the US and the USSR. These global superpowers had now also become regional powers functionally, owing to their previous involvement in the Pacific War and power projection capabilities on the global and regional levels. The outcome was that the process of de-colonization in Northeast Asia was accompanied by civil war and eventual national division, as rival nationalist regimes split along lines of ideology and were backed in their struggles by the competing communist and capitalist superpowers. In China, Japan's defeat enabled the Chinese Communist Party (CCP) and the Kuo Min Tang (KMT, or Nationalist Party) to resume their civil war, resulting in a communist victory and the establishment of the People's Republic of China (PRC) in October 1949, the decampment of the KMT and Republic of China (ROC) governments to Taiwan, and the near *de facto* division of China ever since. In Korea, Japan's defeat was followed by a hasty agreement between the US and the USSR to divide the Korean Peninsula at the 38th parallel into military zones to be administered by them. Although the division of Korea was meant to be temporary, the US and the USSR continued to back respectively anti-communist and communist regimes in the southern and northern halves of the peninsula. The division of Korea was then confirmed by the proclamation of the Republic of South Korea (ROK, or South Korea) on 15 August 1948, and then the Democratic People's Republic of Korea (DPRK, or North Korea) on 9 September 1948.

8.3.iii Cold War bipolarity

In turn, the aftermath of the implosion of Japanese imperialism and the political space that it produced helped to create a geopolitical landscape conducive to the application of bipolarity and the emergence of a new Cold War order in the region. East Asia's integration into the global bipolar structure dominated by the US and the USSR initially lagged behind that of Europe, as the superpowers, although suspicious of each other's intentions, sought at first to scale down their military commitments as far as possible in the region. However, superpower Cold War tensions generated in Europe were eventually transmitted to East Asia, with the effect of underpinning many of the nationalist and civil struggles in the region and creating outlets for 'hot war'. The outbreak of the Korean War in June 1950 was primarily the consequence of civil and revolutionary tensions between the two Koreas (Cumings 1990). Nevertheless, the USSR's apparent blessing of the invasion and arming of North Korea, in conjunction with the US's decision to defend the South Korean regime under UN mandates, and then China's entry into the war in October 1950, broadened the nature of the conflict so that it became a contest of strength between the superpowers and their respective allies.

The response of the US to the Korean War and perceived threat of communist expansion in the region was not only to commit men and war *materiel* to the South, but also to expand its security perimeter by signalling its preparedness in 1950 and again in 1954–5 to interpose the US Seventh Fleet in the Taiwan Straits to prevent any Chinese attempt to invade Taiwan. Thus, these two security crises in Korea and the Taiwan Straits, and the coincidence of superpower global interests with regional national and civil struggles, were to lead to the further solidification of Cold War and bipolar pressures in East Asia along the lines of demarcation established earlier by the fall of Japanese imperialism. The US went on to strengthen its security position by creating a chain of bilateral defensive alliances in East Asia. As was outlined in Chapter 2, Japan was fully integrated into and became the linchpin of this alliance system following the outbreak of the Korean War and the first Taiwan Straits crisis of 1950. Meanwhile, the Soviet side of the emerging bipolar divide in East Asia had already been formed to some degree with the signing of the Sino-Soviet Treaty of Alliance and Mutual Friendship in February 1950, which was predicated upon deterring a resurgence of Japanese imperialism and militarism, and any other country that might align with Japan. The communist alliance system was later consolidated by the decision of both the USSR and China to conclude Treaties of Friendship, Cooperation and Mutual Assistance with North Korea in 1961. Finally, having erected these bilateral alliance systems in East Asia, the superpowers completed the bifurcation of the region with the holding of the Geneva Conference in 1954, called to address the issues of Korea and Indo-China. The conference affirmed the Korean armistice and *de facto* division of the Korean Peninsula, and agreed to the partition of North and South Vietnam. Although the Geneva settlement planned that Vietnam would later be united through elections, the final outcome of the conference was to establish a communist regime in the North oriented towards China and the USSR, and an anti-communist regime in the South reliant upon the US.

The Geneva Conference thus signified the complete integration of the East Asian states into the global and regional bipolar systems centred upon the USSR and the US. The result was to hamper attempts on the part of the East Asian states to remain neutral in the midst of Cold War confrontation or to undertake multilateral dialogue. One rare exception to this was the holding of the first ever Conference of African and Asian nations in Bandung, Indonesia, in April 1955. The Bandung Conference's avowed purpose was to enhance solidarity and cooperation between the newly independent states of Asia and Africa. It was attended by representatives from twenty-nine countries, including Burma, Indonesia, India, Pakistan, China, the Philippines, Thailand and Japan. The US and Western European powers were intentionally not invited, and the Bandung participants used the occasion to rail against the evils of imperialism. Bandung did not succeed in establishing a permanent bloc or organization, but it was an important step in the articulation of Third-World opinion in international affairs and a precursor to the non-aligned movement (NAM) (Yahuda 1996: 53–5). However, much of the spirit of solidarity generated at Bandung and opportunities for multilateral cooperation were later to be undermined by unresolved territorial disputes between China and those Southeast Asian states which attended. The consequence was that regional relations in East Asia in many cases slipped back into a pattern of bilateralism and the reliance by individual states upon political, economic and military support from the external superpowers.

8.3.iv Fragmentation of the East Asian regional political economy

The effect of the rise of the new bipolar order in East Asia was to set the states of the region upon highly-divergent development trajectories. The orientation of the newly independent states towards the external superpowers, and the obstacles to political, economic and security interaction between them created by bipolarity and bilateralism, meant that East Asia once again, as in the imperial world order, ceased to function as an interdependent and integrated regional entity. Moreover, in addition to the continued centripetal attributes of the region as a whole, the individual states on both sides of the bipolar divide developed a wide variety of political and economic systems. Thus, even though all states of the Soviet bloc were necessarily communist in nature, they also displayed dichotomous political economies. The 'orthodox' Marxist–Leninism of the post-revolution USSR clashed strongly with the anti-revisionist, revolutionary and highly nationalist communism of China under Mao Zedong. These doctrinal differences produced differing forms of socialism in the major communist powers, and eventually produced also the conditions for the Sino-Soviet split in the 1960s. In further contrast, the establishment of Kim Il Sung's reclusive communist dictatorship in North Korea produced a model of developmentalism based on an extraordinary amalgam of the principles of revolutionary socialism, anti-colonialism, Confucianism and self-reliance, or *juche* ideology.

Likewise, the US-centred and capitalistic bloc also encouraged diverse economic and political systems at various stages of the Cold War period. In Northeast Asia, Japan was encouraged to develop into an advanced democracy and market economy as a bastion of capitalism in the region, whilst South Korea and Taiwan were essentially developmental authoritarian regimes. In Southeast Asia, the degree of attachment to the US bloc varied, but regimes here ranged from relatively stable authoritarian states in Thailand, Malaysia and Singapore, to less stable and economically weak regimes in the Philippines and South Vietnam. This divergence in East Asia was to persist for much of the Cold War period, although, as will be seen in Chapter 10, the states of the region later experienced some convergence in their political economies under the influence of developmental norms propagated by Japan.

8.3.v Japan's isolation from East Asia

Consequently, it can be seen that the chief repercussion of Japan's involvement in East Asian affairs during the colonial and Pacific War periods was political, economic and security segregation under the newly-emergent Cold War order. Moreover, even though as mentioned above, Japan can be said to be responsible in part for the gradual re-convergence of the region's political economies in the latter stages of the Cold War period and beyond, it was certainly in no position to pick up these fragmented pieces and contribute to East Asian reintegration in the immediate post-war period. Following defeat in the Pacific War and the stripping of its colonies, Japan was treated as a virtual pariah state in the region. Although the citizens and policy-making agents of certain countries such as Burma, Indonesia, Vietnam and Taiwan were relatively tolerant of Japan's presence in the region, the majority of the countries in East Asia remained deeply suspicious of the resurgence of Japanese militarism and imperialism. In particular, China and North and South Korea – which had probably suffered the worst excesses of Japanese imperialism, including in China the rape of Nanking in 1937 and the systematic attempt by Japanese administrators in Korea to eradicate all indigenous culture, language and identity – continued to express virulent anti-Japanese sentiment.

This historical legacy of colonialism and mistrust was reinforced by the nature of Japan's limited participation in the process of de-colonization. As will be seen in Chapters 9 and 10, the Japanese government was obliged under the 1952 San Francisco peace treaty to provide reparations to a number of its former colonies. Nevertheless, Japan's almost instantaneous loss of its colonies in 1945, combined with the return of these colonies to their former Western colonial masters or the colonies' assumption of independence, meant that in practice the Japanese were relieved of direct responsibility for dealing with and making amends for their own colonial past, and rebuilding relations with the newly independent states in East Asia. In turn, Japan's exclusion from the process of de-colonization perhaps helps to explain the notorious reluctance of certain conservative politicians in Japan to address fully the history of their own state's imperialism in East Asia – an issue which has continued to overshadow and often sour relations with the countries of the region even up to the present day.

Japan's distancing from East Asia was compounded by its subjugation to the US during the immediate post-war and Occupation periods. Demilitarization under SCAP and US direction meant that Japan lost all capacity to function as a major power in the region (Iokibe 1996: 23). Even more importantly, Prime Minister Yoshida's policy to accept political, economic and security dependence upon the US, and to sign the US–Japan security treaty as the price for ending the Occupation, as was discussed in Part II, ensured that Japan was isolated even further from a number of states in East Asia. For even though alignment with the US-dominated half of the bipolar divide enabled Japan to achieve the peace settlement with the UN powers in 1952 and brought it access to the material benefits of US hegemony, it also correspondingly isolated it from political, economic and security interaction with the states on the USSR side of the bipolar divide which were not signatories to the peace treaty. Thus, the USSR refused to sign the treaty; communist China was not invited to the peace conference; normal political and economic relations between Japan and China were not established until 1972; and a Sino-Japanese peace treaty was not concluded until 1978. Instead, Japan was obliged at the time of the 1952 San Francisco peace treaty to sign another with Taiwan. It thus maintained relations with the US's ally until 1972, to the exclusion of political relations with China. Similarly, North Korea, the other ex-colony and loosely-associated member of the communist bloc in Northeast Asia, did not sign the treaty. As of 2000, Japan and the DPRK have yet to normalize relations and to settle finally the legacy of colonialism.

8.4 Summary

The above historical overview has demonstrated that by the mid-1950s the legacy of colonialism, national division, the Cold War and bipolarity, and the fractious nature of the political economy had imposed upon Japan four international structural barriers which compounded its isolation from East Asia. They have continued to influence the pattern of its relations with the region ever since. Japanese policy-making agents were thus faced with a massive task in seeking to reintegrate Japan into the region in the Cold War and post-Cold War periods. Having outlined the context of Japan's international relations, Chapters 9, 10 and 11 now set out to demonstrate – drawing on the insights on policy-making and instrumentalization in Chapter 2 – the processes and methods by which Japan's policy-making agents and other political actors have responded to this complex environment, and have gradually re-extended Japan's political, economic and security presence in the region.

Chapter 9

Japan–East Asia political relations

9.1 Overview

Chapter 8 has demonstrated how Japan was excluded from the East Asia region politically following defeat in World War II. The purpose of this chapter is to demonstrate and chronicle how Japanese policy-making agents have mustered power resources in the Cold War and post-Cold War periods in order to reorganize and reintegrate Japan into a new East Asian regional political order, despite the constraints imposed by the structure of the international system. The chapter will deal in turn with Japan's relations with China, the Korean Peninsula and Southeast Asia. Each section begins by reiterating the factors of structure and agency, and is then followed by subsections which demonstrate how these factors interacted with each other to affect at certain critical junctures the development of Japan's political relations with the East Asia region.

9.2 Japan and China

9.2.i *Japan's approach towards China: structure, agency and norms*

In the mid-1950s Japan and China were separated from political, economic and security interaction with each other by the structural boundaries of Cold War bipolarity, together with the legacies of national division and the colonial past. However, as illustrated below, even as structural factors and mutual suspicions continued to limit Japan–China relations in this period and beyond, at the same time Japan has had powerful motives to circumvent the restraints imposed by the structure of the international system and push for gradual engagement. Japanese attempts to engage China have been driven by a variable mix of Asianist and developmental norms and interests. The Japanese state and its people ever since the period of the Chinese world order, as was described in Chapter 2, have felt a sense of cultural affinity and friendship with their massive neighbour, expressed in the phrase *dōbun dōshu* ('same Chinese writing characters, same race'). This Asianist norm has been reinforced by a strong developmental norm and perception of the vital economic importance of China to Japan as a source of raw materials and markets. Beyond that, economic engagement is seen ultimately to produce reform and stability in China. Hence, as Chapter 2 has noted, strong pro-China elements have always been present in the political parties, MOFA and business sectors. These policy-making agents and political actors have exploited all possible diplomatic room for manoeuvre in order to improve relations with China, even whilst attempting to adhere to the general US policy line in East Asia. The outcome during the period of the first Cold War was that Japan was obliged to attempt to instrumentalize the improvement of Sino-Japanese relations through a process of *seikei bunri* and unofficial diplomacy.

9.2.ii Sino-Japanese relations and normalization in the first Cold War period

The first official Sino-Japanese contacts in the post-war era did not come until the 1955 Bandung Conference, referred to in Chapter 8, during which the Chinese side requested improved diplomatic relations. The Japanese government – now under the leadership of Hatoyama Ichirō who was to achieve the normalization of relations with the USSR in 1956 – was receptive to the idea of a general improvement in political and economic ties with China. At the same time, however, Hatoyama remained wary of making any commitment to normalizing relations with China and taking a high-profile position in support of the political aims of Bandung for fear of jeopardizing relations with the US, which at this time was calling for the increased containment of Chinese communism (Ampiah 1997: 39–44). Informal contacts between Japan and China continued to be mediated throughout the 1950s and 1960s by pro-China faction leaders in the LDP (Johnson 1995: 239–40). Nevertheless, the prospects for an improvement in official Sino-Japanese relations were set back following the accession to power of the arch 'Cold War warrior' Kishi in 1957. Prime Minister Kishi's preoccupation with the revision of the US–Japan security treaty, initiation of normalization talks with the US's anti-communist ally South Korea, and staunchly pro-Taiwan position – demonstrated by his official visit to Taipei in June 1957 – served to reinforce the bipolar structural barriers to Sino-Japanese interaction. The response of China was to lambaste the Kishi administration for creating 'two Chinas' and for reviving Japanese militarism, and to cut off all trade with Japan in 1958. The 1960 advent of the Ikeda administration and its emphasis upon economism and the policy of *seikei bunri* enabled the resumption of bilateral trade and the signing of an unofficial trade agreement in November 1962. Still, the administration's public anti-PRC stance – designed to placate the US government and pro-Taiwan factions in the LDP – meant that it stopped short of official efforts to improve political ties.

The Satō administration (1964–72) was clearly aware of the importance of improving relations with China. It laid much of the groundwork for eventual normalization under the Tanaka administration in 1972 through attempts to persevere with the *seikei bunri* policy. As Chapters 4 and 6 have made clear, however, the administration's foreign policy priorities were to gain US assent for the reversion of Okinawa and to demonstrate support for the US's security position in East Asia. Satō presided over the normalization of Japan–South Korea relations in June 1965 and the automatic extension of the security treaty in June 1970; paid an official visit to Taiwan in September 1967 and indicated in the joint communiqué with President Richard Nixon in November 1969 that the 'maintenance of peace and security in the Taiwan area were also important factors for Japan's security'; and he also provided unequivocal public backing for the US intervention in the Vietnam War (Iwanaga 1985: 170–1).

The Chinese government viewed these developments as further evidence of militarism in Japan and its aggressive stance in support of the US's regional allies and containment policy towards China. In response, it launched in Japan itself (despite its own avowed principle of non-interference in the domestic affairs of other states), through pro-China media organizations, LDP factions and opposition parties, a campaign of 'people's diplomacy' designed to mobilize public opinion and break Japan's perceived political dependence on the US. Chinese government leaders informed senior LDP policy-makers visiting Beijing in April 1970 that China would cease to trade with any Japanese companies found to have contravened 'four conditions' relating to the non-assistance of South Korea, Taiwan or US policy in Vietnam and Indo-China. In addition, they were informed that China would only normalize relations with Japan in accordance with the 'three principles' of Japan's recognition of the PRC as the sole legitimate government of all China, that Japan accepted the indivisibility of Chinese territory and Taiwan as a province of China, and that it abandoned official diplomatic ties and the 1952 peace treaty with Taiwan (Tanaka 1991: 68–70). A fierce debate ensued within Japanese policy-making circles over China policy. The pro-China factions of the LDP joined with the Social Democratic Party of Japan (SDPJ), the Democratic Socialist Party (DSP), the Japan Communist Party (JCP) and the Kōmei Party, and with major business interests in the steel, chemical and automobile industries, such as Kawasaki, Sumitomo, Toyota, Nissan and Honda, to lobby the government to normalize relations with China (Welfield 1988: 292–3). Despite the external and internal pressure exerted on the government, however, Satō remained rigidly in support of US policy towards China.

The relative immobilism of the Satō administration's policy towards China was then swept away by fundamental changes in the structure of the international system surrounding Sino-Japanese relations in the early 1970s. These changes subsequently reduced the impediments placed upon the efforts of Japanese policy-making agents and other non-state political actors to engage China politically. The weakening of the bipolar Cold War structure and 'Nixon shocks', as was discussed in Chapter 4, effectively removed US objections to the improvement of Sino-Japanese relations, although, as seen later in this chapter, the US has certainly remained a key factor in Japanese diplomatic calculations concerning China. Japanese policy-makers reacted swiftly to the weakening of international structural restrictions and enhanced diplomatic freedom by seeking early normalization with China. Following an intense struggle within the LDP between pro-China and pro-Taiwan factions, Tanaka Kakuei (1972–4) emerged as Satō's successor and managed to carry overall LDP, MOFA and public opinion with him in favour of normalization. Tanaka journeyed to Beijing in September 1972 and signed a joint communiqué establishing full diplomatic relations (Appendix 9.1). Under the joint communiqué, Japan accepted the 'three principles' of normalization, and thus abandoned official ties with Taiwan. In order to expedite the improvement of bilateral relations, China renounced all claims for war indemnities from Japan, but it declined to discuss the issue of the sovereign of the Senkaku Islands, deferring it to later generations to decide. This left unresolved a potentially-explosive bilateral territorial dispute.

Japan and China then agreed in September 1974 to initiate government-level talks on the conclusion of a peace treaty, during which MOFA as the Japanese government's representative began to take an increasingly important role in the management of diplomacy with China. In the meantime, however, Japanese diplomacy

Plate 9.1 Mr Tanaka goes to Beijing. Following President Richard Nixon's recognition of the PRC as the sole legitimate government of China in February 1972, Prime Minister Tanaka Kakuei travelled to Beijing to meet with Chairman Mao Zedong and announced the normalization of Japan–PRC relations on 29 September 1972.

Source: Courtesy of Mainichi Shimbunsha

towards China was reinforced by the maintenance of contacts between the LDP and opposition parties and Chinese policy-makers. Simultaneously, the Japanese business sector, which was keen to expand economic contacts following China's announcement of its modernization drive in 1976, conducted its own private diplomacy: in 1978 the *Keidanren* (Federation of Economic Organizations) concluded a US$20 billion Long-Term Trade Agreement. The Treaty of Peace and Friendship between Japan and the People's Republic of China was eventually signed in August 1978 (Appendix 9.2; see also Appendix 9.3). During negotiations for the treaty, China indicated privately that it would tolerate Japan's security treaty with the US, and that it was prepared to shelve the issue of whether the 1960 definition of the scope of the US–Japan security treaty covered Taiwan and the question of the sovereignty of the Senkaku Islands.

9.2.iii Sino-Japanese relations in the 1980s

The period from the signing of the peace treaty in 1978 until the Tiananmen Square incident of June 1989 was characterized by the general strengthening of Sino-Japanese ties, although relations were to be hit by a series of bilateral disputes concerning Chinese suspicions of revived Japanese militarism. The onset of the second Cold War globally and in East Asia produced an international environment conducive to Sino-American cooperation versus the USSR, and further lowered US opposition to, and structural constraints upon, Sino-Japanese relations. Japanese policy during this period was directed towards a strategic effort over the long term to deepen political and economic engagement with China in order to strengthen the hand of reformers within the Chinese leadership (Arnold 1990: 125). It also sought to contribute to the general stability of bilateral political, economic and security relations as well as to expand Japanese commercial opportunities (Tanaka 1991: 110–13). Prime Minister Ōhira visited Beijing in December 1979, and, in an example of *omiyage gaikō* (gift-bearing diplomacy), pledged ¥350 billion in yen loans for the support of China's Five Year Plan for 1979–84 (Zhao 1998: 239). This began the process of Japan becoming China's largest international donor of ODA, accentuated the boom in Japanese private sector projects in China, and enhanced Sino-Japanese cultural interchange – up to 1,000 local government organizations forming sister relationships with their counterparts in China (Newby 1988: 65).

Sino-Japanese relations, however, were shaken by the occurrence of the first 'textbook controversy' between June and September 1982 (Rose 1998). Japan's Ministry of Education was accused by liberal and left-wing opinion in Japan itself, as well as by governments and pressure groups in China, South and North Korea, and Thailand, of making revisions to school textbooks in order to distort the true nature of Japanese wartime aggression. Specifically, the Ministry of Education was believed to have ordered that references to the number of Chinese casualties in the 1937 rape of Nanking be deleted, that the term *shinryaku* (invasion) should be substituted for the more neutral term *shinshutsu* or *shinkō* (advance) to describe the activities of the Japanese army in East Asia (*Asahi Shimbun* 24 July 1982; Ijiri 1996: 64–9), and that the Korean independence movement of 1919 be described as nothing more than a 'riot'. The Chinese government launched fierce attacks on the 'handful of rightists' in Japan intent on reviving militarism. Chinese policy-makers were only placated by Prime Minister Suzuki's visit to Beijing in September 1982, during which he offered reassurances that Japan would review the textbook issue and pledged new ODA projects.

Nakasone Yasuhiro's assumption of the premiership (1982–7) initially promised further improvements in Sino-Japanese links. In February 1983 Nakasone acknowledged in the Diet that Japan's war in China had been one of aggression, and in March 1984 he paid a visit to Beijing to unveil a second yen loan package worth ¥470 billion for 1985–90. Nevertheless, bilateral ties were again soon to be strained by changes in the structure of the international system and Chinese concerns about Japanese militarism and relations with Taiwan. Sino-US relations began to cool by the mid-1980s as China became concerned about the Reagan administration's strengthening of the US military presence in East Asia and ties with Taiwan. In turn, China indicated its anxieties about Japan's rapid rise as an economic and potential political and military superpower under Nakasone's leadership, and its close strategic collaboration with the US in this period, as was described in more detail in Chapter 6 and will be further elaborated in Chapter 11. Japan's large trade surplus with China in the mid-1980s appeared as an 'economic invasion', whilst the build-up of Japanese military capacity, both independently and within the framework of the US–Japan security treaty, raised the spectre of renewed Japanese militarism. Consequently, Nakasone's decision to pay an official visit as prime minister to Yasukuni Shintō Shrine on 15 August 1985 – the date of the fortieth anniversary of Japan's defeat in World War II, the shrine being for Japan's 2.5 million war dead, including the wartime prime minister and Class A war criminal Tōjō Hideki – confirmed Chinese and East Asian suspicions of Japan's lack of contrition for its militaristic past. The prime minister's action provoked Chinese government protests, and gave momentum to large-scale anti-Japanese demonstrations by students in China. Chinese concerns about Japanese militarism were raised further because of a second textbook controversy in mid-1986 (Whiting 1989: 51–64).

Nakasone was able to stabilize bilateral relations by his decision not to pay an official visit to Yasukuni in 1986, and by ordering a revision of the offending textbooks. Sino-Japanese ties were then hit by the Taiwan issue. In February 1987, the Osaka High Court recognized Taiwan's ownership of a student dormitory in Kyoto, known as *Kōkaryō* in Japanese. The court's decision drew Chinese protests as an example of Japan's efforts to create 'two Chinas' by violating the spirit of the 1972 joint communiqué and 1978 peace treaty. Chinese rumblings over Japanese economic and past military aggression continued into the late 1980s, but relations recovered as a result of the expansion of Japanese FDI in China and the emergence of a bilateral trade surplus in favour of China by 1988. They improved further as a result of Prime Minister Takeshita Noboru's visit to Beijing in August 1988 and his pledge of a third yen loan package of ¥700 billion for 1990–5. The textbook controversies and other incidents did not alter fundamentally the trend in the overall improvement of Sino-Japanese ties in this period, but were a portend of the types of problems, and in particular the international structural factor of the legacy of history, which were to hamper bilateral relations during the rest of the second Cold War and beyond.

9.2.iv Tiananmen Square incident

Sino-Japanese relations were beginning to enter a stage of economic and even political interdependence by the late 1980s, only for this progress in bilateral ties to be threatened by the Tiananmen Square incident of June 1989. The Japanese government adopted the statement at the G7 summit in Paris in July 1989 condemning the incident as a breach of human rights, and did not oppose the imposition of sanctions by the US and other Western states. Nevertheless, despite the international structural pressure to conform with US and Western opinion as represented by the G7, the Japanese government was more restrained than the other major industrialized states in criticizing and taking official action against China. In part, this was due to continued Japanese guilt about its people's own involvement in human rights abuses in China during the colonial period and fear of a Chinese government backlash. More importantly, however, following an initial tussle between pro-Western and pro-China opinion in MOFA and the LDP (Ōtake 1995: 130–1), Japanese policy-makers had concluded that the optimum policy towards China was to avoid its international ostracism and persist with political and economic engagement. This policy was based on developmentalist norms and designed to assist the Chinese leadership to maintain internal stability and its path of reform and liberalization, and thus lessen the attendant security risks to Japan and the rest of East Asia of China's possible slide into political chaos.

Accordingly, as Chapter 21 will also illustrate, the Japanese government worked behind the scenes at the G7 meeting in Paris in order to persuade the other major industrialized states to introduce into the G7 statement a clause which stressed the need to avoid the international isolation of China. On top of that, Japan itself chose to impose only a limited range of G7 sanctions. The government suspended all high-level diplomatic contacts and ODA loans to China, but did not invoke trade or investment sanctions. In addition, the Japanese government preserved its links with the Chinese leadership through reverting to a process of unofficial LDP, opposition party and private business diplomacy (Zhao 1993: 170–5), and used its influence in the G7 to build quietly a consensus in favour of the progressive removal of sanctions against China. The result of Japan's quiet diplomacy was to secure the US and G7's agreement at the Houston summit in July 1990 to allow Japan to resume its third yen loan programme to China. Japanese policy-makers then proceeded with the restoration of full diplomatic ties with China in 1991, the visit of Prime Minister Kaifu Toshiki to Beijing in August 1991 and the official visit of the Japanese emperor and empress to China in October 1992 – an act of emperor diplomacy (*tennō gaikō*). Thus, by 1992 Japan had managed again to circumvent the constraint imposed by the structure of the international system and the legacy of colonial history. It was able to maintain a careful balancing act between its interests and norms by being simultaneously both a member of the West and East Asia, and of instrumentalizing, through a process of quiet diplomacy and economic engagement, a general recovery in Sino-Japanese relations.

9.2.v Sino-Japanese political relations in the post-Cold War period

Prospects for the rehabilitation of Sino-Japanese relations were raised further in the post-Cold War period and early 1990s owing to the increasing fluidity of the structure of the international system. The winding-down of Cold War tensions in East Asia, the clear commitment of the Chinese leadership to continue with its programme of opening the economy to the outside world, and the US's response under the Bush and Clinton administrations of pursuing a general policy of political and economic engagement with China, all served to lessen barriers to US and

Chinese interaction, and subsequently also US objections to, and international structural barriers upon, Sino-Japanese interaction. Economic interdependency between Japan and China has increased in this period, and the Japanese government has continued to pursue its own engagement policy towards China. The aim of this strategy is to enhance China's integration into regional and international society through encouraging its entry into multilateral institutions such as the ARF, APEC, and then eventually the WTO. Sino-Japanese relations warmed particularly during the Hosokawa administration (1993–4), which was prepared to take a slightly more independent line on foreign policy. Hosokawa was the first non-LDP prime minister to visit China, in March 1994, and he used the occasion to appeal for Chinese diplomatic assistance in restraining North Korea's suspected nuclear programme. He also issued an apology for Japan's 'war of aggression' in China as well as expressing some support for China's position *vis-à-vis* the US on human rights by employing Asianist norms to note the relativity of the concept and the need not to impose 'single standards' in this area (Ijiri 1996: 87).

The closing of international structural pressures and the re-emergence of a range of bilateral issues, however, have hindered the improvement of Sino-Japanese relations in the period from the mid-1990s to the start of the twenty-first century. Sino-US tensions have fluctuated but also have seen an overall increase from the late 1990s onwards, owing to a number of factors. US concerns revolve around China's apparent drive to achieve great power economic and military status in East Asia. China, for its part, has been concerned about the US's renewal of its hegemonic position in East Asia and its possible support for Taiwanese independence, as demonstrated by the US's perceived wavering between engagement and containment policy responses towards China and its concomitant strengthening of its military position in the region via the redefinition of the US–Japan alliance in the 1990s, as will be described in Chapter 11. Japan's own continued rise as a political, economic and military power has produced something akin to an enhanced triangular structure of Japan–US–China political interaction within East Asia (Funabashi 1998: 47, Funabashi 1999: 79–84). However, the nature of the triangular interaction has clearly been asymmetric and inconsistent in this period because the power capabilities of each of the states involved are mismatched – Japan possessing great economic but limited independent military power; the US economic and military power; and China as yet limited but rapidly increasing economic and military power – and because the US and China have tended to focus their energies more on each other than their respective relations with Japan.

In turn, this triangular structure has created both opportunities and obstacles for Japan's relations with China. On one level, the potential for increased Sino-American confrontation and Japan's enhanced political status within the triangular relationship allows it to step in and play a mediating role between the two – the actualization of Japan's vision of its *watashiyaku* diplomacy between the West and East Asia. On another level, however, the triangular relationship poses hazards and dilemmas for Japanese policy-makers. The first hazard is that Japan could be bypassed altogether and left powerless in the face of a Sino-US power struggle, the type of 'Japan-passing' that was mentioned in Chapter 1. This is best illustrated by President Clinton's visit to China in June 1998 when he lavished praise on the Chinese leadership and seemed to indicate that China was becoming the US's partner of choice in the region. Alternatively, the second hazard is that Japan could be caught in the middle of a 'tug of war' between the US and China. In this situation, Japan might be pulled dangerously onto one side or the other and enlisted in a political or even military conflict for which it is not prepared and which it wishes to avoid. Japan's Asianist and developmental norms and interests mean that Japanese policy-making agents clearly wish to obviate conflict with China and to encourage the US to persist with engagement policies. Nevertheless, the strength of the bilateral attachment to the US and Japan's own concerns about the growing power of China provide a strong impulse to cooperate with US policy towards China.

Hence, from the late 1990s onwards, Japanese policy-makers have performed a new and increasingly precarious balancing act between the US and China. The Japanese government has been convinced of the need to redouble its efforts to engage China politically and economically. It has done so by maintaining ODA flows and arguing China's case with the US for its eventual admittance to the WTO – another illustration of its mediating *watashiyaku*. Nevertheless, the slow pace of China's responsiveness to engagement policies as compared with the perceived rapid rise of its military capabilities and ability to disrupt the structure of the international system, appears to be persuading Japanese policy-makers of the need also to hedge against future Chinese power by strengthening Japan's ties with the US *vis-à-vis* China. As Chapter 11 will demonstrate, Japan's policy-makers have been pushed towards this stance by a number of security issues since the mid-1990s, including the lack of transparency of China's defence budget and weapons procurement, the modernization of its nuclear forces and its proactive military activities in the South China Sea. In particular, China's decision to intimidate Taiwan prior to the presidential elections in March 1996 by conducting large-scale military exercises and missile tests in the Taiwan Straits raised Japanese apprehensions about China's willingness to use military power in defence of its national interests.

The Japanese government had already raised some of these issues as early as Hosokawa's visit to China in 1994 and demonstrated concern over Chinese nuclear testing by suspending grant ODA in 1995. Japanese disenchantment with China over a range of bilateral issues has been compounded by changes in the nature of the domestic political actors in Japan. Although the pro-China elements in MOFA and the LDP remain powerful, the collapse of the 1955 system and decline in SDPJ support, the generational change which has seen the emergence of few figures in the LDP with well-established personal connections reminiscent of Prime Minister Tanaka Kakuei, and a resurgent Taiwan lobby encouraged by the process of democratization in Taipei, may weaken political support in Japan for engagement with China (Green and Self 1996: 45–6; Johnstone 1998: 1069). The policy outcome has been that the Japanese government in the late 1990s took an increasingly hard line in negotiations with China, as demonstrated by Prime Minister Obuchi's summit meeting with President Jiang Zemin in Tokyo in December 1998 and in Beijing in July 1999, when he refused to kowtow to China's usual negotiating tactic of raising the issue of the colonial past in order to extract the ritual apology from Japan and exert diplomatic pressure on other issues.

9.3 Japan and the Korean Peninsula

9.3.i *Japan's approach towards North and South Korea: structure, agency and norms*

As in Sino-Japanese relations, Japan's links with the divided Korean Peninsula have been complicated in the post-war era by the structure of the international system. As Chapter 8 has indicated, the first of these structural factors – the legacy of brutal Japanese colonial rule in Korea, and Japan's perceived responsibility for frustrating Korean ambitions for unity and independence by creating the conditions for the division of the Korean Peninsula in 1945 – has left a legacy of historical animosity which ever since has tended to distance North and South Korea from Japan. Throughout the post-war era, anti-Japanese feeling has formed the focus of both North and South Korean nationalism, and has been manifested in concerns about suspected renewed Japanese imperialism and attempts to play the North and South off against each other in order to keep the Korean Peninsula divided and weak – often termed the 'two Koreas' policy. The most important structural factor for Japanese policy towards North and South Korea since 1945, however, has been the combined influence in and around the Korean Peninsula of Cold War and bipolar pressures and the security presence of the US. In Japan–North Korea relations, Japan's support of US containment policy *vis-à-vis* the communist bloc and location of Japan and North Korea on separate sides of the bipolar divide necessarily created barriers to bilateral interaction. In the case of Japan–South Korea relations, the key roles of Japan and South Korea in the US's containment strategy and bilateral alliance systems have meant that the US has maintained a constant interest in pushing its allies towards closer political, economic and eventually limited military cooperation to buttress its security strategy in East Asia.

Japanese policy-making agents have reacted to the constraints and opportunities of the structure of the international system according to their mix of norms and interests, and produced differing policy stances towards North and South Korea. Japan's policy-making norms have generally been compatible with attempts to conform to and overcome respectively the international structural factors of the Cold War and US pressure and the legacy of the colonial past, and to motivate policy-makers actively to improve links with South Korea. The norm of bilateralism and location of Japan's fundamental security interests with the US, and thus by implication with the US's other allies in East Asia and with South Korea, have encouraged policy-makers in factions of the LDP, MOFA, MITI and JDA to promote Japan–South Korea ties in order to stabilize successive authoritarian and democratic regimes in Seoul. The norm of developmentalism and awareness of economic opportunities in South Korean markets and links between economic progress and eventual democratization have also been powerful motives for these groups and the private business sector to seek to engage South Korea. Likewise, Asianist norms and a genuinely-held desire among many policy-making agents and other political actors to correct the mistakes of the colonial past have spurred efforts to improve ties with Japan's closest geographical neighbour.

The flip side to Japan's prioritization of its relations with South Korea has been the circumscribed nature of bilateral links with North Korea. The norms of Asianism and developmentalism to a certain extent have created strong motivations for Japanese attempts to improve bilateral ties, as policy-makers in the LDP, SDPJ and other opposition parties, MOFA, MITI and the private business sector struggle to make amends for the legacy of the colonial past in the same way as with South Korea. They are, of course, increasingly aware of potential economic opportunities in the North as well as the South. As will be demonstrated below, however, these Asianist and developmental norms during the Cold War and beyond have never been strong enough to overcome the international structural barrier of particularly vehement anti-Japanese feeling in North Korea. In any case, they have been overridden themselves by the more powerful norm of bilateralism and the other international structural factor – Japan's strategic alignment with the US. This norm and structure dictates that Japan's principal diplomatic efforts in the Korean Peninsula are directed towards support for the US and South Korean containment of the North.

9.3.ii Japan–South Korea relations in the Cold War period

Following Japan's recovery of its independence in 1952 and the signing of the Korean War armistice in July 1953, the intention of the US was to promote a greater degree of political cooperation between its Japanese and South Korean client states in order to assist its containment strategy in East Asia towards North Korea, China and the USSR. The US insisted on the start of Japan–South Korea normalization talks in 1952, but its hopes for a rapid improvement in bilateral ties were frustrated by deep animosity on both sides over the colonial past and a range of bilateral issues (Welfield 1988: 92). These included: Japan's reluctance to accept the status of South Korea as the only lawful government of Korea, given the existence of another government in the North; its refusal to negotiate South Korean demands for compensation for the colonial or wartime periods, on the grounds that the Japanese annexation of Korea had been recognized under international law in 1910 and that South Korea as a colony had not been a combatant during World War II; and territorial disputes over the sovereignty of the Takeshima Islands and their rich fishing grounds in the Sea of Japan.

Japan had incorporated the two tiny uninhabited Takeshima Islands into Japanese territory in 1905. During the Occupation, SCAP issued an order in 1946 placing the Takeshima Islands outside the operational limits for Japanese fishermen, although at the same time it noted explicitly that this order did not constitute a final ruling on the sovereignty of the islands. No specific mention of the sovereignty of the islands was made in the San Francisco peace treaty. However, South Korea asserted sovereignty over the Takeshima Islands in January 1952, basing its claim on the exclusion of the islands from Japanese jurisdiction in accordance with the SCAP order of 1946. South Korea also unilaterally extended its territorial sovereignty over the continental shelf surrounding the Korean Peninsula for up to 200 nautical miles in places. The Japanese government protested to its South Korean counterpart, which simply responded by occupying the Takeshima Islands with a small garrison in 1953. Japan proposed to bring the territorial dispute to the International Court of Justice in 1954. This move was rejected by South Korea, and the problem of the Takeshima Islands has continued to plague bilateral relations ever since.

The result of these problems was a set of highly acrimonious Japan–South Korea normalization talks which were suspended six times between 1952 and 1965. The conditions for normalization were finally brought about by a mixture of: intensified US structural pressure in the run-up to the Vietnam War for Japan to assist containment policy in East Asia through enhanced cooperation with South Korea; the rise to power of the authoritarian, but relatively pro-Japanese, Park Chung-Hee regime in South Korea; and the growing strength of pro-South Korean policy-making opinion in Japan, including the Kishi faction in the LDP and the private business sector which was increasingly interested in South Korea's markets (Kimura 1989; Bridges 1993: 27–31; Welfield 1988: 202–8). In June 1965, Japan and South Korea signed the Treaty on Basic Relations (hereafter, Basic Treaty). Under the Basic Treaty, Japan recognized South Korea, in accordance with UN resolutions, as the only 'lawful', although not necessarily the only existing, government on the Korean Peninsula. Japan provided no official apology or compensation for the colonial and wartime periods. Instead, in a separate agreement, both governments forged a political compromise and agreed that Japan should provide to South Korea US$500 million in 'economic cooperation'. Another separate agreement was designed to defuse bilateral fishing disputes by the establishment of twelve-nautical-mile exclusive fishing zones, and setting aside certain zones for joint fishing operations. However, this agreement, as seen later in this chapter, did not settle all bilateral tensions over fishing rights and did not deal with the question of sovereignty over the Takeshima Islands.

The provision of economic aid to South Korea following the Basic Treaty initiated a conscious programme on the part of Japanese policy-making agents in the LDP, MOFA and economic ministries to assist in the modernization of the South Korean economy. This programme combined the norms of bilateralism and developmentalism: for it was designed to build up South Korea as an ally of the US and a bastion against communism in the region, as well as to promote economic opportunities for Japanese business interests in South Korean markets, and, over the longer term, to stabilize the South's regime economically and politically and to moderate its authoritarian nature. Japan's provision of economic aid enabled the Park regime to kick-start economic growth in the South, and bilateral trade and investment expanded rapidly throughout the rest of the Cold War period. As a result, the overall trend in bilateral relations was towards economic interdependence and political cooperation.

Japan–South Korea ties, however, were also troubled periodically from the 1970s onwards by a series of political disputes. As explained later in this chapter, the South Korean government became concerned during the period of détente that the Tanaka administration might move to a policy of 'equidistance' between North and South Korea. The Japanese government's vital strategic interest in the security of South Korea meant that it continued to prioritize relations with the South over the North, but for its part it did become concerned about the increasingly authoritarian nature of the Park regime. This was illustrated most vividly by the political furore caused by the Korean Central Intelligence Agency's (KCIA) abduction of the South Korean opposition leader, Kim Dae-Jung, from his hotel room in Tokyo in August 1973 (Welfield 1988: 341–2). President Park's assassination in October 1979 and the subsequent rise of President Chun Doo-Hwan, a new military strongman who took a far more confrontational stance towards Japan (Bridges 1993: 15), combined with the outbreak of the first textbook controversy in 1982, created further strains in bilateral ties and re-emphasized the international structural barrier of the legacy of colonialism. President Chun demanded in 1981 that Japan should provide a massive US$6 billion aid package to South Korea in order to make amends for the colonial past. It was also meant to help the South serve as a 'bulwark' against North Korean communism and thereby assist the defence of Japan at a time when bipolar tensions were rising at the start of the second Cold War. Japanese conservative policy-makers continued to view support for the Seoul regime as the optimum means of ensuring stability on the Korean Peninsula, but at the same time they were concerned at the size of the package and the direct links drawn between Japanese and South Korean security.

Bilateral ties were then put back on track by the efforts of Prime Minister Nakasone. He drew his motivation primarily from the norm of bilateralism which stressed the need for Japan to display greater support for the Reagan administration's security strategy in East Asia and for its South Korean ally. In January 1983, Nakasone paid the first official visit by a Japanese prime minister to South Korea, during which he expressed high regard for South Korean defence efforts, and pledged US$4 billion in ODA. Nakasone also made some attempt to tackle the barrier to improved bilateral relations of the legacy of history by stating his 'deep regret' for the colonial past.

9.3.iii Japan–North Korea relations in the Cold War period

As noted above, the Japanese government continued to acknowledge the practical reality of the existence of the North Korean government throughout the Cold War. Moreover, in line with Asianist and developmental norms, a number of policy-makers in the MOFA, LDP and opposition parties sought to engage North Korea in order to clear up the legacy of colonial history and contribute to the economic development, unification and general stability of the Korean Peninsula. However, the structural factors of the legacy of colonialism, and the Japanese government's attachment to the US half of the bipolar divide and strategic ties with South Korea, meant that it was unable to contemplate with any seriousness the normalization of relations with North Korea during this period and was able to engage the Pyongyang regime only so far as the relaxation of Cold War tensions would permit.

Thus, the brief weakening of the bipolar structure of the international system marked by the restoration of USSR–Japan diplomatic relations in 1956 also encouraged also the growth of Japan–North Korea contacts. Small-scale bilateral trade commenced via Chinese ports in 1956, and Red Cross talks produced an agreement in August 1959 to allow Korean residents in Japan to return permanently to their homeland in North Korea. Between 1959 and 1984, 93,000 Koreans made the trip, including 1,831 Japanese-born spouses of Koreans resident in Japan. The majority of these were women and were to become known as Japanese wives, or *Nihonjinzuma*. As seen later in this chapter, the fate of these *Nihonjinzuma* has become a major humanitarian and bilateral issue between Japan and North Korea in the late 1990s. Further improvement in Japan–North Korea relations was put on hold, however, by the re-escalation of Cold War tensions in the mid-1960s and Japan's normalization of relations with South Korea in 1965 (Appendix 9.4; see also Appendix 9.5; Hughes 1999: 60).

The period of détente in the early 1970s produced the next opportunity for Japan to improve relations with North Korea in much the same way as it had with China. Japan–North Korea ties were first promoted by unofficial political dialogue between, on the one hand, sections of the LDP and opposition parties, and, on the other, North Korean elites represented by the Korean Workers' Party (KWP). An all-party Dietmen's League for the Promotion of Japan–North Korea Friendship was founded in November 1971, which concluded private trade and provisional fishing agreements with the Pyongyang regime in 1972 and 1977 respectively. North Korea at this time was in need of Japanese capital and technology for its modernization drive under its Six-Year Economic Plan for 1971–6. Japan–North Korea trade leaped from US$59 million in 1971 to a high of US$361 million in 1974 (Hughes 1999: 142). The efforts of Japan's non-governmental actors to engage North Korea through a process of quiet diplomacy were supported by the Tanaka administration, which continued to prioritize relations with South Korea, but recognized the practical existence of a government in the North and was keen to foster an atmosphere of détente in the region. However, this policy was often portrayed in South Korea as one of 'equidistance' and as an attempt to play the two Koreas off against each other to keep the Korean Peninsula divided.

Japan–North Korea relations entered another troubled phase in the late 1970s and the 1980s owing to the onset of the second Cold War, the breakdown in dialogue between Seoul and Pyongyang and a series of Japan–North Korea bilateral disputes. These included: North Korea's failure to repay debts to Japanese companies; its alleged involvement in at least seven incidents of the believed abduction of up to ten Japanese citizens to North Korea, known as '*racchi jiken*'; terrorist bombings in Rangoon in October 1983 and of a South Korean airliner in November 1987; and North Korea's incarceration of two crew members from the Japanese fishing vessel *Fujisanmaru-18* in 1983. Thus, by the late 1980s, and despite attempts to instrumentalize improved relations by means of unofficial party-to-party diplomacy and economic engagement (Appendix 9.6), Japanese policy-makers had failed to replicate in North Korea their success in China and to circumvent the structural barriers of bipolarity and the colonial past.

9.3.iv *Japan–South Korea relations in the post-Cold War period*

The end of the Cold War and changes in the structure of the regional system in East Asia in the 1990s offered opportunities for Japan to improve its relations with both Seoul and Pyongyang. These changes in structure were marked by South Korea's normalization of relations with the USSR in September 1990 and with China in August 1992; a brief period of détente between North and South with the signing of a joint Agreement on Reconciliation, Non-Aggression, Exchange and Cooperation in December 1991; and the simultaneous entry of North and South Korea into the UN in September 1991, thereby implying mutual recognition and the official abandonment of respective claims to be the sole legitimate government of Korea.

North Korea's concern about its increasing political and economic isolation following the end of the Cold War led it to engage in eight rounds of normalization talks with Japan between January 1991 and November 1992. These Japan–North Korea normalization talks were acrimonious and ultimately unsuccessful because of various bilateral disputes, discussed later in the chapter; they also threatened to generate tensions in Japan's relations with South Korea. The government of President Roh Tae-Woo became anxious that the Japanese government might normalize relations with North Korea before the South, thereby allowing North Korea to outflank South Korea diplomatically. It also feared that Japan might be prepared to offer North Korea preferential terms on post-war compensation which would exceed the settlement made with the South under the Basic Treaty of 1965, and that Japan was using this to trade North and South off against each other. Moreover, the South Korean government was also increasingly anxious, because of North Korea's suspected development of nuclear weapons, that Japan should only move ahead with normalization if North Korea offered to make progress on allowing International Atomic Energy Agency (IAEA) inspections of its nuclear facilities.

The Japanese government, aware of the crucial strategic importance of South Korea for Japan's own security, and the far greater commonality of norms and interests between Japan and South Korea than between Japan and North Korea, moved to assuage the concerns of President Roh and his successor President Kim Young Sam. MOFA and LDP policy-making agents stressed that Japan would not normalize relations with North Korea without taking into account the South's concerns about the parallel progress in North–South dialogue, compensation and economic aid, and the North's nuclear programme. MOFA termed this as a policy of *renkei*, or linkage between improvements in Japan–North Korea relations and North–South relations, and has maintained that this places no formal diplomatic restriction on Japan engaging the North. Nevertheless, in practice the need to synchronize progress in normalization with progress in general North–South détente has placed a new international structural lock on Japan–North Korea relations.

In fact, Japan's closer coordination with South Korea over its North Korea policy, and shared concerns over North Korea's nuclear programme and development of other weapons of mass destruction, have served as an impetus to strengthen Japan–South Korea political and security cooperation. Japan–North Korea normalization talks eventually broke down over Japanese requests for North Korea to accept IAEA inspections. Japan supported South Korean, and especially US, diplomatic efforts to persuade North Korea to adhere to the Nuclear Non-Proliferation Treaty (NPT). The North Korean nuclear crisis reached its height in mid-1994, when it looked as if the stand-off over nuclear inspections could have provoked a second Korean War. The crisis was eventually defused by US–North Korea talks and the production of an Agreed Framework in October 1994. The agreement committed North Korea to freeze and eventually to dismantle its nuclear reactors, in return for US promises to create an international consortium that would supply the North with two light water reactors (LWR) by 2003 at an estimated cost of US$5 billion. Just as important for the North Korea regime, the US also promised to lift economic sanctions against the North in the future.

The nuclear crisis indicated to the international community the dangers of North Korea's potential involvement in the proliferation of weapons of mass destruction (WMD). It served notice that to a large degree its nuclear brinkmanship and other aggressive military behaviour were a product of its political and economic isolation since the end of the Cold War. Indeed, the fear of some US and South Korean policy-makers has been that North Korea's possible economic collapse – marked by the repetition of near famine conditions in the North since 1995 – could trigger another conflict on the Korean Peninsula. The response of the US and South Korea to the North Korean nuclear and other military crises has been a mixture of deterrence and dialogue. As will be seen in Chapter 11, the US and South Korea have upgraded their military and alliance capabilities to deter perceived North Korean aggression and cope with the military contingency of its collapse. At the same time, in varying degrees they have also pursued a policy of dialogue with the North in an attempt to bring it out of its international isolation, with particular emphasis upon economic engagement and stabilization by the provision of food aid and through bodies such as the Korean Peninsula Energy Development Organization (KEDO), described below; and the initiation since December 1997 of four-party peace talks between South Korea, the US, North Korea and China in an attempt to replace the Korean armistice with a permanent peace treaty.

Japanese policy-makers have been concerned that Japan should not become embroiled directly in a military conflict on the Korean Peninsula, but during and since the nuclear crisis they have expressed strong support for South Korea's stance and increased the number of high-level bilateral meetings. Japan has also backed South Korean engagement policy since the crisis by its agreement to participate in KEDO and provide up to US$1 billion to finance the LWR. Moreover, Japan has maintained its *renkei* policy by stating that Japan–North Korea dialogue will only progress with South–North dialogue and that the four-party talks are the fora for that dialogue. As Chapter 11 will demonstrate, one result of this policy has been the emergence of greater bilateral security contacts between Japan and South Korea in the post-Cold War period within the framework of the US alliance system in East Asia (Appendix 11.1), giving rising to a triangular pattern of Japan–South Korea–US defence cooperation with regard to the Korean Peninsula.

Japan–South Korea cooperation has produced on the whole more mature political relations between the two states. Bilateral relations continue to be hampered by the issue of the Takeshima Islands, and the legacy of colonialism – most notably the demands for compensation from Japan in respect of Korean women forced into prostitution for the Japanese Imperial Army, known euphemistically in Japan as 'comfort women'. Nevertheless, Japanese and South Korean leaders have made considerable progress in beginning to deal with these international structural impediments of the colonial past. The Japanese government denied responsibility over these women, owing to its stance that claims for compensation had been settled under the Basic Treaty, but it did give in to pressure from NGOs in South Korea and Japan and backed the creation of an 'NGO', again termed euphemistically the Peace Foundation for the Women of Asia, to provide up to ¥10 billion for comfort women in Korea and Southeast Asia. Prime Ministers Hosokawa and Murayama offered more explicit apologies for the past, and Japan–South Korea study groups have been established to propagate a correct understanding of Japan's colonial history in both countries, and thus prevent a repeat of the textbook controversies. Moreover, Japanese low and high culture such as food, films, popular songs and *manga* have gained increasing acceptance in South Korea (Bridges 1993: 136–9), and the joint hosting of the 2002 Soccer World Cup by Japan and South Korea has obliged both states to put aside some of the suspicions of the past and find new ways to cooperate.

Indeed, bilateral relations reached a high point with the assumption of Kim Dae-Jung to the South Korean presidency in 1998. Kim Dae-Jung has been motivated to cooperate with Japan in order to enlist support for his engagement, or 'sunshine policy', towards North Korea, and in order to secure financial support for his government's efforts to deal with the impact of the financial crisis which hit South Korea in late 1997, as will be described in more detail in Chapter 10. Kim's accession to the presidency in some ways vindicated the Japanese policy of persisting with economic and political engagement in order to promote greater interdependency between Japan and South Korea and domestic stability in the South, which would eventually create also the conditions for the transition in the South from authoritarianism to a democratic form of government. Kim's official visit to Japan in October 1998 produced a Japan–ROK joint declaration. This confirmed the need to enhance security and political cooperation with regard to North Korea, and called on the two states to cooperate in tackling the East Asian economic crisis by bilateral measures, such as Japanese loan assistance and technology transfer and coordination of activities in multilateral fora such as the WTO, OECD and APEC.

9.3.v Japan–North Korea relations in the post-Cold War period

If Japan succeeded in promoting a higher degree of political and economic interdependence with South Korea by the end of the twentieth century, then once again the reverse side of this improvement of ties with the South has been weaker Japan–North Korea relations. Japan–North Korea normalization talks were initiated following a joint LDP–SDPJ mission to Pyongyang in September 1990, which produced an agreement for the release of the *Fujisanmaru-18* crew, and an LDP–SDPJ–KWP three-party joint declaration on Japan–North Korea relations. The declaration urged the governments of both states to move towards the normalization of relations, and stated that Japan should not only apologize for colonial rule but also provide appropriate compensation for this period and the 'losses' incurred during the forty-five-year gap in bilateral relations since World War II.

The government-level negotiations on normalization, which began in 1991, followed this informal diplomacy. They proved problematic from the outset. North Korea insisted that the Japanese government should adhere to the contents of the above-mentioned joint declaration and provide up to US$10 billion in compensation for the colonial, wartime and post-war periods. MOFA responded by stating that the joint declaration was a non-binding party-to-party statement; that it would not provide compensation; and that it would negotiate only in line with the precedent of the Basic Treaty by providing approximately US$5 billion in the form of 'economic cooperation'. Contributing also to the eventual failure of the talks in 1992 were: issues concerning debt repayments to Japanese companies left over from the 1970s; permission for *Nihonjinzuma* to visit relatives in Japan; Japanese demands for North Korea to investigate individual cases of abductions or *racchi jiken*; and demands for North Korea to adhere to IAEA nuclear inspections.

The experience of the failure of Japan–North Korea normalization talks in 1992 and of the nuclear crisis of 1994, and the international structural lock which Japan has imposed upon itself by linking improvements in its own relations with North Korea to an improvement in North–South relations, which in turn are largely contingent upon improvements in US–North Korea relations, have meant that Japan's ties with North Korea have become further circumscribed from the late 1990s onwards. North Korea's pledge to participate in the four-party talks scheduled for December 1997 produced an opportunity for the Japanese government to negotiate with North Korea in August 1997 an agreement to resume normalization talks in the near future. Japan at the same time agreed to provide US$27 million in food aid, and North Korea agreed to permit the visits of *Nihonjinzuma* to Japan in November 1997 and January 1998, and to investigate the possibility of there being any 'missing' Japanese citizens in the North – a compromise term used to describe the *racchi jiken*. In turn, an LDP–SDP–Sakigake mission was despatched to Pyongyang in November 1997, which confirmed North Korea's desire to restart talks.

Nevertheless, bilateral relations deteriorated again with North Korea's frustration at Japan's reluctance to provide further food aid, its report in June 1998 that it could find no trace of any 'missing' persons in North Korea, and its cancellation of *Nihonjinzuma* visits. Bilateral relations then shifted from bad to worse following North Korea's test launch of a rocket in August 1998 which crossed over Japanese airspace to land in the Pacific Ocean. North Korea claimed it was a satellite launch, whereas the Japanese side declared it to be a Taepodong-1 missile and a reckless challenge to Japan's security. The government responded by suspending its signing of the agreement to fund KEDO and imposing limited sanctions on transportation between Japan and North Korea. Japanese policy-making agents, under pressure from the US and South Korea, eventually agreed that Japan would resume funding for KEDO in early 1999 and indicated that it would seek to resume normalization talks if the North would refrain from further missile tests and make concessions on the *Nihonjinzuma* visits and *racchi jiken*.

However, the North Korea regime largely ignored Japanese objections and persisted with negotiations with the US, managing to secure the Clinton administration's agreement in September 1999 to lift a number of bilateral sanctions in return for North Korea's halting of any missile tests planned for the remainder of 1999. The improvement in US–North Korea relations then placed the onus upon Japan to demonstrate support for US and South Korean attempts to engage North Korea by pushing forward its own relations with the North. The Japanese government agreed to despatch to Pyongyang in December 1999 an all-party mission led by the former prime minister, Murayama Tomiichi, and in the same month in government-level negotiations with North Korea confirmed it would lift its remaining sanctions and investigate the resumption of food aid and normalization talks sometime in early 2000. In return, North Korea once again agreed to investigate the cases of 'missing persons'. At the time of writing (April 2000), however, Japan–North Korea normalization talks have yet to restart.

North Korea undoubtedly remains interested in improved ties with Japan and access to up to US$5 billion in 'economic cooperation' to reconstruct its economy. North Korea's interest in pursuing relations first of all with the US, however, has meant that up until the time of writing it has rejected Japanese diplomatic overtures. Policy-makers have been unable to use Japan's economic power to forge greater engagement and interdependence with North Korea, and thus are unable to influence the development of the North's political economy as they have done with the South. Meanwhile, Japan is left with only KEDO as a new multilateral but ultimately limited framework for economic engagement with North Korea.

The result is that Japan's political ties with the Korean Peninsula remain one-sided. Japanese policy-making agents have succeeded in promoting ever-improving relations with South Korea, but ties with North Korea have deteriorated as the new century starts. Despite Japan's efforts to use quiet diplomacy through party-to-party contacts and the promise of economic aid, bilateral relations with its ex-colony and close neighbour have not improved. North Korea is the only state in the world with which Japan has never maintained diplomatic relations. Moreover, although the Japanese government has professed a desire for greater dialogue with North Korea, as will be examined in Chapter 11, it has in fact switched its policy more to one of deterrence in the dimension of security.

9.4 Japan and Southeast Asia

9.4.i Japan's approach towards Southeast Asia: structure, agency and norms

Chapter 8 has demonstrated how Japan, owing to its defeat in the Pacific War, was effectively driven out of Southeast Asia politically, economically and militarily by the early 1950s, leaving behind it a number of international structural factors which ever since have influenced the pattern of its relations with the region. The legacy of Japanese colonialism and militarism has generated varying degrees of anti-Japanese sentiment in Indo-China and the other states which were later to become members of ASEAN, but in general has worked as a structural barrier to distance Japan from closer relations with Southeast Asia. The legacy of national division, which was initiated by Japan's failed colonial exploits during the Pacific War and then compounded by the application of bipolarity as a result of competition between the USSR and the US during the Cold War, also impacted strongly upon Japan's relations with the region. As in the Korean Peninsula, on the one hand, Japan's attachment to the US half of the bipolar divide created structural impediments to interaction with the communist states of Indo-China. On the other hand, Japan's position within the US camp meant that, throughout the Cold War period, its ally was keen to reopen Japan's access to Southeast Asia, and to encourage Japanese engagement with the capitalist states of the region (Schaller 1985: 178–211).

Japanese policy-making agents during the Cold War and beyond, motivated by various norms and interests, have both exploited and circumvented the opportunities and constraints presented by the structure of the international system, in order to engage Southeast Asia and instrumentalize a general improvement in Japan's relations with the region. The norm of bilateralism has meant that, in many instances, Japan's conservative LDP politicians, MOFA and economic ministries, and the private business sector have been eager to follow US strategy and engage the capitalist states of Southeast Asia so as to resist the spread of communism and promote the general stability of the region. At the same time, however, Asianist and developmental norms have been influential in reinforcing the conviction of Japanese policy-makers that they should not only seek to engage the capitalist states of Southeast Asia in order to make recompense for the colonial past and to secure access to economic resources and markets, but also that they should seek, wherever possible and without undermining their ties with the US, to circumvent or overcome bipolar structural barriers in order to do the same with the communist states of the region. Japanese policy-making agents and other political actors ever since the period of colonial expansion during the Pacific War have been aware of the crucial importance of Southeast Asia to Japan's own economic development, and have attempted to promote the integration of the region as one political and economic unit. Therefore, Japan has cautiously sought to engage the communist states of Vietnam, Cambodia and Laos, and the authoritarian states of Burma and Indonesia, as a means to draw them back into and contribute to the creation of a more complete region. This is based on the belief that, as in China and North and South Korea, over the longer term this will promote economic development, economic interdependence, general political stability in the region, and the smoother transition of the newly independent colonies to statehood and less authoritarian forms of government in the region. In order to instrumentalize this delicate strategy, Japanese policy in the Cold War period and since has been characterized by a typical mix of quiet diplomacy combined with the use of economic power.

9.4.ii Japan and Southeast Asia in the Cold War period

Japan's re-entry into Southeast Asia began in the early 1950s and was marked by a *seikei bunri* approach. In accordance with its obligations under the 1952 San Francisco peace treaty and other separate peace treaties, Japan negotiated reparations agreements with the newly independent states of Burma (November 1954), the Philippines (April 1954), Indonesia (January 1958) and South Vietnam (May 1959) (Mendl 1995: 98). In addition to reparation payments, the start of what can be regarded as Japan's ODA to Southeast Asia came in 1954 with its provision of technical assistance as part of the British Colombo Plan. Japan's principal objective in providing reparations and ODA, and establishing normal relations with the states of Southeast Asia, was more economic than overtly political. As Chapter 10 will reveal in more detail, reparations and ODA were designed to forge new economic links between Japan and the region, as they were made mainly in the form of the transfer of machinery and loans, which led the states of the region to become dependent on Japanese corporations for spare parts, related products and technical assistance (Nester 1992: 122). The *seikei bunri* nature of Japanese policy was demonstrated by the fact that many of the negotiations supposedly covering the diplomatic and political issues of reparations were actually pushed for and even frequently conducted in the government's stead by Japanese private sector economic actors such as the *Keidanren*, illustrating the proxy diplomacy which was introduced in Chapter 2.

Signs of a slightly more assertive Japanese political role in Southeast Asia did not appear until the Kishi administration. Kishi's attachment to the norm of bilateralism meant that he saw the promotion of Japan's ties with the region as an essential means to assist in the US strategy to contain communism in the region and elsewhere. In addition, his pan-Asianist views, derived from his wartime involvement in colonial administration in East Asia, persuaded him that even within the US-defined international structure Japan could assert its rightful position as the political and economic 'leader' of Southeast Asia (Shiraishi T. 1997: 177; Edström 1999: 42–4). Consequently, Kishi made his first overseas trips as prime minister, and the first by any Japanese prime minister in the post-war era, to East Asia in May 1957 rather than to the US in order to demonstrate Japan's commitment to the region.

9.4.iii Japan and the Vietnam War

Kishi's fall as prime minister following the security treaty crisis of 1960 (discussed in Chapter 6) and the increasing bipolar tensions in the region slowed the pace of Japanese overt political re-engagement with Southeast Asia and forced the government to push forward relations under the cover of the *seikei bunri* policy. The chief problem for policy-makers in this period was Japan's position with regard to North and South Vietnam and support for the US war efforts during the Vietnam War. Japan, in line with US interests in Southeast Asia, had established diplomatic relations with the anti-communist regime in Saigon in January 1953, and maintained its recognition of South Vietnam as the sole legitimate government of the country, signing a reparations agreement with it in 1959, as mentioned above. During the height of the Vietnam War from the mid-1960s onwards, the Japanese government under the Satō administration felt obliged as an ally of the US – and intent on securing the return of Okinawa – to continue supporting the US war effort and South Vietnam. As was pointed out in Chapter 4, Satō expressed unreserved public support for the US bombing of Vietnam, much of which was carried out from bases in Okinawa; he visited Saigon in October 1967; and the Satō administration provided significant economic aid to the South Vietnamese regime. However, the Vietnam War was opposed by certain sections of the LDP, including the Afro-Asian Problems Study Association, the opposition parties, and citizens groups such as *Beheiren* (Citizens' League for Peace in Vietnam). These groups, motivated in part by Asianist norms, feared the effect of Japan's support for the US upon efforts to improve relations with communist China, and were appalled at the US's unleashing of modern technological war upon what they viewed as a brave independence movement in Vietnam.

The anti-war movement in Japan proved incapable of overcoming the Satō government's attachment to the norm of bilateralism and its steadfast public support for US policy in Vietnam. At the same time, however, Japan's general adherence to the international structural constraint of the US relationship did not mean that it was averse to attempts to engage North Vietnam on the other side of the bilateral divide. Prior to and during the Vietnam War, aware of the importance of seeking over the longer term to integrate North Vietnam into the Southeast Asia region, the Japanese government was content to pursue something of a *seikei bunri* policy towards the North and to maintain a small bilateral trading relationship with it. After the cease-fire in 1973, Japan continued to recognize the government of South Vietnam and provided it with economic support. Still, the weakening of bipolar tensions, indicated by US defeat in Vietnam and US *rapprochement* with China, enabled the newly-installed Tanaka government to repeat its success in taking advantage of the weakening of international structural pressures to normalize Sino-Japanese relations, by moving also to normalize relations with communist North Vietnam in September 1973. Japan maintained diplomatic links with both North and South Vietnam until the fall of Saigon in 1975 and reunification of Vietnam, when Japan accepted the Hanoi government as the sole legitimate government. Thereafter, Japan concentrated upon building up its economic links with Vietnam, in an attempt, as seen below, to mediate relations between

Vietnam and the newly-emergent ASEAN states. This focus on economic links is illustrated by the Japanese government's decision to pledge US$45 million in aid between 1975 and 1976 for Vietnam's reconstruction (Shiraishi 1990: 51–3).

9.4.iv Japan and the emergence of the Association of Southeast Asian Nations

In the late 1960s and early 1970s, Japan was confronted with new problems in dealing not only with the communist, potentially pro-communist and isolationist states in Southeast Asia, but also with the capitalist states of the region on its own side of the bipolar divide. During this period, Japan intensified its efforts to reintegrate the region, whilst at the same time being careful not to undermine US interests, with the establishment of the Ministerial Conference for Economic Development in Southeast Asia (MEDSEA) in April 1966 and the Asian Development Bank (ADB) in November 1966. The MEDSEA, which continued to meet between 1967 and 1974, was designed to include all ten countries of the region. It can thus be regarded as something of a progenitor of the ASEAN-10. The ADB has focused primarily on development projects in Southeast Asia. However, Japan had designed the MEDSEA as a means to channel mainly US economic assistance to the region, and the ADB, even though it later came to be increasingly dominated by Japan, was founded with US backing and given an equal share of voting rights with Japan. In sum, the MEDSEA and ASEAN revealed Japan's economic commitment to the region, but also its continuing policy of addressing political concerns in Southeast Asia within the international structural restrictions determined by the US (Sudō 1997: 152).

The actual emergence of ASEAN, founded in August 1967 and then comprising Indonesia, Malaysia, Singapore, Thailand and the Philippines, posed particular problems for the previous pattern of Japanese foreign policy towards Southeast Asia (Morrison 1988: 419). Although ASEAN essentially came into being as a security community intended to mitigate internal disputes between its members, the initial fear of MOFA and MITI was that it would conflict with Japan's security and economic interests in the region. MOFA had early concerns about Malaysia's 1971 proposal for a multilateral Zone of Peace, Freedom and Neutrality (ZOPFAN) which appeared to clash with the policy of adhering closely to the US bilateral security system in the region. Similarly, MITI was anxious that ASEAN should not turn itself into an economic bloc which could exclude Japan and the US. At the same time as ASEAN's formation threatened to highlight the bilateral structural obstacles to improved relations between Japan and Southeast Asia, growing dissatisfaction within the ASEAN states themselves with Japan's policy towards the region also threatened to re-emphasize the importance of the legacy of colonialism as a bar to improved ties. Japan's ever-increasing economic penetration of Southeast Asia, marked by its exploitation of the region's natural resources, export of cheap manufactures and supplanting of the US as the chief investor and trade partner for many of the states of the region, had given Japan the image of an 'economic animal'. This sparked off popular boycotts of Japanese goods in the region, and

Plate 9.2 Protests flare. Prime Minister Tanaka Kakuei's visit to Southeast Asia in January 1974 was met with violent protests against the degree of Japanese economic penetration in the region. Angry Indonesian students in Jakarta torch Japanese manufactured cars.

Source: Associated Press

anti-Japanese riots on the occasion of Prime Minister Tanaka's visit to Thailand and Indonesia in 1974. The ASEAN states themselves protested at Japan's apparent over-dependence on US policy in the region and over-emphasis on economics over politics, and began to demand instead a more equal economic *and* political relationship with Japan.

The emergence of ASEAN and these other events exposed for Japanese policy-making agents the limitations of the existing *seikei bunri* policy as a means to overcome the structural barriers of bipolarity and the legacy of colonialism, and to instrumentalize improved relations with Southeast Asia. In response, Prime Minister Fukuda Takeo revealed Japan's 'new look' ASEAN policy during his visit to Southeast Asia in 1977 with the announcement of what became known as the Fukuda Doctrine. This attempted to create a more equal relationship with ASEAN by stating that Japan would: seek to promote ties based on the principle of 'heart-to-heart' understanding on political, economic, social and cultural issues;

continue to eschew a military role in the region; and cooperate with the member states of ASEAN and with Indo-China to contribute to the region's peace and prosperity. The Fukuda Doctrine was accompanied by promises to double Japanese aid to ASEAN; initiate a process of MOFA building a 'special relationship' between Japan and ASEAN; and help to develop new channels for economic and political dialogue between the two (Sudo 1992). Thus, the ASEAN–Japan Forum, ASEAN–Japan Foreign Ministers Conference, and ASEAN–Japan Economic Ministers Conference were established as Japan–ASEAN dialogue bodies in 1977, 1978 and 1979 respectively. The Fukuda administration also made determined efforts to promote stability in the region by engaging Vietnam, maintaining a small but flourishing trade relationship with it throughout the 1980s. It also displayed its *watashiyaku* role by attempting to represent ASEAN's interests to the US and other states of the West at the G7 summit in Bonn in 1978.

Japan's reaction to the onset of the second Cold War in the late 1970s and the reapplication of a more stringent form of bipolarity in Southeast Asia, instigated in part by Vietnam's invasion of Cambodia in December 1978, was to re-adhere to the norm of bilateralism and to increase its burden-sharing efforts for US security strategy in the region. Japan severed all economic aid to Vietnam in 1979, and increased significantly its strategic aid to those US allies and countries 'bordering on areas of conflict' in the early 1980s, namely: Thailand, Indonesia, the Philippines and Malaysia. At the same time, however, Japan still demonstrated the increasingly independent streak of its diplomacy in the region by making quiet diplomatic efforts throughout the 1980s to act as an intermediary between ASEAN and Vietnam, and succeeded in having the Cambodia issue included in the G7 summit statement in 1981. Throughout the rest of the Cold War, the Japanese government continued to express its support for ASEAN opposition to the Vietnamese occupation of Cambodia, and to strengthen links with it through cultural diplomacy and prime ministerial visits to the region. In 1987 Prime Minister Takeshita Noboru visited the ASEAN states and announced a US$2 billion aid initiative entitled, 'Japan and ASEAN: A New Partnership Towards Peace and Cooperation'. Japan's quiet but active diplomacy in Southeast Asia in this period was reinforced by the steady expansion of its trade and investment links in the region, and its emergence as a role model for some of the ASEAN states. Prime Minister Mahathir Mohamad of Malaysia launched his 'Look East' policy in the early 1980s, convinced of the opportunities for Southeast Asia to learn from the development of Japan's political economy.

9.4.v Japan–ASEAN relations in the post-Cold War period

Japan, therefore, had succeeded by the end of the second Cold War in instrumentalizing a general improvement in its political links with ASEAN and had gone a considerable way towards overcoming the international structural restriction of the legacy of the colonial past. The winding-down of Cold War tensions between the major powers in East Asia, marked by Vietnam's announcement in 1988 of the withdrawal of its forces from Cambodia, lowered in turn the bipolar international structural barriers to Japanese interaction with both ASEAN and the Indo-China states, and has since enhanced Japan's freedom to continue its efforts to strengthen its ties with and reintegrate the region politically and economically.

The conditions for the resolution of the Cambodian problem were created by strategic *rapprochement* between the USSR, China and the US, but Japan took advantage of these to play an active role in supporting the actual process of instrumentalizing a peace agreement. Japan sponsored the June 1990 Tokyo Conference concerned with the Cambodian issue and made large financial contributions to the UN Transitional Authority in Cambodia (UNTAC), as will be described in Chapter 19. At a further conference held in Tokyo in June 1992, the Japanese oversaw the collection of US$880 million for Cambodia's reconstruction, with Japan itself offering around one-quarter of this sum. ASEAN's growing acceptance of Japan's political role in Southeast Asian affairs, and Japan's overcoming of the structural impediment of the colonial past, were demonstrated by the general support for the despatch of the SDF to take part in PKO in Cambodia between 1992 and 1993, as will be described in Chapter 19. The resurgence of shared Asianist norms in Japan and the ASEAN states also reflects a degree of increased political solidarity: many Japanese policy-makers refused to insist that certain authoritarian states should observe what are seen as essentially US- and Western-determined standards of human rights. More extreme forms of this revival of Asianist sentiment are typified by Mahathir's statement that Japan should stop apologizing for the past (cited in Elegant 1995: 37) and his co-authorship in 1994 with Ishihara Shintarō of *'No' to Ieru Aija* (The Asia that can say 'no') (Mahathir and Ishihara 1994; Mahathir and Ishihara 1996), which stressed that Japan and East Asia together could resist US influence in the region.

This increasing sense of shared political identity, reinforced by the further strengthening of economic interdependence, as will be described in Chapter 10, prepared the ground for further improvements in ties between Japan and ASEAN, for Japan to play a central role in creating an integrated Southeast Asia region, and for it to begin to be spoken of as a potential political 'leader'. In January 1993, Prime Minister Miyazawa visited the ASEAN states and announced the 'Miyazawa Doctrine' based on the four principles of Japan's active participation in the advancement of region-based political and, for the first time, multilateral security dialogue; the advancement in the Asia Pacific of economic development in step with economic liberalization; the expansion of democratization and the compatibility of development with environmental protection; and cooperation between Japan and ASEAN to improve relations with Indo-China. In January 1997, Prime Minister Hashimoto on his visit to Southeast Asia announced the 'Hashimoto Doctrine', the essence of which was further to strengthen close ties with ASEAN. This was to be achieved by assisting in the maintenance of the region's traditions and culture and by working together with ASEAN to address global issues. Japan's commitment to working with ASEAN was to be tested by the outbreak of the East Asian financial and economic crises from mid-1997 onwards, as will be described in Chapter 10, and Japanese proposals for an Asian Monetary Fund (AMF) under Japan's effective leadership. These Japanese initiatives with their emphasis upon regional and multilateral strategies indicated that, although Japan was certainly not abandoning its attachment to the bilateral norm and the bilateral relationship with the US, these were beginning to be challenged in the minds of Japanese policy-making agents by the resurgent norms of Asianism and internationalism.

In turn, Japan's long-term efforts to achieve the integration of the Southeast Asia region seemed to have been vindicated with Vietnam's accession to ASEAN in 1995, and Laos, Cambodia and Burma's entry as full or observer members into the organization by 1997 – thereby completing the ASEAN-10 and the type of complete regional forum that Japan had envisaged with the MEDSEA proposal of 1966. In particular, Burma's acceptance of observer status seemed to justify Japan's decision to maintain trade and aid relations with the regime as the optimum method to bring it into the ASEAN regional fold, despite a brief suspension of Japanese ODA to Rangoon between 1988 and 1989 in protest at human rights violations, and despite severe international criticism of Japan's policy.

9.4.vi East Asian Economic Caucus

Nevertheless, Japan's emphasis upon political relations with ASEAN and the general 're-Asianization' of its foreign policy detected by certain observers (Funabashi 1993) is still limited by bilateral structural factors in the late 1990s and into the twenty-first century. The ever-present cognition of the bilateral relationship with the US, and the attendant need to present Japanese policy in Southeast Asia as generally compatible with US regional and global aims, have meant that Japanese policy-makers continue to exercise caution in their political initiatives in the region. Japan has been careful not to engage in open efforts to integrate the Southeast and entire East Asia regions to the exclusion of the US, and thus force Japan to choose between its growing Asianist and well-established Western identities. The most notable example of this has been Japan's relatively unenthusiastic response to Prime Minister Mahathir's and ASEAN's proposals for the East Asian Economic Caucus (EAEC). As proposed by Mahathir, EAEC placed Japan as the effective leader of an exclusive economic bloc in East Asia, defined as including the ASEAN-10, South Korea and China, but excluding those states in the region which were racially non-Asian, specifically the US, Australia and New Zealand (Funabashi 1995: 305). The EAEC concept thus sat in direct contravention of the APEC programme supported by the US, as was discussed in more detail in Chapter 5, and threatened to force Japan back into its constant dilemma of choosing between its ties with East Asia and the US. Sections of East Asianist opinion within MITI appreciated the value of EAEC as a means to increase Japan's role in pushing for economic integration in the region and to provide Japan with a counterweight to economic and political dependence on the US, whilst the Southeast Asia Divisions of MOFA were concerned that the rival APEC proposal could undermine Japan's 'special relationship' of economic and growing political interdependence with ASEAN. However, the more serious concern of MITI, derived in part from the norm of bilateralism, was that Japan's participation in the EAEC proposal would damage its relationship with the US and its economic interests in the US market and globally. MOFA was also concerned that EAEC would be viewed by the US as a political project to exclude its influence from the region, which would then have repercussions for Japan's bilateral security relationship.

Thus, in order to avoid an uncomfortable conflict between its interests with the US and those with East Asia, the Japanese government has supported APEC over EAEC, and secured a compromise by acquiescing in the establishment of EAEC within the APEC structure. The Japanese government is convinced that this arrangement will allow it to pursue its norms and interests with both East Asia and the US simultaneously. On the one hand, Japan remains the effective economic leader of East Asia owing to the extensive influence exerted by the economic activities of Japanese TNCs in East Asia. It can push an agenda within APEC of considering the interests of ASEAN and the other East Asian countries in the face of US demands for liberalization by stressing the need for economic development assistance and staged changes to accompany this process. On the other hand, the APEC framework, most vitally, keeps the US engaged in the region, enables Japan to maintain its adherence to the liberal economic trading system and provides a forum for Japan to cooperate with the US to manage regional economic integration. APEC has then once again enabled Japan to navigate its way between its perceived norms and interests with regard to both East Asia and the US.

9.5 Summary

This chapter has demonstrated how in the post-war era Japanese policy-making agents have steadily managed in the dimension of politics to overcome and circumvent in varying degrees the structural barriers to interaction with East Asia imposed by the legacy of colonialism, national division and bipolarity. Sino-Japanese relations are still fraught with difficulties over the colonial past, and Japan is still often forced to stand in the middle between China and the US in the newly-emerging pattern of triangular interaction between these three powers in the post-Cold War period. Nevertheless, Japan has managed at least to create a working political relationship with China – contrasting strongly to the complete disengagement of Japan from China in 1945. Similarly, Japan has also achieved a major turnaround in its post-colonial relations with South Korea, and the two are moving increasingly towards political and economic interdependence. Furthermore, Japan, despite the tribulations of the colonial past, bipolarity and the Vietnam War, has succeeded both in improving its relations with states of ASEAN and Indo-China, once again conjoining politics and economics, and in knitting together a more complete sub-region in Southeast Asia. North Korea thus remains the main black spot on Japan's record of upgrading its ties with East Asia. Japan has instrumentalized this remarkable revival in its political fortunes in the region by the use of economic power, and cautious, quiet diplomacy and leadership.

Chapter 10

Japan–East Asia economic relations

10.1 Overview

Chapter 9 outlined how Japan, during the Cold War and post-Cold War periods, has gradually managed to overcome the international structural barriers of bipolarity, national division and the colonial past, in order to reassert quietly its political presence in East Asia and assist the reintegration of the region as a political unit. This chapter now turns to focus upon how Japan has managed similarly to overcome the international structural barrier to interaction with and between the various East Asian states of the diversity of their economic systems, and to promote a degree of economic convergence and integration between itself and the region. As a result, at the start of the twenty-first century, Japan has re-emerged as the principal, if not wholly unchallenged, economic organizer and leader of a readily identifiable East Asian economic region.

This chapter will concentrate mainly upon an analysis of Japan's links with the East Asian economic region, as divided conventionally into the units of the NIEs-4 (South Korea, Taiwan, Hong Kong and Singapore); the ASEAN-4 (Thailand, Malaysia, the Philippines and Indonesia); and China. The region is divided in this way because each unit represents a set of major economic actors in the region with similar characteristics and at similar stages of development. Hence, even though Singapore shares a political identity with the other ASEAN states, its higher degree of technology and development means that economically it can be located alongside the more industrialized states of Northeast Asia. This chapter does not deal at length with Japan's economic links with the more minor economies of the region, but these are dealt with in more detail in the trade statistics included in Table 1.

10.2 Japan's economic re-entry and presence in East Asia

10.2.i Official Development Assistance

As was noted in Chapter 9, the starting point for Japan's economic re-entry into East Asia was its provision of aid under various reparations agreements signed as part of the 1952 San Francisco peace treaty and the Colombo Plan. Japan became a founding member of the Development Assistance Committee (DAC) of the OECD in 1961; and Japanese ODA expanded rapidly from the mid-1970s onwards under a series of mid-term plans, rising from US$1.42 billion in 1977 to a historic high of US$13.8 billion in 1995, allowing Japan to surpass the US as the world's largest donor of ODA. Japanese ODA had fallen back to around US$9.4 billion by 1998, but Japan remains the number-one donor in the world. In addition, Japan has risen to become the largest ODA donor in the East Asia region. The direction of Japanese ODA diversified in the 1970s and mid-1980s in attempts to guarantee oil supplies from the Middle East and to assist US allies in the Persian Gulf, Horn of Africa, Caribbean and bordering Afghanistan. Despite these changes, however, in 1998 29.4 per cent of Japan's ODA was still directed towards East Asia and the rest of Asia, with the largest proportion of this (around 16 per cent) devoted to Indonesia and China (MOFA 1998b: 105). In 1996 Japan ranked as the main aid donor to these states, as well as to the Philippines, Thailand, Vietnam, Burma, Cambodia and Laos (MOFA 1998b: 106). Furthermore, Japan's position as the main bilateral donor to these states has been reinforced by its central role within the ADB, as was mentioned in Chapter 9, which relies on Japan for up to 50 per cent of its funds (Ming 1995–6: 519).

As Chapter 9 has shown, the provision of ODA to East Asia often had a clear strategic and political purpose, serving as a substitute for military power and helping to draw the states of the region into a relationship of both political and economic interdependency. Reparations aid came primarily in the form of the export of outdated technology and industrial plant, which allowed Japanese companies to re-enter Southeast Asian markets, and to create the technological and production linkages between those countries and Japan. Since then, Japan's economic interests also have been furthered by the 'tying' of ODA to the purchase of Japanese goods and services, especially large infrastructure projects. In 1972, only 28.1 per cent of Japanese ODA was untied at the commitment stage. By 1982 the Japanese government was able to claim that 100 per cent of its ODA was untied, but its allocation of ODA on the basis of *yōseishugi* (principle of request) means that, in practice, much of the aid is still tied (Soderberg 1996: 72–88). This is because in many cases it is Japanese companies which prepare and are awarded ODA projects on behalf of the recipient government making the requests (Soderberg 1996: 72–88). Thus, Japanese ODA can be seen to have supported the penetration of East Asian markets by Japanese TNCs, and, as will be seen later in this chapter, MITI has often conceived of ODA as a means to enhance the vertical integration of the economies of the region into Japan's own economy in order to establish a regional division of labour (Arase 1995: 203; Shiraishi T. 1997: 189–90).

10.2.ii Foreign direct investment

Japanese foreign direct investment (FDI) has performed a function similar to ODA in helping to rebuild the links between Japan and the East Asian economies. Japanese FDI was initiated in the region in the 1950s and 1960s as part of the effort to secure supplies of natural resources, with major investments in resource extraction in Southeast Asia. However, Japanese FDI in this period was also limited by restrictions placed on the convertibility of the yen as a measure designed to preserve Japan's delicate balance-of-payments situation. The first major injection, or 'upsurge', of Japanese FDI in the region came in the late 1960s and early 1970s, triggered by a combination of causes (Table 2). The 'Nixon shocks', described in Chapter 4, led to the end of fixed exchange rates and the appreciation of the yen against the dollar, whilst the first 'oil shock' of 1973 increased energy and production costs for corporations inside Japan, and forced them to restructure and move away from reliance on heavy industry. Added to this were significant rises in labour costs in Japan; pressure from the Japanese public to move heavy and polluting industries offshore; and the ASEAN states' imposition of import restrictions on

Japanese goods as part of their import substitution development policies (Hook 1996b: 177–9; Selden 1997: 306–40). The consequent need for Japanese corporations to avoid import restrictions and find lower-cost production sites, in tandem with the reduced barriers to the convertibility of the yen and movement of Japanese capital, generated an almost fourfold increase in Japanese FDI in East Asia, from US$165 million in 1970 to US$1 billion in 1975 (Table 2). A large proportion of this FDI was concentrated in industries such as textiles (30–40 per cent) and electronics (15–30 per cent), with most production by Japanese TNCs in these states intended for re-export to third countries, and in particular the vital US market (Kanetsuna 1996: 132–46).

The second upsurge of Japanese FDI occurred in the late 1970s and early 1980s. This resulted from the continuing efforts of Japanese TNCs to restructure and seek lower costs, and was characterized by high investment in the metallurgical and chemical industries. The third and largest upsurge in FDI then came in the mid- to late 1980s, as a reaction to renewed US attempts, by the use of currency realignments and other measures, to curb its growing trade deficits and absorption of imports from Japan and the NIEs-4. The Plaza Accord of 1985 raised the value of the yen against the US dollar by up to 70 per cent (Table 4), and the Louvre Accord of 1987 raised also the value of the NIEs-4 currencies. It was followed by the removal of the NIEs-4 from the General System of Preferences. The rapid appreciation of the yen led to a near threefold increase in Japanese FDI worldwide, with the greatest concentration in the US and the EU, as was explained in Chapter 5 and will be elaborated in Chapter 15. Between 1985 and 1989, the share of the NIEs-4, ASEAN-4 and China in Japan's FDI remained steady at around 10 to 15 per cent, but it increased rapidly in value from around US$1.4 billion in 1985 to US$8.1 billion in 1989 (Table 2). Increasingly this FDI was concentrated in electronics, automobiles and manufacturing assembly. The geographical concentration of Japanese FDI also began to shift from the NIEs-4 to the ASEAN-4, reflecting rising wage and currency costs in the NIEs-4, and increasing barriers to exports by Japanese TNCs from production platforms located in the NIEs-4 to markets in third countries within the region and elsewhere in the world (Table 2).

The fourth, and as yet most recent, upsurge of Japanese investment in East Asia occurred in the early 1990s and was brought about by the further appreciation of the yen to around ¥100 to the US dollar. By 1995, Japanese investment in the NIEs-4, ASEAN-4 and China had risen to US$11.7 billion, or 23 per cent of Japan's total world FDI, with ever greater concentrations in the ASEAN-4 (Table 2). Again the majority of Japanese investment was devoted to the manufacturing industry, with between 40 and 60 per cent in the formation of production capital in the electronics, automobile and metallurgy industries (JETRO 1999b: 51).

10.2.iii Trade

The concentration of Japanese ODA and FDI in East Asia has produced a distinctive pattern of trade relations between Japan and the region. Whilst the US has continued to be Japan's largest individual national trading partner, its share has varied significantly over the past three decades, accounting for around 30 per cent of the total in 1970, 21 per cent in 1980, 27 per cent in 1990 and 28 per cent in 1998 (Table 1). Japan's combined trade with the NIEs-4, ASEAN-4 and China has also fluctuated yearly, but the general trend has been upwards, accounting for 19 per cent of the total in 1970, 24 per cent in 1980 and 29 per cent in 1990 (Table 1). Japan's total trade with East Asia came to exceed that with the US in the early 1980s, before falling back again relative to the US. Since 1990, however, the size of Japan–East Asia trade has constantly outstripped Japan–US trade; and by 1998 Japan was the largest national individual trade partner for China and Indonesia, the second largest for South Korea, Taiwan, Thailand, Malaysia and the Philippines, and the third largest for Singapore and Hong Kong (JETRO 1999a: 172, 181, 188, 193, 199, 205, 211, 217, 222). The share of Japan's total exports to these nine states in East Asia increased rapidly from 20 per cent to 33 per cent between 1984 and 1998, and the share of their imports into Japan rose from 21 per cent to 35 per cent over the same period. Furthermore, an increasing proportion of these trade flows consisted of manufactured goods, rising from 25 per cent of total Japanese imports from East Asia in 1984 to 73 per cent in 1998 (JETRO 1999a: 426–7). Hence, it is possible to see that trading links between Japan and East Asia have been strengthening, and that Japan is absorbing a greater proportion of its manufactured imports from the region.

Yet it is also clear that the pattern of trade relations between Japan and East Asia remains somewhat asymmetrical in the late 1990s. The East Asian states have reduced the share of their total exports which goes to Japan to around 10 per cent in 1998, whilst the share of their total imports which comes from Japan remains high at around 17 per cent in 1998 (JETRO 1999a: 428). This indicates that the East Asian economies have been less successful in penetrating Japan's markets than the latter has in penetrating theirs, and ran a combined trade deficit with Japan of around US$31 billion in 1998 (Table 1). The NIEs-4 have the greatest trade deficit with Japan, at around US$49 billion in 1998, but the once favourable balance of trade that the ASEAN states ran with Japan has also moved into deficit, at around US$7 billion in 1997, before recording a slight surplus of US$2 billion in 1998 as a result of the economic downturn in the region brought about by the East Asian financial and economic crises (Table 1). Meanwhile, China is the only state in East Asia which has been able to generate a surplus with Japan, reaching US$17 billion in 1998 (Table 1).

The majority of East Asia's trade deficit with Japan is accounted for by the imbalance in the export and import of manufactured goods. In 1998, nearly 100 per cent of Japan's exports to East Asia consisted of manufactured goods and technology, such as electronics, transport and precision machinery (JETRO 1999a: 425). This created a surplus in manufactured goods close to US$30 billion in 1998, accounting for nearly the entire trade surplus with East Asia (JETRO 1999a: 424–7). It is apparent also that, despite Japan's dominance in many sectors of the East Asian regional economy, a triangular pattern of trade relations still exists between Japan, East Asia and the US. Even though the East Asian states have managed to reduce the share of their total exports which goes to the US from 31 per cent in 1984 to 22 per cent in 1998, the proportion of their exports reliant on the US market is still nearly twice that of Japan (JETRO 1999a: 429). Moreover, the US has also generally accounted for 23 per cent to 35 per cent of the manufacturing exports of each East Asian state, whereas Japan accounts for only 4 per cent to 16 per cent (Bernard and Ravenhill 1995: 205). This suggests that Japan's trade activity in the region has been characterized more by its role as an exporter of technology goods than by its role as an absorber of manufactured goods, and that the US has been an important engine of growth for the export-oriented economies of the region.

10.3 Japan and the economic development of the East Asia region

10.3.i Developmental models

The patterns of Japanese ODA, FDI and trade described in the section above have not only led to the re-emergence of Japan's economic presence in East Asia, but have also influenced the course of the development and integration of the region as a whole. As a result, Japan has been given a central role within this process. The outflow of Japanese investment and the relocation of production by Japanese TNCs have assisted the states of East Asia in their policies to replicate models of development based on Japan's. The models of development are generally characterized by dependence respectively on the demand and supply sides upon export and investment-oriented growth, and by a system of economic governance which involves close cooperation between the state and private economic sectors.

Japanese manufacturing TNCs and financial institutions can be seen to have been directly involved in the transfer to East Asia of a developmental model dependent upon export demand by the setting-up of subsidiaries in the region which serve as production platforms for exports inside the East Asia region, to Japan, and outside the region to Europe and North America. In addition, Japanese corporations, through the *keiretsu*-type links of Japanese manufacturers to subcontractors in the recipient East Asian states which rely for their business on supplying Japanese exporting firms, can be said to have encouraged the growth of indigenous export-oriented industries. Likewise, Japan's manufacturing firms and banks can be seen to have contributed to a model of growth dependent upon the supply side on investment by providing massive injections of FDI which enable the East Asian states to acquire the capital and technology to overcome bottlenecks in production and to raise their international competitiveness, as well as to finance current account deficits without reliance on government borrowing.

The third feature of the developmental model, the close relationship between government and the private sector, can be said to have been transferred to the region by Japan's serving as an example of how an East Asian state can successfully achieve modernization and economic growth in the post-war era. Thus, Japan's management of economic growth – marked by a mixture of government intervention to subsidize declining and nascent export industries; the establishment of government institutions and banks to support the export trade; and the sharing of information between state and private sector economic actors – was taken as a blueprint in certain East Asian states for their own developmental policies. South Korea styled its own economic ministries and *chaebol* industrial conglomerates after MITI and the Japanese *zaibatsu*, and Prime Minister Mahathir's 'Look East' policy (Jomo 1994), inspired by Japan, as has been noted in Chapter 9.

The creation of these 'developmental states', modelled in part upon Japan's own economic success, has been viewed by many Japanese observers as delivering high-speed and sound economic growth to East Asia, and demonstrating Japan's essential role as an economic leader of the region. In particular, the course of development in the region has been explained in terms of a 'flying geese' model. This model was first developed by the Japanese economist Akamatsu Kaname, and later refined in terms of 'production cycles' (Cumings 1984: 1–40; Gangopadhyay 1998: 37; Yamazawa 1992: 1512–29). Both models argue that, as Japan moves up the production cycle in terms of the sophistication of its industrial technology, this is accompanied by shifts in comparative advantage, owing to factors such as rising Japanese labour costs and the appreciation of the yen, and then the transfer of older technology and exporting industries from Japan to East Asia seeking lower production costs. The East Asian states then use these technologies to produce for export to Japan, and in turn move up the production cycle in Japan's wake. Thus, the 'flying geese' model posits a division of labour in East Asia, with Japan constantly occupying the position of the 'lead goose' as the producer and supplier of high technology, and the other East Asian states constantly following behind as they acquire Japan's discarded industries and progress in terms of their technological sophistication.

The predictions of the 'flying geese' model seem in many ways to have been borne out by the recent pattern of development in East Asia and the industrial transformation and high rates of growth, at anything up to 8 per cent to 10 per cent, that many of the states of the region have experienced. Japan itself has made constant progress in its industrial production, moving from textiles, shipbuilding, steel and chemicals in the later 1950s and 1960s; to electronics and automobiles in the 1970s and 1980s; and then to high-technology and computer and information industries in the 1990s. In turn, it would appear that the geographical shifts in Japan's FDI have led to the transfer of older industries, first to the NIEs-4, as shown by South Korea overtaking Japan as the world's leading shipbuilder in the 1970s; then to the ASEAN-4 in the 1980s, as illustrated by Malaysia becoming a major exporter of electronic products; and then finally to China, as it too enters the East Asian production cycle at the bottom of the ladder and begins to export low-tech manufactured goods and then moves up by producing more sophisticated goods for export in the region and beyond.

This industrial transformation has once again been assisted by the presence of Japanese TNCs in the region which have transferred, in varying degrees, technology and production networks to the region. In the electronics industry, Japanese firms have felt less compulsion to expand technology transfer, as local production sites tend to function simply by the operation of automated machinery imported from Japan. In the automobile industry, however, greater technical knowledge is called for in the manufacturing process, which has led to the training of skilled local staff. Moreover, an increasing number of Japanese firms have found it necessary to increase the level of their local procurement of components, research and development and local managers, in order to respond more flexibly to local market conditions (Yamashita 1998: 61–77). The end result of these changes in production practices is to speed the industrial evolution of the NIEs-4 and ASEAN-4, and to increase integration between the Japanese and East Asian economies.

10.3.ii Propagation of developmental norms

The apparent success of the developmental state and 'flying geese' models of growth in East Asia has led MITI and other influential sections of Japanese policy-makers informed by their developmental norms, to adopt and defend these models as the essential means by which to achieve the fuller integration of the region. For MITI and the other economic ministries, Japan's position as the perpetual head of the 'flying geese' model and East Asian economic hierarchy, serves as a convenient justification to view Japan as the natural organizer and leader of an East Asian economic region (Koschmann 1997: 105–6). MITI acknowledges that the East Asian states, like Japan, have had to rely during the initial stages of development on access to the US market to spur economic growth. Thus, this means that the triangular pattern of Japan–East Asia–US economic interaction still continues to some degree, that Japan is not the undisputed leader of the region, and that the region needs to remain 'open' in order to remain engaged with the US and other foreign markets. However, MITI also argues that constantly increasing levels of East Asia intra-regional FDI and trade between Japan, the NIEs-4, ASEAN-4 and China, accounting for close to 36 per cent of total exports in 1998, and the weaning away from dependency on exports to the US, are indicative of the emergence of a self-sustaining 'flying geese' model of growth within the region itself, and that Japan is thus the essential economic leader of East Asia.

Consequently, MITI and the Japanese government have used the device of the 'flying geese' and developmental state models, backed by economic power in the guise of the provision of ODA, in order to propagate their own developmental norms throughout the region and within global institutions as well. For instance, MITI's 1987 new Asian Industrial Development plan aimed to foster, in 'flying geese' fashion, a division of industrial labour between Japan and East Asia by the promotion of export-oriented industries in the region and the transfer of technology and industrial financing. Likewise, MITI's 1992 *White Paper on International Trade 1992* and *Vision 2000 Report* (JETRO 1992: 119–46; Funabashi 1995: 286) attempted to influence the debate on the future of economic development in East Asia within the APEC framework. These reports argued for the importance of the 'flying geese' pattern of development, and that trade and FDI liberalization should be accompanied by cooperation between the state and private sectors to ensure that each APEC member had reached a level of development sufficient to cope with the pressures of increased openness and competition. MITI has also fostered varieties of the developmental state model and its developmental norms within the World Bank (WB), and as a quiet challenge to the existing neo-liberal economic dogma in the WB and other global economic institutions which generally stress the need for development of free trade and FDI regimes that are precluded from government intervention. Accordingly, as will be described in Chapter 20, MITI and the Japanese government funded the production of the WB's *East Asian Miracle* report in 1993, which, against prevailing orthodoxy in the WB, explained the high rate of economic growth in East Asia as in part the outcome of an effective mix of private enterprise and government intervention (World Bank 1993; Wade 1996).

10.3.iii Criticisms of the developmental state model

Japan's promotion of the 'flying geese' and developmental state models in this period clearly did not remain unchallenged, as observers have seen weaknesses in terms of over-reliance on export demand and investment supply, and the nature of governance and management of the East Asian economies. The counter position to the 'flying geese' and production cycles models is that of 'complex production links'. This model argues that, even though in accordance with the outflow of FDI the transfer of production technology may also take place between Japan and East Asia, the costs of industry start-ups and the mastering of new technologies are so great that these countries ultimately remain dependent on Japanese technology and cannot close the production cycles to create their own fully-fledged export industries. Instead, the contention is that Japan has established in East Asia a system of hierarchical complex-production links which are connected vertically backwards to Japan, because of dependence on exports of Japanese technology, and vertically forward to the US, because of its continuing position as a major external export market for East Asian manufactured goods. Thus, in accordance with this view, much of the intra-regional trade and FDI within East Asia can be accounted for not by independent trade between individual firms in finished products in which they enjoy a comparative advantage, but by trade controlled by or linked to Japanese subsidiaries based in East Asia and consisting of products such as components for eventual assembly in Japanese-made manufactured goods which are then exported to other regions (Bernard and Ravenhill 1995; Hatch and Yamamura 1996). The implication of these criticisms of the 'flying geese' model is, then, that it does not deliver complete and rounded economic development to those East Asian states to which FDI is directed, and brings with it an in-built vulnerability and lack of sustainability on the demand side owing to its reliance on the US as the export market of 'last resort'.

Similarly, a few observers in this period criticized the 'flying geese' models and developmental state models as being over-dependent on the supply side upon Japanese and external investment since the Plaza Accord and vulnerable to any drop in its supply (Krugman 1994). Moreover, even if, as seen above, the majority of Japanese FDI is concentrated in the build-up of production capital, the massive inflows of Japanese investment have been seen as likely to create the conditions for speculative bubbles in the region by encouraging the East Asian states to open their financial markets further to the seeming benefits of inflows of foreign capital, and by creating the impression of economic dynamism which attracts volatile 'hot money' portfolio investments from other developed states taking advantage of the dollar-pegged currencies of East Asia and concomitant lack of exchange risk.

Finally, the developmental state model was seen to have weaknesses owing to the nature of its governance, which, although it showed itself capable of building up export industries through state and private sector partnership, could lead also to the state over-protecting inefficient and moribund industries at great cost to the economic fundamentals of the East Asian states (Higgott 1998: 337–40). In a sense, Japan's promotion of developmental norms was seen to be the progenitor of the type of 'crony capitalism' which was to produce endemic corruption in states such as South Korea, Malaysia and Indonesia, and precipitate economic disaster in 1997.

10.4 Japan and the East Asian economic crisis

10.4.i East Asian financial and economic crises

Despite some early criticism of Japanese influence upon the development of the East Asia region, no real challenge to the developmental norms and paradigms of Japan was to come until the advent of the East Asian financial and economic crises from mid-1997 onwards. The East Asian crisis began with a crash in the value of the Thai baht in July 1997. This was the outcome of investor fears that Thailand would be unable to sustain its current account deficit and economic growth owing to declining export demand and declining investment supplies, which led subsequently to the withdrawal of portfolio investments from the country and a reverse outflow of capital. The decline in investor confidence proved to be contagious, causing declines in the Malaysian ringgit, the Philippine peso, the Hong Kong dollar, the Indonesian rupiah and then the South Korean won by November 1997. In reaction to the threatened collapse of the East Asian currencies and economies, the IMF intervened with a series of financial rescue packages in Thailand, Indonesia and South Korea, designed to shore up their currencies and accompanied by a series of conditions. IMF conditionality demanded fundamental restructuring in the management of the East Asian economies in order to restore investor confidence and staunch the outflows of capital. Typical measures included the further liberalization of FDI and trade regimes in the East Asian states, the breaking-up of inefficient manufacturing and financial conglomerates, and removing the links between the state and private sectors. These were all intended, in line with liberal economic orthodoxy, to enhance transparency in the East Asian economies, and to remove what were seen as the distortions in the operation of free markets resulting from government intervention, and thus the causes of declining investor confidence (Nellor 1998: 248). Meanwhile, Malaysia, concerned about the impact of IMF conditions upon its economic sovereignty and social stability, resisted accepting these rescue packages.

The IMF rescue packages did indeed restore a measure of investor confidence in the region and halt the financial crisis as Thailand, Indonesia and South Korea were placed under IMF tutelage. However, the reform measures came at a cost: severe economic recessions in all these states, rising unemployment and social costs, leading to political chaos in Indonesia and the eventual fall of the Suharto government in May 1998. In addition, the East Asian financial crisis and IMF packages marked a challenge to the developmental state model in East Asia and Japanese economic leadership of the region in various ways (Pempel 1999).

10.4.ii Japan's perceived responsibility for the crises

Japanese economic leadership faced two immediate challenges following the onset of the financial crisis: the perceived responsibility of Japan for purveying an inherently vulnerable development model to East Asia because of its over-reliance on export demand (in particular the US market) and investment supply; and, having instigated this model in the region, Japan itself proceeded to bring it crashing down by sweeping away its twin pillars of exports and investment flows.

Japan was seen to have undermined the export side of the model. This was due to the fact that the pattern of trade between Japan and East Asia, characterized by Japan's export to the region of technology goods, but its limited role in absorbing manufactured goods from the region, created chronic current account deficits for states such as Thailand and Malaysia. As a consequence, their ability to earn high-value export remittances to drive growth were limited and they were forced to rely more on traditional export markets in the US and Europe. Moreover, Japan was believed also to have been influential indirectly in reducing the export, and thereby growth, opportunities for East Asian states in these key markets, owing to the fall in the value of the yen by close to 60 per cent against the dollar between April 1995 and April 1996. The depreciation of the yen, following the devaluation of the Chinese yuan in 1994, meant the relative appreciation of the dollar-pegged currencies of the rest of East Asia, and a subsequent decline in the competitiveness of these states' exports versus Japanese and Chinese exports in all key markets. Finally, Japan's own economic recession following the bursting of its bubble economy in 1989 was seen to have compounded the fall-off in demand for East Asian exports. Meanwhile, having created a situation whereby the East Asian states were increasingly unable to fuel growth through exports, Japan was then accused of having choked off the region's supply of investment, again because of its own economic recession and the slackening of FDI flows (Table 2). The end consequence of Japan's reducing the ability of the East Asian states to pay for their current account deficits and to remain afloat economically, by reducing their export and investment potential, was then seen to have become the key trigger for the loss of investor confidence in East Asia in 1997.

10.4.iii Japan's regional response and the Asian Monetary Fund

Dissatisfaction with Japan for its apparent role in creating the conditions for and starting the financial crisis was then compounded by its perceived failure to take effective action to combat and contain the crisis after it had broken out. Japan's first reaction to the crisis was to provide the largest national contribution (US$16 million) to IMF bail-out packages in August 1997 and to support IMF conditionality. However, the seeming reluctance of the US and other developed states to make a major commitment to rescuing the East Asian states led MOF and the Japanese government, drawing on their attachment to developmental and increasingly Asianist and internationalist norms, as was described in Chapter 2, to propose a region-based solution to the crisis. In September 1997, Finance Minister Mitsuzuka Hiroshi proposed the creation of a US$100 billion Asian Monetary Fund (AMF) to organize the region financially, with Japan as its effective head and main financial backer. The AMF proposal was, however, opposed by the US Treasury and the IMF, owing to their concern about the lack of conditionality that might accompany any financial assistance from this quarter, as well as the potential challenge of Japan's region-led response to the US's and the IMF's traditional dominance in global finance (Higgott 1998: 340–6). Japanese policy-makers were yet again faced with a conflict between their norms and interests located in the US and East Asia, with the former once more triumphing as Japan abandoned the AMF proposals and returned to official backing for the IMF reform programmes. The result was that Japan was viewed by certain East Asian states as abdicating its economic leadership in the region. This is illustrated by the comment of Prime Minister Mahathir of Malaysia, at the ASEAN + 3 summit in December 1997, that Japan had lost the will to be the 'lead goose' in the region (*Nikkei Weekly*, 22 December 1997).

In addition to dissatisfaction with Japan for its failed efforts to firefight the outbreak of the crisis in 1997, there was also a perception that Japanese policy-makers and TNCs were either reluctant or simply unable to take any steps to restore the growth by rehabilitating export demand and investment supply in the region. On the export side, the continuing decline of the yen, which reached a new eight-year low of ¥147 to the dollar by August 1998, raised suspicions that Japan's real intention was to allow the yen's fall in value in order to eliminate East Asian competition and to export its way out of its own recession. Moreover, the indications were that Japan had no intention of acting as an absorber of East Asian exports through increases in domestic demand, as MOF showed itself resistant to calls from within the region and the US to launch large-scale stimulus packages because of its desire to limit government spending. Likewise, Japan seemed unable to boost its investment in the region, as its own banks remained mired in financial trouble in the early 1990s.

10.4.iv New Miyazawa Initiative

Japan was perceived by 1998 to have failed both to protect and lead the East Asian states from the onset and prolongation of the financial crisis, and to have allowed its own developmental model and economic apprentices in the region to fall under the influence of US- and IMF-inspired reform packages. However, Japanese policy-makers have clearly been discontent with this image of failure, and since late 1998 have begun, through a series of initiatives, to resuscitate the developmental and 'flying geese' models and to reassert Japan's economic leadership in the region.

Japanese policy-making agents agree with the IMF on the need for a measure of conditionality and financial reform over the short term in order to stamp out further speculative bubbles in the region and manage investment flows more productively. Over the longer term, however, MOF and MITI appear to have rejected the need for large-scale structural reform of the model because sufficient potential is seen to exist for intra-regional export and FDI growth to sustain a revival of the 'flying geese' and developmental state models. Consequently, it can be seen that since late 1998 the chief focus of Japanese economic policy in the region has been to resuscitate existing models of growth. First, on the demand side, Japanese policy-makers have attempted to jump-start East Asian exports by pushing Japan forward as the new principal absorber of the region's exports, marked by Prime Minister Obuchi's announcement in November 1998 of a US$124 billion domestic stimulus package. Second, MITI has issued up to US$22.5 billion in export credits as a means to keep intra-regional exports and trade ticking over during the worst of the crisis. Third, the Japanese government has announced plans to increase the transfer of technology through new ODA projects to the NIEs-4 and the ASEAN-4 in order to allow them to upgrade their industries, move up the ladder of industrial production and 'fly clear' of Chinese competition – so leading to a correct reordering of the 'flying geese' pattern of development in the region.

Regarding the supply side, in October 1998 Minister of Finance Miyazawa Kiichi announced a US$30 billion initiative to provide financial assistance to the region. 'New Miyazawa Initiative' funding has been designated for the guarantee of sovereign bonds in the East Asian states, which can then be used to recapitalize East Asian banks and corporations. In contrast to IMF rescue packages, the New Miyazawa Initiative does not demand significant restructuring of the region's corporations and is intended more as means for them to weather the economic crisis until they can regain sufficient financial strength to resume their old exported-oriented growth.

Hence, the New Miyazawa Initiative has been designed as a means simply to reinvigorate, rather than to reform root and branch, the existing developmental models in the region, and since its announcement has enabled Japan to regain in part its position as the accepted economic leader of the region. Preoccupied with financial contagion in Latin America, the US has been obliged to cede responsibility for dealing with East Asia increasingly to Japan and has not opposed the New Miyazawa Initiative. This is despite the fact that it has provided significant financial assistance to states such as Malaysia which have defied IMF intervention. A number of East Asian states have begun to seek Japanese financial assistance under the plan (Thailand received US$1.9 billion in December 1998; Malaysia,

US$1.5 billion in December 1998 and US$700 million in March 1999; Indonesia, US$2.4 billion in February 1999; the Philippines, US$1.6 billion in March 1999; and South Korea, US$5 billion in January 1999 and US$1 billion in March 1999), and the success of the New Miyazawa Initiative also appears to be reviving calls for some type of region-based financial organization with Japan as its effective head. Thus, in December 1998, Kim Jong-Pil, the South Korean prime minister, called for a new AMF proposal, and the ADB also since 1998 has begun to reconsider the possibility of an AMF. Moreover, the damage produced by pegging the East Asian currencies to the dollar has persuaded a number of influential Japanese policy-makers in the LDP and economic ministries that the states of the region would find more advantages in using a basket of currencies including the yen in order to hedge their exchange risks. The result is likely to be the greater internationalization and use of the yen in East Asia as a trading currency and reserve. Thus, in May 1998 at the APEC finance ministers' meeting, Finance Minister Matsunaga Hikaru announced Japan's first official pledge to work towards the internationalization of the yen.

10.5 Summary

Japan's image as an effective and natural economic leader in East Asia certainly took an extensive battering during the financial crisis. However, as seen above, Japan to some extent has recovered this position and appears to be heading towards yet greater integration with the region at the start of the twenty-first century. The partial substitution of the yen for the dollar is one means of integration, and marks the first official acceptance by Japanese policy-makers since the establishment of the Greater East Asia Co-prosperity Sphere in 1942 of the need to establish the yen as a common unit of currency to bind the region together. Furthermore, even though the financial crisis has been seen to debunk the East Asian 'economic miracle' since 1997 and cooled the ardour of many of the industrialized countries for investments in the region, Japanese policy-making agents' and TNCs' faith in the developmental potential of the region has certainly not been lost and they look set to become still further involved in the region economically. The fall in the value of the currencies of the region has actually increased the attractiveness of the East Asian states as low-cost production and export platforms, and will lead eventually to the further shift of Japanese FDI to the region.

Consequently, this chapter has shown that Japan has attained a position of economic leadership in the East Asia region which has withstood even the shock of the financial and economic crises of 1997. Japan has created an economic region centred upon itself, and has instrumentalized this policy through the use of economic power, and, increasingly, the promotion of region-based multilateral economic frameworks and institutions. In the economic dimension, then, Japan has without doubt succeeded in reintegrating itself into and reorganizing the region in its own image, and generated an East Asian cooperation area, if not co-prosperity sphere (Yamashita 1998: 64).

Chapter 11

Japan–East Asia security relations

11.1 Overview

Chapter 8 elaborated how Japan was excluded from political, economic and security interaction with East Asia at the start of the post-war era. In turn, Chapters 9 and 10 examined the ways in which Japan has begun to reintegrate and reassert a position of leadership over an emergent East Asia region in the dimensions of politics and economics. This chapter now moves on to the dimension of security, in order to examine the extent to which Japan has been able to fulfil a similar role in reintegrating and leading a security region in East Asia, instrumentalized by means of both military and economic power. The discussion begins by looking at the structure, agency and norms factors which have influenced the nature of Japan's security role in the region, and then considers Japan's changing bilateral and multilateral links with the East Asian states during the Cold War and post-Cold War periods.

11.2 The pattern of Japan's security policy in East Asia

11.2.i Structure, agency and norms in Japan's security role in East Asia

Japan's security links with East Asia in the post-war era, both during and after the Cold War, have been determined predominantly by the international structural factors of the legacy of colonialism and bipolarity, and their associated norms of anti-militarism and bilateralism. By contrast, and as seen below, the norms of internationalism, developmentalism and Asianism have until recently played only a minor part in Japan's regional security policy.

As was indicated in Chapter 8, Japan's defeat in the Pacific War, the driving of its forces from its colonies on the East Asian continent and elsewhere, the atomic bombings of Hiroshima and Nagasaki and the state's total demilitarization planned during the initial period of the Occupation meant that Japan was to be removed, physically and psychologically, from East Asia as a major security actor in the immediate aftermath of the war. Defeat in East Asia, and the bitter process of the rapid acquisition and loss of colonies, engendered fear of Japanese militarism in the East Asian states, and raised once again the international structural barrier of the legacy of colonialism to security interaction between Japan and the newly independent states of the region. In turn, the structural barrier of the colonial past was reinforced by the emergent norms of anti-militarism, and, to a certain extent, internationalism. Accordingly, as Chapters 3 and 6 elucidated and Chapter 19 will elaborate, the initial intention following World War II was that Japan's defence and security policy would be centred on the principles of Article 9 of the 1947 Constitution and the UN Charter, precluding a significant role for Japan in either East Asian regional or global security. Nevertheless, as was outlined in Chapter 8, the onset of Cold War pressures in the late Occupation period, and then the twin crises of the outbreak of the Korean War in 1950 and the Taiwan Straits in 1954–5, meant that both US and conservative Japanese policy-makers became convinced that the security of Japan and East Asia, and the containment of a potential communist threat, could best be served by Japanese integration into the US half of the bipolar divide and the US bilateral alliance system. As a consequence, Japan's security policy towards, and links with, the East Asia region were to be determined, not only by the structural factor of the legacy of colonialism and the norm of anti-militarism, but also, and often more powerfully, by the international structural factor of bipolarity and the norm of bilateralism.

The mix of these international structural barriers and norms produced a distinctive pattern to Japan's military security policy in East Asia during the Cold War. The memory of the disastrous end to Japan's colonial and military exploits in East Asia during the Pacific War, cognizance of the legacy of colonialism, and anti-militarism norms and constitutional prohibitions, convinced conservative LDP politicians and government officials that Japan should avoid further damaging military entanglements and direct intervention on the East Asian continent, and rely instead for military security upon the US. Likewise, the East Asian states themselves, fearful of Japanese militarism, were wary of any direct Japanese involvement in regional military affairs and the expansion of Japan's military capabilities, and viewed the US–Japan alliance as a means with which actually to suppress or act as the 'cork in the bottle' of Japanese militarism. Thus, it can be seen that the legacy of colonialism and anti-militarist norms combined to restrain Japanese policy-making agents from attempts to establish direct military contact with, and make a direct contribution to, East Asian military security during the Cold War.

Instead, as shown below, Japan's adherence to the US half of the bipolar divide determined that its contribution to East Asian security would be made indirectly through the framework of the US–Japan alliance and support for the US overall alliance system in the region, and would be legitimized primarily pursuant to the norm of bilateralism. One consequence of this, as outlined later, has been to hinder Japan's participation in multilateral security arrangements in the region.

11.2.ii Japan's alternative security agenda

However, the adherence of Japan's LDP and government policy-makers to the bilateral military alliance with the US and the norms of bilateralism did not mean that they viewed this as the only dimension or avenue by which Japan could instrumentalize its own security and make a contribution to the stability of East Asia. As Chapter 2 demonstrated, although Japanese policy-makers in the government ministries and LDP have acquiesced since the onset of the Cold War in the need to rely on US military power in the Cold War period in order to assist in the defence of Japan, at the same time the awareness of the costs of war and anti-militarist norms have instilled in them an awareness of the limitations of military power as a means to deal with many forms of security. The result is that Japanese policy-making agents have developed alternative conceptions of security policy designed to supplement or even be substituted for military power in various instances. In particular, the notion of comprehensive security policy, as described in Chapter 2, has emphasized that Japan can contribute to regional security by reliance, not just upon the US–Japan alliance, but also upon the extension of economic power in the form of ODA and economic cooperation, and thereby address the root economic causes of social and political instability which often generate military conflict in the first place. As was seen in Chapter 8 and also below, Japan has been able to extend its economic power for security ends both in conformity with and by support for the US bilateral alliance system in the region, but also independently, as a non-military contribution to stability in the region which is not subject to the same international structural and normative barriers to interaction.

11.3 Japan and East Asian security in the Cold War period

11.3.i Japan and Southeast Asia

As noted in Chapter 9, the ASEAN states are of crucial strategic importance to Japan as sources of raw materials and markets, and because of their geographical position along the sea lines of communication (SLOC) which link Japan to the oil supplies of the Middle East. Hence, since 1980 the JDA's *White Paper on Defence* has reiterated that the 'security of the ASEAN countries is essential to Japan's own' (Bōeichōhen 1980: 78).

Still, despite the growth of economic interdependence and of shared strategic interests between Japan and the ASEAN states during the Cold War, the legacy of colonialism ensured that Japan's military contribution to the region's stability in this period was to be entirely indirect and made through the mechanism of the US–Japan alliance. As was outlined in Chapter 9, the Satō administration, in accordance with the US–Japan security treaty, supported the US war effort in Vietnam by the provision of bases. Nevertheless, at the same time Japanese policy-makers were also careful to prevent Japan from becoming embroiled directly in any military operations in Vietnam, as had been the case with the US's other allies in East Asia, South Korea and also Australia. Indeed, even after the US's commitment to East Asian security was seen to wane following the announcement of the Guam Doctrine in 1969 and the US withdrawal from Vietnam, Japan continued to stress to the ASEAN states, in line with the 1977 Fukuda Doctrine, that it would not seek to play a major military role in the region, and thus would not compensate for the declining military power of the US. The Japanese position, instead, was that Japan would endeavour to make a direct contribution to ASEAN security by diplomacy and economic means. Japan's active role in pushing for a resolution to the Cambodia problem and its expansion of ODA supplies to Thailand as a 'state bordering the area of conflict' during the onset of the second Cold War have been noted in Chapter 9.

The only military contact which took place between Japan and the ASEAN states in the Cold War period was the agreement between Singapore and Thailand in 1981 to send a limited number of personnel for training at the Japanese National Defence Academy; and the only bilateral consultations on security matters were generally cases of Japanese leaders during visits to Southeast Asia being forced to defend Japan against accusations of renewed militarism, one example being Prime Minister Nakasone Yasuhiro's visit in 1983 following the first textbook controversy of 1982 (Hughes 1996: 236).

11.3.ii Korean Peninsula

Chapter 9 has elucidated Japan's interest in ensuring stability on the Korean Peninsula, and the strategic rationale for Japanese and South Korean security cooperation in order to contain the perceived military threat from North Korea during the Cold War. The legacy of colonialism and South Korean suspicions of Japanese militarism ensured, however, that Japan's contribution to Korean Peninsula security was once again indirect and channelled predominantly through the agency of the US–Japan bilateral alliance.

As was explained in Chapter 6, the signing of the US–Japan security treaty in 1951 and then the revised security treaty in 1960 bound Japan into US containment strategy *vis-à-vis* North Korea, obligated as it was (after prior consultation in accordance with the 1960 exchange of notes between Prime Minister Kishi and the US secretary of state, Christian Herter) to provide bases for the US to use for the projection of its military power onto the Korean Peninsula. The revised security treaty further highlighted Japan's role in assisting the US to contain North Korea and maintain stability on the Korean Peninsula, with Prime Minister Kishi Nobusuke's definition of the scope of the operation of the security treaty in 1960 including South Korea (see Chapter 6).

Japan's underpinning of the US security presence in Northeast Asia, via the mechanism of the revised security treaty, thus constituted an indirect contribution to the security of the Korean Peninsula and South Korea in this period. During the late 1960s, as the US became progressively committed to military intervention in Vietnam, its policy-makers began to pressure Japan to assume more of the burden for ensuring stability in Northeast Asia and on the Korean Peninsula, and to draw a more direct link between Japanese and South Korean security. The first secret meeting between Japanese Ground Self-Defence Force (GSDF) chief, General Sugita Ichiji, and the South Korean defence minister, General Song Hyo Chan, was held in Tokyo in June 1961; and, as was explained in Chapter 6, the strategic importance of South Korea to Japan was also made clear by the 1969 joint communiqué between Prime Minister Satō Eisaku and President Richard Nixon in which the Japanese government stated that the 'security of the ROK was essential to Japan's own'. The possibility of Japanese direct military intervention on the Korean Peninsula in support of US forces was also raised for the first time by the uncovering of the 'Three Arrows Study' incident (*Mitsuya Kenkyū*) in February 1965. SDPJ member Okada Haruo revealed in the Diet that the SDF's confidential 1963 General Defence Plan of Operation contained provisions for Japan to assist the US in the event of a military crisis in East Asia provoked by a North Korean or Chinese invasion of South Korea. Included among these provisions were statements that Japan would necessarily act as an integral part of US security strategy in the Far East in order to contain the crisis; that US, Taiwanese, South Korean and Japanese troops would conduct joint training exercises; that Japan's MSDF would assist the US to blockade the eastern coast of China; and that the SDF could be despatched to act as a reserve force in South Korea and Manchuria. Prime Minister Satō at first denied the existence of the plan, but then later acknowledged its existence and defended it on the grounds that it was merely a theoretical study by the SDF (Hughes 1999: 113; Matsueda and Moore 1967; Wakamiya 1994: 126–49; Tanaka A. 1997: 215–16).

Nevertheless, despite the pressure that the US placed upon Japan and South Korea during the Cold War to cooperate on military security matters, the structural barrier of the legacy of colonialism ensured that neither of the US's allies was prepared to contemplate the establishment of direct security links with the other, and that both remained convinced that their security interests could best be guaranteed through their respective bilateral alliances with the US and the maintenance of the US military presence in and around the Korean Peninsula. As a result, Japan and South Korea combined to exert political pressure on the Carter administration to abandon its 1977 plan to withdraw US ground troops from South Korea (Murata 1998). Japan in this period, however, was prepared to make a direct contribution to South Korean stability through the extension of its economic power and the provision of ODA, as was described in Chapter 9.

11.3.iii China

Japan's security relations with China during the Cold War were determined by its role in assisting US containment policy through the mechanism of the US–Japan security treaty. Under provisions similar to those in respect of the Korean Peninsula, Japan was obligated by the security treaty to provide bases for US forces to defend Taiwan. Its pivotal position in US military strategy *vis-à-vis* China was subsequently highlighted following the revision of the security treaty in 1960 and Prime Minister's Kishi statement at the same time that Taiwan was included within its scope; and again prior to the 1970 automatic extension of the security treaty, with the statement in the 1969 Nixon–Satō communiqué that, alongside South Korea, 'the Taiwan area was also a most important factor for the security of Japan'.

Japan's integration into the US bilateral alliance system in East Asia necessarily precluded direct military contacts between Japan and China and generated Sino-Japanese security tensions. China's government condemned the signing of the security treaty in 1951, and its renewal and extension in 1960 and 1970, as attempts by the leaders of the US and Japan to perpetuate the national division of China, and to revive Japanese militarism in support of US hegemony in East Asia. In particular, China viewed the announcement of the Guam Doctrine in 1969, as was discussed in Chapter 6, with its emphasis upon the need for East Asian states to take a greater burden for their own defence, as a ploy to create a US-backed and Japan-headed counter-revolutionary coalition in East Asia. According to the Chinese official media, the US intended to 'unleash Japanese militarism' and to use

Japan as a 'gendarme in Asia and the fugleman in opposition to the Chinese, Koreans, Vietnamese, and all the other peoples of Asia' (Wang and Wu 1998: 13). Japanese policy-making agents were also concerned about the implications of the security treaty for political and economic relations with China and that military containment should not be the only option pursued. Chapter 9 indicated that even staunch anti-communists, such as Prime Ministers Yoshida, Kishi and Satō, viewed China's military capabilities in this period as very limited compared to those of the USSR, and were prepared to contemplate economic engagement rather than military containment as the optimum policy to ensure that China did not become a destabilizing factor in East Asian security. Moreover, Japanese policy-makers and opposition parties were aware that the obligation under the security treaty to provide bases for the US could involve Japan being dragged into a costly and unwelcome conflict between the US and China over the status of Taiwan.

However, despite the awareness of Japanese policy-makers that there were alternative or supplementary policies to military containment, and that support for the US military presence in East Asia carried risks, their calculation was that the US–Japan security treaty worked for overall stability in security relations between Japan and China. For even though Japanese policy-makers were aware that the US had imposed upon East Asia a bipolar security structure which contained sources of Sino-US conflict and by implication also possible Sino-Japanese conflict owing to Japan's integral position in support of US military strategy, they also expressed relative confidence that the sheer weight of US military hegemony in the region would prevent these sources of conflict from ever escalating into a full-blown military contingency. Thus, China's development and deployment of nuclear weapons from 1964 onwards, in reaction to the perceived threat from US and Soviet nuclear weapons, was not perceived by Japanese policy-makers to be a significant strategic threat, owing to their continued faith in the US nuclear umbrella (Welfield 1970). In addition, overwhelming US naval and air power in East Asia in effect barred any attempt by China to threaten Taiwan militarily, ensured that Taiwan remained largely inert as a security issue in this period, and meant that Japan's resolve to support US efforts to defend Taiwan never had to be tested. Similarly, although Japan and China continued to assert quietly their legal claims to the Senkaku Islands during the first Cold War period, the US's control of the islands as part of the territory of Okinawa prior to 1972 meant that this territorial dispute did not become a major Sino-Japanese security issue.

The advent of détente, *rapprochement* between the US and China, and normalization of Sino-Japanese relations eased the security tensions between China, the US and Japan in the 1970s and 1980s. China's decision to enlist US support in order to counterbalance the perceived Soviet threat meant that it was prepared to tolerate the existence of the US–Japan security treaty. As was touched on in Chapter 4, the US acceptance of the principle of the existence of 'one China' and that Taiwan was an integral part of it in the February 1972 Shanghai communiqué, and Japan's similar acceptance of a 'one China' policy by establishing relations with the PRC and abandoning the Japan–Taiwan peace treaty as a result of the normalization of bilateral issues later in 1972, lessened also the importance of

Taiwan as a security issue. The terms of the Sino-Japanese peace treaty of 1978 emphasized that it would not affect the treaties or relations of either signatory with a third party, and China indicated at the time of the treaty's negotiation that it was prepared to shelve the issue of whether Taiwan came within the scope of the US–Japan security treaty.

Sino-Japanese security relations during the rest of the Cold War period remained relatively stable, although indications surfaced of problems brewing throughout the second Cold War period of the 1980s. Despite the eventual normalization of Sino-US relations in January 1979, the insistence of the US Congress on passing in tandem with it in April 1979 the Taiwan Relations Act, which committed the US to selling arms to Taiwan sufficient to guarantee its own defence, and the determination of the Reagan administration to regain military dominance in East Asia, re-emphasized for China's leadership the dangers of US hegemony and a 'two Chinas' policy. In a similar fashion, the advent of the Nakasone administration and its build-up of Japan's quantitative and qualitative military strength in support of US strategy in East Asia raised once again Chinese fears of renewed Japanese militarism. The shelved issues of Japan's position with regard to support for US military intervention in Taiwan and the sovereignty of the Senkaku Islands also remained potentially explosive bilateral security problems between Japan and China.

11.3.iv *Japan and multilateral security in East Asia in the Cold War period*

During the Cold War period, Japan took no direct part in, and in fact shied away from, proposals for regional and multilateral security cooperation or dialogue. As was seen in Chapter 6, the norm of bilateralism precluded for Japanese policy-makers any type of multilateral security which might be seen to undermine the bilateral relationship with the US as the foundation of Japan's security. Hence, Japan was unenthusiastic about ASEAN's ZOPFAN concept, which seemed designed to exclude US influence from the region; Japan rejected proposals from President Leonid Brezhnev of the USSR in 1969 for a collective security system in East Asia, and then President Mikhail Gorbachev's proposal for a region-wide security community in 1988. These were all seen as Soviet attempts to drive a wedge between the US and its bilateral alliance partners, including Japan (Fukushima 1999: 140). Moreover, even when the build-up of Japan's defence commitments carried implications for the security of other states in Northeast and Southeast Asia, such as the issue of Japan assuming responsibility in 1981 for patrolling 1,000 nautical miles of SLOC around Japan, this was carried out entirely within the US–Japan bilateral framework. The result was that in this period, and as was outlined in Chapter 6, Japan's multilateral contribution to East Asian stability entirely took the form of quiet diplomatic initiatives in conjunction with ASEAN to deal with the Cambodia issue, and proposals for economic cooperation and limited political dialogue via concepts such as Pacific Trade and Development in 1968, and the Pacific Economic Cooperation Conference (PECC) in 1978 (Korhonen 1994: 167–81; Deng 1997: 36).

11.4 Japan and East Asian security in the post-Cold War period

11.4.i Changes in the post-Cold War international structure

The gradual winding-down of Cold War tensions in East Asia in the late 1980s and early 1990s – marked by the reduction of the Soviet military presence in the region, normalization of USSR–China relations in 1989, and the perceived decline of US military commitment to the region following its withdrawal from military bases in the Philippines in 1991–2 – removed many of the bipolar structural barriers to interaction amongst the region's states. At the same time, the imperatives for regional cooperation on security matters increased as the reduction of US and Soviet power reactivated a series of bilateral and multilateral disputes between the states of East Asia which previously had been suppressed under the weight of their competing military blocs during the Cold War. In particular, receding Cold War ideological confrontation gave way to the re-emergence of disputes centred on national divides and territorial sovereignty, which could spark a military conflict and require security approaches on the bilateral and multilateral levels for a successful resolution. In Northeast Asia, these issues included the competition for legitimacy and survival between the divided states of North and South Korea, and between China and Taiwan; and the territorial disputes amongst China, Taiwan and Japan over the Senkaku Islands, between South Korea and Japan over the Takeshima Islands, and between the USSR (later Russia) and Japan over the Northern Territories. In Southeast Asia, disputes re-emerged concerning competing claims in the South China Sea: between China and Vietnam over the Paracel Islands, and amongst China, Taiwan, Vietnam, Malaysia and the Philippines over the Spratly Islands (Valencia 1995). China is involved in nearly all these bilateral and multilateral disputes. The perceived increase in its military capabilities, and its willingness to deploy force in the service of its national aims since the end of the Cold War, have also convinced many states in the region that they need to counter, or at least temper, China's growing power by engaging China in various forms of bilateral and multilateral security frameworks so as to prevent it from becoming a destabilizing factor in regional security.

11.4.ii Complexity of the post-Cold War security agenda

In addition to these 'traditional' military problems and approaches to security, the rationale for region-wide and multilateral security cooperation in the post-Cold War period has been boosted by the course of the economic development of the region. East Asia's enhanced economic growth and economic interdependence in the late and post-Cold War periods has created the conditions for both enhanced friction and cooperation between the states of the region. On the one hand, economic interdependency creates friction as states and TNCs compete for energy and other natural resources, generates environmental destruction, and also can lead to economic dislocation and social disruption – as happened in the East Asian currency crisis; all of these threaten stability amongst the states of the region and the security of their individual citizens. On the other hand, economic interdependency creates an imperative for states and TNCs to cooperate to maximize wealth generation; it also creates a demand for multilateral bodies, which can coordinate the economic integration of the region and prevent economic dislocation and its attendant security problems. In turn, the initiation of multilateral economic bodies in the region, such as APEC, although not designed specifically to deal with political and military security issues, has indicated to the policy-makers of the region the necessity and potential of some type of multilateral security dialogue in order to assist in the resolution of the national and territorial disputes identified above.

11.4.iii Japan's bilateral security links with East Asia in the post-Cold War period

Japan's response to this weakening of the bipolar barriers to security interaction with the rest of the states of East Asia, and the new security challenges it and growing economic interdependency have engendered in the post-Cold War period, has been to pursue limited bilateral and multilateral security dialogue across the region. As examined in more detail below in the discussion of its participation in multilateral security, Japan's extension of bilateral security linkages in this period has been viewed as a means to supplement rather than to supplant the existing bilateral security relationship with the US, and, indeed, has in many cases really only been made possible and initiated in conjunction with the US policy on regional security.

The Japanese government announced officially for the first time in 1995 that it would exploit the new opportunities offered to it by the ending of the Cold War to begin to overcome the legacy of colonialism in the region and to augment security dialogue and confidence-building measures with the states of the region. In fact, the JDA and MOFA had already begun to extend these links in the late 1980s to the ASEAN states, South Korea and China. Appendix 11.1 demonstrates the development and nature of these links, and that the success of Japan's policy has varied. In the case of ASEAN, Japan made remarkable progress towards dispelling some of the suspicion in Southeast Asia concerning its militaristic past, especially since the SDF's participation in UNPKOs in Cambodia in 1993, which represented the first direct contribution that Japan's military had made to East Asian security since the end of the Pacific War. Progress in Japan–South Korea bilateral security relations has also been remarkable, with various personnel exchanges and training exercises since 1992. These have taken place in spite of the fact that the South Korean government continued to warn against renewed Japanese militarism up until 1991. As seen in the last section of this chapter, Japan–South Korea bilateral dialogue has, however, been pushed along in the main by mutual concerns about the North Korean security threat, and in conjunction with the US, which has looked to build up a pattern of triangular US–Japan–South Korea security cooperation in order to counter any military contingency on the Korean Peninsula (Yamaguchi 1999: 3–24). In October 1998, for instance, following the North Korean missile launch, the Japan–ROK joint declaration pledged increased defence exchanges and consultations.

By contrast, Sino-Japanese security dialogue has not progressed so smoothly, even though the Japanese government has been attempting to engage China on a number of security concerns since the mid-1980s (Whiting 1989: 132). In particular, bilateral security dialogue has been hampered by Japan's concern that China should increase the transparency of its military budget and capabilities, curb its exports of missile technology in line with the Missile Technology Control Regime(MCTR), and cease nuclear weapon testing. Bilateral dialogue was interrupted in 1989 following the Tiananmen Square incident, and again following China's nuclear tests in 1995. Japanese officials are constantly looking to engage China on a range of security issues, but, as will be seen in section 11.4.v on Japan and the US alliance, growing anxieties about China's military intentions and the Taiwan Straits crisis of March 1995 have worked fully to reintegrate Japan back into the US alliance system, and to ensure that its principal security interaction with China remains within the framework of the bilateral US–Japan security treaty.

11.4.iv Japan and multilateral security in East Asia in the post-Cold War period

As Chapters 8 and 9 and the sections above have indicated, during the Cold War period the East Asia region was characterized predominantly by bilateral security arrangements, but in the post-Cold War period the necessary conditions have begun to emerge for the initiation of multilateral security dialogue. Gorbachev's 1988 proposal has already been noted, and this was followed by separate proposals from the foreign ministers of Canada and Australia in 1990 for the creation of a Conference on Security and Cooperation in Asia, modelled on the example of the Conference on Security and Cooperation in Europe (CSCE). The major military powers in East Asia were at first against any proposals for multilateral security arrangements. The US viewed multilateral security arrangements as ineffective in the region, preferring its bilaterally-based 'hubs and spokes system'; and China was concerned that multilateral discussion of issues such as the Spratly Islands in the South China Sea might undermine its claims to exclusive territorial sovereignty. ASEAN was also concerned that any region-wide multilateral security arrangement might weaken its legitimacy and overshadow it. Japan's position was similar to that of the US: namely, it was concerned that any multilateral arrangement might undermine the bilateral security frameworks in the region which had seemingly been so successful in ensuring stability in the past (Leifer 1996: 16–20, 23–4, 37–8; Nishihara 1994: 63–5). Thus, in July 1990 Prime Minister Kaifu stated that it was too early for any type of multilateral security arrangement in the region.

Nevertheless, by June 1991 the ASEAN Institutes of Strategic and International Studies (ASEAN ISIS) had begun to consider proposals that the ASEAN Post-Ministerial Conference (ASEAN PMC) be used as a forum for multilateral dialogue in the region, concerned as they were to consider some security framework in the region which could hedge against any possible decline in US military commitment to the region, or the growing military assertiveness of China. Japanese policy-makers also moved towards acceptance of the principle of multilateral dialogue following Gorbachev's visit to Japan in April 1991 and then the eventual break-up of the USSR in December 1991, all of which indicated the possibility of improvement in Russo-Japanese relations and signalled that the USSR and Russia no longer posed an effective threat to the bilateral alliance with the US. Accordingly, Foreign Minister Nakayama Tarō launched an initiative at the July 1991 ASEAN PMC, proposing that in the future the meeting should become 'a forum for political dialogue ... designed to improve the sense of mutual security' amongst East Asian states. Nakayama's proposal was at first greeted coolly by the ASEAN states, but it succeeded in helping to move the US towards official acceptance of the principle of multilateral dialogue by 1993, and, along with the 1991 ASEAN ISIS proposals, became the basis for the agreement to create the ARF in July 1993. Since 1994, the ARF has met annually after each ASEAN PMC. It is committed to a three-stage evolution: from confidence-building measures, to preventive diplomacy, to conflict resolution; it also takes an evolutionary approach, stating that progress from one stage to the next is dependent upon securing the consensus of all ARF members. The ARF inter-governmental process is also supported by a 'track-two' process (that is, involving non-governmental as well as governmental representatives) of contacts between academics and government officials from across the region in bodies such as the Council for Security Cooperation in the Asia-Pacific (CSCAP). By the time of the sixth ARF in 1999, membership had grown to encompass the ASEAN-10, Japan, China, South Korea, Mongolia, Russia, Papua New Guinea, Australia, New Zealand, Canada and the US. China dropped its objection to the ARF in order to influence the process from within and has attended all the ARF meetings since 1994. As of 2000, the stage of preventive diplomacy had not been reached: the completion of this stage and progression to the next had been blocked by China's reluctance to accept the working definitions of preventive diplomacy.

Japan has taken a full role in both the inception and the running of the ARF since the Nakayama proposal in 1991. The concept of the ARF is an attractive one for Japan because it espouses cooperative security based on attempts to build up a structure of peaceful relations amongst its members that are neither confrontational nor coercive, and does not designate any specific threat. Cooperative security emphasizes security with, rather than against, other members, and political and diplomatic more than military means (Kamiya 1997: 23–4). In addition, it does not demand any type of formal commitment to defend other members as with a collective security arrangement. Thus, Japan's participation in the ARF does not clash with its anti-militarist norms and constitutional prohibitions, or with its attachment to bilateralism and the US–Japan security treaty, yet it provides a political and diplomatic multilateral avenue for it to contribute to the region's security. As a consequence, Japanese MOFA and JDA officials have taken part in ARF senior officials meetings and inter-sessional meetings on PKO held prior to the ARF working sessions themselves, and co-chaired with Indonesia in 1997 inter-sessional support groups on confidence-building measures. Japanese academics and policy-makers have also taken part in the CSCAP process (Dobson 1999b). Meanwhile, in a separate process from the ARF, the Japanese government has conducted regular Asia-Pacific security seminars since 1994, inviting uniformed officers from a number of countries, including China, South Korea, Russia and the US, to discuss regional security matters and confidence-building measures. The Japanese government has further dabbled in multilateral security concepts in the region by suggesting since 1997 the possibility of a four-way dialogue on security amongst Japan, the US, Russia and China, and that Japan and Russia could be added to the four-way peace talks over the Korean Peninsula to create a six-way peace framework.

Japan's support for the ARF is certainly an important development in its security policy within the region, but nevertheless clear limits exist as to how far it is prepared to commit itself to a multilateral security framework and to depart from its adherence to the bilateral US–Japan alliance. The first consideration is that, even though Japan has been influential in persuading the US to back multilateral security dialogue in the region and has taken a rare diplomatic lead over the US in this instance, it has only ever been able to contemplate multilateral security dialogue in the knowledge that the ARF process in no way threatens to supplant but only to supplement the existing bilateral relationship with the US (Hook 1998: 182). The second consideration is that Japanese policy-makers in the JDA and MOFA perceive the ARF to have only a limited use in ensuring security in the region. This is because the ARF is purely a forum for cooperative dialogue rather than any type of collective security action, and owing to Chinese objections and North Korea's absence from the forum (North Korea finally joined in mid-2000) has a limited mandate to discuss such pressing security issues as the Spratly Islands, Taiwan and North Korea's proliferation of WMD (Yamakage 1997: 302). The third and related consideration is that Japanese policy-making agents remain wedded to the norm of bilateralism and to the US–Japan security treaty as the foundation of Japan's security. In part, this is due to US pressure on Japan not to expand its role in multilateral security bodies: for as Chapter 6 has made clear, the attempts by the Prime Minister's Advisory Group on Defence in 1994 to prioritize multilateral security arrangements over the US–Japan alliance were quashed by US objections. More important, however, it has been security concerns surrounding the Korean Peninsula and the Taiwan Straits which have reaffirmed for Japanese policy-makers the indispensability of the bilateral security treaty for Japan's security. Their principal diplomatic efforts and contribution to East Asian security have thus been devoted to shoring up the US–Japan alliance and US military presence in the region.

11.4.v United States–Japan alliance and regional security in the post-Cold War period

As Chapter 8 made clear, Japan's initial integration into the US bilateral alliance system in East Asia was occasioned by the twin crises of the Korean War and the Taiwan Straits. In the mid-1990s, the re-emergence of crisis situations on the Korean Peninsula and in the Taiwan Straits once again led to Japan's further integration into the US alliance system in the region. Chapters 4, 5 and 6 have shown how in the early post-Cold War period the US commitment to the bilateral alliance with Japan was seen to be threatened by disputes over trade, Japan's perceived reluctance to make a 'human contribution' to the Gulf War, and uncertainty over the future status of US bases in Okinawa – all of which seemed to augur for Japan's possible move away from exclusive dependence upon the US in matters of security. In turn, the events of the North Korean nuclear crisis of 1994, as was outlined in Chapter 9, were to compound the concerns in the minds of Japanese policy-makers about the future viability of the US–Japan alliance. Under Article VI of the US–Japan security treaty, Japan is obligated, after prior consultation with the US, to provide to it bases to be used for the maintenance of security in the region, which according to the Japanese government's own 1960 definition included South Korea. In the run-up to the nuclear crisis in mid-1994, the US's natural expectation was that in a new Korean conflict, it would be able to reinforce its military presence in South Korea with the despatch of military forces from bases in Japan. The Japanese government was uncomfortable with the prospect of even this indirect involvement in another Korean War, but as the nuclear crisis escalated it also began to receive US requests for more active and direct support for the US military position in South Korea. Specifically, the US asked the Japanese government to provide various forms of rear-end logistical support such as intelligence-gathering, facilities for the repair of US warships in Japan, and the use by the US military of Japanese civilian harbours and airports. In addition, the US military appealed for SDF participation in a naval blockade of North Korea and for the despatch of MSDF minesweepers to Korean waters (Hughes 1999: 93–6; George Mulgan 1997: 148).

The Japanese government, however, was unable to respond effectively to US requests for assistance. The 1978 Guidelines for US–Japan Defence Cooperation, which were discussed in Chapter 6, had not produced sufficient research on plans for Japan to support the US in the event of an emergency situation in East Asia, and concerns were raised among policy-makers that any direct involvement in Korean Peninsula security could contravene constitutional prohibitions on the exercise of the right of collective self-defence. Therefore, the Japanese government was forced to communicate to the US government that, although it was prepared to allow US forces to use bases in Japan to support its military operations in South Korea, it would be unable to provide logistical support or participate in blockade and minesweeping operations. Japanese policy-makers were aware that their response would appear inadequate to their US counterparts, and feared that, as in the Gulf War, US opinion would begin to question the value of an alliance under which Japan enjoyed the benefits of US protection, but in return was seemingly unable even to contribute to rear-end logistical operations to support its ally's forces engaged in a conflict close to Japan and with implications for Japan's own security (Hughes 1999: 94–5). Fortunately, the North Korean nuclear crisis was averted by the diplomatic intervention of the ex-president of the US, Jimmy Carter, and Japan's resolve to support its ally during a military contingency in the East Asia region was not fully tested. Nevertheless, the crisis did induce considerable political trauma in the US–Japan alliance, and raised questions in the minds of US and Japanese policy-makers about the future utility of the alliance. The eventual response of Japanese policy-makers to this Korean Peninsula crisis, informed by their bilateral norms, was to look to restore confidence in the alliance as the foundation of Japan's security in much the same way as at the time of the Korean War in 1950. As was seen in Chapter 6, this was carried out by the issuing of the US–Japan Joint Declaration on Security in April 1996, and then the conduct of research into and the passing of the revised Guidelines for US–Japan Defence Cooperation in May 1999.

In conjunction with the situation on the Korean Peninsula, the other crisis which worked to reintegrate Japan into the US bilateral alliance system in East Asia was that of the Taiwan Straits in March 1996. As noted in Chapter 9 and earlier in this chapter, Japanese policy-makers along with those of many other states in the region have become increasingly concerned in the post-Cold War period by the rising military power of China. In particular, Japan has been concerned about China's nuclear testing and export of missile technology, and the fact that the modernization of its military forces means that with even a small blue-water naval capacity it can disrupt Japan's SLOCs in the South China Sea. To some extent, Japanese concerns about China's military intentions were confirmed by its military intimidation of Taiwan with missile tests and military exercises in the run-up to the presidential elections on the island in March 1996, which drew the response from the US of the despatch of the aircraft carrier *Independence* based in Japan to the Taiwan Straits in order to illustrate US resolve to intervene in any conflict involving Taiwan. This crisis demonstrated to Japanese policy-making agents the potential threat that China's expanding military power could pose to East Asian security, and the possibility of renewed Sino-US conflict over the Taiwan issue in the post-Cold War period. Japanese policy-makers have remained conscious of the risks of being dragged into a Sino-US conflict owing to Japan's position as the provider of bases for the US to employ in the defence of Taiwan. Above all, however, the crisis in 1996 reinforced for them the continuing need to hedge against any future Chinese military threat by strengthening the US military presence in the region, thus creating further momentum for the review of the Guidelines.

The impact of the North Korean and Taiwan Straits security crises has been, then, to persuade Japanese policy-makers in MOFA, the JDA and political parties to prioritize the strengthening of Japan's bilateral security links with the US rather than the development of its multilateral links with the other states of the region. The subsequent effect of Japan's reconfirmation and redefinition of its bilateral links with the US has been to create new triangular patterns of security interaction amongst Japan, South Korea and the US, as well as amongst Japan, China and the US, which have made for cooperation and conflict respectively. In tandem with the strengthening of the US–Japan alliance in order to deal with any security contingency involving North Korea, Japan and South Korea have stepped up their bilateral cooperation, as was indicated in Chapter 9 and in previous sections of this chapter, and the US–Japan–South Korea interaction has also created new frameworks for security cooperation. The degree of actual Japan–South Korea security cooperation, even within a trilateral forum involving the US, necessarily continues to be limited by the legacy of colonialism, South Korean opposition to Japan playing any direct role in Korean Peninsula security such as the despatch of the

Plate 11.1 'Who will make him listen?' The US, Japan, South Korea and China ponder ways to persuade Kim Il Sung's North Korea to halt its nuclear programme. The 1994 crisis marked the emergence of US–Japan–South Korea security cooperation, whilst China has remained ambivalent.

Source: Cartoon by Yamada Shin published in the *Asahi Shimbun*, 31 March 1994. Copyright 1994, Asahi Shimbunsha. Reprinted with permission

SDF, and Japanese constitutional prohibitions on collective security. Still, as well as diplomatic consultation between the three states at trilateral summits and at international summits such as APEC as was outlined in Chapter 9, since 1997 regular JDA–ROK Ministry of Defence–US Department of Defense discussions have taken place, and since 1999 a Trilateral Coordination and Oversight Group on North Korea, consisting of senior foreign ministry officials, has been initiated. These official government talks have been further reinforced by track-two dialogue amongst Japanese, South Korean and US research institutes.

With regard to Sino-Japanese security interaction, the outcome of the revised Guidelines has been to increase security tensions to some degree. As Chapter 6 made clear, the most controversial item in the revised Guidelines bill passed in

May 1999 was the definition of *shūhen*, or range of action of US–Japan security cooperation under the Guidelines, as situational rather than geographical in nature. This represents an attempt by the Japanese government to move away from its 1960 definition of the scope of the US–Japan security treaty as broadly geographical in nature and including the area north of the Philippines, South Korea and Taiwan. This shift in emphasis from geographical to situational carries two apparent advantages for Japanese security planners. First, it allows the government, when required (based on the concept of situational need), to expand the range of action of the US–Japan alliance beyond the traditional geographical limits of East Asia and the security treaty as defined in 1960, and to encompass the entire Asia-Pacific region as envisaged in the US–Japan Joint Declaration. Second, the concept of situational need introduces for Japanese policy-makers a valuable element of strategic ambiguity into the coverage of the US–Japan security treaty. It offers the particular advantage of leaving vague the position of China as an object of the Guidelines. In line with the 1960 definition of the Far East, Taiwan is covered by the US–Japan security treaty, and the events of 1996 demonstrated that China–Taiwan tensions are still a major concern for the US–Japan alliance. However, as noted previously, the policy of the US and Japan appears to be to hedge against a possible military contingency involving China by strengthening the bilateral alliance, but also to avoid the designation of China as a threat for fear of antagonizing it and endangering the general policy of engagement. The concept of situational need seems to be ideally designed for this policy as it enables the US and Japan to de-emphasize the clear-cut geographical specification of Taiwan as part of *shūhen* and a concern of the US–Japan security treaty and the Guidelines, but at the same time retains for the alliance the option to operate in the Taiwan Straits if necessary. However, China has clearly not been convinced by the obfuscating language of the revised Guidelines and has continually denounced them as an attempt to interfere in internal Chinese politics between the mainland and Taiwan. Moreover, the Chinese government has become concerned that Japan's participation in the TMD programme, as was described in Chapter 6, has been designed as a means to negate China's nuclear deterrent and ballistic missiles in any future conflict over the Taiwan Straits, further raising Chinese suspicions that Japan might assist the US to enable Taiwan to declare its independence. The result has been rising Sino-Japanese security tensions since the initiation of the Guidelines review. As a consequence, bilateral summits have often been marred by wrangling between Japan and China over the coverage of the Guidelines and Japan's security relations with the US.

11.4.vi Japanese economic power and security policy in the post-Cold War period

The above discussion has demonstrated that a large proportion of Japanese policy-making energy in the post-Cold War period has been devoted to traditional military security concerns and the redefinition of the US–Japan alliance. Nevertheless, it is not the case that Japan's only contribution to East Asian security has been and continues to be via military means. As the earlier sections in this chapter have indicated, Japan's conception of security in the region also extends to include non-military and economic aspects, as derived from the norm of developmentalism and the belief that economic progress and interdependence can become the ultimate guarantors of peace and security. Consequently, it is in this area of security that it is possible to view Japan as more directly engaged with the region. In particular, the East Asian financial crisis and the problems of social degradation and environmental destruction that it has triggered have produced a 'human security' agenda, which can only be addressed effectively by the extension of economic power.

Japanese policy-makers have been criticized for their slow response to the economic problems arising from the East Asian financial crisis, but have responded to the security problems it has engendered with the announcement by Prime Minister Obuchi at the Japan–ASEAN summit in Hanoi in December 1998 of an initiative on 'human security'. Under this initiative Japan emphasized that its financial aid to the region would be devoted not just to economic restructuring but also to meeting the food and medical needs of the crisis-hit populations of the region (JCIE and ISEAS 1998). In this sense, then, it can be seen that Japan's anti-militarist norms continue to push Japan to instrumentalize a direct security role in the region based on economic rather than military power.

11.5 Summary

The preceding sections have demonstrated how the pattern of Japan's security interaction with East Asia has been conditioned by the international structural legacies of bipolarity and colonialism, and the norms of bilateralism and anti-militarism. During the Cold War period, these structure and agency factors combined to cordon off Japan from direct security relations with other East Asian states and ensured that its military contribution to regional security was indirect and channelled through the agency of the US–Japan alliance. Japan did not participate in multilateral security arrangements and instead its principal and direct security contribution to East Asia was made by the extension of its economic power.

In the post-Cold War period, the change in the structure of the international system has enabled Japan to experiment with multilateral forms of security dialogue in East Asia. The norm of bilateralism, however, has meant that Japan's main contribution to military security has remained indirect and located within the framework of the bilateral alliance with the US. Thus, in many ways the dimension of military security continues to be the missing link in Japan's relations with the region. Even though Japan has made major progress in overcoming the structural barriers – of the colonial past, national division, and bipolarity – to interaction with the states of East Asia in the post-war era, its military security ties remain predominantly with the US as in 1952. However, the continuing lack of multilateral security links with the East Asia has, at the same time, obliged Japan to pursue an innovative, and often highly effective, security policy based on economic power and oriented to the new post-Cold War challenges of human security.

Chapter 12

Conclusion

12.1 Association of Southeast Asian Nations + 3 revisited

Chapter 8 presented the ASEAN + 3 summit meeting in 1997 as a striking example of the progress made in the political, economic and security integration of the East Asia region in the post-Cold War period and Japan's central role within this process. As noted in Chapter 8, this turnaround in the status of the region as a whole, and Japan's place within it, appeared even more remarkable in the light of our knowledge of the fractured nature of the region's political economy in the post-war era, and the rejection of Japan's legitimacy as a regional actor following its failed efforts to unite the region under its imperial auspices in the years prior to and during the Pacific War. Given these developments in the region, the overall objective of Chapters 9, 10 and 11 was to examine – in the interrelated dimensions of politics, economics and security – the nature of Japan's relations with East Asia in the post-war era, and the extent to which Japan has functioned to reintegrate the region and succeeded in regaining a central, or even leading, position within it.

12.2 Japan's reconstruction of an East Asia region

Japan has managed largely to overcome post-war international structural barriers – bipolarity, legacy of colonialism, national division, fragmented political economy – to interaction with China, the Korean Peninsula and the ASEAN states. Japanese policy-making agents have been motivated in this regionalist project by a mix of norms. Bilateralism and anti-militarism have played a significant role, but it has been developmentalism and Asianism which have most consistently driven Japan's policy forward. These have emerged as the dominant norms in its East Asian policy in the post-Cold War period. Japan's pursuit of these developmental and Asianist norms has been instrumentalized by a process of long-term and quiet diplomacy – probing the limits of US bipolarity and the international structure – and characterized by the application of economic power.

As a result of Japan's policy, the groundwork has been laid for improved bilateral relations between Japan and its East Asian neighbours; to promote the integration of all the East Asian states in such a way that it is now possible for them to consider the construction of region-wide political, economic and security frameworks in the post-Cold War period; and for Japan to reach the point where it is now considered by some states as an appropriate leader for the region. Hence, in the post-Cold War period, Japan has assumed a pivotal role, whether behind the scenes or by more overt diplomatic initiatives, in the creation of nascent regional institutions. In the political sphere, the emergence of the EAEC concept has posited Japan as the potential leader of an exclusively East Asian economic and, consequently, political bloc; in the economic sphere, the AMF designated Japan as the main provider of financial public goods in the region; and in the security sphere, the ARF offers Japan a potential regional security role outside of the framework of the US–Japan alliance.

Clearly, Japan's position and the legitimacy of its leadership do not remain uncontested in the region by either China or the US, or indeed other regional actors, as shown by the fact that the EAEC and AMF concepts have been held in abeyance. Japanese policy-makers themselves also remain reluctant to exercise leadership from the front; to exploit the opportunities of Asianism and internationalism to the full; and to endorse frameworks which could form an exclusive regional body centred upon Japan, and which would generate tensions with China, the US and other states in the region.

Nevertheless, Japan, through a policy of careful re-engagement and quiet diplomacy with East Asian states in the post-war era, has undoubtedly succeeded in manoeuvring itself into a position whereby it has regained the ability to construct and lead a latent East Asia region. Even the failed or deferred projects of EAEC and the AMF are more representative as examples of Japan's increasing long-term influence in the region, rather than as evidence of an irrecoverable deficit in Japan's leadership capacity: for it is apparent that, even though neither of them has yet come to fruition, both ascribe a leadership role for Japan and have planted the seeds of enhanced Asianist sentiment in Japan and the other states in the region – the outcome of which can only be to propel Japan and East Asia closer together over the long term.

Thus, the story of the 'what', 'why' and 'how' of Japan's relations with East Asia in the post-war era has been one of a cautious, yet determined, strategy to rebuild its links with other East Asian states and to reintegrate them into a coherent political, economic and security region. Japan's task in binding together the region is clearly not finished, but without doubt can be raised that its patient efforts have made a major contribution towards making possible the institutionalization of region-wide dialogue in the form of the ASEAN + 3 summit, and have enabled it to reassume an East Asian identity and to interact with its neighbours in this regional and multilateral forum.

Part IV

JAPAN–EUROPE RELATIONS

Chapter 13

Introduction

13.1 Obuchi calls for a new currency era

On 1 January 1999 the EU launched its single currency, the euro. By 6 January, Japanese Prime Minister Obuchi Keizō had arrived in Paris to begin a week-long tour of the major EU capitals and to solicit support for a new financial order centred upon the dollar, the euro and the yen. To be framed within a loose exchange rate grid, this new order would, it was hoped, prevent the marginalization of the yen in the global marketplace (*Financial Times*, 6 January 1999). Finance Minister Miyazawa Kiichi and Foreign Minister Kōmura Masahiko were equally active in promoting this trilateral initiative, and in emphasizing the likely international political as well as economic impact (MOFA 1999a).

Why should this Japanese attention to Europe be so startling? After all, the EU in 1999 numbered some 370 million people and supported a gross domestic product (GDP) of over US$24,000 per capita (compared with US$34,000 for the US). In addition, the EU's fifteen member states were already engaged in dialogue with six 'fast-track' countries (namely Cyprus, the Czech Republic, Estonia, Hungary, Poland and Slovenia), primarily from Central and Eastern Europe, in the first round of accession negotiations, whilst at least a further four were waiting in the wings. As a result, the early decades of the twenty-first century could witness the formation of a union of more than twenty-five countries. These impressive figures notwithstanding, Japan rarely showed much interest in Europe during the post-war era and even in 2000 only a small number of Japanese politicians, bureaucrats, journalists and business people were engaged regularly with their European counterparts. For many Japanese people, 'Europe' remains only an interesting holiday destination.

Nevertheless, changes are taking place. In the economic realm, the Single European Market (SEM) project of 1992 has become a reality and the impact of integrated economic structures is being felt throughout the rest of the world. Japanese business concerns have not remained unaffected by prospects of 'fortress Europe', and investors such as Toyota have put themselves at the forefront of activity in responding to changes deriving from the new single currency. Politically, too, the EU has become more visible on the international stage, to the extent that it now speaks regularly as a group in several international fora in which Japanese officials also participate. These include bodies of the UN, the ARF, the ASEAN PMC and ASEM. As far as security issues are concerned, in spite of the presence of NATO on European soil, since the revival of the Western European Union (WEU) in 1984, repeated attempts have been made to create a greater security role for the EU *per se*. Japan's closer relations with NATO combine with growing mutual concerns over security in Russia and former Yugoslavia to ensure that activities in this field, too, have now become a component of Japan–Europe affairs. Whilst the cumulative impact of these proliferating engagements remains paltry when compared with Japan's well-established relations with the US and its long, if often contentious, interaction with the rest of East Asia, developments between Japan and Europe are becoming more important. This and the following chapters will show how Japan–Europe relations, which were once characterized by neglect, misunderstanding and mistrust (Wilkinson 1981; Daniels and Drifte 1986), and diverted by the norm of bilateralism, have over time become influenced by the norm of trilateralism in the context of a changing world order.

In order to understand how Japanese observers and practitioners view the different levels of actors who combine to constitute 'Europe', the following chapters will examine the changing nature of Japan's relations with the member states of the European Community (EC)/Union; with the key organs of the EU itself; and with the major countries of Central and Eastern Europe. By examining the pattern of Japan's relations with Europe in the political, economic and security dimensions (the 'what' question) this part will assess why particular forms of behaviour have been adopted (the 'why' question). The means and method of Japan's actions (the 'how' question) will be shown to inform these orientations. In addition, it will be demonstrated that Japan's approaches towards, and responses to, Europe have been influenced by dominant bilateral norms that have given way over time to trilateral norms. Prior to addressing these questions, the remainder of this chapter provides an overview which focuses in particular upon Japan–Europe relations since 1945.

13.2 From early encounters to defeat in World War II

Japan's early encounters with Europe came in the sixteenth century, when Portuguese and subsequently Spanish missionaries came armed with bibles and muskets to introduce Western culture to the Japanese (Storry 1982). Following the reopening of Japan during the 1850s, its newly created government adopted much of its knowledge from European models, which were used as a 'guide to Western-style modernization in all its aspects' (Beasley 1990: 87). The Iwakura Mission of 1862, for example, visited Great Britain, France, Belgium, Holland, Germany, Russia and some Mediterranean countries in addition to the US, in order to learn about societal structures, including government systems, military establishments, churches, museums, banks, schools, factories, law courts and parliaments. Japan's relationship with the European imperialists, however, was not always a smooth one. Following the Treaty of Shimonoseki to end the Sino-Japanese war in April 1895, the Japanese were indignant about the 'triple intervention' shortly thereafter by France, Germany and Russia, which 'advised' the Japanese government, *inter alia*, to abandon claims to the Liaotung Peninsula so as not to threaten the 'peace of the Far East' (Storry 1982: 127). The psychological effects of this action were tremendous and left a negative impression in Japan towards the European early-starters for many decades to follow.

After the successful revocation of the so-called 'unequal treaties' with several European powers by the turn of the century, the signing of the 1902 Anglo-Japanese Alliance was prompted by fear of continuing Russian advancement southward and a guarantee that Japan would receive a free hand in Korea. These events went some way towards restoring national pride and served as a major boost for Japanese credibility. This agreement ensured for the Japanese that

Plate 13.1 Unlikely allies? This commemorative postcard marks the signing of the Anglo-Japanese Alliance in January 1902. The bilateral alliance lasted until 1923 and demonstrates Japan's strategy of 'piggy-backing' with the great power of the day.

Source: Courtesy of Neil Pedlar and Japan Library

British neutrality could be secured in the event of war with Russia. It also demonstrated the retreat by Great Britain from its policy of 'splendid isolation'. Later, this Anglo-Japanese Alliance would be cited by Japan in its claim for former German territories in China during World War I. Relations with this imperial power were important in promoting Japan's international status during the early twentieth century. Japan's victory in its war with Russia (1904–5) further reinforced its newly-acquired imperialist status, when the vanquished agreed to recognize Japan's 'paramount political, military and economic interests' in Korea, to transfer the lease of the Liaotung Peninsula and railway line from Port Arthur to beyond Mukden, and to cede half of Sakhalin with special fishing rights. However, Japan as a late-starter felt that it had been under-rewarded for its war success.

Initial clashes in East Asia did not bring Europeans into the Japanese war. Whilst the Anti-Comintern Pact of 1936 committed Japan to cooperate with Germany against international communism, the Tripartite Pact with Germany and Italy in September 1940 brought the Japanese much more closely into line with the fascist powers. As a result, Japanese relations with other European powers were weakened, and when the US froze Japanese assets in July 1941, other West European powers followed.

Following Japan's defeat in the Pacific War, the terms of surrender created a greater distance between Japan and Western Europe, especially since the arrival of the Supreme Command for the Allied Powers (SCAP) ensured the development of Japan's closer relations with the US (see Chapters 3 and 4). Growing calls for independence by former colonies, and concerns with domestic and regional affairs, drew European powers away from this region and further consolidated the distancing of the European early-starter powers from East Asia generally.

13.3 Core states of Europe

At the end of the war, Japan found no opportunity to renew relations with the major industrial powers of Europe. The states of Western Europe were eager to pool much-needed post-war resources and to draw Germany into a regional community, thereby focusing upon the affairs of their own continent. Further afield, events such as the 1956 Suez Crisis consumed the energies of the UK and France. The roles of Austria and Germany in Europe paralleled in some ways the role of Japan in East Asia. All were occupied by Allied forces and were of regional strategic significance. However, unlike in the Occupation of Japan, occupation policies in Europe were led by the UK, France and the USSR in conjunction with the US. Austria, viewed as a potential satellite by the USSR, was also rocked by pro-communist coup attempts in 1947 and 1950. Thus, again unlike Japan, it was caught in the middle of the early Cold War in a most direct way, although, paradoxically, this direct involvement was to lead to a settlement ensuring Austrian neutrality. Germany, by contrast, was separated into four occupation zones at the end of the World War II and eventually came to be divided into East and West, with the USSR controlling the East. The Eastern part became known as the German Democratic Republic (GDR) and claimed to be the legitimate successor to the former German state. West Germany, or the Federal Republic of Germany (FRG), for its part, was rehabilitated through its central role in the European Economic Community (EEC) that was established from 1 January 1958 by the Treaty of Rome (1957). Germany's politics, economics and security were subsumed within this regional grouping. As a result, it did not have to push for its own re-entry into the international community, in the way that Japan did after regaining independence.

The rising power of the US, and the US-dominated Occupation of Japan from 1945 to 1952, meant that Japan's relationship with the major industrial powers of Europe diminished. The development of Western European groupings, closely associated with the US, polarized Europe as the USSR led the breakaway communist response. With these concerns, Europe in the 1950s had little time for Japan. Japanese policy-makers, for their part, were consumed with internal economic development and the need to shelter under the umbrella of the US–Japan security treaty (see Chapter 6). Japan and Europe, it seemed, had little or nothing to offer one another (Gilson 2000a).

The task of rebuilding war-torn Europe was never going to be an easy one, since the continent lay in economic and physical ruins and the rebuilding thereof was inextricably linked to the growing divisions between the US and USSR (Black *et al.* 1992: 48). The loss of life had been substantial, and included between sixteen and twenty million Soviet deaths, four-and-a-half million German, over half a million French, and just under that number in both Italy and the UK. The agricultural and industrial output of Europe after the war had declined to about half its pre-war level. Simultaneously, the national debt across European states had increased, and the huge problem of providing shelter for the approximately fifty million uprooted people of the continent plagued attempts at controlling recovery. In Central Europe and the USSR, where most of the fighting had taken place, nearly half of all urban residential areas and three-quarters of rural homes had been destroyed completely. What is more, the victors could no longer find solace for their economic woes in their colonies, since these were calling for their own independence (Black *et al.* 1992: 45, 48).

13.4 Divided continent

Winston Churchill made his famous 'Iron Curtain' speech in March 1946 in Fulton, Missouri. This speech portended the ideological as well as physical division of a huge continent which would remain separated until the fall of the Berlin Wall in 1989. The speech angered President Harry Truman of the US, who regarded it as an aggressive posture towards the USSR. However, he himself was later to be the architect of the so-called 'Truman Doctrine' of March 1947, by which a programme of economic and military aid for Greece and Turkey was established in recognition of US fears of Soviet expansion. This was followed shortly afterwards by the Marshall Plan of June 1947, which offered aid to the whole of Europe. Stalin's rejection of this aid in June was to seal the division of the continent. Between 1948 and 1952, the so-called 'Stalinization' of East European satellites took place, whereby Eastern European governments came to be imposed or controlled directly by Moscow. The Soviet blockade of Berlin of March 1948 to June 1949 led to a military airlift by the Western powers and precipitated the signature of the North Atlantic Treaty Organization (NATO) in April 1949.

13.5 European Economic Community

The major industrial powers of Western Europe were consumed with the need to cooperate in the immediate post-war years. Established by the Treaty of Rome 1957 with effect from 1 January 1958, the EEC was set up in order to provide a frontier-free zone for the people, goods and services of the original six members (namely Belgium, France, Germany, Italy, Luxemburg and the Netherlands). The debate surrounding the establishment of the EEC promoted two possible means of developing cooperation so as not to facilitate a return to war. For their part France,

Italy and the Benelux countries (Belgium, the Netherlands and Luxembourg) sought close integration in order to rehabilitate their economies, gain a greater international voice and draw Germany in particular into a pan-European structure. The UK, in contrast, advocated a looser grouping of states in the form of a European Free Trade Association (EFTA). As Japan had, historically, a particularly close relationship with the UK, which was resuscitated in the 1950s and 1960s, it followed this process with interest. The US, for its part, keen to reintegrate the European countries with one another and to have them assume their own economic burdens, supported the closer form of integration. For this reason, Japan, too, supported the establishment of the EEC in 1957 (which the UK did not join) and pledged to develop relations with the new Community. The practicalities of this policy, however, have never been easy to achieve. The EEC represented an explicitly political project (especially from the point of view of Germany and France) with only a limited trade mandate in its formative years. For this reason, Japanese policy-making agents, business and a limited number of other actors continued to develop their bilateral relations with the individual member states as well as the UK, whilst viewing with some scepticism the grander European project.

The Community, in turn, paid little attention to Japan, until the latter's GDP reached such high proportions that it was seen as an international economic threat during the early 1950s. As they began to view Japan as a direct threat to the European economy, the countries of the Community and the UK initially opposed Japanese entry to the General Agreement on Tariffs and Trade (GATT) and insisted on implementing safeguard clauses in their bilateral trade relations (Rothacher 1983).

In terms of the dimension of security, it soon became clear to the Europeans (particularly Churchill) that they needed to keep the US interested in Europe, as well as militarily engaged (Lane 1985: 30). Thus, attention to this area of affairs was focused upon the (unsuccessful) attempts to build a European Defence Community (EDC) which would complement NATO's role in the region. This Eurocentric consideration ensured that the prospect of establishing any kind of security relationship with East Asia was not entertained seriously.

13.6 Summary

By the end of the 1950s, the Cold War agenda had materialized and Japan's place within it was firmly established. The structure of the international system ensured that Japan's relations with the US remained paramount, and yet it was within this structure that Japan resumed relations with the Western European powers. The following chapters will examine how Japan's bilateral relations altered over time to accommodate trilateral norms of behaviour, and will assess the extent to which these alternative norms are shaping Japan's foreign policy orientation towards Europe in the first decade of the twenty-first century.

Chapter 14

Japan–Europe political relations

14.1 Overview

Speaking at the opening Diet session in September 1978, Prime Minister Fukuda Takeo of Japan emphasized the need to strengthen the trilateral relations of Japan, Europe and the US (Rothacher 1983: 253). This form of trilateral cooperation would incorporate economic and political dialogue within a broad three-way framework. In spite of occasional areas of cooperation in the political dimension of the relationship during the 1970s and 1980s, however, the overall relationship continued to be dominated by economic concerns and bilateral negotiations. Only at the end of the 1980s did a change in the structure of the international system facilitate a new role for trilateralism. Japan and Europe altered the parameters of their own relations as a result of these structural changes.

Even in rhetorical statements promoting the development of trilateral political relations during the 1970s and 1980s, 'political dialogue' remained an ill-defined concept, and only since the beginning of the 1990s have Japan and Europe begun to sketch out the limits of such a dialogue. Indeed, since the signature of the Hague Declaration between Japan and the EC in 1991 (Appendix 14.1), political dialogue has been a formal and integral part of Japan's relations with Europe.

The current political relationship represents the culmination of many changes during the post-war era. For, whilst Japanese responses to Europe from the 1950s to 1970s were influenced most extensively by US policy, incremental steps towards improving mutual relations were taken. In the wake of changes in the structure of the international system after 1989 in particular, these small steps provided the foundation for the development of a new kind of relationship.

The first section in this chapter examines the 'what' of Japan–Europe political relations, by assessing the structural constraints that formerly impeded them. The second section determines the 'how', by illustrating the actors within Japan responsible for developing and influencing those relations. In so doing, they show why the pattern of relations between Japan and Europe differs from that witnessed *vis-à-vis* the US and East Asia. The third section examines how domestic norms and institutional structures have shaped Japan's relations with Europe within the context of the changing structure of the international system. In particular, it shows how, in response to the need to balance tensions between structure and agency in the post-Cold War period and within a changing international system, Japan's approach to Europe is informed increasingly by the impact of the emergent norm of trilateralism.

14.2 Japan and the community of Europe

Chapter 13 has provided a brief historical overview of Japan's relations with the EEC/EC/EU. It has illustrated how, largely in the shadow of the US, the countries of Western Europe and Japan itself for most of the post-war era left their foreign-policy orientations to be governed by directions from the US. During this time, the need for mutual engagement over specific (mostly trade) issues led to the development of *ad hoc* channels of dialogue between Japan and Europe. The deepening of European integration during the 1980s and a period of 'Japan-bashing' by the US provided further stimuli for mutual engagement. However, it was the ending of the Cold War after 1989 and the structural transformations it heralded which altered more significantly Japan's relations with Europe.

14.2.i Fall of the Berlin Wall

On 9 November 1989, a major event took place in Europe that was to change dramatically the lives of the people on this continent. The Berlin Wall, which had not only separated East from West Berlin since 1961, but had symbolized the physical and ideological division of the whole European continent, was torn down. This momentous occasion was followed rapidly over the next few months and years by calls for the ending of communism in other countries of Central and Eastern Europe. From 1989, countries such as Poland, Hungary and Czechoslovakia renounced their communist heritage. It was not long before the USSR itself broke up in 1991.

This definitive ending of the Cold War in Europe wrought significant changes to Japan's relations with the major industrial powers of Europe. Not only did Europe appear frequently in Japanese press coverage and the government become involved almost immediately in the reconstruction of Europe's eastern flank, but the very idea of what 'Europe' was changed, too. As the cornerstone of modern, capitalist Europe, the EC had to be taken seriously by outsiders, as both an economic and a political entity. Moreover, the continuing internal changes within the Community provided the Japanese with clear 'European' interlocutors to add to Japan's national member state counterparts.

14.2.ii Consolidating links with the European Community

In July 1991, the prime minister of Japan, Kaifu Toshiki, the president of the European Commission, Jacques Delors, and the president of the Council of Ministers of the EC, Ruud Lubbers, signed a joint declaration in The Hague (known as the 'Hague Declaration'; see Appendix 14.1). The purpose of this declaration was to consolidate existing meetings and consultations between the Japanese government and the EC member states, as well as to introduce new initiatives, most notably an annual summit meeting amongst the leaders of Japan, the European Commission and the Council presidency. It also set out a timetable for lower-level meetings, including the Japan–EU Troika Foreign Ministers Meeting and the Japan–EU Political Directors Meeting, as well as issue-specific consultations. The declaration made it clear that relations would be promoted in economic as well as political dimensions, and should be conducted at government, business and academic levels. In many ways, the Hague Declaration did no more than clarify and codify the set of *ad hoc* arrangements already in place between Japan and the EC.

At the same time, however, it created a recognizable institutional structure within which all Japan–EC affairs would be conducted from that time (Gilson 2000a).

Clearly, economic gains could accrue from Japan's deepening involvement in newly-emerging European markets and much of the momentum to deal with Europe came from Japanese industry (see Chapter 15). At the same time, the opportunity to enhance political relations with the growing European body, as well as to promote Japan's own profile on this distant continent in the wake of continuing US withdrawal from East Asia and economic tensions with the US, should not be underestimated. Recent years have also witnessed a more issue-based approach to cooperation, with conferences, workshops and symposia focusing on specific issues of interest or concern to Japan and its EU counterparts, such as the environment and the international trafficking of drugs. Indeed, the notion of political dialogue now embraces a host of different activities, as listed in the Hague Declaration. These include the promotion of intellectual and ministerial personnel exchanges, and cooperation over energy provision and nuclear safety, as well as mutual concern over the future of Russia and China.

The EC became the European Union (EU) through the Treaty on European Union (TEU, or 'Maastricht Treaty') of February 1992. Since 1992, the deepening and widening processes underway within the EU itself have made it impossible for Japan or any other major industrial power to ignore the current and future potential of this highly-populated region. The TEU clarified the 'three-pillar' system of European economic and political behaviour. The first pillar deals with the EC treaties and recognizes the European Commission's right of initiative and mandate to negotiate on behalf of the member states in the field of economic affairs. Issues of common foreign and security policy (CFSP) are dealt with at an inter-governmental level within pillar two, whilst pillar three (also inter-governmental) covers justice and home affairs. This division of labour often makes it difficult for an external interlocutor to appreciate fully the internal mechanisms of the Union. As the EU continues to grow in membership and to deepen its responsibilities, the political potential for Europe is likely to develop further. It is noteworthy that when the euro was launched in January 1999, Foreign Minister Kōmura Masahiko of Japan praised the political will of his European counterparts for engaging in this economic and political project. At the same time, it should be noted that growing dialogue with the EU as such has not prevented the deepening of Japan's bilateral relations with its key allies in the Union, as examined in section 14.4.

14.3 Policy-making actors

Within the changing structural parameters outlined above, Japanese policy-making agents, business people, non-governmental organizations and other political actors have formulated their own approaches to Europe in the 1990s and at the beginning of the twenty-first century. At the official level, only a handful of elite political representatives stand out with regard to the promotion of relations with Europe. Their contributions have, nevertheless, been important.

Although earlier calls for trilateral cooperation had been made by Japanese prime ministers such as Ikeda Hayato and Fukuda Takeo, it was not until the late 1980s that the political elite focused on the role of Japan–Europe relations specifically within that framework. The structures of the Cold War and the enduring impact of the US–Japan security treaty (see Chapter 6) ensured that Japanese and European politicians paid each other little attention, except through the interface of US policy-makers.

14.3.i Policy-making agents

After the fall of the Berlin Wall, Prime Minister Kaifu arrived in Europe as early as January 1990, where he discussed with Jacques Delors, president of the European Commission, the potential for Japan's contribution to the reconstruction of Central and Eastern Europe, through participation in the then Conference on Security and Cooperation in Europe (CSCE) (which later became the Organization for Security and Cooperation in Europe (OSCE)) and the G24 programme of assistance. This unprecedented high level of Japanese interest in events on the European continent encouraged the deepening of bilateral relations at all levels, which in turn led to the signing of the Hague Declaration. Negotiations over the declaration itself were facilitated by the involvement of the then deputy vice-minister of MOFA, Owada Hisashi. His own proposal had initiated the whole declaration and his personal intervention during often difficult negotiations between Japanese ministries, on the one hand, and with an inchoate European body, on the other, were important for the final outcome. On a different level, a fellow Europhile, the former prime minister Hata Tsutomu, has recently been engaged in the promotion of Japanese relations with the EC, particularly through the six-monthly meetings of the Japan–EC Interparliamentary Delegation, which bring together members of the European Parliament and Diet members to discuss a range of issues. Moreover, since the Hague Declaration, Japanese prime ministers have been careful to place Europe on their international schedules and to respond actively and promptly to changes within the Community itself. Thus, following the ratification of the TEU, Prime Minister Hosokawa Morihiro sent his congratulations to President Jacques Delors and made it clear that it would be in Japan's interests to cooperate with its European counterparts in their bilateral dialogue as well as in regional and global fora. In the absence of public and media attention to Japan's relations with Europe, these high-profile figures are important in developing dialogue. They also act as norm entrepreneurs, to the extent that they shape the types and intensity of dialogue which the Japanese have chosen with their European counterparts.

Although the Japanese prime minister may occasionally show an interest in improving relations with his European counterparts, it is at the level of bureaucratic activity that Japan maintains and develops its European policy. Compared with government bureaux which deal with US and Asian affairs, those concerned with Europe have never held a high profile in the ministries. Moreover, the division of labour within MOFA means that, despite this ministry's responsibility for the overall conduct of relations with Europe, it does not retain a single unified division for devising Japan's strategy. In addition, contemporary political dialogue involves a range of different issues, so that relations with Europe are often discussed within other divisions, such as the United Nations and International Peace Cooperation Divisions within the Foreign Policy Bureau, the Science and Nuclear Energy Division within the Directorate-General for Arms Control and Scientific Affairs, as well as the Global Issues Division in the Multilateral Cooperation Department. As it becomes increasingly difficult to distinguish political from economic activity, responsibilities within and between ministries overlap, with the result that the Economic Affairs Bureau within MOFA deals with WTO and OECD issues, which are also covered by more powerful MITI bureaux (Rothacher 1983: 58). Other ministries dealing with Europe in respect of trade issues include MITI, especially through its West European–African–Middle East division of the Industrial Policy Bureau and International Trade Policy Bureau, and the Ministry of Finance (MOF) through its International Finance Bureau.

14.3.ii Political parties

Political parties within Japan differ only in nuance with regard to relations with Europe. In general terms, the Liberal-Democratic Party (LDP) has viewed Western Europe as a partner in its engagement within a US-led Western order. For the same reason, the Social Democratic Party of Japan (SDPJ) has often voiced discontent over Europe's willingness to follow the US agenda. The changing view of the SDPJ with regard to the US–Japan security treaty also means that its foreign policy manifesto today emphasizes the need to work alongside Europe, particularly over concerns such as preventive diplomacy. In addition, the variety of political models available in Europe offers potential partners for all the major parties in Japan. Thus, the political right during the 1980s followed closely the policy-making agenda and style of Prime Minister Margaret Thatcher of Britain, whilst parties of the left have followed with interest the progress of Prime Minister Lionel Jospin of France and Chancellor Gerhard Schröder of Germany.

14.3.iii Business interests

Chapter 15 will deal in more detail with the role of Japanese business representatives in the development of relations with Europe. It is worth noting here, however, that the *Keidanren*, which represents big business, has been instrumental in certain cases in influencing the government's agenda on Europe. In addition, business representatives take on a political role by participating in major government missions to Europe. The most (in)famous is the so-called 'Dokō mission' of 1976, which returned to Japan with an extensive list of Europe-wide complaints against restrictive Japanese trade practices (Rothacher 1983: 66–7). In addition to the *Keidanren*, Japanese Chambers of Commerce and representatives from large general trading companies (*sōgo shōsha*) gather information which is subsequently collated and used by the Japanese government.

The extent to which economic issues have become entwined with the political agenda can be seen in the vocal role played by Japanese industrialists with regard to the euro. Companies such as Toyota and Nissan have called for the UK government, for example, to make clear its position with regard to entry into the euro-zone (see Chapter 15). This kind of involvement, moreover, has resulted in transnational cooperation between non-governmental business actors and interest groups.

14.3.iv Non-governmental organizations

Non-governmental activities in Japan are influenced more and more by activists based in Europe, a phenomenon aided considerably by the availability of information through the Internet. Examples include Amnesty International, Greenpeace and Human Rights Watch, which are all highly active in Europe and have a growing number of chapters in Japan. Smaller NGOs have also been affected. For instance, the Association to Aid Refugees, Japan (AARJ) not only conducts many of its activities in Europe (as in Bosnia) but also adopts symbols from Europe, such as its use of footage of, and statements by, a member of Britain's royalty, the late Diana, Princess of Wales, in its anti-landmines campaign. All these activities are assisted by a proliferation of Japanese media coverage of Europe, which, although still not at a significant level, has gained important ground. This tends to be promoted as a result of events occurring in Europe (such as the fall of the Berlin Wall, the war in former Yugoslavia and the 1999 earthquake in Turkey) rather than through a sense that Japan's relations with Europe are growing.

14.3.v The European Commission Delegation in Tokyo

The Japanese have also become more exposed to EC-level representation on their own soil, where the Delegation of the European Commission to Japan has been particularly important in developing relations with the Japanese and in disseminating information regarding the role of the EC/EU itself. Through daily interaction with MOFA, MITI and other ministries, the Delegation is able to distribute and collect information as a *de facto* European 'embassy' that is much better resourced than many of the member state embassies themselves. In recent years, through events such as 'Cooperation Week' in autumn 1997, it has been able to bring together national interests of EU member states under the banner of EU cooperation. In this way, and despite continuing suspicion and scepticism on the part of several member state representatives, a recognizable EU identity has developed within Japan itself (Gilson 2000a).

As illustrated here, small groups of policy-making agents and other political actors in Japan tend to make decisions based upon specific issues and needs with regard to Europe, and little evidence exists of an overall Japanese strategy towards Europe. Japanese and European governments have found common ground since the late 1970s over specific events, such as the Soviet invasion of Afghanistan in 1979 and the Iranian hostage crisis in 1980. Subsequently, the rise of the Solidarity movement in Poland, the question of the boycotting of the Moscow Olympics, and the Middle East peace process have all been discussed by Japan with its EC counterparts. This era of increasing mutual interest led to the development of ministerial-level meetings between Japan and the EC from 1983 and set the foundations for the political dialogue that would continue into the following decade and beyond. Before examining the changing nature of Japan–Europe relations within its trilateral context, the following sections illustrate some of the complexities of dealing with 'Europe' as an entity.

14.4 Divide and rule? Japan and the European Union member states

In addition to growing Japan–EU ties, Japanese policy-makers have also continued to cultivate political relations with their key bilateral allies in Europe. Principal among their number are the UK, France and Germany, although other member states are engaged for specific fields of discussion and interest. The nature of the EU itself also ensures that member states play different roles according to the issues under consideration. Japan is able to instrumentalize its individual bilateral political relations in a way not possible in the economic dimension, since the European Commission represents the member states in matters pertaining to the Single European Market, but holds no such authority in the political dimension. As a result, the Japanese government retains different types of arrangements with different member states for reasons explored below.

14.4.i Japan's promotion of shared interests with the European Union

First, the Japanese government will frequently promote relations with countries which share particular international problems or interests with Japan. Thus, in its bilateral relations with the UK, Japanese policy-makers acknowledge a long history of bilateral interaction and the most important European destination for Japanese foreign direct investment (FDI, see Chapter 15). Meanwhile, the Japanese government has promoted its ties with Germany as part of its pursuit of a permanent seat on the UNSC. Moreover, its relationship with Germany, which remained distant for most of the post-war era, has been strengthened since German reunification and owing to the central role of the deutschmark (DM) within the European monetary union (Bridges 1999: 46). In contrast, the Japanese still view France as potentially the most hostile European country (Bridges 1999: 47), and problems have been exacerbated by French nuclear testing in the Pacific in 1995 and the anti-Japanese attitude of Prime Minister Edith Cresson of France between 1989 and 1991. In spite of this, Japanese representatives have undertaken a variety of cooperative initiatives with their French counterparts, which include: Japanese peacekeeping troops working alongside French troops in Cambodia and Goma; the joint hosting of the International Committee for the Restoration of Cambodia; the establishment of a convention for a forum on Global

Development in Indo-China; and the construction of an AIDS centre in Uganda. This positive attitude has been enhanced by the approach and many visits to Tokyo of Japanophile President Jacques Chirac of France.

14.4.ii Japan's promotion of multilevel engagements with the European Union

Second, in addition to high-level meetings, personnel exchanges take place between Japanese and European foreign ministries, whilst consultations between representatives of their diplomatic missions in third countries and visits through friendship associations of parliamentary exchange ensure a range of engagements at a number of additional levels. Meetings at the official level include gatherings to discuss specific subjects, such as: the Japanese–German Joint Committee on Cooperation in Science and Technology; meetings of the Japanese Environment Agency and member state ministries for the environment; aid policy consultations; government consultations on pension agreements; and meetings of joint cultural committees. These are accompanied by non-governmental programmes, which include an exchange programme for social services, youth exchanges and trainee exchanges. In the private sector, too, fora such as the German–Japanese Cooperation Council for High-Technology and Environmental Technology bring together experts from specific industries.

14.4.iii Standardized approach to the European Union

The Japanese state and its people have begun to implement a standardized approach to their bilateral relations. Thus, the idea of organizing a summit of heads of state, as well as ministerial meetings, is common to many of these bilateral relations. The similarity of approach derives from the fact that Japan shares a common Cold War experience under the wing of the US with its Western European counterparts and from the deepening of European integration: for, whilst the EU has yet to formulate one foreign policy for all its member states, its *de facto* political weight presents a need to address the EU as a unit on some level. These structural dimensions caused the Japanese government to redefine its political relations with Europe from the late 1980s and ensure that an 'EU' factor lies behind all bilateral relations with EU member states in the twenty-first century. In addition, the types of political issues discussed in bilateral fora tend to be similar, and today include support for UN reform, the promotion of non-nuclear proliferation, the abolition of anti-personnel landmines and various cultural projects to promote Japan's image in Europe. 'Japan 2001' in the UK is the latest in a line of national government efforts to promote Japan within Europe and has been replicated elsewhere (see www.japan2001.org.uk).

As well as provoking changes in the nature of traditionally significant bilateral relations with key member states, greater Japanese attention to the EU during the 1990s has also created opportunities for new dialogues with countries formerly ignored by Japan. As a result, membership of the EU and the rotating responsibility of EU Council presidency mean that capitals such as Helsinki and Lisbon are now more frequently visited by Japanese policy-making agents and other political actors than they were before becoming members of the Union. Although these developments have not yet translated into major new bilateral political initiatives or major investment opportunities, they still contribute towards a consolidation of Japan's approach to the EU as a whole.

14.5 Japan and peripheral Europe

Japan continues to retain strong ties with its key counterparts in Europe, whilst at the same time it deals increasingly with the EU as a coherent bloc. This central focus on Western Europe has implications for relations with what might be termed 'peripheral Europe', namely the countries of Central and Eastern Europe that have been undergoing major political and economic reforms since the breakdown of the Cold War international structures after 1989. It is the Japanese business community that has paid most attention to this region. Since the beginning of the 1990s in particular, however, the Japanese government has begun to play a more significant political role in Central and Eastern Europe, as illustrated by its involvement with many of the institutional arrangements in that part of the region and in conjunction with the EU. Chapter 16 will examine the purpose of Japan's growing role in the CSCE, which invited the Japanese government to Budapest in December 1994 for its summit meeting on the future of Central and Eastern Europe, and in which it became a Partner for Cooperation in 1998. Similarly, Chapter 15 will look at the Japanese government's involvement in the European Bank for Reconstruction and Development (EBRD). As will be shown in Chapter 16, moreover, Japan's participation in the Steering Committee of the Peace Implementation Council for Bosnia-Herzegovina, and its direct contributions to the resolution of the crisis in Kosovo in 1999, further demonstrate Japan's growing role in Europe.

It is important to note three general factors pertaining to Japan's relations with Central and Eastern Europe. First, owing to the proximity of many of these countries to the EU, as well as their likely membership of that Union, they have become attractive targets of Japanese inward investment (Darby 1996; see Chapter 15). Second, relations with Central and Eastern Europe have also been important in helping to define a new kind of multilateral engagement in the security dimension, since Japanese peacekeepers have participated in the post-conflict occupation of Bosnia-Herzegovina and Kosovo, and the Japanese government and non-governmental organizations have provided financial and humanitarian assistance to these regions. This side of relations will be dealt with in Chapter 16. Third, the support (mostly through international fora) for reform in Central and Eastern Europe has provided an opportunity for the Japanese government to instrumentalize in a proactive way its quiet diplomacy. This activity is demonstrated, for example, by Prime Minister Kaifu's active use of Japan's economic diplomacy in 1990 to promote the development of former communist societies and economies, in order to gain a stronger foothold in the major institutions in the region. In so doing, the Japanese are able to carve out a new kind of diplomatic role in a new geographical region.

14.6 Expanding dialogue with Europe

Japan benefits from greater representation in Europe in several ways. First, it increases its profile in the economically and politically important region of Europe. Second, it assuages in this way claims (most vocally articulated by the US) that it is not sharing the international burden. Moreover, in formulating responses to European concerns, the Japanese can be seen to be acting on behalf of the whole East Asia region. Third, the participation of Japanese policy-makers in these processes allows them to see at first hand the development of regional coordination measures which may hold lessons for East Asian political and security cooperation. In particular, the Japanese government has been carefully following moves towards preventive diplomacy, arms control and disarmament, which give concrete meaning to the anti-militarist norm. Finally, these channels serve to deepen Japan–Europe relations, by fulfilling the pledges laid down in the Hague Declaration, and thus the 'third side of the triangle' itself is strengthened.

14.7 Cooperating in regional fora

Not only do Japanese policy-making agents and other political actors interact with their European counterparts on an individual member state level and within a Japan–EU dialogue, but they also encounter European officials and non-governmental representatives in a number of regional and global fora. Chapters 19, 20 and 21 will deal specifically with many of the issues raised by multilateral levels of engagement. This section introduces the role and significance of Japan's relations with Europe in larger fora, especially the Asia-Europe Meeting (ASEM).

14.7.i Multilateral opportunities

Japanese and European interlocutors began to create important networks and coalitions in the 1990s within fora as varied as the United Nations, the OSCE, KEDO, the ASEAN PMC, the ARF and ASEM. Cooperation at these levels of engagement now constitutes a fundamental component of Japan–Europe relations. These fora serve two principal purposes: they provide additional formal channels through which Japanese policy-makers become acquainted with their European counterparts; and they provide the Japanese government with the potential to exercise power both over other members of the given community as well as over states and regions which lie outside it.

Plate 14.1 Asia and Europe link hands. The first ASEM meeting in Bangkok in March 1996 included, on the Asian side, representatives of the ASEAN states alongside China, South Korea and Japan; and on the European side, representatives of the fifteen EU member states alongside the European Commission president.

Source: Associated Press

14.7.ii Asia-Europe Meeting

The Asia-Europe Meeting is the newest multilateral forum in which Japanese policy-makers can meet with their European counterparts. It began with a summit of heads of state in Bangkok in 1996 and, as its name suggests, brings together representatives from the two regions of East Asia and Europe. The East Asian bloc comprises seven of the member states of ASEAN alongside China, South Korea and Japan (see Chapter 8), whilst the Europeans include representatives of the fifteen EU member states together with the European Commission president. At Bangkok in 1996, it was decided that the second summit meeting would be held in London in 1998 and the third in Seoul in 2000. The heads of state meeting itself represents the apex of a range of ASEM-related activities which spans the three key dimensions of politics, economics and culture. Some concrete activities have arisen as a result of the establishment of ASEM, although mostly in the economic dimension (see Chapter 15). With regard to the political dimension, ASEM by the beginning of 2000 has offered little more than pledges to respect general democratic principles (Bridges 1999). It nevertheless forms an additional dimension for Japan–Europe relations and is used by Japanese policy-makers in their relations with Europe in several ways.

First, ASEM promotes directly the exact interests discussed between Japan and the EU bilaterally and thereby provides an additional forum to air such issues and concerns. In addition, it allows for the discussion of these interests in a forum which embraces three of Japan's most important regional neighbours. Moreover, it also provides a way for Japan to play a greater international political role without military implications, because its primary focus is upon trade matters and other non-military topics of contemporary interest. In the political dimension, the most salient issues under discussion in ASEM include UN reform, international terrorism and drugs trafficking, conventional and nuclear arms control and regional stability in Europe and Asia. As such, it has been used by Japanese policy-makers as a forum in which to emphasize the development of quiet diplomacy (*Nikkei Weekly* 12 April 1999; see Chapter 23).

Second, the ASEM format enables the Japanese government to instrumentalize its relations with Europe to support its policy towards East Asia. Thus, Japanese policy-makers employ proxy diplomacy by getting the EU to voice some of its regional proposals without raising East Asian fears regarding Japanese motives. At the same time, they are able to instrumentalize Japanese international relations with the rest of East Asia in areas of common concern with the EU. For this reason, however, the forum may also be used by the other members as a means to exert pressure on Japan, as was seen in London when Japanese policy-makers were urged to play a bigger role in the resolution of the East Asian financial and economic crises (see Chapter 10). In addition, the Japanese government uses ASEM to respond to the growing regional and global dimension of Japan–Europe relations more generally (Maull *et al.* 1998: 171).

Third, Japanese policy-makers have used ASEM as a means of strengthening its relations with the rest of East Asia (Gilson 1999). The unique characteristic of this forum is that it sets one region alongside another: Europe and East Asia. In so doing, Japan is able not only to develop further its regional relations without creating tension between its neighbours, but also to sit around a table with other East Asian powers. Indeed, Japanese participation in various pre-ASEM Asian-side discussions also prompted US criticism that the plans of Prime Minister Mahathir of Malaysia, for an East Asian Economic Caucus (EAEC), were being realized, and that Japan was adopting a uniquely Asian stance in the whole meeting (see Chapter 9).

Fourth, ASEM is the most important forum in which Japan and Europe meet one another in the absence of the US. For this reason, it can act not only as a counterbalance to the role played by the US in the East Asia region, but also to establish an agenda which does not prioritize US concerns (as occurs in the WTO and APEC, for example). In this way, ASEM may also create a long-term relationship in which there is greater scope for reciprocity over different issues and within both East Asia and Europe (Keohane 1986b: 5). Similarly, the overarching framework of ASEM means that Japan can address European concerns within this forum and participate on the European continent, and in return can expect European cooperation in East Asia. The promotion of KEDO in this context is dealt with in Chapters 9 and 16.

Finally, as a 'bilateral' (Asia–Europe) dialogue, ASEM contributes to the deepening of relations between the two weakest sides of the Japan–US–Europe triangle. This trilateral dimension has also become more salient within Japan–Europe relations themselves, such that the 2000 G7/8 meeting in Okinawa pledged to expand relations between East Asia and Europe, and to establish a Japan–Europe Millennium Partnership to help keep the US committed to its multilateral engagements (*Financial Times*, 14 January 2000). In this way, ASEM also expands the 'Japan' pole to include other major East Asian players, in recognition not only of the growth of the other two interlocutors within the triangle (whereby the US incorporates NAFTA and the EU has expanded and integrated further), but also of the growth of regions within the globalizing political economy (see Chapter 24).

These illustrations have shown how trilateral motivations have become more than a rhetorical foil for action between Japan and Europe, and how, rather, they have become the basis of concrete proposals and activities. The next section examines the role of trilateralism as an emergent norm underpinning Japan's relations with Europe.

14.8 Emerging norms: new trilateralism

The changing structures of the international system provided the background to the signing of the Hague Declaration and subsequent developments in Japan–Europe relations. In addition to the relaxing of the strict Cold War framework, which had constrained Japan and Western Europe to follow a US agenda, the traditional substance of Japan–EC relations entered the mainstream of international political debate. In these conditions, the framework of trilateral relations between Japan, the US and Europe served to facilitate Japan's relations with Europe after 1989.

14.8.i Trilateral Commission

Trilateral relations of the 1990s and the first decade of the twenty-first century differ qualitatively from those of the early 1970s, which were most notably represented by the Trilateral Commission (TC) (Gill 1990). This earlier triangular incarnation was designed to coordinate institutionalized Western high politics and to socialize an elite stratum through conferences, discussions and mutual informal contacts (Dent 1999; Thurow 1992). This form of trilateralism was designed to support a US, anti-communist agenda, and in the so-called 'trilateral administration' of President Jimmy Carter of the US, it became an important vehicle by which the US could 'socialize' its Cold War partners into the same view of the world (Rothacher 1983: 199). In addition to this Cold War orientation, specific issues dealt with by the TC, such as OPEC and détente, were relevant to that particular historical juncture. The two-versus-one structure embodied in the TC ensured almost invariably that the US, at the triangle's apex, retained a dominant position over the other two, which subsequently hindered the development of their mutual relations.

14.8.ii New trilateralism

In some ways, the contemporary form of trilateralism which is emerging and beginning to take hold in Japan–Europe relations parallels its previous format. Most obviously, the two-versus-one arrangement can still be seen frequently. This structure therefore enables Japan to request a codified dialogue with the EC to match that of the Transatlantic Agreement (a 1990 agreement between the US and the EC to reinforce their dialogue at a number of levels); President Clinton to pressure his European and East Asian counterparts to play greater burden-sharing roles; and Japan and Europe to come together in ASEM to strengthen the 'third side of the triangle'. In its current form, however, this two-versus-one format reflects a shifting set of alliances, which interchange between the three parties.

At the same time, new trilateralism is qualitatively different. Most significantly, the very nature of the three 'poles' of the triangle have altered in the light of changes in the structure of the international system. The US, whilst often referred to as the lone superpower is, nevertheless, no longer assumed to act unilaterally as global guardian of the international order, as was discussed in Part II of this book. The EU has now developed into a fifteen-member organization which incorporates not only economic integration through its single market programme, but also political dialogue through a growing common foreign and security policy, and even a security dimension, through closer association with the mechanisms of the WEU. For its part, Japan's attempts to deepen relations with its East Asian neighbours (see Chapter 9), external pressure for it to assume regional responsibilities, and multiplying assertions in multilateral fora that Japan is acting as the East Asian representative, have all expanded the third 'pole' to include Japan as part of a broader East Asian group.

In addition to the changing nature of the three poles of the triangle, the nature of issues now covered within the developing trilateral structure has changed. With Cold War structures now largely obsolete in Europe, the rationale for Europeans and Japanese to follow US policy as a matter of course has diminished. As a result, many of the subjects now addressed on a trilateral scale would not fit with the 'high politics' agenda of the TC. Instead, issues that have formed the basis of Japan's and the EU's non-military dialogue up to 2000 have now gained salience in most international organizations and multilateral fora. These, as noted above, include concerns relating to environmental degradation, the trafficking of drugs and human welfare.

Finally, trilateralism has begun to take its place among the multilevel structures which are being formulated in response to trends towards a globalized political economy. This theme will be taken up in more detail in Chapter 24, but suffice it to note here that the trilateral structure of the 1970s was explicitly bilateral-enhancing, in the sense that it reinforced US-dominated notions of capitalist versus communist ideologies. By contrast, the new trilateralism is multilateral-enhancing, in its recognition that post-Cold War problems can only be solved through cooperative engagements undertaken by a number of different actors. From among some of the major industrialized powers of the world, Europe and Japan have assumed collectively the mantle of that trilateral responsibility. This type of behaviour befits attempts by the Japanese government to adopt supplemental strategies in its foreign policy (see Chapter 23).

New trilateralism, then, should be clearly distinguished from its old form. It is the trilateralism that can be found to resonate in fora as diverse as regional engagements such as the ARF, at inter-regional encounters such as ASEM, and in global entities such as the WTO and the UN. This is not, then, the 'skewed triangle' (Bridges 1999: 41), but a new triangle that impacts upon Japan's relations with Europe and the US, and which provides the 'checks and balances' for these relations (CAEC 1997: 38). Whilst it is not a fully-fledged norm, it can nevertheless be viewed as an emergent norm which informs relations between Japan and Europe (see Dent 1999: 96). Its impact on Japan–Europe relations is examined in the next section.

14.9 Summary

Policy-making agents and other political actors from Japan and Europe now encounter one another in a range of different fora, from governmental summits to business exchanges and non-governmental meetings. The political realm in which they meet now encompasses a range of issues relating to sub-national, national, regional and global agendas. What is more, the bilateral Japan–EU dialogue now also serves to underpin positions and to discuss issues debated within wider fora to which both belong. These include the UN, the G7/8, the ARF and ASEM.

The Japanese government has been able to pursue its growing relations with Europe for a number of ends. The development of a political dialogue with Europe (especially in the codified form of the Hague Declaration) demonstrates Japan's own commitment to assuming international responsibilities commensurate with its economic power and thereby seeking to respond to criticisms such as those levelled at Japan during the 1990–1 Gulf War (see Chapters 1 and 18). In addition, growing contacts with Europe enable Japan to set a firmer footing in this region and thereby garner support on international issues of mutual concern. In so doing, Japanese policy-makers and other political actors are able to externalize further the norm of economism, by enhancing relations with a counterpart regarded as having a similar approach to international political and economic behaviour.

The tensions in Japan's attempts to balance its bilateral and multilateral approaches to Europe are resolved through the application of trilateralism: for, in its new form, trilateralism both constrains and facilitates the growth of their mutual relations. On the one hand, it provides a stable framework within which these three major industrialized powers/regions of the world can address issues of contemporary concern. It functions, moreover, by ensuring that the US remains central to the respective policy concerns of Japan and Europe, with the result that their bilateral relationship is not presented in opposition either to bilateral relations with the US or to international obligations. On the other hand, trilateralism in the twenty-first century permits Japan and Europe to oppose the US jointly without jeopardizing their respective relations with it.

Trilateralism thus enables the development of Japan–Europe dialogue in the face of continuing processes of globalization. The changing structure of the international system has not only altered the very nature of the trilateral participants themselves and the issues they address, but has also begun to inform the norms and institutions upon which contemporary relations between states and non-state actors are based. The future of political dialogue between Japan and the countries of Europe will depend upon the extent to which trilateralism becomes embedded as a globally-recognized norm.

Chapter 15

Japan–Europe economic relations

15.1 Overview

Chapter 13 began with reference to Japan's interest in the euro, which was launched in January 1999. It is this interest in the economic dimension of Japan–Europe relations which has been at the core of the overall relationship since it restarted in the 1950s after the end of World War II. In particular, the development of the European Economic Community (EEC), and the rapid growth of Japan from the late 1950s, drew attention to both Japan and Europe as economic powers. This chapter examines the path that Japan has taken in pursuing bilateral trade with the major European powers alongside a developing economic relationship with the EEC. It demonstrates how these developments have been driven by changes in the structure of the international system from the 1970s and particularly from the 1980s, as well as by specific policy-making agents. Changes brought about by the Nixon shocks of 1971 and by the oil crisis of 1973 caused Japan to review its international economic relations, particularly those with the US. In the early 1970s, the expanded EC attempted not only to develop its own monetary union, but also to deal with external economic affairs as a unitary actor. As a result, the European Commission began to deal with Japan on behalf of the EC. International conditions, however, also led to a decline in Japan–Europe relations at the end of the 1970s. At that time, the oil crisis of 1979, combined with economic stagnation in the EC, began to slow down attempts to deal with Japan in the economic dimension. It was only in the 1980s that a strong yen and a revitalized EC prompted Japan and the EC once again to pay attention to one another's economic development. Since that time, their economic relations have been constantly refined and reinforced. In the 1990s, the development of a Single European Market (SEM), and moves towards a single European currency, intensified this trend. In discussing these developments up to the beginning of the twenty-first century, this chapter will examine structure and agency as well as the norms which now underpin economic relations between Japan and the countries of Europe.

15.2 Economic relations with the European Union

15.2.i Japan as an emerging challenge during the 1970s and 1980s

Compared with Japanese trading activity with the US and other parts of East Asia during the 1970s, Japanese economic interest in Europe during that decade was limited. This apparent lack of interest notwithstanding, the first boom in foreign direct investment (FDI) by Japanese companies in 1972–3 (FDI in the EC rising from US$29 million in 1971 to US$113 million in 1972) caused consternation within European industries, which lobbied the Japanese government and the *Keidanren* for the implementation of voluntary export restraints (VERs) by Japanese companies in specific sectors. Although many European industries at that time appealed to their national governments to take action against this Japanese penetration, by the time of the visit to Europe of the *Keidanren* mission led by Dokō Toshio in 1976 it was evident that a Europe-wide hostility towards Japanese trade practices had taken root (Rothacher 1983). It was also clear that the European Commission had become involved in addressing these issues directly on behalf of European companies and industries.

In the wake of the second oil crisis and the ending of a global recession towards the end of the 1970s, Japanese FDI picked up significantly in the early part of the 1980s, and by 1985 FDI exceeded US$12 billion, a figure that was to increase by more than US$10 billion by 1986 (Akimune 1991: 11; Table 2). During this second boom period, although more than half of Japanese FDI was still directed at the US, the EC's share nearly doubled from 11 per cent to 21 per cent between 1980 and 1989 (Table 2). Trade between Japan and the EC in the mid-1980s was mostly in industrial products, and Japan exported mainly office machinery, electronic consumer goods, telecommunications equipment, chemicals, manufactured rubber products, paper, textiles, manufactured mineral goods, steel products, machinery and precision instruments to the European continent. The EEC/EC's trade balance with Japan moved from a small deficit of US$183 million in 1970 to a deficit of US$18 billion by 1990 (Grewlich 1994: 100; Table 1), a situation which gave cause for concern to Japan's European trading partners, and forced the Japanese to respond to EC criticism of Japanese trade practices.

The Japanese, for their part, had come to realize by the early 1980s that the forces of globalization necessitated a broader investment approach by Japanese businesses. As the decade wore on and the US Congress adopted increasingly stringent trade measures directed at the Japanese in particular, the need for diversification became ever more apparent: Europe offered a growing market for trade and investment, and in January 1980 MITI announced that Japanese automobile manufacturers would increase their production by 10 per cent, and that other industries were likely to follow. As a result, the 1980s saw a growth in manufacturing investment, which added to existing FDI in service industries (Akimune 1991: 5). European financial centres had also become popular because they provided major markets for international finance, and existed within the dynamic framework of the market unification programme (Kitamura 1991). This trend formed part of a Japanese global approach, which saw more proactive behaviour by Japanese transnational corporations and investors (Dent 1999: 84).

In September 1985, the Plaza Accord was signed by the G5 governments of Japan, the United States, France, the UK and West Germany (see Chapter 5). In signing the accord, these governments agreed to drive down the value of the US dollar by appreciating that of the yen. The plan was to reduce the growing US trade deficit and to stoke domestic demand in Japan. When the yen subsequently fell against the dollar, its fall against European currencies was less marked, with the result that many Japanese companies changed their export emphasis from the US to the EC. Moreover, since no amount of short-term savings could fully accommodate the yen's fall against the dollar, and, since Japan had become the country with the highest wages, major Japanese exporters shifted more and more of their final assembly operations to Western markets, in order to take advantage of lower labour costs and to reduce transport charges, as well as to minimize import duties and tax penalties (James 1989: 57; Steven 1991: 51). The ensuing inflow of Japanese FDI into the EC leaped from US$1.8 billion in 1985 to US$3.4 billion in 1986 (Table 2). Although EC member states voiced concern about the rapid growth of Japanese FDI, the measures taken to protect industry against it were not surrounded by the same intense anti-Japan sentiments that were spreading throughout the US (Yoshitomi 1991: viii). By 1989, the EC received 21 per cent of total worldwide Japanese FDI, compared with 48 per cent for the US and 12 per cent for East Asia (Table 2).

15.2.ii Responding to structural changes

Whilst Japanese investors and manufacturers took advantage of beneficial market conditions in the EC, the Japanese government simultaneously was forced to respond to structural changes imposed by the European Commission. Significantly, these structural changes derived from the expansion of the EC, which had increased to twelve member states by the early 1980s and was geared to become a Union of fifteen during the 1990s. This 'widening' of membership was accompanied by efforts to 'deepen' the structures of the EC. Having largely ignored the EC during its period of 'Eurosclerosis' in the early 1980s, the launch of the Single European Market programme during the mid-1980s precipitated a rapid increase in Japanese FDI in preparation for the 1992 deadline for completion of the programme. To many Japanese companies, the prospect of a single European market brought with it the possibility of a 'fortress Europe' structure (Ramazotti 1996: 152; cf. Tanaka 1992: 353). Later plans for the introduction of the euro were to provoke a similar reaction. At the same time, the three-pillar structure introduced by the TEU in 1992 ensured that the economic dimension of the EU's foreign policy remains the best coordinated and offers the clearest channels of communication for the Japanese business sector and the Japanese government in their dealings with the EU (see Chapter 14). In these ways, the EU has become an international economic actor which the Japanese government and Japanese industry now have to deal with as an integral unit, in addition to their relations with individual member states.

The interests of Japanese policy-makers, business and other actors on the European continent during the second half of the 1980s were not only altered by the challenges brought about by increasing European economic integration, but were also affected by European structural restrictions. From a European perspective, the greater penetration of the region by Japanese investors was not always welcome, and countries with protected industries (such as the automobile sectors in France, Italy and Germany) lobbied the European Commission to take preventive action against Japan. Measures, from VERs on specific sectors (such as automobiles and semi-conductors) to anti-dumping complaints and GATT cases, testified to Western Europe's concern over Japanese regional penetration. Moreover, press reports began to claim that Japanese business jeopardized domestic employment levels, since Japanese manufacturing investment often acted merely as a substitute for those areas of employment being replaced.

What is more, some falls in the employment levels of specific sectors, such as consumer electronics (which fell from 250,000 in 1975 to 120,000 in 1985) were attributed to increased Japanese competition (James 1989: 130). Such pressures gave rise to the implementation of a number of different measures to restrict Japanese imports, which in the 1980s included the emergence of VERs and Prior Community Surveillance, by which imported products could be released for free circulation within the EC only on production of a licence (Oppenheim 1991: 277). The most often cited measure of the 1980s became the anti-dumping mechanism. Although not aimed solely at Japan (countries such as China and South Korea were also frequent targets), this measure was nevertheless a major trade impediment which the Japanese had, perforce, to address.

15.2.iii Anti-dumping

The initiation of anti-dumping cases against Japan in 1983 by the European Commission was based upon a 1968 piece of legislation (revised in 1988), and deemed a product to have been dumped 'if its export price to the Community is less than the "normal value" of the like product on its home market' (Oppenheim 1991: 278). Between 1983 and 1986, the EC imposed punitive anti-dumping duties against Japanese companies in ten major product categories (James 1989: 27), whilst other sectors also came under investigation (Kume and Totsuka 1991: 30). If the companies were found guilty of the dumping charge, duties were imposed on the product in question.

In order to address these criticisms and circumvent many of the penalties imposed by the European Commission, Japanese industries began to locate manufacturing sites in the EC itself. In addition, European Commission investigations took such inordinate amounts of time that it was quicker for Japanese companies to invest directly in European local production (Kume and Totsuka 1991: 32). This phenomenon of Japanese FDI in Europe during the 1980s has also been called 'global localization', whereby the activities of Japanese manufacturers become embedded in foreign markets (Morris 1991: 2–3). In the process, many companies moved from assembly to full manufacture within both Western and Eastern Europe, as well as to a greater use of local suppliers and the transfer to some local management.

By the end of the 1980s, Japanese FDI had reached between US$47 billion and US$68 billion annually (Table 2). Reflecting the scale of these investments, during the latter part of that decade Japanese companies were arriving in Europe at a rate of 200 per year (Wells and Rawlinson 1994: 13 and 174), whilst the number of mergers and acquisitions also increased approximately threefold between 1986 and 1989 (Akimune 1991: 6, 13). With a greater number of obstacles in their way, Japanese manufacturing companies began to shift their production platforms into these markets, in order to maintain or enlarge their market share (Akimune 1991: 12). By establishing a larger manufacturing base in Europe, Japanese companies could not only counter some of the trade friction, but could also gain comparative advantage of local production, in the face of growing EC restrictions on non-EC imports (Yoshitomi 1991: ix). Even after setting up local production, however, Japanese companies faced further structural barriers within Europe.

15.2.iv 'Screwdriver' problems

The increase of Japanese production facilities on European soil prompted European producers to lobby the European Commission yet again in 1987. Their actions resulted in accusations against Japanese 'screwdriver plants'. These were factories which supposedly imported so many of their parts that the workers were left only with the task of screwing them together. In the face of this new phenomenon, the European Commission gave itself the remit of extending anti-dumping provisions to EC production operations, and subsequently new regulations were introduced (later to be declared illegal by GATT). These allowed action to be taken against EC-based factories belonging to companies against which anti-dumping cases had succeeded, and where 60 per cent or more of the components were being imported from the 'dumping' country for assembly within the EC. This effectively meant that any product from a Japanese-owned EC factory with a final value which included only a small percentage of imported components could, nevertheless, be subject to duties (Oppenheim 1991: 287).

Local content requirements have been a source of contention in Japan–Europe economic relations since, on this question, national differences can be especially pronounced. The EC defines a product as being of Community origin if the last substantial process or operation that is economically justified was performed in the EC and represented an important stage in the product's manufacture (James 1989: 229; Wells and Rawlinson 1994: 58). This vague definition has allowed plenty of room for disagreement over what local content actually does and should mean. A loose agreement was made in 1986 that a product with 60 per cent EC-sourced content qualifies for free circulation within the EC, but disagreement over the appropriate level of local content persisted between member states which had been negotiating individually with Japan. For example, the UK, in a typical response to Japan, gave Nissan a five-year period to reach the 60 per cent local content requirement (James 1989: 233). Further national differences are examined below.

15.3 Post-Cold War economic relations

These trade problems continued into the 1990s, by which time many large Japanese companies had established monitoring offices in Brussels, in order to keep abreast of the latest developments in EC law and regulation. Following completion of the single market in 1992, however, and the subsequent recession in the EC economies, attention by Japanese companies to this part of the world dwindled. Signs of European recovery from the second half of 1996 did combine with favourable overseas demand, stable prices and exchange rates, and falling interest rates to encourage renewed investment in the continent. In addition, growth in Japanese imports owing to economic recovery in the EU relieved some of the previous trade tensions as the bilateral deficit was reduced. However, it was not until the late 1990s that repeated overtures began to be made by Japanese businesses for action to be taken in Europe to stabilize external trade. Moves towards the launch of the single currency prompted Japanese companies to shift to full manufacturing in Europe rather than just assembly plants; to adopt a greater use of EU-sourced components; and to commence moves towards a larger research and development base within the EU. At the same time, changes within Japan also affected economic relations, in particular because Japan's 'big bang' deregulation of its financial industry, and new WTO negotiations on financial services which ended in December 1997, led to a spate of mergers and acquisitions.

In Brussels in May 1998, it was confirmed that eleven of the fifteen EU member states were eligible and ready to adopt the euro from 1 January 1999. When the euro was launched, Foreign Minister Kōmura Masahiko of Japan recognized the significant economic and political potential its existence could exert on Japan. He joined Finance Minister Miyazawa Kiichi in stressing the desire for a trilateral economic structure based upon the three strong currencies of the US dollar, the euro and the yen, a premise which resonated in Japan's promotion of the New Miyazawa Initiative in 1999 (launched in 1998; see Chapter 10). This period also witnessed other forms of agreement in the economic dimension, such as the Japanese government's response at the G8 1999 summit to the new EU–Japan Mutual Recognition Agreement (MRA). This agreement was established to promote trade between Japan and the EU by their mutually recognizing conformity assessment in several specific sectors. Indeed, this was regarded as the first major international agreement between Japan and the EU (MOFA 1999a), and heralded important recognition for the EU as a serious economic partner with a range of new and efficient networks for the Japanese to work with (Sazanami and Kawai 1999: 45). The response by domestic policy-making agents and other actors to these structural changes has shaped much of Japan's contemporary economic agenda on Europe.

15.4 Domestic actors

Japan's economic relations with Europe involve disparate groups of policy-making agents and actors, who engage at a variety of levels with their European counterparts. This section examines some of the key contributors to the formulation of Japan's economic policy towards Europe to date.

15.4.i Policy-making agents

MOFA is responsible for the overall coordination of Japan's relations with the EU. However, a close examination of economic interests demonstrates that this dimension involves a complex interplay of different actors. Most notably, MOFA has been in constant exchange – sometimes in agreement but often in opposition –

with the two key economic ministries of MITI and MOF, since the re-establishment of economic relations with EC countries in the 1950s and 1960s.

These ministries have been instrumental in guiding the direction of Japan's EC trade policy and have played different and varied roles to that end. MITI, especially through the West European–African–Middle East division of the Industrial Policy Bureau and International Trade Policy Bureau, has applied various pressures to domestic industries which have both favoured and hindered trade relations with the EC. In particular, through its application of 'administrative guidance', a system whereby 'advice' and various kinds of incentives are given directly to key businesses by the ministry (Shindō 1992), MITI has both increased and stemmed the flow of Japan–EC trade. In 1975, for example, MITI discussed with the top six Japanese steelmakers ways of introducing self-regulation on exports to the EC. After several rounds of negotiations between MITI and the European Coal and Steel Community (ECSC) and business-to-business consultations, the industry eventually created a cartel-like control over the level of exports to the EC in this sensitive field. In this way, administrative guidance has served to aid the European Commission in implementing its own aims in the past, as was also the case when in October 1978 MITI suddenly cut automobile exports to the EC in the face of a threat of a total ban on Japanese automobile imports by the Europeans. Nevertheless, administrative guidance can also produce negative effects, such as the rumour that MITI requested importers to cut their imports of ski-boots from the EC in 1976, resulting in threats of retaliatory action from Europe (Rothacher 1983: 235 and 255).

This influential ministry has maintained a turbulent relationship with the other major ministries in Japan and in turn this has affected relations with Europe in different ways. In the early 1960s, for example, MITI was opposed to the requirements of entry to the OECD and – in support of its powerful Domestic Industry Bureau – rejected the idea of freed capital imports, a move which it felt might pave the way for foreign takeover of areas controlled by the ministry (Rothacher 1983: 106). Similarly, MITI was vehemently opposed to MOFA's plans to offer a safeguards clause to the Europeans in return for most-favoured nation (MFN) treatment, as well as to the ending of certain GATT opt-out clauses, fearing that such a move might lead to similar demands by the US. MITI has also been influential through its meetings with the ECSC which were set up in September 1965, and later VER agreements were directed through MITI. The traditional leadership role played by MITI has waned over time as Japan's foreign policy orientation has become more visible internationally, and as the deepening integration of Europe makes it more difficult for the Japanese to play off the member states against one another, as will be seen later in this chapter. Nevertheless, MITI has remained abreast of economic integration within Europe through, *inter alia*, its JETRO offices which are located in the major European capitals. JETRO acts in this way as an important purveyor of the latest information regarding the European market, whilst simultaneously disseminating within Europe information about specific industries and opportunities in particular prefectures in Japan. JETRO's comprehensive surveys of Japanese manufacturing in Europe also enable Japanese businesses and the government to chart the progress of Japan's overall trade approach to the region (Bourke 1996: 166). Other initiatives, such as the EC–Japan Centre for Industrial Cooperation set up in 1987, bring together the European Commission, MITI and private Japanese and European firms in both Tokyo and Brussels, with the aim of running training programmes and promoting two-way business.

Similarly, MOF, notably through its International Finance Bureau, has also demanded a say in relations with Europe. In 1977, MOF opposed unilateral tariff cuts and lowered taxes, a move that was overturned with regard to such items as automobiles, computers and photographic film. As with MITI, MOF was vehemently opposed to MOFA's *Japan's EEC Policy* publication of 1962 and its subsequent proposal for the introduction of a permanent safeguards clause. Aligning itself most often with MITI, this ministry has adopted a generally hard line with regard to Europe.

15.4.ii Other policy-making actors

State guidance and the nature of state–business relations in Japan mean that non-governmental actors, such as private firms, often work closely with the government or within parameters set by the government. One clear example of such a relationship can be seen in the agreements reached in 1980 between the Japanese Automobile Manufacturers' Association (JAMA) and the European Society of Motor Manufacturers and Traders (SMMT), which together decided the restricted levels of Japanese imports to the UK. Other countries instituted similar VERs with Japan. Thereafter, VERs were agreed through annual negotiations and other guidelines were established for bilateral, sector-specific issues (McLaughlin and Maloney 1999: 163). JAMA and MITI have retained close cooperative links in regard to this particular European concern. On a wider level, the *Keidanren* has also been important in setting limits for relations with Europe, and since the early 1970s has been instrumental in dealing directly with the European Commission to decide upon VERs and import quotas.

The automobile sector has brought together collective sectoral interest groups within Japan and Europe, notably JAMA and the SMMT, which have provided important lobbying points for automobile manufacturers in both regions. In particular, during the mid-1980s, Japanese automobile manufacturers became concerned that the development of regulations for the single market would replace verbal agreements made with national industries by JAMA. In the event, this decade saw the growth of a more prominent role for the European Commission, as it attempted to produce an EC-wide understanding whilst negotiating member state interests. In 1988 and 1989, for instance, the European Commission favoured an approach which was to combine an EC-wide understanding on moderation with a transitional period for protected markets gradually to lessen their quotas (McLaughlin and Maloney 1999: 164). The European Commission was also instrumental in negotiating with MITI in the early 1990s to resolve the problem of Japan's penetration of the European automobile market. It became clear in the 1990s that the widespread penetration of the Japanese automobile production sector brought host governments and investors into a closely-linked relationship (McLaughlin and Maloney 1999: 171). As a result of direct dealings between the European Commission and MITI, a July 1991 understanding, known as the 'Elements of Consensus', agreed to a transitional period of seven years, during which time the Japanese share of the EU market was allowed to increase from 12 per cent in 1991 to 16 per cent by 1999. In 1992, in the light of a recession in the EC automobile market, MITI and the European Commission agreed eventually to a 6 per cent reduction in direct imports from Japan (McLaughlin and Maloney 1999: 178). Thus, this major sector involves important agreements between the European Commission and MITI, which bypass both the automobile manufacturers as well as the respective governments. In working closely alongside various European contacts, the Japanese government and business sectors are able to exploit the norms of developmentalism and economism whilst at the same time encouraging their European counterparts to become the norm entrepreneurs in this economic dimension.

15.4.iii Business interests

The role of major Japanese companies in building a European strategy cannot be overlooked. Following the slow decades of the 1960s and 1970s, during which only a few Japanese producers, such as the YKK zip manufacturer, ventured into Europe, and following several famous joint-venture disasters during the 1980s (such as that between Hitachi and GEC and Toshiba and Rank), Japanese firms moved into Europe carefully.

Companies such as Sony, Nissan, Honda and Toyota became household names in Europe during the 1980s, and represented both the threat of foreign penetration and opportunities for employment. During the 1980s, Sony's colour television operations stretched from Bridgend in North Wales to Stuttgart in Germany, Bayonne and Dax in France, Barcelona in Spain, Anif in Austria and Roverto in Italy, and all formed part of an extensive integrated production network (Morris 1991: 5). Japanese firms used their operations in Europe to diversify the products manufactured, to use a variety of local sources and suppliers (whose number increased as EC local content rules became more stringent), and to transfer some of their research and development activities. They approached the market in two ways: through original equipment manufacture, producing equipment for existing European firms; and through branded products, whereby Japanese products were sold under their own name, and by which method Japanese products were to penetrate the European market-place. Increasingly, such companies adopted their own strategies to cope with greater European competition and stiff European legislation during the 1980s. These are dealt with later in this chapter. In the 1990s, however, it had become clear that Japan's presence on European soil presented not only economic challenges but also direct political influence, as illustrated by the spate of Japanese business leaders lining up to voice their opinions on the euro in 1999 and 2000. During those years following the launch of the euro, and, with regard to the UK's position outside the eleven-member euro-zone in particular, high-profile calls were made for clearer signals to be given regarding the future of European economic integration (*Financial Times*, 4 October 1999). When Toyota's chief executive officer, Okuda Hiroshi, called on the UK to be more forthright in its policy towards membership of the euro-zone so as not to lose Japanese investment there, the political influence of business, and that accruing from Japan's global economic position, were brought into sharp relief. Whilst some observers regard this kind of action as political interference (*The Guardian*, 18 January 2000), it demonstrates, in fact, how the Japanese government and businesses have learned to exercise their economic power in Europe to instrumentalize their political ends.

15.5 National differences of perception and reception

A range of different approaches has emerged in Japan's export behaviour and direct investment in the different member countries of the EC, owing to the qualitatively and quantitatively different economic relations that Japan maintains with each of them and to the different economic conditions prevailing within them. A brief overview of specific national issues illustrates the difficulty inherent in Japanese attempts to formulate a response to Europe as a whole. In January 1981, France decided (through the European Commission) to restrict the import of several Japanese products, including colour television sets. The following month, Greece raised its tariff rates on the import of those and other products, and imposed quota restrictions on machine tools. Simultaneously, Italy (also through the European Commission) restricted the import of Japanese video recorders and certain vehicles, and then in March 1981 announced import quotas for some Japanese products for the period from October 1980 to September 1981. In October 1981, the UK issued a twenty-point proposal for rectifying its trade imbalance with Japan, which was followed by the European Commission's own fourteen-point plan regarding the expansion of EC exports to Japan (El-Agra 1988: 114). This small sample illustrates how specific products, trading histories and national impediments pose barriers to Japan's formation of a Europe-wide trade approach. As is shown below, however, this diversified approach to Europe brings both advantages and disadvantages. Japanese businesses have focused on different investment sites in Europe for a variety of reasons, the principal ones of which are examined here.

15.5.i Types of market

In spite of attempts to standardize EU economic behaviour, the fifteen member states retain different economic cultures and offer Japanese investors and traders a variety of market types. Germany, the strongest and largest of the European economies, whose deutschmark lies at the heart of the euro, is Japan's number-one European trading partner because of its economic performance. In contrast, the UK is the location for most of Japan's FDI in the region. With its own failing economy and haphazard development of manufacturing, the UK was more apt to be open to inward investment during the 1980s and to protect that investment as its own (McLaughlin and Maloney 1999: 70, 85). As a result, the investment of £50 million in assembly facilities by Nissan in the UK in 1981 – the first major production facility in the UK by a Japanese automobile company – was welcomed by the British government. By 1992, Nissan had invested over £600 million, with a production capacity of over 300,000 vehicles per year. In 1997, the company drew up plans to build a third model in the UK, whilst Toyota and Honda followed with similar strategies (McLaughlin and Maloney 1999: 71). By the same token, when market conditions worsen, such locations are open to cuts and restructuring. Nissan's actions in the 1990s are a case in point: forced to restructure because of falling market share, an unattractive range of models and financial problems, the company initiated a realignment between manufacturers, component suppliers and dealers that was replicated in other sectors (*Financial Times*, 19 October 1999). Dismembering much of the 'Japanese style' it had formerly imposed, Nissan went into partnership with Renault (which purchased a 36.8 per cent stake in the company) and brought in Carlos Ghosn, otherwise known as 'le cost killer', as the first non-Japanese chief operating officer (*Financial Times*, 19 October 1999). As this example shows, market forces leave only few possibilities for intervention by host governments, although their input has been important.

15.5.ii Reception by host government

Japanese companies have faced a variety of national attitudes towards investment in Europe, extending from a warm UK welcome to hostile French protectionism, and, as a result, have had to formulate different strategies for each country in Europe. The obstacles they have to negotiate range from structural national restrictions which affect all imported goods and services to high-profile hostility directed towards the Japanese in particular. The French government and business circles have for a long time been infamous for their condemnation of Japanese trade practices, as illustrated most pointedly by an outburst by Edith Cresson in her role as minister of trade and industry (1983–6), when she criticized the Japanese for wanting to 'conquer the world' (cited in McIntyre 1994: 61). In France, Japanese inward investors also faced a country with a tradition of close government–industry involvement, especially in sectors such as automobile manufacturing, where traditional French companies were struggling in the face of major Japanese penetration of the home market. As a result of particular problems with France, the Japanese government and Japanese companies have lobbied the European Commission to promote the EC-wide implementation of Community decisions, whilst at the same time, French concerns have resulted in the application of EC-wide rules and VERs. In both cases, Japanese investors have been forced as a result to deal with France through the European Commission. In spite of former difficulties, national conditions within France have changed, and Japanese investors have profited from the low average labour costs of French workers and the size of the French market to increase their dealings there.

Plate 15.1 Off with her head! The Japanese extreme right-wing organization, Issuikai, 'decapitates' a mannequin of Prime Minister Edith Cresson of France in July 1991 after she publicly dubbed the Japanese as ants planning to take over the world.

Source: Corbis Sygma

In Germany, Japanese businesses have been welcomed, although not with the zeal found in the UK. Following a period of mutual avoidance during the early post-war era, the Japanese sought to reconstruct relations with Germany by engaging their respective economic strengths. Germany since 1962 has been Japan's largest trading partner in Europe, taking approximately one-third of Japan's European trade (Table 2). The Japanese have promoted this trade relationship for several reasons. First, Germany is located at the heart of the growing European market and therefore offers opportunities for Japanese traders to distribute to a wide area of consumers. Second, Germany's form of capitalism shares some similarities with Japan's, being less state-centric than that of France without being *laissez-faire* like the UK. Third, and most important, the German deutschmark lies at the core of the euro and Germany, for now, remains the economic powerhouse of the EU. However, although Germany is host to over 1,000 Japanese companies, and is favoured for having a positive view of industrial relations, a skilled labour force and, like France, a central geographical position, Japanese growth in the newly-reunified nation has been 'unspectacular' (Bridges 1999: 34). This is largely because high labour costs have often made it less attractive than other areas in Europe. What is more, Japanese companies traditionally have preferred export substitution in Germany, since German management is heavily based on institutional arrangements which differ markedly from Japanese practices (Kumar 1991: 231).

Japanese businesses have taken full advantage of the warm welcome they have received in the UK, where their European FDI is greatest. Since the Thatcher government in the UK in the 1980s, the British government has consistently offered financial inducements for Japanese companies to locate themselves there. Japanese investors are not only attracted by low wage costs, the use of English for negotiations, the ability to implement 'no strike' policies in their manufacturing operations (Drifte 1996:109) and the possibility of exporting their own management and production styles to the UK, but have also received major incentives from local and national government to invest in the UK. The case of Nissan illustrates this type of inducement: in the late 1980s, Nissan received £100 million in British central and regional government grants towards building the second phase of its car assembly plant in the UK (James 1989: 138), and in 1999, the British government offered a further £5 million in regional assistance to encourage the Japanese company to invest in a new generation of Primera cars to be built at its Sunderland plant (*Financial Times*, 22 October 1999). In the financial sector, Japanese traders and investors take advantage of the deregulated nature of the vast financial centre in London (Drifte 1996: 98). This interest in the UK notwithstanding, many Japanese business representatives have raised doubts about maintaining this special relationship with the UK if the latter fails to join the euro-zone in the medium term.

15.5.iii Links with the European Union

One key issue in Japanese investment decisions since the 1980s, and especially since the 1990s, has been the 'EU factor', which has penetrated even Japan's special relationship with the UK. Not only is the geographical centrality of French and German markets crucial to Japanese interests there, but the UK, too, is attractive precisely because of its membership of the EU (McLaughlin and Maloney 1999: 84). The current structure of the EU market offers Japanese businesses two key advantages: it benefits them by standardizing and harmonizing certain incentives and investment subsidies; and its lack of harmonization in other areas has enabled Japanese companies to play one member state off against the others.

On the one hand, the structural changes of the EU since the mid-1980s have offered Japan an additional point of reference for trade discussions with Europe. Japanese interest in the EC has been encouraged, not only directly by the European Commission, which became an active lobbyist and coordinator for inward investment, but also by the recovery of the European economy in the mid-1980s combined with promises of tax harmonization, customs simplification, the harmonization of standards and the formation of EC-level policies in specific sectors (such as automobiles), all of which make the European continent increasingly attractive for Japanese investors and exporters. These EC-level policy opportunities allow for the harmonization of Japanese business approaches to Europe as a whole. The example of FDI in financial affairs is illustrative of this trend, for the

EU provides both major markets for international finance, as well a potentially international dynamism in trade and finance (Kitamura 1991: 106). Market unification also enables Japanese companies to make long-term investment commitments to this region. On the other hand, the levels of member state tax incentives and subsidies differ from one country to another, which allows Japanese companies to select the optimal location for their business ventures. The threat by some major Japanese companies to relocate from the UK to alternative euro-zone locations if the UK does not adopt the euro is one salient example of this trend. Japanese responses to this EU level of negotiation have been threefold.

Despite continuing confusion within Japan regarding the development of the EU (Bourke 1996: 48), current evidence suggests that Japanese businesses have benefited from this disarray, by diversifying their activities according to the market conditions obtaining in each individual state, in spite of EU-wide rules. Thus, during the 1980s the UK accommodated a new £12.5 million Komatsu assembly plant and a £6 million investment by Matsushita in an electronic typewriter and printer assembly plant. The companies hoped in this way to avoid EC anti-dumping duties on imported excavators, and import duties on Japanese electronic typewriters, respectively (James 1989: 74). The list continues. In this way, Japanese companies can move around in order to minimize the import duties and tax penalties they have to bear. At the same time, Japan benefits from internal trade rows over Japanese penetration of Europe, such as that which flared up over the issue of local content prior to 1992, in which the UK championed Japanese rights in the face of French and Italian hostility (James 1989: 9).

The role of the European Commission has gradually expanded in the face of often nebulous European arrangements. Since the early 1980s, the European executive has monitored imports and investment in areas such as automobiles, and demonstrated a longer-term intention to create an EC-wide trade policy in this sector. It has also negotiated compromises between competing European interests, as occurred with the Elements of Consensus, thereby gaining support from major interests represented by the newly-created Association des Constructeurs Européens d'Automobiles. In this and other sectors, the European Commission has become increasingly the key policy actor with which the Japanese have to deal (McLaughlin and Maloney 1999: 183).

Finally, in dealing with a more coherent and vociferous EU, Japan has been forced to respond to criticisms levelled at its own trade practices. As a result of diplomatic pressure, Japan has partially liberalized its market restrictions, and since the 1980s has been the target of greater EC legislation, as noted above.

15.6 Peripheral Europe

During the 1990s, many countries in Central and Eastern Europe began economic and political reforms designed to facilitate their eventual entry into the EU. As such, these countries offer new and alternative destinations for Japanese investment and exports. Indeed, countries such as Poland and Hungary have received most-favoured nation (MFN) status from the EC since the late 1980s and, owing to the signature of the PHARE (Poland, Hungary Aid for Reconstruction) programme of G24 assistance to them, the EC has agreed to shorten the time required to eliminate all quotas placed on imports from them (Mason and Turay 1994: 116). Reforms undertaken by these and other aspiring members of the EC include privatization laws, price liberalization, wage controls, import liberalization, exchange rate and interest rate liberalization, banking, money, capital market reforms and budget reforms, all of which make it easier for Japanese businesses to enter and expand within these markets (Mason and Turay 1994: 117).

These agreements offer Japanese businesses more opportunities in a developing region with key channels of access to EC markets: they offer production sites for goods destined for those markets in increasingly politically and economically stable locations; and provide a pool of cheap but relatively high-skilled labour. Since 1994 in particular, noteworthy improvements have been made in the economies of these former communist states, which have resulted in increased investment overall. Some privatization of public services in this region after 1995 also encouraged Western companies to begin large-scale investment, whilst the control of inflation there has led to a rise in real incomes and the growth of domestic consumption. In addition, in 1996 Japanese-affiliated companies already present within Western Europe began moving into Eastern Europe in order to secure sources for parts supplies in the face of a strengthening yen, a move which also made Japanese companies keener to invest directly in this region. Agreements made by the EC/EU with Poland, Hungary, the Czech Republic, Slovakia, Romania and Bulgaria mean that these countries have been lowering tariffs on trade with the EU in stages. The biggest driving force behind increasing direct investment by Japan in the region since 1997 has been the expansion of investment in plants by those Japanese and Western European automobile manufacturers already present.

In spite of new opportunities, this region still poses problems for Japanese business. Whilst Slovakia, now separated from the richer Czech Republic, remains politically unstable, foreign investment has started to experience slumps in Hungary, and rampant inflation in Bulgaria has made it difficult for outside investors. What is more, in many Central and Eastern states, there remains a need for outside suppliers to provide energy, machinery and equipment. Host governments also narrow opportunities: the Czech Republic and Poland have directed their attention to the promotion of large-scale projects (such as automobile production and communication); and a reduction in investment in Bulgaria and Romania has led to their governments promoting medium- to large-scale projects to the disadvantage of smaller ones. Some positive steps towards attracting outside investment have been taken, and include: privatization laws adopted in Bulgaria and Romania in 1995, which aimed to attract new investment; and a new emphasis by Hungary and Romania on offering preferential treatment to large investors. The Czech Republic, Poland and Hungary, which have all joined the OECD since 1995, have also received initial and additional investment from Germany and the US to promote their development. Yet this remains a slow process and ensures that Japan has to approach these countries on a case-by-case basis.

Japan's initial approach to the region was made through joint ventures or Japanese affiliates based there. However, from 1996, signs of full-scale investment in manufacturing industries have become more widespread as, for example, with Matsushita Electric's announcement of a fully-owned factory in the Czech Republic and Sony's similar plans in Slovakia. It is no coincidence that these are the countries to be found on the fast track to EU membership. What is more, Agenda 2000, launched by the European Commission in July 1997 to address EU expansion, not only designated Poland, Hungary, the Czech Republic, Estonia, Slovenia and Cyprus for entry negotiations, but also pledged that Common Agricultural Policy issues would be discussed and subsidies for regional development would be cut. These and other changes will benefit outside investors.

15.7 Institutions

Japan engages in economic dialogue with the countries of Europe through a number of institutions in addition to its bilateral frameworks. These include mutual membership of the OECD, the EBRD, as well as other international fora which will be examined in Chapter 16. The current section will highlight only the EBRD, in order to illustrate the role of broader fora in instrumentalizing Japan's economic relations in the region.

The EBRD, which Japan joined as a founding member in 1991, has been a frequent conduit for Japanese engagement with the economies of the European continent. Events such as the annual Investment Promotion Seminar for Central and Eastern Europe, held since 1998, bring Japanese private businesses and the Export–Import (Exim) Bank of Japan together with the EBRD and heads of investment-related ministries and agencies from Bulgaria, the Czech Republic, Hungary, Poland, Romania, Slovakia and Slovenia. These seminars are designed for delegates to share expertise in the investment environment and economic situation in the region and to broaden opportunities for investment there. As such, they are important points for gathering up-to-date information about the investment climate here. Indeed, these seminars are held in London because many Japanese companies deal in Central and Eastern Europe via their London offices. In addition, the EBRD has now extended its remit in order to lend also to industrialized economies. The funding of the rail link between central London and nearby Heathrow airport was the first such project, and brings the Japanese government into greater proximity with decisions taken regarding developed and developing European countries alike (Drifte 1996: 99). With regard to the broader agenda, the Asia-Europe Meeting (ASEM), as was seen in Chapter 14, also serves to enhance economic dialogue. These bring benefits to the Japan–Europe relationship as part of a broader framework.

15.8 Trilateralism

As was noted in Chapter 14, the notion of trilateralism is not new. The growth of this emergent norm of trilateralism has been in evidence in the political dimension in particular since the early 1990s when Japan and the EC framed their relations within institutionalized parameters. More recently, it has been evident in government-level discussions of economic affairs. It was within this framework, for instance, that Prime Minister Obuchi toured Europe in early January 1999 to promote a new era of triadic economic cooperation between the US dollar, the new euro and the yen. In drawing upon the emergent norm of trilateralism, Prime Minister Obuchi demonstrated how Japan has the capacity to become a trilateral entrepreneur in the economic dimension of international relations. Not only does this form of trilateralism serve to provide two-versus-one leverage for its members, it also acts as a formula by which Japan exerts an influence upon the construction of the post-Cold War economic order. In so doing, it makes no claims to replace US–Japan or US–EU relations, or to provide an overarching framework for the new international political economy. Nevertheless, more and more of the economic activities of Japan and Europe are undertaken in an effort to strengthen the 'weak side of the triangle', which now frequently includes Japan as part of East Asia. For the Japanese government and Japanese businesses, therefore, trilateralism has come to supplement bilateral activities in the dimension of economic relations.

15.9 Summary

In 1998, the EU fifteen together accounted for 30 per cent of worldwide GNP, whilst equivalent figures for Japan and the US were 16 per cent and 26 per cent respectively (Asahi Shimbunsha 1999: 80; JETRO 1999a: 7–8). In 1998, the EU accounted for 40 per cent of world exports and 40 per cent of world imports, compared with 8 per cent and 5 per cent for Japan, and 13 per cent and 18 per cent for the US (JETRO 1999a: 7–8). It is clear from this chapter that Japan and Europe can no longer ignore one another. Structural developments and individual initiatives have ensured that their economic futures will overlap. In terms of structure, the changing international system, the onset of globalization (see Chapter 24) and the rise of regional integration require broader and diversified trade orientations. At the same time, in its own dealings with Europe, Japan has sought to counter trade frictions arising from the structural changes within Europe itself. Decisions to base operations in Europe have derived from the comparative advantage of local production, whilst the selection of specific trading partners and investment sites has been decided on the basis of host country conditions and historical relations.

This move into Europe demonstrates not only that Japan–EC relations are primarily concerned with economic affairs, but also shows how Japanese actors have been able to use economic diplomacy to exercise power in Europe so as to promote a broader agenda. The bargaining positions obtained by Japanese companies through their direct presence in Europe, and by the Japanese government through its participation in regional institutions have, moreover, been improved by their ability to deal increasingly with one representative interlocutor on European soil. These developing economic relations, moreover, enable Japanese policy-making agents and other actors to promote their domestically embedded norms of economism and developmentalism within an internationally-visible relationship. It remains to be seen whether the continuing effects of globalization will enhance Japan's ability to exploit this normative position further.

Chapter 16

Japan–Europe security relations

16.1 Overview

MOFA's 1999 *Diplomatic Bluebook* examined the course of Japanese foreign policy during 1998. Two distinct trends were clear: the pursuit of security interests with bilateral counterparts (such as the US, Russia, China and South Korea) which gave particular prominence to military matters; and the promotion of an alternative security paradigm as a 'demonstration of comprehensive and proactive leadership' (MOFA 1999b). Chapters 6 and 11 have shown how relations with the US and East Asia continue to be dominated by traditional security concerns. Security relations with Europe and within the United Nations (see Chapter 19), however, demonstrate a new kind of behaviour by Japan: the articulation of quiet diplomacy. It is a form of diplomacy which emphasizes issues such as support for nuclear non-proliferation and peacekeeping activities across the world, and is embodied in Prime Minister Obuchi Keizō's pledge at the end of 1998 to advocate 'human security' in pursuit of peace and stability (see Chapter 11). Two points are important to note in the context of Japan–Europe relations: quiet diplomacy has provided the mainstay of their bilateral relations throughout the post-war period; and, as this type of security dialogue becomes more prominent, Japan and the EU have a clear alternative path of bilateral diplomacy to follow. Such a path eschews notions of military security in favour of a broader concept of human and civil security. This dialogue has been adopted frequently in bilateral and multilateral engagements between Japan and its European counterparts.

With the pursuit of just such a policy in mind, in 1999 the Japanese government played an important, if largely unnoticed, role in the Kosovo crisis in Europe. Statements by MOFA officials and the prime minister himself emphasized that Japan's contribution to the resolution of this crisis would be channelled through multilateral fora (most notably the UN and the G8), and that its attention would focus in particular on civilian needs as part of the efforts towards post-crisis reconstruction. This policy orientation also stresses the need to bring together Japanese and European non-governmental organizations (NGOs), and to publicize this type of security agenda within the public domain.

This chapter will examine the gradual development of a multifaceted security dialogue between Japan and Europe, despite the constraints of the norm of bilateralism on Japanese security policy during the Cold War. Indeed, it will show how the development of new trilateralism has served to reinforce a certain kind of security behaviour between Japan and Europe, which is based, moreover, on the support of one of Japan's strongest domestic norms: namely, anti-militarism.

16.2 Cold War structures

During the Cold War, Japan's security interests were dominated by relations with the US, as well as by concerns within East Asia (see Chapters 6 and 11). Europeans, for their part, were preoccupied with the question of Germany: first, with the issue of integrating the defeated Germany into a Europe-wide political and security framework; then, once the Iron Curtain descended, with ways to ensure that West Germany remained in the anti-communist bloc of states and within a pan-European community. During the 1950s, moreover, it became clear that the US-dominated NATO would feature at the centre of European security concerns. As a result, internal preoccupations of both Japan and Europe, combined with a geographic distance, kept them, for the most part, out of one another's spheres of interest and influence.

This understanding of the early post-war relationship between Japan and Europe should not be viewed as the *status quo* for the entire Cold War period. In fact, whilst the US remained at the forefront of their respective foreign policies, Japan and the member states of the EC did begin to develop their own means of achieving dialogue in the security dimension of international relations. The norm of bilateralism served to define the external boundaries of their relationship: mutual relations would thus be either directly supportive of the United States in the security dimension, or else Japan–Europe dialogue would focus on an altogether different conceptualization of security. As a result, there developed between Japan and its European counterparts an incremental growth in often *ad hoc* engagements which paved the way for their post-Cold War mutual interests in broader definitions of security. It is upon this incrementally-established redefinition of security that the norm of trilateralism has come to be based in the wake of the ending of the Cold War. As a result, the alternative types of security interest that Japan and Europe were seen to promote after the end of the Cold War (such as Japanese participation in Kosovo) are essentially a consequence of embedding these anti-militarist norms within their bilateral (Japan–Europe) relations.

In terms of the military concerns, discussions by the Japanese government with European counterparts have generally taken place only within the context of NATO, in which the United States retains an overarching presence. Moreover, Prime Minister Nakasone Yasuhiro's remarks at the 1983 Williamsburg summit (see Chapter 21) were interpreted in Russia as a move towards Japanese participation in an aggressive Western alliance (Robertson 1988: 103). For this reason, greater Japanese involvement with Europe through NATO was approached with some trepidation by the Japanese government, and the US continued to provide security structures for Japan.

Chapter 15 has shown that economic issues formed the core of Japan–Europe relations during the Cold War period. To the extent that bilateral military issues were considered, they should be understood in this context. Thus, for example, by mid-1973 European firms, along with their US counterparts, began to put MITI under pressure to allow them access to Japan's potentially huge arms market (Green 1995: 67). This economic pursuit of military interests continued into the following decades, as illustrated by the Japanese government's decision in the early 1980s to exercise economic power, by playing off US against European producers of fighter planes in order to influence US policy interests in the development of Japan's own indigenous aircraft. In the early 1990s, the surprise alliance between Daimler-Benz and the Mitsubishi Group, French attempts to sell cheap fighter planes to Japan during the FSX controversy (see Chapter 6), and the Japanese purchase of search-and-rescue aircraft from British Aerospace, all pointed to two further developments in this strategy: a new willingness on the part of the Japanese to look beyond the US for its military purchases; and an ability to play off one European country against others in the face of internal European competition in this field (Green 1995: 148).

16.3 Post-Cold War changes

The ending of the Cold War precipitated a number of important changes within the security dialogue between Japan and Europe. First, the Cold War concluded in Europe with the fall of the Berlin Wall in 1989. Signalling not only the cessation of divisions in Europe, its collapse also resulted in a rethinking by European countries of their whole security framework. Put simply, as former Soviet bloc countries began to join Western European organizations, 'Europe' after 1989 began to embrace both Eastern and Western states within the same 'European' structures. The Japanese government was quick to express its desire to be involved in assisting states such as Poland and Hungary to make the requisite transitions, through participation in the G24 process and the European Bank for Reconstruction and Development (EBRD) (see Chapter 15). One further significant step came with the signature of the Treaty on European Union (TEU) in 1992, which associated the security forum of the WEU with the EU framework (see Chapter 14). The appointment in 1999 of the former NATO secretary-general, Javier Solana, to the post of 'high representative' of the CFSP (and his additional role as head of the WEU) brings this coherence into greater relief. In these ways, the very nature of the European interlocutor in security issues has changed since the end of the Cold War.

Second, these new structural conditions prompted a subtle change in Japan's orientation towards Europe; that is, Japanese policy-making agents gradually came to exercise economic power in order to instrumentalize new kinds of security goals. Japan's non-military participation in Bosnia and Kosovo is a case in point (Gilson 2000b). Third, this new framework has facilitated the growth of multilateral fora, such as the G24, in which Japan has been able to promote more actively its own ideas of security. Fourth, these alternative forms of security have found echoes in Europe, where similar developments towards quiet diplomacy have also been evident at the EU level, as the Union continues to wrestle with its ambivalent security identity. Trilateralism has underpinned many of these changes.

16.4 Facing a converging European security agenda

Whilst there is growing recognition that Japan and Europe share concerns over security issues, clearly areas of difference do exist in Japan's relations with the individual states of the EU. As in other dimensions of its foreign policy, Japanese policy-makers and other actors are able to make use of differing EU approaches, whilst also dealing more and more with the structures of the EU over matters in the dimension of security.

16.4.i Shared security interests

Although Japan retains bilateral relations with EU member states, some subjects are common to their various meetings. These include, for instance, promoting the joint combating of international terrorism and cooperation towards the most comprehensive response possible to the Register of Conventional Arms Transfers, as well as the reform of the Convention on Conventional Weapons protocol on anti-personnel landmines. Moreover, considerable common ground exists within Europe with regard to the promotion of a conclusion to the Comprehensive Test Ban Treaty (CTBT) and universal adherence to the Nuclear Non-Proliferation Treaty (NPT), as well as support for the full implementation of principles and objectives for Nuclear Non-Proliferation and Disarmament as agreed at the 1995 Review and Extension Conference of the Parties to the NPT, and in emphasizing the importance of bringing the Chemical Weapons Convention into force as soon as possible. Joint support for the four-party talks over the search for a Korean Peninsula peace treaty has also been a familiar topic in recent bilateral dialogues, as has the promotion of the use of multilateral fora, such as the UN and the G7/8 (see later and Chapters 19 and 21).

Particular interests are also pursued at the bilateral level. For example, in its security dialogue with the UK, Japan's MOFA, the JDA and institutions such as the National Institute for Defence Studies in Tokyo have worked with the UK's Ministry of Defence and the Foreign and Commonwealth Office to sponsor joint initiatives and share information. In addition, the UK has supported Japan's requests for a permanent seat on the UNSC and for general UN reform, as well as Japan's observer status to the OSCE. On the other hand, the Japanese government has supported British cooperation within the Korean Peninsula Energy Development Organization (KEDO) and the UK's claims to an independent (that is, non-EU) seat at the table of the ASEAN Regional Forum (ARF). It should be noted, too, that support by the British prime minister, Tony Blair, for a more coherent European-level security role (in contrast to a more ambivalent British stance on the euro) has also placed the UK – in conjunction with France – at the forefront of developing EU security interests. In this capacity, Blair has sought to promote stronger links amongst the EU, NATO and the WEU. This position reinforces Japan's reasons for maintaining its bilateral security dialogue with the UK.

In Germany, Japan has long recognized a partner similarly 'burdened with constitutional and emotional sensitivities about overseas military action' (Bridges 1999: 46). With this in mind, Japan and Germany have worked closely together in PKO, and both have been active in sponsoring cooperation in the development of the peaceful use of nuclear energy and the promotion of nuclear safety. In addition, given their close mutual interest in the Russian Federation, Japan and Germany have established a joint dialogue on this subject and in support of reforms in Russia and in the newly independent states (Maull *et al.* 1998: 173). In their joint approach to UN reform, Japan and Germany also share a desire to become permanent members of the Security Council, as expressed officially by Germany in September 1992 and by Japan in 1993.

Specific areas of interest for Japan and France tend to concern the former colonies of the French. Thus, Japanese staff cooperated with French troops in Cambodia following the 1991 peace settlement there, and subsequently Japan and France jointly hosted the International Committee for Restoration of Cambodia. However, particular problems arose with regard to the French government, following its resumption of nuclear testing in the Pacific in 1995, which had the effect of rocking the whole structure of Japan–Europe security relations more generally. Thus, problems with one member state tend to affect the whole of the EU, since Japan now views its future as linked with this growing European partner, even in this dimension.

16.4.ii Peacekeeping operations

Joint PKO initiatives have become an integral part of Japan's security engagement with its European counterparts. Not only has this led to a sustained government-led dialogue, such activity has also emphasized support for the actions of non-government actors in this field. To this end, seminars, training initiatives and joint symposia have been held between Japan and various European states, in order to discuss, for instance, post-conflict nation-building in Africa, the participation of Japanese personnel in PKO map exercises and other measures to develop more effective means of training peacekeepers and more effective instruments of preventive diplomacy. Peacekeeping efforts have also been promoted by Japan's participation on the Peace Implementation Council Steering Board for Bosnia-Herzegovina, a forum which provides the Japanese government with direct involvement in security affairs on European soil. This type of dialogue has also sought to promote cooperation between representatives of NGOs from Japan and Europe.

16.5 Bilateral security dialogue

As a first step towards a coordinated security dialogue, the Hague Declaration of 1991 between Japan and the EC set out the principal security interests of the two parties. This included the promotion of negotiated solutions to international or regional tensions, the strengthening of the UN and other international organizations, the enhancement of policy consultation and, wherever possible, policy coordination on international issues that might affect world peace and stability. It also emphasized adopting a cooperative stance in the face of transnational challenges (such as the conservation of resources and energy, terrorism and international criminal activity). As is clear from this list, relations with individual member states tend to mirror this kind of agenda.

One area of particular interest to Japan and its European counterparts is the question of Russia, a geographical expanse which separates them and in respect of which they have mutual concerns. From the move to *perestroika* (openness) from 1985 onwards, and especially following the 1991 break-up of the USSR and the rise to power of President Boris Yeltsin, the Japanese government began to seek common positions with its European counterparts with regard to Russia. In particular, the problems posed by the threat of economic disintegration in Russia, and by the need to dismantle nuclear weapons and maintain or close down nuclear power stations (in Russia and beyond) enabled Japan and Europe to define a mutual interest in the geographical area between them.

16.6 Peripheral Europe

The Hague Declaration itself pledged joint cooperation in dealing with Central and Eastern Europe, as well as the countries of Asia. In this way, the idea that Eastern Europe belongs to the EU's backyard and is therefore its own responsibility, and that East Asia is Japan's concern, is being broken down.

Most notably, Japanese policy-makers have used the conflicts in the Balkans to demonstrate their willingness to participate in burden-sharing away from East Asia. Foreign Minister Obuchi travelled to Bosnia and Herzegovina in April 1998, in order to illustrate the high level of Japan's commitment to the promotion of peace implementation there. In November 1999, the Japanese government despatched foreign ministry officials for a seven-month mission to former Yugoslavia and a six-month spillover mission to Skopje, in order, according to official reports, to improve the situation in the region and to deepen Japan–Europe relations. The Japanese government also became a member of the Steering Committee of the Peace Implementation Council for Bosnia-Herzegovina, and subsequently sent sixty-five supervisors and observers in addition to US$3.5 million to support the 1996–7 elections. For the September 1998 elections it sent thirty observers and US$1 million to cover costs of activities such as ballot printing.

In the Kosovo crisis of 1999, Japan was also involved by participating in the G8 foreign ministers' meeting in Cologne, Germany in May 1999 and by pledging US$200 million in assistance for Kosovo, of which US$60 million was destined to be given over two years to the neighbouring countries of Macedonia and Albania for refugee assistance. During this crisis, Prime Minister Obuchi travelled to Washington in April and May 1999, where he met with Russia's special envoy, Viktor Chernomyrdin. Japanese support for a political solution to the crisis and its appreciation of Russian mediation demonstrated a willingness by the Japanese government to act as a bridge (*kakehashi*) between Russian and Western interests, as was seen in Part III with regard to the US and East Asia. In addition, Foreign Minister Kōmura visited refugee camps in the Republics of Macedonia, Azerbaijan and Uzbekistan in April 1999, in order to highlight the plight of refugees and Japanese commitment to easing their problems (Gilson 2000b).

These actions not only demonstrate a commitment to its European counterparts in the dimension of security; they also illustrate Japan's engagement in a *proactive* policy of quiet diplomacy. Much of this diplomacy is channelled consciously through multilateral fora.

16.7 Multilateral cooperation

The joint Japan–EC Hague Declaration emphasized the multilateral aspect of relations between Japan and Western Europe. Applying a multilateral approach to the security dimension of Japan–Europe relations enables Japanese policy-makers to demonstrate their international commitment, and increasingly to conduct in a positive way Japan's quiet diplomacy (see Chapter 2). In this way, the Japanese government is seeking to use multilateral fora as a conduit for proposing new forms of security diplomacy. For this reason, too, many of the security issues concerning Japan and Europe can be found in UN debates. Many of these fora will be examined in Chapters 19, 20 and 21, but the current section outlines some of the ways in which multilateral frameworks serve to enhance and constrain Japan–Europe security relations.

16.7.i North Atlantic Treaty Organization

With regard to military activity, Japanese policy-makers use the structures of NATO to keep up to date with events in Europe. Since 1990, the annual NATO–Japan Security Conference has enabled Japanese policy-makers to confer with their NATO counterparts on issues of mutual interest. Such issues include their respective relations with Russia, concerns over arms proliferation and the need to strengthen and support the role of the UN. Japanese diplomats also occasionally attend NATO seminars, whilst NATO officials travel to Japan (Drifte 1996: 83).

As demonstrated during the Kosovo crisis of 1999, when NATO led bombing raids against Serbia, Japan's current level of links with NATO provide two principal advantages. In the first place, the Japanese government was party to some of the detailed information about the bombings; in the second place, Japan's non-membership of NATO enabled it to play a neutral role with regard to the military campaign. By liaising with this grouping, the Japanese government is able to pursue a non-military stance within a military forum.

16.7.ii Organization for Security and Cooperation in Europe

Known as the OSCE since 1995 (formerly the CSCE), this organization comprises almost all European countries, together with the US and Canada. It was designed as a series of conferences to discuss cooperation in the fields of, *inter alia*, security in Europe, economic and environmental affairs, and humanitarian assistance. Its principal objectives have become early warning for conflicts, conflict management and crisis management. It now addresses a whole gamut of regional trouble spots, from Bosnia-Herzegovina to Nagorno-Karabakh.

During the 1980s, as Japan's financial assistance was solicited by this forum, the Japanese government began to request representation within it. This was achieved in December 1995, when the Permanent Council of the OSCE agreed that Japan and South Korea could become 'Partners for Cooperation' (Yasutomo 1995: 330). Within this special category, Japan is a non-participating state at meetings of the Permanent Council, a status that allows the Japanese government to be involved in exchanges of information with representatives in Europe over a range of security-related issues (Bridges 1999). By allowing Japan to become associated with the organization, moreover, the Japanese government's financial assistance is slowly opening doors for Japanese policy-makers to become more involved in the decision-making capabilities of this and other fora. In a similar way, Japan gained observer status to the Council of Europe in 1996.

The OSCE has proved to be an important forum for promoting Japan's credentials as a quiet diplomat, and the Japanese government recognizes its value as a channel for confidence-building measures, which are designed to encourage dialogue and to facilitate preventive diplomacy. Japanese activities to date within the OSCE have included the provision of financial assistance to the OSCE Mission in Sarajevo which was established in June 1994 to monitor and set up elections, record human rights' violations, and promote further measures for regional stabilization. In July 1996, the Japanese Diet also decided to provide US$2 million through the OSCE as grant-in-aid to Bosnia for purchases relating to the setting-up of local elections, and in February 1998 Japan sent an expert to the OSCE Mission in Croatia. Japanese policy-makers, especially those within MOFA, watch with interest the 'OSCE first' principle, whereby it tries to resolve intra-regional disputes before going to the UN, because the OSCE offers a potential model for the ASEAN Regional Forum (ARF) in East Asia.

16.7.iii United Nations

Various agencies of the UN have offered Japan and Europe the opportunity to work together on a number of issues, and in particular to promote a joint stance on non-military contributions to conflict prevention and post-conflict management. Two issues exemplify the types of cooperation that the two sides have undertaken in this organization to date: the 1992 UN Register of Conventional Arms Transfers; and cooperation in Kosovo (Gilson 2000b).

A draft resolution entitled 'Transparency in armaments' was introduced to the United Nations General Assembly (UNGA) by The Netherlands on behalf of the Community together with Japan, in November 1991 (Gilson 2000a). Following its introduction, Japanese and the EC policy-makers worked to ensure agreement from other member states until the Arms Register resolution was adopted as a confidence-building measure in December 1991. This resolution was important in consolidating existing discussions within Japan's bilateral dialogue with the core countries of Europe over the nature and importance of confidence-building measures as a means of conflict prevention. It has remained a frequently-reiterated theme in their bilateral security agenda since that time.

Various crises on the European continent, from Bosnia to Kosovo, have increased Japanese direct financial and personnel involvement there. In the name of Japan's Law on Cooperation in UN Peacekeeping and Other Operations of 1992 (see Chapter 19), the Japanese government and NGOs began to participate in the reconstruction of former Yugoslavia in 1998. In the case of Kosovo, the Japanese government contributed financially to the G7/8, the UN's High Commission for Refugees, to the United Nations Children's Fund and to the World Health Organization. It also sent personnel to the OSCE's Kosovo Verification Mission and to the UN Mission in Kosovo, and has supported activities of a number of aid agencies such as the AARJ.

Of particular importance with regard to this final issue was the implementation of post-crisis assistance in the form of high-level personnel and the financing of clearly-targeted projects, in particular the return of refugees and displaced persons. Given Japan's professed desire to gain a permanent seat on the UN Security Council, Japanese policy-makers had an opportunity to develop in more concrete terms Japan's commitment to international cooperation based on non-military criteria (see also Chapter 19). Prime Minister Obuchi's proposal for a Fund for Human Security within the UN, and Japan's US$200 million package of aid (the highest amount paid by any participating member) towards the resolution of the Kosovo crisis, should be seen in this context.

16.7.iv G7/8

The importance of the G7/8 forum for Japan was illustrated during the Kosovo crisis of 1999. The Japanese government agreed to assist in the resolution of the crisis 'as a responsible member of the G8'. This participation in the G7/8 summit was important, because it stipulated the creation of a strictly civil presence to complement a security role for the UN. Activities undertaken within this framework were to include election monitoring, economic support, humanitarian and disaster relief, and the maintenance of order, and fitted well with Prime Minister Obuchi's concern for human security as part of his government's foreign policy. The G8 (with the presence of Russia as a second non-NATO state) on this occasion facilitated the development of the notion that an alternative path to cooperation could be followed, namely, by providing humanitarian assistance in the promotion of civil security, as opposed to military security. At the G7/8 summit in Okinawa in 2000, the Japanese government proposed the establishment of a Japan–Europe conflict prevention cooperation, and thereby used once again a major international forum in order to further bilateral dialogue, and to pursue quiet diplomacy (*Financial Times*, 14 January 2000).

16.7.v ASEAN Regional Forum

As well as activities on the European continent, Japan and the countries of Europe also meet in East Asia-based fora, which include ASEAN's Post-Ministerial Conference (PMC) and the ASEAN Regional Forum (ARF), both of which have been dealt with in Chapter 11. This section examines their particular contribution to the development of Japan–Europe relations.

The development of the ARF in the 1990s provided Japan with a forum in which new approaches to security could be raised without arousing regional concerns about renewed Japanese militarism. For Japan and the EU, the ARF provides a further channel for consultation on East Asian issues such as disarmament, the NPT, the UN, and human rights, and places particular emphasis on security concerns (European Commission 1994; Fujizaki 1995: 6). In addition, the ARF provides a forum for discussing issues of military concern in Europe (such as Bosnia-Herzegovina) in a setting meant to promote deeper understanding on security matters.

On the one hand, the ARF ensures a continued US presence in the region by strengthening multilateral ties and, on the other, it balances the growing political strength of Japan and China. In terms of its institutional development, creating the ARF as the 'PMC +' not only saved on transaction costs by employing existing fora, but also ensured its credibility by linking the new grouping with a successful institution. Moreover, the Japanese were aware of the advantages of using a pre-existing and well-tried institution in developing a new form of interaction, since it offered an established *modus operandi*, defined membership, and useful precedents for activities in the new forum. Therefore, the ARF is important for both Japan and the EU because its novel mode of discussion allows contemporary issues to be debated in non-Cold War language, by applying new terms to security and political discourse (Evans and Dibb 1994: 1).

16.7.vi Korean Peninsula Energy Development Organization

KEDO is another security forum in which Japan meets its European counterparts (see Chapter 11). It is important in demonstrating how Japan and key states in Europe have become involved in activities in one another's part of the world.

Given its own financial commitments to KEDO, and under pressure from the US, the Japanese government was active in seeking additional participation on the board of KEDO. As a result it turned to the EU. It also wanted to spread its own political burden and make it easier to facilitate the making of domestic decisions regarding financial contributions (Maull *et al.* 1998: 181). The EU finally confirmed KEDO as a joint actor with the CFSP in December 1995 (Gilson 2000a) and agreed to contribute to the organization as a member of the executive board. The most important role of the EU in KEDO for the Japan–EU relationship, however, was as a vehicle for the promotion of reciprocal concerns regarding human security in East Asia and Europe. In addition, the participation of the EU in KEDO provides the Japanese government with further credibility when it attempts to garner domestic support for Japanese participation in this project. In terms of the nature of involvement, KEDO-related actions reinforce the validity of the concept of quiet diplomacy, through mutual emphasis on non-military solutions to regional problems. Difficulties remain in achieving EU-wide consensus over security (Maull *et al.* 1998: 182), but fora such as KEDO provide possible blueprints for future EU activities in this dimension. For the Japanese government, participation with its European counterparts demonstrates their increasing interdependence in security matters. The implications for this growing joint approach to alternative forms of security activities will be analysed further in Chapter 23.

16.8 Domestic actors

16.8.i Policy-making agents

As has been shown, security concerns between Japan and Europe focus in particular on elements of civil participation in the resolution of, and post-conflict restoration following, regional and global crises. For this reason, whilst the JDA is instrumental in implementing specific and limited military exercises with some of its European counterparts, most of this dimension of Japan–Europe relations is conducted through various departments within MOFA. However, as is the case with political dialogue, MOFA does not adopt a coordinated approach to security affairs with Europe, since relations with the member states of the EU are dealt with by two different divisions of the European and Oceania Affairs Bureau. As a result, the type of issue addressed will determine (although not always in a clear-cut way) the locus of responsibility. The case of the UN Register of Conventional Arms Transfers, for example, came under the responsibilities of various agents responsible for arms and disarmament, and which include MOFA's UN Bureau and the JDA.

In the pursuit of alternative forms of security, the role of the prime minister and other high-level policy-making agents has been of particular importance. In addition to making statements in support of Japan's quiet diplomatic stance, such as Prime Minister Murayama's support of his European counterparts over the abolition of anti-personnel landmines, Japanese leaders have begun to articulate a more sustained set of principles regarding this type of action. Prime Minister Obuchi has provided the clearest examples of this approach, from his sustained concern over refugees and displaced persons resulting from landmine threats in Bosnia to the Serbian expulsion of Kosovars; to his announcement in the UNGA in 1998 of a 'human security' agenda, and a Fund for Human Security. Not only does the Japanese government use the discussion of such topics to provide tangible evidence of its quiet diplomacy, but such discussion also illustrates how this position fits closely with Japan's long-held norm of anti-militarism (see Chapter 23).

16.8.ii Non-governmental organizations

It is in the security dimension of Japan–Europe relations that NGOs have become most active. In many ways, their activities have come to embody the type of human security stance that the Japanese government is trying to promote. In the case of the Kosovo crisis, for instance, Japanese NGOs active in the area included the Association of Medical Doctors for Asia, the AARJ, Japan Emergency NGOs and the Japanese Red Cross. Medical specialists were also sent through the Japan International Cooperation Agency (JICA) to Kosovo. Indeed, during the Kosovo crisis, much of Japan's financial assistance was channelled through Japanese NGOs working with their counterparts in Europe, an illustration of the proxy channels of diplomacy referred to in Chapter 2. Following the cessation of the bombing, the Japanese government sent its counsellor at the Japanese embassy in India and an official of MOFA's UN Administration Division to the UN Mission in Kosovo (UNMIK), to work alongside the chief of staff of the Mission, to assist in UNMIK's remit to rebuild infrastructure, including housing, and to carry out the safe return of refugees. It is no surprise that during the Kosovo crisis private Japanese aid groups reacted more quickly than the Japanese government to the problems suffered by local populations, since they are able to respond in an apolitical manner to urgent and localized humanitarian needs.

These NGOs serve two purposes. First, some, such as the Japanese Red Cross, receive independent financing from their main headquarters and depend upon charitable donations and membership fees. This type of NGO can interact easily with its overseas counterparts. At the same time, semi-independent (such as the AARJ) and government-sponsored (such as JICA) NGOs receive some or all of their financing from the Japanese government. Each of these serves its purpose: the former provide the Japanese government with evidence of both a more internationalist and more independent response to global issues; whilst the latter enable the government to prioritize particular areas for diplomatic action, such as refugees.

The NGO sector stands at the forefront of human security, and the Japanese government is instrumentalizing its activities for its own purposes, thereby promoting the norm of anti-militarism proactively and internationally. These increasingly visible Japanese NGOs have been encouraged further by the high-level participation of Ogata Sadako and Akashi Yasushi, head of the UNHCR and the former UN secretary-general's special representative in the Balkans, respectively. Both of them have lobbied for Japanese government support in the resolution of the crises in Kosovo and Yugoslavia and ensured that this European issue gained considerable Japanese press coverage. Responses to European events by the Japanese government and Japanese NGOs have increasingly overlapped, for example, following the earthquake in Izmit in Turkey in August 1999. The Japanese government immediately sent a 37-man rescue team and a 16-man medical team (Japan Disaster Relief Team), as well as an 8-man earthquake-proofing study expert team to examine the earthquake resistance of buildings, civil engineering structures and lifelines in stricken areas, and to give advice to the disaster headquarters. This intertwining of activities is one way in which the

Japanese government is able to promote its growing international credibility as an international aid donor and humanitarian paramedic. In so doing, it deploys power in line with the norm of anti-militarism.

16.9 Changing security norms

Japan's security dialogue with Europe is qualitatively distinct from its security relations with the US and East Asia. It represents a change in security policy by the Japanese government towards a more assertive articulation of quiet diplomacy in formal channels of diplomacy and away from informal channels (see Chapter 2). This type of diplomacy prioritizes specific non-military agendas that emphasize issues of human welfare within multilateral and bilateral fora. Quiet diplomacy involves the incorporation of financial and personnel participation in specific international fora and crises (such as KEDO and Kosovo), on the basis of clearly-defined non-military goals and in support of a set of humanitarian principles. It is most explicitly articulated in the security dimension, but is applied by the Japanese government and non-governmental actors to a growing degree in politics and economics, too. In particular, quiet diplomacy incorporates NGO as well as business actors within state-level foreign policy-making, as illustrated by Japan's attempts to join the UN's permanent Security Council. The implications of this type of diplomacy will be considered at length in Chapters 23 and 24.

In the security dimension, quiet diplomacy, which as discussed in Chapter 2 has roots in the domestically embedded norm of anti-militarism, needs to be balanced with Japan's long-standing bilateral security links with the US. In doing this, the Japanese government and its people have begun to exploit the emergent norm of trilateralism to reconcile these external and domestic demands. The 1998 *Diplomatic Bluebook* (MOFA 1999b) states how trilateralism offers a supplemental arrangement to bilateralism, and explains that it involves cooperation between members of the 'minilateral' grouping of the US, Japan and Europe within a variety of fora, several of which were examined above. Whilst not as pronounced as in its economic relations, a nascent trilateralist norm is underpinned and made formal by tangible modes of cooperation, such as the Japan–US–Europe Diet Members' League for Comprehensive Security (*Nichibeiō Sōgō Anzen Hoshō Giin Renmei*). In this trilateral structure, moreover, relations with Europe not only offer a counterbalance to bilateral ties with the United States (ASEM in particular is viewed in this light), but also allow for greater interaction in one another's regions. In addition, the changes in the structure of the international system both permit a broader interpretation of what security can be, and bring into the mainstream of debate over security questions those subjects which have long lain at the heart of Japan–Europe dialogue. Thus, questions over sustainable development, environmental degradation and human welfare have become part of high-level agendas on security matters in the twenty-first century.

At present, this emergent trilateralist norm is developing with European consent, since Europe, too, espouses anti-militarist norms and the EU as such currently retains no military structure. However, the future integration of the WEU into the framework of the EU, and the clarification of the WEU's role versus that of NATO, will determine the extent to which Japan and Europe continue to share these principles in the security realm. At present, the trilateral framework sets important parameters for Japan–Europe security affairs: by constraining and facilitating action.

On the one hand, the trilateral framework locks Japan and Europe into a security agenda set initially by the US, and which continues to view Japan (through its security treaty with the US) and Europe (through NATO) as secondary contributors to a US-led structure. This structure ensures that debates continue in Japan over the retention of Article 9 of the Constitution and that Europe is reluctant and unable to set an independent security agenda. On the other hand, trilateralism as an emergent norm offers opportunities to redefine the very nature of security, in order to incorporate space for the articulation of a human security agenda. In these ways, Japan's relations with Europe offer the ideal site for the promotion of Japan's quiet diplomacy.

16.10 Summary

This chapter has shown how a security dialogue between Japan and Europe is important in several ways. First, because of the lack of military relations with Europe, Japanese policy-makers are able to pursue a human security dialogue with this interlocutor, and in so doing to promote at an international level quiet diplomacy. The Japanese government, therefore, is able to exploit fully its relations with the EU in order to extend the areas covered by the term 'security', such that humanitarian and civil agendas are included, and to develop its foreign policy through a variety of channels outside the purely military. For this reason, Japan and the EU jointly promote issues such as human 'safety nets' against globalization and other welfare concerns within security fora.

Second, the more visible and assertive articulation of quiet diplomacy now promoted by the Japanese government represents the externalization of domestic norms into a coherent foreign policy orientation. Its domestic origins, moreover, make it easier for the government to gain popular support for this kind of international activity, whilst the government's cooperation with, and support of, NGOs and international agencies gives still greater credibility to this norm in the eyes of the Japanese public and external observers alike.

Third, the broader dialogue in which the pursuit of this alternative security agenda is located enables Japan and the EU to engage in a long-term relationship even in terms of security issues. In this context, a situation of reciprocity ensues, to the extent that Japan and the EU are able to expect some element of mutual concern in their affairs. Thus, Japan participates in Kosovo, whilst the EU joins the KEDO project. This formula is also extended by the fact that humanitarian security issues may arise anywhere and encompass a range of transnational concerns.

Fourth, this joint cooperation in the security dimension enables Japan and the EU to keep in balance the position of the US with regard to global security concerns. In the case of Kosovo, cooperation in Europe on a humanitarian scale enabled the Japanese government to avoid having to condone the actions of the US, and facilitated support of China after the embassy bombing in May 1999. This was all achieved without jeopardizing bilateral relations with the US.

Finally, by locating their security dialogue within this trilateral approach, Japanese policy-making agents are able to move away from the US government's position on a range of subjects, by gaining support from Japan's European counterparts within international fora, such as the G7. This form of trilateralism mirrors debates taking place in the economic dimension (see Chapter 15) and serves to balance US military concerns at the apex with a growing alternative link between the other two members of the triangle.

Chapter 17

Conclusion

17.1 Trilateral agenda

Chapter 13 observed Prime Minister Obuchi Keizō arriving in Paris in January 1999. The aim of his trip was to obtain support for a trilateral financial order, in the wake of the launch of the single currency in eleven states of the EU. This proposal aimed to prevent the yen from becoming marginalized on the periphery of international financial activities. A similar process can be seen in the dimensions of politics and security, in which the Japanese government and its people have sought a central role in contemporary international relations. Chapters 14, 15 and 16 have shown how the emergent norm of trilateralism underpins these dimensions of Japan's relations with Europe in different ways and with different implications.

17.2 Balancing relations

Chapter 14 examined how the political dimension of Japan's relations with Europe has become increasingly formalized, and how the Japanese government has succeeded in using this relationship as part of its wider political agenda. First, it demonstrated how this bilateral relationship came to be sustained by a set of formal structures during the 1990s. As codified in the Hague Declaration of 1991, these structures facilitate regular dialogue between Japanese policy-makers and the Council of Ministers of the EU, and demonstrate how the Japanese government has come to recognize the key role of the EU as an international actor with which it shares common interests.

Second, the Japanese government and its people have come not only to recognize how the 1992 Treaty on European Union (TEU) integrated the political and economic agenda of the Union, but also to promote the EU's status as a legitimate trilateral pole in order to balance their own relations with the US. Whilst the US remains the key international partner for Japan, therefore, Japanese policy-making agents have begun to cultivate relations with Europe as part of a strategy of diversification in their foreign policy.

Third, the ending of the Cold War and flux within alliances inside multilateral fora offer Japan the possibility of using its trilateral relations to form a core group around which contemporary international agendas are formulated. In these ways, Japanese policy-makers are able provide Japan with a position as a key political actor without raising concerns about its regional and global role among its trilateral counterparts or those outside the triangle.

17.3 Tripolar competition

Economic dialogue has been the mainstay of Japan's relations with Europe throughout the post-war era. Whilst much of that time has seen Japan in conflict with one or more EU member state over economic issues (such as anti-dumping), the lengthy history of their economic interaction and the coherent role of the

EC/EU in the economic dimension have ensured the continued development of this dimension to relations. Trade relations have also enabled the Japanese government and business community to play a direct part in European affairs, as the many Japanese production operations in Europe show. In addition, growing fears of a potential 'fortress Europe' during the 1980s precipitated major relocation by Japanese companies on Western European soil, as well as direct investment projects within the cheaper labour markets of Central and Eastern Europe.

Within this dimension, as Chapter 16 has shown, the trilateral norm is becoming firmly embedded, particularly in view of the launch of the euro as a major currency with future potential to rival the US dollar and the Japanese yen. In this dimension, moreover, the Japanese have used their economic power to situate themselves at the heart of a new international economic order. This positioning has served several purposes. First, trilateralism in the economic dimension enables Japan to counterbalance not only the role of the dollar, but also the potential future role of the euro. Prime Minister Obuchi's proposed trilateral financial order represented an attempt to counterbalance growing European financial influence alongside the existing role of the dollar. Second, in order to do that, the Japanese have become actively engaged in the international fora which set the rules for economic behaviour. In this context, Japan's position at the G8 meeting in 1998, in the wake of the East Asian financial and economic crises, demonstrated how Japan has also assumed the mantle of responsibility for the East Asia region. Third, the trilateral framework affords Japanese exporters and investors the possibility of adopting two-versus-one alliances in fora such as the WTO, in order to gain more leverage against the trilateral partner in opposition. Obviously, this two-versus-one structure often places Japan in opposition to a US–Europe alliance. Fourth, Japan's growing economic relations with Europe ensure that Japanese businesses now take up opportunities in Europe and, through their own chambers of commerce as well as direct business-to-business dialogue with their European counterparts, are at the forefront of economic developments in Europe. In that position, they have not only enjoyed privileged opportunities within the borders of the Community, but have also played an increasingly significant role in voicing an opinion over the direction of EC/EU economic policy agendas themselves. In these ways, the Japanese government and its people are able to influence European economic policy both directly and indirectly.

17.4 Triangular unity

Military security issues have never been at the forefront of Japan's relations with the EU. That is not to say, however, that no security dialogue has taken place at all, since the respective concerns of Japan and the EU over issues such as nuclear non-proliferation, humanitarian and environmental problems, and post-crisis society-building have been reformulated into joint bilateral efforts to follow an alternative path towards security issues. As a result, the security dimension with Europe has been instrumentalized by Japanese policy-makers in order to present an innovative approach to these issues, which now forms a new and dynamic pillar of their relationship. Two factors are important to note with regard to security: the role of multiple actors; and the search for legitimacy for this kind of approach to security.

First, this dimension of bilateral relations has benefited from growing direct contact between Japanese and European NGOs, since they are at the forefront of activities such as aiding conflict zones and campaigning to abolish anti-personnel landmines. The Japanese government has encouraged and promoted the development of such informal channels in the pursuit of security dialogue, in order both to persuade the domestic audience that security issues are led by the people, and to demonstrate to the outside world that Japan's security policy is neither based upon military propositions nor solely the domain of policy-making agents.

Second, Japanese policy-makers have formulated their human security proposals within multilateral fora to gain legitimacy for them. By linking their strategy to trilateral efforts, moreover, the Japanese are able to garner support from Europe which contains several militarily neutral countries and which as the EU does not have a standing army.

17.5 Supplemental strategy

All three dimensions of Japan's relations with Europe have been affected by particular changes during the 1980s and 1990s. First, the level of European integration itself has provided a driving force for the strengthening of relations, by giving Japan a more coherent counterpart in Europe, and also by causing Japanese policy-makers to respond to particular EU developments (such as the euro). Second, the perceived decline of the US as world superpower has combined with the US government's own exhortations for Japan and Europe to play greater burden-sharing roles on the international stage. These factors have enabled Japan and Europe each to pursue a more proactive policy within a trilateral framework that does not jeopardize their respective relations with the US, but seeks to supplement them. Third, pursuit of this emergent trilateralist norm ensures that Japan does not become marginalized in international affairs, by placing it at the heart of post-Cold War policy-making structures in all three dimensions of politics, economics and security.

These examples demonstrate how relations with Europe as part of this emergent norm of trilateralism not only support Japan's domestic norms of economism and anti-militarism, but also provide an additional means of engagement in a period of complex international relations. The growing EU is a major economic, political and security counterpart to Japan, and enables Japan to supplement its bilateralist norm with bilateralist-supporting trilateralism. This supplementalist approach, moreover, lies at the core of Japan's quiet diplomacy, as will be seen in Chapter 23.

Part V

JAPAN–GLOBAL INSTITUTIONS

Chapter 18

Introduction

18.1 Renewed internationalism

On 24 April 1991 a decision to despatch four minesweepers to the Persian Gulf was made at an extraordinary meeting of the Japanese Cabinet. These four minesweepers (*Yurishima*, *Hikoshima*, *Awashima* and *Sakushima*), one flagship (*Hayase*), and a support ship (*Tokiwa*) departed two days later with Captain Ochiai Taosa hurriedly appointed commander of the task force. One day before the despatch, faced with civil groups protesting near the JDA, some peacefully, some torching vehicles, Prime Minister Kaifu Toshiki underlined to the House of Representatives' Steering Committee on Foreign Affairs the peaceful objectives behind these extraordinary events: 'it is quite important for those countries [which are capable of contributing to peacekeeping in the Persian Gulf] to cooperate in safety in the region' (*Japan Times*, 26 April 1991). This intent was reinforced by the farewell address given by Ōshima Tadamori, deputy director-general of the JDA, who went to great pains to characterize the despatch as part of an international contribution. Fortunately for all parties concerned, this minesweeper episode came quietly to an end on 31 October 1991 with the return of the whole task force to the port of Kure after having detonated thirty-four mines without incurring any casualties.

For a state which renounced the maintenance of any war-making capability and has not despatched its Self-Defence Forces (SDF) abroad since their creation in 1954 (although Japanese minesweepers were involved in the Korean War prior to the SDF's formal creation), these events seem anomalous. The immediate causes can be found in the first crisis of the post-Cold War period, when Iraqi tanks rapidly occupied Kuwait on 2 August 1990. This was construed by President George Bush and other political leaders around the world as a direct challenge to the emerging world order. For the Japanese state and its people, it heralded a rollercoaster political ride involving an initially rapid response, criticisms thereafter of immobilism, and the eventual despatch of the four minesweepers, the flagship and support ship to the Persian Gulf. Thereafter, Japan's commitment to the UN increased and the SDF began to participate in UNPKO. However, at first the Iraqi invasion of Kuwait posed a challenge for the Japanese people and the quiet, chiefly economic, diplomatic approach to international relations the government had adopted up until this point. The government of Prime Minister Kaifu Toshiki came under pressure both domestically and internationally, especially from the US, to make more than the financial and minimal contribution espoused by the Yoshida Doctrine and conditioned by the norms of economism and anti-militarism. Eventually the Japanese government settled upon financial support totalling US$13 billion, although this sum was not forthcoming initially and failed to satisfy demands from the Allies in the Gulf for Japan's human contribution to the crisis in the Middle East, which is a region of vital concern to Japan owing to its dependence on oil imports. The two most salient effects were the introduction of legislation enabling the first despatch of Japanese military personnel abroad since 1954, and the Tokyo Declaration of January 1992, issued during the brief revival period in the UN's post-Cold War role by which Bush and Prime Minister Miyazawa

Plate 18.1 Chequebook diplomacy? Prime Minister Kaifu Toshiki responds to international pressure and criticism during the 1990–1 Gulf War by providing financial contributions.

Source: Cartoon by Taylor Jones published in the *Los Angeles Times*, 1991. Copyright 1991. Los Angeles Times Syndicate. Reprinted with permission

Kiichi committed 'their resources and the talents of their peoples to the purposes of the United Nations Charter [and agreed to] cooperate to reinvigorate the UN Organization' (Immerman 1994: 182).

US interest in the UN's post-Cold War role in Somalia (and generally) withered as a result of the failure of the operation. Quarrels over the US's budgetary contributions provided a further nail in the coffin of post-Cold War UN activism. However, Japan's recent role in UNPKO, its desire to acquire a permanent seat on the UNSC, and continued financial support for the UN system still give cause for optimism amongst those who seek to shape a new internationalist and multilateral role in the world for Japan, in contrast to its traditional reliance upon a bilateral relationship with the regional or global hegemon. With these issues in mind, the following three chapters will examine Japan's participation in a number of global institutions, namely the UN, the WB, the IMF and GATT – the post-World War II family of organizations created at the Bretton Woods Conference of 1944–5 – and the WTO and the G7/8. Issues will be highlighted which have dominated Japan's political, economic and security relationships with these institutions (the 'what' question); the aims and objectives behind Japan's participation (the 'why' question); and the manner in which Japan has attempted to address these issue-areas (the 'how' question). The immediate origins of Japan's first post-Cold War dilemma – namely, the 1990–1 Gulf War – have been described above. However, in order to gain a more nuanced understanding of how this string of cataclysmic events developed and the influence of both structure and internationally and domestically embedded norms in shaping Japan's responses, it is necessary to return to the beginning of the twentieth century and Japan's interactions with the international order of the day.

18.2 From Versailles to the San Francisco peace treaty

Since Japan opened its doors to the early-starters of the West in the mid-nineteenth century, the experience of the state and its people of dealing with the world on a multilateral basis has been severely constrained, and the emphasis in its foreign relations has been placed upon bilateral relations especially with the dominant power in the international system. This can been seen in the Anglo-Japanese Alliance (1902–23); the Tripartite Pact with Germany (1940–5, the Italian side of the alliance undeveloped to the degree that it was, in effect, a bilateral relationship (Dobson 1999a)); and the US–Japan security treaty (1951 to date, see Part II). Japan's first substantial interface with the world on a multilateral basis was throughout World War I and resulted in participation as a victorious power in the creation of the League of Nations at the Paris Peace Conference of 1919. It was a remarkable achievement to be seated among the great powers of the time for a state and its people which had only fifty years previously embarked upon the path of modernization sparked by the Meiji restoration. Thereafter, the inter-war period did witness Japan's participation in various schemes for international cooperation under the initiative of Foreign Minister Shidehara Kijūrō. The eponymously titled 'Shidehara Diplomacy' stressed cooperation with particularly the US and Britain, including participation in and ratification of international conventions such as the Kellogg–Briand Pact of 1928 and the London Naval Treaty of 1930. For a time it appeared that the Japanese government was aspiring to behave as a responsible member of the international system promoting, in the words of Niitobe Inazō, Japan's under-secretary of the League, 'the maintenance of peaceful relations with the rest of the world' (Howes 1995).

Despite such sentiments, Japan's failure to persuade the early-starters to write a clause on racial equality into the Covenant of the League of Nations ensured that this honeymoon period was short-lived and that Japan's first impressions of the League were tarnished irrevocably (Shimazu 1998). This initiative was resisted by the US, Great Britain and its dominions, particularly Australia, which suspected the proposal to be an attempt to sanction unchecked Japanese immigration. Thus, from the outset, the great Western powers of the day created the impression that Japan was regarded as a racially inferior *parvenu*. As a result, the political mood in Japan perceived the post-World War I international system as a self-serving construction of the West intended to maintain the pre-war *status quo*. Thus, the structural constraints imposed on Japan as a latecomer to the Western imperial world order were patently evident. The immediate post-war reflections of the Shōwa emperor (1926–89), upon the symbolic importance of the rejected racial equality proposal, demonstrated these misgivings:

> If one asks about the causes of the war in the Far East, they can be found concealed in the contents of the peace treaty signed after World War I. Factors such as the rejection by the powers of the racial equality proposal advocated by Japan, the continuation of discriminatory sentiments between white races and yellow races, and the rejection of immigrants in California were enough to cause resentment among the Japanese people.
>
> (Bungei Shunjū 1990: 100)

The phenomenon of Japan growing in status whilst chaffing against the confinements of the Western imperial world order was neatly summed up by politician Itō Miyoji's statement to the Foreign Affairs Deliberation Committee in February 1919 that:

> the League may prove convenient for increasing despotic action on the part of countries such as England and America, but it be [*sic*] a real obstacle to countries now struggling for future progress and development …
>
> (Hosoya 1965–8: 19)

This negative perception of multilateral fora was further coloured by the Washington Conference and Four Power Treaty of December 1921. The treaty stipulated the ratios for replacement tonnage of capital ships for the five leading naval powers (the US, Great Britain, Japan, France and Italy) at 5:5:3:1.75:1.75 respectively. Although seeking to promote arms limitation and stability, the treaty failed to acknowledge Japan's original demands for a higher proportion and locked Japan's navy into an inferior position compared to the US and Great Britain. Hence, despite the existence of a number of influential internationalists or norm entrepreneurs, such as Shidehara and Niitobe, occupying positions of responsibility and influence within the Japanese government and the League, and working actively for their promotion, Japan's participation in the fledgling organization was ultimately a failure. It came to a sudden end in March 1933 when Japan withdrew pre-emptively from the multilateral body owing to anticipated international criticism based on the findings of the Lytton Commission (despatched by the League to report on the Japanese establishment of the puppet state of Manchukuo in the aftermath of the Kwantung Army-engineered Manchurian Incident of 1931). Thereafter, the concepts of internationalism and civilian control in Japan continued to be eroded by a militarist clique as the state turned away from its former allies, joined with the revisionist powers of Germany and Italy, and abandoned internationalism for a period of over twenty years, in favour of expansion and regional hegemony in East Asia (Nish 1993).

After defeat in World War II, Occupation under SCAP and the consequent adherence to strict bilateralism with the US, the Japanese state and its people were:

> defeated in battle, and under allied occupation she [*sic*] had no choice but to stand on the sidelines as the UN made its debut. To Japan stripped of membership qualifications, and in a state of spiritual prostration, the UN was, indeed, a distant entity.
>
> (Hosoya 1965–8: 18)

However, it was already becoming evident that, despite Japan's exclusion, the roles both of Japan in the UN system, and of the UN system in guaranteeing Japan's security in relation to Article 9 of the 1947 Constitution, were beginning to be debated in the Diet most vehemently by Shidehara, Yoshida Shigeru and Nanbara Shigeru, later president of the University of Tokyo (Dore 1997: 52–9). Moreover, the virtues of the UN system were debated in the Japanese media, academic circles and domestic society. The *Yomiuri Shimbun* declared on 13 January 1946 that, 'in comparison to the League, the UN organization is markedly more powerful, leaving almost no opportunity for a renewal of aggression'. Even with the onset of the Cold War, these hopes remained alive, as seen in the *Asahi Shimbun*'s declaration of 25 October 1949 that, 'the world's hopes are linked by the fact that the UN remains very much an active reality'. Clearly, this represented a distinctly different reaction in contrast to that which greeted the creation of the League of Nations. In fact, based upon the Constitution and Japan's renunciation of any war-making capacity, there was a short-lived expectation within these circles, until the onset of a bipolar structure to the international system, that the UN would be the future and logical guarantor of Japan's security.

18.3 Post-war reintegration of Japan

Despite this initial exclusion from the international institutions set in place by the early-starters of the West, Japan's next substantial experience of internationalism came with admission to the UN in December 1956 at a time when, as was seen in Chapter 4 on the normalization of relations with the Soviet Union under Prime Minister Hatoyama Ichirō, the Cold War was showing signs of thawing. A number of previous attempts, initiated as soon as Japan regained its sovereignty and was able to apply for UN membership, had been vetoed by the Soviet Union, fearful of adding what it regarded as a servile follower of the US to this nascent international organization. Eventual admission was greeted at home with an overwhelming display of public support, even euphoria, in line with an immediate post-war gadarene rush into other UN agencies like the Universal Postal Union (July 1948),

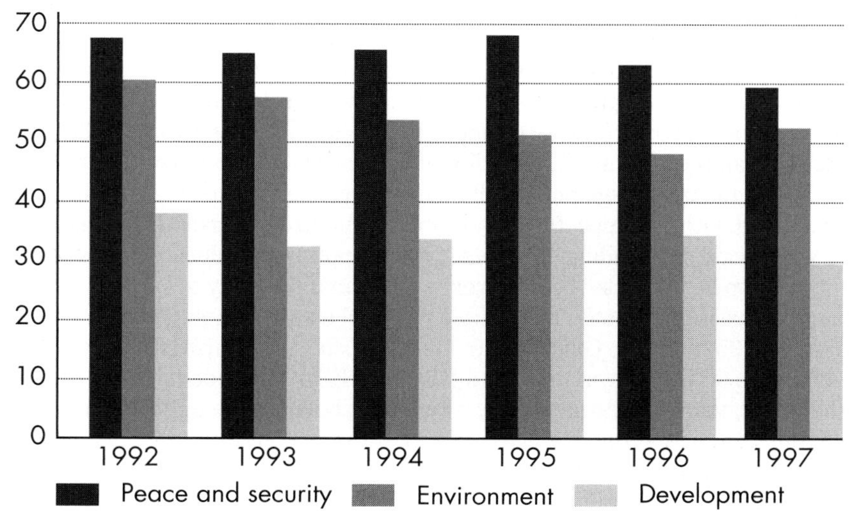

Figure 18.1 Japanese public opinion on the major role for Japan to undertake in the UN

Source: Naikaku Sōri Daijin Kōhōshitsu 1998

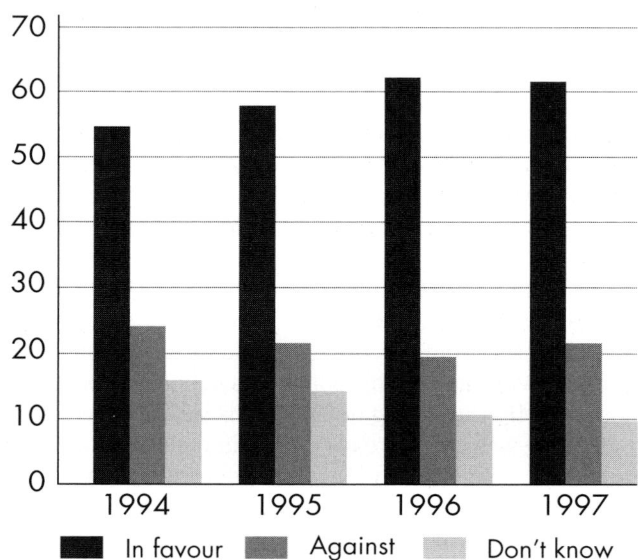

Figure 18.2 Japanese public opinion on a permanent seat for Japan on the UN Security Council

Source: Naikaku Sōri Daijin Kōhōshitsu 1998

the World Health Organization (WHO, May 1951), the United Nations Educational, Scientific and Cultural Organization (UNESCO, July 1951), and the International Court of Justice (ICJ, April 1954). In fact, throughout the Cold War and post-Cold War periods the UN system and its work have continued to command high levels of support from the Japanese public (see Figures 18.1 and 18.2). Even today in Japan the National Federation of UNESCO and the Japan Committee for UNICEF command a large public following. It has been argued that this popularity is connected with the impact these organizations made in Japan in the immediate post-war period in providing emergency food supplies and education programmes, but it can also be linked to the preference of domestic society to support a range of organizations seeking as far as possible peaceful means to solve human problems (Fujiyama 1952: 66–74; Obana 1976: 78–81). Especially during the period when membership of the UN was denied to Japan, UNESCO provided a sense of linkage to the world, thanks to its ideal that, 'since wars begin in the minds of men, it is in the minds of men that the defences of peace must be constructed'. This tenet both created and embedded a 'UNESCO spirit' in Japanese society.

Upon Japan's admission to the UN in December 1956, Foreign Minister Shigemitsu Mamoru both mimicked the Preamble to Japan's 1947 Constitution and placed an idealistic emphasis upon international cooperation through various global institutions:

> We have determined to preserve our security and exist, trusting in the justice and faith of peace-loving peoples of the world. We desire to occupy an honored place in an international society striving for the preservation of peace. Japan is gratified that, together with the maintenance of peace, the United Nations places great importance on humanitarianism. It has taken up the problem of disarmament as a major task in the pursuit of its objective of maintaining peace. Being the only country which has experienced the horrors of the atomic bomb, Japan knows its tragic circumstances.
>
> (*Asahi Shimbun*, 19 December 1956)

Indeed, since 1957 the Japanese government's annual *Diplomatic Bluebook* has repeatedly espoused a UN-centred foreign policy. However, owing to the constraining influence of the Cold War international structure and the overarching bilateral relationship with the US, this policy was stillborn at best. Similarly in the WB, GATT and the IMF, the sibling organizations which were established within the UN system, Japan was initially excluded from membership. The WB and the IMF were proposed at the Bretton Woods Conference of July 1944 in order to assist global post-war reconstruction. The goals of the WB were to 'assist in the reconstruction and development of members and to promote private foreign investment and the long-range balanced growth of international trade'. The IMF was created to aid the WB and 'assist in the establishment of a multilateral system of payments in order to facilitate international trade' (Vadney 1987: 66–7). The extent to which these organizations were embedded within the international system designed by the US can be seen in the fact that one-third of the seed money for the organizations was provided by the US, which thus acquired one-third of the voting rights. In addition, the headquarters were established in New York and predominantly staffed by US citizens. GATT, however, came into being in a more muted style. There was a general consensus on some mutual reduction of trade barriers in a multilateral forum, but this could not be realized until the US's allies were economically strong enough to adopt a multilateral approach. Reconstruction was their priority. In this atmosphere, Japan did not accede to GATT until July 1955 (effective from September 1955), owing to the opposition of some members, such as the UK, because of concern over certain Japanese commercial practices. Japan's eventual admission was sponsored by the US in line with Japan's subservient position taken under the Yoshida Doctrine. Thus, the international structure of bipolarity and Japan's dedication to the norm of bilateralism was from the outset dictating Japan's role.

Nevertheless, a greater opportunity for independence existed within the G7 summit created in 1975 by President Valéry Giscard d'Estaing of France and Chancellor Helmut Schmidt of Germany. As finance ministers, they had both been frustrated by the IMF and WB, finding the parallel, informal sessions with their American, British and Japanese counterparts more satisfying. Thus, a more intimate organization of major powers came into being that recognized, unlike previous global institutions, Japan's status in the world. Despite this belated recognition, however, the original and unfortunate beginning to Japan's historical experience of internationalism provides the background to understanding the Japanese government's and people's reaction to the 1990–1 Gulf War.

18.4 Summary

After defeat in World War II, the Japanese state and its people joined an international system created by the early-starters, the partisan nature of which was institutionalized by the UN and Bretton Woods global economic institutions. The following chapters will demonstrate that, slowly but surely, a variety of norms has both encouraged and constrained Japan in its realization of the ideal of promoting multilateral solutions to global problems. In order to gauge the extent to which Japan has overcome the obstacles outlined above and risen to the status of a responsible international actor concomitant with its global economic stature in the dimensions of politics, economics and security, this Part V will deal only with institutions possessing a truly global reach. For the sake of clarity, this three-pronged tool of analysis will be maintained within each chapter rather than in Part V as a whole. In Chapter 19, Japan's participation in the immediate offspring of the League of Nations, that is, the UN, will be examined in the areas of voting patterns, personnel, budget reform and UN peacekeeping. Thereafter, the following two chapters will focus on the sibling organizations of the UN: the IMF, the WB, GATT and the WTO (Chapter 20); and the G7/8 and its offshoot organizations (Chapter 21). Accompanying this elaboration of what Japan has done will be an enquiry into the aims and objectives behind these activities, to fashion an understanding of why Japan has behaved in this way, as well as an exploration of the instrumentalization of Japanese policy, that is, how Japan has undertaken its UN policy initially as a dependant of the US and a latecomer to the US-dominated international system. In concluding, and with this chapter in mind, appraisals of whether Japan has achieved an 'honored place in an international society striving for the preservation of peace', as stated in the Preamble to the Constitution, will be made in order to evaluate the level of Japanese proactivism.

Chapter 19

Japan–United Nations

19.1 Overview

Upon admission to the UN in 1956, the Japanese government advocated ebulliently a 'UN-centred diplomacy'. Kishi Nobusuke reiterated this in February 1957 (when he was still foreign minister), stating that Japan's policy would revolve around the three pillars of: cooperation with other democracies; maintaining a position as a member of Asia; and UN-centrism. However, beyond the rhetoric the Japanese government was unable, and unwilling, to push forward with such a proactive policy in a Cold War world divided structurally by East–West ideological conflict. Instead, it located itself firmly in the Western, capitalist camp, displaying overriding preferences for economism and minimum security commitments that accompanied bilateral cooperation with the US. These were articulated in the Yoshida Doctrine. Thus, for the first few decades of Japan's UN membership, the concept of UN-centred diplomacy was a hollow one compromised by the structural constraints imposed by the international order which limited policy to meeting budget contributions to the UN, joining various organs of the UN system, as was seen in Chapter 18, serving occasionally as a non-permanent member of the UNSC, and maintaining bilateralism by voting until the early 1970s in line with the US on issues such as support for Taiwan as the Chinese representative in the UN.

During the 1970s, the composition of the UN changed dramatically, concomitant with the process of decolonization. This created new, non-Western power bases within the General Assembly, as represented by the non-aligned movement (NAM). As a consequence, the US began to relinquish dominance, and then interest, in the UN. In this atmosphere, the Japanese government was presented with the structural freedom to realize the concept of UN-centrism and participate more independently of the US, at least in global institutions and multilateral fora. For example, on the Palestine issue Japan abstained in the 'Zionism equals Racism' General Assembly Resolution 3379 of November 1975. Japan also, despite opposition from the US, departed from an equidistant position between Israel and the Arab states by beginning to endorse UN resolutions inviting the Palestine Liberation Organization (PLO) to the General Assembly as the representative of the Palestinian people, and by recognizing the right of self-determination for Palestinians in 1976. Moreover, because supply for Japan's energy needs was, and remains, highly dependent upon Middle Eastern oil, the issues of energy and the *status quo* in the Middle East enabled Japan to play a more independent role in the UN. This confirms the conclusion reached in Chapter 7 regarding Japanese willingness, within the bilateral relationship with the US, to take a stand when its own interests are paramount.

The 1980s witnessed continued US disillusionment with the UN and the Reagan administration's policy of non-cooperation with several organs of the UN system. Despite the strength of bilateralism, this created a political environment within which the Japanese government found it increasingly difficult to support the aggressive, anti-UN line of the US. Hence, the modicum of independence and proactivism in Japan's UN diplomacy, which began in the 1970s, continued to develop with the aim of promoting reconciliation between the US and UN through re-

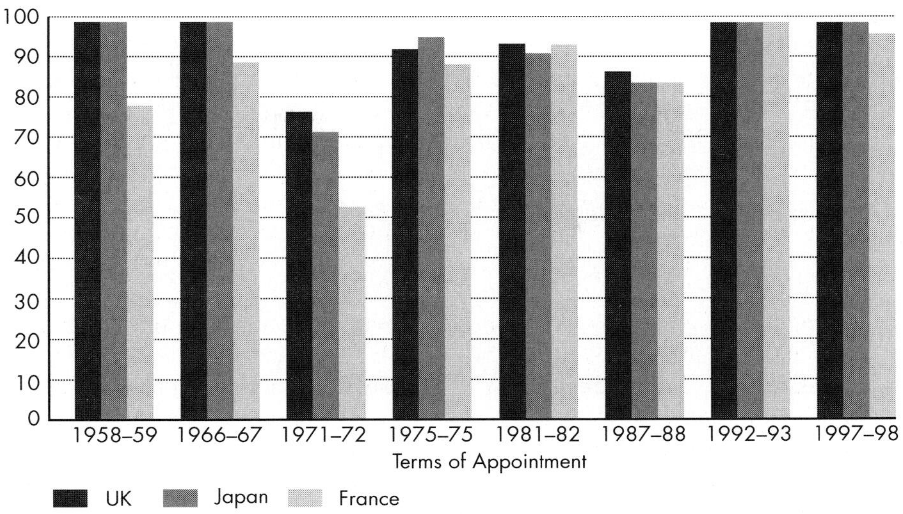

Figure 19.1 Coincidence of voting with the US in the UN Security Council
Source: United Nations various years

form of the UN. This was exemplified by Japan remaining in UNESCO, despite the departures of the US and – in apostolic fashion – the UK and Singapore, which paid further testament to the independent line being developed by the Japanese government during these years. Moreover, voting patterns reflect the extent to which Japan was beginning to move away from obedient endorsement of US voting (see Figures 19.1 and 19.2). It was thus only in the 1980s, owing to structural changes in the international system, that concrete, rather than rhetorical, proactivism began to accompany the espousal of UN-centrism. In a number of fields, as will be seen in the following sections, this fledgling proactivism in Japan's UN policies has continued to develop expeditiously.

19.2 United Nations reform

19.2.i United Nations Security Council

Today, the issue of permanent membership of the UNSC demonstrates the power of the domestically embedded norm of developmentalism and Japan's desire to be recognized as a first-class country (*ittō koku*). This has been an explicit policy goal since the Meiji restoration of 1868 and was tied to the UN specifically in 1968 and 1969 when Foreign Minister Aichi Kiichi, at the 23rd and 24th Sessions of the General Assembly, made comments interpreted at the time as representing the Japanese government's desire to become a permanent UNSC member. In 1973, a

Session	Year	Japan	UK	France
51st Session	*1996*	46.1%	61.8%	53.3%
50th Session	*1995*	42.9%	62.0%	53.6%
49th Session	*1994*	41.5%	68.8%	61.9%
48th Session	*1993*	35.9%	54.7%	47.6%
47th Session	*1992*	27.0%	51.4%	39.7%
46th Session	*1991*	34.7%	54.8%	45.1%
45th Session	*1990*	32.1%	58.0%	55.1%
44th Session	*1989*	25.4%	56.1%	34.5%
43rd Session	*1988*	25.9%	50.4%	43.7%
42nd Session	*1987*	28.7%	52.6%	43.7%
41st Session	*1986*	29.9%	61.2%	51.7%
40th Session	*1985*	34.7%	62.3%	51.4%
39th Session	*1984*	42.7%	57.8%	50.0%
38th Session	*1983*	37.5%	62.3%	52.4%
37th Session	*1982*	38.0%	58.9%	47.8%
36th Session	*1981*	44.4%	65.4%	52.6%
35th Session	*1980*	44.4%	75.0%	69.8%
34th Session	*1979*	48.4%	78.2%	66.4%
33rd Session	*1978*	55.0%	81.7%	71.8%
32nd Session	*1977*	55.2%	82.1%	64.2%
31st Session	*1976*	46.0%	73.5%	64.7%
30th Session	*1975*	33.3%	76.5%	41.2%

Figure 19.2 Coincidence of voting with the US in the UN General Assembly
Source: United Nations various years

joint communiqué issued by Prime Minister Tanaka Kakuei and President Richard Nixon touched on this issue and declared that 'a way should be found to assure permanent representation in that council [the UNSC] for Japan, whose resources and influence are of major importance in world affairs' (Ogata 1983: 30–1). Japan's claim is reinforced by the fact that only it and Brazil have served as non-permanent members of the UNSC on a record eight separate occasions, most recently from 1997 to 1998 (the other occasions are 1958–9, 1966–7, 1971–2, 1975–6, 1981–2,

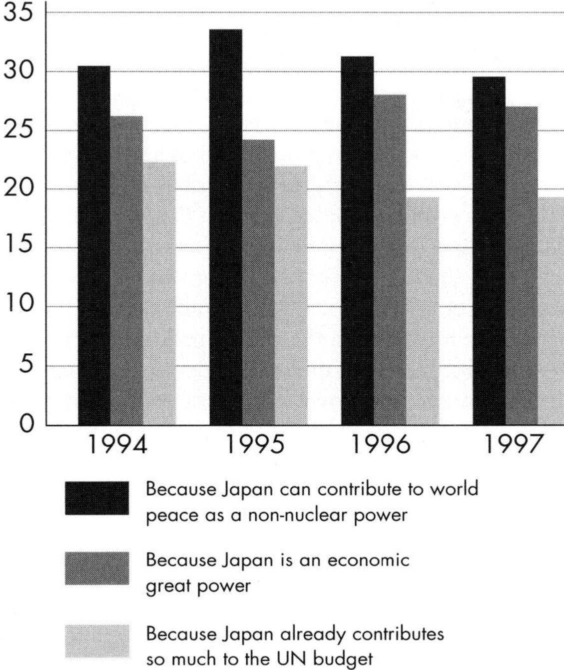

Figure 19.3 Reasons behind Japanese public opinion support for Japan's entry to the UN Security Council
Source: Naikaku Sōri Daijin Kōhōshitsu 1998

1987–8 and 1992–3). However, Japan has no automatic claim to this position, as demonstrated by the 1978 election, when Japan lost the vote to Bangladesh for a non-permanent seat on the UNSC. In this way, it would appear from a realist perspective that the chief incentives for the Japanese government to join the UNSC are fourfold: first, to dispense with the need to run for election; second, to promote Japanese representation befitting its financial contribution; third, to procure the influential veto that automatically goes with a permanent UNSC seat; and fourth, to acquire information on various issues facing the UNSC. The Japanese government and MOFA commonly agree on the point postulated by the former foreign minister, Kakizawa Kōji, that even though Japan pays the second largest amount in the UN budget, it has no more ability to make its voice heard than a country with a population of 40,000–50,000 and that this imbalance needs to be resolved (Ishida 1998: 126). Moreover, public opinion polls in Japan support these assertions (see Figure 19.3).

The effects of this issue of representation have filtered down to Japanese domestic society and demonstrate the pluralist nature of the Japanese policy-making process. Combined with a need to address the immobilism seen at the time of Japan's response to the 1990–1 Gulf War, the issue of UNSC representation was the catalyst to create MOFA's Foreign Policy Bureau. Its aim, based on the activities of the UN Office of MOFA, is to oversee Japan's diplomacy in the post-Cold War world and the creation of a new world order, responding both to internationalist and bilateral norms. Its first head, Yanai Shunji, has attempted to paint a picture of harmonious relations between MOFA and the LDP-led coalition government over the issue of Japan's inclusion as a permanent member of the UNSC (Gaikō Fōramu 1994). Similarly, in line with MOFA, some politicians seeking to influence the policy-making process, such as the LP leader and chief norm entrepreneur, Ozawa Ichirō, called for inclusion in the UNSC as the right and natural direction for Japan in the process of becoming a 'normal state' able to exercise military power unhindered by the norm of anti-militarism. This points to the role of sectional bureaucratic interests in the policy-making process.

Nevertheless, anti-militarism, embedded deeply in Japanese domestic society, remains of crucial importance, owing to fears expressed within the Japanese government (Prime Minister Hosokawa Morihiro's administration being the most vocal example) and society, and even reflecting those of the JDA, that a permanent UNSC seat would result in an expanded peacekeeping role, possibly including peace-enforcement duties. Japanese representatives have repeatedly voiced their readiness to assume the responsibilities of a permanent member, but 'in accordance with its basic philosophy of the non-resort to the use of force prohibited by its Constitution' (Obuchi 1997). In addition, socialist and communist opposition parties in Japan argue that Japan's role in the UN should be primarily economic and social, not military. These fears are also expressed in East Asia, especially by both South and North Korea, and China, which all regard any increase in Japan's peacekeeping role as silent or creeping remilitarization, as was discussed in Part III.

19.2.ii *Japanese initiatives*

Nevertheless, MOFA has repeatedly underscored the seriousness of UNSC reform:

> The issue which brings us here today, the reform of the Security Council, is an issue which can determine the future of the world. It would be no exaggeration to say that our future will depend upon whether we are going to succeed in creating a new United Nations and its new Security Council, capable of effectively dealing with the issues that the present-day world is expected to face.
>
> (Owada 1997)

In this way, Japan's inclusion in the UNSC is regarded as one aspect of a wider reform of the UN system aimed at reflecting the realities and power configurations of the post-Cold War world, rather than those of the post-World War II world. A variety of plans for restructuring the UNSC exists. However, the opinions of leading Japanese policy-making agents reflect Japan's attempt to respond to the exigencies of the post-Cold War world and reinforce international structures by centring upon the need for far-reaching and long-term reform, rather than a quick fix, in order to enable the UN to face an expanded security agenda in the new century. This suggests a more proactive role for Japan in the twenty-first century. However, MOFA fears that to support an expanded UNSC could see a second General Assembly being created and dilution of the influence and prestige of membership of the UNSC. In addition, there is no desire in Japan to downplay the importance of established members such as the UK and France, whose international significance may have declined relatively since 1945, yet which still occupy key positions in the UN and other global institutions and enjoy the ability to exert influence. In any case, it is unlikely that either would simply acquiesce in the reduction of their central role in the UN. A regional and cultural *mélange* is seen to be necessary but not at the risk of fundamentally weakening the UNSC. Hence, owing to domestic norms based on anti-militarism and the structural impediments faced by Japanese policy-makers in carving out a role for Japan in international organizations dominated by the West, MOFA promotes a degree of conservatism combined with an attempt to include in any future UNSC the rising global and regional powers.

In the meantime, Japanese diplomatic style has been to promote conciliatory measures aimed at blurring the line between UNSC members and non-members. Prime examples of this include daily briefing sessions for non-members by the president of the council, and the increasing availability to non-members of papers from informal UNSC consultations. The manner in which Japanese diplomats have kept the issue of Japan's inclusion alive – by finding a middle way to resolve the problem – illustrates Japan's quiet diplomacy.

Other political issues complicate reform of the UNSC. Rewording the text of the UN Charter would be a necessary condition for Japan's entry into the family of UNSC members. The choice of the name, 'United Nations', itself is a relic from the wartime alliance against Germany and Japan (fortunately translated into Japanese as International Confederation, *Kokusai Rengō*, not the direct translation of the words 'united' and 'nations', *Rengōkoku*, which is tantamount to meaning 'allied nations', thus avoiding any association with the World War II Allies). A more serious issue than titular concerns is the enemy clauses (Articles 53 and 107) within the UN Charter. Article 53 is of particular symbolic importance in that it sanctions regional security organizations to take peace enforcement actions without the approval of the UNSC in the event of the World War II Allies' former enemies renewing their aggression. The chief importance of the two clauses is in their psychological weight. The Charter, created by the early-starters of the West, continues to brand anachronistically the Japanese state as an enemy within an organization that is propped up financially by Japanese contributions, and in which Japan is gaining an increasingly high profile and making a commitment to its internationalist norms.

19.3 Representation

19.3.i Personnel

In most organs of the UN system Japanese representation has been traditionally lowkey. What is more, there is a scarcity of qualified Japanese international public servants, owing to its coming late to the UN, language limitations, and a tendency towards a system of lifelong employment at home as opposed to short-term UN contracts. As a result of these drawbacks in the promotion of Japanese nationals, in 1994 Japan despatched fewer staff to the UN than did the other major industrialized powers (see Figure 19.4). Furthermore, the quantitative problem of Japanese personnel was compounded by (especially US) criticism of and opposition to the re-election of Nakajima Hiroshi, director-general of the World Health Organization (WHO) in 1992 (the opposition was ultimately unsuccessful). However, recently, through individuals such as Ogata Sadako in the UN High Commission for Refugees (UNHCR), Akashi Yasushi as secretary-general and special representative in Cambodia and the former Yugoslavia, Owada Hisashi, Japan's permanent representative to the UN, and the first campaign to elect a Japanese national to the post of director-general of UNESCO in 2000, Japan's reputation has risen qualitatively. Although the reality of a Japanese national as UN secretary-general may be a long way off, the idea of Ogata Sadako occupying the recently-created post of deputy secretary-general was touted, especially by UN Secretary-General Kofi Annan (*The Times*, 12 January 1998). The Japanese government is aware of personnel-related issues and attempts to raise its profile at the UN to a muted degree within the constraints of the structural anachronisms within the UN founded upon the norms of the Western early-starters.

Despite strong support for, and endorsement of, the UN's norms and activities within Japan, there is a large discrepancy in Japan's staffing levels. This is shown by the statistic that, despite the desired level of Japanese staffing at 226–305 (with an average of 265), in 1998 only 104 Japanese were employed by the UN, despite the best efforts of the organization and the Japanese government to recruit more. In comparison, countries such as the US, the UK, France and Germany have managed by and large to meet their required staffing levels, with Russia even fielding twice as many as is required (Ise 1998: 62). Once these figures are analysed more closely, however, it becomes clear that the issue is not so clear cut. In fact, Japanese personnel are well represented at the lower junior staff levels (P2 and P3). In 1998, 33 Japanese P2 and 35 P3 staff members were employed, compared with respectively 19 and 32 German staff members and 32 and 86 Americans. Still, the problem of understaffing is undeniable at higher levels (P5, D1, D2 – that is, section chiefs). Japan's representation starts to lag behind with only 12 Japanese citizens at this level compared with 33 French, 36 German, 31 UK and 132 US citizens. Various factors, in addition to those mentioned above, such as the level of competence, language ability, work methods, specialities, and place of appointment suggest a lack of movement upward from the younger levels, which is simply regarded as an examination to pass and an experience to garner,

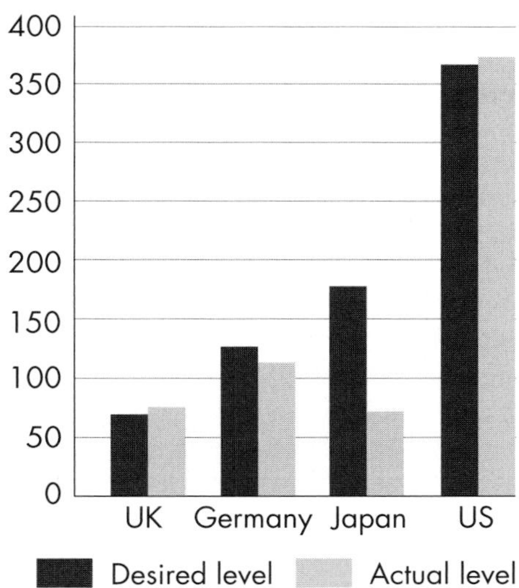

Figure 19.4 Comparative staffing levels of UN member nations
Source: United Nations 1994

rather than a long-term career move. In seeking to enhance its international role, a future task for the Japanese government identified by policy-making agents in MOFA is to improve the upward mobility of the large numbers of young Japanese who pass the initial lower-level entrance exams so that over the next ten to fifteen years the statistics of staffing levels can begin to reflect these rises up the UN career ladder (Akashi 1998: 72–4). In this way, Japanese representation can overcome the obstacles of the international order created by the early-starters and into which Japan entered as part of its post-World War II rehabilitation.

The role of Japanese personnel working within the UN re-emerged as an issue after the murder of Akino Yutaka, UN employee and associate professor of Tsukuba University, in July 1998 in Tajikistan. In Japan, the media questioned whether the nature of Japan's international role was appropriate. However, the government both rode out and responded to waves of opposition and criticism and has continued to sponsor the recognition and enforcement of the Convention on the Safety of United Nations and Associated Personnel adopted by the General Assembly in December 1994. The convention came into effect on 15 January 1999 owing to Japan's active role in its promotion (Japan became the second contracting state to the convention on 6 June 1995). Japan was concerned to ensure the safety of its UN personnel, but its promotion of the convention is also, in the aftermath of the Akino incident, a response to the norm of internationalism, and to domestic revulsion at despatching Japanese personnel into dangerous areas rooted in the norm of anti-militarism. At the same time, it provides another example of domestic actors attempting to shape events, rather than be shaped by the structure of the international order.

19.3.ii United Nations University

Another area in which Japan has promoted actively both its own and the UN's ideals is in the creation of the United Nations University (UNU). The Japanese government was swift to provide the fledgling institution with a home, offering temporary headquarters in 1975. The UNU was created to be 'an international community of scholars and an academic arm of the United Nations system' (Sezaki 1991). The university now occupies impressive headquarters in central Tokyo built with financial contributions from Japan's central government and the Tokyo metropolitan government. The Japanese government has strongly supported the UNU, promoting it as 'a reservoir of ideas' for the UN system. It provides another example of Japan's understated or quiet approach to its UN diplomacy (Owada 1996). This has created a highly visible and positive symbol of the UN among the Japanese, and especially Tokyo, population. Moreover, Japan's activism in line with the norms of internationalism can be seen in the fact that the post of senior adviser to the rector has always been held by a Japanese national (Katō Ichirō, Okita Saburō, Nagai Michio, Okamura Sōgo, Inoguchi Takashi, Satō Hideo).

Nevertheless, problems have arisen over the UNU's purpose, owing to a vaguely-defined template from its inception as to whether it would be a teaching or a research establishment. This has meant that the UNU has sought to define itself through a process of trial and error (Nagai 1981: 344–6). Furthermore, it has had problems attracting good-quality academic staff from outside of the West, causing Third-World scholars to regard it as a 'university run by the US using Japanese money' (Hayashi 1981: 350–1). Moreover, the case of the UNU provides another example of Japan constrained by domestic anti-militarist norms in the contribution it can make, its fear of international isolation and its recourse to financial contributions to give voice to its role as a responsible international actor, sandwiched within the Cold War ideological conflict at the time of the UNU's creation. Still, all these human issues demonstrate a continuation of Japan's methods of making an international commitment through what has been termed traditionally 'cheque-book diplomacy', but is regarded here as an extension of the domestically embedded norm of economism, and is illustrative of Japan's quiet diplomacy. However, in addition, a burgeoning human contribution can be discerned.

19.4 Economics

19.4.i Funding

Japan's contribution to the UN regular budget has demonstrated a steadily growing financial commitment since its admission in December 1956. At that time Japan paid a modestly-assessed contribution of 2.19 per cent of the UN budget. In

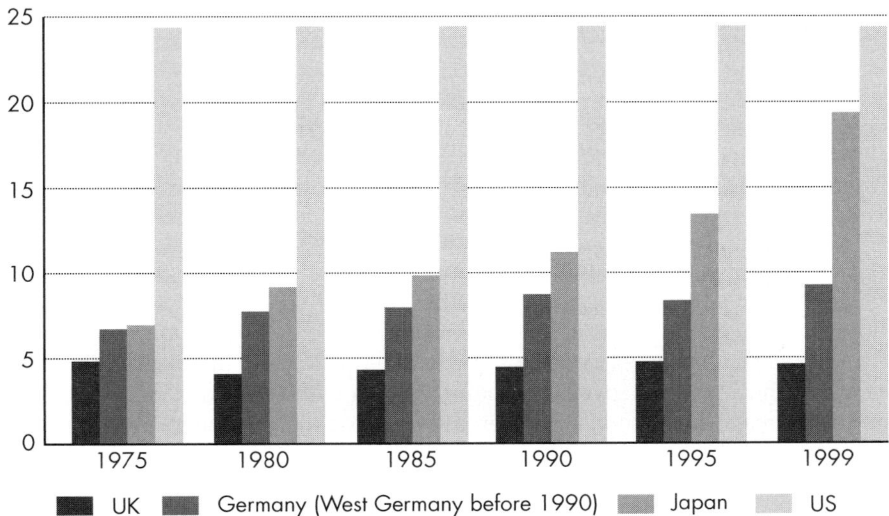

Figure 19.5 Comparison of percentage contributions to the UN regular budget

Source: United Nations 1998

line with Japan's growth in GNP, the state's contribution has increased rapidly to overtake not only Germany, but also the permanent UNSC members – the UK, France and the Soviet Union/Russia (see Figure 19.5). Japan's contribution has risen recently from 16.75 per cent in 1997 and 1998 to 19.984 per cent in 1999, and then to 20.573 per cent in the year 2000, so that the US and Japan are separated by only a 4.5 per cent difference. Moreover, considering that the US has been withholding its payments since 1980, Japan is in effect the number-one contributor to the UN budget. Thus, in response to its international commitments and with the goal of a permanent seat on the UNSC, Japan has proved to be a financially-responsible member of the UN system by instrumentalizing its foreign policy through financial means. In other words, although gaining a seat can be interpreted in purely realist terms of enhancing Japan's national interests, the position taken here is that this represents the commitment of the government wherever possible to appeal to international norms and to deal with issues in a non-violent way.

Instrumentalization of foreign policy through financial means was also evident in the past when Japan provided regular reserve funds to assist the UN when funding was in short supply. For example, its voluntary contributions to the UN Peacekeeping Force in Cyprus (UNFICYP) operation are surpassed only by the US and four European states. Japan is not only the second largest contributor to the general UN budget but is also the second largest contributor to the peacekeeping budget: it made large donations to the UN interventions in Iraq, Cambodia, Somalia, Bosnia and Kosovo. It was a Japanese initiative which set up the Peacekeeping Reserve Fund under General Assembly Resolution A47/217 'to ensure the availability of resources for start-up costs of new operations' (Hatano 1994); and it was Japan that recently established a US$70,000 trust fund charged with the objective of disseminating public information on UN peacekeeping activities (Owada 1998). Japan has often had to make up shortfalls in US contributions, in a sense reflecting a hidden aspect of bilateralism, and has regularly made sizeable voluntary contributions to various UN agencies. In 1963, Japan purchased US$5 million in UN bonds; special contributions amounted to US$2.5 million in 1966 and US$10 million in 1974; and in 1987, Japan made an unsolicited donation of US$15 million to assist in the establishment of UNPKO in Afghanistan and between Iran and Iraq. Japan became the second largest contributor to the UNHCR in 1979, the UN Environment Programme in 1981 and the UN Development Programme in 1984.

Japanese foreign policy has also extended to taking up the role of promoting reform of the UN's controversial funding system with the two objectives of promoting its image as a responsible international actor and, as seen above, to prevent the isolation, and encourage the accommodation, of the US. In the 1980s, US attitudes towards the UN were coloured by the Kassebaum amendment which demanded the introduction of a weighted voting system on budgetary matters and introduced a 20 per cent ceiling on US contributions to the UN budget. Rather than align itself with this uncooperative stance, Japanese policy-makers continued to develop a degree of independence and proactivism with the aims of promoting reconciliation between the US and the UN, and reforming the UN. This was exemplified by Foreign Minister Abe Shintarō's proposal of 1985 tabled at the 40th Session of the UN General Assembly (UNGA Resolution 40/237 December 1985). This proposal sought to create the 'Group of 18', also known as the Group of High-Level Intergovernmental Experts, to review administrative and financial procedures in order to regain the trust, participation and funds of the US and major contributing countries. This demonstrates again Japan's overriding commitment to the universal principles and norms of the UN, rather than promotion of Japan's own narrow interests as a realist interpretation would suggest. Ogata described the proposal as 'a group of eminent persons for a more efficient United Nations so that the world body and its specialized agencies will function efficiently into the twenty-first century' (Ogata 1987: 957). This group met four times in 1986 with Japan's UN ambassador, Saitō Shizuo, acting as vice-chairman and submitted a 71-point report to the 41st Session of the General Assembly (UNGA Resolution 41/213 December 1986). This report, adopted by the 41st Session, included a consensus principle on budgetary matters and was taken by the US to be a conciliatory measure judging by the immediate but partial relaxation of the Kassebaum amendment.

In this understated manner, Japan has sought to promote the UN and reconcile it with the US, thereby demonstrating commitment to both internationalism and its most important bilateral relationship. Recently, MOFA has sought to supplement the principle of 'capacity to pay' with the concept of 'responsibility to pay', which takes into account the special responsibilities and privileges of the permanent members of the Security Council. Thus, again with the limited commitment of the US in the UN since the 1980s and the restructuring of the Cold War international system, Japan has attempted to address shortfalls in the UN budget and maintain its economic viability, rather than promoting solely its own interests within the organization, as the norm of internationalism gains ground.

19.4.ii Development

Japan has also begun to behave proactively in dealing with problems of development in the developing world through the UN, believing it to be the only global organization capable of tackling the issues as part of a broader definition of security. This definition encompasses non-military issues to which Japan can contribute, unconstrained by the anti-militarist norm. Moreover, the unique Japanese experience of development is seen as a significant example for the developing world. With this in mind, Japan has emphasized the necessity of embracing and integrating developing countries into the global economic and financial order and is also grasping the opportunity to promote its own model of development as it has done in East Asia (see Chapter 10). The Japanese delegation has advocated since 1993 a 'new development strategy', which was endorsed by the OECD in 1996. It includes a 'comprehensive approach' to development stressing the importance of trade, private investment and market access, not solely ODA, in encouraging development, and developing a solid socio-economic infrastructure to support growth (Kawada 1998: 45–7).

Concretely, Japan's proactive contribution has been through the First Tokyo International Conference on African Development (TICAD-I) held in October 1993 and the Second Tokyo International Conference on African Development (TICAD-II) held in October 1998. The aim of these two conferences was to react to the economic and social crises on the African continent during the 1980s by taking the successful development examples of East Asian success and elucidating the lessons that African states can learn. Although both were non-pledging conferences, the main agenda points of the consequent Tokyo Declaration stressed assisting:

> African countries in improving people's lives, and promoting peace and stability, through self-help of sub-Saharan countries with them playing a proactive and responsible role in their own development (the concept of 'ownership'), and cooperation with the countries outside the region blurring the distinction between developing and developed countries with development an issue for all (the concept of 'partnership').
>
> (MOFA 1998a)

The two conferences advocated political and economic reforms allowing a stronger role for domestic society; improving the quality of governance; respecting human rights; encouraging entrepreneurship; promoting a multilateral open trading system; and providing East Asian assistance in Africa's development.

These meetings were held in Tokyo and the Japanese government has been instrumental in having the recommendations adopted in the Development Partnership Strategy adopted by the OECD. Japan has played a pivotal role in Africa's development (specifically in sub-Saharan Africa), providing 17 per cent (US$1.1 billion) of the total global ODA in 1996, making it the largest donor (MOFA 1996). Japan has contributed to a number of educational and training projects in Africa including the Japan Overseas Cooperation Volunteers, assisting in the sectors of agricultural, manufacturing, fishery, health and sport. In addition, at the opening of TICAD-II in October 1998, Prime Minister Obuchi committed Japan to provide greater assistance under the TICAD-II process to education, health and sanitation; bring African citizens to Japan for technical training; inject growth into the private sector in Africa through trade and investment; and fund landmine clearance on the African continent (MOFA 1998a). In a similar vein, Foreign Minister Kōmura Masahiko pledged ¥90 billion in grants to realize the social and humanitarian goals of TICAD-II in addition to the creation of regional bases in Kenya and Ghana to fight the spread of disease and an Asia–Africa Investment Information Centre to attract investment into the African private sector. Thus, a leadership role is apparent not only in the form of financial contributions but also with Japan acting as an 'ideas-man' with its own experience of development in mind.

19.4.iii Environmental issues

Environmental issues are linked to development and have also given Japan the opportunity to take a proactive stance with the UN acting as a conduit. This is an issue which has grown in importance within Japan in response to the awareness of the negative effects of economism and developmentalism, as experienced in a number of pollution cases in the 1960s. In December 1997, the Third Conference of the Parties to the UN Framework Convention on Climate Change was held in Kyoto with the aim of limiting gas emissions. Prime Minister Hashimoto Ryūtarō, working closely with MITI, proposed the Comprehensive Strategy for the Prevention of Global Warming, or Green Initiative, consisting of green technology, which involves the development and dissemination by developed countries of energy-conserving technology; the introduction of non-fossil energy sources; promotion of afforestation and preservation of forests; and green aid, which uses ODA and private finance resources to cope with global warming (Hashimoto 1997). This would suggest that MITI has been forced to reinvent itself and expand the remit of its influence as Japan's economy matures into a post-developmental stage and the Japanese state is expected to provide leadership and guidance to developing states. With the promotion of green aid in mind, Japan exceeded its target amount of ODA agreed at the Earth Summit (3–14 June 1992) by 40 per cent to ¥1.44 trillion (US$13.3 billion). This suggests clearly how Japan's environmental policies have provided a potential leadership role for Japan, and signifies also the pluralist nature of the policy-making process in Japan with various international and domestic NGOs, MOFA, MITI and the Environment Agency all vying for influence (Schreurs 1997: 150–6).

Thus, Japan's international financial contribution has been considerable and motivated by a patchwork of reasons, including a palpable sense of duty to other countries, increasingly dependent upon yen contributions, as detailed above. This sense of duty is demonstrated by the Japanese government's launch of a ¥120 million project in conjunction with the UN Economic and Social Commission for Asia and the Pacific. This is aimed at alleviating poverty in Asia by providing stable employment and health services; it is also indicative of a self-seeking desire, especially within MOFA, for recognition as a major power through UNSC representation. Moreover, structural constraints have played their part in confining Japan's contribution chiefly to the financial sphere during the Cold War, and then encouraging both a human contribution and the role for Japan of 'ideas-man'. This is typical of the trend towards quiet diplomacy, including the introduction of initiatives in the post-Cold War order – a trend which is even more manifest in the security dimension.

19.5 Security

19.5.i Peacekeeping

Although the greatest change in Japan's peacekeeping policy came in the post-Cold War period, Japan's participation within UNPKO was a smouldering issue from the moment of Japan's admission to the UN. In 1958, UN Secretary-General Dag Hammarskjöld attempted, albeit unsuccessfully, to solicit the despatch of the newly-created SDF to the Lebanon. During the Cold War, Japan's support for UNPKO was purely financial. With the relaxation of East–West tensions in the late 1980s, however, human (civilian) contributions by Japan to UNPKO began: twenty-seven civilians were sent to Namibia in October 1989 as part of the United Nations Transition Assistance Group. Thereafter, six Japanese civilians joined UNPKO overseeing the Nicaraguan and Haiti elections in 1989–90. Yet, owing to the legacy of World War II and constitutional restrictions on Japan's right to belligerency, backed by the norm of anti-militarism embedded in domestic society, these were purely non-military operations arousing little controversy over remilitarization within Japan or among its East Asian neighbours.

As was seen in Chapter 18, the 1990–1 Gulf War demonstrated the immobility of the Japanese policy-making process and acted as the catalyst for a reconsideration of Japan's contribution of military personnel to UNPKO. Within the Japanese government, the UN became accepted as the chief conduit for playing an international role in response to the conflicting constraints upon Japan: the pressure to make a human contribution to UNPKO; and the fears of East Asian countries that a unilateral contribution would be tantamount to remilitarization. Before hostilities had even begun the government presented the short-lived United Nations Peace Cooperation Bill to the Diet in October 1990. The bill failed to pass the Diet not only because of the lack of public and political support both inside and outside the government, but also because of the haste with which it was prepared in response to outside pressure (*gaiatsu*) arising from Japan's dedication to bilateralism. The debate over how best to contribute did continue, however, and

Plate 19.1 No overseas despatch. Anti-PKO demonstrators, including SDPJ leaders Doi Takako and Murayama Tomiichi, protest against the first overseas despatch of the Self-Defence Forces in September 1992.

Source: Kyōdō News

in September 1991 the Japanese government proposed the Law on Cooperation in UN Peacekeeping and Other Operations (known as the PKO Bill in the Japanese media and hereafter).

The PKO Bill facilitated the participation of Japanese personnel in a number of peacekeeping duties, including: observing and supervising elections and ensuring fair balloting; providing bureaucratic advice and guidance, such as police administration; medical care; transportation, communications and construction work; and humanitarian work including the assistance, rescue and repatriation of war refugees. Also, out of respect for the Constitution of Japan and the domestic norm of anti-militarism, the bill banned Japanese participation in peacekeeping operations involving the monitoring of cease-fires; stationing troops in and patrolling demilitarized zones; controlling the influx of weapons; collecting, storing and disposing of abandoned weapons; assisting disputants in settling borders; and assisting with the exchange of prisoners of war. This ban can only be lifted after a government review. Moreover, five conditions, influenced by the anti-militarist norm, were introduced in respect of any use of the SDF. These require a cease-fire between all the parties involved in the conflict; each party's consent to the deployment of Japanese forces; the deployed force to remain impartial; the use of weapons to be limited to self-defence; and the Japanese government to remove its forces if any of the previous conditions are not met. This second bill was ultimately successful

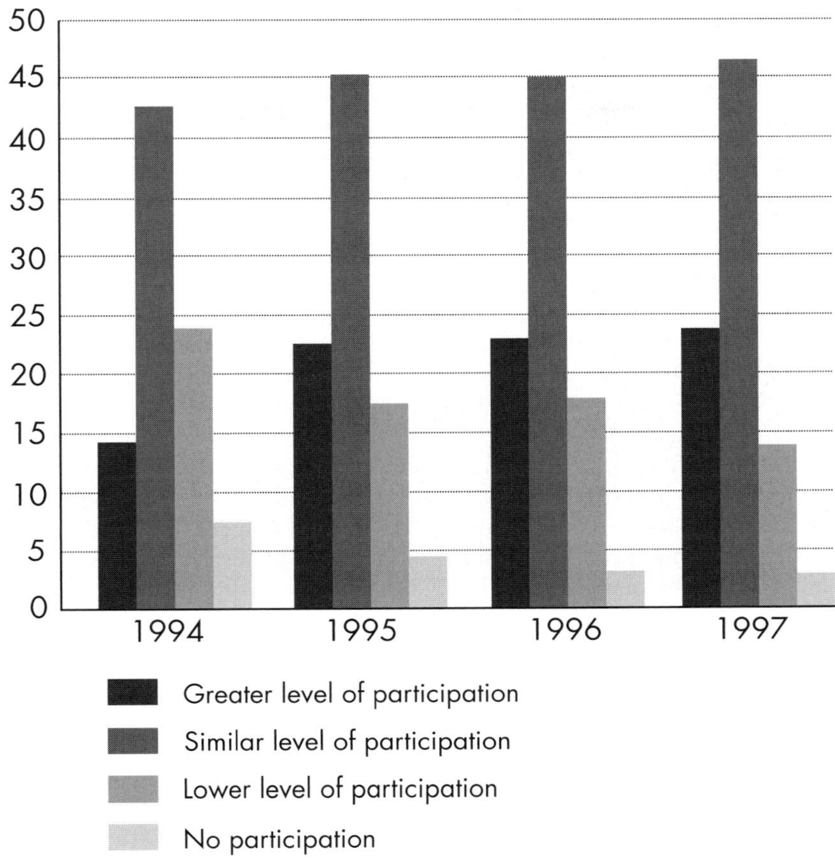

Figure 19.6 Japanese public opinion on Japan's UN peacekeeping operations role

Source: Naikaku Sōri Daijin Kōhōshitsu 1998

owing to the fact that the international climate and domestic public opinion had changed dramatically (Hook 1996a: 100–26). Resistance at home and in East Asia relaxed after the Japanese government made clear what kinds of UNPKO the SDF could, and could not, participate in, and that Japan's contribution would be conducted in accordance with UN resolutions (see Figure 19.6). Thus, the norm of anti-militarism embedded in Japanese society and resistance to Japanese militarization in East Asia had to be circumnavigated with reference to internationalism.

Japan's first despatch overseas of the SDF since its creation in 1954 was to the UN Transitional Authority in Cambodia (UNTAC) operation, although as noted earlier Japan had played a role in minesweeping during the Korean War, before the SDF's formal creation (Dobson 1998). The despatch consisted of 600

SDF personnel employed as engineers engaged chiefly in repairing roads and bridges in areas where the use of force would be unlikely. Despite these precautions, hostilities did continue, particularly with the Khmer Rouge faction refusing to honour the terms of the Paris Peace Accords. As a result, Japan experienced its first UNPKO casualties when Nakata Atsuhito, a Japanese UN volunteer, was killed in April 1993 and Takata Haruyuki, a Japanese civilian police officer, was shot and killed one month later. These events were met by calls at home, prompted by the domestically embedded norm of anti-militarism, to bring back all Japanese personnel in the face of an evidently ineffective cease-fire. Nevertheless, the government weathered the storm, with the normative support of some of its East Asian neighbours and the UN, by contending that the cease-fire was generally holding, the Japanese presence ought to remain, and that a certain number of casualties was to be expected as a result of participation in UNPKO. In this way, the Japanese government demonstrated its attachment to the norm of internationalism.

Having fulfilled its Cambodian duties, Japan found domestic and regional opposition to its peacekeeping role weakened. Thus, it was considerably less controversial to despatch SDF contingents as staff officers, movement control units and electoral observers to the UN Operation in Mozambique (ONUMOZ) between May 1993 and January 1995. Further contributions came in January 1996 when Japan despatched SDF troops to the UN Disengagement Observer Force (UNDOF) in the Golan Heights to provide secondary support for staff and transportation. In between these two commitments, Japan despatched its first SDF contingent on a humanitarian relief effort to Goma, Zaire, in order to provide medical assistance, sanitation, water supplies and air transport for refugees. Participation in these operations encountered little opposition at home and abroad in comparison to operations during the 1990–1 Gulf War and in Cambodia. Moreover, Japanese personnel participated in the UN Mission in Kosovo (UNMIK) in support of providing humanitarian and reconstruction assistance. Furthermore, in August 1999 three Japanese police officers were despatched to the East Timor referendum on independence, although no human contribution was made to the attempt to prevent the resulting chaos that followed, owing to the anti-militarist preference for financial contributions initially totalling US$2 million. However, despite these advances in Japan's UNPKO role, certain obstacles need to be tackled before Japan can shoulder greater responsibilities. These issues include the legally-required and lengthy government review necessary to remove the restricted peacekeeping activities of the SDF under the PKO Bill; the use of force within UNPKO; and the number of operations in which Japan will participate simultaneously. Undoubtedly, UNPKO has proved to be one of the hottest issues in Japan's post-Cold War foreign and security policy enabling norm entrepreneurs, such as Ozawa Ichirō, to promote Japan as a 'normal' state no longer shackled by anti-militarist and constitutional restrictions in the post-Cold War world. In addition, the tentative nature of Japan's foreign policy is evident in the evolutionary and, for some, frustratingly slow development of Japan's international contribution.

19.5.ii Disarmament

The Japanese government has pursued the other main security issue, disarmament, principally within the framework of the UN since its admission, in line with the maintenance of the three non-nuclear principles and the norm of anti-militarism, growing in part out of the A-bomb experience (see Chapters 3 and 6). In September 1957, the Japanese delegation submitted a resolution addressing the banning of nuclear tests, which was rejected because of the bipolar stand-off between the East and the West in the UN. Japan joined the Conference of the Committee on Disarmament in 1969 through which it attempted to promote an early resolution of the Comprehensive Test Ban Treaty; signed up to the NPT in 1970 (but did not ratify it until 1976); and has encouraged the extension of the Strategic Arms Reduction Treaty (START) processes. Still, at times the Japanese government has dragged its feet over disarmament issues. As the Japanese government was 'sandwiched' between commitments to US bilateralism, as symbolized by the tacit acceptance of port calls by US ships carrying nuclear weapons (see Chapter 6), and multilateral compunctions to address disarmament issues, along with domestic concerns over nuclear energy, it took six years to ratify the NPT.

It is evident that non-governmental organizations have sought to influence Japan's policy in the UN. In June 1964, seven and a half years after Japan joined the organization, the Hiroshima–Nagasaki Peace Pilgrimage presented a petition to Secretary-General U Thant for a 'UN commission to investigate the realities of A-bomb damages in Hiroshima, Nagasaki, and Bikini; and for the results to be disseminated throughout the world to help achieve a ban on nuclear weapons' (Shono 1981: 165). Global anti-nuclear movements culminated in the first Special Session on Disarmament (SSD-I) in 1978 and the second session (SSD-II) in 1982. A large number of Japanese NGOs petitioned both of these meetings, including the Japan Council against Atomic and Hydrogen Bombs (*Gensuikyō*), the New Union of Japanese Religious Organizations (*Shinkyūren*), *Sōka Gakkai* and the Japanese Catholic Organization. It seemed that there was a boom of anti-nuclear groups (*hankaku būmu*) at the time (Ōnishi 1985: 174). This boom was manifest in two of the largest rallies organized in the post-war period in 1982 in Hiroshima and Tokyo attracting 186,000 and 406,000 protestors respectively. Eighty million signatures were also delivered to the SSD-II. Japanese peace movements, opposed to the recognition the NPT extended to the *status quo* on the possession of nuclear weapons, also attempted to prevent the indefinite extension of the NPT in 1995, including an appeal by the NPT Research Association to Prime Minister Miyazawa Kiichi and a similar appeal by Hiraoka Takashi, Mayor of Hiroshima, at the UN NGO Special Session. The NPT Research Association also appealed to Hosokawa but with little result as he supported the indefinite extension of the NPT yet opposed the perpetual possession of nuclear weapons. In cooperation with other peace movements, specifically the International Physicians for the Prevention of Nuclear War (IPPNW), the NPT Research Association gained currency in the NAM's sponsorship of a resolution calling on the WHO in 1993 to request a judgement by the International Court of Justice

(ICJ) over the legality of the use of nuclear weapons: 'in view of the health and environmental effects, would the use of nuclear weapons by a state in war or other armed conflict be a breach of its obligations under international law including the WHO Constitution?' (Shono *et al.* 1993: 187).

All these NGO activities have played two important roles: first, imbued with the anti-militarist norm, they have sustained public awareness within Japan of disarmament issues; and second, their efforts have internationalized through the UN this anti-militarism norm. The Japanese government has also addressed the issue of landmines, as was seen in Chapter 16, in similar fashion to peacekeeping and disarmament, as one to be resolved through multilateral means and shaped by the participation of NGOs.

19.6 Summary

Within the UN system, the three issues of UNSC representation, funding and peacekeeping have demonstrated most clearly the ambition 'to occupy an honored place in an international society striving for the preservation of peace'. All these three aspects of Japan's participation in the UN system are entwined deeply with each other. Hence, MOFA's goal of a UNSC permanent seat can be fulfilled through increased peacekeeping and budgetary contributions. In turn, increased budgetary contributions bring demands both domestically and internationally for Japan to be more visibly represented within the UN.

Foreign Minister Kōmura's 1999 address to the UN General Assembly succinctly summarized Japan's attitude to the UN:

> fully recognizing the significance of the Organization, the people of Japan regarded its admittance to the membership of the United Nations as their country's reinstatement in the international society after World War II. They have been supporting and contributing to the activities of the United Nations ever since.
>
> (Komura 1999)

Returning to the League of Nations, Hosokawa reinforced this claim at the UN with a quotation from Niitobe Inazō: 'an international mind is not the antonym of a national mind ... The international mind is an expansion of the national mind, just as philanthropy or charity ... should begin at home' (Hosokawa 1994).

An examination of Japan's experience in the UN has made evident a break with the traditional low-profile, low-risk, US-dependent foreign policy of Prime Minister Yoshida, which had served Japan so well in the Cold War period. In the post-Cold War world, Japan is demonstrating signs of having emerged from the cocoon of the Yoshida Doctrine, and is developing cautiously a degree of international leadership. It is adjusting its previous emphasis on bilateral relations, especially with the US, and supplementing it with multilateral relations and the development of a greater emphasis on human contributions. In particular, Japan's

UNPKO experience has demonstrated an incrementally-active multilateral role leading to greater international commitment, imbued with a greater sense of responsibility which can only be understood with reference to, and yet challenges, the immediate post-war norms of economism and anti-militarism.

Chapter 20

Japan–economic institutions

20.1 Overview

The Japanese state and its people have renounced the military option of solving global human problems and have stressed instead the economic contribution they can make. Thus it would be natural to expect that Japan has played a role in global financial institutions commensurate with its global economic standing. The indicators which were cited in Chapter 1 of Japan's importance in the international political economy demonstrate in raw, quantitative terms, the undeniable importance of Japan in the global political economy. However, aspersions have been cast over the quality of, and ambitions behind, Japan's leadership in the economic dimension of its international relations. The US has been compared to the Tokugawa-period samurai who, although allowed to bear arms, was impoverished. Japan is equated to the merchants (*chōnin*) who possessed no political power, yet accumulated vast fortunes. During the Meiji restoration, modern government was built upon leadership provided by the lower-class samurai, whilst the merchants supplied financial resources but provided no leadership (Hamada 1994: 144). In the light of this metaphor, a common belief emerged in the major industrialized powers in the immediate post-Cold War period that Japan had 'displayed an inexplicable inability to discern its own national interest' (Johnson 1993: 54). Moreover, 'Japan must overcome a widespread feeling at the World Bank and the International Monetary Fund (IMF) that despite its ambitions it has no real set of policies it wants to carry out at the two institutions' (*The Japan Times*, 4 October 1989). Thus, Japan's normative commitment to the creation and articulation of multilateral solutions to human problems has been questioned.

The other norms, introduced in Chapter 2, are of equal importance in the economic dimension and their interplay has caused tensions to surface recently. As was seen in Chapter 10, the IMF's role in the East Asian economic and financial crises has been to impose what the former vice-minister of MOF Sakakibara Eisuke (dubbed 'Mr Yen' by the media) has followed others in calling the 'Washington consensus' of 'free markets and sound money' upon the economies of East Asia in a policy of 'blind application of the universal model on emerging economies' (Associated Free Press, 23 January 1999). Still, this fracas was not framed purely in terms of the IMF imposing the US's agenda upon East Asia; it also implied that the traditional norm of bilateralism would suffer:

> First, American dominance which seemed assured for some time after the demise of socialism seems to be declining both on political and economic grounds – partly because of the unification of Europe and partly because of potential anti-American sentiment in various parts of the world that has arisen in recent years.
>
> (Associated Free Press, 23 January 1999)

Thus, within multilateral financial and economic fora, the tensions between Japan's position in East Asia and its traditional adherence to the US under the

Yoshida Doctrine have become tangible. What is more, in the post-Cold War world, issues such as democratization, environmental degradation, AIDS, terrorism, nuclear testing and drugs require consultation at a multilateral level but still often require implementation on a bilateral basis. Thus, in these remaining chapters on Japan's role in global institutions, the focus will be on the tensions for Japan in its multilateral and bilateral commitments which have recently, and will continue to, come into relief.

20.2 Historical context

Upon regaining its sovereignty, Japan joined the IMF in 1952 with the initial aims of gaining international recognition and rehabilitation, in addition to encouraging Japan's economic reconstruction and responding to the norm of developmentalism. At that time Japan ranked only ninth in its share of voting rights in the IMF. Since the early post-Cold War period, as will be seen later and in line with catching up with the early-starter economies of the West, it has ranked second to the US. The year 1952 also witnessed Japan's continued international rehabilitation by its entry into the WB. Japan started as one of the major recipients of loans from the WB, which assisted its rapid post-war economic growth and specifically helped in the 1960s to finance the building of the bullet train (*shinkansen*), Tōmei expressway and Kurobe (Kuroyon) Dam – three symbols of Japan's rapid post-war growth. Additionally, the policy of being the biggest borrower from the WB deflected criticisms of dependence upon US bilateral aid. As is discussed below, however, concomitant with the growth of its economy, Japan's contribution to the WB grew.

Japan's membership of the World Trade Organization (WTO), which came into being in January 1995, was decided during the Uruguay Round of GATT trade talks, when a further lowering of tariffs and the establishment of the WTO to replace GATT were decided. Japan formally applied for GATT membership in 1952 but faced strong opposition from the early-starter economies, particularly from the UK and the British Commonwealth. Japan eventually entered GATT in 1955 with the support of the US but faced criticisms that Japan's 'low wages' rendered it an unfair competitor and resulted in several European powers' refusal (the UK, Belgium and France) to extend most-favoured nation (MFN) treatment by invoking GATT Article 35. This meant that Article 1, mandating non-discrimination, was not applicable to trade with Japan – a long-running issue which was taken up by the Japanese media at the time (Wilkinson 1983: 169). As a result, Japan was forced to start making bilateral trade agreements with a variety of countries which maintained protectionist policies against Japanese exports. Equally, throughout the 1950s Japan was pressurized by the US both to reduce trade barriers and to conform to GATT in the first half of the decade, and then to curb its increasing exports of textiles in violation of the spirit of GATT. Thus, a global institution was being used as a tool of bilateralism by the US to promote its hegemonic role. Only with Japan's admission to the OECD was Europe encouraged to revoke Article 35 of GATT. However, it still maintained selective safeguards which forced Japan to adopt a number of discriminatory export restraints. GATT failed to address this rift in Japan–Europe relations which made Japanese policy-makers feel victimized by the structure of the international system created by the early-starters. Only Germany and Italy granted MFN status to Japan.

Since then, Japan has been committed to maintaining and strengthening a free and non-discriminatory multilateral trading system through active participation in the Kennedy Round, Tokyo Round and Uruguay Round of multilateral trade negotiations. Japan is an original signatory to all the WTO Multilateral Trade Agreements and to the Agreement on Government Procurement and, as a result, the Japanese government applies MFN status to all but six countries and customs territories (Albania, Equatorial Guinea, Lebanon, Nepal, North Korea and Vietnam). Japan was also a signatory to the Negotiations on Basic Telecommunications, the Declaration on Trade in Information Technology Products and Financial Services Negotiations. Japan participates in the WTO Working Groups on Trade and Investment and Trade and Competition Policy, and has also been actively involved in the WTO dispute settlement provisions both as complainant and respondent.

20.3 Financial contributions

In contrast to the position in the US, the growing contribution and importance of the WB to Japan are evident. The US share of the capital of the WB has declined from 34.9 per cent in 1945 to 16.98 per cent in 1999. However, Japan's share has increased from 2.8 per cent in 1952 to 8.14 per cent in 1999. By the early 1980s, Japan was already the principal co-financier of WB loans, the number-two shareholder in the International Development Association (IDA, the WB's soft-loan facility). In 1984, Japan became the second biggest shareholder in the WB after the US. In 1990, Japan became the second biggest shareholder in the International Finance Corporation (IFC, the WB's affiliate for private sector lending). In the early post-Cold War period, Japan surpassed the US as the world's largest manufacturing economy and accounted for half of the world's total net savings (US savings accounting for 5 per cent) and became the world's largest source of foreign investment. These figures demonstrate the decreased functional importance of the WB for the US, and its increased importance for Japan. Today Japan is the second largest contributor after the US. Moreover, Japan's voluntary contributions have been significant with ¥19.6 billion contributed in 1997 to the WB (World Bank 1999).

These contributions can be interpreted as demonstrating leadership and support for institutions that Japan regards as particularly important in order to address global human problems. Furthermore, they provide a means to promote Japanese thinking on development. As is adumbrated later in this chapter and was seen in Chapters 1, 2 and 10, Japan has promoted understanding of East Asian development through the WB report on the *East Asian Miracle*. In addition, the contributions allow for the promotion of an understanding of Japan abroad through scholarship schemes and training programmes (Omura 1997: 47–8). The WB has provided a way for Japan to supplement its bilateral contributions and deflect criticisms that aid was proffered chiefly for Japan's own commercial gain. MOF policy-making agents have admitted that they prefer to channel funds through global institutions as bilateral aid is much more politicized in Japan, making the process of giving easier and depersonalized. Especially in the 1980s when the recycling of Japan's large current account surplus was necessary, MOF began to impute the WB with more positive meaning. However, Japan does not want to replace the US at the WB, preferring instead to supplement its bilateral relationship with the US in a multilateral setting, reflecting the rising Asianist norm. Thus, prediction of a new Cold War between Japan and the US over forms of capitalism is not necessarily correct. Equally, a scenario is unlikely where Japan and the US share hegemony. As was seen in other parts of this book, Japan has at different times tapped into its East Asian identity, as illustrated by the creation of the Asian Development Bank (ADB) in 1966. As in the case of the Asian Monetary Fund (AMF), this is regarded as a supplementary measure to, and not as a rival to, WB orthodoxy. The president of the ADB is always Japanese and has always come from MOF (with only one exception from the Bank of Japan), 'this may result in Japan – and specifically the Finance Ministry, which oversees relations with multilateral financial institutions – exercising the kind of effective control over the ADB which the US Treasury exerts over the World Bank' (*Far Eastern Economic Review*, 7 May 1992).

20.4 Japanese representation

20.4.i World Bank

In all of these institutions, Japanese staffing levels have yet to catch up with the government's financial contributions. Despite Japan being the second largest shareholder in the WB since 1984, MOF policy-making agents have felt that often the US does not want Japan to play a more active role in taking initiatives and thus have been reluctant to demand a rise in Japan's voting rights in the WB. Moreover, a large proportion of what Japan contributes is in co-financing, which is not included in the assessment of voting rights. The Japanese government has attempted to promote Japanese policy-makers in the WB and to this end has conducted a recruitment drive and despatched opinionated, young MOF officials to the WB. Although the WB does not publish the nationality of its staff, a Japanese newspaper reported in the early post-Cold War period that the bank employed only 86 Japanese citizens out of 6,700, that is, 1.3 per cent. This is considerably below the desired level of 145 to 197 (Lincoln 1993: 139). In addition, the average age of employment in the WB is 42. Thus, most Japanese employees are already committed to their company and find difficulty in shifting to a new organization. Still, the problem is not faced only by Japan. The WB needs to find more non-US staff members to address the imbalance caused by its location in Washington. Similar reasons behind the scarcity of Japanese personnel in the UN can be cited with the existing international structure weighted against Japan.

The Japanese government began in the 1980s to use unusually aggressive methods to secure a second-place position for Japan in the WB's voting share. It did this by tying its WB contributions to its IDA contributions, in respect of which Japan in 1999 held 10.72 per cent of voting rights in comparison to the US at 14.96 per cent. US support was gained by acceding to various bilateral liberalization measures, thus demonstrating the importance of the bilateral relationship. As a result, reshuffling in the WB in 1984 saw the US's share drop minimally from 21.78 per cent to 20.91 per cent, and Japan's rise to number two from 4.94 per cent to 5.19 per cent, slightly exceeding Germany on 5.17 per cent. Japan's voting share stood in 1999 at 7.93 per cent, in comparison to the US at 16.52 per cent and Germany at 4.53 per cent (World Bank 1999: 12–14).

20.4.ii International Monetary Fund

In the IMF, Japan's contribution by 1999 stood at 6.33 per cent of the whole, with the US's standing at 17.68 per cent. The IMF provides another example of Japan seeking to obtain international recognition for its financial contributions and to live up to the status of a world power (for a more detailed discussion of the events surrounding Japan's campaign for recognition, see Rapkin *et al.* 1997). From the 1988 IMF/WB meeting in Berlin, Japan adopted a proactive role in the IMF with the avowed goal within the MOF of increasing its quota of voting rights from 4.7 per cent to 8 per cent (*Japan Times*, 9 February 1989). Sumita Satoshi, the governor of the Bank of Japan, made an appeal at the meeting to improve Japan's standing in the IMF, declaring that he would be 'hard-pressed to say that [Japan's current quota position in the IMF] accurately or adequately reflects Japan's current standing in the world economy', and claiming that recent quota increases had taken Japan 'further away from' rather than nearer to its 'legitimate position' in the fund (*Far Eastern Economic Review*, 13 October 1988; cited in Rapkin *et al.* 1997). Then Finance Minister Hashimoto Ryūtarō warned that this issue of Japan's representation within the IMF, if not resolved by raising Japan to 'a proper-ranking to reflect our economic power' would make it difficult for the LDP to pass bills in the Japanese Diet sanctioning contributions to the IMS (*Japan Times*, 28 February 1989). In the IMF, there was strong resistance to an increase in Japan's subscription quota, with opposition coming mainly from the UK and France during the 1987–90 negotiations based on doubts about Japan's ability to lead, and the decline that their own voting power would face from a reduced quota (Hirono 1991: 178).

Nevertheless, the Japanese government pressed for increased voting rights in the late 1980s in the IMF in line with its high levels of foreign investment, trade and foreign aid. Up to that point Japan was fifth in the distribution of voting rights with 4.47 per cent (US 18.9 per cent, UK 6.55 per cent, Germany 5.72 per cent, France 4.75 per cent). However, in 1990 Japan was elevated to joint second place with Germany on 5.65 per cent (Lincoln 1993: 133). By 1999, the US held 17.35

per cent of the votes in the IMF, with Japan second on 6.23 per cent and Germany third on 6.08 per cent (International Monetary Fund 2000). This is clearly disproportionate with the size of their economies. It is telling that constitutional change in the IMF requires an 85 per cent majority vote, which means that the US retains *de facto* veto power over major IMF decisions.

The inequality in this global institution demonstrates the favourable position held by the early-starter economies that created the international system and resonates with the idea of institutional lag (Rapkin *et al.* 1997: 172). MOF policy-makers were satisfied, but being ranked jointly with Germany made the victory somewhat 'bittersweet' (*Japan Times*, 9 May 1990). The new quotas in 1990 were referred to by Finance Minister Theo Waigel of Germany as creating 'two silver and two bronze medals', that is Japan and Germany coming in at joint second place, and UK and France equal in third place (*Japan Times*, 8 May 1990). This sense of developmentalism was most clearly demonstrated by comments made by MOF policy-makers likening this battle to 'the struggle over the revision of the unequal treaties in the Meiji period' (Ogata 1989: 18; cited in Rapkin *et al.* 1997: 176). In February 2000, with the nomination of the former vice-minister of finance for international affairs, Sakakibara Eisuke, to the post of managing director of the IMF, Japan's commitment to promoting Japanese representation in the IMF continued to be evident.

20.4.iii World Trade Organization

At the highest level of the WTO, Japan has played an active role in the contest over the successor to Renato Ruggiero as secretary-general of the WTO fought between the deputy prime minister of Thailand, Supachai Panitchpakdi, and the former prime minister of New Zealand, Mike Moore. The latter candidate was favoured by the US, who feared that the former, favoured by the countries of Asia and Africa, would be more likely to be influenced by Japanese policy-making agents. The Thai ambassador to Japan, Sakthip Krairiksh, was reported as having declared that, 'without the strong support of Japan, which was Thailand's number one ally, we would have lost the WTO race a long time ago' (*Daily Yomiuri*, 6 August 1999). Japan prioritized the Asianist norm and emphasized its East Asian identity. It supported the Thai candidate, managing to win an unprecedented compromise of each candidate serving three years of the full six-year term of appointment. This illustrates the point made in Part III of this book: that Japan is beginning to assume a stronger East Asian identity, sometimes at the cost of the traditional norm of US bilateralism. More interestingly, however, it demonstrates the way in which Japan instrumentalizes policy through proxies, as discussed in Chapter 2. Unable to voice clear opposition to the US owing to the overbearing norm of US bilateralism, Japan has been able to use the Thai representative for its own ends as much as for those of East Asia.

This phenomenon of Japan's own interests and the Asianist norm overlapping at the expense of US bilateralism is similarly evident over the issue of China's entry into the organization. Since the inception of the WTO Japan has been supportive of China's entry into the WTO. Finance Minister Takemura Masayoshi was asked by the Chinese vice-premier, Zhu Rhongi, to support China's bid. He expressed support for China's entry as a developing state – an issue that was undermined by US complaints about Chinese trade policies, specifically as regards intellectual property rights and financial liberalization (*Japan Times*, 10 January 1995).

This provides another illustration of the norm of US–Japan bilateralism weakening as Japan promotes an East Asian identity and pursues its own interests over and above aspects of the bilateral relationship. These interests include engaging a potential rival and regional hegemon in a number of multilateral organizations and the fact that China is the largest recipient of Japanese ODA and is obliged to repay to Japan about ¥40 billion a year for loans dating back to 1979. More recently, talks between the US and China collapsed after the US bombing of the Chinese embassy in Belgrade during the Kosovo crisis and over suspicions that China had acquired classified information on US nuclear weapons' technology. Japan's position was to support the entry of China at the earliest possible stage and avoid any linkage with the bombing of the Chinese embassy. Prime Minister Obuchi Keizō offered his good offices as a go-between in the resolution of strained relations between China and the US, thereby maintaining Japan's role as a *kakehashi* between the East and West. It is clear that Japan wishes to continue its policy of 'constructive engagement' and ensure that China becomes embedded in global and regional institutions.

20.5 Japan as a norm entrepreneur

In attempting to address the perceived lack in its role as an 'ideas-man', Shiratori Masaki of MOF has called on Japan to make a greater intellectual contribution, stating that: 'Japan's experience should be useful to developing countries and indeed these countries are wanting to learn from Japanese experience' (Awanohara 1995: 178). The regional leadership role which accompanies this intellectual contribution is apparent and has been accepted by various East Asian neighbours, even China, despite a traditional wariness of anything that smacks of Japanese proactivism in foreign policy. Feng Zhaokui of the Chinese Academy of Social Sciences said that:

> [Reagan and Thatcher] were too *laissez-faire*. Nor should we go the way of Russia, where a strict planned economy system was suddenly abolished, leading to chaos. There is much we should learn from the Japanese experience in which the government has played a key role in directing and guiding the economy since 1945.
>
> (Awanohara 1995: 179)

Thus, in March 1999 Foreign Minister Miyazawa Kiichi proposed that the WB establish a development award for academic achievement in the creation of new development models or for progress in solving issues such as poverty, health, education and the environment: 'I hope that the establishment of such an award will encourage all concerned in development, whether it is in theory or practice, and I would like to explore the possibility for assisting such an initiative' (*Yomiuri Shimbun*, 2 March 1999).

The WB is evidently in need of structural reform: 'the [World] Bank, at least until 1996, was organized in an extraordinarily segmented way, so that knowledge did not actually flow from one part of the bank to another' (Robert Wade, cited in the *Daily Yomiuri*, 20 June 1999). To this end Japan has proposed the AMF as a supplement to the IMF, not a rival organization, in order to counterbalance the weight and influence of the US in managing the crisis. Finance Minister Miyazawa Kiichi, in reference to the East Asian financial and economic crises, said, 'The IMF, which was created in the days of limited capital flows, has not fully attuned itself to addressing this type of crisis' (*Yomiuri Shimbun*, 20 June 1999). At the Hong Kong WB/IMF meeting of September 1997, Japan launched the AMF plan with provisos stressing the complementary work of the AMF and the IMF. Thus, despite fears among US policy-makers that the AMF would *undermine* the work of the IMF, from the beginning the plan was that the AMF would *supplement* the work of the IMF, suggesting the bilateral, Asianist and international norms influencing Japanese foreign policy (Hamada 1999: 33). Nevertheless, US and Asian opposition essentially sank the Japanese proposal, demonstrating the extent to which the US can still silence opposing voices in the IMF and the WB – the global institutions it took the lead in creating.

Japan's intellectual leadership came with emphasis placed upon the role of the state as well as the market in development. This ran against the international consensus in the 1980s and post-Cold War period. This issue, and conditional privatization, two-step loans, infrastructural development and protectionism at the early stages of development, all came from Japan's own experience of development. Thus, Japan was attempting to instrumentalize the norm of developmentalism in its intellectual leadership role. This manifested itself in the publication of *The East Asian Miracle* report, which is addressed in the next section. Within the WTO, Japan has called upon members to introduce anti-monopoly laws and cooperate to identify unfair trading practices. This proposal, which originated in MITI, was aimed at developing countries introducing legislation for fair business competition, since only half of the WTO's members have laws equivalent to Japan's Anti-Monopoly Law or the US's Anti-Trust Law. Suggested policies included the outlawing of price cartels, contract bid-rigging and preference for domestic companies and transparency in administrative procedures. Again in this field, as in debt relief, Japan is closer to Europe in outlook than to the US, its traditional bilateral partner.

20.6 *The East Asian Miracle* report

A battle in the WB for influence is also a battle for leadership in the global political economy, which during the 1980s saw neo-classicism in the ascendant. Japan took a line independent from the ideas of the WB and the IMF (and, as a result, independent from the ideas of the linchpin of the international system, the US) regarding the role of state intervention in development. The result was to create tensions as the WB and the IMF criticized Japanese aid programmes for undermining their work. In this context, rather than reacting obediently to criticisms, Japan sought to stake its claim to the leadership role with its differing ideas of development and set out the stall of the East Asian development model. This leadership attempt came to fruition in September 1993 with the publication of the WB report *The East Asian Miracle: Economic Growth and Public Policy* (World Bank 1993). The promotion of this report in the WB was taken on by MOF and its Overseas Economic Cooperation Fund (OECF), Japan's largest aid agency. The key figures involved, Shiratori Masaki and Kubota Isao, had been responsible for the OECF report of October 1991 entitled *Issues Related to the World Bank's Approach to a Structural Adjustment: Proposals from a Major Partner*, which aimed to stress the positive role of government intervention in economic development (Wade 1996: 10–11).

The ideological battle was decided in the 1980s when the WB underwent an enormous shift to the right in its basic philosophy, in line with the free-market economic policies of President Ronald Reagan and Prime Minister Margaret Thatcher. This shift in ideology was criticized at the WB/IMF meeting in Bangkok in 1991 by MOF policy-making agents from the OECF. Japanese criticism of the new philosophical bent in the WB and the IMF centred specifically upon the necessity for these global institutions to examine and learn from the alternative East Asian economic experience; the WB/IMF policy of tying multilateral aid for China to human rights; and the free-market reform strategy of the WB/IMF in the former Soviet Union. Key policy-making agents, such as the governor of the Bank of Japan, Mieno Yasushi, stressed instead the 'Asian experience', which paid due respect to the role of the private sector but also emphasized the need 'for the government to complement the market mechanism and create the kind of environment in which free markets can function effectively' (Awanohara 1995: 168). This criticism led to the call for a study of the East Asian developmental experience and engendered a belief that it was not the WB itself which was necessarily at fault, but rather the dominance of US staff in the organization.

In contrast to Japan's position in the Gulf War, as was seen in Chapter 18, when Japan was criticized for not providing 'sweat and blood', MOF policy-makers talked of providing people (*hito*) and wisdom (*chie*) to the WB. This touted provision of wisdom was fulfilled in October 1991 with the publication by MOF ideologues of the above-mentioned *Issues Related to the World Bank's Approach to a Structural Adjustment: Proposals from a Major Partner*. This report stressed the need to promote and sustain growth through government-propelled investment measures, the need for well-selected infant industry protection measures, the careful use of subsidized interest rates and a more cautious approach to privatization. The report questioned the universal application by the WB of measures such as the reduction of subsidies, liberalization of financial markets, dismantling of barriers to imports and foreign investment, and privatization of public corporations. Criticisms continued when Shiratori, then executive-director at the WB, promoted the publication of a study of the industrial strategies of South Korea,

Indonesia and Thailand. This concluded that the WB needed to pay more attention to the successful role of government intervention in these cases. Despite considerable opposition from the neo-classic economists within the WB, following Shiratori's protestations to the bank's president, Lewis Preston, the report was published. Shiratori has been characterized as one of the more argumentative and combative MOF policy-makers, especially because of his excellent command of the English language (Wade 1996).

The sense of alienation was also evident during the writing of the report on the East Asian miracle. Japan paid for the research, with the WB having to fund only its own staff. The staff appointed included Lawrence Summers, a vocal critic of the East Asian model, and a number of like-minded free-market supporters with PhDs chiefly from Anglo-American universities and no adult experience of living and working in East Asia. The only input from a scholar with East Asian experience came at the editorial stage from Lawrence MacDonald of the *Asia Wall Street Journal*, who argued for cultural factors to be included. However, this was rejected by the research team as too vague and possibly encouraging accusations of racism. The degree of cultural myopia can be seen in the fact that the vice-president for East Asia, Gautam Kaji, had to confess at a board meeting that he did not know of the report. The researchers were also aware of Japanese interest in the conclusions, and the importance of Japan to the WB as its second largest shareholder. As a result, they tried to steer a middle course between government intervention and market-friendly policies. Again the structure of the international system worked against the late-starter, Japan.

20.7 Policy-making process

20.7.i Ministry of Finance

To a degree, the reasons behind Japan's recent proactivism in multilateral organizations can be located within the Japanese policy-making process. Within MOF, there is a deeply-rooted ideological belief in the virtues of government intervention rather than 'market-friendly' approaches, which reflects Japan's own developmental experience and the utility of this model to East Asia, as was seen in Chapters 2 and 10. Additionally, MOF seeks to promote the use of its development strategy based on directed credit, which is the means by which Japan instrumentalized economic development in East Asia. MOF does not want to see the WB criticize its policy methods as being moribund. Moreover, nationalist sentiments based on pride and status are an impetus for activity. The Japanese government wants to be recognized for its intellectual and political leadership as well as for its economic leadership. In the WB, US citizens have been greatly over-represented in comparison to their contributions, easily outnumbering other nationalities, and the vast majority of staff (80 per cent) have been trained at Anglo-American universities. As a result, the Japanese sense of being an outsider has been magnified.

As the content of *The East Asian Miracle* report, published on 26 September 1993 at the annual meeting of the IMF and the WB, was a compromise, separate parties were able to take what solace they required from the report, whether it be support for state intervention or the validation of the market (*Japan Times*, 27 and 28 September 1998).

However, Japan did manage to ensure that its own ideas on economic policy were gradually promoted within the WB. A parallel report was commissioned at the time through the Japan Development Bank to feed into the WB report. Moreover, the Educational Developmental Institute of the WB undertook a study of the Japanese civil service. Suddenly in the post-Cold War period, Japan and its developmental model surfaced as a hot topic for WB economists.

MOF is in charge of operations at multilateral development banks and has rarely been constrained by the Japanese Diet when it comes to the provision of ODA. However, there have been segments of Japanese society opposed to aid-giving for its 'alleged self-centred commercialism, politically corrupting and environmentally degrading effects, and its excessive focus on infrastructure building (to the neglect of basic human needs)' (Awanohara 1995: 165). It has been argued by these groups that Japanese aid has no philosophy behind it. Yet MOF policy-makers have argued that with emphasis placed on the role of the state, the encouragement of self-help through responding to recipients' requests and the provision of loans, not grants, Japan does promote a philosophy. On a smaller scale, MOF's Institute of Fiscal and Monetary Policy sponsors' meetings where representatives of developing economies are invited to Tokyo for briefings on Japan's economic and financial system. Similarly, Japanese policy-making agents have used proxy channels to direct aid through a third party, such as Singapore, in order to introduce personnel from Southeast Asia to Japanese developmentalist norms.

20.7.ii Other actors

In the early post-Cold War period, MOF and MOFA began to work together on the issue of Japan's role in global economic institutions despite the traditional rivalries between the two. With MOF targeted for administrative reform, MOFA has tended to gain ground in promoting its *kao ga mieru* (visible) multilateral aid at the expense of MOF's more apolitical *kao ga mienai* (invisible) policy. MOF has also suffered from recent scandals involving its role in the WB. One scandal involved the use of a Japanese trust fund for the training of MOF officials, leading to accusations of bias. Another incident concerned the dismissal of two Japanese WB officials receiving kickbacks for awarding a procurement project to a Japanese firm (*Japan Times*, 17 July and 6 September 1998). Thus, within the policy-making process MOF has lost ground to MOFA. Also, with the appointment at the WB of dynamic Japanese representatives from MOF, such as Shiratori and Gyōten Toyō, the two ministries have begun to coordinate, rather than compete over, policy.

Demonstrative of the pluralism of the policy-making process in Japan, Japanese aid agencies have interacted with global financial institutions to improve the provision of aid. The two sides meet regularly and exchange ideas on a local level. By supporting institutions in their preparation of activities, voluntary contributions promote co-financing between the institutions and Japanese aid agencies, and put the institutions' know-how to practical use. Co-financing is a factor when a project is only partially funded by the institution and the remainder is provided by other lending institutions, commercial banks and bilateral aid programmes of the donors. Over half of WB projects have been co-financed in recent years. Significantly, Japan has been the main source of co-financing in recent years (Lincoln 1993: 137–8). This process involves considerable negotiation between the multilateral agency and the national donor, giving policy-making agents in the donor country the opportunity to shape the project. Through the promotion of co-financing, Japanese public and private sector institutions have worked in order to solve debt relief problems. The first Miyazawa Initiative announced in 1987 at the IMF/WB meeting in Berlin is an example of the Japanese government proposing this approach (see also Chapter 10).

Bilateral relations with the US remained a factor, however, external pressure being brought by the US government when it wanted concessions from its trading partners. Japan was the focus of Congress's rage in the run-up to the Uruguay Round of GATT trade negotiations in 1984 as it held US$37 billion of the US$123 billion US trade deficit. Upon Prime Minister Nakasone Yasuhiro's announcement of a 25 per cent increase in auto exports to the US in March 1985, Congress threatened the introduction of a 20 per cent surcharge on imports from states which allowed an 'unreasonable' trade imbalance with the US. Although this threatened surcharge was later dropped, the desired effect upon Japan was achieved. Nakasone admitted that he had underestimated Congress's fury and that he had committed an 'error in judgement' (Wiener 1995: 99–100), thus demonstrating the importance of bilateral relations with the US and also the plurality of actors involved in the policy-making process.

20.8 Trade conflict

The Japanese government has brought three cases against the US in the WTO: over measures based on sections 301 and 304 of the US Trade Act of 1974, which imposed a 100 per cent tax on imported Japanese luxury cars; in respect of the Massachusetts State Procurement Law limiting procurement from companies trading with Myanmar; and over three clauses of the 1916 US Anti-Dumping Law. The US has taken Japan to the WTO over alcohol tax; copyright; measures connected with printing paper and photographic film used by consumers; measures connected with circulation services; and measures connected with the quarantine of agricultural items. The US Department of Trade, moreover, announced on 1 April 1999 a report on barriers to foreign trade which condemned the closed nature of Japan's security markets and suggested a policy appeal to the WTO. This all demonstrates friction in the bilateral relationship, as was seen in Chapter 5. Despite this, a number of trade disputes have been resolved on both a bilateral and multilateral basis, thus demonstrating the functional utility of global institutions to Japan. This was clear in the declaration of MITI Minister Hashimoto Ryūtarō, upon the conclusion of negotiations with the US trade representative, Mickey Kantor, that the agreement was not only a victory for the US and Japan, but also for the newly-created WTO (Ōhara 1999: 20).

In May 1995, US–Japan friction reached crisis level, as was seen in Chapter 5, with the US threatening 100 per cent punitive tariffs on Japanese imports of luxury cars unless markets were opened to foreign markets. Whereas a 'Japan problem' is often highlighted, with the US and Europe citing the tolerance of unfair trading practices or 'inappropriate measures to limit imports of cars and car parts', a 'US problem' is equally in evidence in May 1995. The US broke two GATT principles at a time when the WTO was attempting to establish itself as a fledgling organization. First, GATT members can only apply tariffs negotiated with another signatory of the treaty, and the US had previously agreed with Japan to apply tariffs of no more than 2.5 per cent. Second, equal treatment is to be accorded to all GATT members, which would force the US to apply similar tariffs on other GATT members (*Financial Times*, 23 May 1995). So, while the WTO was still considering the US's claims of Japanese unfair trading practices, the US was threatening tougher measures (running against GATT principles) of the 100 per cent tariff. In this way, the US government was undermining the global institution in its infancy. It also failed to obtain the support of the EU and East Asian states for sanctions against Japan (owing to the levels of ODA provided by the Japanese government and Japanese business presence in East Asia) and faced isolation on this issue (*Asahi Shimbun*, 30 May 1995).

Since the time of Japan's admission to GATT, Japanese policy-making agents in the governing parties (the LDP mostly), as well as in MOFA, MITI, MOF and other ministries, have been forced to respond to international pressures, especially *beiatsu*, for Japan to open its markets. The Kennedy Round of trade negotiations held from 1964 to 1967 resulted in tariff reductions to be put into effect from 1968 to 1972. Six countries brought these tariff cuts into effect ahead of schedule: Argentina, Canada, Iceland, Ireland, Switzerland and Japan. The WTO has attempted to encourage Japan to reduce tariffs specifically in the fields of fishery products, certain wood products and petroleum. State regulations remain in place for items such as rice, barley, wheat, milk products, raw silk, salt and leaf tobacco. Japan has maintained an average rate in tariffs of 9.4 per cent in 1997 with 60 per cent of all tariffs at 5 per cent or below. In exceptional cases, tariffs shoot up to 920 per cent. Japan does not belong to any free trade bloc or customs union and, although it has played a leading role in APEC and ASEM, policy-makers baulked at the idea when one was mooted in the form of EAEC, as was seen in Chapter 9. Japan has maintained a number of bilateral agreements with the US covering, *inter alia*, semi-conductors, the automobile industry, financial services and insurance. On this bilateral basis, Japan has undertaken to increase access to Japanese markets and sales opportunities for foreign automobiles and automobile parts. In 1996, it also created the Global Government Forum to discuss issues facing the semi-conductor industry in a multilateral, rather than a bilateral, context.

At the same time, however, Japanese policy has been in line with WTO agreements, as illustrated by the change in government procurement policy to one of open tendering, and respect for intellectual property legislation by the strengthening of copyright laws in Japan in 1996. Since 1995, Japan has abolished nine of eleven export cartels. As regards the Uruguay Round negotiations, Japanese policy-makers can be said to have attempted to implement the results of the talks: average tariff rates were reduced to 1.5 per cent for industrial products, 1 per cent for forestry products, 4.1 per cent for fisheries' products and 9.3 per cent for agricultural products. The average tariff rate for non-agricultural products was reduced to an overall 1.7 per cent level – one of the lowest in the world. Japan also contributed to the successful conclusion of the Information Technology Agreement at the WTO Singapore Ministerial Conference in 1996. Japan implemented in 1997 the first tariff reductions, and planned to eliminate customs tariffs on information technology products by the end of 2000. Japan also reviewed the tariff lines on pharmaceutical products to cover 400 products in July 1997. Moreover, GATT has been supportive of Japan's position in relation to the US. In August 1988, for instance, the Omnibus Trade and Competitiveness Act was passed by the US House of Representatives maintaining the Gephardt Amendment which allowed for mandatory retaliation on states that maintained an 'excessive and unwarranted' trade surplus with the US and failed to reduce it by 10 per cent annually. This was targeted at the then high-growth economies of East Asia as well as particularly Japan. These measures were met with criticism from GATT, which stated that the main source of the trade deficit was the US budget deficit.

Nevertheless, GATT has also been used as a tool in policy instrumentalization by Japan for its own interests. For instance, MOFA policy-makers criticized France for discriminating against Japanese car imports, and protested that:

> The French government has withheld giving type certificates for new Japanese cars since July 1980, making it impossible to sell them in France. If this move is aimed at keeping Japanese cars' share of the French market within 3 per cent, it constitutes undue discrimination against Japan, which runs counter to the spirit of GATT.
>
> (Ishikawa 1990: 26)

Hence, GATT, created by the early-starter economies as a means to preserve and enhance their interests against Japan and other late-starters, was now being used by a late-starter economy as a means to preserve and enhance Japan's interests in relation to Europe.

20.9 Summary

The international relations of Japan during the post-war era have been compared to those of the US during the first half of the twentieth century when isolationist and internationalist groups lobbied to influence the direction of the US's role in the world. The battle was fought between Wilsonian internationalists, such as J. P. Morgan Jr., who supported the League of Nations and cancellation of Germany's war debt, and Republican isolationist sections. Japan today stands in the same position; the debate in international and domestic society is nothing new. Within Japan, the policy-making agents who favour a more active, visible role encompassing Asianist and internationalist norms include many in MOFA, major Japanese banks and corporations with global interests. Ministries such as MOFA, as well as the major business players, are the groups that are especially willing to trade off domestic for foreign goals, as seen in their support for deregulation and the maintenance of a strong yen. Those groups that are wary of this role include MOF and the construction industry, as well as the wholesale and retail sectors, which depend chiefly on the domestic market and cannot compete internationally. The influence of these small and medium-sized businesses has traditionally been supported by the ruling LDP. As big business has become more international, these policy-making agents and other political actors have come into greater competition. The influence of the internationalists is now increasing, as the weight of small business and farmers declines in favour of urban voters, the LDP leadership imposes policy on unruly backbenchers, and the globalization of the Japanese economy and society proceeds within multilateral organizations in response to a variety of norms, as adumbrated in this chapter (Frieden 1993: 423–7). In addition, the comparison with the US extends to Japan's recent use of global institutions in order to instrumentalize its own policy ends in much the same way the US has done.

Chapter 21

Japan–G7/8

21.1 Overview

With the collapse of the Bretton Woods system in 1971, Japan reacted positively to President Valéry Giscard d'Estaing's invitation to attend the inaugural G7 summit in 1975. Since its first meeting at Rambouillet in France in November 1975 to discuss economic policy in light of the Nixon shocks of August 1971 and the oil shock of 1973, the G7 system has undergone a considerable transformation (see Appendix 21.1). Of greatest significance has been the expansion in both the number of participants, from five members to eight, and the remit of its concerns – originally purely economic, but now embracing the security dimension of international relations. The original six (the US, the UK, France, Germany, Italy and Japan) metamorphosed rapidly into the G7 with the addition of Canada in 1987. From 1998 Russia was included officially as a member of the G8. Japan was excluded from much of the institutional machinery for global policy coordination up until the creation of the G7, a situation which continues to some extent even today, especially in the security dimension. Notwithstanding this, however, Japan has become a central member of the G7 system, and is now recognized within the international system created by the early-starter economies. As a result, the issues of voting rights and representation within the G7 have not been so problematic in comparison to Japan's participation in other global institutions (see Chapters 19 and 20). In fact, the G7 has taken on a special significance for Japan.

Japan's global importance, owing to its remarkable post-war economic growth and its massive current account surplus, ensured that from the outset Japan was regarded as an equal among the early-starter economies of the West in an organization dominated by the West, especially Europe. Moreover, Japan has taken a more proactive role and shown greater willingness to shoulder its global responsibilities in the G7 than in other global institutions. Prime Minister Miki Takeo attended the first meeting, indicating that Japan could no longer be ignored as it occupied one pole in the developing tripolar global political economy. He soon found the summit an effective arena in which to combat his weak position within the ruling LDP and increase his domestic popularity. Thus, his support rose from 36 per cent to 43 per cent in August 1975 following his return from a preparatory meeting for the first G7 summit with President Gerald Ford. At the Williamsburg summit in May 1983, Prime Minister Nakasone Yasuhiro took the lead among the G7 leaders, discussing not only the economic dimension but also global security problems as part of his foreign policy. As was seen in Chapter 4, this strengthened the Ron–Yasu relationship and the idea of Japan as a member of the West (*nishigawa no ichiin*) or an international state (*kokusai kokka*). Thus, as well as promoting discussion of sustainable growth with no inflation and currency stability through a multilateral observation mechanism, the Nakasone administration tied Japan to the West in the security dimension by accepting the common threat posed by the USSR's installation of SS-20 nuclear missiles in Europe. Nakasone was the most vocal supporter of the US and stressed the inseparability of Western security (*anzen no fukabun*).

Thus, as Chapters 19 and 20 have done in the context of the UN, the IMF, the WB, GATT and the WTO, this chapter will adumbrate those of the norms analysed in Chapter 2 that exert their influence in the G7. The first norm, Asianism, is clearly discernible in Japan's G7 policy, for Japanese policy-makers have a history of promoting East Asian ideals and interests in the G7 as Japan is the only East Asian representative in an organization dominated by the early-starter economies of the West. The Venice summit of 1987 witnessed the G7's economic declaration referring to the successful economic growth of the newly industrialized economies (NIEs) and the need to promote exchange rate stability and accelerate market liberalization. Before the 1988 Toronto summit, Prime Minister Takeshita Noboru visited the ASEAN states and conducted a telephone discussion with President Roh Tae-Woo of South Korea, which led to Japan being dubbed as the representative of Asia (*Ajia no Daihyō*). Thus, Japanese policy-makers responded to the developmentalist norm by explaining the purpose of aid to the Philippines and promoting dialogue with the NIEs, which can be interpreted as anticipating Japan's post-Cold War diplomacy (Iokibe 1999: 216).

The norm of internationalism can be seen in the way Japan has also used the G7 to instrumentalize its ideas of managing global security and economics. In addition, as Prime Minister Hashimoto Ryūtarō attempted to do at the 1997 Denver meeting, policy-making agents have promoted the credentials of Japan as a permanent member of the UNSC. Thus, the interplay of both domestic and external norms is readily discernible. The policy-making process at the G7 demonstrates the influence of a plurality of actors. More interesting is the distinction between the Western world order implied by the term 'G7' and the post-Cold War order suggested by the term 'G8' and the inclusion of Russia. As demonstrated later in this chapter, this structural distinction had serious implications for Japan's multilateral foreign policy, and at times forced Japan to behave in a proactive manner in order to protect its interests.

21.2 Economic issues

21.2.i Management of the global economy

Managing the global economy was the original main *raison d'être* for the G7. With the aim of boosting the world economy after the first oil crisis, the 1977 London summit advanced the idea of the 'locomotive theory'. Thereafter, the locomotive theory metamorphosed into the 'convoy theory' at the Bonn summit of 1978, but remained essentially the same: that is, the major economies of Japan, the US and Germany would pull forward the other troubled economies of the world. This policy highlighted the perceived trilateral structure of the global political economy. Japan also responded to a multilateral approach by accepting a higher growth target of 7 per cent, in an attempt to stimulate its economy in a manner that would boost the world economy. This led to a domestic outcry against Prime Minister Fukuda Takeo for accepting such a sacrifice at a time of tight budgetary constraints when additional growth could only be stimulated by huge deficit financing. However, at the Bonn summit in 1978 Japanese policy-makers also made serious efforts to conclude the Tokyo Round of trade negotiations, in contrast to the Munich summit of 1992 where Japan almost abandoned trade negotiations. To this extent, the Bonn summit of 1978 has been described by Owada Hisashi as one of the most successful summits for Japan (Owada 1994).

The G7 has recognized Japan's critical role in tackling instability in the world's economies and has long encouraged Japan to continue in its efforts to stimulate its own domestic economy and make structural reforms. This was a salient issue at the 1999 Cologne summit, which also promoted a free-trade system based around the WTO. The hope was that this would ensure the stability of the global economy, encourage reform of the global financial system and assist in relieving the debt burden. Japanese policy-makers have been swayed by the opinions of the other G7 members – there are regular statements in G7 communiqués calling on Japan to stimulate domestic demand and avoid instability in exchange rates. This was believed to be the reason behind the BOJ's decision to step in to halt a surge in the value of the yen in June 1999, as such an upswing threatened nascent economic growth in the Japanese economy. The US has also used the G7 to encourage the Japanese government to exploit 'all available tools to support strong domestic demand-led growth' (*Yomiuri Shimbun*, 28 April 1999). This means the introduction of effective fiscal, tax and financial measures in line with supply-side structural reforms to bring about a full-scale recovery of the Japanese economy as expressed at the 1999 G7 meetings. However, divisions have appeared between MOF and the Bank of Japan (BOJ) over how to implement G7 suggestions for the achievement of stable exchange rates. Matsushima Masayuki, director of the BOJ, has stated that, although there have been exchanges of opinion with MOF, there is no consensus on how to achieve stable exchange rates. The BOJ stresses the connection between stability in prices and stability in currency. No policy-maker has suggested actually sacrificing stability in prices (*Yomiuri Shimbun*, 22 February 1999), but MOF is more willing to *risk* stability in prices in order to achieve stability in the currency markets in cooperation with other members of the G7. Division within the policy-making process in Japan over this issue illustrates the pluralistic nature of policy-making, as discussed in Chapter 2.

21.2.ii Debt relief

Debt relief also has become a major issue in the global political economy of the post-Cold War period: Japan alone has extended loans in respect of about 44 per cent of the total debt in the world. Japan, like France, has insisted upon attaching certain conditions to debt relief in an effort to secure fairness among creditor states, and ensure repayment and economic reform efforts by debtors in order to minimize their future reliance on international financial support. With the establishment of funds to write off debts, Japan and France have argued that the UK and other states, whose ODA loans are minimal, ought to contribute to the funds in order to make the individual burdens of industrialized powers more equitable (*Yomiuri Shimbun*, 10 June 1999). Japan's position, as presented to the meeting of G8 foreign and finance ministers in Cologne, is to stress that highly-indebted poor countries should be trained to handle debt by themselves. Suggestions included reducing debt burdens by extending the borrowing term and varying the terms of repayment through the provision of technical assistance. Thus, Japan's policy emphasizes that waiving debt is not enough and that technical advice on debt management is essential in order to promote self-management (*Yomiuri Shimbun*, 3 June 1999). In order to tackle the controversy over hedge funds, Japan, along with its European counterparts, has called for the direct monitoring of the flow of speculative funds by setting certain criteria. Accordingly, Japanese policy-making agents have tackled the chief issues facing the major industrialized powers within a multilateral context. A similar trend can be seen in a new round of multilateral talks which the G8 finalized at Cologne, when a three-year round of negotiations was agreed to deal with issues beyond the agricultural and service sectors.

21.3 Expanding the G7

21.3.i Russian reconstruction

It has been asserted that Japan's whole policy towards the former Soviet Union became multilateral in the period between the 1989 Paris summit and the 1993 Tokyo summit of the G7 (Yasutomo 1995: 151–76). In dealing with the reconstruction of the former Soviet Union, Japanese policy-makers found it effective to provide aid in small amounts and, most important, through multilateral organizations. At the Houston summit of 1990, Japan opposed large-scale aid to Russia and favoured the resumption of large-scale ODA to China after the Tiananmen Square incident. Japanese policy was not to oppose aiding Russia *per se*, but to maintain small levels of aid; to respond to a Japanese public which is traditionally anti-Russian; and to moderate the enthusiasm of its Western partners for large-scale aid to Russia. From the beginning, Japanese aid to Russia, including assistance after the Chernobyl incident, which had to be funnelled through the proxy channel of the Red Cross, was going to 'remain small scale rather than large scale, humanitarian rather than developmental, semi-official rather than official, and multilateral rather than purely bilateral' until the Northern Territories issue (see Chapters 3 and 4), the thorn in the side of Russo-Japanese relations, was resolved successfully (Yasutomo 1995: 154).

From an early stage Japanese policy-makers were vocally opposed to writing off large amounts of East European and Russian debt. The Japanese position was encapsulated by one official: 'Russia is not an advanced economy [and should not join the G7]. The West should demand that Russia help itself' (*Far Eastern Economic Review*, 16 July 1992). This wariness in providing aid to Russia extended to preventing President Mikhail Gorbachev or any Russian

Plate 21.1 Japan walks tall. Shoulder to shoulder with the big powers, Prime Minister Nakasone Yasuhiro occupies a central position during the G7 summit meeting at Williamsburg, Virginia, 28–30 May 1983.

Source: Kyōdō News

representative from joining the G7 process. Kaifu strongly opposed the idea when it was first mooted at the G7 London summit of 1991. Equally, Japan also opposed Russia's membership of the IMF and the World Bank. After the August *coup* (against Gorbachev) in 1991, Japan did concede and supported a meeting of the G7 to address the problem, but was keen to avoid the G7 becoming overly-concerned with the 'Russian problem'.

Japanese policy-making agents were more keen, for historical reasons, to develop relationships with the Central Asian Republics (CARs) of Kazakhstan, Kyrgyzstan, Tajikistan, Turkmenistan and Uzbekistan. This was part of Japan's emerging post-Cold War 'Silk Road' diplomatic effort (Gaikō Fōramu 1998). The willingness of MOFA to give voice to the Asianist norm is illustrated by the comments made by one senior minister who stated: 'of course, providing assistance to Russia is regarded as a top priority. But as an Asian nation, we would like to lend greater support to the former Soviet states in the Asian region' (*Japan Times*, 20 October 1992; cited in Yasutomo 1995: 157). This was a move equally favoured by MOF, which undertook a fact-finding mission to the CARs in October 1992 and then invited government representatives to Tokyo for briefings in February 1993. The Japanese government pressed to have all the CARs placed on the OECD's Development Assistance Committee list of developing economies, despite the opposition of the US. Thus, Japan's policy exhibited aspects of bilateralism coexisting alongside a multilateral approach to the Russian problem, and the Asianist norm was extended beyond the confines of East Asia.

Eventually, in the ministerial meeting of April 1993 prior to the Tokyo summit of 1993 a decision was made on aid for Russia, so that Moscow was supplied with a US$43 billion package out of which US$1.82 billion came from Japan. The extent of US pressure exerted at the time is illustrated by Secretary of State Warren Christopher's comments that 'we are urging all the members of the G7 – Japan included – to participate in these two new programs that we've outlined [funds to promote the privitization of Russian state industries and help Russia dismantle its nuclear weapons]', and he praised Japan for managing to 'delink' the Northern Territories issue from the aid issue (*Japan Times*, 16 April 1993). As far as Japan was concerned, both formal and informal channels of diplomacy using the G7 could be effective in this regard.

21.3.ii From G7 to G8

The issue of Russia's participation in an expanded G8 forum demonstrates a variety of influences at work. Divisions within Japanese policy-making circles were evident as MOFA acted quickly to deny Warren Christopher's comments and stress that Japan opposed the participation of the former Soviet Union in the G7 process. The importance of the US bilateral relationship with Japan over the Russian issue in the G7 is also evident. As European criticism of Japanese intransigence over Russia increased, President Bill Clinton met with President Boris Yeltsin in April 1993 and took a line different from the Europeans, stressing that 'the Japanese have been very forthcoming as the leaders of the G7. This is their year to lead and they are leading' (*Japan Times*, 5 April 1993; cited in Yasutomo 1995: 159).

The Japanese government came close to 'un-inviting' Yeltsin to the 1993 Tokyo G7 summit after he cancelled a trip to Japan earlier that year, and displayed intransigence over changing the date for the summit to accommodate Russian participation. Foreign Minister Watanabe Michio stressed that, 'although some G7 countries are calling for earlier talks, we, as the country that holds the chairmanship, are not considering having another summit to discuss aid for Russia. We [the G7] may have the Russian lieder brief us on the Russion economic and political situations' (*Japan Times*, 17 March 1993). Japan's argument extended to the fact that the G7 was meant to involve aid donors, not recipients. One MOFA official stated that 'it seems difficult to expand G7 to G8 by granting full membership to Russia because that country is not a world leading country in terms of economics' (*Japan Times*, 13 May 1994).

Japanese policy was constrained in this instance by domestic policy-makers opposed to developing closer relations with Russia whilst the Northern Territories dispute continued. Moreover, Japan regarded the G7 as the forum in which the Northern Territories dispute could be addressed. The 1990 Houston summit was an important meeting for Japan as it was the first time that support was extended by the G7 to Japan over the Northern Territories issue. Secretary of State James Baker stated that 'we support the early resolution of the Northern Territory issue as an essential step leading to the normalization of Japan–Soviet relations'. In addition, the norm of the bilateral relationship with the US in Japanese foreign policy can be seen in James Baker's second statement that the US was raising the issue 'every time we sit down with them [the Soviets]' (*Japan Times*, 12 July 1990). The different direction of US policy was also evident in President Clinton's initiative to allow Russia to join the G7 forum in 1997, using Russian membership to ease any fears over expanded NATO membership. Japan hoped that support from its G7 partners might force a conclusion to the problem. However, this became a difficult position to maintain because, as seen above, the G7 was keen to proceed with large-scale aid to Russia and regarded Japan as tardy and self-centred. This left the Japanese fearful of diplomatic isolation but unable to shift their position drastically owing to domestic opposition to a compromise on the Northern Territories issue. However, Obuchi was able to obtain Yeltsin's reaffirmation at the 1999 Cologne summit that he would visit Japan by the end of 1999 in order to conclude a peace treaty with Japan by 2000. What with Yeltsin's decision to step down, and the victory of Vladimir Putin in the March 2000 presidential elections, a solution to the territorial issue in 2000 was not realizable. Thus, Japan has used multilateral fora in order to instrumentalize its national interests and has attempted to globalize the issue of the Northern Territories through the G7 process.

21.4 Japan, East Asia and the G7/8

21.4.i Japan as regional leader

From the start of the G7 summits, Japan has used summitry to develop and promote an East Asian perspective. Miki arrived at the first Rambouillet meeting with the plans of creating an East Asian version of the Lomé Convention, tripling ODA and contributing funds to the UN's Food and Agriculture Organization. Despite support from MOFA, these plans were eventually jettisoned because of financial constraints imposed by MOF. Such bureaucratic disputes, as mentioned in the discussion of policy-making in Chapter 2, were to erode Miki's opportunity to promote North–South issues and Japan's East Asian identity at this first summit. Be that as it may, this trend of Japan promoting East Asian regional issues developed further under Prime Minister Suzuki Zenkō. At the 1982 Versailles summit, he called for the promotion of a stable Sino-Japanese relationship as the key to peace and prosperity in East Asia. To this end, he conducted meetings with Prime Minister Zhao Ziyang of China prior to the G7 summit. Nakasone also used pre-summit diplomacy to continue carving out Japan's role as an East Asian regional representative. Thus, prior to the 1983 Williamsburg summit he visited the ASEAN capitals in order to gain support for Japan's position at the G7, to propose aid programmes to them and soothe fears of Japanese remilitarization (*Asahi Shimbun*, 19 May 1983). Significantly, Nakasone ensured that the assertion that the countries of 'the dynamic Pacific region were drawing even closer together' was included in the declaration of the 1985 Bonn summit.

21.4.ii East Asian participation

In reaction to the policies of the other major industrialized powers, in particular Europe's near obsession with the inclusion of Russia in the G7 system, in Japan the Asianist norm has come to the fore in G7 policy. A senior member of the Mitsuzuka faction of the governing LDP called for the government to petition for the participation of China in the 1993 G7 summit: 'we cannot ignore China in discussing Asia. We should consider having China attend the [Tokyo] summit as an observer'. Equally a MOFA official regarded the issue of Russia's participation as a spur to the discussion of China's inclusion (*Japan Times*, 19 July 1991). Japan's embrace of this new East Asian identity can be seen in Miyazawa attempting to give the 1993 Tokyo G7 summit an East Asian feel and emphasis by announcing an official tour of Southeast Asia for January 1993 (*Japan Times*, 14 November 1992). Moreover, requests came from Indonesia that Japan convey in the G7 the views of East Asian countries and the non-aligned movement (NAM). With reference specifically to the dimension of security (but the quote could be applied to other fields), Miyazawa stated that Japan 'will think and act together' with ASEAN (*Japan Times*, 17 January 1993). To a degree, the Japanese government found itself in the common position of being a bridge between East and West and having to balance the bilateralist and Asianist norms. Japan's Western counterparts were opposed to the participation of President Suharto of Indonesia in the 1993 Tokyo summit, leading the Japanese government to regard the chances of his invitation as 'quite slim'. MOFA, in contrast, stated, 'Japan will do its utmost diplomatically up to the last minute to realize Suharto's dialogue with some of the G7 leaders in Tokyo' (*Japan Times*, 17 June 1993). Ultimately, MOFA policy-making agents succeeded in securing Suharto's invitation to a pre-summit meeting with Prime Minister Miyazawa and President Clinton, but not to the actual G7 meeting itself.

MOFA was clearly concerned with the West's preoccupation regarding assistance for the former Soviet Union and Eastern Europe: one MOFA official declared that 'the G7 members, especially the United States, are more concerned about aiding Russia and have lost interest in the developing nations. We want to correct that' (*Japan Times*, 10 July 1993; cited in Yasutomo 1995: 169). Four years later an editorial in the *Japan Times* encapsulated the issue of the inclusion of Russia and non-inclusion of China by stating, 'at least the Japanese raised the issue of why Russia had been invited, courted and all but canonized, when of course China was out of sight and almost out of mind except for Hong Kong' (*Japan Times*, 28 June 1997). As was seen in Chapter 9, Japan sought to provide another point of view on the implications of the Tiananmen Square incident and how the West should deal with China. Thus, without alienating China and maintaining a policy of constructive engagement, Japanese policy-makers sought to play the role of *kakehashi* between East and West in the G7. Most significantly, this clearly shows Japanese policy-makers reacting to and appealing to the Asianist norm and attempting to integrate China into a variety of multilateral fora.

21.5 Promotion of security

21.5.i Traditional security

Japan has tabled proposals addressing the resolution of the 1999 war in Kosovo within the G7 system but Japan's role has been limited by both domestically and internationally embedded norms (Gilson 2000b). MOFA has tried to enhance its economic post-conflict reconstruction role in the settlement of the dispute and to this end has contributed US$200 million to the resettlement of refugees. This was in addition to its tabling of a proposal, which was adopted at the June 1999 G8 summit in Cologne, to create the infrastructure necessary to repatriate refugees and secure aid for the province's reconstruction. To achieve this, Japanese political leaders and MOFA have sought international approval as embodied by the G7/8 and especially the UN. The importance of approval by the UN has been stressed by Japan in any post-war settlement. The absence of such approval during the bombing of Kosovo generated strong misgivings among Japanese policy-making agents. The June 1999 meeting of the G8 concentrated on the issue of Kosovo. Constrained by the domestically embedded norm of anti-militarism, Japanese policy-making agents opted to contribute financially to international efforts to implement the peace plan, support reconstruction efforts and assist the return of Albanian refugees. In terms of human contribution, Japan sent civilian assistance to Kosovo as part of the international effort with the PKO Bill's ban on participation in a peacekeeping force still in effect, as discussed earlier in this Part V and in Part IV. The LDP and the LP have expressed their desire to remove the ban, but coalition politics is hampering this initiative as the Kōmei Party and its lay Buddhist following still have misgivings.

However, security issues in East Asia, namely, North Korea and its missile programme, as discussed in Chapter 11, led the G8 to state in the 1999 Cologne communiqué that they would consider taking individual or joint action depending on the policy pursued by North Korea. Obuchi pushed the point that G8 leaders should express 'deep concern' in the final G8 communiqué over the development of nuclear weapons and missile delivery systems in North Korea. Japanese policy-makers also promoted the G8's support for the 'sunshine policy' of President Kim Dae-Jung of South Korea, in line with Japan's agreement with the US and South Korea to pursue a 'dialogue and deterrence' policy towards North Korea, as discussed in Chapter 9. In this way, Japanese policy-makers have attempted to promote policies within multilateral fora and with international backing. To this end, the Cologne communiqué called upon the UN to strengthen its crisis-prevention role. China and Russia agree with this call, as a way for the UN to act as a check upon the US. The Japanese government is of the same mind as China and Russia, but for different reasons: it seeks to enhance the role of the UN and promote Japan's inclusion in the UNSC. This demonstrates that Japan is attempting to resolve its security problems not unilaterally, but multilaterally through global institutions.

In the field of disarmament, Japanese policy-makers have attempted to pursue policies within a multilateral forum. In June 1999, the government decided to extend approximately US$200 million in assistance to Russia to finance the dismantling of nuclear weapons built during the Soviet period. The plan to provide money for the disposal of plutonium was announced at the G8 meeting in line with the 'reduction of threat' initiative put forward by President Clinton. Thus, Japan has supplemented its bilateral diplomacy towards Russia. This can be seen in the adoption of a multilateral approach through the approved G8 initiatives, as illustrated by Foreign Minister Kōmura Masahiko's May 1999 visit to Russia and the agreement on three points for the disassembly of nuclear submarines, transfer of military technology and the disposal of plutonium from nuclear weapons. During the India–Pakistan stand-off over nuclear tests in May 1998, the G8 played a minimal role. Japan played a bilateral role in applying economic sanctions and then encouraging both sides to come to the negotiating table, resulting in a conference in Tokyo in August 1998. The restoration of aid to Iran, Burma and Vietnam was achieved through bilateral means, not multilateral, against the will of the US. In this sense, Japanese policy-making agents do not opt for a clear-cut division between bilateral and multilateral engagements, but adopt a much more nuanced multilevel approach, as discussed in Chapter 2.

21.5.ii New security challenges

During the Cold War, Japan attempted to promote traditional military security links as a Cold War warrior tied to the norm of US bilateralism. Nakasone promoted links at the Williamsburg summit with the slogan that 'security is indivisible' in light of the Soviet decision to deploy SS-20 nuclear missiles in Europe and East Asia. With the end of the Cold War, however, newer and broader definitions of the term 'security' have been promoted within various global institutions. The 1978 Bonn summit saw Fukuda promote the insertion of the broader definition in the final statement of a denunciation of international terrorism (*Mainichi Shimbun*, 17 July 1978). This concern with terrorism continued into the post-Cold War period. As a result of the sarin gas attack in the Tokyo subway of March 1995 and related attacks by the Aum Shinrikyō (Supreme Truth) cult (Hughes 1998), Prime Minister Murayama Tomiichi sought at the Halifax meeting of the G7 in June 1995 to call upon the G7 to address terrorism.

Food security has been another issue promoted by Japanese policy-makers, in view of which the Houston summit communiqué of June 1990 included a statement on Japan's concerns with food security. Hence, Japan's definition of security has extended from one solely based on military concerns to include Japan's rice markets and the tradition of self-sufficiency – clearly a desire to protect Japanese markets from competition with the West, and a reflection of the developmentalist norm. Domestic pressures are also noteworthy in this issue-area. As one observer stated: 'since rice is a highly domestic problem, I doubt Miyazawa can ignore the fierce opposition from farmers and some politicians and immediately open the markets' (cited in the *Japan Times*, 31 October 1991). Thus, as was suggested in Chapter 2, which policy-maker is involved in a specific policy will depend on the policy issue-area.

Again, an extended interpretation of security can be discerned in Japan's landmine policy and proposed landmine conference in June 1996 within the G7. Hashimoto regarded the security issues within the G7 as one area where he could 'display leadership qualities on global issues' with regard to UN peacekeeping and the reconstruction of Bosnia-Herzegovina. At the same time, as mentioned in Part III, Hashimoto responded to the Asianist norm by wanting 'to avoid isolating China and to continue dialogue to foster the process of economic opening' (*Japan Times*, 13 May 1996). Japanese policy-making agents have urged an environmental role for the G7 in an expanded sense of security but also with an East Asian bent in response to the Asianist norm. This has included an emphasis on monitoring acid rain in East Asia and making it a priority to avoid pollution whilst promoting development in the region. In a similar way to that described in Chapter 19 on the work of the UN in Africa, Japan has drawn on its own experience to address environmental issues, giving East Asia, for instance, the benefit of Japan's knowledge of such well-known problems of pollution as Minamata disease (an illness affecting muscular and other human functions, which spread to the local inhabitants of Minamata through their consumption of mercury-contaminated fish caught off the coast of Minamata, Kyūshū).

21.6 Policy-making process

21.6.i Ministry of Foreign Affairs and Ministry of Finance

It is clear that MOFA lies at the core of Japan's G7 policy-making process, and that MOFA took a tough line against the Soviet Union throughout the Cold War as a result of the Soviet violation of the Neutrality Pact, the occupation of the Northern Territories and an anti-communist world view (Yasutomo 1995: 170). As was seen in Chapter 4, however, changes in personnel as well as the rise up the ranks of younger more flexible members of the Soviet Desk have prompted a review of Japan's policy towards Russia regardless of the pressure placed on Japan by the G7. MOF was a mere observer of MOFA's activities until the Soviet Union disintegrated, when there arose the issues of funnelling aid to the former Soviet Union and opportunities in the CARs. As in MOFA, a strong suspicion of Russia's inability effectively to use assistance led MOF to promote a multilateral policy in addition to opposing Russian membership of various international organizations. MOFA and MOF began to work together on issues such as approaching the CARs and began to share a common approach, especially with the rise of the 'Asian Mafia' in MOF between 1992 and 1993 (Yasutomo 1995: 171). Coordination between MOFA and MOF extended to the assistance Japan agreed to provide to Russia with the grants overseen by MOFA, whereas the World Bank and IMF contributions would be overseen by MOF.

21.6.ii Ministry of International Trade and Industry and Bank of Japan

Other ministries have exerted influence depending on the issue-area. Nakasone's project, the Human Frontier Science Programme, proposed at the 1987 Venice summit, led to bitter infighting between MOF and MITI. MITI had been developing the project for some time previous to the summit and aimed to promote state-of-the-art scientific and technological research in Japan to compensate for a perceived lack of creativity (*Asahi Shimbun*, 12 June 1987). MOF was not willing to provide the ¥1 trillion required to fund this twenty-year project. The legitimacy the G7 extended to Nakasone's proposal enhanced MITI's position relative to MOF. Thus, the G7 was used to resolve domestic policy disputes. Within the G7 process, MOF and the BOJ have traditionally been financially stringent compared to the commitments that have been made by MOFA at the summits. In 1999, the BOJ decided to assert its independence and resist outside pressure by not relaxing monetary policy any further. This undermined the government's attempt to gain US approval for market intervention in order to stem the appreciation of the yen at the G7 finance ministers' meeting in Washington in September 1999 – another example of Japan implementing its policy through bilateral and multilateral means (*Daily Yomiuri*, 23 and 27 September 1999).

21.6.iii Big business and opposition parties

The *zaikai* has also been able to influence Japan's G7 policy. Before the Rambouillet summit, for instance, heads of the *Keidanren* and *Nisshō* met Prime Minister Miki and petitioned him to promote the Tokyo Round of trade negotiations to curb protectionism. The conclusion of the Tokyo Round by 1977 was promoted by Miki and ultimately the date was written into the final statement as a proposed target. Opposition parties within Japan, especially the SDPJ and JCP, have traditionally been against summitry and the G7. By the use of proxy diplomacy and other informal channels, however, the opposition parties have exerted influence in building a consensus on Japan's G7 policy (*Asahi Shimbun*, 23, 27 and 28 April 1985).

21.6.iv Prime minister

In the context of the G7, the prime minister, premier or president plays an important role. Where once economic policy was purely the preserve of the finance minister, the head of the executive has become increasingly important. At the G7 summits in particular, personal diplomacy has been regarded as an important factor. For example, Prime Minister Kaifu Toshiki is seen as having placed the Northern Territories on the agenda at the 1990 Houston summit. In seeking to improve the environment for dealing with the USSR, he also persuaded the JDA to drop references to the 'Soviet threat' from defence white papers (*Bōei Hakusho*). In addition, Miyazawa was seen to resist European and American demands for assistance to Russia. However, this freedom to exert an influence can be constrained by domestic factors. For instance, Miki's role at the 1976 San Juan (Puerto Rico) summit was curtailed by opposition within his own party to his sanctioning of a full investigation into the Lockheed Scandal. Fukuda's pledge at the 1978 Bonn summit to meet a 7 per cent growth rate in line with the 'locomotive theory' (see section 21.2.i), which was generally recognized as, and proved to be, unattainable, provided his rival and successor Ōhira Masayoshi with an opportunity to take political advantage of the situation. Thus, what was promised as an international commitment could be renounced by a change in the executive head. An active prime minister is in a position to promote his own ideas. At the 1981 Ottawa summit, Prime Minister Suzuki was able to insert the concept of harmony (*wa* or *chōwa*) in the policy-making process into the final statement. In addition, under Nakasone a new pattern developed of assertiveness and major policy announcements properly publicized and leaked in advance, so as to avoid major confrontations at the actual summit, or the kind of 'bombshell' announcements made by Giscard d'Estaing at the 1979 Tokyo summit on oil imports. In that instance, Ōhira was compromised owing to his dual role as chair of the summit and representative of Japan. The central role of the prime minister can lead to activism or reactivity depending on the ability of the politician in question.

This does not completely negate the role of bureaucratic policy-making agents. Japan's voice within the G7 has traditionally been muted and Japanese leaders presume that decisions have been made in advance by bureaucrats, simply to be rubber-stamped at the summit. This began at Rambouillet when Ushiba Nobuhiko, a former MOFA policy-maker, preferred predictable outcomes rather than spontaneity at the summit. The 'sherpa' system of bureaucrats literally guiding the summit agenda in the preparatory stages does lead to the top political leadership just rubber-stamping the work already done. The 'sherpas' tend to come from MOFA. Typically, in the extraordinary circumstances created by the sudden death of Prime Minister Ōhira in June 1980 immediately prior to the 1980 Venice summit, it was Foreign Minister Okita Saburō and Finance Minister Takeshita Noboru, neither a member of the Diet or of the LDP, who played key roles at this summit. As Okita was not sanctioned to make any binding commitments that would compromise the incoming government, however, there was little long-term impact resulting from bureaucrats setting the agenda (including the vetoing of Ōhira's plan to double ODA over five years) and settling the wording for the final statement (*Mainichi Shimbun*, 15 June 1980).

21.6.v Domestic issues

The importance of domestic issues in Japan's G7/8 policy was evident in the summer of 2000 when the G8 meeting of heads of state and government took place in Okinawa prefecture. On all the previous occasions that Japan acted as the summit's host – 1979, 1986 and 1993 – Tokyo was chosen as the venue, despite competition from major cities such as Osaka. Thus, the choice of Okinawa was symbolic not only because it was the first time that the Japanese government hosted a summit outside the capital, but also because of the peculiar position of Okinawa within Japan.

With the approach of the 2000 G8 summit, the Japanese government began to make money available with an initial payment of ¥16 billion to improve infrastructure within Okinawa prefecture (*Daily Yomiuri*, 23 June 1999). The prime minister's strategy was twofold. First, Obuchi sought to provide Okinawa, which has historically suffered from abandonment by the capital, with a much-needed economic stimulus. Second, despite the misgivings of the US government over the choice of venue, he attempted to intertwine the norms of US bilateralism and internationalism in dealing with a prefecture known to be one of the bastions of the anti-militarist norm, as was seen in Chapter 6. In this way, the summit focused world attention on the prefecture, highlighting its different culture and the heavy presence of US military facilities there, as was elaborated in Chapter 6. The Okinawan prefectural government and citizens' groups in Okinawa also viewed the summit as an opportunity to inform the world of the cultural differences and the problems the prefecture faces with the presence of US bases. In addition, the summit was an attempt to change the image abroad of Japan's diplomacy as purely 'chequebook diplomacy'. Thus, summitry has played a role in Japan's domestic politics, as well as enabling Japan to play a role in and shape the G7/8 process.

21.7 Summary

Japanese policy-makers have been willing to promote the objectives and interests of the state and its people through multilateral organizations. Japan is now recognized within the global institutions under examination as an important participant, thereby satisfying Japan's desire for international recognition conditioned by the norm of developmentalism. It has responded to the internationalist norm and has deflected criticism of dependence upon the bilateral relationship with the US. Equally important is the fact that Japan is the sole East Asian participant in a predominantly Western-oriented summit. As part of its pre-summit diplomacy, Japan has generally reached a consensus with its East Asian neighbours on policy goals and has reported back to them after the summit. Also, the role of the prime minister, notably, in this area of foreign policy, is paramount. The prime minister has been a key policy-making agent and has been able to bypass internal conflict and input his own vision into G7 policy. In contrast to the brusque style of the French and Italians in threatening to walk out of summits, Japan's style has emphasized the 'sherpa' system, pre-summit *nemawashi* and even compromising its national interests for the sake of harmony at the summit. Thus, 'summitry is a place for compromise rather than conflict as far as Japan is concerned' (Sakurada 1988: 102–3).

Chapter 22

Conclusion

22.1 Assuming global responsibilities

Chapter 18 began by describing the watershed decision by the Japanese government to despatch minesweepers to the Persian Gulf and thereafter personnel on UN-sanctioned peacekeeping operations. Building upon this jarring image, Chapters 19, 20 and 21 have demonstrated the dichotomy between Japan's traditional low-key, financial contributions and its growing visible and human contribution to the various global institutions. In short, and as the vignette in Chapter 18 illustrated, Japan has begun to behave internationally as a recognized and responsible actor, both despite and because of the norms of bilateralism and Asianism.

Chapter 19 on Japan and the UN showed that, as Japan has grown in economic power during the post-war era, its role and influence in the UN has grown in tandem. With the end of the Cold War, however, Japan's desire for recognition of its role has increased, and Japan has started to chafe against the constraints imposed by the early-starter economies of the West. Nowhere is this more evident than in Japan's avowed aim of acquiring a permanent seat on the UN Security Council. As the concluding chapters in Part VI will discuss, despite the growth in Japan's financial power and the end of the Cold War, structural obstacles still exist to Japan taking its place as a perceived responsible member of global institutions. Although Japanese contributions have increased and evolved, the kind of constraints which frustrated Japan's representatives at the Paris Peace Conference in 1919 still inform the norm of developmentalism to which the Japanese government and people have responded. The other norms of anti-militarism, bilateralism and Asianism also came under the spotlight throughout this Part V, and in Chapter 23 will be related to issues covered in other chapters. Although the UN-centred policy espoused by Prime Minister Kishi Nobusuke has yet to be realized, with obstacles still remaining, the Japanese state and its people have played, and will continue to play, a central role within the UN.

Chapter 20 demonstrated how Japan has used its economic power in order to instrumentalize the multilateral management of the global political economy. Thus, not only is the policy-making process pluralistic, but also the role of norms which have constrained and encouraged Japan's role is complex – a further theme which will be taken up in Chapter 23. Nevertheless, it was also clear that Japan was not willing to compromise its own interests unless absolutely necessary. Accordingly, Japan has sought, with a degree of success, to increase its representative rights within the IMF and the WB. Moreover, it has played the role of norm entrepreneur and has championed non-Western ideas as witnessed by the publication of the report *The East Asian Miracle: Economic Growth and Public Policy*, despite the objections of the early-starter Western economies. Japan has taken on the mantle of a potential leader of East Asia in global institutions. The example of the election of the secretary-general of the WTO demonstrates both the norms and tensions which mould Japan's role in financial and economic global institutions.

In Chapter 21 issues of representation and the norm of developmentalism were of less importance, as the G7 from its inception recognized and included Japan as one of its key members. Hence, Japan was accorded the international recognition it has sought since the Meiji restoration. Instead, Japan has increasingly reflected the Asianist norm by promoting regional issues at G7 meetings through close pre- and post-summit consultation with East Asian policy-makers, and by attempting to shift the focus of the G7 to the region, as seen in the support for the inclusion of President Suharto and China within the summit process. Once again, the policy-making process is adumbrated as pluralistic, with the prime minister in particular playing a pivotal role in G7 summitry. In addition, the changing structure of the international system has been a key impulse to Japanese policy after the end of the Cold War, along with the need to accommodate Russia within the summit process.

22.2 Internationalist future?

These chapters have evinced an admixture of norms, structure and agency in changing proportions and have expounded a number of points which will be interwoven in the concluding chapters with points made in previous chapters. These can be summarized as: the recent importance of internationalist and multilateral approaches to Japan's foreign policy; the continued importance of the US within these approaches but not at the expense of Japan's national interest; Asianism in Japan's policy; a tendency towards the role of mediator or quiet diplomat; and the importance of a plurality of domestic and external inputs as both liberating and constraining factors in understanding how policy is made in Japan. What is chiefly noticeable from Part V is that Japan has begun, with the end of the Cold War and the end to the structure of bipolarity, to pursue more clearly multilateral approaches to its international relations. As was seen in Chapter 18, this renewed internationalism is rooted in Japan's experience in the League of Nations. It has been both emboldened and restricted by all of the other norms elaborated in Chapter 2 and also accelerated with the processes of globalization and the end of the Cold War – themes that will be developed in the concluding chapters which follow.

Part VI

JAPAN'S INTERNATIONAL RELATIONS

WHAT NEXT?

Chapter 23

Japan explained

23.1 Japan: no longer an enigma

Japan's International Relations has been written on the premise that, not only does Japan matter, as asserted in the Preface, but also it can, and needs to be, explained. To this end, this book has presented a comprehensive understanding of the role of the Japanese state and its people in the Cold War and post-Cold War periods through an examination of Japan's involvement in the three key dimensions (politics, economic and security) and the four key sites (the US, East Asia, Europe and global institutions) of its international relations. As a result, Japan's appearance as a major player on the world stage during the post-World War II era has been traced and the most significant issues it has faced in the post-Cold War period have been evaluated with reference to a number of explanatory variables – the structure of the international system, agency in the policy-making process, and embedded and emerging norms. In this way, Japan has been explained and, as a result, no longer presents itself as anomalous or abnormal. This constitutes the contribution, both theoretical and empirical, that *Japan's International Relations* makes to the literature.

The purpose of this chapter is to summarize each part of the book, reflect upon these findings, and then bring together the tri-dimensional approach of politics, economic and security, as used for analytical purposes throughout this book, in order to provide an holistic understanding of Japan's international relations. The chapter then returns to the central question of why it is important to study Japan. Japan's approach to the global political economy is underscored and characterized. The final section proposes that, with the renewed domestic and global relevance after the end of the Cold War of the structure and norms which have shaped Japan's foreign policy, Japanese policy-making agents and domestic society have responded effectively to a complex web of international, regional and bilateral challenges since 1945 and at the start of the new millennium. The structural phenomenon of globalization and the implications of an integrated global political economy will be addressed in the final chapter.

23.2 Japan–United States relations

23.2.i What?

Part II examined the development of Japan's relations with the US as a result of the combination of the US's direct engagement with Japan in the immediate post-war period and the consequences of the bipolar structure of the international system thereafter. Within this system, Japan not only institutionalized its relations with the US, but also came to embed the norm of bilateralism at the heart of its foreign policy-making process. Put simply, it became impossible for the Japanese government to consider its foreign policy in relation to other regions and global institutions independent of its security relationship with the US. By examining the political, economic and security dimensions of the bilateral US–Japan relationship,

Part II illustrated how this bilateral relationship provided both a cocoon for Japan's remarkable economic growth in the post-World War II era, as well as a straitjacket preventing, for the most part, concerted Japanese efforts to forge an independent role in the world. However, with the perceived decline in US hegemony and with the collapse of bipolarity, US policy-making agents have been keen to encourage a more proactive role for Japan in the political and security dimensions. Thus, the US has provided not only a traditional constraint, but also an impetus for Japan to assume a higher profile.

23.2.ii Why?

Changes in the structure of the international system engendered by the end of the Cold War have played a crucial role in problematizing Japan's traditional post-1945 methods of instrumentalizing its international relations. During the Cold War, with the more immediate threat of the Soviet Union and the perceived threat from the expansion of communism, the US and the international community at large were willing to indulge Japan and create a 'greenhouse' for Japan's economic growth which played down the necessity for Japan to contribute to regional and global security. Thus, economism, centring on a steady increase in GNP, became embedded in the years after the end of the war, particular in the 1960s. However, with the end of the Cold War and the US's withdrawal from the role of the world's 'policeman', so-called 'mercantile states' such as Germany and Japan have each come under mounting pressure not only to maintain (and expand) their economic contribution, which is suited to the resolution of a range of problems faced by the post-Cold War world, but also to expand the human side of their contribution. In this way, the legacy of the Yoshida Doctrine and Japan's traditional reliance on instrumentalizing its international relations via the medium of economic power have gained greater acceptance over recent years as contributing to the resolution of both political and security issues. As was seen in Japan's initial reaction to the 1990–1 Gulf War, however, Japan's economic contributions have been misunderstood as 'free riding' and Japan has been censured for its provision of economic, at the expense of human, aid.

In the post-Cold War period, relations with the US continue to be central in determining many of the foreign policy coordinates charted by Japanese policy-making agents. At the same time, it has become clear that these bilateral relations increasingly have to adapt to, and compete with, growing Japanese commitments to other regions of the world, as well as to global institutions. The value of a strict interpretation of the bilateralist norm in an interdependent environment in which multilateral activities have proliferated has been diluted. Also, given that the Cold War is now over, Japan's security treaty relationship has come to be regarded by some as nothing more than an anachronism. It is certain that responses to these changes will prompt a new kind of relationship between Japan and the US in the twenty-first century and that tensions between bilateralist constraints and a new regionalist and internationalist agenda will have implications for Japan's whole foreign policy-making process and orientation to other regions and global institutions.

23.2.iii How?

Japan's relations with the US have been characterized by a mixture of frank exchanges and subtle, behind-the-scenes negotiations. Throughout the Cold War period, with the US providing for Japan's security concerns, it became accepted practice for Japan to devote itself to economic activity informed by the norms of economism and developmentalism. However, as seen in the automobile negotiations in Chapter 5, Japan has been willing to stand its ground and state a firm 'no' to the US. In addition, although the bilateralist norm remains relevant in the post-Cold War period, Japan has clearly instrumentalized its international relations through other levels of activity. With its admission to a number of multilateral institutions on the global, regional and inter-regional levels, Japanese policy-makers have taken the opportunity to develop a more textured foreign policy which still gravitates towards the US but not to the exclusion of the multiple levels available. Thus, Japan has been able to address its relationship with the US at the multilateral level, as seen in the government's proposed reforms of the UN in the 1980s in order to reintegrate Japan into international society (see Chapter 19). Japanese policy-making agents have shown considerable skill in shifting between these various levels, as demonstrated in their support for APEC. This has been used by policy-making agents as a means to maintain the bilateral relationship with the US within the framework of a multilateral organization, whilst at the same time promoting Japan's East Asian identity in a less threatening stance than that offered by the closed regional project EAEC, as was seen in Chapter 5.

23.3 Japan–East Asia relations

23.3.i What?

Part III addressed Japan's relations with its East Asian neighbours, examining the key developments at bilateral and multilateral levels between Japan and the countries of China, South Korea, North Korea and the ASEAN during the Cold War decades and post-Cold War period. It then demonstrated how Japan's role in the region has changed over time as a result of these developments, and the degree to which Japan has returned as a political player in the region, following its economic penetration of East Asia. Nevertheless, Japan has yet to create and exploit fully opportunities in the political and security dimensions, owing to the weight of history and the strength of the anti-militarist norm domestically, which is reinforced at the regional level by a remaining distrust of and resistance to Japan playing a full military role.

23.3.ii Why?

The post-Cold War years have witnessed changes in the structure of the international system together with a continuation of the growth of regionalism and regionalization. When combined with the perceived decline of the US, these structural factors constitute processes pushing Japan towards filling the gap left by the US in East Asia. What is more, with an incremental decline in the strength of the anti-militarist norm within Japanese domestic society, and the decline in resistance to Japan playing a military role in East Asia, particularly Southeast Asia, there are fewer obstacles to a more active role for Japan in the political and security dimensions. These chapters have offered convincing evidence of the growing norm of Asianism, at different levels of penetration depending on the dimension in question. Frequently, this has overlapped with other dimensions of Japan's international relations. For example, Japan's internationalist agenda now displays a high degree of Asianism as seen in Japan acting as the East Asian spokesperson in the G7. Japanese norm entrepreneurs have over the decades attempted to embed this norm of behaviour within domestic society. Both in the 1950s under Prime Minister Kishi Nobusuke and in the first decade of the twenty-first century under Governor Ishihara Shintarō of Tokyo, the Asianist norm has been actively promoted. These norm entrepreneurs also play a role outside Japan. As Part III showed, Japan has been provided with the opportunity, constrained by the norm of bilateralism, to promote the rallying cry of 'Asia for the Asians' with the encouragement of East Asian leaders such as Prime Minister Mahathir Mohamad of Malaysia, and to consolidate a leadership role in East Asia. Both of these sources provide a possible counterbalance in the future to overt dependence upon the US and the bilateralist norm.

23.3.iii How?

Part III raised questions regarding the type of role Japan is playing in the region in terms of its broader policy approach: it elicited issues of how Japanese foreign policy-makers can and will be able to reconcile the Asianist norm with the constraints and opportunities of bilateralism. On the one hand, as Part III demonstrated, Japan has worked within the framework of the US–Japan security treaty to develop closer relations with its East Asian neighbours. To this end, Japanese policy-making agents have shown a continued reluctance to play a high-profile role in the region seemingly still constrained by the norms of bilateralism and anti-militarism. Thus, Japan's role in the region in the post-World War II era has been chiefly that of an economic model. Nevertheless, on the other hand, Japan has played an active role through informal and proxy channels of diplomacy. Thus, a number of actors have exerted an influence upon the policy-making process, as seen in opposition party politicians visiting North Korea and the emperor's visit to China. Similarly, Japanese policy-making agents have been active in promoting region-building institutions, such as the ARF and the AMF, and have worked in the shadows to gain their acceptance.

23.4 Japan–Europe relations

23.4.i What?

Part IV examined Japan's relations with the various countries of Europe, focusing in particular on the members of the European Union (EU). By demonstrating the incremental development of a broad dialogue with Europe over a host of political, economic and security issues and, once again, the structural changes engendered by the end of the Cold War, this part offered evidence that a new set of relations is being established. On the one hand, the continuing integration and expansion of the EU itself provides the Japanese government, as well as business interests and non-governmental actors, with an opportunity to find alternative approaches to foreign policy-making. This orientation towards the EU has been intensified since the ending of the Cold War. On the other hand, Japan–EU relations themselves have been placed on a more institutional footing, with the result that dialogue can now be sustained at the highest levels.

23.4.ii Why?

It is clear from the evidence presented that as a result of changes in the structure of the international system, Europe offers an alternative route for Japan, by locating US–Japan relations in a broader, trilateralist framework that encompasses key European partners. Thus, the growth of a new norm of trilateralism is evident. This is not to suggest that Japanese policy-making agents and other political actors view the EU as a potential replacement in the role previously played by the US. Still, as this important economic and increasingly political relationship grows, and indeed (particularly in terms of a widened definition of security) offers a new dimension to Japan's foreign policy orientation, it is difficult to see how this can be accommodated fully within the traditional constraints of the US–Japan relationship.

23.4.iii How?

The interest of Japanese policy-making agents in the EU has been chiefly economic, with the political and security dimensions being of secondary importance. However, Japan–EU relations have been promoted by new methods with the end of the Cold War, including the use of multilateral institutions. Part IV demonstrated how both Japan and the EU have used these fora to articulate a trilateralist political agenda. Global institutions, such as the UN, embrace countries beyond the confines of the US–Japan–Europe triangle and offer Japan the opportunity to counterbalance its relations with the US. In response, Japanese policy-makers have managed to manoeuvre between these levels of activity with some success. Japan's relations with Europe have also undergone a steady build-up, from the 1991 Hague Declaration to the more recent addition of non-economic issues to the Japan–EU agenda. These include nuclear non-proliferation, humanitarian and environmental problems, and post-crisis society building. As Part IV revealed, a new non-military, civil approach to global human problems constitutes a new direction to the Japan–EU relationship which includes both Japanese and European non-governmental organizations.

23.5 Japan–global institutions

23.5.i What?

Part V focused on Japan's participation in global institutions. It demonstrated how the Japanese – at the governmental as well as societal level – have begun to play a growing international role in the resolution of problems related to human needs. Japanese participation is now visibly evident and welcomed within major institutions such as the UN, the G7 and the World Bank. This growing commitment to becoming involved in global affairs of all kinds has enabled Japan to articulate an alternative, internationalist strategy towards its foreign policy responsibilities.

Whilst this reformulation of the very nature of foreign policy responsibility has encouraged Japan to become a recognized and accepted member of international society, it has done so in the context of changing bilateral and international engagements: most noticeably, and controversially, in the dimension of security. In this case, the internationalist norm has merged with the anti-militarist norm so that Japan's UNPKO contribution is now acceptable, both domestically and in East Asia, provided that it is contained within the framework of the UN. It remains, therefore, unclear as to where this internationalist agenda resides in relation to Japan's other normative commitments.

23.5.ii Why?

The growth in internationalist activity after the end of the Cold War, as exemplified by the burgeoning number of multilateral projects in the UN, the G7 and regional projects such the ARF and APEC, provided the impetus for Japan to assume a more active multilateral role. In the light of the perceived decline of US hegemony and the public declaration of US policy-makers that the US could not and would not fulfil the role of the world's policeman, together with the re-evaluation of the use and efficacy of military power after events in Somalia and the former Yugoslavia, it has become clearer in the post-Cold War period that economic power is of vast importance and is no longer exercised only unilaterally, but also multilaterally. This provides Japan with a highly influential role. Growing disillusionment in US society and government circles with the UN and its peacekeeping activities has led to a domestic backlash against the activities of this multilateral organization, which stands in contrast to the appeal the UN continues to possess in Japanese society. This appeal has been the target of norm entrepreneurs, such as Ozawa Ichirō, who are attempting to promote a more active role for Japan in the UN.

23.5.iii How?

Japan's role in global institutions has been pushed forward by a number of policy-making agents and other political actors. These include, most notably, MOFA, in its promotion of Japanese norms and interests in the UN, and also MOF, in its consolidation of Japan's position in global financial institutions. The promotion of Japan's role is also evident in the prime minister's prominent position in the G7 summit process. In addition, non-state actors have influenced the Japanese state, as seen in the issue of disarmament in the UN. Other political actors have been brought into play by Japan's use of proxies to make its statements for it, as illustrated by the election of the WTO secretary-general in 1999 (see Chapter 20). These actors have all instrumentalized a variety of non-military methods that favour economic activity above Japan's political or security role. Thus, financial contributions to the budgets of global institutions have traditionally constituted Japan's role in the UN, the IMF and the WB. After the 1990–1 Gulf War, Japan began to build upon its economic power through participation in a highly-circumscribed role in UN peacekeeping activities which stresses humanitarianism, self-defence and peaceful resolution of conflict.

23.6 Japan: the *aikidō* state

> *Aikidō* is non-violence. In *aikidō* we never attack. If you want to strike first to gain the advantage over someone, that is proof your training is insufficient, and it is really you yourself who has been defeated. Let your partner attack, and use his aggression against him. Do not cower from an attack; control it before it begins. Non-violence is the true practice of *aikidō*.
>
> Ueshiba Morihei (1883–1969), founder of *aikidō* (Ueshiba 1994)

The idea of a non-violent martial art seems at first to be as paradoxical as Japan is commonly seen to be, as was outlined in Chapter 1. In addition, any attempt to connect the role of the Japanese state and its people in the world to the practice of *aikidō* may appear, at first glance, trite and frivolous. However, as *aikidō* is both defensive and non-aggressive in its philosophy and techniques, and yet versatile and practical, it provides a highly germane metaphor by which the essence of Japan's international relations can be captured. Moreover, in an attempt to avoid the negative connotations of previous characterizations of Japan's foreign policy in the existing literature, such as 'leadership by stealth', this metaphor seeks to connect both quiet diplomacy and activism in Japan's role in the world. In other words, '*aikidō* state' seeks to highlight certain characteristics of Japanese diplomacy that are obfuscated by other metaphors.

Practitioners of *aikidō* do not attempt to initiate attacks, win fights or defeat opponents. Instead, they seek to control and neutralize an attack, not through sheer physical strength, but rather through connected movements that blend with the energy of an attack and redirect that energy back against the attacker. Attacks are neutralized by the use of various wristlocks, armpins and tactical retreats, rather than crippling kicks or blows. *Aikidō* does not necessarily require physical strength. Much of the practice involves techniques for defending against attacks. This all, ultimately, allows *aikidō* students to practise a powerful martial art which operates at a variety of levels in an active, yet non-violent, manner.

With this definition of *aikidō* in mind, the appropriateness of the metaphor now becomes evident. Japan's quiet diplomacy is characterized by the norm of economism and restricted by the anti-militarist norm and has accordingly imputed economic activity above military activity with positive meaning. Thus, for Japan it has been *de rigueur* to exercise economic power to attain its national interests or contribute to international society. Japanese policy-makers have used economic power to achieve other goals, such as the expansion of Japanese influence throughout East Asia as an exemplary model of economic development and alternative to Western capitalism. Equally, economic power has been deployed to counter accusations of burden-shirking in the relationship with the US and stake the claim for Japan's active burden-sharing. Thus, in the UN Japan has stressed its prompt contributions to the UN budget – second only in share to the irregular payments of the US – and its oft-ignored financial support for the international community's efforts in Kosovo and East Timor.

In short, the power that Japan deploys is not dependent on sheer physical strength. There is a preference for non-violent approaches as seen in the continuing strength of the anti-militarist norm and the importance given to economic activity. The metaphor continues to work when the modes of Japan's quiet diplomacy are examined. Japan does not attempt to initiate attacks, win fights or defeat opponents. Rather, Japanese policy-making agents attempt to foster an atmosphere of cooperation by acting as a *kakehashi* between East and West influenced by the norms of both bilateralism and Asianism. Also, Japan supplements its power by employing a number of other tools and operating on a number of levels in the instrumentalization of its foreign policy. Ultimately, as has been demonstrated throughout this book, Japan operates in an active, yet non-militaristic, way in the global political economy and employs a variety of modes in the conduct of its quiet diplomacy – acting in different sites through a variety of agents and proxies, operating on multiple levels and displaying a long-term temporal perception.

23.6.i Crisis and long-term policy-making

It is recognized that, in times of crisis, Japan often acts erratically and unpredictably which results in immobilism. Japan's reaction to the 1990–1 Gulf War or the East Asian financial and economic crises starting in 1997 need only be cited here to reinforce this point. Although this book has not sought to deny this tendency towards immobilism, it has attempted at the same time to build upon it by suggesting that, just as patience and stamina are required in *aikidō*, similarly the Japanese state and its people demonstrate a different perception of time. In a number of instances Japanese policy-makers have shown themselves not to be subject to the pressures which exist in the West to provide a 'quick fix'. The Japanese state and its people have demonstrated a longer-term, incremental approach which allows problematic issues to be shelved. A case in point is the normalization of Japan's relations with China in 1972, when the territorial dispute over the Senkaku Islands was left for future generations to solve, as seen in Chapter 9. Equally, Japan's refusal to give up the idea of the AMF during the East Asian financial and economic crises, despite the initial veto of the US and the IMF, as was seen in Chapter 10, demonstrates this longer-term approach.

23.6.ii Formal, informal and proxy channels

This book has demonstrated how Japanese policy-makers have employed public, unequivocal declarations of their policy in tandem with less easily discerned manoeuvring. As noted in Chapter 2, the Japanese words *omote* (surface or explicit) and *ura* (back or implicit) exemplify Japan's formal and informal approaches to the implementation of its power. The example of Japan operating out in the open and acting in a surprisingly forceful and frank manner by asserting itself has been seen in Chapter 5, when Prime Minister Hosokawa Morihiro firmly said 'no' to US pressure in automobile negotiations. The second aspect of *ura* is probably best illustrated by behind-the-scenes bargaining. The domestic Japanese practice of *nemawashi* has been extended on to an international scale as seen in the G7 summit process. Japan has regarded the G7 summit as an opportunity to represent East Asia and, to this end, the prime minister has regularly toured East Asia to acquire a consensus of what issues Japan should raise at the actual meeting on behalf of East Asia. Thus, Japan operates both very evidently out in the open and in a more removed manner employing a number of channels.

A further question related to formal and informal and proxy channels that has been addressed throughout *Japan's International Relations* is that of agency. In other words, in the same way that it is unclear whose power the student of *aikidō* is using, the content of 'Japan' remains unclear. All the chapters have demonstrated a move within Japan towards a more encompassing idea of the state. The traditional interpretation of Japanese foreign policy-making as an 'iron triangle' reinforcing solidarity between the three poles of the bureaucracy, LDP politicians and big business is ultimately of only limited use in understanding how specific policy-making processes work. This is not to deny that these three poles occupy a crucial position in foreign policy formulation. Rather, this book has promoted a deeper understanding of two areas.

On the one hand, clear tensions exist both between the poles of the triangle and within each pole. Thus, MOFA and MOF have disagreed vehemently over Japan's position with the G7 *vis-à-vis* the Russian problem, as was seen in Chapter 21. Equally MOFA and the JDA have quarrelled over the level of participation in UNPKO. On the other hand, the number of policy-making agents and other political actors involved in any policy issue-area has expanded to include a broad gamut of influences at work. These policy-makers often act as proxies for the Japanese state. To a degree, this is inevitable with economic globalization through the activities of TNCs and the staggering increase in the number of NGOs which have influenced decisions in the cases of Japan's policy towards the China and nuclear disarmament respectively. What is more, different epithets have been coined to capture this plurality of actors from *tennō gaikō* (emperor diplomacy) in the case of China to *kōjin gaikō* (individual diplomacy) in the case of North Korea. This increased pluralism has made the study of IR and Japan more complicated, but also more rewarding when attempting to locate influence and power in the policy-making process. In addition, this increased pluralism has acted to redefine the purported role of the state.

Equally, the Japanese concept of a *kagemusha* has been exploited in the foreign policy field, as seen in the promotion by Japan of the deputy prime minister of Thailand, Supachai Panitchpakdi, as secretary-general of the WTO and as the representative of East Asia. This offers a contrastive strategy to the traditional Western approach personified by the US-backed candidate, the former prime minister of New Zealand, Mike Moore. In this way, Japan often operates on the periphery and uses other states as proxies to make its statements for it. Thus, Japan can circumvent the restrictive nature of the anti-militarist norm, that is, the sensitivity which exists in Japanese society and East Asia towards an explicit leadership role that may involve the military. Accordingly, Japan's position stands in direct contrast to the highly- visible and central role that has been the wont and defining quality in the West of traditional great power status.

23.6.iii Bilateral, regional and multilateral levels

This book has demonstrated that Japan deploys its power on a variety of levels (bilateral, regional and multilateral) and has been skilful at both manoeuvring amongst the levels and employing, or supplementing, them at the same time. This is an approach which has been facilitated by the increasing globalization of the world – a theme which will be taken up in the next chapter. This conclusion challenges the idea that Japan's era of bilateralism may be over and that Asianism or internationalism have come to replace it. Rather, the evidence presented in this work suggests powerfully that the characteristics of the era in which the norm of anti-militarism often clashed with the norm of bilateralism have been modified: increasingly, different types of norms are applied to different functional realities. In this sense, both bilateralism and internationalism may jointly constitute Japanese foreign policy.

Nevertheless, such a supplemental strategy does not provide complementarity between a range of diverse activities. As the previous chapters have made clear, tensions are developing between the various norms which have shaped the perceptions of policy-makers and public opinion within Japan. It is not being argued here that a paradigm shift is taking place, which would see the dominance of one norm over another – for example, the ascendancy of Asianism over bilateralism. Clearly, bilateralism constrains Japanese action *vis-à-vis* Europe, with the result that a two-versus-one structure often prevails in trade issues and political dialogue. At the same time, Japanese policy-makers also participate in ASEM, an arrangement designed in part, at least, to counter American dominance in the region, as was seen in Part IV. Equally, Japan's participation on the multilateral level in the UN and APEC has been informed by its goal of including, not excluding, the US. With the end of the Cold War, the Yoshida Doctrine's emphasis upon bilateralism with the US is no longer enough to guarantee Japan's political, economic and security interests.

23.7 Summary

Thus, *Japan's International Relations* has contributed to the extant literature both empirically and theoretically. Empirically, a comprehensive review of Japan's post-war international relations has been undertaken to include the oft-neglected topics of Europe and global institutions, thereby filling in a Japan-shaped lacuna in our knowledge and understanding. Theoretically, the book has drawn on a number of existing theories and adopted an innovative and balanced approach, acknowledging the importance of structure and norms as well as the pluralistic nature of the parties involved in the policy-making process. Hence, Japan's singular role in the world has been explained in addition to its specific style of leadership, stressing economic power, a preference for functioning on the periphery and not in the limelight (which marks Western ideals of success), and its preference for a *mélange* of bilateral, regional and multilateral initiatives, instead of unilateral ones. In this way, Japan, the *aikidō* state, has altered the orthodox understanding of how a great power behaves.

Nevertheless, Japanese policy-making agents and other political actors are currently wrestling with the tensions between the norms explored in this book. It is the process of consolidating these norms which renders Japan capable, at the beginning of the new millennium, to act in an increasingly interdependent world. In this sense, the tensions between these domestically and internationally embedded norms can lead to cooperation as well as conflict. At the same time, these norms are encouraging the Japanese state and its people to pursue a different kind of approach to the world, an approach which has emerged in the form of quiet diplomacy. The lesson of this book is that, in the light of a whole range of factors, Japan stands in the position of being able to offer the world a different foreign policy orientation with the end of the Cold War. It has created new opportunities in new regions and global institutions, and encouraged diversification in its foreign policy options in contrast to the traditional strict bilateralism with the US or simply aligning itself with the major power of the day.

For all that, it could still be argued that essentially it is not Japan that has changed. The dominant themes which have been prevalent within Japan during the post-World War II era have become more prominent and been co-opted into international society with the end of the Cold War. The process of globalization has spurred this trend. The norms which informed Japan's foreign policy have become externalized and have become those of international society. The use of military might to solve human problems in international society has been increasingly confined to multilateral actions, and economic power has become accepted as a legitimate policy tool of greater importance than (as was the former view) just one tool of many in the armoury of a big state, as in the use of economic sanctions in the build-up to war. As with all states, Japan's international relations are a composite of success, as in making the transition from latecomer to join the ranks of the major industrialized powers, and failure, as in the disastrous Pacific War. Over the longer term, however, the Japanese state and its people have successfully achieved the twin goals pursued by most states, namely, peace and prosperity.

As was stated in Chapter 1, the image of the US's role in the world is one of policing the globe, the UK is 'punching above its weight', France is maintaining a distance from entanglement with the US, and Germany is leading the 'European Project'. In the case of Japan, although at first glance there seems to be no clear impression of its role or strategy, the overriding image throughout this volume is of a state whose international relations are influenced by a variety of structural and normative factors in addition to a plurality of agents. As a result, Japan appears to be bursting at the seams of a now antiquated post-World War II straitjacket. Japan is far from being a reactive or rudderless state, but rather possesses a foreign policy orientation of great relevance to the post-Cold War world and pursues these international relations in an original and novel manner. However, can this approach retain its efficacy in a globalizing world? This is a question which will be addressed in the final chapter.

Chapter 24

Japan: the challenge of globalization

24.1 Overview

The previous chapter has illustrated the inherent tensions between the domestic and international norms which the Japanese state and its people face at the beginning of the twenty-first century. This final chapter assesses the ways in which globalization is likely to shape how those tensions are resolved, and will determine whether and how Japan as a foreign policy actor is equipped to stand up to the forces it unleashes. Chapter 2 offered a definition of globalization and highlighted the divergent views on its meaning. This chapter examines how globalization imposes constraints and at the same time offers opportunities for the Japanese state and its people at the cusp of the twenty-first century.

On the one hand, the processes of globalization alter the very structure of the international system, whilst the Japanese government continues to seek a greater role within its older state-to-state form and to be seen to be playing the role of a 'normal' state within that system. At the same time, non-state actors offer important sites of resistance against the fragmentation that globalization is seen to create. On the other hand, globalization provides greater opportunities for all Japanese policy-making agents and other political actors to promote new approaches to foreign policy. It does so, not only by creating new opportunities for participation at different levels within the structure of the international system, but also by facilitating the adoption and pursuit of new norms of behaviour. These contending forces are examined here in the light of the case studies presented throughout this book, in order to demonstrate how the Japanese state and its people are optimally placed to address the various trends towards globalization.

24.2 Globalization and the tri-dimensional approach

24.2.i Political dimension

In the political dimension, the disappearance of the bipolar Cold War structures that ensured the primacy of Japan's bilateral relationship with the US has resulted in a more fluid set of international relations. The calls by the US for greater burden-sharing on the part of its allies and an apparent weakening of the US as global hegemon have led the Japanese to begin to respond to the new structural realities of the post-Cold War world. In so doing, they have begun to consolidate formal, informal and proxy channels through the promotion of multilateral initiatives, and to participate in political dialogue within fora as varied as the UN, the G7, the ASEAN Regional Forum and in bilateral summit meetings of heads of state. The forces of globalization have ensured that formerly issue-specific fora, such as the G7 and APEC, have become repositories of more comprehensive discussions. As a result, clear divisions between economic and political dialogue are hard to distinguish. In addition, Japanese policy-makers also channel their diplomatic affairs through a whole range of interactive structures. Finally, the uncertainty created by globalization increases the need to diversify relations, and in response Japanese policy-making agents and other political actors have begun to supplement bilateral relations with regional, trilateral and global interaction.

24.2.ii Economic dimension

Globalization has brought down temporal and spatial barriers to economic interaction, through the advent of new technologies and the Internet age. Whether understood as a world without borders in which TNCs act in the three core regions of the global political economy; as the spread of a US-led liberalist political project which forces the removal of protective national and regional barriers to global trade; or as the fragmentation of economic interests and the growth of sites of resistance to global economic trends, changes in the economic structures in which Japanese economic actors must operate have forced them to adopt a global view in their economic strategies. As a result, recourse to national protection for trade and industrial interests is becoming increasingly hard to maintain. Instead, the Japanese state and its businesses face the prospect of greater global competition, global communication and open trading. Whilst some domestic economic restructuring has begun in order to counter accusations of burden-shirking in the relationship with the US and to redress trade imbalances, globalization will intensify this pressure from without as well as from business interests within Japan itself.

24.2.iii Security dimension

The Japanese state and its people have been locked in a tight security relationship with the US for most of the post-war era. The salience of the norm of bilateralism ensured that Japan contributed indirectly rather than directly to military security by deferring largely to US leadership and the US presence in military concerns within its region. Globalization has changed this *status quo* in two ways. First, the growth in transparency and multilateral networks for the discussion of security interests has ensured that the same set of security interests becomes important for all participating states. This has engendered a broader interpretation of security. Thus, not only do Japanese policy-makers discuss the question of the Korean Peninsula in the UN, the G7, the ARF and KEDO, but they also introduce issues such as 'human security' which focus upon humanitarian rather than military concerns. Second, security concerns are no longer restricted to behaviour in a state's own region nor do they only pertain directly to a state's own interests. Thus, Japan's involvement in Bosnia and Kosovo is difficult to understand without taking account of the globalization of security concerns. All of these changing structural factors have precipitated original responses to them and have therefore impacted upon the nature of agency itself.

24.3 Globalizing agents

24.3.i Political dimension

State-centred diplomacy has formed the core of Japanese political behaviour during the past fifty years. The process of globalization has challenged the state's position and facilitated a more important role for non-state actors. It is clear from the examples provided throughout this book that the Japanese state no longer dominates all sites of political activity and that it must instead function alongside business and NGO agents who maintain their own independent, global networks. If the processes of globalization continue to intensify, the roles of TNCs such as Toyota and Japanese branches of international NGOs such as Amnesty International and Greenpeace are likely to influence further policy decisions within and beyond Japan. Whilst the Japanese state is not about to wither, it is going to be forced to incorporate and work alongside these non-state actors. Indeed, in certain cases, the Japanese state uses these agents as proxies.

24.3.ii Economic dimension

As was seen in Chapter 2, Japan is famous for the model of an 'iron triangle' policy-making elite, which guides the pattern of its economic behaviour. This notion has been waning for some time, and Japan has deregulated, removed trade barriers and become more transparent in some sectors, in response to *gaiatsu* (more specifically, *beiatsu*) and to the influence of international fora such as the WTO. Globalization adds to this trend in two ways: by forcing Japan to assume a more proactive role within multilateral economic fora; and by promoting participation by proxy. In the first case, the Japanese government has, for instance, encouraged the establishment of a new Millennium Round of WTO talks and has shown itself to be the champion of East Asian concerns in fora such as the G7. In the second case, the Japanese government has used indirect means to enhance its influence in such fora, as occurred when it supported Supachai Panitchpakdi, the deputy prime minister of Thailand, to become the WTO's secretary-general, as was mentioned in Chapter 23. Globalization not only affects policy-making elites, but also gives greater salience to the role of the business actors in shaping Japan's foreign economic policies. This phenomenon is most evident in the examples of Japanese TNCs such as Nissan, Toyota, Sony and Matsushita, which affect economic decisions made by the Japanese government and even their foreign counterparts. In addition, non-governmental actors have expanded in number as people seek to construct institutions to govern aspects of their daily lives in the face of exposure to global economic and political forces.

24.3.iii Security dimension

For most of the post-war era military security has remained the preserve of the Japanese government which itself acted under US tutelage. However, the government has begun to use the broadened agenda provided by globalization to propose its own concept of security, one which suits the particular constitutional constraints imposed on Japanese policy-makers. The three non-nuclear principles suggest how these can impinge on Japanese security policy. It can also be seen in Japan's request for a permanent seat on the UN Security Council, whereby the Japanese government pledges to offer an approach to security different from that of the members of the UNSC who possess nuclear weapons. In so doing, Japan promotes itself as a new kind of agent within major international fora. At a non-governmental level, sub-state actors have become central to the debate over security, by raising issues in mainstream fora which were previously ignored. These include involvement in internal conflicts; burden-sharing with regional organizations; and a delineation of peacekeeping duties into preventive peacekeeping and peace enforcement. Not only does this involvement by different actors reshape debates over security, but it also leads to the rise of new norms of behaviour.

24.4 Globalizing norms

24.4.i Political dimension

For most of the post-war period, diplomatic interaction has been conducted between states in recognition of the salience of national identity. Collective action was undertaken in order to benefit participating states. Globalization has altered this balance, by giving greater significance to the rise of the competing norms of universalism (in which everyone comes to share the same values) and globalism (whereby a dominant set of values is imposed upon everyone). Whether viewed negatively or positively, these norms redefine the borders of Japanese participation, and require Japanese policy-making agents and other political actors to consider the global consequences of their actions across a range of different issues. Such behaviour can be seen in Japanese advocacy of East Asian affairs within the G7 and the UN. Responding to the potential for each of these norms to become embedded more deeply, the Japanese state and its people have begun to articulate more explicitly and in a wide variety of international fora the domestically embedded norms of developmentalism and anti-militarism which have been confined to understandings of the Japanese state itself until now. By refining the goals of its ODA to incorporate more ethical requirements, and by promoting a new kind of UNSC behaviour that eschews the possession of nuclear weapons, Japan is in the process of defining a new kind of foreign policy orientation.

24.4.ii Economic dimension

In the economic dimension, globalization heralds for some a new emphasis on liberalism, on the breaking down of internal, regional and global barriers to trade and investment in order to create an equitable and open trading system at the global level. For others, globalization signifies greater disparities between the haves and have-nots and gives rise to groups within Japan which oppose its further development. These trends conflict with Japanese norms of economism and developmentalism, which have directed national economic planning and policy without attention to their global implications. The Japanese have responded to this challenge by playing a greater role in international fora and by setting their own economic agenda (such as the proposed AMF). If the processes of globalization continue to deepen, it will fall to Japanese policy-making agents and other actors to globalize their domestic norms by combining them with the internationally embedded norms of Asianism, trilateralism and internationalism. At the same time, globalization prompts changes within Japan towards the adoption of new kinds of norms. The growing role of NGOs and the transnational nature of Japanese business within a globalizing system will enable them to play a larger role in determining the norms which underpin Japanese foreign policy.

24.4.iii Security dimension

Security is no longer a question of military hardware alone. The globalization of the security agenda has prompted two kinds of responses from Japan to date. On the one hand, the idea of globalization as a universal phenomenon has prompted the Japanese actors, particularly NGOs but increasingly at the level of head of state, to assume a leading role in propagating ideas such as 'human security' and collective security. In particular, the new norm of environmentalism is a rising global norm which fits particularly well with long-held domestically embedded norms, and is therefore welcomed by the Japanese people. The Kyoto conference on the environment is one such example. On the other hand, the phenomenon of fragmentation has also promoted a growing trend towards neo-nationalism, with the result that the Japanese, whilst asserting a greater multilateral purpose, are also consolidating domestic notions of Japanese identity with calls for remilitarization and for Japan to become militarily 'normal' in the conventional sense of deploying the military as a legitimate instrument of state power.

24.5 Globalization and quiet diplomacy

The previous sections examined how Japan has begun to respond to signs of globalization in the three dimensions of politics, economics and security at the heart of this study and the key agents and norms under consideration throughout this book. This section assesses whether and how Japan will be able to employ its quiet diplomacy (see Chapter 2) in order to instrumentalize this task in the longer term.

First, the formal, informal and proxy channels used in Japan's foreign relations enable policy-makers to adopt both an explicit and an implicit position *vis-à-vis* particular concerns. Prime Minister Obuchi may have been confident in promoting human security without fear of US criticism or East Asian suspicion, but Japanese posturing over regional security issues and economic affairs often takes place behind the scenes. To the extent that globalization functions through multilateral fora, it is not necessary for Japanese policy-making agents to act as sole agents with regard to most issues. However, if globalization continues to require a more energetic policy commitment from Japan within the East Asia region (and particularly if the US presence there continues to decline), other East Asian states may look to Japan for greater leadership.

Second, the Japanese state and its people are already engaged in global affairs through participation in a whole range of bilateral, regional, inter-regional and global fora. As a quiet diplomat, Japan seeks to use these different levels simultaneously. However, the interests represented in one type of forum are rarely identical to those elsewhere. Japan's failure in the short term to establish the AMF in the light of IMF objections is one example of dissonance between the different levels. So long as Japanese policy-makers are forced to defend different interests in different fora, no clear policy strategy to deal with globalization will be allowed to emerge.

Third, Japan as the quiet diplomat can employ various agents or actors within Japan in the pursuit of its perceived interests and norms. The promotion of state goals through NGOs, for instance, has become more salient in recent years. In an era of globalization, this ability will become more important, as negotiations are held between groups within different states without recourse to state-level frameworks themselves. The Japanese government has only just begun to adopt this strategy, whilst the NGOs themselves have still to adopt a fully-international outlook. In addition, the ability of these various groups within Japan to promote their aims by proxy will become more important as guaranteed post-war alliances decline and issue-specific alliances rise in their place.

Finally, Japan's temporal framework, in which issues are decided within a long-term outlook for foreign relations, will be promoted by globalization. In an era when issues and positions are less clearly discernible, the ability to lock Japan into long-term relationships will become fundamentally important for securing long-term gains.

As a quiet diplomat, then, Japan has many of the facets which will enable it to deal with the new concerns created by globalization. Japanese policy-making agents and other actors will now have to begin to externalize their domestic responses to globalization in order to play a leading role in the emerging regional and global orders.

24.6 Challenges for Japan

Japan–US relations have undergone major changes since the 1980s, and reflect the changing nature of the structure of the international system itself. Similarly, Japan's relations with East Asia demonstrate how structural developments have facilitated a greater role for Japan in the region and how new agents have been engaged to promote that role, through the rising salience of the norm of Asianism. Relations with Europe similarly reflect the greater engagement of non-state actors and illustrate an emerging supplement to bilateralism and Asianism in the form of trilateralism. Finally, internationalism is promoted by Japanese state and non-state actors through participation in global institutions. Globalization ensures that these sites cannot be isolated from one another and that Japan must provide a multi-actor and multilevel response to all of them simultaneously.

This chapter has examined some of Japan's possible responses to globalization. The Japanese state and its people will have to adapt their foreign policy according to the ways in which the tensions caused by globalization are resolved. Both within the Japanese state as well as in domestic society, strong forces remain opposed to globalization. These divergent responses to globalization suggest that the nature of the policies adopted will depend on whether those for, or those against, globalization predominate. Whilst it would seem that support for globalization is growing, the political parties have not yet coalesced around one or the other viewpoint, and opposing and supporting groups conflict with one another within the ministries. The agenda for Japan, therefore, remains a complex one. However it is addressed, three key areas will be affected.

First, the Japanese state and its people will have to address the *locus* of foreign policy engagement. There are already signs that Japanese policy-makers have moved from a predominantly US-centred framework to a US-supplemented framework. Second, policy-making agents will have to determine the *tools* of their engagement, in order to incorporate the growing role of non-state actors which will lead to a more comprehensive foreign policy machinery. Third, they will have to renegotiate the very *terms* of engagement, as the importance of their domestically and internationally embedded norms continues to change as globalization sinks roots. The case studies presented in this book have demonstrated how some of these processes have already begun, but it remains to be seen how they will be formulated in future to resolve some of the tensions created by the impact of globalization.

It is instructive to return to the original question posed in Chapter 1 of *Japan's International Relations*: why study Japan? Two conclusions are clear from this assessment of the impact of globalization. First, the nature of Japan as participant, and the dimensions of its foreign policy activities, will exert a major influence upon Japan's future ability to play a leading global role. Japan's potential responses to the global structures of the twenty-first century and the capacity of its domestic actors for implementing those responses make it a fascinating case study in national reactions to globalization. Second, an understanding of such responses is incongruous with the traditional perceptions of the Japanese role in the world.

This calls for a reconsideration of the traditional definitions of power. In reconciling its internal tensions with the external forces of globalization, Japan has created a *different* kind of approach to the world, one that might well be capable of dealing with the structures of a globalizing era.

This approach to Japan contributes to our understanding of IR and IPE theory, by addressing the 'what', 'why' and 'how' questions relating to Japan through the integration of norms with structure and agency. In so doing, it has become possible to understand Japan not simply as a reactive state, but as an alternative form of international actor, a quiet diplomat or *aikidō* state, which holds the tools to deal effectively with the changing systemic conditions of this new millennium. These theoretical and empirical findings clearly demonstrate one thing: Japan does indeed matter.

Chronology of Japan and world affairs 1933–2002

Year	*Japan*			*World*		
1933	Mar	27	Japan withdraws from League of Nations			
1941	Dec	7	Japan attacks Pearl Harbor			
1945	Aug	6	Atomic bomb dropped on Hiroshima			
1945	Aug	9	Atomic bomb dropped on Nagasaki			
1945	Aug	15	Emperor announces end of the war	Aug	15	World War II ends
1945	Aug	17	PM Higashikuni Naruhiko assumes office			
1945	Aug	30	Allied Occupation of Japan begins			
1945	Sep	2	GCHQ established			
1945	Oct	9	PM Shidehara Kijūrō assumes office			
1945				Oct	24	UN established
1946				Mar	3	Winston Churchill delivers 'Iron Curtain' speech
1946	May	3	Tokyo war crimes trials begin			
1946	May	22	PM Yoshida Shigeru assumes office			
1946				Jul	4	Philippines granted independence
1946	Nov	3	New Constitution promulgated			
1947				Mar	12	President Harry S. Truman of the US announces 'Truman Doctrine'

Year	Japan			World		
1947	May	3	New Constitution comes into effect			
1947	May	24	PM Katayama Tetsu assumes office			
1947				Jun	5	Marshall Plan announced
1948				Jan	4	Burma granted independence
1948	Jan	6	US military commander announces intention to make Japan a bulwark against communism in the Far East – start of 'reverse course'			
1948	Mar	10	PM Ashida Hitoshi assumes office			
1948				Apr	1	USSR begins isolation of Berlin
1948				May	14	1st Middle East War begins (until 1949, Feb 24)
1948				Jun	26	Berlin airlift begins
1948				Aug	15	ROK established
1948				Sep	9	DPRK established
1948	Oct	15	PM Yoshida Shigeru assumes office			
1948	Nov	12	Tokyo war crimes trial ends			
1949	Feb	1	Joseph Dodge arrives in Japan as SCAP special economic adviser			
1949				Apr	4	NATO treaty signed
1949				May	6	FRG established
1949				May	12	USSR ends isolation of Berlin
1949				Sep	24	USSR successfully detonates its own nuclear device
1949				Oct	1	PRC established
1949				Oct	7	GDR established
1949				Dec	7	KMT decamps to Taiwan
1949				Dec	27	Indonesia achieves independence
1950				Feb	14	Sino-Soviet Treaty of Alliance and Mutual Friendship signed
1950				Jun	25	Korean War begins
1950	Jul	8	General Douglas MacArthur approves establishment of NPR			

Year	Japan			World		
1950				Oct	25	China intervenes in Korean War
1950	Dec		SDPJ determines three peace principles as the basis of its foreign policy			
1951	May	2	Japan joins WHO			
1951	Jul		Japan joins UNESCO			
1951				Aug	30	US–Philippines Mutual Defence Treaty signed
1951				Sep	1	ANZUS Treaty signed
1951	Sep	8	San Francisco peace treaty signed. US–Japan security treaty signed			
1951	Jan	18	Japan–Indonesia reparations agreement signed			
1952				Jan	18	South Korea declares 'Rhee Line'
1952	Feb	15	Japan–ROK normalization talks begin			
1952	Apr	28	Allied Occupation of Japan ends			
1952	Apr	28	Japan–ROC Peace Treaty signed			
1952	Apr	28	San Francisco peace treaty comes into force			
1952	Apr	28	US–Japan security treaty comes into force			
1952	Aug	13	Japan joins the IMF and WB			
1952				Oct	3	UK conducts atom bomb test
1952				Nov	1	US conducts hydrogen bomb test
1953	Jan	10	Japan restores diplomatic relations with Vietnam, Cambodia and Laos			
1953				Feb	27	ROK claims sovereignty over Takeshima Islands
1953				Mar	5	President Josef Stalin of USSR dies
1953				Jul	27	Korean War armistice signed
1953				Aug	12	USSR conducts hydrogen bomb test
1953				Oct	1	US–ROK Mutual Defence Treaty signed
1953	Oct	21	Japan–ROK normalization talks suspended			
1954	Apr	2	Japan joins ICJ			

Year	Japan			World		
1954	Apr	15	Japan–Philippines reparations agreement signed			
1954				Apr	26	Geneva Conference convened (until Jul 21)
1954				Apr	28	Vietnam granted independence
1954	Jun	2	House of Councillors imposes ban on overseas despatch of SDF			
1954	Jun	9	SDF Law promulgated			
1954				Sep	8	SEATO Treaty signed
1954	Sep	25	Japan seeks ROK agreement to submit problem of sovereignty of Takeshima Islands to ICJ. Rejected by ROK on Oct 28			
1954	Sep	26	PM Yoshida Shigeru visits Canada, France, FRG, Italy, Vatican City, UK and US (until Nov 17)			
1954	Oct	5	Japan joins Colombo Plan			
1954	Nov	5	Japan–Burma reparations agreement signed			
1954	Dec	10	PM Hatoyama Ichirō assumes office			
1954				Dec	2	US–ROC Mutual Security Treaty signed
1955				Apr	18	Asia–Africa Conference convened, Bandung, Indonesia
1955				May	14	Warsaw Pact signed
1955	Sep	10	Japan membership of GATT comes into effect			
1956				Feb	14	President Nikita Khrushchev criticizes Stalin in 'Secret Speech' at USSR Communist Party 20th Congress
1956	Oct	7	PM Hatoyama Ichirō visits USSR (until Nov 11)			
1956	Oct	19	Japan–USSR Joint Declaration			
1956				Oct	24	USSR intervenes in Hungary
1956				Oct	29	2nd Middle East War begins (Suez Crisis) (until Nov 6)
1956	Dec	12	Japan–USSR relations normalized			

Year	Japan			World		
1956	Dec	18	Japan joins UN			
1956	Dec	23	PM Ishibashi Tanzan assumes office			
1957	Feb	25	PM Kishi Nobusuke assumes office			
1957				Mar	25	Treaty of Rome signed,EEC established (with effect from Jan 1 1958)
1957				May	15	UK conducts hydrogen bomb experiment
1957	May	20	PM Kishi Nobusuke visits Burma, India, Pakistan, Ceylon, Thailand and Taiwan (until Jun 4)			
1957	May	20	Basic Policy on National Defence adopted			
1957	Jun	3–4	PM Kishi Nobusuke visits Taiwan			
1957	Jun	16	PM Kishi Nobusuke visits US (until Jul 1)			
1957				Aug	26	USSR announces successful testing of ICBM
				Oct	4	USSR launches *Sputnik-1*
1957	Nov	18	PM Kishi Nobusuke visits South Vietnam, Cambodia, Laos, Malaya, Singapore, Indonesia, Australia, New Zealand and Philippines (until Dec 8)			
1958	Jan	17	Japan–Indonesia reparations agreement			
1958	Oct	15	Japan–Laos economic cooperation agreement signed			
1958				Dec	17	US successfully tests Atlas ICBM
1958–9			Japan serves as a non-permanent member of the UNSC			
1959	Mar	2	Japan–Cambodia economic cooperation agreement signed			
1959	May	13	Japan–South Vietnam reparations agreement signed			

Year	Japan			World		
1959	Jul	11	PM Kishi Nobusuke visits UK, FRG, Austria, Italy, Vatican City, France, Brazil, Argentina, Chile, Peru and Mexico (until Aug 11)			
1959				Aug	25	PRC–India border conflict
1960	Jan	19	Revised US–Japan security treaty signed			
1960				Feb	13	France conducts atom bomb test
1960	Jul	19	PM Ikeda Hayato assumes office			
1960				Jul	20	US conducts SLBM test
1961				Jul	6	USSR–DPRK Treaty of Friendship, Cooperation and Mutual Assistance signed
1961				Jul	11	PRC–DPRK Treaty of Friendship, Cooperation and Mutual Assistance signed
1961	Jul	19–30	PM Ikeda Hayato visits US and Canada			
1961				Aug	13	Berlin Wall constructed
1962	Nov	16–30	PM Ikeda Hayato visits Pakistan, India, Burma and Thailand			
1962				Oct	20	PRC–India border conflict begins
1962				Oct	24	US Navy imposes embargo on Cuba (Cuban missile crisis)
				Oct	28	President Nikita Khrushchev of USSR announces withdrawal of missiles from Cuba
1962	Nov	4–25	PM Ikeda Hayato visits FRG, France, UK, Belgium, Vatican City and Netherlands			
1962	Nov	9	Japan–PRC unofficial Long-Term Trade Agreement signed, Beijing			
1963				Aug	5	US, UK and USSR sign partial nuclear test ban treaty
1964	Apr	28	Japan joins OECD			
1964				Aug	2	Gulf of Tonkin incident, Vietnam
1964	Oct	10	Tokyo Olympics begin			

Year	Japan			World		
1964				Oct	16	PRC conducts first atom bomb test
1964	Nov	9	PM Satō Eisaku assumes office			
1965				Feb	7	US commences bombing of North Vietnam
1965	Feb	10	Three Arrow incident revealed in House of Representatives			
1965	Jun	22	Japan–ROK Treaty on Basic Relations signed – diplomatic relations normalized			
1965				Sep	1	2nd India–Pakistan conflict begins (until Sep 22)
1966	Apr	4	1st MEDSEA meeting held in Tokyo			
1966				May	16	Cultural Revolution begins in PRC
1966				Oct	27	PRC conducts first nuclear missile test
1966–7			Japan serves as a non-permanent member of the UNSC			
1967	Apr	21	Ban on the export of arms			
1967				Jun	5	3rd Middle East War begins (until Jun 9)
1967				Jul	1	EC established
1967				Aug	8	ASEAN established
1967	Sept	7–9	PM Satō Eisaku visits Taiwan			
1967	Sept	20–30	PM Satō Eisaku visits Burma, Malaysia, Singapore, Thailand and Laos			
1967	Oct	8–21	PM Satō Eisaku visits Indonesia, Australia, Philippines and South Vietnam			
1968				Jan	23	DPRK seizes USS *Pueblo* information ship
1968	Jan	27	PM Satō Eisaku announces three non-nuclear principles as part of four nuclear principles			
1968				May	13	Vietnam peace talks, Paris
1968				Jul	1	NPT treaty signed
1968				Aug	20	USSR intervenes in Czechoslovakia
1969				Mar	2	USSR–PRC border clashes

Year	Japan			World		
1969				Jul	25	President Richard M. Nixon of US announces 'Nixon/Guam' Doctrine
1969	Nov	21	Joint communiqué between PM Satō Eisaku and President Richard M. Nixon of US			
1970	Jan	14	Nakasone Yasuhiro appointed director-general of JDA			
1970	Feb	3	Japan signs NPT			
1970				Mar	5	NPT comes into effect
1970	Mar	31	Yodo hijacking incident – hijackers given asylum in DPRK			
1970	Apr	19	LDP delegation visits Beijing			
1970	Jun	23	US–Japan security treaty extended automatically			
1970	Sep	17	European Commission opens trade negotiations with Japan			
1970	Oct	20	Japan publishes first Defence White Paper			
1970	Oct	24	PM Satō Eisaku visits US			
1970	Nov	25	Novelist Mishima Yukio commits suicide at SDF base, Tokyo			
1971	Jun	17	Agreement on reversion of Okinawa to Japan signed			
1971				Jul	9	US National Security Advisor Henry Kissinger's secret mission to Beijing
1971				Aug	15	US President Nixon announces abandonment of gold standard and the introduction of an import surcharge – creates 'Nixon shocks'
1971				Oct	25	UNGA expels Taiwan and invites PRC membership
1971	Nov	16	Dietmen's League for the Promotion of Japan–North Korea Friendship founded			
1971				Nov	27	ZOPFAN agreement signed
				Dec	3	3rd India–Pakistan conflict
1971–2			Japan serves as a non-permanent member of the UNSC			
1972	Jan	7	PM Satō Eisaku and President Nixon joint communiqué			

Year	Japan			World		
1972	Jan	23	Japan–DPRK unofficial provisional fishing agreement signed			
1972	Feb	12–18	European Commission President Malfatti visits Japan			
1972				Feb	28	President Nixon of US makes official visit to China – US–PRC joint communiqué
1972	May	15	Administrative authority over the Ryūkyūs (Okinawa and the Senkaku Islands) reverts to Japan			
1972				May	26	President Nixon of US visits USSR, SALT I and ABM treaties signed
1972				Jul	3	India–Pakistan peace agreement signed
1972	Jul	7	PM Tanaka Kakuei assumes office			
1972	Aug	31	PM Tanaka Kakuei visits US			
1972	Sep	29	PM Tanaka Kakuei visits PRC – Japan–PRC diplomatic relations normalized			
1972				Dec	21	GDR–FRG Basic Treaty signed
1973				Jan	27	Vietnam peace treaty signed
1973				Jan	28	Vietnam War cease-fire
				Mar	29	US completes withdrawal of military forces from Vietnam
1973				Jan	1	UK, Ireland and Denmark join the EEC – EEC becomes EC
1973	Apr	28	Foreign Minister Ōhira Masayoshi visits Yugoslavia, Belgium and EC Commission (until May 6)			
1973	May	4	Foreign Minister Ōhira Masayoshi conducts first high-level consultations between Japan and the EC			
1973	Aug	29	Kim Dae-Jung abducted from Tokyo by KCIA			
1973	Sep	21	Japan–North Vietnam normalize diplomatic relations			

Year	Japan			World		
1973	Sep	26	PM Tanaka Kakuei visits France, UK, FRG and USSR (until Oct 11)			
1973				Oct	6	4th Middle East War begins (until Oct 25)
1973	Oct	8	Japan–USSR leaders' summit, Moscow			
1973				Oct	17	1st oil shock begins
1974	Jan	7–17	PM Tanaka Kakuei visits Philippines, Thailand, Singapore, Malaysia and Indonesia – encounters anti-Japanese protests in Indonesia on Jan 17			
1974	Jan	7–18	MITI Minister Nakasone Yasuhiro visits Iran, UK, Bulgaria and Iraq as part of 'resource diplomacy'			
1974				May	18	India conducts first underground nuclear test
1974	Jul		European Commission Delegation opens in Tokyo			
				Jul	3	President Nixon of US visits USSR – treaty limiting underground nuclear tests signed
1974	Aug	19	PM Tanaka Kakuei visits ROK			
1974	Sep	12–27	PM Tanaka Kakuei visits Mexico, Brazil and US			
1974	Oct	28	PM Tanaka Kakuei visits New Zealand, Australia and Burma			
1974	Dec	9	PM Miki Takeo assumes office			
1975				Apr	30	Saigon falls to North Vietnam forces
1975				Aug	1	CSCE established
1975	Aug	2–11	PM Miki Takeo visits US – Japan–US Joint Declaration announced Aug 6			
1975	Aug		Yasser Arafat, PLO leader, visits Tokyo			
1975				Nov	15–17	1st G5 meeting, Rambouillet, France
1975	Nov	10	Japan abstains in the 'Zionism equals Racism' General Assembly Resolution 3379			
1975–6			Japan serves as a non-permanent member of the UNSC			

Year	Japan			World		
1976	Feb		PM Miki Takeo administration strengthens ban on arms exports – introduces restrictions on export of defence-related technology			
1976	Jun	8	Japan ratifies NPT			
1976				Jun	27–28	G7 meeting in San Juan, US. Canada joins G7
1976				Jul	2	Socialist Republic of Vietnam officially established
1976				Aug	18	US servicemen killed at Panmunjon by DPRK soldiers, ROK
1976				Sep	9	Mao Zedong dies
1976	Oct	29	National Defence Programme Outline (NDPO) adopted			
1976	Oct	15–31	*Keidanren* 'Dokō' trade mission to Europe			
1976	Nov	5	PM Miki administration introduces 1 per cent ceiling on defence spending			
1976	Dec	24	PM Fukuda Takeo assumes office			
1977	Feb		Opening of PLO office in Tokyo			
1977	Mar	19–25	PM Fukuda Takeo visits US			
1977				May	7–8	G7 meeting, London, UK. EC joins G7
1977	May		Orderly Market Agreement restricting export of Japanese colour televisions to US market			
1977				Jun	30	SEATO dissolved
1977	Aug	6–18	PM Fukuda Takeo visits Malaysia, Burma, Indonesia, Singapore, Thailand and Philippines – announces 'Fukuda Doctrine' (Aug 18)			
1978	May	3–4	PM Fukuda Takeo visits US			
1978	May	11	JDA Director General Kanemaru Shin announces financial support for US forces in Japan (*omoiyari yosan*)			
1978	Jul		1st Japan–EC inter-parliamentary meeting			
1978				Jul	16–17	G7 meeting, Bonn, West Germany

Year	Japan			World		
1978	Aug	12	Sino-Japanese Treaty of Peace and Friendship signed			
				Sep	7	Camp David Agreement
1978	Nov	27	1st US–Japan joint military exercises			
1978	Nov	27	Guidelines for US–Japan Defence Cooperation adopted			
1978	Dec	7	PM Ōhira Masayoshi assumes office			
1978				Dec	16	US–ROC Mutual Defence Treaty annulled
1978				Dec	25	Vietnam invades Cambodia
1979				Jan	1	US–PRC relations normalized
1979				Feb	1	Iranian revolution
1979				Feb	17	PRC–Vietnam conflict (until Mar 5)
1979				Mar	26	Egypt–Israel Peace Treaty signed
1979	Apr	30	PM Ōhira Masayoshi visits US (until May 6)			
1979	May	9–11	PM Ōhira Masayoshi visits Philippines			
1979				Jun	18	SALT II treaty signed
1979				Jun	28–29	G7 meeting, Tokyo, Japan
1979				Oct	26	ROK President Park Chung-Hee assassinated
1979	Nov	26	Japan–ASEAN Economic Ministers Conference established			
1979	Dec	5–9	PM Ōhira Masayoshi visits PRC			
1979	Dec		Revision of Japan's Foreign Exchange Law			
1979				Dec	27	USSR invades Afghanistan
1980	Jan	15	PM Ōhira Masayoshi visits Australia, New Zealand and Papua New Guinea			
1980	Feb	26	MSDF participates in RIMPAC exercises for first time (until Mar 18)			
1980				Apr	11	USSR–PRC Treaty of Peace and Friendship lapses

Year	Japan			World		
1980	Apr	30	PM Ōhira Masayoshi visits US, Mexico and Canada (until May 4)			
1980				May	18	PRC conducts first ICBM test towards South Pacific
1980				Jun	22–23	G7 meeting, Venice, Italy
1980	Jul	17	PM Suzuki Zenkō assumes office			
				Sep	22	Iran–Iraq War begins
1980	Dec	1	Comprehensive Security Cabinet Committee established			
1981	Jan	8–20	PM Suzuki Zenkō visits ASEAN-5			
1981	May	4–8	PM Suzuki Zenkō visits US and Canada – announces Japan is willing to assume responsibility for patrolling SLOC up to 1,000 nautical miles surrounding Japan on May 8			
1981	May		VER on Japanese automobiles			
1981	Jun	9–21	PM Suzuki Zenkō visits Italy, Vatican City, Switzerland, Belgium, UK and Netherlands– meets EC Commission president			
1981				Jul	20–21	G7 meeting, Ottawa, Canada
1981	Oct	20–6	PM Suzuki Zenkō visits Mexico			
1981–2			Japan serves as a non-permanent member of UNSC			
1982				Apr	2	Falklands War begins (until Jun 14)
1982				Jun	6	Israeli army advances into Lebanon
1982				Jun	29	US–USSR START I talks commence
1982				Jun	4–6	G7 meeting, Versailles, France
1982	Jun	10–18	PM Suzuki Zenkō visits Peru and Brazil			
1982	Jun		1st textbook controversy begins (until Sep)			
1982	Sep	26	PM Suzuki Zenkō visits PRC (until Oct 1)			

Year	Japan			World		
1982				Oct	12	PRC conducts first SLBM test
1982	Nov	27	PM Nakasone Yasuhiro assumes office			
1983	Jan	11–12	PM Nakasone Yasuhiro visits ROK			
1983	Jan	17–21	PM Nakasone Yasuhiro visits US. Reported in US press as declaring on Jan 19 that Japanese archipelago is 'unsinkable aircraft carrier'			
1983				Mar	23	President Ronald Reagan of US announces SDI initiative
1983	Apr	30	PM Nakasone Yasuhiro visits Indonesia, Thailand, Singapore, Philippines, Malaysia and Brunei (until May 10)			
1983	Apr		1st Japan–EC ministerial meeting			
1983				May	28–30	G7 meeting, Williamsburg, US
1983				Sep	1	USSR shoots down ROK airliner
1983				Oct	9	Rangoon bombing incident
1983				Oct	25	US leads invasion of Grenada
1983	Nov	4	DPRK detains crew of *Fujisanmaru 18*			
1983	Nov	9–12	President Ronald Reagan of US visits Japan			
1983	Nov		The Exchange of Technology Agreement between Japan and the United States			
1984	Mar	23–6	PM Nakasone Yasuhiro visits PRC			
1984	Apr	30	PM Nakasone Yasuhiro visits Pakistan and India			
1984				Jun	7–9	G7 meeting, London, UK
1985	Jan	1–5	PM Nakasone Yasuhiro visits US			
1985	Jan	13–20	PM Nakasone Yasuhiro visits Fiji, Papua New Guinea, Australia and New Zealand			
1985				Mar	11	President Mikhail Gorbachev assumes office in USSR

Year	Japan			World		
1985				May	2–4	G7 meeting, Bonn, West Germany
1985	Jul	13–19	PM Nakasone Yasuhiro visits France, Italy, Belgium and European Commission			
1985	Aug	15	PM Nakasone Yasuhiro visits Yasukuni Shrine			
1985				Sep	22	Plaza Accord
1985	Oct	19–26	PM Nakasone Yasuhiro visits US and UN			
1985	Nov		Membership of the Tokyo Stock Exchange opened to foreign firms			
1985	Dec		Abe proposal at the 40th Session of the General Assembly of the UN seeking to review administrative and financial procedures			
1986	Jan	12–15	PM Nakasone Yasuhiro visits Canada			
1986	Apr	12	PM Nakasone Yasuhiro visits US			
1986				Apr	26	Chernobyl nuclear accident
1986	Apr		Maekawa Report published			
1986				May	4–6	G7 meeting, Tokyo, Japan
1986	Sep		1st US–Japan Semi-conductor Accord signed			
1986	Sep	9	PM Nakasone Yasuhiro administration agrees to participate in SDI research			
1986	Sep	20	PM Nakasone Yasuhiro visits ROK			
1986				Oct	11	US–USSR summit, Reykjavik, Iceland
1986	Nov	8–9	PM Nakasone Yasuhiro visits PRC			
1987	Jan	10	PM Nakasone Yasuhiro visits Finland, GDR and Yugoslavia			
1987				Feb	21	Louvre Accord
1987	Feb	26	Ōsaka High Court recognizes Taiwan's ownership of a student dormitory in Kyoto, known as *Kōkaryō*			

Year	Japan			World		
1987	Mar	27	US takes retaliatory action against Japan for infringement of Semi-conductor Accord			
1987	Apr	29	PM Nakasone Yasuhiro visits US (until May 4)			
1987				Jun	8–10	G7 meeting, Venice, Italy
1987				Jul		EC Single European Act comes into effect
1987	Sep	19–22	PM Nakasone Yasuhiro visits US to address UNGA			
1987	Nov	6	PM Takeshita Noboru assumes office			
1987				Nov	29	Korean airliner terrorist bombing incident
1987				Dec	8	INF Treaty signed
1987	Dec	15–16	PM Takeshita Noboru visits Philippines			
1987–8			Japan serves as a non-permanent member of the UNSC			
1988	Jan	12–20	PM Takeshita Noboru visits US and Canada			
1988	Feb	24–5	PM Takeshita Noboru visits ROK			
1988				Mar	14	PRC–Vietnam forces clash in South China Sea
1988				May	29	US–USSR leaders' summit, Moscow – exchange agreements on ratification of INF Treaty
1988	Apr	29	PM Takeshita Noboru visits Italy, Vatican City, UK and FRG (until May 9)			
1988				Jun	19–21	G7 meeting, Toronto, Canada
1988	Jul	1–5	PM Takeshita Noboru visits Australia			
1988				Aug	20	Iran–Iraq War cease-fire concluded
1988	Aug	23	US Omnibus Trade and Competitiveness Act signed into law			
1988	Aug	25	PM Takeshita Noboru visits PRC			
1988	Sep	16–17	PM Takeshita Noboru visits ROK			

Year	Japan			World		
1988	Nov	29	US–Japan memorandum of understanding on FS-X signed			
1989	Jan	7	Emperor Hirohito dies			
1989				Feb	15	USSR completes withdrawal of military forces from Afghanistan
1989	Feb	29	PM Takeshita Noboru visits ASEAN			
1989				May	17	USSR–PRC leaders' summit, Beijing – normalization of USSR–PRC relations
1989	Jun	3	PM Uno Sōsuke assumes office			
1989				Jun	4	Tiananmen Square incident, Beijing
1989	Jun	28	US–Japan SII talks end			
1989				Jul	14–16	G7 meeting, Paris, France
1989	Aug	10	PM Kaifu Toshiki assumes office			
1989			Collapse of Japanese 'bubble economy'			
1989	Aug	30	PM Kaifu Toshiki visits US and Canada			
1989	Sep	4	US–Japan SII talks commence			
1989	Oct	26	Japan despatches twenty-seven civilians to Namibia as part of the UNTAG operation			
1989				Nov	6–7	Inaugural meeting of APEC, Canberra, Australia
1989				Nov	9	GDR permits free travel to West, initiates process leading to fall of Berlin Wall
1989				Dec	2–3	US–USSR summit, Malta
1990	Jan	8–18	PM Kaifu Toshiki visits FRG, Belgium, France, UK, Italy, Vatican City, Poland, Hungary and European Commission			
1990	Mar	2–4	PM Kaifu Toshiki visits US			
1990	Apr	29	PM Kaifu Toshiki visits India, Pakistan, Bangladesh, Sri Lanka and Indonesia (until May 6)			
1990	Jun	4–5	Tokyo Conference on Cambodia			
1990				Jul	9–11	G7 meeting, Houston, US

Year	Japan			World		
1990				Jul	30–1	2nd APEC ministerial meeting, Singapore
1990				Aug	2	Iraq invades Kuwait
1990	Aug	17–25	Foreign Minister Nakayama Tarō visits Saudi Arabia, Jordan, Turkey, Egypt and Oman			
1990	Aug	30	Japan announces US$1 billion assistance for activities to restore peace in Persian Gulf			
1990	Sep	14	Japan announces extra US$2 billion assistance to three Gulf states for activities to restore peace in Persian Gulf			
1990	Sep	24–8	LDP–SDPJ delegation to Pyongyang, and LDP–SDPJ–KWP three-party declaration			
1990				Sep	30	USSR–ROK diplomatic relations normalized
1990	Oct	2–9	PM Kaifu Toshiki visits Egypt, Jordan, Turkey, Saudi Arabia, Oman and US			
1990				Oct	3	German unification
1990	Oct	16	United Nations Peace Cooperation Bill submitted to the Diet			
1990	Nov	2–4	1st Japan–DPRK preparatory normalization talks, Beijing			
1990	Nov	10	United Nations Peace Cooperation Bill rejected in the Diet			
1990	Nov	17	2nd Japan–DPRK preparatory normalization talks, Beijing			
1990	Dec	15–17	3rd Japan–DPRK preparatory normalization talks, Beijing			
1991	Jan	9–10	PM Kaifu Toshiki visits ROK			
1991	Jan	30–1	1st Japan–DPRK full normalization talks, Pyongyang			
1991	Mar	11–12	2nd Japan–DPRK full normalization talks, Tokyo			
1991	Apr	4–6	PM Kaifu Toshiki visits US			
1991	Apr	5	Japan restores full diplomatic relations with PRC			
1991	Apr	24	Japan decides to despatch four minesweepers to the Persian Gulf			

Year	Japan			World		
1991	Apr	27	PM Kaifu Toshiki visits Malaysia, Brunei, Thailand, Singapore and Philippines			
1991	May	20–2	3rd Japan–DPRK full normalization talks, Beijing			
1991				Jun	25	Croatia and Slovenia declare independence from Yugoslavia
1991				Jul	10	Boris Yeltsin assumes presidency of Russia
1991				Jul	15–17	G7 meeting, London, UK
1991	Jul	18	1st Japan–EC summit, Japan–EC Hague Declaration signed			
1991	Jul	22–4	Foreign Minister Nakayama Tarō launches an initiative at the July 1991 ASEAN PMC, proposing that in the future the meeting should become 'a forum for political dialogue ... designed to improve the sense of mutual security'			
1991				Jul	31	US–USSR summit, Moscow. START I signed
1991	Aug	10–14	PM Kaifu Toshiki visits Mongolia			
1991	Aug	30	4th Japan–DPRK full normalization talks, Beijing (until Sep 2)			
1991				Sep	6	Baltic Republics achieve independence from USSR
1991				Sep	17	ROK–DPRK simultaneous entry into UN
1991	Sep	19	Japanese government proposes Law on Cooperation in UN Peacekeeping and Other Operations			
1991	Nov	5	PM Miyazawa Kiichi assumes office			
1991				Nov	13–14	3rd APEC ministerial meeting, Seoul
1991	Nov	18–20	5th Japan–DPRK full normalization talks, Beijing			
1991				Dec	31	ROK–DPRK Agreement on Reconciliation, Non-Aggression, Exchange and Cooperation

Year	Japan			World		
1992	Jan	31	Japan–USSR summit meeting, UNHQ			
1992	Jan	7–10	President George Bush of US visits Japan – Prime Minister Miyazawa Kiichi and President Bush announce Tokyo Declaration			
1992	Jan	16–18	PM Miyazawa Kiichi visits ROK			
1992	Jan	30	6th Japan–DPRK full normalization talks, Beijing (until Feb 2)			
1992				Feb	7	EC signs Maastricht Treaty
				Feb	25	PRC announces law on national waters stating Senkaku Islands are Chinese territory
1992	Apr	29	PM Miyazawa Kiichi visits France and Germany			
1992	May	13–15	7th Japan–DPRK full normalization talks, Beijing			
1992				May	23	US, Russia, former USSR republics sign START I
1992	Jun	22	Ministerial conference on Cambodian reconstruction adopts 'Tokyo Declaration'			
1992	Jun	30	PM Miyazawa Kiichi visits US and UK (until Jul 10)			
1992				Jul	6–8	G7 meeting, Munich, Germany
1992				Aug	24	PRC–ROK normalize diplomatic relations
1992				Sep	10–11	4th APEC ministerial meeting, Bangkok
1992	Sep	17	SDF despatched to Cambodia PKO			
1992	Oct	23	Emperor and empress of Japan official visit to PRC			
1992	Nov	5	8th Japan–DPRK full normalization talks suspended			
1992				Nov	9	CFE Treaty comes into force
				Nov	24	US completes withdrawal of military forces from Philippines
1992–3			Japan serves as a non-permanent member of the UNSC			

Year	Japan			World		
1993				Jan	3	US–Russia summit meeting, Moscow. START II signed
1993	Jan	11–18	PM Miyazawa Kiichi visits Indonesia, Malaysia, Thailand and Brunei – announces 'Miyazawa Doctrine' Jan 16			
1993				Mar	12	DPRK announces withdrawal from NPT
1993	Apr	8	Nakata Atsuhito, a Japanese UN volunteer, killed in Cambodia			
1993	Apr	16	PM Miyazawa Kiichi visits US			
1993	May	4	Takata Haruyuki, a Japanese civilian police officer, killed in Cambodia			
1993				May	4	UNOSOM II assumes responsibilities of multinational forces deployed in Somalia
1993	May	27	Cabinet decides to despatch SDF to ONUMOZ operation, Mozambique (until Jan 1995)			
1993				Jun	11	DPRK announces suspension of decision to withdraw from NPT following talks with US
1993				Jul	24	ARF established
1993				Jul	7–9	G7 meeting, Tokyo, Japan
1993	Jul		US–Japan Framework Talks on Bilateral Trade announced			
1993	Aug	9	PM Hosokawa Morihiro assumes office			
1993	Aug		MOFA's Foreign Policy Bureau established			
1993				Sep	1	US Department of Defense announces 'Bottom-Up Review'
1993				Sep	13	Israel and PLO sign agreement on provisional autonomy
1993	Sep	27	PM Hosokawa Morihiro visits US			
1993				Sep		Publication of the WB report *The East Asian Miracle: Economic Growth and Public Policy*
				Oct	3	Eighteen US Marines killed in UNOSOM II operations

Year	Japan			World		
				Oct	4	President Boris Yeltsin uses forces to expel opposition forces from Russian Duma
1993	Oct	5–6	TICAD-I, Tokyo			
1993				Nov	1	Maastricht Treaty comes into forces, EC becomes EU
1993	Nov	6	PM Hosokawa Morihiro visits ROK			
1993				Nov	17–19	5th APEC ministerial meeting, Seattle
1993	Nov	30	SDF despatched to Mozambique PKO			
1994				Jan	1	NAFTA launched
1994				Jan	14	NATO adopts PFP agreement
1994	Feb	11	PM Hosokawa Morihiro visits US			
1994	Feb	23	Prime Minister's Advisory Group on Defence established			
1994				Mar	3	Lapsed Super 301 provision of the 1988 US Omnibus Trade and Competitiveness Act revived
1994				Mar	3–14	IAEA conducts inspection of DPRK nuclear facilities
1994	Mar	20–1	PM Hosokawa Morihiro visits PRC			
1994				Mar	25	US completes withdrawal of military forces from Somalia
1994	Apr	28	PM Hata Tsutomu assumes office			
1994	May	2–6	PM Hata Tsutomu visits Italy, France, Germany, Belgium and European Commission			
1994	Jun	10–26	Emperor Akihito's first official visit to US			
1994				Jun	14	DPRK informs US of its decision to withdraw from IAEA
				Jun	17	Ex-president Jimmy Carter meets President Kim Il Sung, DPRK
1994	Jun	30	PM Murayama Tomiichi assumes office			
1994				Jul	8	President Kim Il Sung dies

Year	Japan			World		
1994				Jul	8–10	G7 meeting, Naples, Italy
1994	Jul	23	PM Murayama Tomiichi visits ROK			
1994				Jul	25	1st ARF, Bangkok, Thailand
1994	Aug	12	Prime Minister's Advisory Group on Defence reports to PM Murayama Tomiichi			
1994	Aug	23–30	PM Murayama Tomiichi visits Philippines, Vietnam, Malaysia and Singapore			
1994				Aug	31	Russia completes withdrawal of military forces from Germany and Baltic Republics
1994	Sep	17	SDF despatched to Kenya to assist in Rwanda PKO			
1994				Oct	21	US–DPRK 'Agreed Framework' concluded
1994				Sep	11–12	6th APEC ministerial meeting, Jakarta
1994				Dec	18	Russia commences military operations in Chechnya
1995				Jan	1	OSCE established
1995	Jan	10–13	PM Murayama Tomiichi visits US			
1995	Jan	17	Kobe earthquake			
1995				Feb	9	Philippines reveals aerial photographs of PRC construction of buildings on 'Mischief Reef' in South China Sea
1995				Feb	27	US Department of Defense announces EASR ('Nye Report')
1995				Mar	9	KEDO established
1995	Mar	20	Aum Shinrikyō sarin attack on Tokyo subway			
1995	May	2–6	PM Murayama Tomiichi visits PRC			
1995				May	11	NPT extended indefinitely
1995	Jun	18–19	PM Murayama Tomiichi visits France for Japan–EU summit			
1995	Jun	28	US–Japan reach agreement under Japan Framework Talks on bilateral trade			
1995				Jun	15–17	G7 meeting, Halifax, Canada

Year	Japan			World		
1995				Jul	11	President Bill Clinton announces normalization of US–Vietnam relations
1995				Jul	28	Vietnam joins ASEAN
1995				Aug	1	2nd ARF, Darussalam, Brunei
1995	Aug	28	Japan suspends grant ODA to PRC			
1995	Sep	4	Three US military personnel rape an Okinawan schoolgirl. Widespread protests against US bases follow			
1995	Sep	12	PM Murayama Tomiichi visits Saudi Arabia, Egypt and Syria			
1995	Oct	19	APEC summit, Osaka, Japan			
1995	Oct		US–Japan auto-talks			
1995				Nov	1–21	Bosnia Peace Conference, Dayton, US
1995				Nov	16–17	7th APEC ministerial meeting, Osaka
1995	Nov	28	New NDPO announced			
1995				Nov	14	Bosnian Peace Accord signed, Paris
1996	Jan	11	PM Hashimoto Ryūtarō assumes office			
1996				Jan	27	France conducts nuclear tests
1996	Jan	31	SDF despatched to the UNDOF operation, Golan Heights			
1996	Feb	25	PM Hashimoto Ryūtarō visits US. Discusses Okinawa issue with President Bill Clinton			
				Mar	1–2	1st ASEM, Bangkok, Thailand
1996				Mar	8–25	PRC conducts missile and military exercises close to Taiwan, creates Taiwan Straits crisis
1996				Mar	23	Taiwan presidential election
1996	Apr	15	US–Japan ACSA signed			
1996				Apr	16	US and ROK propose four-party peace talks on Korean Peninsula

Year	Japan			World		
1996	Apr	17	PM Hashimoto Ryūtarō and US President Clinton sign 'Japan–US Joint Declaration on Security: Alliance for the 21st Century', reaffirming US–Japan security treaty			
1996	Jun	23	PM Hashimoto Ryūtarō visits ROK			
1996				Jun	27–9	G7 meeting, Lyon, France
1996	Jun	28	US–Japan commence review of Guidelines for Defence Cooperation			
1996				Jul	23	3rd ARF, Jakarta, Indonesia
1996				Jul	29	PRC conducts underground nuclear tests
1996	Aug	24	PM Hashimoto Ryūtarō visits US			
1996	Sep	8	Okinawa plebiscite			
1996				Sep	10	UNGA adopts CTBT
1996				Sep	18	DPRK submarine beached in ROK territorial waters
1996				Oct	3	Russia–Chechnya cease-fire agreed
1996				Nov	5	Bill Clinton re-elected as president of US
1996				Nov	22–3	8th APEC ministerial meeting, Manila
1996	Nov		Prime Minister Hashimoto Ryūtarō's announces 'big bang' financial deregulation package			
1996	Dec	2	US–Japan produce final report on reduction and consolidation of bases on Okinawa			
1997	Jan	7–14	PM Hashimoto Ryūtarō visits Brunei, Malaysia, Indonesia, Vietnam and Singapore. Announces 'Hashimoto Doctrine'			
1997				Jan	20	Bill Clinton begins second term in office as president of US
1997				Feb	19	Deng Xiaoping dies
1997				Apr	22	Peruvian special forces successfully free hostages from Japanese Embassy, Lima, Peru

Year	Japan			World		
1997	Apr	24–6	PM Hashimoto Ryūtarō visits US			
1997	Apr	28	PM Hashimoto Ryūtarō visits US, Australia and New Zealand (until May 1)			
1997	May	10	PM Hashimoto Ryūtarō visits Peru			
1997				Jun	20–2	G7 meeting, Denver, US
1997				Jul	2	Thai baht allowed to float – beginning of East Asian financial crisis
1997				Jul	23	Laos and Burma join ASEAN
1997				Jul	27	4th ARF, Subang Jaya, Malaysia
1997				Aug	5–7	1st four-party preparatory peace talks, New York
1997	Aug	15	IMF Tokyo summit			
1997				Aug	19	KEDO begins construction of LWRs in DPRK
1997	Aug	21	Japan agrees to resume normalization talks with DPRK			
1997	Sep	4–7	PM Hashimoto Ryūtarō visits PRC			
1997	Sep	10	Japan proposes AMF			
1997	Sep	23	US–Japan adopt revised Guidelines for Japan–US Defence Cooperation			
1997				Oct	8	Kim Jong-Il appointed general secretary of KWP
1997	Nov	1–2	PM Hashimoto Ryūtarō visits Russia			
1997	Nov	8–10	PM Hashimoto Ryūtarō visits Saudi Arabia			
1997				Nov	24–5	9th APEC ministerial meeting, Vancouver
1997	Dec	1–10	3rd Conference of the Parties to the United Nations Framework Convention on Climate Change held in Kyoto			
1997				Dec	3	Anti-Personnel Landmines Treaty signed, Ottawa, Canada
1997				Dec	9–10	Four-party peace talks begin, Geneva, Switzerland

Year	Japan			World		
1997				Dec	14–16	1st ASEAN + 3 summit, Kuala Lumpur, Malaysia
				Dec	16	Czech Republic, Hungary, Poland sign treaty to join NATO
1997	Dec	25	Mayor of Nago City, Okinawa, accepts floating heliport plan			
1998	Feb	6	Ōta Masahide, governor of Okinawa, rejects floating heliport plan			
1998				Feb	25	Kim Dae-Jung assumes office as president of ROK
1998	Mar	14–15	PM Hashimoto Ryūtarō visits Indonesia			
1998				Apr	2–4	2nd ASEM, London, UK
1998				Apr	6	UK and France ratify CTBT
1998	Apr		WTO settlement of Eastman Kodak and Fuji Photo Film dispute			
1998	Apr		Liberalization of Japan's Foreign Exchange Law			
1998	May	8	Finance Minister Matsunaga Hikaru announces official Japanese commitment to internationalization of the yen			
1998				May	15–17	G8 meeting, Birmingham, UK. Russia officially included in G7 meetings as part of G8 process
1998				May	21	President Suharto government falls in Indonesia
1998				May	30	Pakistan repeats underground nuclear test
1998	Jun		Diet passes 'big bang' financial deregulation package			
1998				Jun	27	President Bill Clinton of US visits PRC (until Jul 3)
1998	Jul	30	PM Obuchi Keizō assumes office			
1998				Jun	30	US launches missile attacks on Iraq
1998				Jul	27	5th ARF, Manila, Philippines

Year	Japan			World		
1998	Jul	20	Akino Yutaka, UN employee and associate professor of Tsukuba University, murdered while participating in UN operation in Tajikistan			
1998				Aug	7	Simultaneous bomb attacks on US embassies in Mozambique and Kenya
1998				Aug	20	US launches air raids on terrorist bases in Afghanistan
1998				Aug	31	DPRK test-fires suspected Taepodong-1 ballistic missile over Japanese airspace
1998	Aug	31	Japan refuses to provide final financing for KEDO			
1998	Sep	1	Japan freezes negotiations on the restart of normalization talks with DPRK			
1998				Sep	5	Kim Jong-Il appointed chief of National Defence Council
1998	Sep	20–3	PM Obuchi Keizō visits US to address UNGA			
1998	Oct	3	Finance Minister Miyazawa Kiichi announces 'New Miyazawa Initiative'			
1998	Oct	7–10	ROK President Kim Dae-Jung visits Japan – Japan–ROK joint declaration			
1998	Oct	19	TICAD-II, Tokyo			
1998	Oct	21	Japan agrees to sign KEDO financing agreement			
1998	Nov	11–13	PM Obuchi Keizō visits Russia			
1998				Nov	14–15	10th APEC ministerial meeting, Kuala Lumpur
1998	Nov	15	Ōta Masahide defeated in Okinawan gubernatorial elections			
1998	Nov	16	Japan announces US$124 billion domestic stimulus package			
1998				Nov	16	2nd ASEAN + 3 meeting, Hanoi, Vietnam
1998	Nov	19–20	President Bill Clinton of US visits Japan			

Year	Japan			World		
1998	Nov	28	PM Kim Jong-Pil (ROK) visits Japan – expresses support for AMF proposal			
1998	Dec	16–18	PM Obuchi Keizō visits Vietnam to attend ASEAN summit – announces 'human security' initiative			
1998				Dec	17–20	US and UK conduct air raids on Iraq
1998	Dec	25–30	PRC President Jiang Zemin visits Japan			
1999				Mar	12	NATO commences air raids on Yugoslavia
1999	Mar	19	PM Obuchi Keizō visits ROK			
1999	Mar	24	DPRK 'mysterious ships' enter Japanese territorial waters. MSDF responds by firing warning shots			
1999	Mar		Japanese interest rates reduced to zero			
1999				Apr	30	Cambodia joins ASEAN
1999				May	7	PRC embassy in Belgrade, Yugoslavia – destroyed by NATO bomb attack
1999				May	20	US inspectors enter DPRK underground facilities at Kumgang-ni
1999	May	24	Diet passes legislation to implement revised Guidelines for US–Japan Defence Cooperation, revised ACSA, and revised SDF law			
1999				Jun	4	Yugoslavia accepts US–EU–Russia Kosovo peace plan
1999				Jun	18–20	G8 meeting, Cologne, Germany
1999	Jul	8–10	PM Obuchi Keizō visits PRC			
1999				Jul	26	6th ARF, Singapore
1999	Aug	16	US–Japan sign agreement on cooperative research into technological feasibility of TMD			
1999	Sep	9	Legislation to make Kimigayo and Hinomaru the national anthem and flag passed in Diet			

Year	Japan			World		
1999				Sep	9–12	11th APEC ministerial meeting, Auckland, New Zealand
1999				Sep	17	US agrees to lift selective sanctions on DPRK
1999				Nov	28	3rd ASEAN + 3 meeting, Manila
1999	Dec	3–4	Ex-PM Murayama Tomiichi leads cross-party political mission to DPRK			
2000	Jan	12	PM Obuchi Keizō visits Laos			
2000	Apr	4	Japan–DPRK full normalization talks resume			
2000	Apr	5	PM Mori Yoshirō assumes office			
2000	May	14	Ex-PM Obuchi Keizō dies			
2000				Jun	21–3	G7 meeting, Okinawa/Kyushu, Japan
2000				Nov	12–13	12th APEC ministerial meeting, Darussalam, Brunei
2002			Japan and ROK host World Cup Soccer Championships			

Bibliography

English

Newspapers and Magazines

Economist
Euromoney
Far Eastern Economic Review
Financial Times
Japan Times
The Guardian
The Times
Yomiuri Shimbun

Articles and Books

A-Bomb Committee (The Committee for the Compilation of Materials on Damage Caused by the Atomic Bombs in Hiroshima and Nagasaki) (1979) *Hiroshima and Nagasaki: The Physical, Medical, and Social Effects of the Atomic Bombings* (trans. Eisei Ishikawa and David Swain), Tokyo: Iwanami Shoten.

Abo, Tetsuo (1998) 'Changes in Japanese automobile and electronic transplants in the USA: evaluating Japanese-style management and production systems', in Harukiyo Hasegawa and Glenn D. Hook (eds) *Japanese Business Management: Restructuring for Low Growth and Globalization*, London: Routledge, 80–106.

Akimune, Ichiro (1991) 'Overview: Japan's direct investment in the EC', in Masaru Yoshitomi (ed.) *Japanese Direct Investment in Europe*, Aldershot: Avebury, 1–25.

Albrow, Martin (1996) *The Global Age: State and Society beyond Modernity*, Oxford: Polity Press.

Alperovitz, Gar (1995) *The Decision to Use the Atomic Bomb and the Architect of an American Myth*, New York: A. A. Knopf.

Ampiah, Kweku (1997) *The Dynamics of Japan's Relations with Africa: South Africa, Tanzania and Nigeria*, London: Routledge.

Arase, David (1995) *Buying Power: The Political Economy of Japanese Foreign Aid*, Boulder: Lynne Rienner.

Arnold, Walter (1990) 'Political and economic influences in Japan's relations with China since 1978', in Kathleen Newland (ed.) *The International Relations of Japan*, London: Macmillan, 121–46.

Asahi Shimbunsha (1998) *Japan Almanac*, Tokyo: Asahi Shimbunsha.

—— (1999) *Japan Almanac*, Tokyo: Asahi Shimbunsha.

Awanohara, Susumu (1995) 'The US and Japan at the World Bank', in Peter J. Katzenstein, Takashi Inoguchi and Courtney Purrington (eds) *United States–Japan Relations and International Institutions after the Cold War*, San Diego: Graduate School of International Relations and Pacific Studies, University of California, 155–82.

Beasley, W. G. (1987) *Japanese Imperialism 1894–1945*, Oxford: Clarendon Press.

—— (1990) *The Rise of Modern Japan*, Tokyo: Charles E. Tuttle.

Bernard, Mitchell and Ravenhill, John (1995) 'Beyond product cycles and flying geese: regionalization, hierarchy and the industrialization of East Asia', *World Politics* 47, 2: 171–209.

Berger, Thomas U. (1998) *Cultures of Antimilitarism: National Security in Germany and Japan*, Baltimore: Johns Hopkins University Press.

Black, Cyril E., Helmreich, Jonathan E., Helmreich, Paul C., Issawi, Charles P. and McAdams, A. James (1992) *Rebirth: A History of Europe since World War II*, Boulder: Westview.

Bourke, Thomas (1996) *Japan and the Globalisation of European Integration*, Aldershot: Dartmouth.

Bridges, Brian (1993) *Japan and Korea in the 1990s: From Antagonism to Adjustment*, Aldershot: Edward Elgar.

—— (1999) *Europe and the Challenge of the Asia Pacific*, Cheltenham: Edward Elgar.

Calder, Kent E. (1988a) 'Japanese foreign economic policy formation: explaining the reactive state', *World Politics* 40, 4: 517–41.

—— (1988b) *Crisis and Compensation: Public Policy and Political Stability in Japan, 1949–1986*, Princeton: Princeton University Press.

—— (1993) *Strategic Capitalism: Private Business and Public Purpose in Japanese Industrial Finance*, Princeton: Princeton University Press.

—— (1997) 'The institutions of Japanese foreign policy', in Richard L. Grant (ed.) *The Process of Japanese Foreign Policy: Focus on Asia*, London: Royal Institute of International Affairs, 1–24.

Callon, Scott (1997) *Divided Sun: MITI and the Breakdown of Japanese High-Tech Industrial Policy, 1975–1993*, Stanford: Stanford University Press.

Carr, Edward H. (1946) *The Twenty Years' Crisis, 1919–1939: An Introduction to the Study of International Relations*, London: Macmillan.

Chapman, John M. W., Drifte, Reinhard and Gow, Ian T. M. (1983) *Japan's Quest for Comprehensive Security: Defence, Diplomacy, Dependence*, London: Pinter.

Choate, Pat (1990) *Agents of Influence*, New York: Alfred A. Knopf.

Clarke, Michael and White, Brian (eds) (1989) *Understanding Foreign Policy*, Aldershot: Edward Elgar.

Council for Asia–Europe Cooperation (CAEC) (1997) *The Rationale and Common Agenda for Asia–Europe Cooperation*, Tokyo: JCIE.

Cox, Robert W. with Sinclair, Timothy (1996) *Approaches to World Order*, Cambridge: Cambridge University Press.

Cumings, Bruce (1984) 'The origins of the Northeast Asian political economy: industrial sectors, product cycles and political consequences', *International Organization* 38, 1: 1–40.

—— (1990) *Origins of the Korean War Volume II: The Roaring of the Cataract*, Princeton: Princeton University Press.

Curtis, Gerald (1988) *The Japanese Way of Politics*, New York: Columbia University Press.

Daniels, Gordon and Drifte, Reinhard (eds) (1986) *Europe and Japan: Changing Relationships since 1945*, Ashford: Paul Norbury.

Darby, James (ed.) (1996) *Japan and the European Periphery*, London: Macmillan.

Deng, Yong (1997) *Promoting Asia–Pacific Economic Cooperation: Perspectives from East Asia*, London: Macmillan.

Dent, Christopher (1999) *The European Union and East Asia: An Economic Relationship*, London: Routledge.

Desmond, Edward W. (1995) 'Reformer at bay', *Foreign Affairs* 74, 5: 117–31.

Destler, I. M., Fukui, Haruhiro and Sato, Hideo (1979) *The Textile Wrangle: Conflict in Japanese–American Relations, 1969–71*, Ithaca: Cornell University Press.

Dobson, Hugo (1998) 'Japan and the world: from bilateralism to multilateralism', in Patrick Heenan (ed.) *The Japan Handbook*, London: Fitzroy Dearborn, 260–70.

—— (1999a) 'The failure of the Tripartite Pact: familiarity breeding contempt between Japan and Germany, 1940–1945', *Japan Forum* 11, 2: 179–90.

—— (1999b) 'Regional approaches to peacekeeping activities: the case of the ASEAN Regional Forum', *International Peacekeeping* 6, 2: 152–71.

Dore, Ronald F. (1997) *Japan, Internationalism and the UN*, London: Routledge.

Dower, John W. (1979) *Empire and Aftermath: Yoshida Shigeru and the Japanese Experience, 1878–1954*, Cambridge, MA: Harvard University Press.

—— (1989) 'Occupied Japan and the Cold War in East Asia', in M. J. Lacey (ed.) *The Truman Presidency*, Cambridge: Cambridge University Press, 366–409.

—— (1999) *Embracing Defeat: Japan in the Wake of World War II*, New York: W. W. Norton.

Drifte, Reinhard (1986) *Arms Production in Japan: The Military Applications of Civilian Technology*, Boulder: Westview.

—— (1990) *Japan's Foreign Policy*, London: Routledge.

—— (1996) *Japan's Foreign Policy in the 1990s: From Economic Superpower to What Power?*, London: Macmillan.

—— (1998) *Japan's Foreign Policy for the Twenty-First Century: From Economic Superpower to What Power?* (2nd edn of 1996 work), London: Macmillan.

Edström, Bert (1999) *Japan's Evolving Foreign Policy Doctrine: From Yoshida to Miyazawa*, London: Macmillan.

El-Agra, Ali M. (1988) *Japan's Trade Frictions*, London: Macmillan.

Elegant, Simon (1995) 'Memory and apathy', *Far Eastern Economic Review* 158, 38: 36–8.

Emmott, Bill (1989) *The Sun Also Sets: Why Japan Will Not Be Number One*, New York: Simon and Schuster.

—— (1991) *Japan's Global Reach: The Influences, Strategies and Weaknesses of Japan's Multinational Companies*, London: Century.

European Commission (1994) *Bulletin of the European Union* 7/8, Brussels: European Commission.

Evans, Gareth and Dibb, Paul (1994) *Australian Paper on Practical Proposals for Security Cooperation in the Asia Pacific Region*, Canberra: Australian National University Press.

Fairbank, John F. (ed.) (1968) *The Chinese World Order*, Cambridge, MA: Harvard University Press.

Farley, Maggie (1996) 'Japan's press and the politics of scandal', in Susan J. Pharr and Ellis S. Krauss (eds) *Media and Politics in Japan*, Honolulu: University of Hawaii Press, 133–63.

Feldman, Ofer (1993) *Politics and the News Media in Japan*, Ann Arbor: University of Michigan Press.

Fingleton, Eammon (1995) 'Japan's invisible leviathan', *Foreign Affairs* 74, 2: 69–85.

Finnemore, Martha and Sikkink, Katherine (1998) 'International norm dynamics and political change', *International Organization* 52, 4: 887–917.

Frankel, Jeffrey A. and Kahler, Miles (eds) (1993) *Regionalism and Rivalry: Japan and the United States in Pacific Asia*, Chicago: University of Chicago Press.

Frieden, Jeffry A. (1993) 'Domestic politics and regional cooperation: the United States, Japan, and Pacific money and finance', in Jeffrey A. Frankel and Miles Kahler (eds) *Regionalism and Rivalry: Japan and the United States in Pacific Asia*, Chicago: University of Chicago Press, 423–44.

Fujiyama, Aiichiro (1952) 'Report on the UNESCO movement', *Contemporary Japan* 21, 1: 66–74.

Fukui, Haruhiro (1972) 'Economic planning in postwar Japan: a case study in policy-making', *Asian Survey* 12, 4: 238–47.

Fukushima, Akiko (1999) *Japanese Foreign Policy: The Emerging Logic of Multilateralism*, London: Macmillan.

Fukuyama, Francis (1992) *The End of History and the Last Man*, London: Hamish Hamilton.

Funabashi, Yoichi (1991–2) 'Japan and the new world order', *Foreign Affairs* 70, 5: 58–74.

—— (1993) 'The Asianization of Asia', *Foreign Affairs* 72, 5: 75–85.

—— (1998) 'Thinking trilaterally', in Morton I. Abramowitz, Yoichi Funabashi and Wang Jisi (eds) *China–Japan–US: Managing the Trilateral Relationship*, Tokyo: JCIE, 47–60.

—— (1999) *Alliance Adrift*, New York: Council on Foreign Relations.

Gamble, Andrew and Payne, Anthony (eds) (1996) *Regionalism and World Order*, London: Macmillan.

Gangopadhyay, Partha (1998) 'Patterns of trade, investment and migration in the Asia-Pacific region', in Grahame Thompson (ed.) *Economic Dynamism in the Asia-Pacific: The Growth of Integration and Competitiveness*, London: Routledge, 20–54.

Garby, Craig C. and Brown Bullock, Mary (eds) (1994) *Japan: A New Kind of Superpower?*, Baltimore: Johns Hopkins University Press.

George Mulgan, Aurelia (1997) 'The US–Japan security relationship in a new era', in Denny Roy (ed.) *The New Security Agenda in the Asia Pacific Region*, London: Macmillan, 237–96.

Giddens, Anthony (1991) *Modernity and Self-Identity: Self and Society in the Late Modern Age*, Oxford: Polity Press.

Gill, Stephen (1990) *American Hegemony and the Trilateral Commission*, Cambridge: Cambridge University Press.

Gill, Stephen and Law, David (1988) *The Global Political Economy: Perspectives, Problems and Policies*, New York: Harvester Wheatsheaf.

Gills, Barry K. (1997) '"Globalisation" and the politics of "resistance"', *New Political Economy* 2, 1: 11–15.

Gilpin, Robert (1987) *The Political Economy of International Relations*, Princeton: Princeton University Press.

Gilson, Julie (1999) 'Japan's role in the Asia-Europe Meeting: establishing an interregional or intraregional agenda?', *Asian Survey* 34, 5: 736–52.

—— (2000a) *Japan and the European Union: A Partnership for the Twenty First Century?*, London: Macmillan.

—— (2000b) 'Japan in Kosovo: lessons in the politics of "complex engagement"', *Japan Forum* 12, 1: 65–76.

Green, Michael J. (1995) *Arming Japan: Defense Production, Alliance Politics, and the Postwar Search for Autonomy*, New York: Columbia University Press.

Green, Michael J. and Self, Benjamin L. (1996) 'Japan's changing China policy', *Survival* 38, 2: 35–58.

Grewlich, Klaus W. (1994) 'The impact of "Europe 1992" on Japan's relations with Europe: a German view', in T. David Mason and Abdul M. Turay (eds) *Japan, NAFTA and Europe*, New York: St Martin's Press, 93–107.

Hamada, Koichi (1994) 'Japan's prospective role in the international monetary regime', in Craig Garby and Mary Brown Bullock (eds) *Japan: A New Kind of Superpower?*, Baltimore: Johns Hopkins University Press, 143–58.

—— (1999) 'From the AMF to the Miyazawa Initiative: observations on Japan's current diplomacy', *The Journal of East Asian Affairs* 8, 1: 1–32.

Hamashita, Takeshi (1997) 'The intraregional system in East Asia in modern times', in Peter J. Katzenstein and Takashi Shiraishi (eds) *Network Power: Japan and Asia*, Ithaca: Cornell University Press, 113–35.

Hara, Yoshihisa (1987) 'The significance of the US–Japan security system to Japan: the historical background', *Peace and Change* 12, 3/4: 29–38.

Hartcher, Peter (1999) *The Ministry: The Inside Story of Japan's Ministry of Finance*, London: HarperCollins.

Hashimoto, Ryutaro (1997) 'Special Session of the General Assembly for the Overall Review and Appraisal of the Implementation of Agenda 21'. Online. Available at: http://www.undp.org/missions/japan/s_0623_7.htm.

Hatano, Yoshio (1994) '48th Session of the United Nations General Assembly', *Statements Delivered by Delegates of Japan*, Tokyo: United Nations Bureau, Ministry of Foreign Affairs.

Hatch, Walter and Yamamura, Kozo (1996) *Asia in Japan's Embrace: Building a Regional Production Alliance*, Cambridge: Cambridge University Press.

Havens, Thomas R. H. (1987) *Fire Across The Sea: The Vietnam War and Japan 1965–1975*, Princeton: Princeton University Press.

Hayao, Kenji (1993) *The Japanese Prime Minister and Public Policy*, Pittsburgh: University of Pittsburgh Press.

Hayashi, Takeshi (1981) 'UNU – The Japanese experience', *Japan Quarterly* 28, 3: 348–54.

Hayes, Peter, Zarsky, Lyuba and Bello, Walden (1986) *American Lake: Nuclear Peril in the Pacific*, Harmondsworth: Penguin.

Hellman, Donald C. (1969) *Japanese Foreign Policy and Domestic Politics: The Peace Agreement with the Soviet Union*, Berkeley: University of California Press.

—— (1988) 'Japanese politics and foreign policy: elitist democracy within an American greenhouse', in Takashi Inoguchi and Daniel I. Okimoto (eds) *The Political Economy of Japan Volume 2: The Changing International Context*, Stanford: Stanford University Press, 345–78.

Higgott, Richard (1998) 'The Asian economic crisis: a study in the politics of resentment', *New Political Economy* 3, 3: 333–56.

Higgott, Richard, Leaver, Richard and Ravenhill, John (eds) (1993) *Pacific Economic Relations in the 1990s: Cooperation or Conflict?*, Boulder: Lynne Rienner.

Hirono, Ryokichi (1991) 'Japan's leadership role in the multilateral development institutions', in Shafiqul Islam (ed.) *Yen for Development: Japanese Foreign Aid and the Politics of Burden-Sharing*, New York: Council on Foreign Relations, 171–88.

Hook, Glenn D. (1986) *Language and Politics: The Security Discourse in Japan and the United States*, Tokyo: Kuroshio Shuppansha.

—— (1988) 'The erosion of anti-militaristic principles in contemporary Japan', *Journal of Peace Research* 25, 4: 381–94.

—— (1996a) *Militarization and Demilitarization in Contemporary Japan*, London: Routledge.

—— (1996b) 'Japan and the construction of the Asia-Pacific', in Andrew Gamble and Anthony Payne (eds) *Regionalism and World Order*, London: Macmillan, 169–206.

—— (1998) 'Japan and the ASEAN Regional Forum: bilateralism, multilateralism or supplementalism?', *Japanstudien* 10: 159–88.

—— (1999a) 'The East Asian Economic Caucus: a case of reactive subregionalism?', in Glenn D. Hook and Ian Kearns (eds) *Subregionalism and World Order*, London: Macmillan, 223–45.

—— (1999b) 'Japan and microregionalism: constructing the Japan Sea Rim Zone', in Yoshinobu Yamamoto (ed.) *Globalism, Regionalism and Nationalism: Asia in Search of its Role in the 21st Century*, Oxford: Blackwell Publishers, 126–41.

—— and McCormack, Gaven (2001) *Japan's Contested Constitution: Documents and Analysis*, London: Routledge.

Horsley, William and Buckley, Roger (1990) *Nippon New Superpower: Japan since 1945*, London: British Broadcasting Corporation.

Hosokawa, Morihiro (1994) '48th Session of the United Nations General Assembly', *Statements Delivered by Delegates of Japan*, Tokyo: United Nations Bureau, Ministry of Foreign Affairs.

Hosoya, Chihiro (1965–8) 'Japan and the United Nations', *Japan Institute of International Affairs Annual Review* 4:18–36.

Howes, John F. (ed.) (1995) *Niitobe Inazo: Japan's Bridge across the Pacific*, Boulder: Westview.

Hughes, Christopher W. (1996) 'Japan's subregional security and defence linkages with ASEAN, South Korea and China in the 1990s', *The Pacific Review* 9, 2: 229–50.

—— (1998) 'Japan's Aum Shinrikyo, the changing nature of terrorism, and the post-Cold War security agenda', *The Pacific Review: Peace, Security and Global Agenda* 10, 1: 39–60.

—— (1999) *Japan's Economic Power and Security: Japan and North Korea*, London: Routledge.

—— (2000) 'Japanese policy and the East Asian currency crisis: abject defeat or quiet victory?', *Review of International Political Economy* 7, 2: 219–53.

Hummel, Hartwig (1996) 'Japan's military expenditure after the Cold War: the "realism" of the peace dividend', *Australian Journal of International Affairs* 50, 2: 137–55.

Huntington, Samuel P. (1993) 'The clash of civilizations', *Foreign Affairs* 72, 3: 22–49.

Igarashi, Takeshi (1985) 'Peace-making and party politics: the formation of the foreign-policy system in postwar Japan', *Journal of Japanese Studies* 11, 2: 323–56.

Ijiri, Hidenori (1996) 'Sino-Japanese controversy since 1972', in Christopher Howe (ed.) *China and Japan: History, Trends and Prospects*, Oxford: Clarendon Press, 60–82.

Immerman, Robert M. (1994) 'Japan in the UN', in Craig Garby and Mary Brown Bullock (eds) *Japan: A New Kind of Superpower?*, Baltimore: Johns Hopkins University Press, 181–92.

Inada, Juichi (1990) 'Japan's aid diplomacy: economic, political or strategic?', in Kathleen Newland (ed.) *The International Relations of Japan*, London: Macmillan, 100–20.

Inoguchi, Takashi (1988) 'The ideas and structures of foreign policy: looking ahead with caution', in Takashi Inoguchi and Daniel I. Okimoto (eds) *The Political Economy of Japan, Volume 2: The Changing International Context*, Stanford: Stanford University Press, 23–63.

Inoguchi, Takashi and Okimoto, Daniel I. (eds) (1988) *The Political Economy of Japan, Volume 2: The Changing International Context*, Stanford: Stanford University Press.

International Institute for Strategic Studies (various years) *The Military Balance*, London and Oxford: Brassey's and Oxford University Press.

—— (1998) *The Military Balance 1998/99*, Oxford: Oxford University Press.

—— (1999) *The Military Balance 1999–2000*, Oxford: Oxford University Press.

International Monetary Fund (2000). Online. Available at: http://www.imf.org/external/np/sec/memdir/members.htu.

Ishihara, Shintaro (1991) *The Japan that Can Say No* (trans. Frank Baldwin), New York: Simon and Schuster.

Ishikawa, Kenjiro (1990) *Japan and the Challenge of Europe*, London: Pinter.

Islam, Shafiqul (1993) 'Foreign aid and burdensharing: is Japan free riding to a coprosperity sphere in Pacific Asia?', in Jeffrey A. Frankel and Miles Kahler (eds) *Regionalism and Rivalry: Japan and the United States in Pacific Asia*, Chicago: University of Chicago Press, 321–90.

Ito, Takatoshi (1993) 'US political pressure and economic liberalization in East Asia', in Jeffrey A. Frankel and Miles Kahler (eds) *Regionalism and Rivalry: Japan and the United States in Pacific Asia*, Chicago: University of Chicago Press, 391–420.

James, Barrie G. (ed.) (1989) *Trojan Horse: The Ultimate Japanese Challenge to Western Industry*, London: Mercury.

JCIE and ISEAS (1998) *The Asian Crisis and Human Security: An Intellectual Dialogue on Building Asia's Tomorrow*, Tokyo: JCIE.

JETRO (1992) *White Paper on International Trade 1992*, Tokyo: Ōkurashō Insatsukyoku.

Johnson, Chalmers (1986) *MITI and the Japanese Miracle: The Growth of Industrial Policy*, Tokyo: Charles E. Tuttle.

—— (1993) 'History restarted: Japanese–American relations at the end of the century', in Richard Higgott, Richard Leaver, John Ravenhill (eds) *Pacific Economic Relations in the 1990s: Cooperation or Conflict?*, Boulder: Lynne Rienner, 39–61.

—— (1995) *Japan: Who Governs? The Rise of the Developmental State*, New York: W. W. Norton.

Johnson, Chalmers and Keehn, E. B. (1995) 'The Pentagon's ossified East Asia strategy', *Foreign Affairs* 74, 4: 2–23.

Johnstone, Christopher B. (1998) 'Japan's China policy: implications for US–Japan relations', *Asian Survey* 38, 11: 1067–85.

Jomo, K. S. (ed.) (1994) *Japan and Malaysian Development: In the Shadow of the Rising Sun*, London: Routledge.

Jones, R. J. Barry (1995) *Globalisation and Interdependence in the International Political Economy: Rhetoric and Reality*, London: Pinter.

Kahn, Herman (1971) *The Emerging Japanese Superstate: Challenge and Response*, London: Deutsch.

Kamiya, Matake (1997) 'The US–Japan alliance and regional security cooperation: toward a double-layered security system', in Ralph A. Cossa (ed.) *Restructuring the US–Japan Alliance: Toward a More Equal Partnership*, Washington, DC: CSIS, 19–28.

Kamo, Takehiko (1994) 'The internationalization of the state: the case of Japan', in Yoshikazu Sakamoto (ed.) *Global Transformation. Challenges to the State System*, Tokyo: United Nations University, 102–33.

Katz, Richard (1998) *Japan, the System that Soured: The Rise and Fall of the Japanese Economic Miracle*, New York: M. E. Sharpe.

Katzenstein, Peter (1996a) *Cultural Norms and National Security: Police and Military in Postwar Japan*, Ithaca: Cornell University Press.

—— (ed.) (1996b) *The Culture of National Security: Norms and Identity in World Politics*, New York: Columbia University Press.

Keddell, Joseph P. Jr (1993) *The Politics of Defence in Japan: Managing Internal and External Pressures*, London: M. E. Sharpe.

Keohane, Robert O. (1986a) *Neo-Realism and its Critics*, New York: Columbia University Press.

—— (1986b) 'Reciprocity in international relations', *International Organization* 40, 1: 1–27.

Kitamura Toshiharu (1991) 'Investment in financial services', in Yoshitomi Masaru (ed.) *Japanese Direct Investment in Europe*, Aldershot: Avebury, 86–117.

Koh, Byung Chul (1989) *Japan's Administrative Elite*, Berkeley: University of California Press.

Komura, Masahiko (1999) 'Statement at the 54th Session of the General Assembly of the United Nations – Issues in the Twenty-First Century and the Role of the United Nations'. Online. Available at: http://www.mofa.go.jp/announce/announce1999/9/927-2.html.

Korhonen, Pekka (1994) *Japan and the Pacific Free Trade Area*, London: Routledge.

Koschmann, Victor J. (1997) 'Asianism's ambivalent legacy', in Peter J. Katzenstein and Takashi Shiraishi (eds) *Network Power: Japan and East Asia*, Ithaca: Cornell University Press, 83–110.

Kumar, B. Nino (1991) 'Japanese direct investments in West Germany: trends, strategies, and management problems', in Jonathan Morris (ed.) *Japan and the Global Economy*, London: Routledge, 213–32.

Kume, Gorota and Totsuka Keisuke (1991) 'Japanese manufacturing investment in the EC: motives and locations', in Masaru Yoshitomi (ed.) *Japanese Direct Investment in Europe*, Aldershot: Avebury, 26–56.

Krugman, Paul (1994) 'The myth of Asia's miracle', *Foreign Affairs* 73, 6: 62–78.

LaFeber, Walter (1997) *The Clash: A History of US–Japan Relations*, New York: W. W. Norton.

Lane, Peter (1985) *Europe since 1945: An Introduction*, London: Batsford Academic and Educational.

Leifer, Michael (1983) *Indonesia's Foreign Policy*, London: Allen and Unwin.

—— (1996) *The ASEAN Regional Forum: Extending ASEAN's Model of Regional Security*, Oxford: Oxford University Press.

Leitenberg, Milton (1996) 'The participation of Japanese military forces in UN peacekeeping operations', *Asian Perspective* 20, 1: 5–50.

Lincoln, Edward J. (1993) *Japan's New Global Role*, Washington, DC: Brookings Institution.

McCargo, Duncan (1996) 'The political role of the Japanese media', *The Pacific Review* 9, 2: 251–64.

McIntyre, John R. (1994) 'Europe 1992 and Japan's relations with Western Europe', in T. David Mason and Abdul M. Turay (eds) *Japan, NAFTA and Europe*, New York: St Martin's Press, 58–92.

McLaughlin, Andrew M. and Maloney, William A. (1999) *The European Automobile Industry: Multi-Level Governance, Policy and Politics*, London: Routledge.

Macridis, Roy (ed.) (1992) *Foreign Policy in World Politics: States and Regions*, Englewood Cliffs: Prentice Hall.

Mahathir, Mohamad and Ishihara, Shintaro (1996) *The Voice of Asia: Two Leaders Discuss the Coming Century*, Tokyo: Kōdansha International.

Malcolm, James D. (1998) 'The political economy of financial globalisation: does Japan's "Big Bang" herald convergence?', PhD dissertation, University of Sheffield.

Mashiki, Tomi (1999) 'Opposition to the heliport: alternatives for local development in Nago city', *AMPO: Japan Asia Quarterly Review* 29, 1: 24–8.

Mason, T. David and Turay, Abdul M. (1994) (eds) *Japan, NAFTA and Europe*, New York: St Martin's Press.

Masumi, Junnosuke (1995) *Contemporary Politics in Japan*, Berkeley: University of California Press.

Matsueda, Tsukasa and Moore, George A. (1967) 'Japan's shifting attitudes towards the military: Mitsuya Kenkyu and the Self Defence Forces', *Asian Survey* 7, 8: 614–25.

Maull, Hanns W. (1990–1) 'Germany and Japan: the new civilian powers', *Foreign Affairs* 69, 5: 91–106.

Maull, Hanns W., Segal, Gerald and Wanandi, Jusuf (eds) (1998) *Europe and the Asia Pacific*, London: Routledge.

Mendl, Wolf (1990) 'Stuck in a mould: the relationship between Japan and the Soviet Union', in Kathleen Newland (ed.) *The International Relations of Japan*, London: Macmillan, 174–205.

—— (1995) *Japan's Asia Policy: Regional Security and Global Interests*, London: Routledge.

Menju, Toshiro with Aoki, Takako (1996) 'The evolution of Japanese NGOs in the Asia Pacific context', in Tadashi Yamamoto (ed.) *Emerging Civil Society in the Asia Pacific Community*, Tokyo: JCIE, 143–60.

Miles, Rufus (1985) 'Hiroshima: the strange myth of half a million lives saved', *International Security* 10, 2: 121–40.

Military Base Affairs Office (1999) *US Military Bases on Okinawa: Current Situation and Issues*, Naha: Okinawa Prefectural Government.

Mills, C. Wright (1956) *The Power Elite*, Oxford: Oxford University Press.

Milner, Helen V. (1998) 'Rationalizing politics: the emerging synthesis of international, American, and comparative politics', *International Organization* 52, 4: 759–86.

Ming, Wan (1995–6) 'Japan and the Asian Development Bank', *Pacific Affairs* 68, 4: 509–28.

Ministry of National Defence Republic of Korea (1998) *Defence White Paper*, Seoul: Ministry of National Defence Republic of Korea.

MOFA (1996) 'Tokyo declaration on African development "towards the 21st Century"'. Online. Available at: http://www.infojapan.org/regiona/africa/ticad2/ticad22.html.

—— (1998a) 'Tokyo international conference on African development II' (TICAD-II). Online. Available at: http://www.infojapan.org/announce/announce/1998/7/703–3.html.

—— (1998b), *Japan's Official Development Assistance 1998*, Tokyo: Association for Promotion of International Cooperation.

—— (1999a) Online. Available at: http://www.mofa.go.jp/region/europe/germany/agenda/htm.

—— (1999b) Online. Available at: http://www.mofa.go.jp/other/bluebook/1999/I-a.html.

Morris, Jonathan (1991) *Japan and the Global Economy*, London: Routledge.

Morrison, Charles (1988) 'Japan and the ASEAN countries: the evolution of Japan's regional role', in Takashi Inoguchi and Daniel I. Okimoto (eds) *The Political Economy of Japan, Volume 2: The Changing International Context*, Stanford: Stanford University Press: 414–45.

Muramatsu, Michio and Krauss, Ellis S. (1987) 'The conservative policy line and the development of patterned pluralism', in Yamamura Kozo and Yasuba Yasukichi (eds) *The Political Economy of Japan Volume One: The Domestic Transformation*, Stanford: Stanford University Press, 516–54.

Nagai, Michio (1981) 'Reaching for a global institution', *Japan Quarterly* 28, 3: 339–47.

Nagatomi, Yuichiro (1988) *Masayoshi Ohira's Proposal to Evolve the Global Society*, Tokyo: Foundation for Advanced Information and Research.

Nakamura, Masanori (1992) *The Japanese Monarchy: Ambassador Joseph Grew and the Making of the 'Symbol Emperor System', 1931–1991*, New York: M. E. Sharpe.

Nellor, David C.L. (1998) 'The role of the International Monetary Fund', in Ross H. McCleod and Ross Garnaut (eds) *East Asia in Crisis: From Being a Miracle to Needing One?*, London: Routledge, 227–44.

Nester, William (1990) *The Foundation of Japanese Power: Continuities, Changes, Challenges*, New York: M. E. Sharpe.

—— (1992) *Japan and the Third World: Patterns, Power, Prospects*, New York: St Martin's Press.

Newby, Laura (1988) *Sino-Japanese Relations: China's Perspective*, London: Routledge.

Nish, Ian (1993) *Japan's Struggle with Internationalism: Japan, China, and the League of Nations*, London: K. Paul International.

Nishihara, Masashi (1976) *The Japanese and Sukarno's Indonesia: Tokyo–Jakarta Relations, 1951–1966*, Honolulu: University of Hawaii Press.

Noda, Makito (1995) 'Research institutes in Japan: from the perspective of the Asia Pacific intellectual network', in Tadashi Yamamoto (ed.) *Emerging Civil Society in the Asia Pacific Community*, Tokyo: JCIE, 384–401.

Nye, Joseph S. (1988) 'Neorealism and neoliberalism', *World Politics* 40 2: 235–51.

—— (1990) 'Soft power', *Foreign Policy* 80: 155–71.

—— (1992) 'What New-World order', *Foreign Affairs* 71, 2: 83–96.

—— (1999) 'Redefining the national interest', *Foreign Affairs* 78, 4: 22–41.

Obana, Tamaki (1976) 'The UNESCO movement in Japan', in *Peace Research in Japan 1976*, Tokyo: Tokyo University Press, 78–81.

Obuchi, Keizo (1997) 'UN General Assembly 52nd Session'. Online. Available at: http://www.undp.org/missions/japan/s_0923_7.htm.

Ogata, Sadako (1983) 'The changing role of Japan in the UN', *Journal of International Affairs* 37, 1: 29–42.

—— (1987) 'Japan's United Nations Policiy in the 1980s', *Asian Survey* 27,9: 957–72.

—— (1989) 'Shifting power relations in multilateral development banks', *Journal of International Studies* 22: 1–23.

—— (1995) 'Japan's policy towards the United Nations', in Chadwick F. Alger, Gere M. Lyons and John E. Trent (eds) *The United Nations System: the Policies of Member States*, Tokyo: UN University Press.

Ogino, Hiroshi (1998) 'Bureaucratic prestige imperiled by selective administration', *Japan Quarterly* 41, 2: 4–10.

Ohmae, Kenichi (1990) *The Borderless World*, London: Collins.

Okawara, Yoshio (1993) 'Japan's global responsibilities', in Danny Unger and Paul Blackburn (eds) *Japan's Emerging Role*, Boulder: Lynne Rienner, 55–67.

Omura, Masaki (1997) 'Development aid and development finance institutions', *Kinyu Journal*, (October): 43–9.

Onuf, Nicholas (1985) *World of our Making: Rules and Rule in Social Theory and International Relations*, Columbia: University of South Carolina Press.

Oppenheim, Phillip (1991) *The New Masters: Can the West Match Japan?*, London: Business Books.

Orr, Robert, M. (1990) *The Emergence of Japan's Foreign Aid Power*, New York: Columbia University Press.

Owada, Hisashi (1994) 'A Japanese perspective on the role and future of the G-7', in *The International Spectator: Special Issue, The Future of the G-7 Summits* 29, 2: 95–112.
—— (1996) '51st Session of the United Nations General Assembly', *Statements Delivered by Delegates of Japan*, Tokyo: United Nations Bureau, Ministry of Foreign Affairs.
—— (1997) 'UN General Assembly 52nd Session'. Online. Available at: http://www.undp.org/missions/japan/s_1204_7.htm.
—— (1998) 'Special Committee on Peacekeeping Operations'. Online. Available at: http://www.undp.org/missions/japan/s_0331_8.htm.
Ozaki, Robert (1985) 'The political economy of Japan's foreign relations', in Robert Ozaki and Walter Arnold (eds) *Japan's Foreign Relations: A Global Search for Economic Security*, Boulder: Westview, 1–12.
Ozawa, Ichiro (1994) *Blueprint for a New Japan* (trans. Louisa Rubinfen, ed. Eric Gower), Tokyo: Kodansha.
Packard, George (1966) *Protest in Tokyo: The Security Treaty Crisis of 1960*, Princeton: Princeton University Press.
Patrick, Hugh and Rosovsky, Henry (eds) (1976) *Asia's New Giant: How the Japanese Economy Works*, Washington, DC: Brookings Institution.
Pempel, T. J. (1979) 'Japanese foreign economic policy: the domestic bases for international behaviour', *International Organization* 31, 4: 723–74.
—— (1987) 'The unbundling of "Japan Inc": the changing dynamics of Japanese policy formation', *The Journal of Japanese Studies* 13, 2: 271–306.
—— (1998) *Regime Shift: Comparative Dynamics of the Japanese Political Economy*, Ithaca: Cornell University Press.
—— (1999) *Politics of the Asian Economic Crisis*, Ithaca: Cornell University Press.
Pharr, Susan J. (1993) 'Japan's defensive foreign policy and the policies of burden sharing', in Gerald L. Curtis (ed.) *Japan's Foreign Policy*, New York: M. E. Sharpe, 235–63.
Pharr, Susan J. and Krauss, Ellis S. (eds) (1996) *Media and Politics in Japan*, Honolulu: University of Hawaii Press.
Prestowitz, Clyde V. (1988) *Trading Places: How We Allowed Japan to Take the Lead*, New York: Basic Books.
Ramazotti, Paolo (1996) 'Italy and Japanese investment: the influence of the European monetary system', in James Darby (ed.) *Japan and the European Periphery*, London: Macmillan, 149–66.
Ramseyer, J. Mark and McCall Rosenbluth, Frances (1993) *Japan's Political Marketplace*, Cambridge, MA: Harvard University Press.
Rapkin, Daniel P. (1990) 'The limits of hegemony', in Daniel P. Rapkin (ed.) *World Leadership and Hegemony*, Boulder: Lynne Rienner, 191–212.
Rapkin, Daniel P., Elston, Joseph U. and Strand, Jonathan R. (1997) 'Institutional adjustment to changed power distributions: Japan and the United States in the IMF', *Global Governance* 3, 2: 171–95.
Reischauer, Edwin O. (1986) *My Life between Japan and America*, New York: Harper and Row.
Risse-Kappen, Thomas (1995) *Co-operation among Democracies: European Influence on U.S. Foreign Policy*, Princeton: Princeton University Press.
Rix, Alan (1993a) *Japan's Foreign Aid Challenge: Policy Reform and Aid Leadership*, London: Routledge.
—— (1993b) 'Japan and the region', in Richard Higgott, Richard Leaver and John Ravenhill (eds) *Pacific Economic Relations in the 1990s. Cooperation or Conflict?* St Leonards (Australia): Allen and Unwin, 62–82.

Robertson, Myles L. C. (1988) *Soviet Policy towards Japan: An Analysis of Trends in the 1970s and 1980s*, Cambridge: Cambridge University Press.

Robertson, Roland (1992) *Globalisation*, London: Sage Publications.

Rose, Caroline (1998) *Interpreting History in Sino-Japanese Relations*, London: Routledge.

Rosecrance, Richard (1986) *The Rise of the Trading State: Commerce and Conquest in the Modern World*, New York: Basic Books.

Rosenau, James N. (1980) *The Scientific Study of Foreign Policy* (2nd edn), London: Pinter.

Rothacher, Albrecht (1983) *Economic Diplomacy between the European Community and Japan 1959–1981*, Aldershot: Gower.

Ruigrok, Winfried and Tulder, Rob van (1995) *The Logic of International Restructuring*, London: Routledge.

Saito, Shiro (1990) *Japan at the Summit: Its Role in the Western Alliance and Asian Pacific Cooperation*, London: Routledge.

Sakurada, Daizo (1988) 'Japan and the management of the international political economy: Japan's seven power summit diplomacy', *Country Study Series No. 6*, Toronto: University of Toronto, Centre for International Studies.

Samuels, Richard J. (1987) *The Business of the Japanese State: Energy Markets in Comparative and Historical Perspective*, Ithaca: Cornell University Press.

—— (1996) *Rich Nation, Strong Army: National Security and the Technological Transformation of Japan*, Ithaca: Cornell University Press.

Sazanami, Yoko and Kawai, Hiroki (1999) 'An empirical analysis of Japanese multinational corporate strategies in Europe, Asia and North America', in Sang-Gon Lee and Pierre Bruno Ruffini (eds) *The Global Integration of Europe and East Asia*, Cheltenham: Edward Elgar, 37–53.

Schaede, Ulrike (1995) 'The "old boy" network and government–business relationship in Japan', *The Journal of Japanese Studies* 21, 2: 293–317.

Schaeffer, Robert K. (1997) *Understanding Globalization: The Social Consequences of Political, Economic, and Environmental Change*, Oxford: Rowman and Littlefield.

Schaller, Michael (1985) *The American Occupation of Japan: The Origins of the Cold War in Asia*, Oxford: Oxford University Press.

—— (1997) *Altered States: The United States and Japan since the Occupation*, Oxford: Oxford University Press.

Schonberger, Howard B. (1989) *Aftermath of War: Americans and the Remaking of Japan, 1945–52*, Kent, OH: Kent State University Press.

Schoppa, Leonard J. (1999) 'The social context in coercive international bargaining', *International Organization* 53, 2: 307–42.

Schreurs, Miranda A. (1997) 'Japan's changing approach to environmental issues', *Environmental Politics* 6, 2: 150–6.

Schwartz, Frank J. (1998) *Advice and Consent: The Politics of Consultation in Japan*, Cambridge: Cambridge University Press.

Selden, Mark (1997) 'The regional political economy of East Asia', in Peter J. Katzenstein and Takashi Shiraishi (eds) *Network Power: Japan and Asia*, Ithaca: Cornell University Press, 306–40.

Sellek, Yoko (2000) *From Workers to Social Beings: Japanese Migration in a Globalized Economy*, London: Macmillan.

Sezaki, Katsumi (1991) '45th Session of the United Nations General Assembly', *Statements Delivered by Delegates of Japan*, Tokyo: United Nations Bureau, Ministry of Foreign Affairs.

Shigemitsu, Mamoru (1956) '11th Session of the United Nations General Assembly', *Statements Delivered by Delegates of Japan*, Tokyo: United Nations University.

Shikata, Toshiyuki (1995) 'The expanding role of Japan: opportunities and problems', in Trevor Taylor and Seizaburo Sato (eds) *Future Sources of Global Conflict*, London: Royal Institute of International Affairs, 107–23.

Shimazu, Naoko (1998) *Japan, Race and Equality: The Racial Equality Proposal of 1919*, London: Routledge.

Shiraishi, Masaya (1990) *Japan's Relations with Vietnam 1951–1987*, Ithaca: Cornell University Press.

Shiraishi, Takashi (1997) 'Japan and Southeast Asia', in Peter J. Katzenstein and Takashi Shiraishi (eds) *Network Power: Japan and Asia*, Ithaca: Cornell University Press, 169–94.

Shiraishi, Saya S. (1997) 'Japan's soft power: Doraemon goes overseas', in Peter J. Katzenstein and Takashi Shiraishi (eds) *Network Power: Japan and Asia*, Ithaca: Cornell University Press, 234–74.

Shono, Naomi (1981) 'A-bomb related research activities and antinuclear movements of Japanese scientists', *Hiroshima Peace Science* 4: 155–75.

Shono, Naomi, Matsuo, Masatsugu and Kumao, Kaneko (1993) 'Japan's role for the abolition of nuclear weapons', *Hiroshima Peace Science* 16: 175–204.

Soderberg, Marie (1996) 'Japanese ODA: the business perspective', in Marie Soderberg (ed.) *The Business of Japanese Foreign Aid: Five Cases from Asia*, London: Routledge, 72–88.

Stephan, John J. (1974) *The Kuril Islands: Russo-Japanese Frontier in the Pacific*, Oxford: Oxford University Press.

Steven, Rob (1991) 'Structural origins of Japan's direct foreign investment', in Jonathan Morris (ed.) *Japan and the Global Economy*, London: Routledge, 45–59.

Stockwin, J. A. A. (1988) 'Dynamic and immobilist aspects of Japanese politics', in J. A. A. Stockwin, Alan Rix, Aurelia George, James Horne, Daiichi Ito and Martin Collick, *Dynamic and Immobilist Politics in Japan*, London: Macmillan, 1–21.

—— (1998) 'The political system: stability and change', in Patrick Heenan (ed.) *The Japan Handbook*, London: Fitzroy Dearborn, 19–30.

—— (1999) *Governing Japan: Divided Politics in a Major Economy*, Oxford: Blackwell Publishers.

Stokes, Bruce (1996) 'Divergent paths: US–Japan relations towards the twenty-first century', *International Affairs* 72, 2: 281–92.

Storry, Richard (1982) *A History of Modern Japan*, London: Penguin.

Strange, Susan (1987) 'The persistent myth of lost hegemony', *International Organization* 41, 4: 551–74.

—— (1988) *States and Markets: An Introduction to International Political Economy*, London: Pinter.

Stubbs, Richard (1994) 'The political economy of the Asia-Pacific region', in Richard Stubbs and Geoffrey D. Underhill (eds) *Political Economy of and the Changing World Order*, London: Macmillan, 366–77.

Sudo, Sueo (1992) *The Fukuda Doctrine and ASEAN: New Dimensions in Japanese Foreign Policy*, Singapore: ISEAS.

Tanaka, Toshiro (1992) 'The EC 1992 and Japan: opportunity for co-operation', *Keio Hogaku Kenkyu* 65: 338–56.

Thrift, Nigel (ed.) (1994) *Globalisation, Institutions and Regional Development in Europe*, Oxford: Oxford University Press.

Thurow, Lester (1992) *Head to Head: The Coming Economic Battle among Japan, Europe and America*, London: Nicholas Brealey.

Ueno, Makiko (1998) 'Think tanks in Japan', in Diane Stone, Andrew Denham and Mark Garnett (eds) *Think Tanks across Nations: A Comparative Approach*, Manchester: Manchester University Press, 188–201.

Ueshiba, Morihei (1994) in John Stephens, Kissomaru Ueshina and Eric Chaline (eds) *The Essence of Aikido: Spiritual Teaching of Morihei Ueshiba*, Tokyo: Kodansha International.

United Nations (various years) *Index to Proceedings of the Security Council*, New York: United Nations.

—— (1994) UN Document A/49/527: Report of the Secretary General (17 October), New York: United Nations.

—— (1998) *The United Nations Handbook*, Wellington: New Zealand Ministry of Foreign Affairs and Trade 1975–1997.

US Department of Defense (1992) *East Asian Strategic Initiative*, Washington, DC: US Department of Defense.

Vadney, Thomas E. (1987) *The World since 1945*, London: Penguin.

Valencia, Mark J. (1995) *China and the South China Sea Disputes*, Oxford: Oxford University Press.

Vogel, Ezra (1979) *Japan as Number One: Lessons for America*, New York: Harper and Row.

—— (1986) 'Pax Nipponica?', *Foreign Affairs* 64, 4: 752–67.

Vogel, Stephen K. (1997) *Bargaining with Japan: What American Pressure Can and Cannot Do*, New York: Columbia University Press.

Wade, Robert (1996) 'Japan, the World Bank and the art of paradigm maintenance: the East Asian Miracle in political perspective', *New Left Review* 217: 3–36.

Waltz, Kenneth N. (1979) *Theory of International Politics*, Reading, MA: Addison-Wesley.

Wang, Jianwei and Wu, Xinbo (1998) *Against Us or with Us? The Chinese Perspective of America's Alliances with Japan and Korea*, Stanford: Asia-Pacific Research Center, Stanford University.

Watanabe, Osamu (1993) 'Nakasone Yasuhiro and post-war conservative politics: an historical interpretation', *Nissan Occasional Paper Series* 18.

Weiss, Linda (1998) *The Myth of the Powerless State: Governing the Economy in a Global Era*, Oxford: Polity Press.

Welfield, John (1970) *Japan and Nuclear China: Japanese Reactions to China's Nuclear Weapons*, Canberra: Australian National University Press.

—— (1988) *An Empire in Eclipse: Japan in the Postwar American Alliance System*, London: Athlone.

Wells, Peter, and Rawlinson, Michael (1994) *The New European Automobile Industry*, New York: St Martin's Press.

Wendt, Alexander (1992) 'Anarchy is what states makes of it: the social construction of power politics', *International Organization* 46, 2: 391–425.

—— (1994) 'Collective identity formation and the international system', *American Political Science Review* 88, 2: 384–96.

White, James W. (1970) *The Sokagakkai and Mass Society*, Stanford: Stanford University Press.

Whiting, Allen S. (1989) *China Eyes Japan*, Berkeley: University of California Press.

Wickens, Peter (1987) *The Road to Nissan*, London: Macmillan.

Wiener, Jarrod (1995) *Making Rules in the Uruguay Round of the GATT: A Study of International Leadership*, Aldershot: Dartmouth.

Wilkinson, Endymion (1981) *Misunderstanding: Europe versus Japan*, Tokyo: Chūō Kōronsha.

—— (1983) *Japan versus Europe: A History of Misunderstanding*, London: Penguin.

Williams, David (1994) *Japan: Beyond the End of History*, London: Routledge.

van Wolferen, Karel G. (1986/7) 'The Japan problem', *Foreign Affairs* 65, 2: 288–303.

—— (1990) *The Enigma of Japanese Power*, New York: Albert A. Knopf.

Woo-Cumings, Meredith (1995) 'The Asian Development Bank and the politics of development in East Asia', in Peter Gourevitch, Takashi Inoguchi and Courtney Purrington (eds) *United States–Japan Relations and International Institutions after the Cold War*, San Diego: Graduate School of International Relations and Pacific Studies, University of California, 227–49.

World Bank (1993) *The East Asian Miracle: Economic Growth and Public Policy*, Oxford: Oxford University Press.

—— (1999) 'World Bank financial statement' (30 June). Online. Available at: http://www.worldbank.org.

Woronoff, Jon (1991) *Japan as – Anything but – Number One*, London: Macmillan.

Yahuda, Michael (1996) *The International Politics of the Asia-Pacific, 1945–1995*, London: Routledge.

Yamaguchi, Noboru (1999) 'Trilateral security cooperation: opportunities, challenges and tasks', in Ralph A. Cossa (ed.) *US–Korea–Japan Relations: Building a 'Virtual Alliance'*, Washington, DC: CSIS, 3–24.

Yamakage, Susumu (1997) 'Japan's national security and Asia Pacific's regional institutions in the post-Cold War era', in Peter J. Katzenstein and Takashi Shiraishi (eds) *Network Power: Japan and Asia*, Ithaca: Cornell University Press, 275–308.

Yamashita, Shoichi (1998) 'Japanese investment strategy and technology transfer in East Asia', in Harukiyo Hasegawa and Glenn D. Hook (eds) *Japanese Business Management: Restructuring for Low Growth in Globalization*, London: Routledge, 61–79.

Yamazawa, Ippei (1992) 'On Pacific integration', *The Economic Journal* 102: 1519–29.

Yanaga, Chitose (1968) *Big Business in Japanese Politics*, New Haven: Yale University Press.

Yasutomo, Dennis T. (1986) *The Manner of Giving: Strategic Aid and Japanese Foreign Policy*, Lexington: Lexington Books.

—— (1995) *The New Multilateralism in Japan's Foreign Policy*, London: Macmillan.

Yoshitomi, Masaru (1991) *Japanese Direct Investment in Europe*, Aldershot: Avebury.

Zhao, Quansheng (1993) *Japanese Policymaking: The Politics behind Politics, Informal Mechanisms and the Making of China Policy*, Oxford: Oxford University Press.

—— (1998) 'Japan and China', in Patrick Heenan (ed.) *The Japan Handbook*, London: Fitzroy Dearborn, 236–45.

Japanese

Newspapers and Magazines

Asahi Shimbun
Mainichi Shimbun
Nihon Keizai Shimbun
Yomiuri Shimbun

Articles and Books

Akashi, Yasushi (1998) 'Nihon no wakamono yo, kokusai shakai ni habatake', *Gaikō Fōramu* 123 (November): 72–4.

Asahi Shimbunshahen (1999) *Japan Almanac 1999*, Tokyo: Asahi Shimbunsha.
Asai, Motofumi (1989) *Nihon Gaikō: Hansei to Tenkan*, Tokyo: Iwanami Shoten.
—— (1992) *Watakushi no Heiwagaikōron*, Tokyo: Shin Nihon Shuppansha.
—— (1995) *Taikoku Nippon no Sentaku: Kokuren Anzen Hoshōrijikai to Nippon*, Tokyo: Rōdōjunhosha.
—— (1997) *Koko ga Mondai: Shin Gaidorain Q&A*, Tokyo: Aoki Shoten.
Bōei Handobokku (1997) *Bōei Handobokku*, Tokyo: Asaguma Shimbunsha.
—— (1999) *Bōei Handobokku*, Tokyo: Asagumo Shimbunsha.
Bōei Kenkyūjo (various years) *Higashi Ajia Senryaku Gaikan*, Tokyo: Ōkurashō Insatsukyoku.
Bōeichōhen (various years) *Bōei Hakusho*, Tokyo: Ōkurashō Insatsukyoku.
—— (1980) *Bōei Hakusho*, Tokyo: Ōkurashō Insatsukyoku.
Bungei Shunjū (1990) *'Shōwa Tennō no dokuhaku hachi jikan: taiheiyō sensō nozenbō o kataru'*, Bungeishunjū 68,13: 94–145.
Eda, Kenji (1999) *Dare no Sei de Kaikaku o Ushinau ka?* Tokyo: Shinchōsha.
Fujiwara, Osamu (1992) 'Nihon no heiwa undō' (1), *Tokyo Keizai Daigaku Kaishi* 176: 15–39.
Fujizaki, Ichirō (1995) 'Aijia no jidai wo kangaeru', *Gaikō Jiho* 136: 4–13
Fukushima, Eiichi (1995) *NAFTA to Nihon Kigyō e no Eikyō*, Tokyo: JETRO.
Funabashi, Yōichi (1995) *Ajia Taiheiyō: APEC to Nihon*, Tokyo: Chūō Kōronsha.
—— (1997) *Dōmei Hyōryū*, Tokyo: Iwanami Shoten.
Gaikō Fōramu (1994) 'Intabyu: henkakuki ni okeru Nihon gaikō no yakuwari. Sōgō Gaikō Seisaku Kyoku sōsetsu ni atatte', *Gaikō Fōramu* (January): 59–66.
—— (1998) 'Shiruku rōdo gaikō', *Gaikō Fōramu* 124 (December): 12–62.
Gomi, Hisatoshi (1999) *Gurōbaru Kyapitalizumu to Ajia Shihonshugi. Chūgoku, Ajia Shihonshugi no Taitō to Sekai Shihonshugi no Saihen*, Tokyo: Hihyōsha.
Hahei Chekku Henshū Iinkai (1997) *Kore ga Beigun e no 'Omoi yari Yosan' da*, Tokyo: Shakai Hyōronsha.
Handa, Shigeru (1999) '"Muda na heiki" jieitai kara hihan sareru TMD sanka', *Gunshuku Mondai Shiryō* 230: 38–41.
Hara, Yoshihisa (1988) *Sengo Nihon to Kokusai Seiji*, Tokyo: Chūō Kōronsha.
Haraguchi, Kōichi (1995) 'Nichibei hōkatsu keizai kyōgi: haikei, keiei, kadai', *Kokusai Mondai* 419: 63–77.
Hatoyama, Yukio (1999) 'Jieitai o guntai to mitomeyo', *Bungei Shunjū* 77, 10: 262–73.
Hōgaku Seminā Henshū Bu (1999) 'Shin gaidorain kanrenhō no seiritsu wa nani o motarasuka', *Hōgaku Seminā* 536: 6–7.
Igarashi, Takeshi (1999) *Nichibei Kankei to Higashi Ajia. Rekishiteki Bunmyaku to Mirai no Kōsō*, Tokyo: Tokyo Daigaku Shuppankai.
Inoguchi, Takashi and Iwai, Tomoaki (1987) *Zoku Giin no Kenkyū: Jimintō Seiken o Gyūjiru Shuyakutachi*, Tokyo: Nihon Keizai Shimbunsha.
Iokibe, Makoto (1996) 'Kokusai kankyō to Nihon no sentaku', in Aruga Tadashi, Uno Shigeru, Kido Shigeru, Yamamoto Yoshinobu and Watanabe Akio (eds) *Nihon no Gaikō*, Tokyo: Tokyo Daigaku Shuppankai, 19–52.
—— (1999) *Sengo Nihon Gaikōshi*, Tokyo: Yūhikakusha.
Ise, Momoyo (1998) 'Kokuren no jinji to Nihon: kiki ni tatsu kokusai kōmin seido', *Kokusai Mondai* 465: 54–68.
Ishibashi, Masashi (1980) *Hibusō Chūritsu Ron*, Tokyo: Nihon Shakaitō Chūō Honbu Kikanshikyoku.
Ishida, Hiroshi (1975) *Koji Seigo Kotowaza Jiten*, Tokyo: Yūzankyaku.
Ishida, Ken (1998) 'Nihon kara mita Kokuren Kaikakuron no Sanchōryū', *Chiba Daigaku Hōgaku Ronshū* 23, 3: 123–45.

Ishihara, Shintarō and Morita, Akio (1989) *'No' to Ieru Nippon*, Tokyo: Kōbunsha (an unofficial translation of this Japanese version, which differs from that published in English listed in the English bibliography, appeared in 1989 in the United States under the title, *The Japan that Can Say 'No': The New US–Japan Relations Card*, Washington, DC).

Ishiyama, Toshihiko (1985) 'Hikaku Kobe kō no jikken', in Masaru Nishida (ed.) *Hikaku Jijitai Undō no Riron to Jissai*, Tokyo: Orijin Shuppan Sentā.

Itō, Takeshi (1985) *Hiroshima Nagasaki kara Mirai e*, Tokyo: Keisō Shobo.

Iwanaga, Kenichirō (1985) *Sengo Nihon no Seitō to Gaikō*, Tokyo: Tokyo Daigaku Shuppankai.

JETRO (various years) *Sekai to Nihon no Chokusetsu Tōshi*, Tokyo: Ōkurashō Insatsukyoku.

—— (1999a) *JETRO Bōeki Hakusho*, Tokyo: JETRO.

—— (1999b) *JETRO, Jettoro Tōshi Hakusho*, Tokyo: JETRO.

Kaminishi, Akio (1986) *GNP 1% Waku*, Tokyo: Kadokawa Shoten.

Kan, Hideki (1992) *Beisō Reisen to America no Ajia Seisaku*, Kyoto: Mineruva Shobo.

Kanetsuna, Motoyuki (1996) 'Nihon kigyō no gurobaru netowōku', in Masaki Yokoyama and Hideyuki Wakui (eds) *Posuto Reisen to Ajia: Ajia no Kaihatsushugi to Kankyō, Heiwa*, Tokyo: Chūō Keizaisha, 129–64.

Kawada, Tsukasa (1998) 'Kokuren kaikaku to Nihon: kaikaku no keii to kongo no hōkōsei', *Kokusai Mondai* 465: 38–53.

Kawakami, Tamio (1994) *Shakaitō no Gaikō: Atarashii Jidaizukuri no tame ni*, Tokyo: Saimaru Shuppankai.

Kimura, Masato (1989) 'Nihon no taikankokuminkan keizai gaikō', *Kokusai Seiji* 92: 116–31.

Kitaoka, Shinichi (1995) *Jimintō. Seikentō no 38 nen*, Tokyo: Yomiuri Shimbunsha.

—— (2000) '"Omoiyari Yosan" no Sakugen', *Chūō Kōron* (March): 42–5.

Kokusai Higashi Ajia Kenkyū Sentā (ed.) (1995) *Kenshō: Kankōkai Keizaiken. Kyokuchi Keizaiken no Keisei ni Mukete*, Kitakyūshūshi: Kokusai Higashi Ajia Kokusai Sentā.

Kōsaka, Masataka (1963) 'Genjitsushugisha no heiwaron', *Chūō Kōron* (January): 38–49.

Kusano, Atsushi (1993) 'Taigaiseisaku kettei no kōsō to katei', in Tadashi Aruga, Shigeaki Uno, Shigeru Kido, Yoshinobu Yamamoto, and Akio Watanabe (eds) *Nihon no Gaikō*, Tokyo: Tokyo Daigaku Shuppankai.

Mahathir, Mohamad and Ishihara, Shintarō (1994) *'No' to Ieru Ajia: Tai Ōbei e no Hōsaku*, Tokyo: Kōbunsha (an English translation of this Japanese version is cited in the English bibliography: Mahathir and Ishihara 1996).

Murata, Kōji (1998) *Daitōryō no Zasetsu: Kātā Seiken no Zaikan Biegun Tettai Seisaku*, Tokyo: Yūhikakusha.

Muroyama, Yoshimasa (1992) *Nichibei Anpōtaisei* (jō), Tokyo: Yūhikakusha.

Nagasu, Kasuji and Sakamoto, Yoshikazu (eds) (1983) *Jijitai no Kokusai Kōryū*, Tokyo: Gakuyū Shobo.

Naikaku Sōri Daijin Kōhōshitsu (1997) *Gaikō ni kan suru Yoron Chōsa* (May), Tokyo: Naikaku Sōri Daijin Kanbōshitsu.

—— (1998) *Gaikō ni kan suru Yoron Chōsa* (May), Tokyo: Naikaku Sōri Daijin Kanbōshitsu.

Nakajima, Kuniko (1999) 'Nihon no gaikō seisaku kettei yōin ni okeru Jiyū Minshutō Seimu Chōsakai no yakuwari', in Hashimoto Kōhei (ed.) *Nihon no Gaikō Seisaku Kettei Yōin*, Tokyo: PHP Kenkyūjo, 70–105.

Nakamura, Kenichi (1985) 'Soren kyōiron kara no dakkyaku', *Sekai* (April): 56–73.

Nihon Ginkō (various years), *Keizai Tōkei Nenpō*, Tokyo: Nihon Ginkō.

Nihon Hōsō Kyōkai (NHK) (1991) *Gendai Nihonjin no Ishiki Kōzō*, Tokyo: NHK Books.

Nihon Keizai Shimbunsha (ed.) (1995) *Dokyumento. Nichibei Jidōsha Kyōgi*, Tokyo: Nihon Keizai Shimbunsha.

Nihon Seijigakkai (ed.) (1996) *55 nen Taisei no Hōkai. Nenpō Seijigaku 1996*, Tokyo: Iwanami Shoten.
Nihon Toshi Sentā (ed.) (1995) *Toshi Gaikō. Jijitai no Kokusai Kōryū*, Toyko: Nihon Toshi Sentā.
Nishihara, Masashi (1994) 'Ajia taiheiyō chiiki to takokukan anzen hoshō kyōryoku wakugumi: ASEAN Chiiki Fōramu o chūshin ni', *Kokusai Mondai* (October): 60–74.
Ōhara, Yoshio (1999) 'Nichibei bōeki kōshō to WTO', *Kokusai Mondai* 470: 16–28.
Oka, Yoshitake (1958) *Gendai Nihon no Seiji Katei*, Tokyo: Iwanami Shoten.
Okinawa Taimususha (ed.) (1997) *Okinawa kara. Beigun Kichi Mondai Dokkyumento*, Tokyo: Asahi Shimbunsha.
Ōnishi, Hitoshi (1985) 'Nihon no hankaku undō: 1982-nen zenhan no SSDII Kokumin Undō Suishin Renkaku Kaigi no undō ochūshin ni' (jō), *Hōgaku* (Tōhoku University) 49, 2: 167–200.
Ōtake, Isshō (1995) 'Tenanmon jiken to Nihon gaikō: genkaika nokagami toshite no Nihon', in Tomoyuki Kojima (ed.) *Ajia Jidai no Nicchū Kankei: Kakō to Mirai*, Tokyo: Saimaru Shuppankai, 119–35.
Ozawa, Ichirō (1999) 'Nihon koku kenpō kaisei shian', *Bungeishunjū* 77, 9: 94–106.
Sakamoto, Yoshikazu (1959) 'Chūritsu Nihon no bōei kōsō', reprinted in Yoshikazu Sakamoto (1982) *Kakujidai no Kokusai Seiji*, Tokyo: Iwanami Shoten, 3–29.
Satō, Seizaburō and Matsuzaki, Tetsuhisa (1984) 'Jimintō chōchōki Seiken ni kaibai', *Chūōkōron* (November): 86–94.
Seisaku Jihōsha (1999) *Seikan Yōran* 17, 35.
Shindō, Muneyuki (1992) *Gyōsei Shidō*, Tokyo: Iwanami Shoten.
Sudō, Sueo (1997) 'Nihon gaikō ni okeru ASEAN no chii', *Kokusai Seiji* 116: 147–64.
Suzuki, Ikutarō (1998) 'Hokubei shijō senryaku', in Masaharu Inabetsu (ed.) *Honda no Beikoku Genchi Keiei. HAM no Sōgō Kenkyū* (new edn), Tokyo: Bunshindō, 141–59.
Takenaka, Heizō (1994) 'Kulintonseiken no shinsenryaku "NAFTA to APEC no nerai"', *Ushio* 419 (February): 106–15.
Takii, Mitsuo (1996) 'NAFTA to Nihon kigyō no taiō', in Takeshi Aoki and Keiichi Umada (eds) *Nichibei Keizai Kankei. Arata na Wakugumi to Nihon no Sentaku*, Tokyo: Keisō Shobo, 105–29.
Tamura, Shigenobu (1997) *Nichibei Anpo to Kyokutō Yūji*, Tokyo: Nansōsha.
Tanaka, Akihiko (1991) *Nicchū Kankei 1945–1990*, Tokyo: Tokyo Daigaku Shuppankai.
—— (1997) *Anzen Hoshō: Sengo 50nen no Mosaku*, Tokyo: Yomiuri Shimbunsha.
Tanaka, Hiroto (1997) 'Ruwanda nanmin kinkyū enjo to NGO', in Hisakazu Usui and Mikio Takase (eds) *Minsai Gaikō no Kenkyū*, Tokyo: Sanrei Shobo, 249–70.
Tōkai Daigakuhen (Tōkai Daigaku Heiwa Senryaku Kokusai Kenkyūjohen) (1997) *Nichibei Anpo to Okinawa Mondai. Bunseki to Shiryō*, Tokyo: Shakai Hyōronsha.
Tōyō Keizai Shimbunsha (1999) *Seikai Kanchō Jinjiroku*, Tokyo: Tōyō Keizai Shimbunsha.
Tsuchiya, Motohiro (1995) 'Nichibei handōtai masatsu no bunseki', *Hōgaku Seijigaku Ronkyū* (Keiō University) 25: 343–72.
Tsūshō Sangyōshō (various years) *Tsūshō Hakusho*, Tokyo: Ōkurashō Insatsukyoku.
—— (1976) *Tsūshō Hakusho*, Tokyo: Ōkurashō Insatsukyoku.
—— (1986) *Tsūshō Hakusho*, Tokyo: Ōkurashō Insatsukyoku.
Wada, Haruki (1999) *Hoppo Ryōdo Mondai*, Tokyo: Asahi Shimbunsha.
Wakamiya, Yoshibumi (1994) *Wasurerarenai Kokkai Ronsen*, Tokyo: Chūkō Shinsho.
Yamashita, Masamitsu, Takai, Susumu and Iwata, Shūichiro (1994) *TMD. Seiki Dandō Misairu Bōei*, Tokyo: TBS Britannia.

Tables

Table 1 Japan's trade 1950–98 (US$ millions)

	1950	1955	1960	1965	1970	1975	1980	1985	1990	1995	1996	1997	1998
WORLD													
Exports	820	2,011	4,055	8,452	19,318	55,753	129,807	175,638	286,948	442,937	410,872	420,896	387,958
Imports	974	2,471	4,491	8,169	18,881	57,863	140,528	129,539	234,799	336,094	349,124	349,124	280,505
Total	1,794	4,482	8,546	16,621	38,199	113,616	270,335	305,177	521,747	779,031	759,996	770,020	668,463
Trade balance	–154	–460	–436	283	437	–2,110	–10,721	46,099	52,149	106,843	61,748	71,772	107,453
US													
Exports	179	449	1,083	2,479	5,940	11,149	31,367	65,278	90,322	120,859	111,855	117,092	118,429
% of total exports	21.8	22.3	26.7	29.3	30.7	20.0	24.2	37.2	31.5	27.3	27.2	27.8	30.5
Imports	427	773	1,545	2,366	5,560	11,608	24,408	25,793	52,369	75,408	79,376	75,693	67,026
% of total imports	43.8	31.3	34.4	29.0	29.4	20.1	17.4	19.9	22.3	22.4	22.7	21.7	23.9
Total trade	628	1,244	2,655	4,874	11,531	22,777	55,799	91,108	142,722	196,294	191,258	192,813	185,486
% total trade	35.0	27.8	31.1	29.3	30.2	20.0	20.6	29.9	27.4	25.2	25.2	25.0	27.7
Trade balance	–248	–324	–462	113	380	–459	6,959	39,485	37,953	45,451	32,479	41,399	51,403
EAST ASIA													
Exports	254	474	863	1,794	4,595	13,632	33,383	42,275	87,978	186,546	174,262	170,840	128,666
% total exports	31.0	23.6	21.3	21.2	23.8	24.5	25.7	24.1	30.7	42.1	42.4	40.6	33.2
Imports	214	520	636	1,288	2,692	10,261	31,396	33,041	62,428	115,519	122,855	117,680	98,014
% total imports	22.0	21.0	14.2	15.8	14.3	17.7	22.3	25.5	26.6	34.4	35.2	33.7	34.9
Total trade	468	994	1,499	3,082	7,287	23,893	64,779	75,316	150,406	302,065	297,117	288,520	226,680
% total trade	26.1	22.2	17.5	18.5	19.1	21.0	24.0	24.7	28.8	38.8	39.1	37.5	33.9
Trade balance	40	–46	227	506	1,903	3,371	1,987	9,234	25,550	71,027	51,407	53,160	30,652
CHINA													
Exports	20	29	3	245	569	2,259	5,078	12,477	6,130	21,931	21,806	21,689	20,105
% total exports	2.4	1.4	0.1	2.9	2.9	4.1	3.9	7.1	2.1	5.0	5.3	5.2	5.2
Imports	40	81	21	225	254	1,531	4,323	6,483	12,054	35,922	40,370	41,846	37,085
% total imports	4	3.3	0.5	2.8	1.3	2.6	3.1	5.0	5.1	10.7	11.6	12.0	13.2
Total trade	60	110	24	470	823	3,790	9,401	18,960	18,184	57,853	62,176	63,535	57,190
% total trade	3.3	2.5	0.3	2.8	2.2	3.3	3.5	6.2	3.5	7.4	8.2	8.3	8.6
Trade balance	–20	–52	–18	20	315	728	755	5,994	–5,924	–13,991	–18,564	–20,157	–16,980

	1950	1955	1960	1965	1970	1975	1980	1985	1990	1995	1996	1997	1998
NIEs-4													
Exports	123	251	445	810	2,641	6,972	19,186	22,491	59,667	111,036	101,403	101,140	78,314
% total exports	15.0	12.5	11.0	9.6	13.7	12.5	14.8	12.8	20.8	25.1	24.7	24.0	20.2
Imports	55	113	120	266	659	2,764	7,365	9,839	25,947	41,218	40,827	35,227	28,804
% total imports	5.6	4.6	2.7	3.3	3.5	4.8	5.2	7.6	11.1	12.3	11.7	10.1	10.3
Total trade	178	364	565	1,076	3,300	9,736	26,551	32,330	85,635	152,279	142,255	129,665	107,530
% total trade	9.9	8.1	6.6	6.5	8.6	8.6	9.8	10.6	16.4	19.5	18.7	16.8	16.1
Trade balance	68	138	325	544	1,982	4,208	11,821	12,652	33,720	69,818	52,066	59,626	49,411
South Korea													
Exports	18	40	100	180	818	2,248	5,368	7,097	17,457	31,291	29,338	26,086	15,401
Imports	16	10	19	41	229	1,308	2,996	4,092	11,707	17,269	15,955	14,590	12,117
Total trade	34	50	119	221	1,047	3,556	8,364	11,189	29,164	48,560	45,293	40,676	27,518
Trade balance	2	30	81	139	589	940	2,372	3,005	5,750	14,022	13,383	11,496	3,284
Taiwan													
Exports	38	64	102	218	700	1,822	5,146	5,025	18,430	28,969	25,953	27,552	25,602
Imports	38	81	64	157	251	812	2,293	3,386	8,496	14,366	14,971	12,506	10,237
Total trade	76	145	166	375	951	2,634	7,439	8,411	26,926	43,335	40,924	40,058	35,839
Trade balance	0	–17	38	61	449	1,010	2,853	1,639	9,934	14,603	10,982	15,046	15,365
Hong Kong													
Exports	53	88	156	288	700	1,378	4,761	6,509	13,072	27,775	25,337	27,241	22,529
Imports	0.5	6	23	35	92	245	569	767	2,173	2,739	2,576	2,252	1,733
Total trade	54	94	179	323	792	1,623	5,330	7,276	15,245	30,514	16,315	22,791	24,674
Trade balance	53	82	133	253	608	1,133	4,192	5,742	10,899	25,036	14,251	18,702	20,697
Singapore													
Exports	14	59	87	124	423	1,524	3,911	3,860	10,708	23,001	20,775	20,261	14,782
Imports	0	16	14	33	87	399	1,507	1,594	3,571	6,844	7,325	5,879	4,717
Total trade	14	75	101	157	510	1,923	5,418	5,454	14,279	29,845	28,100	26,140	19,499
Trade balance	14	43	73	91	336	1,125	2,404	2,266	7,137	16,157	13,450	14,382	10,065

	1950	1955	1960	1965	1970	1975	1980	1985	1990	1995	1996	1997	1998
ASEAN-4													
Exports	111	194	415	739	1,385	4,401	9,119	7,307	22,181	53,579	51,053	48,011	30,247
% exports	13.5	9.6	10.2	8.7	7.2	7.9	7.0	4.2	7.7	12.1	12.4	11.4	7.8
Imports	119	326	495	797	1,779	5,966	19,708	16,719	24,427	38,379	41,658	40,607	32,125
% imports	12.2	13.2	11.0	9.8	9.4	10.3	14.0	12.9	10.4	11.4	11.9	11.6	11.5
Total trade	230	520	910	1,536	3,164	10,367	28,827	24,026	46,608	91,958	92,711	88,618	62,372
% total trade	12.8	11.6	10.6	9.2	8.3	9.1	10.7	7.9	8.9	11.8	12.2	11.5	9.3
Trade balance	–8	–132	–80	–58	–394	–1,565	– 10,589	–9,412	–2,246	15,200	9,395	7,404	–1,878
Thailand													
Exports	43	63	118	219	449	959	1,917	2,030	9,126	19,715	18,285	14,613	9,347
Imports	44	63	72	131	190	724	1,119	1,027	4,147	10,134	10,213	9,574	8,170
Total trade	87	126	190	350	639	1,683	3,036	3,057	13,273	29,849	28,498	24,187	17,517
Trade balance	–1	0	46	88	259	235	798	1,003	4,979	9,581	8,072	5,039	1,177
Malaysia													
Exports	4	14	32	75	166	566	2,061	2,168	5,511	16,795	15,326	14,519	9,331
Imports	39	93	194	263	419	691	3,471	4,330	5,402	10,549	11,746	11,382	8,687
Total trade	43	107	226	338	585	1,257	5,532	6,498	10,913	27,344	27,072	25,901	18,018
Trade balance	–35	–79	–162	–188	–253	–125	–1,410	–2,162	109	6,246	3,580	3,137	644
Philippines													
Exports	18	52	155	240	454	1,026	1,683	937	2,504	7,098	8,390	8,691	7,267
Imports	23	89	159	254	533	1,121	1,951	1,243	2,157	3,482	4,513	5,022	4,427
Total Trade	41	141	314	494	987	2,147	3,634	2,180	4,661	10,580	12,903	13,713	11,694
Trade balance	–5	–37	–4	–14	–79	–95	–268	–306	6,818	14,062	3,877	3,669	2,840
Indonesia													
Exports	46	65	110	205	316	1,850	3,458	2,172	5,040	9,971	9,052	10,188	4,302
Imports	13	81	70	149	637	3,430	13,167	10,119	12,721	14,214	15,186	14,629	10,841
Total trade	59	146	180	354	953	5,280	16,625	12,291	17,761	24,185	24,238	24,817	15,143
Trade balance	33	–16	40	56	–321	–1,580	–9,709	–7,947	–7,681	–4,243	–6,134	–4,441	–6,539
North Korea													
Exports	0	0	1	17	23	181	374	247	176	255	227	179	175
Imports	0	0	0.008	15	34	65	180	179	300	340	291	302	219
Total trade	0	0	1	32	57	246	554	426	476	595	518	481	394
Trade balance	0	0	1	2	–11	116	194	68	–124	–85	–64	–123	–44

	1950	1955	1960	1965	1970	1975	1980	1985	1990	1995	1996	1997	1998
Brunei													
Exports	0	0	0	0	10	34	88	90	86	131	132	149	62
Imports	0	0	0	0	1	1,021	3,245	1,892	1,262	1,349	1,393	1,407	1,028
Total trade	0	0	0	0	−10	−34	−88	−90	1,348	1,480	1,525	1,556	1,090
Trade balance	0	0	0	0	10	−987	−3,157	−1,802	−1,176	−1,218	−1,261	−1,258	−966
Vietnam													
Exports	—	—	—	—	—	—	113	149	214	921	1,136	1,278	1,333
Imports	—	—	—	—	—	—	49	65	595	1,716	2,012	2,189	1,748
Total trade	—	—	—	—	—	—	162	214	809	2,637	3,148	3,467	3,081
Trade balance	—	—	—	—	—	—	64	84	−381	−795	−876	−911	−415
North Vietnam													
Exports	—	—	6	4	5	43	—	—	—	—	—	—	—
Imports	—	—	10	12	6	27	—	—	—	—	—	—	—
Total trade	—	—	16	16	11	70	—	—	—	—	—	—	—
Trade balance	—	—	−4	−8	−1	16	—	—	—	—	—	—	—
South Vietnam													
Exports	—	—	62	37	146	39	—	—	—	—	—	—	—
Imports	—	—	5	7	5	15	—	—	—	—	—	—	—
Total trade	—	—	67	44	151	54	—	—	—	—	—	—	—
Trade balance	—	—	57	30	141	24	—	—	—	—	—	—	—
Cambodia													
Exports	—	—	14	13	11	0.1	25	2	5	77	56	58	45
Imports	—	—	8	8	6	0.6	0.6	0.4	3	7	7	13	16
Total trade	—	—	22	21	17	0.7	25.6	2.4	8	84	63	71	61
Trade balance	—	—	6	5	5	−0.5	24.4	1.6	2	70	49	45	29
Laos													
Exports	—	—	2	1	7	4	12	12	20	29	39	29	19
Imports	—	—	0	0	0.049	1	6	1	5	30	24	21	20
Total trade	—	—	2	1	7.049	5	18	13	25	59	63	50	39
Trade balance	—	—	2	1	6.951	3	6	11	15	−1	15	8	−1

	1950	1955	1960	1965	1970	1975	1980	1985	1990	1995	1996	1997	1998
Indo-China (Vietnam, Laos, Cambodia)													
Exports	2	37	—	—	—	—	—	—	—	—	—	—	—
Imports	2	6	—	—	—	—	—	—	—	—	—	—	—
Total trade	4	43	—	—	—	—	—	—	—	—	—	—	—
Trade balance	0	31	—	—	—	—	—	—	—	—	—	—	—
Burma													
Exports	16	38	65	76	39	61	214	184	101	157	254	211	187
Imports	18	46	13	26	13	25	76	35	41	94	103	99	89
Total trade	34	84	78	102	52	86	290	219	142	251	357	310	276
Trade balance	–2	–8	52	50	26	36	138	149	60	63	151	112	98
REST OF EAST ASIA													
Exports	18	75	150	148	241	362	826	684	602	1,570	1,844	1,904	1,821
% exports	2.2	3.7	3.7	1.8	1.2	0.6	0.6	0.4	0.2	0.4	0.4	0.5	0.5
Imports	20	52	36	68	65	1,155	3,557	2,172	2,206	3,536	3,830	4,031	3,120
% imports	2.1	2.1	0.8	0.8	0.3	2.0	2.5	1.7	0.9	1.1	1.1	1.2	1.1
Total trade	38	127	186	216	306	1,517	4,383	2,856	2,808	5,106	5,674	5,935	4,941
% total trade	2.1	2.8	2.2	1.3	0.8	1.3	1.6	0.9	0.5	0.7	0.7	0.8	0.7
Trade balance	–2	23	114	80	176	–793	–2,731	–1,488	–1,604	–1,966	–1,986	–2,127	–1,299
EEC/EC/EU													
Exports	0	0	174	484	1,302	5,675	17,195	20,017	53,519	70,289	62,927	65,502	71,481
% total exports	0.0	0.0	4.3	5.7	6.7	10.2	13.2	11.4	18.7	15.9	15.3	15.6	18.4
Imports	0	0	209	392	1,119	3,371	7,879	8,893	35,030	48,812	49,306	44,970	39,056
% total imports	0.0	0.0	4.7	4.8	5.9	5.8	5.6	6.9	14.9	14.5	14.1	12.9	13.9
Total trade	0	0	383	876	2,421	9,046	25,074	28,910	88,549	119,101	112,233	110,472	110,537
% total trade	0.0	0.0	4.5	5.3	6.3	8.0	9.3	9.5	17.0	15.3	14.8	14.3	16.5
Trade balance	0	0	–35	92	183	2,304	9,316	11,124	18,489	21,477	13,621	20,532	32,425
EEC													
Exports	—	—	174	484	1,302	—	—	—	—	—	—	—	—
Imports	—	—	209	392	1,119	—	—	—	—	—	—	—	—
Total trade	—	—	383	876	2,421	—	—	—	—	—	—	—	—
Trade balance	—	—	–35	92	183	—	—	—	—	—	—	—	—

	1950	1955	1960	1965	1970	1975	1980	1985	1990	1995	1996	1997	1998
EC													
Exports	—	—	—	—	—	5,675	17,195	20,017	53,519	—	—	—	—
Imports	—	—	—	—	—	3,371	7,879	8,893	35,030	—	—	—	—
Total trade	—	—	—	—	—	9,046	25,074	28,910	88,549	—	—	—	—
Trade balance	—	—	—	—	—	2,304	9,316	11,124	18,489	—	—	—	—
EU													
Exports	—	—	—	—	—	—	—	—	—	70,289	62,927	65,502	71,481
Imports	—	—	—	—	—	—	—	—	—	48,812	49,306	44,970	39,056
Total trade	—	—	—	—	—	—	—	—	—	119,101	112,233	110,472	110,537
Trade balance	—	—	—	—	—	—	—	—	—	21,477	13,621	20,532	32,425
France													
Exports	10	12	16	49	127	699	2,021	2,083	6,128	6,067	5,381	5,625	6,197
Imports	5	15	32	63	186	501	1,296	1,324	7,590	6,696	6,259	5,771	5,737
Total trade	15	27	48	112	313	1,200	3,317	3,407	13,718	12,763	11,640	11,396	11,934
Trade balance	5	–3	–16	–14	–59	198	725	759	–1,462	–629	–878	–146	460
Belgium + Luxemburg													
Exports	5	10	24	49	156	510	1,426	1,493	3,860	4,867	4,325	4,142	4,734
Imports	5	9	13	25	75	162	375	484	1,617	2,391	2,364	1,846	1,530
Total trade	10	19	37	74	231	672	1,801	1,977	5,477	7,258	6,689	5,988	6,264
Trade balance	0	1	11	24	81	348	1,051	1,009	2,243	2,476	1,961	2,296	3,204
Netherlands													
Exports	0	27	39	119	277	726	2,061	2,071	6,165	9,915	9,255	9,791	10,860
Imports	0	12	28	43	104	214	380	439	1,170	2,178	2,104	1,956	1,839
Total trade	0	39	67	162	381	940	2,441	2,510	7,335	12,093	11,359	11,747	12,699
Trade balance	0	15	11	76	173	512	1,681	1,632	4,995	7,737	7,151	7,835	9,021
Italy													
Exports	0	8	29	52	192	334	955	1,117	3,409	4,063	3,389	3,786	4,260
Imports	0	13	13	38	134	365	938	1,050	5,008	6,364	6,769	5,934	5,099
Total trade	0	21	42	90	326	699	1,893	2,167	8,417	10,427	10,158	9,720	9,359
Trade balance	0	–5	16	14	58	–31	17	67	–1,599	–2,301	–3,380	–2,148	–839
Germany													
Exports	10	25	66	215	550	1,661	5,756	6,938	17,782	20,317	18,212	17,982	19,091
Imports	7	46	123	223	620	1,139	2,501	2,928	11,487	13,705	14,169	12,414	10,711
Total trade	17	71	189	438	1,170	2,800	8,257	9,866	29,269	34,022	32,381	30,396	29,802
Trade balance	3	–21	–57	–8	–70	522	3,255	4,010	6,295	6,612	4,043	5,568	8,380

	1950	1955	1960	1965	1970	1975	1980	1985	1990	1995	1996	1997	1998
UK													
Exports	26	61	121	205	480	1,473	3,782	4,723	10,786	14,141	12,476	13,706	14,599
Imports	6	38	99	163	395	810	1,954	1,817	5,239	7,151	7,166	7,183	5,849
Total trade	32	99	220	368	875	2,283	5,736	6,540	16,025	21,292	19,642	20,889	20,448
Trade balance	20	23	22	42	85	663	1,828	2,906	5,547	6,990	5,310	6,523	8,750
Ireland													
Exports	0	4	8	9	15	58	221	257	944	2,068	1,911	2,171	2,415
Imports	0	0	0	2	11	34	78	209	636	1,984	2,100	2,283	2,184
Total trade	0	4	8	11	26	92	299	466	1,580	4,052	4,011	4,454	4,599
Trade balance	0	4	8	7	4	24	143	48	308	84	–189	–112	231
Denmark													
Exports	0	6	13	44	64	214	428	758	969	913	807	790	825
Imports	0	2	5	15	30	146	321	579	1,126	1,930	1,708	1,708	1,440
Total trade	0	8	18	59	94	360	749	1,337	2,095	2,843	2,515	2,498	2,265
Trade balance	0	4	8	29	34	68	107	179	–157	–1,017	–901	–918	–615
Greece													
Exports	0	4	43	48	307	337	545	577	824	660	797	664	891
Imports	0	1	4	7	13	40	36	63	149	107	90	92	73
Total trade	0	5	47	55	320	377	581	640	973	767	887	756	964
Trade balance	0	3	39	41	294	297	509	514	675	553	707	572	818
Spain													
Exports	0	3	3	22	104	302	410	605	2,092	2,274	2,063	2,080	2,649
Imports	0	12	17	20	28	115	389	350	793	1,437	1,461	1,283	1,140
Total trade	0	15	20	42	132	417	799	955	2,885	3,711	3,524	3,363	3,789
Trade balance	0	–9	–14	2	76	187	21	255	1,299	837	602	797	1,509
Portugal													
Exports	0	0	9	3	37	88	264	173	560	726	755	806	974
Imports	0	1	3	6	9	25	54	55	215	223	190	168	151
Total trade	0	1	12	9	46	113	318	228	775	949	945	974	1,125
Trade balance	0	–1	6	–3	28	63	210	118	345	503	565	638	823

	1950	1955	1960	1965	1970	1975	1980	1985	1990	1995	1996	1997	1998
Austria													
Exports	0	2	6	6	25	87	400	473	1,616	1,197	969	992	1,008
Imports	0	1	7	6	16	52	170	180	705	905	963	875	614
Total trade	0	3	13	12	41	139	570	653	2,321	2,102	1,932	1,867	1,622
Trade balance	0	1	–1	0	9	35	230	293	911	292	6	117	394
Sweden													
Exports	7	13	37	61	99	384	793	1,094	1,954	1,695	1,438	1,630	1,595
Imports	6	5	11	34	89	199	463	441	1,292	2,586	2,798	2,559	1,955
Total trade	13	18	48	95	188	583	1,256	1,535	3,246	4,281	4,236	4,189	3,550
Trade balance	1	8	26	27	10	185	330	653	662	–891	–1,360	–929	–360
Finland													
Exports	0	4	3	18	54	127	387	489	1,046	1,386	1,149	1,337	1,383
Imports	0	1	1	3	11	33	120	217	441	1,155	1,165	898	734
Total trade	0	5	4	21	65	160	507	706	1,487	2,541	2,314	2,235	2,117
Trade balance	0	3	2	15	43	94	267	272	605	231	–16	439	649

Source: Tsūshō Sangyōshō various years.

Notes

'East Asia' consists of: China, NIEs-4 and ASEAN-4.

'Rest of East Asia' consists of: North Korea, Brunei, Indo-China and Burma until 1955; North Korea, Brunei, South and North Vietnam, Cambodia, Laos and Burma until 1975; North Korea, Brunei, Vietnam, Cambodia, Laos and Burma from 1975 to 1998.

'EEC' consists of: France, Belgium, Luxemburg, Netherlands, Italy and Germany.

'EC' consists of: France, Belgium, Luxemburg, Netherlands, Italy, Germany, UK, Ireland and Denmark until 1979; France, Belgium, Luxemburg, Netherlands, Italy, Germany, UK, Ireland, Denmark and Greece from 1980 until 1985; and France, Belgium, Luxemburg, Netherlands, Italy, Germany, UK, Ireland, Denmark, Greece, Spain and Portugal from 1981 until 1994.

'EU' consists of: France, Belgium, Luxemburg, Netherlands, Italy, Germany, UK, Ireland, Denmark, Greece, Spain, Portugal, Austria, Sweden and Finland from 1995 onwards.

Table 2 Japan's FDI 1951–97 (US$ millions)

	1951–64	*1965*	*1970*	*1975*	*1980*	*1985*	*1986*	*1987*	*1988*	*1989*	*1990*	*1995*	*1996*	*1997*
WORLD														
FDI to	790	159	904	3,280	4,693	12,217	22,320	33,364	47,022	67,540	56,911	50,694	48,019	53,972
FDI from	0	0	0	0	299	930	940	2,214	3,243	2,860	2,778	3,837	6,841	5,527
Total FDI	790	159	904	3,280	4,992	13,147	23,260	35,578	50,265	70,400	59,689	54,531	54,860	59,499
Balance	790	159	904	3,280	4,394	25,364	21,380	31,150	43,779	64,680	54,133	46,857	41,178	48,445
US														
FDI to	187	33	94	846	1,484	5,395	10,165	14,704	21,701	32,540	26,128	22,193	22,005	20,769
% to world	23.7	20.8	10.4	25.8	31.6	44.2	45.5	44.1	46.2	48.2	45.9	43.8	45.8	38.5
FDI from	0	0	0	0	104	413	488	938	1,774	1,642	806	1,843	2,122	1,237
% from world	0.0	0.0	0.0	0.0	34.8	44.4	51.9	42.4	54.7	57.4	29.0	48.0	31.0	22.4
Total FDI	211	54	104	872	1,620	5,852	10,699	15,686	23,521	34,230	26,980	24,080	24,173	22,044
Balance	187	33	94	846	1,380	4,982	9,677	13,766	19,927	30,898	25,322	20,350	19,883	19,532
EAST ASIA														
FDI to	138	32	165	1,077	1,176	1,414	2,310	4,836	5,526	8,120	6,946	11,763	10,997	11,094
% to world	26.3	26.3	26.3	26.3	25.1	11.6	10.3	14.5	11.8	12.0	12.2	23.2	22.9	20.6
FDI from	0	0	0	0	40	39	57	36	44	63	62	245	1,215	604
% from world	0.0	0.0	0.0	0.0	13.4	4.2	6.1	1.6	1.4	2.2	2.2	6.4	17.8	10.9
Total FDI	138	32	165	1,077	1,216	1,453	2,367	4,872	5,570	8,183	7,008	12,008	12,212	11,698
Balance	138	32	165	1,077	1,136	1,375	2,253	4,800	5,482	8,057	6,884	11,518	9,782	10,490
CHINA														
FDI to	0	0	0	0	12	100	226	1,226	296	438	349	4,473	2,510	1,987
% to world	0.0	0.0	0.0	0.0	0.3	0.8	1.0	3.7	0.6	0.6	0.6	8.8	5.2	3.7
FDI from	0	0	0	0	0	0	0	0	0	0	0	13	5	5
% from world	0.0	0.0	0.0	0.0	0.0	0.0	0.0	0.0	0.0	0.0	0.0	0.3	0.1	0.1
Total FDI	0	0	0	0	12	100	226	1,226	296	438	349	4,486	2,515	1,992
Balance	0	0	0	0	12	100	226	1,226	296	438	349	4,460	2,505	1,982

	1951–64	1965	1970	1975	1980	1985	1986	1987	1988	1989	1990	1995	1996	1997
NIEs-4														
FDI to	33	5	60	277	378	718	1,531	2,580	3,264	4,900	3,355	3,179	3,539	3,411
% to world	4.2	3.1	6.6	8.4	8.1	5.9	6.9	7.7	6.9	7.3	5.9	6.3	7.4	6.3
FDI from	0	2	0	0	40	39	57	36	44	63	62	230	1,199	599
% from world	0.0	0.0	0.0	0.0	13.4	4.2	6.1	1.6	1.4	2.2	2.2	6.0	17.5	10.8
Total FDI	33	5	60	277	418	757	1,588	2,616	3,308	4,963	3,423	3,415	4,738	4,010
Balance	33	5	60	277	338	679	1,474	2,544	3,220	4,837	3,293	2,949	2,340	2,812
South Korea														
FDI to	0	0	17	93	35	134	436	647	483	606	284	445	416	442
FDI from	0	0	0	0	0	0	0	0	0	0	0	94	71	69
Total FDI	0	0	17	93	35	134	436	647	483	606	284	539	487	511
Balance	0	0	17	93	35	134	436	647	483	606	284	351	345	373
Taiwan														
FDI to	9	1	25	24	47	114	291	367	372	494	446	457	521	450
FDI from	0	0	0	0	1	0	0	0	0	0	0	104	19	40
Total FDI	9	1	25	24	48	114	291	367	372	494	446	561	540	490
Balance	9	1	25	24	46	114	291	367	372	494	446	353	502	410
Hong Kong														
FDI to	9	2	9	105	156	131	502	1,072	1,662	1,898	1,785	1,125	1,487	695
FDI from	0	0	0	0	39	39	57	36	44	63	62	26	155	334
Total FDI	9	2	9	105	195	170	559	1,108	1,706	1,961	1,847	1,151	1,642	1,029
Balance	9	2	9	105	117	92	445	1,036	1,618	1,835	1,723	1,099	1,332	361
Singapore														
FDI to	15	2	9	55	140	339	302	494	747	1,902	840	1,152	1,115	1,824
FDI from	0	0	0	0	0	0	0	0	0	0	0	6	954	156
Total FDI	15	2	9	55	140	339	302	494	747	1,902	840	1,158	2,069	1,980
Balance	15	2	9	55	140	339	302	494	747	1,902	840	1,146	161	1,668
ASEAN-4														
FDI to	105	27	105	800	786	596	553	1,030	1,966	2,782	3,242	4,111	4,948	5,696
% to world	13.3	17.0	11.6	24.4	16.7	4.9	2.5	3.1	4.2	4.1	5.7	8.1	10.3	10.6
FDI from	0	0	0	0	0	0	0	0	0	0	0	2	11	0
% from world	0.0	0.0	0.0	0.0	0.0	0.0	0.0	0.0	0.0	0.0	0.0	0.1	0.2	0.0
Total FDI	118	44	117	824	803	601	555	1,033	1,970	2,786	3,248	4,121	4,969	5,707
Balance	105	27	105	800	786	596	553	1,030	1,966	2,782	3,242	4,109	4,937	5,696

	1951–64	1965	1970	1975	1980	1985	1986	1987	1988	1989	1990	1995	1996	1997
Thailand														
FDI to	33	6	13	14	33	48	124	250	859	1,276	1,154	1,224	1,403	1,867
FDI from	0	0	0	0	0	0	0	0	0	0	0	0	0	0
Total FDI	33	6	13	14	33	48	124	250	859	1,276	1,154	1,224	1,403	1,867
Balance	33	6	13	14	33	48	124	250	859	1,276	1,154	1,224	1,403	1,867
Malaysia														
FDI to	13	5	14	52	146	79	158	163	387	673	725	573	572	791
FDI from	0	0	0	0	0	0	0	0	0	0	0	0	9	0
Total FDI	13	5	14	52	146	79	158	163	387	673	725	573	581	791
Balance	13	5	14	52	146	79	158	163	387	673	725	573	563	791
Philippines														
FDI to	24	0	29	149	78	61	21	72	134	202	258	718	559	524
FDI from	0	0	0	0	0	0	0	0	0	0	0	0	2	0
Total FDI	24	0	29	149	78	61	21	72	134	202	258	718	561	524
Balance	24	0	29	149	78	61	21	72	134	202	258	718	557	524
Indonesia														
FDI to	35	16	49	585	529	408	250	545	586	631	1,105	1,596	2,414	2,514
FDI from												2	0	0
Total FDI	35	16	49	585	529	408	250	545	586	631	1,105	1,598	2,414	2,514
Balance	35	16	49	585	529	408	250	545	586	631	1,105	1,594	2,414	2,514
North Korea														
FDI to	0	0	0	0	0	0	3	2	13	10	1	0	1	0
FDI from	0	0	0	0	0	0	0	0	0	0	0	0	0	0
Total FDI	0	0	0	0	0	0	3	2	13	10	1	0	1	0
Balance	0	0	0	0	0	0	3	2	13	10	1	0	1	0
Brunei														
FDI to	1	0	0	1	0	1	1	0	0	0	0	0	0	0
FDI from	0	0	0	0	0	0	0	0	0	0	0	0	0	0
Total FDI	1	0	0	1	0	1	1	0	0	0	0	0	0	0
Balance	1	0	0	1	0	1	1	0	0	0	0	0	0	0

	1951–64	1965	1970	1975	1980	1985	1986	1987	1988	1989	1990	1995	1996	1997
Vietnam														
FDI to	—	—	—	—	0	0	0	0	0	0	0	197	319	311
FDI from	—	—	—	—	0	0	0	0	0	0	0	0	0	0
Total FDI	—	—	—	—	0	0	0	0	0	0	0	197	319	311
Balance	—	—	—	—	0	0	0	0	0	0	0	197	319	311
North Vietnam														
FDI to	0	0	0	0	—	—	—	—	—	—	—	—	—	—
FDI from	0	0	0	0	—	—	—	—	—	—	—	—	—	—
Total FDI	0	0	0	0	—	—	—	—	—	—	—	—	—	—
Balance	0	0	0	0	—	—	—	—	—	—	—	—	—	—
South Vietnam														
FDI to	0	0	0	0	—	—	—	—	—	—	—	—	—	—
FDI from	0	0	0	0	—	—	—	—	—	—	—	—	—	—
Total FDI	0	0	0	0	—	—	—	—	—	—	—	—	—	—
Balance	0	0	0	0	—	—	—	—	—	—	—	—	—	—
Cambodia														
FDI to	—	—	0	0	0	0	0	0	0	0	0	0	3	0
FDI from	—	—	0	0	0	0	0	0	0	0	0	0	3	0
Total FDI	—	—	0	0	0	0	0	0	0	0	0	0	6	0
Balance	—	—	0	0	0	0	0	0	0	0	0	0	0	0
Laos														
FDI to	—	—	0	0	0	0	0	0	0	0	0	0	0	0
FDI from	—	—	0	0	0	0	0	0	0	0	0	0	0	0
Total FDI	—	—	0	0	0	0	0	0	0	0	0	0	0	0
Balance	—	—	0	0	0	0	0	0	0	0	0	0	0	0
Burma														
FDI to	0	0	0	0	0	0	0	0	0	0	1	0	0	0
FDI from	0	0	0	0	0	0	0	0	0	0	1	0	0	0
Total FDI	0	0	0	0	0	0	0	0	0	0	2	0	0	0
Balance	0	0	0	0	0	0	0	0	0	0	0	0	0	0

	1951–64	1965	1970	1975	1980	1985	1986	1987	1988	1989	1990	1995	1996	1997
REST OF ASIA														
FDI to	1	0	0	1	0	1	4	2	13	10	2	197	323	311
% to world	0.1	0.0	0.0	0.0	0.0	0.0	0.0	0.0	0.0	0.0	0.0	0.4	0.7	0.6
FDI from	0	0	0	0	0	0	0	0	0	0	1	0	3	0
% from world	0	0.0	0.0	0.0	0.0	0.0	0.0	0.0	0.0	0.0	0.036	0	0.04	0
Total FDI	1	0	0	1	0	1	4	2	13	10	3	197	326	311
Balance	1	0	0	1	0	1	4	2	13	10	1	197	320	311
EEC/EC/EU														
FDI to	15	4	35	190	521	1,760	3,324	6,245	8,329	14,011	13,305	7,908	6,648	10,930
% to world	1.9	2.5	3.9	5.8	11.1	14.4	14.9	18.7	17.7	20.7	23.4	15.6	13.8	20.3
FDI from	0	0	0	0	67	216	118	200	491	498	1,121	2,371	2,099	3,777
% from world	0.0	0.0	0.0	0.0	22.4	23.2	12.6	9.0	15.1	17.4	40.4	61.8	30.7	68.3
Total FDI	15	4	35	190	588	1,976	3,442	6,445	9	14,509	14,426	10,279	8,747	14,707
Balance	15	4	35	190	454	1,544	3,206	6	7,838	13,513	12,184	5,537	4,549	7,153
EEC														
FDI to	15	4	35	—	—	—	—	—	—	—	—	—	—	—
FDI from	0	0	0	—	—	—	—	—	—	—	—	—	—	—
Total FDI	15	4	35	—	—	—	—	—	—	—	—	—	—	—
Balance	15	4	35	—	—	—	—	—	—	—	—	—	—	—
EC														
FDI to	—	—	—	190	521	1,760	3,324	6,281	8,329	14,031	13,305	—	—	—
FDI from	—	—	—	0	68	216	118	200	491	498	1,121	—	—	—
Total FDI	—	—	—	190	589	1,976	3,442	6,481	8,820	14,529	14,426	—	—	—
Balance	—	—	—	190	453	1,544	3,206	6,081	7,838	13,533	12,184	—	—	—
EU														
FDI to	—	—	—	—	—	—	—	—	—	—	—	7,908	6,648	10,930
FDI from	—	—	—	—	—	—	—	—	—	—	—	2,371	2,070	3,777
Total FDI	—	—	—	—	—	—	—	—	—	—	—	10,279	8,718	14,707
Balance	—	—	—	—	—	—	—	—	—	—	—	5,537	4,578	7,153
France														
FDI to	5	0	9	15	83	67	152	330	463	1,136	1,257	1,524	503	1,736
FDI from	0	0	0	0	25	22	17	20	27	25	74	114	93	76
Total FDI	5	0	9	15	108	89	169	350	490	1,161	1,331	1,638	596	1,812
Balance	5	0	9	15	58	45	135	310	436	1,111	1,183	1,410	410	1,660

	1951–64	1965	1970	1975	1980	1985	1986	1987	1988	1989	1990	1995	1996	1997
Belgium + Luxemburg														
FDI to	3	2	20	45	77	384	1,142	1,834	821	980	591	358	89	88
FDI from	0	0	0	0	0	0	0	0	0	0	0	0	0	0
Total FDI	3	2	20	45	77	384	1,142	1,834	821	980	591	358	89	88
Balance	3	2	20	45	77	384	1,142	1,834	821	980	591	358	89	88
Netherlands														
FDI to	0	0	1	42	41	613	651	829	2,359	4,547	2,744	1,509	1,099	3,295
FDI from	0	0	0	0	8	108	19	78	157	248	734	561	713	1,192
Total FDI	0	0	1	42	49	721	670	907	2,516	4,795	3,478	2,070	1,812	4,487
Balance	0	0	1	42	33	505	632	751	2,202	4,299	2,010	948	386	2,103
Italy														
FDI to	3	1	1	4	8	32	23	59	108	314	217	120	109	139
FDI from	0	0	0	0	0	0	0	0	0	0	0	2	1	34
Total FDI	3	1	1	4	8	32	23	59	108	314	217	122	110	173
Balance	3	1	1	4	8	32	23	59	108	314	217	118	108	105
Germany														
FDI to	4	1	4	35	110	172	210	403	409	1,083	1,242	547	571	732
FDI from	0	0	0	0	27	25	47	53	195	144	259	167	423	450
Total FDI	4	1	4	35	137	197	257	456	604	1,227	1,501	714	994	1,182
Balance	4	1	4	35	83	147	163	350	214	939	983	380	148	282
UK														
FDI to	2	1	290	46	186	375	984	2,473	3,956	5,239	6,806	3,445	3,438	4,118
FDI from	0	0	0	0	7	61	35	49	112	81	54	117	360	364
Total FDI	2	1	290	46	193	436	1,019	2,522	4,068	5,320	6,860	3,562	3,798	4,482
Balance	2	1	290	46	179	314	949	2,424	3,844	5,158	6,752	3,328	3,078	3,754
Ireland														
FDI to	1	0	0	3	14	81	72	58	42	133	49	340	397	566
FDI from	0	0	0	0	0	0	0	0	0	0	0	0	0	0
Total FDI	1	0	0	3	14	81	72	58	42	133	49	340	397	566
Balance	1	0	0	3	14	81	72	58	42	133	49	340	397	566

	1951–64	1965	1970	1975	1980	1985	1986	1987	1988	1989	1990	1995	1996	1997
Denmark														
FDI to	0	0	0	0	2	1	1	6	2	24	7	0	0	0
FDI from	0	0	0	0	1	0	0	0	0	0	0	0	0	0
Total FDI	0	0	0	0	3	1	1	6	2	24	7	0	0	0
Balance	0	0	0	0	1	1	1	6	2	24	7	0	0	0
Greece														
FDI to	0	0	0	1	0	35	0	0	1	0	4	0	0	0
FDI from	0	0	0	0	0	0	0	0	0	0	0	0	0	0
Total FDI	0	0	0	1	0	35	0	0	1	0	4	0	0	0
Balance	0	0	0	1	0	35	0	0	1	0	4	0	0	0
Spain														
FDI to	0	0	4	9	22	91	86	283	161	501	320	51	318	232
FDI from	0	0	0	0	0	0	0	0	0	0	0	0	0	0
Total FDI	0	0	4	9	22	91	86	283	161	501	320	51	318	232
Balance	0	0	4	9	22	91	86	283	161	501	320	51	318	232
Portugal														
FDI to	2	0	0	2	1	0	3	6	7	74	68	5	5	8
FDI from	0	0	0	0	0	0	0	0	0	0	0	0	0	0
Total FDI	2	0	0	2	1	0	3	6	7	74	68	5	5	8
Balance	2	0	0	2	1	0	3	6	7	74	68	5	5	8
Austria														
FDI to			0	0	1	5	41	23	22	18	38	0	0	0
FDI from			0	0	0	0	0	0	0	0	0	0	0	0
Total FDI	0	0	0	0	1	5	41	23	22	18	38	0	0	0
Balance	0	0	0	0	1	5	41	23	22	18	38	0	0	0
Sweden														
FDI to	0	0	0	0	1	0	2	1	4	10	11	9	10	6
FDI from	0	0	0	0	4	0	0	0	0	0	0	0	70	0
Total FDI	0	0	0	0	5	0	2	1	4	10	11	9	80	6
Balance	0	0	0	0	– 3	0	2	1	4	10	11	9	– 60	6

	1951–64	1965	1970	1975	1980	1985	1986	1987	1988	1989	1990	1995	1996	1997
Finland														
FDI to	0	0	0	0	0	0	0	1	0	2	0	0	109	10
FDI from	0	0	0	0	0	0	0	0	0	0	0	0	0.3	1
Total FDI	0	0	0	0	0	0	0	1	0	2	0	0	109	11
Balance	0	0	0	0	0	0	0	1	0	2	0	0	109	9

Source: JETRO various years.

Notes

'East Asia' consists of: China, NIEs-4 and ASEAN-4.

'Rest of East Asia' consists of: North Korea, Brunei, Indo-China and Burma until 1955; North Korea, Brunei, South and North Vietnam, Cambodia, Laos and Burma until 1975; and North Korea, Brunei, Vietnam, Cambodia, Laos and Burma from 1975 to 1997.

EEC consists of: France, Belgium, Luxemburg, Netherlands, Italy and Germany.

EC consists of: France, Belgium, Luxemburg, Netherlands, Italy, Germany, UK, Ireland and Denmark until 1979; France, Belgium, Luxemburg, Netherlands, Italy, Germany, UK, Ireland, Denmark and Greece from 1980 until 1985; and France, Belgium, Luxemburg, Netherlands, Italy, Germany, UK, Ireland, Denmark, Greece, Spain and Portugal from 1981 until 1994.

EU consists of: France, Belgium, Luxemburg, Netherlands, Italy, Germany, UK, Ireland, Denmark, Greece, Spain, Portugal, Austria, Sweden and Finland from 1995 onwards.

Table 3 Japan's defence expenditure 1975–99

Year	*¥ billions*	*US$ millions*	*% GNP*	*% annual government expenditure*
1975	1,273.3	4,484	0.84	6.23
1976	1,512.4	5,058	0.90	6.22
1977	1,690.6	6,100	0.88	5.93
1978	1,901.0	8,570	0.90	5.54
1979	2,094.5	10,080	0.90	5.43
1980	2,230.2	8,960	0.90	5.24
1981	2,400.0	11,500	0.91	5.24
1982	2,586.1	10,360	0.93	5.21
1983	2,754.2	11,617	0.98	5.47
1984	2,934.6	12,018	0.99	5.80
1985	3,137.1	14,189	0.997	5.98
1986	3,343.5	20,930	0.933	6.18
1987	3,517.4	25,420	1.004	6.50
1988	3,700.3	28,850	1.013	6.53
1989	3,919.8	30,090	1.006	6.49
1990	4,159.3	28,122	0.997	6.28
1991	4,386.0	32,890	0.954	6.23
1992	4,551.8	34,300	0.941	6.30
1993	4,640.6	39,710	0.937	6.41
1994	4,683.5	42,100	0.959	6.41
1995	4,723.6	53,800	0.959	6.65
1996	4,845.5	45,100	0.977	6.45
1997	4,941.4	42,900	0.958	6.39
1998	4,929.0	35,200	0.948	6.35
1999	4,920.1	41,100	0.991	6.01

Sources: Bōei Handobokku 1999; International Institute for Strategic Studies various years.

Table 4 Yen–dollar rate 1949–99 (average annual rate, yen per dollar)

Year	*Yen to dollar rate*
1949–70	360.0
1971	308.0
1972	303.8
1973	272.18
1974	292.06
1975	296.84
1976	296.49
1977	268.32
1978	210.11
1979	219.47
1980	226.45
1981	220.83
1982	249.26
1983	237.61
1984	237.61
1985	238.05
1986	168.03
1987	144.52
1988	128.2
1989	138.11
1990	144.88
1991	134.59
1992	126.62
1993	111.06
1994	100.0
1995	80.0
1996	108.3
1997	123.4
1998	131.3
1999	114.1

Source: Nihon Ginkō various years.

Appendices

Note The appendices are numbered according to the chapter to which they relate.

Appendix 0.1

INTERNET SOURCES

These website addresses were current as of February 2001.

Japanese

Newspapers and news sources

Asahi Shimbun http://www.asahi.com
Mainichi Shimbun http://www.mainichi.co.jp
Yomiuri Shimbun http://www.yomiuri.co.jp/index-j.html
Nihon Keizai Shimbun http://www.nikkei.co.jp
Sankei Shimbun http://www.sankei.co.jp
Nihon Hōsō Kyōkai (NHK) http://www.nhk-group.co.jp
Kyōdō News http://www.kyodo.co.jp

Diet

House of Representatives http://www.shugiin.go.jp
House of Councillors http://www.sangiin.go.jp
National Diet Library http://www.ndl.go.jp

Prime Minister

Prime Minister's Residence http://www.kantei.go.jp

Cabinet

Cabinet Office http://www.cao.go.jp
Cabinet Legislation Bureau http://www.clb.admix.go.jp
National Personnel Authority http://www.jinji.admix.go.jp/top.htm
Prime Minister's Office http://www.sorifu.go.jp
Fair Trade Commission http://www.jftc.admix.go.jp
National Police Agency http://www.npa.go.jp
Management and Coordination Agency http://www.somucho.go.jp
Okinawa Development Agency http://www.oda.go.jp
Japan Defence Agency http://www.jda.go.jp
Economic Planning Agency http://www.epa.go.jp
National Land Agency http://www.nla.go.jp
Ministry of Justice http://www.moj.go.jp
Ministry of Foreign Affairs http://www.mofa.go.jp/mofaj
Ministry of Finance http://www.mof.go.jp
Ministry of the Environment http://www.env.go.jp
Ministry of Health, Labour and Welfare http://www.mhlw.go.jp

Ministry of Agriculture, Forestry and Fisheries http://www.maff.go.jp
Ministry of Economy, Trade and Industry http://www.meti.go.jp
Ministry of Transport http://www.motnet.go.jp
Ministry of Construction http://www.moc.go.jp
Ministry of Home Affairs http://www.mha.go.jp
Ministry of Public Management, Home Affairs, Posts and Telecommunications http://www.soumu.go.jp
Ministry of Education, Culture Sports, Science and Technology http://www.mext.go.jp
Ministry of Land, Infrastructure and Transport http//www.mlit.go.jp
Statistics Bureau and Statistics Centre http://www.stat.go.jp
Agency of Industrial Science and Technology http://www.aist.go.jp
Patent Office http://www.jpo.go.jp
Small and Medium Size Enterprise Agency http://www.sme.ne.jp

Political parties

Liberal-Democratic Party http://www.jimin.or.jp
Liberal Party http://www.jiyuto.or.jp
Kōmei Party/New Kōmei Party http://www.komei.or.jp
Democratic Party of Japan http://www.dpj.or.jp
Japanese Communist Party http://www.jcp.or.jp
Social Democratic Party of Japan http://www.sdp.or.jp
New Party Sakigake http://www.coara.or.jp/~sakigake

Universities

University of Tokyo http://www.u-tokyo.ac.jp/index-j.html
Kyoto University http://www.kyoto-u.ac.jp/
Nagoya University http://www.nagoya-u.ac.jp
Osaka University http://www.osaka-u.ac.jp
Kyūshū University http://www.kyushu-u.ac.jp
Tōhoku University http://www.tohoku.ac.jp/index-j.html
Hokkaidō University http://www.hokudai.ac.jp
Hitotsubashi University http://www.hit-u.ac.jp
Waseda University http://www.waseda.ac.jp/index-j.html
Keiō University http://www.keio.ac.jp/index-jp.html
Hōsei University http://www.hosei.ac.jp
Chūō University http://www.chuo-u.ac.jp/index-j.html

Others

Supreme Court http://www.courts.go.jp
Bank of Japan http://www.boj.or.jp/index.html
Keidanren http://www.keidanren.or.jp/indexj.html
Tokyo Metropolitan Government http://www.metro.tokyo.jp
Tokyo Stock Exchange http://www.tse.or.jp/index.html

English

Newspapers and news sources

Daily Yomiuri http://www.yomiuri.co.jp/index-e.htm
Asahi News http://www.asahi.com/english/english.html#top
Mainichi Daily News http://www.mainichi.co.jp/english/index.html
Nihon Keizai Shimbun http://www.nni.nikkei.co.jp
Japan Times http://www.japantimes.co.jp
Japan Echo http://www.japanecho.co.jp
Far Eastern Economic Review http://www.feer.com
Nihon Hōsō Kyōkai (NHK) http://www.nhk.or.jp/index-e.html
Kyōdō News http://home.kyodo.co.jp
Japan Documentation Center http://lcweb.loc.gov/rr/jdc

Diet

House of Representatives http://www.shugiin.go.jp/itdb_main.nsf/html/index_e.htm
House of Councillors http://www.sangiin.go.jp/eng/index.htm
National Diet Library http://www.ndl.go.jp/index-e.html

Prime Minister

Prime Minister's Residence http://www.kantei.go.jp/foreign/index-e.html

Cabinet

Cabinet Legislation Bureau http://www.clb.admix.go.jp/english/index.htm
National Personnel Authority http://www.jinji.admix.go.jp/top_e.htm
Prime Minister's Office http://www.sorifu.go.jp/english/index.html
Fair Trade Commission http://www.jftc.admix.go.jp/e-page/f_home.htm
National Police Agency http://www.npa.go.jp/police_e.htm
Management and Coordination Agency http://www.somucho.go.jp
Japan Defence Agency http://www.jda.go.jp/e/index_.htm
Economic Planning Agency http://www.epa.go.jp/e-e/menu.html
Environment Agency http://www.eic.or.jp/eanet/en/index.html
National Land Agency http://www.nla.go.jp/welcome-e.html
Ministry of Justice http://www.moj.go.jp/english/preface.htm
Ministry of Foreign Affairs http://www.mofa.go.jp/index.html
Ministry of Finance http://www.mof.go.jp/english/index.htm
Ministry of Education, Science, Sports and Culture http://www.monbu.go.jp/emindex.html
Ministry of Health and Welfare http://www.mhw.go.jp/english/index.html
Ministry of Agriculture, Forestry and Fisheries http://www.maff.go.jp/eindex.html
Ministry of International Trade and Industry http://www.miti.go.jp/index-e.html
Ministry of Transport http://www.motnet.go.jp/mthome.htm
Ministry of Posts and Telecommunications http://www.mpt.go.jp/index-e.html
Ministry of Labour http://www.mol.go.jp/english/index.htm

Ministry of Construction http://www.moc.go.jp/eng/eng/index.htm
Ministry of Home Affairs http://www.mha.go.jp/eng/index.html

Political parties

Liberal-Democratic Party http://www.jimin.or.jp/jimin/english/e-index.html
Liberal Party http://www.jiyuto.or.jp/index_e.htm
Kōmei Party/New Kōmei Party http://www.komei.or.jp/english/index.htm
Democratic Party of Japan http://www.dpj.or.jp/english
Japanese Communist Party http://www.jcp.or.jp/english/index.html
New Party Sakigake http://www.coara.or.jp/~sakigake/eng/guide/index.html

Universities

University of Tokyo http://www.u-tokyo.ac.jp/index.html
Kyoto University http://www.kyoto-u.ac.jp/english
Nagoya University http://www.nagoya-u.ac.jp/english/index.html
Osaka University http://www.osaka-u.ac.jp/english/index.html
Kyūshū University http://www.kyushu-u.ac.jp/english/index-e.htm
Tōhoku University http://www.tohoku.ac.jp
Hokkaidō University http://www.hokudai.ac.jp/index-e.html
Hitotsubashi University http://www.hit-u.ac.jp/foreigner/index.htm
Waseda University http://www.waseda.ac.jp
Keiō University http://www.keio.ac.jp/index.html
Hōsei University http://www.hosei.ac.jp/english/index.html
United Nations University http://www.unu.edu/index.htm

International organizations

Association of Southeast Asian Nations http://www.aseansec.org
World Bank http://www.worldbank.org
G7 http://www.g7.utoronto.ca
World Trade Organization http://www.wto.org
International Monetary Fund http://www.imf.org
Asian Development Bank http://www.adb.org
Asia-Europe Meeting http://asem.inter.net.th
United Nations http://www.unu.org
United Nations Educational, Scientific and Cultural Organization (UNESCO) http://www.unesco.or.jp/english/index_e.htm
European Union http://www.europa.eu.int

Others

Supreme Court http://www.courts.go.jp/english/ehome.htm
Bank of Japan http://www.boj.or.jp/en/index.htm
Keidanren http://www.keidanren.or.jp
Tokyo Metropolitan Government http://www.seikatubunka.metro.tokyo.jp/english/englishindex.htm
Tokyo Stock Exchange http://www.tse.or.jp/eindex.html

Appendix 1.1

CONSTITUTION OF JAPAN – PREAMBLE AND ARTICLE 9

Preamble

We, the Japanese people, acting through our duly elected representatives in the National Diet, determined that we shall secure for ourselves and our posterity the fruits of peaceful cooperation with all nations and the blessings of liberty throughout this land, and resolved that never again shall we be visited with the horrors of war through the action of government, do proclaim that sovereign power resides with the people and do firmly establish this constitution. Government is a sacred trust of the people, the authority for which is derived from the people, the powers of which are exercised by the representatives of the people, and the benefits of which are enjoyed by the people. This is a universal principle of mankind upon which this constitution is founded. We reject and revoke all constitutions, laws, ordinances, and rescripts in conflict herewith.

We, the Japanese people, desire peace for all time and are deeply conscious of the high ideals controlling human relationship, and we have determined to preserve our security and existence, trusting in the justice and faith of the peace-loving peoples of the world. We desire to occupy an honored place in an international society striving for the preservation of peace, and the banishment of tyranny and slavery, oppression and intolerance for all time from the earth. We recognize that all peoples of the world have the right to live in peace, free from fear and want.

We believe that no nation is responsible to itself alone, but that laws of political morality are universal; and that obedience to such laws is incumbent upon all nations who would sustain their own sovereignty and justify their sovereign relationship with other nations.

We, the Japanese people, pledge our national honor to accomplish these high ideals and purposes with all our resources.

Article 9

Aspiring sincerely to an international peace based on justice and order, the Japanese people forever renounce war as a sovereign right of the nation and the threat or use of force as means of settling international disputes.

In order to accomplish the aim of the preceding paragraph, land, sea and air forces, [illegible]ll as other war potential, will never be maintained. The right of belligerency [illegible]t be recognized.

Appendix 1.2

POST-WAR PRIME MINISTERS OF JAPAN

Higashikuni Naruhiko 17 August 1945 to 9 October 1945
Shidehara Kijūrō 9 October 1945 to 22 May 1946
Yoshida Shigeru 22 May 1946 to 24 May 1947
Katayama Tetsu 24 May 1947 to 10 March 1948
Ashida Hitoshi 10 March 1948 to 15 October 1948
Yoshida Shigeru 15 October 1948 to 16 February 1949
Yoshida Shigeru 16 February 1949 to 30 October 1952
Yoshida Shigeru 30 October 1952 to 10 December 1954
Hatoyama Ichirō 10 December 1954 to 22 November 1955
Hatoyama Ichirō 22 November 1955 to 23 December 1956
Ishibashi Tanzan 23 December 1956 to 25 February 1957
Kishi Nobusuke 25 February 1957 to 19 July 1960
Ikeda Hayato 19 July 1960 to 9 November 1964
Satō Eisaku 9 November 1964 to 7 July 1972
Tanaka Kakuei 7 July 1972 to 9 December 1974
Miki Takeo 9 December 1974 to 24 December 1976
Fukuda Takeo 24 December 1976 to 7 December 1978
Ōhira Masayoshi 7 December 1978 to 17 July 1980
Suzuki Zenkō 17 July 1980 to 27 November 1982
Nakasone Yasuhiro 27 November 1982 to 27 December 1983
Nakasone Yasuhiro 27 December 1983 to 15 August 1986
Nakasone Yasuhiro 15 August 1986 to 6 November 1987
Takeshita Noboru 6 November 1987 to 3 June 1989
Uno Sōsuke 3 June 1989 to 10 August 1989
Kaifu Toshiki 10 August 1989 to 5 November 1991
Miyazawa Kiichi 5 November 1991 to 9 August 1993
Hosokawa Morihiro 9 August 1993 to 28 April 1994
Hata Tsutomu 28 April 1994 to 30 June 1994
Murayama Tomiichi 30 June 1994 to 11 January 1996
Hashimoto Ryūtarō 11 January 1996 to 30 July 1998
Obuchi Keizō 30 July 1998 to 5 April 2000
Mori Yoshirō 5 April 2000 to present

ndix 1.3

RITY TREATY BETWEEN THE UNITED STATES JAPAN

8 September, 1951

s this day signed a Treaty of Peace with the Allied Powers. On the coming
e of that Treaty, Japan will not have the effective means to exercise its
t right of self-defense because it has been disarmed. There is danger to
this situation because irresponsible militarism has not yet been driven
world. Therefore, Japan desires a Security Treaty with the United States
ica to come into force simultaneously with the Treaty of Peace between
ed States of America and Japan. The Treaty of Peace recognizes that Japan
ereign nation has the right to enter into collective security arrangements,
her, the Charter of the United Nations recognizes that all nations possess
ent right of individual and collective self-defense.

cise of these rights, Japan desires, as a provisional arrangement for its
, that the United States of America should maintain armed forces of its own
bout Japan so as to deter attack upon Japan.

ited States of America, in the interest of peace and security, is presently
o maintain certain of its armed forces in and about Japan, in the expecta-
wever, that Japan will itself increasingly assume responsibility for its own
against direct and indirect aggression, always avoiding any armament
ould be an offensive threat or serve other than to promote peace and secu-
ccordance with the purposes and principles of the United Nations Charter.

ngly, the two countries have agreed as follows:

Japan grants, and the United States of America accepts the right, upon
e coming into force of the Treaty of Peace and of this Treaty, to dispose
nited States land, air, and sea forces in and about Japan. Such forces may be
ilized to contribute to the maintenance of the international peace and secu-
ty in the Far East and to the security of Japan against attack from without,
cluding assistance given at the express request of the Japanese Govern-
ent to put down large-scale internal riots and disturbances in Japan, caused
rough instigation or intervention by an outside Power or Powers.

II During the exercise of the right referred to in Article I, Japan will not
rant, without the prior consent of the United States of America, any bases
any rights, power, or authority whatsoever, in or relating to bases or the
ght of garrison or of maneuver, or transit of ground, air, or naval forces to
ny third Power.

Article III The conditions which shall govern the disposition of armed forces of the United States of America in and about Japan shall be determined by administrative agreements between the two Governments.

Article IV This Treaty shall expire whenever in the opinion of the Governments of the United States of America and of Japan there shall have come into force such United Nations arrangements or such alternative individual or collective security dispositions as will satisfactorily provide for the maintenance by the United Nations or otherwise of international peace and security in the Japan Area.

Article V This Treaty shall be ratified by the United States of America and Japan and will come into force when instruments of ratification thereof have been exchanged by them at Washington.

IN WITNESS WHEREOF the undersigned plenipotentiaries have signed this Treaty.

DONE in duplicate at the city of San Francisco, in the English and Japanese languages, this eighth day of September, 1951.

endix 1.4

ATY OF MUTUAL COOPERATION AND :URITY BETWEEN THE UNITED STATES D JAPAN

Signed at Washington, DC, January 19, 1960

Jnited States of America and Japan,

:ing to strengthen the bonds of peace and friendship traditionally existing een them, and to uphold the principles of democracy, individual liberty, and ule of law,

ring further to encourage closer economic cooperation between them and to 10te conditions of economic stability and well-being in their countries,

firming their faith in the purposes and principles of the Charter of the United ons, and their desire to live in peace with all peoples and all governments,

gnizing that they have the inherent right of individual or collective defense as affirmed in the Charter of the United Nations,

sidering that they have a common concern in the maintenance of international e and security in the Far East,

ng resolved to conclude a treaty of mutual cooperation and security,

:efore agree as follows:

:le I The Parties undertake, as set forth in the Charter of the United Nations, to settle any international disputes in which they may be involved by peaceful means in such a manner that international peace and security and justice are not endangered and to refrain in their international relations from the threat or use of force against the territorial integrity or political independence of any state, or in any other manner inconsistent with the purposes of the United Nations.

The Parties will endeavor in concert with other peace-loving countries to strengthen the United Nations so that its mission of maintaining international peace and security may be discharged more effectively.

:le II The Parties will contribute toward the further development of peaceful and friendly international relations by strengthening their free institutions, by bringing about a better understanding of the principles upon which these institutions are founded, and by promoting conditions of stability and well-being. They seek to eliminate conflict in their international economic policies and encourage economic collaboration between them.

Article III The Parties, individually and in cooperation with each other, by means of continuous and effective self-help and mutual aid will maintain and develop, subject to their constitutional provisions, their capacities to resist armed attack.

Article IV The Parties will consult together from time to time regarding the implementation of this Treaty, and, at the request of either Party, whenever the security of Japan or international peace and security in the Far East is threatened.

Article V Each Party recognizes that an armed attack against either Party in the territories under the administration of Japan would be dangerous to its own peace and safety and declares that it would act to meet the common danger in accordance with its constitutional provisions and processes.

Any such armed attack and all measures taken as a result thereof shall be immediately reported to the Security Council of the United Nations in accordance with the provisions of Article 51 of the Charter. Such measures shall be terminated when the Security Council has taken the measures necessary to restore and maintain international peace and security.

Article VI For the purpose of contributing to the security of Japan and the maintenance of international peace and security in the Far East, the United States of America is granted the use by its land, air, and naval forces of facilities and areas in Japan.

The use of these facilities and areas as well as the status of the United States armed forces in Japan shall be governed by a separate agreement, replacing the administrative Agreement under Article III of the Security Treaty between the United States of America and Japan, signed at Tokyo on February 28, 1952, as amended, and by such other arrangements as may be agreed upon.

Article VII This Treaty does not affect and shall not be interpreted as affecting in any way the rights and obligations of the Parties under the Charter of the United Nations or the responsibility of the United Nations for the maintenance of international peace and security.

Article VIII This Treaty shall be ratified by the United States of America and Japan in accordance with their respective constitutional processes and will enter into force on the date on which the instruments of ratification thereof have been exchanged by them in Tokyo.

Article IX The Security Treaty between the United States of America and Japan signed at the city of San Francisco on September 8, 1951, shall expire upon the entering into force of this Treaty.

Article X This Treaty shall remain in force until in the opinion of the Governments of the United States of America and Japan there shall have come into force such United Nations arrangements as will satisfactorily provide for the maintenance of international peace and security in the Japan area.

vever, after the Treaty has been in force for ten years, either Party may give ce to the other Party of its intention to terminate the Treaty, in which case the aty shall terminate one year after such notice has been given.

VITNESS WHEREOF the undersigned plenipotentiaries have signed this aty.

NE in duplicate at Washington in the English and Japanese languages, both ally authentic, this 19th day of January, 1960.

Appendix 2.1

CONSTITUTION OF JAPAN – ARTICLE 66

The cabinet shall consist of the Prime Minister, who shall be its head, and other Ministers of State, as provided for by law.

The Prime Minister and other Ministers of State must be civilians.

The cabinet shall, in the exercise of executive power, be collectively responsible to the Diet.

ppendix 4.1

LATERAL VISITS BETWEEN JAPAN AND THE NITED STATES

pan to United States

vember 1954 Prime Minister Yoshida visits the United States
ne/July 1957 Prime Minister Kishi visits the United States
y 1961 Prime Minister Ikeda visits the United States
uary 1965 Prime Minister Satō visits the United States
vember 1967 Prime Minister Satō visits the United States
vember 1969 Prime Minister Satō visits the United States
tober 1970 Prime Minister Satō visits the United States
gust 1975 Prime Minister Miki visits the United States
rch 1977 Prime Minister Fukuda visits the United States
y 1979 Prime Minister Ōhira visits the United States
uary 1983 Prime Minister Nakasone visits the United States
uary 1985 Prime Minister Nakasone visits the United States
ril 1986 Prime Minister Nakasone visits the United States
uary 1988 Prime Minister Takeshita visits the United States
ril 1993 Prime Minister Miyazawa visits the United States
oruary 1994 Prime Minister Hosokawa visits the United States
ril 1997 Prime Minister Hashimoto visits the United States
ptember 1998 Prime Minister Obuchi visits the United States
y 1999 Prime Minister Obuchi visits the United States

nited States to Japan

vember 1974 President Ford visits Japan
vember 1983 President Reagan visits Japan
uary 1992 President Bush visits Japan
ril 1996 President Clinton visits Japan
vember 1998 President Clinton visits Japan

Appendix 6.1

JAPAN–US JOINT DECLARATION ON SECURITY: ALLIANCE FOR THE 21ST CENTURY

17 April 1996

1 Today, the Prime Minister and the President celebrated one of the most successful bilateral relationships in history. The leaders took pride in the profound and positive contribution this relationship has made to world peace and regional stability and prosperity. The strong Alliance between Japan and the United States helped ensure peace and security in the Asia-Pacific region during the Cold War. Our Alliance continues to underlie the dynamic economic growth in this region. The two leaders agreed that the future security and prosperity of both Japan and the United States are tied inextricably to the future of the Asia-Pacific region.

The benefits of peace and prosperity that spring from the Alliance are due not only to the commitments of the two governments, but also to the contributions of the Japanese and American people who have shared the burden of securing freedom and democracy. The Prime Minister and the President expressed their profound gratitude to those who sustain the Alliance, especially those Japanese communities that host US forces, and those Americans who, far from home, devote themselves to the defense of peace and freedom.

2 For more than a year, the two governments conducted an intensive review of the evolving political and security environment of the Asia-Pacific region and of various aspects of the Japan–US security relationship. On the basis of this review, the Prime Minister and the President reaffirmed their commitment to the profound common values that guide our national policies: the maintenance of freedom, the pursuit of democracy, and respect for human rights. They agreed that the foundations for our cooperation remain firm, and that this partnership will remain vital in the twenty-first century.

The regional outlook

3 Since the end of the Cold War, the possibility of global armed conflict has receded. The last few years have seen expanded political and security dialogue among countries of the region. Respect for democratic principles is growing. Prosperity is more widespread than at any other time in history, and we are witnessing the emergence of an Asia-Pacific community. The Asia-Pacific region has become the most dynamic area of the globe.

t the same time, instability and uncertainty persist in the region. Tensions con-ıue on the Korean Peninsula. There are still heavy concentrations of military rce, including nuclear arsenals. Unresolved territorial disputes, potential gional conflicts, and the proliferation of weapons of mass destruction and their eans of delivery all constitute sources of instability.

he Japan–US Alliance and the Treaty of lutual Cooperation and Security

The Prime Minister and the President underscored the importance of promoting stability in this region and dealing with the security challenges facing both countries.

In this regard, the Prime Minister and the President reiterated the significant value of the Alliance between Japan and the United States. They reaffirmed that the Japan–US security relationship, based on the Treaty of Mutual Cooperation and Security between Japan and the United States of America, remains the cornerstone for achieving common security objectives, and for maintaining a stable and prosperous environment for the Asia-Pacific region as we enter the twenty-first century.

(a) The Prime Minister confirmed Japan's fundamental defense policy as articulated in its new 'National Defense Program Outline' adopted in November, 1995, which underscored that the Japanese defense capabilities should play appropriate roles in the security environment after the Cold War. The Prime Minister and the President agreed that the most effective framework for the defense of Japan is close defense cooperation between the two countries. This cooperation is based on a combination of appropriate defense capabilities for the Self-Defense Forces of Japan and the Japan–US security arrangements. The leaders again confirmed that US deterrence under the Treaty of Mutual Cooperation and Security remains the guarantee for Japan's security.

(b) The Prime Minister and the President agreed that continued US military presence is also essential for preserving peace and stability in the Asia-Pacific region. The leaders shared the common recognition that the Japan–US security relationship forms an essential pillar which supports the positive regional engagement of the US. The President emphasized the US commitment to the defense of Japan as well as to peace and stability in the Asia-Pacific region. He noted that there has been some adjustment of US forces in the Asia-Pacific region since the end of the Cold War. On the basis of a thorough assessment, the United States reaffirmed that meeting its commitments in the prevailing security environment requires the maintenance of its current force structure of about 100,000 forward deployed military personnel in the region, including about the current level in Japan.

(c) The Prime Minister welcomed the US determination to remain a stable and steadfast presence in the region. He reconfirmed that Japan would continue appropriate contributions for the maintenance of US forces in Japan, such as through the provision of facilities and areas in accordance with the Treaty of Mutual Cooperation and Security and Host Nation Support. The President expressed US appreciation for Japan's contributions, and welcomed the conclusion of the new Special Measures Agreement which provides financial support for US forces stationed in Japan.

Bilateral cooperation under the Japan–US security relationship

5 The Prime Minister and the President, with the objective of enhancing the credibility of this vital security relationship, agreed to undertake efforts to advance cooperation in the following areas.

(a) Recognizing that close bilateral defense cooperation is a central element of the Japan–US Alliance, both governments agreed that continued close consultation is essential. Both governments will further enhance the exchange of information and views on the international situation, in particular the Asia-Pacific region. At the same time, in response to the changes which may arise in the international security environment, both governments will continue to consult closely on defense policies and military postures, including the US force structure in Japan, which will best meet their requirements.

(b) The Prime Minister and the President agreed to initiate a review of the 1978 Guidelines for Japan–US Defense Cooperation to build upon the close working relationship already established between Japan and the United States. The two leaders agreed on the necessity to promote bilateral policy coordination, including studies on bilateral cooperation in dealing with situations that may emerge in the areas surrounding Japan and which will have an important influence on the peace and security of Japan.

(c) The Prime Minister and the President welcomed the April 15, 1996 signature of the Agreement Between the Government of Japan and the Government of the United States of America Concerning Reciprocal Provision of Logistic Support, Supplies and Services Between the Self-Defense Forces of Japan and the Armed Forces of the United States of America, and expressed their hope that this Agreement will further promote the bilateral cooperative relationship.

(d) Noting the importance of interoperability in all facets of cooperation between the Self-Defense Forces of Japan and the US forces, the two governments will enhance mutual exchange in the areas of technology and equipment, including bilateral cooperative research and development of equipment such as the support fighter (F-2).

(e) The two governments recognized that the proliferation of weapons of mass destruction and their means of delivery has important implications for their common security. They will work together to prevent proliferation and will continue to cooperate in the ongoing study on ballistic missile defense.

The Prime Minister and the President recognized that the broad support and understanding of the Japanese people are indispensable for the smooth stationing of US forces in Japan, which is the core element of the Japan–US security arrangements. The two leaders agreed that both governments will make every effort to deal with various issues related to the presence and status of US forces. They also agreed to make further efforts to enhance mutual understanding between US forces and local Japanese communities.

In particular, with respect to Okinawa, where US facilities and areas are highly concentrated, the Prime Minister and the President reconfirmed their determination to carry out steps to consolidate, realign, and reduce US facilities and areas consistent with the objectives of the Treaty of Mutual Cooperation and Security. In this respect, the two leaders took satisfaction in the significant progress which has been made so far through the 'Special Action Committee on Okinawa' (SACO), and welcomed the far reaching measures outlined in the SACO Interim Report of April 15, 1996. They expressed their firm commitment to achieve a successful conclusion of the SACO process by November 1996.

Regional cooperation

The Prime Minister and the President agreed that the two governments will jointly and individually strive to achieve a more peaceful and stable security environment in the Asia-Pacific region. In this regard, the two leaders recognized that the engagement of the United States in the region, supported by the Japan–US security relationship, constitutes the foundation for such efforts.

The two leaders stressed the importance of peaceful resolution of problems in the region. They emphasized that it is extremely important for the stability and prosperity of the region that China play a positive and constructive role, and, in this context, stressed the interest of both countries in furthering cooperation with China. Russia's ongoing process of reform contributes to regional and global stability, and merits continued encouragement and cooperation. The leaders also stated that full normalization of Japan–Russia relations based on the Tokyo Declaration is important to peace and stability in the Asia-Pacific region. They noted also that stability on the Korean Peninsula is vitally important to Japan and the United States and reaffirmed that both countries will continue to make every effort in this regard, in close cooperation with the Republic of Korea.

The Prime Minister and the President reaffirmed that the two governments will continue working jointly and with other countries in the region to further develop multilateral regional security dialogues and cooperation mechanisms such as the ASEAN Regional Forum, and eventually, security dialogues regarding Northeast Asia.

Global cooperation

8 The Prime Minister and the President recognized that the Treaty of Mutual Cooperation and Security is the core of the Japan–US Alliance, and underlies the mutual confidence that constitutes the foundation for bilateral cooperation on global issues.

The Prime Minister and the President agreed that the two governments will strengthen their cooperation in support of the United Nations and other international organizations through activities such as peacekeeping and humanitarian relief operations.

Both governments will coordinate their policies and cooperate on issues such as arms control and disarmament, including acceleration of the Comprehensive Test Ban Treaty (CTBT) negotiations and the prevention of the proliferation of weapons of mass destruction and their means of delivery. The two leaders agreed that cooperation in the United Nations and APEC, and on issues such as the North Korean nuclear problem, the Middle East peace process, and the peace implementation process in the former Yugoslavia, helps to build the kind of world that promotes our shared interests and values.

Conclusion

9 In concluding, the Prime Minister and the President agreed that the three legs of the Japan–US relationship – security, political, and economic – are based on shared values and interests and rest on the mutual confidence embodied in the Treaty of Mutual Cooperation and Security. The Prime Minister and the President reaffirmed their strong determination, on the eve of the twenty-first century, to build on the successful history of security cooperation and to work hand-in-hand to secure peace and prosperity for future generations.

April 17, 1996 Tokyo

Prime Minister of Japan — President of the United States

Appendix 9.1

JOINT COMMUNIQUÉ OF THE GOVERNMENT OF JAPAN AND THE GOVERNMENT OF THE PEOPLE'S REPUBLIC OF CHINA

September 29, 1972

Prime Minister Kakuei Tanaka of Japan visited the People's Republic of China at the invitation of Premier of the State Council Chou En-lai of the People's Republic of China from September 25 to September 30, 1972. Accompanying Prime Minister Tanaka were Minister for Foreign Affairs Masayoshi Ōhira, Chief Cabinet Secretary Susumu Nikaidō and other government officials.

Chairman Mao Tse-tung met Prime Minister Kakuei Tanaka on September 27. They had an earnest and friendly conversation.

Prime Minister Tanaka and Minister for Foreign Affairs Ōhira had an earnest and frank exchange of views with Premier Chou En-lai and Minister for Foreign Affairs Chi Peng-fei in a friendly atmosphere throughout on the question of the normalization of relations between Japan and China and other problems between the two countries as well as on other matters of interest to both sides, and agreed to issue the following Joint Communiqué of the two Governments:

Japan and China are neighboring countries, separated only by a strip of water with a long history of traditional friendship. The peoples of the two countries earnestly desire to put an end to the abnormal state of affairs that has hitherto existed between the two countries. The realization of the aspiration of the two peoples for the termination of the state of war and the normalization of relations between Japan and China will add a new page to the annals of relations between the two countries.

The Japanese side is keenly conscious of the responsibility for the serious damage that Japan caused in the past to the Chinese people through war, and deeply reproaches itself. Further, the Japanese side reaffirms its position that it intends to realize the normalization of relations between the two countries from the stand of fully understanding 'the three principles for the restoration of relations' put forward by the Government of the People's Republic of China. The Chinese side expresses its welcome for this.

In spite of the differences in their social systems existing between the two countries, the two countries should, and can, establish relations of peace and friendship. The normalization of relations and development of good-neighborly and friendly relations between the two countries are in the interests of the two peoples and will contribute to the relaxation of tension in Asia and peace in the world.

1 The abnormal state of affairs that has hitherto existed between Japan and the People's Republic of China is terminated on the date on which this Joint Communiqué is issued.

2 The Government of Japan recognizes that Government of the People's Republic of China as the sole legal Government of China.

3 The Government of the People's Republic of China reiterates that Taiwan is an inalienable part of the territory of the People's Republic of China. The Government of Japan fully understands and respects this stand of the Government of the People's Republic of China, and it firmly maintains its stand under Article 8 of the Potsdam Proclamation.

4 The Government of Japan and the Government of People's Republic of China have decided to establish diplomatic relations as from September 29, 1972. The two Governments have decided to take all necessary measures for the establishment and the performance of the functions of each other's embassy in their respective capitals in accordance with international law and practice, and to exchange ambassadors as speedily as possible.

5 The Government of the People's Republic of China declares that in the interest of the friendship between the Chinese and the Japanese peoples, it renounces its demand for war reparation from Japan.

6 The Government of Japan and the Government of the People's Republic of China agree to establish relations of perpetual peace and friendship between the two countries on the basis of the principles of mutual respect for sovereignty and territorial integrity, mutual non-aggression, non-interference in each other's internal affairs, equality and mutual benefit and peaceful co-existence.

The two Governments confirm that, in conformity with the foregoing principles and the principles of the Charter of the United Nations, Japan and China shall in their mutual relations settle all disputes by peaceful means and shall refrain from the use or threat of force.

7 The normalization of relations between Japan and China is not directed against any third country. Neither of the two countries should seek hegemony in the Asia-Pacific region and each is opposed to efforts by any other country or group of countries to establish such hegemony.

8 The Government of Japan and the Government of the People's Republic of China have agreed that, with a view to solidifying and developing the relations of peace and friendship between the two countries, the two Governments will enter into negotiations for the purpose of concluding a treaty of peace and friendship.

9 The Government of Japan and the Government of the People's Republic of China have agreed that, with a view to further promoting relations between the two countries and to expanding interchanges of people, the two Govern-

ments will, as necessary and taking account of the existing non-governmental arrangements, enter into negotiations for the purpose of concluding agreements concerning such matters as trade, shipping, aviation, and fisheries.

DONE at Peking, September 29, 1972

Prime Minister of Japan Premier of the State Council of the People's Republic of China

Minister for Foreign Affairs of Japan Minister for Foreign Affairs of the People's Republic of China

Appendix 9.2

TREATY OF PEACE AND FRIENDSHIP BETWEEN JAPAN AND THE PEOPLE'S REPUBLIC OF CHINA

12 August 1978

Japan and the People's Republic of China, recalling with satisfaction that, since the Government of Japan and the Government of the People's Republic of China issued a joint communiqué in Peking on 29th September 1972, the friendly relations between the two Governments and the peoples of the two countries have developed greatly on a new basis, confirming that the above mentioned joint communiqué constitutes the basis of the relations of peace and friendship between the two countries and that the principles enunciated in the joint communiqué should be strictly observed, confirming that the principles of the Charter of the United Nations should be fully respected, hoping to contribute to peace and stability in Asia and in the world, for the purpose of solidifying and developing the relations of peace and friendship between the two countries, have resolved to conclude a Treaty of Peace and Friendship and for that purpose have appointed as their plenipotentiaries:

Japan Minister for Foreign Affairs — Sunao Sonoda

People's Republic of China Minister for Foreign Affairs — Huang Hua

who, having communicated to each other their full powers, found to be in good and due form, have agreed as follows:

Article 1

1 The contracting parties shall develop relations of perpetual peace and friendship between the two countries on the basis of the principles of mutual respect for sovereignty and territorial integrity, mutual non-aggression, non-interference in each other's internal affairs, equality and mutual benefit and peaceful coexistence.

2 The contracting parties confirm that, in conformity with the foregoing principles of the Charter of the United Nations, they shall in their mutual relations settle all disputes by peaceful means and shall refrain from the use or threat of force.

Article 2

The contracting parties declare that neither of them should seek hegemony in the Asia-Pacific region or in any other region and that each is opposed to efforts by any other country or group of countries to establish such hegemony.

Article 3

The contracting parties shall, in good-neighborly and friendly spirit and in conformity with the principles of equality and mutual benefit and non-interference in each other's internal affairs, endeavor to further develop economic and cultural relations between the two countries and to promote exchanges between the peoples of the two countries.

Article 4

The present Treaty shall not affect the position of either contracting party regarding its relations with third countries.

Article 5

1 The present Treaty shall be ratified and shall enter into force on the date of the exchange of instruments of ratification which shall take place at Tokyo. The present Treaty shall remain in force for ten years and thereafter shall continue to be in force until terminated in accordance with the provisions of paragraph 2.

2 Either contracting party may, by giving one year's written notice to the other contracting party, terminate the present Treaty at the end of the initial ten year period or at any time thereafter.

IN WITNESS WHEREOF the respective plenipotentiaries have signed the present Treaty and have affixed thereto their seals.

Appendix 9.3

JAPAN–CHINA JOINT DECLARATION ON BUILDING A PARTNERSHIP OF FRIENDSHIP AND COOPERATION FOR PEACE AND DEVELOPMENT

26 November 1998

In response to an invitation extended by the Government of Japan, President Jiang Zemin of the People's Republic of China made an official visit to Japan as a State Guest from 25 to 30 November 1998. On the occasion of this historically significant first visit to Japan by a President of the People's Republic of China, President Jiang met with His Majesty the Emperor of Japan, and held an intensive exchange of views with Prime Minister Keizō Obuchi on the international situation, regional issues and the overall Japan–China relationship. They attained a broad common view and, based on the success of this visit, declared as follows:

I Both sides shared the view that as the world in the post-Cold War era continues to undergo great changes toward the creation of a new international order, further economic globalization is deepening interdependence and security dialogue and cooperation are making constant progress. Peace and development remain major issues facing the human society. It is therefore the common wish of the international community to build a new international political and economic order which is fair and rational, and to strive for a peaceful international environment in the twenty-first century that is even more firmly rooted.

Both sides reaffirmed that the principles of mutual respect for sovereignty and territorial integrity, mutual non-aggression, non-interference in each other's internal affairs, equality and mutual benefit and peaceful co-existence, as well as the principles of the Charter of the United Nations, are the basic norms for relations between states.

Both sides positively evaluate the efforts made by the United Nations to preserve world peace and to promote the economic and social development of the world, and believe that the United Nations should play an important role in building and maintaining a new international order.

Both sides express support for the reforms of the United Nations including the reform of the Security Council, in order for the United Nations to further embody the common wish and collective will of all Members in its activities and policy decision making process.

Both sides stress the importance of the ultimate elimination of nuclear weapons, and oppose the proliferation of nuclear weapons in any form whatsoever, and furthermore, strongly call upon the nations concerned to cease all nuclear testing and nuclear arms race, in order to contribute to the peace and stability of the Asian region and the world.

Both sides believe that both Japan and China, as nations influential in the Asian region and the world, bear an important responsibility for preserving peace and promoting development.

Both sides will strengthen coordination and cooperation in the areas such as international politics, international economy, and global issues, thus positively contributing to the endeavor for the peace and development of the world aimed at the progress of humanity.

II Both sides believe that, after the Cold War, the Asian region has continued to move toward stability and the regional cooperation has deepened further. In addition, both sides are convinced that this region will exert greater influence on international politics, economics and security and will continue to play an important role in the coming century.

Both sides reiterate that it is the unshakable fundamental policy of the two countries to maintain the peace of this region and to promote its development, and that they will not seek hegemony in the Asian region and settle all disputes by peaceful means, without recourse to the use or threat of force.

Both sides expressed their great interest in the current financial crisis in East Asia and the ensuing difficulties for the Asian economy. At the same time, both sides recognize that the economic foundation of this region is sound, and firmly believe that by advancing rational adjustment and reform based on experiences, as well as by enhancing regional and international coordination and cooperation, the economy of Asia will definitely overcome its difficulties and continue to develop. Both sides affirmed that they would positively meet the various challenges that they faced, and would respectively make their utmost efforts toward promoting the economic development of the region.

Both sides believe that stable relations among the major nations of the Asia-Pacific region are extremely important for the peace and stability of this region. Both sides shared the view that they would actively participate in all multilateral activities in this region, such as the ASEAN Regional Forum, promote coordination and cooperation, and support all measures for enhancing understanding and strengthening confidence.

III Both sides reviewed the bilateral relationship since the normalization of relations between Japan and China, and expressed satisfaction with the remarkable development in all areas, including politics, economics, culture and personnel exchanges. Further, both sides shared the view that under the current situation cooperation between the two countries is growing in importance, and that further strengthening and developing the friendly and cooperative relations between the two countries not only serve the fundamental interests of their peoples, but also positively contribute to the peace and development of the Asia-Pacific region and the world as a whole. Both sides reaffirmed that the Japan–China relationship is one of the most important bilateral relationships for the respective country, deeply recognized the role and responsibility of both countries in achieving peace and development, and expressed their resolve to establish a partnership of friendship and cooperation for peace and development toward the twenty-first century.

Both sides restated that they will observe the principles of the Joint Communiqué of the Government of Japan and the Government of the People's Republic of China, issued on 29 September 1972 and the Treaty of Peace and Friendship between Japan and the People's Republic of China, signed on 12 August 1978, and reaffirmed that the above-mentioned documents will continue to be the most important foundation for the bilateral relations.

Both sides are of the view that Japan and China share a history of friendly exchanges spanning more than 2,000 years, as well as a common cultural background, and that it is the common desire of the peoples of the two countries to continue this tradition of friendship and to further develop mutually beneficial cooperation.

Both sides believe that squarely facing the past and correctly understanding history are the important foundation for further developing relations between Japan and China. The Japanese side observes the 1972 Joint Communiqué of the Government of Japan and the Government of the People's Republic of China and the 15 August 1995 Statement by former Prime Minister Tomiichi Murayama. The Japanese side is keenly conscious of the responsibility for the serious distress and damage that Japan caused to the Chinese people through its aggression against China during a certain period in the past and expressed deep remorse for this. The Chinese side hopes that the Japanese side will learn lessons from the history and adhere to the path of peace and development. Based on this, both sides will develop long-standing relations of friendship.

Both sides shared the view that expanding personnel exchanges between the two countries is extremely important for advancing mutual understanding and enhancing mutual trust.

Both sides confirmed an annual visit by a leader of either country to the other, the establishment of a Tokyo–Beijing hotline between the two Governments, and the further enhancement of personnel exchanges at all levels, in particular among the younger generation who will shoulder the heavy burden of the future development of the two countries.

Both sides shared the view that, based on the principles of equality and mutual benefit, they will formulate long-term, stable, cooperative economic and trade relations, and will further expand cooperation in such areas as high technology, information, environmental protection, agriculture and infrastructure. The Japanese side reiterated that a stable, open and developing China is significant for the peace and development of the Asia-Pacific region and the entire world, and restated its policy of continuing cooperation and assistance for the economic development of China. The Chinese side expressed its gratitude for the economic cooperation extended by Japan to China. The Japanese side reiterated that it will continue to support China's efforts for the early accession to the WTO.

Both sides positively evaluated the beneficial role played by their bilateral security dialogue in increasing mutual understanding, and shared the view that they would further strengthen this dialogue mechanism.

The Japanese side continues to maintain its stand on the Taiwan issue which was set forth in the Joint Communiqué of the Government of Japan and the Government of the People's Republic of China and reiterates its understanding that there is one China. Japan will continue to maintain its exchanges of private and regional nature with Taiwan.

Both sides affirmed that, based on the principles of the Joint Communiqué of the Government of Japan and the Government of the People's Republic of China and the Treaty of Peace and Friendship between Japan and the People's Republic of China, and following the spirit of seeking common major benefits while setting aside minor differences, they would work to maximize their common interests and minimize their differences, and, through friendly consultations, appropriately handle the issues, differences of opinion and disputes which currently exist and may arise in the future, thereby avoiding any restraint or obstacle to development of friendly relations between the two countries.

Both sides believe that through establishment of a partnership of friendship and cooperation for peace and development, the bilateral relations will enter a new level of development. To this end, a wide range of participation and sustained effort not only of both Governments, but also of the peoples of both countries, is essential.

Both sides firmly believe that, if the peoples of both countries, hand-in-hand, thoroughly demonstrate the spirit shown in this Declaration, it will not only contribute to the friendship of the peoples of both countries for generations to come, but also make an important contribution to the peace and development of the Asia-Pacific region and of the world.

Appendix 9.4

TREATY ON BASIC RELATIONS BETWEEN JAPAN AND THE REPUBLIC OF KOREA

Tokyo, 22 June 1965

Japan and the Republic of Korea,

Considering the historical background of relationship between their peoples and their mutual desire for good neighborliness and for the normalization of their relations on the basis of the principle of mutual respect for sovereignty;

Recognizing the importance of their close cooperation in conformity with the principles of the Charter of the United Nations to the promotion of their mutual welfare and common interests and to the maintenance of international peace and security; and

Recalling the relevant provisions of the Treaty of Peace with Japan signed at the city of San Francisco on September 8, 1951 and the Resolution 195(III) adopted by the United Nations General Assembly on December 12, 1948;

Have resolved to conclude the present Treaty on Basic Relations and have accordingly appointed as their Plenipotentiaries,

Japan:

Etsusaburō Shiina, Minister for Foreign Affairs of Japan

Shinichi Takasugi

The Republic of Korea:

Tong Won Lee, Minister of Foreign Affairs of the Republic of Korea

Dong Jo Kim, Ambassador Extraordinary and Plenipotentiary of the Republic of Korea

Who, having communicated to each other their full powers found to be in good and due form, have agreed upon the following articles:

Article I

Diplomatic and consular relations shall be established between the High Contracting Parties. The High Contracting Parties shall exchange diplomatic envoys with the Ambassadorial rank without delay. The High Contracting Parties will also establish consulates at locations to be agreed upon by the two Governments.

Article II

It is confirmed that all treaties or agreements concluded between the Empire of Japan and the Empire of Korea on or before August 22, 1910 are already null and void.

Article III

It is confirmed that the Government of the Republic of Korea is the only lawful Government in Korea as specified in the Resolution 195(III) of the United Nations General Assembly.

Article IV

(a) The High Contracting Parties will be guided by the principles of the Charter of the United Nations in their mutual relations.

(b) The High Contracting Parties will cooperate in conformity with the principles of the Charter of the United Nations in promoting their mutual welfare and common interests.

Article V

The High Contracting Parties will enter into negotiations at the earliest practicable date for the conclusion of treaties or agreements to place their trading, maritime and other commercial relations on a stable and friendly basis.

Article VI

The High Contracting Parties will enter into negotiations at the earliest practicable date for the conclusion of an agreement relating to civil air transport.

Article VII

The present Treaty shall be ratified. The instruments of ratification shall be exchanged at Seoul as soon as possible. The present Treaty shall enter into force as from the date on which the instruments of ratification are exchanged.

IN WITNESS WHEREOF, the respective Plenipotentiaries have signed the present Treaty and have affixed thereto their seals.

DONE in duplicate at Tokyo, this twenty-second day of June of the year one thousand nine hundred and sixty-five in the Japanese, Korean, and English languages, each text being equally authentic. In case of any divergence of interpretation, the English text shall prevail.

FOR JAPAN	FOR THE REPUBLIC OF KOREA
Etsusaburō Shiina	Tong Won Lee
Shinichi Takasugi	Dong Jo Kim

AGREEMENT BETWEEN JAPAN AND THE REPUBLIC OF KOREA CONCERNING FISHERIES

Tokyo, 22 June 1965

Japan and the Republic of Korea,

Desiring that the maximum sustained productivity of the fishery resources in waters of mutual interest be maintained;

Firmly believing that the conservation of such resources and their rational exploitation and development will serve the interests of both countries;

Confirming that the principle of freedom of the high seas shall be respected unless otherwise prescribed by special provisions in the present Agreement;

Recognizing the desirability of eliminating the causes of disputes which may arise from their geographical proximity and the intermingling of their respective fisheries; and

Desiring mutual cooperation for the development of their fisheries,

Have agreed as follows:

Article I

1 The High Contracting Parties mutually recognize that each High Contracting Party has the right to establish a sea zone (hereinafter 'fishery zone'), extending not more than 12 nautical miles from its respective coastal base line, over which it will have exclusive jurisdiction with respect to fisheries. However, in case either High Contracting Party uses the straight base line for the establishment of its fishery zone, the straight base line shall be determined through consultation with the other High Contracting Party.

2 The High Contracting Parties shall not present objections when one Party excludes the fishing vessels of the other Party from engaging in fishing operations in its fishery zone.

3 Areas where the fishery zones of the High Contracting Parties overlap shall be divided in two by straight lines joining the ends of the overlapping areas with the midpoints of straight lines drawn across the areas at their widest points.

Article II

1 The High Contracting Parties shall establish a joint control zone encircled by the lines described below (excluding territorial waters and the Republic of Korea's fishery zone).

(a) A line north on the 124th E meridian north of 37° 30' N.

(b) Thence, a line joining the following coordinates in order:

(I) 37° 30' N, 124° E
(II) 36° 45' N, 124° 30' E
(III) 33° 30' N, 124° 30' E
(IV) 32° 30' N, 126° E
(V) 32° 30' N, 127° E
(VI) 34° 34' 30? N, 129° 2' 50? E
(VII) 34° 44' 10? N, 129° 8' E
(VIII) 34° 50' N, 129° 14' E
(IX) 34° 30' N, 130° E
(X) 37° 30' N, 131° 10' E
(XI) High peak of Uamnyong

Article III

Until conservation measures necessary for maintaining the maximum sustained productivity of fishery resources are implemented on the basis of exhaustive scientific research, the provisional fishery control measures listed in the Annex [not reproduced here], which forms an integral part of this Agreement, shall be enforced in the joint control zones with respect to dragnet fishing and surrounding net fishing, and mackerel fishing by fishing vessels of not less than 60 tons. (Ton represents gross ton. The tonnage shall be indicated by deducting the tonnage permitted for improving living quarters on the vessels.)

Article IV

1 The right of control (including the right to halt and inspect vessels) and jurisdiction in waters outside the exclusive fishery zone shall be exercised only by the High Contracting Party to which the ship belongs.

2 The High Contracting Parties shall exercise appropriate guidance and supervision in order to guarantee the faithful observance of the provisional fishery control measures by their own nationals and fishing vessels, and shall carry out domestic measures, including appropriate penalties against violations thereof.

Article V

Joint resources survey zones shall be established outside of the joint control zones. The scope of the said zones and the surveys to be conducted within these zones shall be determined through consultation between the two High Contracting Parties, on the basis of recommendations made by the Joint Fisheries Commission provided for in Article VI.

Article VI

1 The High Contracting Parties shall establish and maintain the Japan–Republic of Korea Joint Fisheries Commission (hereinafter referred to as the 'Commission') in order to realize the purposes of this Agreement.

2 The Commission shall be composed of two national sections, each consisting of three members appointed by the Governments of the respective High Contracting Parties.

3 All resolutions, recommendations, and other decisions of the Commission shall be made only with the concurrence of the national sections.

4 The Commission may decide upon and revise, as occasion may require, rules for the conduct of its meetings.

5 The Commission shall meet at least once each year and, in addition, it may meet as requested by one of the national sections. The date and place of the first meeting shall be determined by agreement between the High Contracting Parties.

6 At its first meeting, the Commission shall select a Chairman and Vice-Chairman, one from each national section. The Chairman and Vice-Chairman shall hold office for a period of one year. During the succeeding years selection of a Chairman and a Vice-Chairman from the national sections shall be made in such a manner as will provide each High Contracting Party in turn with representation in those offices.

7 A standing secretariat shall be established under the Commission to carry out the business of the Commission.

8 The official languages of the Commission shall be Japanese and Korean. Proposals and data may be presented in either official language, or, if necessary, they may be presented in English.

9 In the event that the Commission concludes that joint expenses are necessary, such expenses shall be paid by the Commission through contributions made by the High Contracting Parties in the form and proportion recommended by the Commission and approved by the High Contracting Parties.

10 The Commission may delegate the disbursement of funds for the joint expenses of the Commission.

Article VII

1 The Commission shall perform the following functions:

(a) The Commission shall make recommendations to the High Contracting Parties concerning scientific research for the purpose of studying the fishery resources in the sea areas of mutual interest and concerning control measures within the joint control zones to be carried out on the basis of the results of such research and study;

(b) The Commission shall make recommendations to the High Contracting Parties on the scope of the joint resources survey zones;

(c) When it is deemed necessary, the Commission shall review matters concerning provisional fishery control measures and make recommendations to the High Contracting Parties concerning measures to be taken as a result of such review (including the revision of the provisional control measures);

(d) The Commission shall review necessary matters concerning safe operations and order among the fishing vessels of the High Contracting Parties and general policies for settling accidents occurring at sea between the fishing vessels of the High Contracting Parties, and shall make recommendations to the High Contracting Parties concerning measures to be taken as a result of such review;

(e) The Commission shall compile and study data, statistics, and records which the High Contracting Parties submit at the request of the Commission;

(f) The Commission shall consider and make recommendations to the High Contracting Parties concerning the enactment of schedules of equivalent penalties for violations of this Agreement;

(g) The Commission shall submit annually its business report to the High Contracting Parties; and

(h) The Commission shall study the various technical questions arising in connection with the implementation of this Agreement, and shall, when it is deemed necessary, make recommendations to the High Contracting Parties on the steps to be taken.

2 The Commission may establish such subsidiary organs as it deems necessary for the performance of its functions.

3 The Governments of the High Contracting Parties shall respect to the extent possible the recommendations made by the Commission in accordance with the provisions of paragraph 1.

Article VIII

1 The High Contracting Parties shall take measures as may be appropriate to guarantee the observance of international practices concerning navigation by their nationals and fishing vessels, to promote safe operations between the fishing vessels of the High Contracting Parties, to maintain proper order among them, and to achieve smooth and speedy settlements of accidents arising at sea between the fishing vessels of the High Contracting Parties.

2 In order to achieve the objective of paragraph 1, the authorities concerned of the two High Contracting Parties shall maintain as closely as possible mutual contact and cooperation.

Article IX

1 Any dispute between the High Contracting Parties concerning the interpretation or implementation of this Agreement shall be settled primarily through diplomatic channels.

2 Any dispute which cannot be settled under the provision of paragraph 1 shall be submitted for decision to an arbitration Commission of three arbitrators; one to be appointed by the Government of each High Contracting Party within a period of thirty days from the date of receipt by the Government of either High Contracting Party from that of the other High Contracting Party of a note requesting arbitration of the dispute; and the third to be agreed upon by the two arbitrators so chosen or to be nominated by the Government of a third power as agreed upon by the two arbitrators within a further period of thirty days. However, the third arbitrator must not be a national of either High Contracting Party.

3 If, within the periods respectively referred to, the Government of either High Contracting Party fails to appoint an arbitrator, or the third arbitrator of the third nation is not agreed upon, the arbitration commission shall be composed of one arbitrator to be nominated by the Government of each of two

nations respectively chosen by the Government of each High Contracting Party within a period of thirty days, and the third arbitrator to be nominated by the Government of a third power decided upon by agreement between the Governments so chosen.

4 The Governments of the High Contracting Parties shall accept decisions rendered by the arbitration commission established in accordance with the provisions of this Article.

Article X

1 The present Agreement shall be ratified. The instruments of ratification shall be exchanged at Seoul as soon as possible. This Agreement shall enter into force as from the date on which the instruments of ratification are exchanged.

2 The present Agreement shall continue in force for a period of five years and thereafter until one year from the day on which a High Contracting Party shall give notice to the other High Contracting Party of an intention to terminate the Agreement.

IN WITNESS WHEREOF, the undersigned, duly authorized by the respective Governments, have signed the present Agreement.

DONE in duplicate at Tokyo, this twenty-second day of June of the year one thousand nine hundred and sixty-five in the Japanese and Korean languages, each text being equally authentic.

FOR JAPAN	FOR THE REPUBLIC OF KOREA
Etsusaburō Shiina	Tong Won Lee
Shinichi Takasugi	Dong Jo Kim

AGREEMENT BETWEEN JAPAN AND THE REPUBLIC OF KOREA CONCERNING THE SETTLEMENT OF PROBLEMS IN REGARD TO PROPERTY AND CLAIMS AND ECONOMIC COOPERATION

Tokyo, 22 June 1965

Japan and the Republic of Korea,

Desiring to settle problems regarding the property of both countries and their peoples and the claims between both countries and between their peoples; and

Desiring to promote economic cooperation between the two countries,

Have agreed as follows:

Article I

1 Japan shall supply the Republic of Korea with:

(a) Products of Japan and the services of Japanese people, free of charge, the total value of which will be so much in yen as shall be equivalent to three hundred million United States dollars ($300,000,000), at present computed at one hundred and eight billion yen (¥108,000,000,000), within a period of ten years of the date on which the present Agreement enters into force. The supply of products and services each year shall be limited to so much in yen as shall be equivalent to thirty million United States dollars ($30,000,000), at present computed at ten billion eight hundred million yen (¥10,800,000,000); when the supply of any one year falls short of this amount, the remainder shall be added to the amount for the next and subsequent years. However, the maximum amount supplied for any one year may be increased by agreement between the Governments of the High Contracting Parties.

(b) Long-term and low-interest loans up to so much in yen as shall be equivalent to two hundred million United States dollars ($200,000,000), at present computed at seventy-two billion yen (¥72,000,000,000), which are requested by the Government of the Republic of Korea and which will be covered by procuring the products of Japan and the services of Japanese people necessary for implementing the enterprises to be decided upon in accordance with arrangements to be concluded under paragraph 3 within a period of ten years of the date on which the present Agreement enters into force. These loans shall be extended by the Overseas Economic Cooperation Fund of Japan, and the Government of Japan shall take the necessary measures to enable the Fund to secure the funds for equal annual loans. The aforesaid supply and loans must serve the economic development of the Republic of Korea.

2 There shall be established a Joint Committee composed of representatives of the two Governments as an organ for consultation between them, with the power to make recommendations on matters concerning the implementation of the present Agreement.

3 The two Governments of the High Contracting Parties shall take measures necessary for the implementation of this Article.

Article II

1 The High Contracting Parties confirm that the problems concerning property, rights, and interests of the two High Contracting Parties and their peoples (including juridical persons) and the claims between the High

Contracting Parties and between their peoples, including those stipulated in Article IV(a) of the Peace Treaty with Japan signed at the city of San Francisco on September 8, 1951, have been settled completely and finally.

2 The provisions of this Article shall not affect the following (excluding those which become the objects of special measures taken by either of the High Contracting Parties prior to the date of the signing of the present Agreement):

(a) The property, rights, and interests of the people of either High Contracting Party who have ever resided in the territory of the other High Contracting Party in the period between August 15, 1947, and the date of the signing of the present Agreement; and

(b) The property, rights, and interests of either High Contracting Party and its people which were acquired or brought under the control of the other High Contracting Party in the course of ordinary contacts after August 15, 1945.

3 As a condition to comply with the provisions of paragraph 2 above, no claims shall be made with respect to the measures relating to the property, rights, and interests of either High Contracting Party and its people which were brought under the control of the other High Contracting Party on the date of the signing of the present Agreement, or to all the claims of either High Contracting Party and its people arising from the causes which occurred prior to that date.

Article III

1 Any dispute between the High Contracting Parties concerning the interpretation or the implementation of this Agreement shall be settled primarily through diplomatic channels.

2 Any dispute which cannot be settled under the provision of paragraph 1 above shall be submitted for decision to an arbitral commission of three arbitrators; one to be appointed by the Government of each High Contracting Party within a period of thirty days from the date of receipt by the Government of either High Contracting Party from that of the other High Contracting Party of a note requesting arbitration of the dispute; and the third to be agreed upon by the two arbitrators so chosen or to be nominated by the Government of a third power as agreed upon by the two arbitrators within a further period of thirty days. However, the third arbitrator must not be a national of either High Contracting Party.

3 If, within the periods respectively referred to, the Government of either High Contracting Party fails to appoint an arbitrator, or the third arbitrator or the third nation is not agreed upon, the arbitral commission shall be com-

posed of one arbitrator to be nominated by the Government of each of two nations respectively chosen by the Government of each High Contracting Party within a period of thirty days, and the third arbitrator to be nominated by the Government of a third power decided upon by agreement between the Governments so chosen.

4 The Governments of the High Contracting Parties shall accept decisions rendered by the arbitral commission established in accordance with the provisions of this Article.

Article IV

The present Agreement shall be ratified. The instruments of ratification shall be exchanged at Seoul as soon as possible. The present Agreement shall enter into force as from the date on which the instruments of ratification are exchanged.

IN WITNESS WHEREOF, the undersigned, duly authorized thereto by their respective Governments, have signed the present Agreement.

DONE in duplicate at Tokyo, this twenty-second day of June of the year one thousand nine hundred and sixty-five in the Japanese and Korean languages, each text being equally authentic.

FOR JAPAN	FOR THE REPUBLIC OF KOREA
Etsusaburō Shiina	Tong Won Lee
Shinichi Takasugi	Dong Jo Kim

AGREEMENT BETWEEN JAPAN AND THE REPUBLIC OF KOREA CONCERNING THE LEGAL STATUS AND TREATMENT OF THE PEOPLE OF THE REPUBLIC OF KOREA RESIDING IN JAPAN

Tokyo, 22 June 1965

Japan and the Republic of Korea,

Considering the fact that the nationals of the Republic of Korea residing in Japan for many years have come to possess a special relationship with Japanese society; and

Recognizing that enabling the nationals of the Republic of Korea to lead a stabilized life under the Japanese social order will contribute to the promotion of friendly relations between the two countries and their peoples,

Have agreed as follows:

Article I

1 The Government of Japan will permit a national of the Republic of Korea falling under any one of the following categories to reside permanently in Japan if within five years of the date on which the present Agreement enters into force he applies, in accordance with the procedures determined by the Government of Japan for the implementation of the present Agreement, for permission for permanent residence:

(a) A person who resided in Japan prior to August 15, 1945, and who has continuously resided there until the application has been filed; and

(b) A person who is born on or after August 16, 1945, and within five years of the date on which the present Agreement enters into force, who is a lineal descendant of a person mentioned in (a) above, and who has continuously resided in Japan therefrom until the application has been filed.

2 The Government of Japan will permit a national of the Republic of Korea, born after the lapse of five years from the date on which the present Agreement enters into force, and who is the child of a person permitted to reside permanently in Japan in accordance with the provisions of paragraph 1 above, to reside permanently in Japan when permission for permanent residence is applied for within sixty days of the date of his birth in accordance with the procedures determined by the Government of Japan for the implementation of the present Agreement.

3 The term within which application for permission for permanent residence is to be filed for a person falling under paragraph l(b) above and who is born after the lapse of 4 years and 10 months from the date on which the present Agreement enters into force shall be 60 days beginning from the date of his birth notwithstanding the provisions of paragraph 1 above.

4 No fee shall be levied on the aforesaid application and permission.

Article II

1 The Government of Japan agrees to enter into consultations, if requested by the Government of the Republic of Korea, within 25 years of the date on which the present Agreement enters into force, with a view to the residence in Japan of a national of the Republic of Korea born in Japan as a lineal descendant of a person who has been permitted to reside permanently in Japan in accordance with the provisions of Article I.

2 In the consultations under paragraph I above, the spirit and purposes which form the basis of the present Agreement shall be respected.

Article III

A national of the Republic of Korea who has been permitted to reside permanently in Japan in accordance with the provisions of Article I shall not be forcibly deported from Japan unless after the date on which the present Agreement enters into force he commits an act whereby he falls under any one of the following categories:

(a) A person who has been punished with a penalty heavier than imprisonment in Japan for crimes concerning insurrection or crimes concerning foreign aggression (excluding a person whose sentence has been suspended or one who has been punished on charges of joining in an insurrection);

(b) A person who has been punished with a penalty heavier than imprisonment in Japan for crimes relating to diplomatic relations, and a person who has been punished with a penalty heavier than imprisonment for criminal acts against the chief of State, a diplomatic envoy, or a diplomatic mission of a foreign country and thereby causing an injury to the important diplomatic interests of Japan;

(c) A person who has been punished with penal servitude or imprisonment for life or for not less than three years (excluding a person whose sentence has been suspended) on charges of violation of Japanese laws and ordinances concerning control of narcotics for the purpose of gain, and a person who has been punished three or more times (twice or more for one who has been punished three or more times for acts committed prior to the date on which the present Agreement enters into force) on charges of violation of Japanese laws and ordinances; and

(d) A person who has been punished with penal servitude or imprisonment for life or for seven or more years on charges of violation of Japanese laws and ordinances.

Article IV

The Government of Japan will give due consideration to the following matters:

(a) Matters concerning the education, livelihood protection, and national health insurance in Japan for a national of the Republic of Korea who has been permitted to reside permanently in Japan in accordance with the provisions of Article I; and

(b) Matters concerning the carrying of property and the remitting of funds to the Republic of Korea in the case of a national of the Republic of Korea who has been permitted to reside permanently in Japan in accordance with the provisions of Article I (including one who is qualified to apply for permission for permanent residence in accordance with the provisions of the same Article), who has abandoned the intention to reside permanently in Japan, and who returns to the Republic of Korea.

Article V

It is confirmed that a national of the Republic of Korea who has been permitted to reside permanently in Japan in accordance with the provisions of Article I shall be subject to the application of Japanese laws and ordinances applicable equally to all aliens, concerning all matters including emigration, immigration, and residence, except for the cases specifically prescribed in the present Agreement.

Article VI

The present Agreement shall be ratified. The instruments of ratification shall be exchanged at Seoul as soon as possible. The present Agreement shall enter into force thirty days after the date on which the instruments of ratification are exchanged.

IN WITNESS WHEREOF, the undersigned, being duly authorized thereto by their respective Governments, have signed the present Agreement.

DONE in duplicate at Tokyo, this twenty-second day of June of the year one thousand nine hundred and sixty-five in the Japanese and Korean languages, each text being equally authentic.

FOR JAPAN	FOR THE REPUBLIC OF KOREA
Etsusaburō Shiina	Tong Won Lee
Shinichi Takasugi	Dong Jo Kim

[Agreed minutes interpreting the Agreement are not reproduced.]

Appendix 9.5

JAPAN–REPUBLIC OF KOREA JOINT DECLARATION: A NEW JAPAN–REPUBLIC OF KOREA PARTNERSHIP TOWARDS THE 21ST CENTURY

8 October 1998

1 President Kim Dae-Jung of the Republic of Korea and Mrs Kim paid an official visit to Japan as State Guests from 7 October 1998 to 10 October 1998. During his stay in Japan, President Kim Dae-Jung held a meeting with Prime Minister Keizō Obuchi of Japan. The two leaders conducted an overall review of past relations between Japan and the Republic of Korea, reaffirmed the current friendly and cooperative relations, and exchanged views on how the relations between the two countries should be in the future.

As a result of the meeting, the two leaders declared their common determination to raise to a higher dimension the close, friendly and cooperative relations between Japan and the Republic of Korea which have been built since the normalization of their relations in 1965 so as to build a new Japan–Republic of Korea partnership towards the twenty-first century.

2 The two leaders shared the view that in order for Japan and the Republic of Korea to build solid, good-neighborly and friendly relations in the twenty-first century, it was important that both countries squarely face the past and develop relations based on mutual understanding and trust.

Looking back on the relations between Japan and the Republic of Korea during this century, Prime Minister Obuchi regarded in a spirit of humility the fact of history that Japan caused, during a certain period in the past, tremendous damage and suffering to the people of the Republic of Korea through its colonial rule, and expressed his deep remorse and heartfelt apology for this fact. President Kim accepted with sincerity this statement of Prime Minister Obuchi's recognition of history and expressed his appreciation for it. He also expressed his view that the present calls upon both countries to overcome their unfortunate history and to build a future-oriented relationship based on reconciliation as well as good-neighborly and friendly cooperation.

Further, both leaders shared the view that it was important that the peoples of both countries, the young generation in particular, deepen their understanding of history, and stressed the need to devote much attention and effort to that end.

3 The two leaders shared the recognition that Japan and the Republic of Korea, which have maintained exchanges and cooperation throughout a long history, have developed close, friendly and cooperative relations in various areas since the normalization of their relations in 1965, and that such cooperative relations have contributed to the development of both countries. Prime Minister Obuchi expressed his admiration for the Republic of Korea which, through the untiring efforts of its people, has achieved dramatic development and democratization and has grown into a prosperous and mature democratic state. President Kim highly appreciated the role that Japan has played for the peace and prosperity of the international community through it security policies, foremost its exclusively defense-oriented policy and three non-nuclear principles under the postwar Japanese Peace Constitution, its contributions to the global economy and its economic assistance to developing countries, and other means. Both leaders expressed their determination that Japan and the Republic of Korea further develop their cooperative relationship founded on such universal principles as freedom, democracy and the market economy, based on broad exchanges and mutual understanding between their peoples.

4 The two leaders shared the view that there was a need to enhance the relations between Japan and the Republic of Korea in a wide range of areas to a balanced cooperative relationship of a higher dimension, including in the political, security and economic areas as well as in personnel and cultural exchanges. They also shared the view that it was extremely important to advance the partnership between the two countries, not only in the bilateral dimension but also for the peace and prosperity of the Asia-Pacific region and the international community as a whole, and in exploring in various ways to achieve a society in which individual human rights are better respected, and a more comfortable global environment.

In order to bring the relationship between Japan and the Republic of Korea in the twentieth century to a fitting conclusion as well as to build and develop the partnership between the two countries as a common goal based on true mutual understanding and cooperation, the two leaders therefore concurred on the following. They formulated the action plan annexed to this Joint Declaration in order to give concrete form to this partnership.

The two leaders decided that the Ministers for Foreign of Affairs of their countries would serve as the overall supervisors of this Japan–Republic of Korea partnership and that their Governments would review regularly the state of progress in the cooperation based on it and strengthen the cooperation as necessary.

5 Both leaders shared the view that consultations and dialogue between the two countries should be further promoted in order to develop the present Japan–Republic of Korea relationship to a higher dimension.

Based on this view, the two leaders decided to maintain and strengthen the mutual visits and the close consultations between them, to conduct these visits and consultations regularly and to further enhance Minister-level consultations in various areas, in particular those between their Foreign Ministers. They also decided that a gathering of Ministers of the two countries would be held as soon as possible to provide an occasion for a free exchange of views among the concerned Ministers responsible for policy implementation. In addition, the two leaders expressed appreciation for the positive results of exchanges among parliamentarians of Japan and the Republic of Korea, and welcomed the positions of the Japan–Republic of Korea and the Republic of Korea–Japan parliamentarian friendship leagues to expand their activities, and decided that they would encourage increased exchanges among young parliamentarians who will play a prominent role in the twenty-first century.

6 The two leaders shared the view that it was important for Japan and the Republic of Korea to cooperate on and to participate actively in international efforts to build a more peaceful and safer international order in the post-Cold War world. They shared the view that the role of the United Nations should be strengthened in order to respond more effectively to the challenges and tasks in the twenty-first century and that this could be achieved through strengthening the functions of the Security Council, increasing the efficiency of the United Nations Secretariat, ensuring a stable financial base, strengthening United Nations peace-keeping operations, cooperation for economic and social development in developing countries and other means.

Bearing these views in mind, President Kim Dae-Jung expressed appreciation for Japan's contributions to and the Japanese role in the international community, including the United Nations, and expressed the expectation that these kinds of contributions and role will be increased in the future.

The two leaders also stressed the importance of disarmament and non-proliferation. In particular, they emphasized that all kinds of weapons of mass destruction and their proliferation posed a threat to the peace and security of the international community, and decided to further strengthen cooperation between Japan and the Republic of Korea in this field.

The two leaders welcomed the security dialogue as well as the defense exchanges at various levels between the two countries and decided to further strengthen them. The leaders also shared the view on the importance of both countries to steadfastly maintain their security arrangements with the United States while at the same time further strengthen efforts on multilateral dialogue for the peace and stability of the Asia-Pacific region.

7 The two leaders shared the view that in order to achieve peace and stability on the Korean Peninsula, it was extremely important that North Korea pursue reform and openness and take through dialogue a more constructive attitude. Prime Minister Obuchi expressed support for the policies of Presi-

dent Kim Dae-Jung regarding North Korea under which the Republic of Korea is actively promoting reconciliation and cooperation while maintaining a solid security system. In this regard, both leaders shared the view that the implementation of the Agreement on Reconciliation, Nonaggression, Exchanges and Cooperation between the South and North, which entered into force in February 1992, and the smooth progress of the Four-Party Talks are desirable. Furthermore, both leaders confirmed the importance of maintaining the Agreed Framework signed in October 1994 between the United States of America and North Korea and the Korean Peninsula Energy Development Organization (KEDO) as the most realistic and effective mechanisms for preventing North Korea from advancing its nuclear program. In this connection, the two leaders shared the concern and regret expressed by the President of the United Nations Security Council on behalf of the Security Council over the recent missile launch by North Korea, as well as the view that, North Korea's missile development, if unchecked, would adversely affect the peace and security of Japan, the Republic of Korea and the entire Northeast Asian region.

The two leaders reaffirmed the importance of close coordination between the two countries in conducting their policies on North Korea, and shared the view that policy consultations at various levels should be strengthened.

8 The two leaders agreed that in order to maintain and develop the free and open international economic system and revive the Asian economy which is facing structural problems, it is important that Japan and the Republic of Korea further strengthen their mutual cooperative relations in the economic field in a balanced manner while each overcomes its respective economic difficulties. For this end, the two leaders shared the view that they would further strengthen bilateral economic policy consultations as well as to further promote policy coordination between the two countries at such multilateral fora as the World Trade Organization (WTO), the Organization for Economic Cooperation and Development (OECD) and the Asia-Pacific Economic Cooperation (APEC).

President Kim appreciated the economic assistance to the Republic of Korea from Japan in the past in a wide range of areas including finance, investment and technological transfer, and explained the efforts of the Republic of Korea to resolve its economic problems. Prime Minister Obuchi explained the various measures for reviving the Japanese economy and the economic assistance which Japan is providing to assist in overcoming the difficulties faced by Asian economies, and expressed Japan's intention to continue support for the efforts being made by the Republic of Korea to overcome its economic difficulties. Both leaders welcomed that a basic agreement was reached on loans from the Export–Import Bank of Japan to the Republic of Korea which properly utilizes the fiscal investment and loan program.

The two leaders sincerely welcomed that the negotiations on the new Japan–Republic of Korea fisheries agreement, which had been a major outstanding issue between the two countries, had reached basic agreement, and expressed the hope that under the new fishing order based on the United Nations Convention on the Law of the Sea, relations between Japan and the Republic of Korea in the area of fisheries would develop smoothly.

The two leaders also welcomed the signing of the new Japan–Republic of Korea Tax Convention.

They shared the common view that they would enhance cooperation and exchanges in various areas including trade and investment, industrial technology, science and technology, telecommunications and exchanges between governments, employers and workers, and to exchange information and views on their respective social welfare systems at an appropriate time in the future, bearing in mind the probable conclusion of a Japan–Republic of Korea Agreement on Social Security.

9 The two leaders shared the view that both Governments would cooperate closely on resolving various global issues which transcend national borders and which are becoming new threats to the security and welfare of the international community. They also shared the view that both countries would promote Japan–Republic of Korea environmental policy dialogue in order to strengthen their cooperation on various issues concerning the global environment, such as reducing greenhouse gas emissions and countermeasures against acid rain. They further shared the determination to promote bilateral coordination further on overseas assistance so as to strengthen their support for developing countries. In addition, the two leaders shared the view that both Governments would commence talks on concluding a Japan–Republic of Korea Extradition Treaty and further strengthen cooperation on countermeasures against international organized crime such as on illicit narcotics and stimulants.

10 Recognizing that the foundation for effectively advancing cooperation between Japan and the Republic of Korea in the areas mentioned above lies not only in intergovernmental exchanges but also in profound mutual understanding and diverse exchanges among the peoples of the two countries, the two leaders shared the view that they would expand cultural and personnel exchanges between the two countries.

The two leaders shared their determination to support cooperation between the peoples of Japan and the Republic of Korea for the success of the 2002 Soccer World Cup and to use the occasion of this event to further promote cultural and sports exchanges.

The two leaders decided to promote exchanges among various groups and region at various levels in the two societies, inter alia, researchers, teachers, journalists, civic circles and other diverse groups.

The two leaders decided to continue the ongoing measures to simplify visa requirements as a means to create a foundation on which to promote such exchanges and mutual understanding. The two leaders agreed that, in order to contribute to the expansion of exchanges and to the furthering of mutual understanding between Japan and the Republic of Korea, efforts would be made to enhance governmental programs for the exchange of students and youths including the introduction of such programs for junior and senior high school students, and that both Governments would introduce a working holiday program for youths of both countries from April 1999. Recognizing that Korean nationals residing in Japan could serve as a bridge for mutual exchanges and understanding between the peoples of Japan and the Republic of Korea, the two leaders also shared the determination to continue ongoing consultations between the two countries for the enhancement of their social status.

The two leaders highly appreciated the significance of intellectual exchanges between Japan and the Republic of Korea being conducted by the concerned individuals and groups such as the Japan–Republic of Korea Forum and the Japan–Republic of Korea Joint Committee to Promote Historical Research, and decided to continue support for such efforts.

President Kim Dae-Jung conveyed his policy of opening the Republic of Korea to Japanese culture. Prime Minister Obuchi welcomed this policy as contributing to true, mutual understanding between the peoples of Japan and the Republic of Korea.

11 Prime Minister Obuchi and President Kim Dae-Jung expressed their shared faith that the new Japan–Republic of Korea partnership towards the twenty-first century can be enhanced to an even higher dimension through the broad-based participation and untiring efforts of the peoples of the two countries. The two leaders called on the peoples of both countries to share the spirit of this Joint Declaration and to participate in joint efforts to build and develop a new Japan–Republic of Korea partnership.

Prime Minister of Japan President of the Republic of Korea

Tokyo, 8 October 1998

Appendix 9.6

JOINT DECLARATION ISSUED BY KOREAN WORKERS' PARTY, LIBERAL-DEMOCRATIC PARTY AND JAPAN SOCIALIST PARTY

28 September 1990

Delegations of the LDP and the JSP visited the Democratic People's Republic of Korea from Sep. 24 to 28, 1990.

President Kim Il Sung, General Secretary of the Central Committee of the Korean Workers' Party, received the delegations.

On the occasion, Kanemaru Shin and Tanabe Makoto who were heading the delegations conveyed personal letters of President of the LDP Kaifu Toshiki and Chairwoman of the Central Executive Committee of the JSP Doi Takako to President Kim Il Sung, General Secretary of the Central Committee of the Korean Workers' Party.

During the visit, a series of joint talks were held between the KWP delegation led by Secretary of the Party Central Committee Kim Young Sun, the LDP delegation led by member of the House of Representatives Kanemaru Shin and the JSP delegation led by Vice Chairman of the Central Executive Committee Tanabe Makoto.

Considering that to normalize and develop Korea–Japan relations on the basis of the idea of independence, peace and friendship conforms to the interests of the peoples of the two countries and would contribute to peace and prosperity of a new Asia and the world, the delegations of the three parties declare as follows:

1 The three parties consider that Japan should fully and officially apologize and compensate to the Democratic People's Republic of Korea for the enormous misfortunes and miseries imposed upon the Korean people for 36 years and the losses inflicted upon the Korean people in the ensuing 45 years after the war. In his personal letter to President Kim Il Sung, President Kaifu Toshiki of the LDP admitted that there was an unfortunate past imposed by Japan upon Korea and expressed the hope to improve the DPRK–Japan relations, saying: 'Former Prime Minister Takeshita expressed deep remorse and regret over such unfortunate past at the Diet in March last year. I, as a prime minister, share his view.'

   Head of the delegation of the LDP Kanemaru Shin, member of the House of Representatives, too, expressed the same apology for Japan's past colonial rule over the Korean people. The three parties consider that in connection with the establishment of the diplomatic relations, full compensation should be made by the Japanese government for the past 36-year-long colonial rule and the losses inflicted upon the DPRK people in the ensuing 45 years.

2 The three parties consider that the abnormal state between the DPRK and Japan must be eliminated and diplomatic relations be established as soon as possible.

3 The three parties consider that, for the improvement of relations between DPRK and Japan, it is necessary to develop exchanges between them in various domains including politics, economy and culture and, for the present, to use satellite communications and open direct air services between the two countries.

4 The three parties consider that the Koreans in Japan must not be discriminated against, their human rights and all national rights and legal status be respected and the Japanese government should guarantee them by law. The three parties regard it necessary for the Japanese authorities to remove the entries made in the Japanese passport as regards the DPRK.

5 The three parties consider that Korea is one and that the peaceful reunification through north–south dialogue accords with the national interests of the Korean people.

6 The three parties consider that it is necessary for them to make joint efforts for the building of a peaceful and free Asia and eliminate nuclear threats from all regions on the globe.

7 The three parties agreed to strongly recommend the start of inter-governmental negotiations for the realization of the establishment of diplomatic relations and the solution of all the outstanding problems within November 1990.

8 The three parties agreed to strengthen party relations and further develop mutual cooperation between the KWP, and the LDP and between the KWP and the JSP in conformity with the desire of the two peoples and in the interests of peace in Asia and the world.

Agreed on Sep. 28, 1990 in Pyongyang

by

Kim Yong Sun on behalf of the KWP

Kanemaru Shin on behalf of the LDP

Tanabe Makoto on behalf of the JSP

Appendix 11.1

DEFENCE EXCHANGES: JAPAN AND EAST ASIA

Japan–ROK defence exchanges 1979–99

1979

Jul 25–26	Director-General JDA visits ROK

1990

Dec	Director-General JDA visits ROK

1994

Apr 26	Minister of National Defence ROK visits Japan
Nov 9	1st Japan–ROK Defence Policy Working-Level Meeting (Seoul)
Dec 20–23	ROK navy training ship flotilla visits Japan

1995

Feb	Chairman of Joint Chiefs of Staff SDF visits ROK
Sep 22	Director General JDA visits ROK
Oct	2nd Japan–ROK Defence Policy Working-Level Meeting (Tokyo)

1996

Jul 12	Chief of Combined General Staff ROK visits Japan – talks with Director-General JDA; Vice-Minister for Administrative Affairs JDA; Chairman of Joint Chiefs of Staff SDF
Sept 2–6	MSDF training ship flotilla visits ROK
Sept 23–24	Vice-Minister for Political Affairs JDA visits ROK
Oct 16–19	3rd Japan–ROK Defence Policy Working-Level Meeting (Seoul)
Nov 25–Dec 3	Chief of Air Force Staff ROK visits Japan
Dec 8–10	Chairman of Joint Chiefs of Staff SDF visits ROK
Dec 12–15	ROK navy training ship flotilla visits Japan

1997

Apr 28	Director-General JDA visits ROK – explanation of Guidelines review
Jun 12–13	Chief of Army Staff ROK visits Japan – talks with Director-General JDA; Chairman of Joint Chiefs of Staff SDF
Jul 13–17	Japan–ROK Joint Conference on Defence (Tokyo)
Aug 8	4th Japan–ROK Defence Policy Working-Level Meeting
Sep 2–6	Chief of Staff ASDF visits ROK
Oct 8–10	Deputy Director-General of Defence Bureau JDA visits ROK – US–Japan Guidelines review explanation
Oct 27–Nov 1	28 GSDF cadets visit ROK

1998

Feb 2–4	Chief of Staff ASDF visits ROK
Apr 1	Head Officer of JDA Intelligence HQ visits ROK
May 16–17	Chief of Defence Bureau JDA visits ROK – talks with National Defence Policy Adviser ROK
Jun 25	5th Japan–ROK Defence Policy Working-Level Meeting (Seoul)
Jun 26	1st Japan–ROK Security Policy Committee Meeting (Seoul) – defence and foreign ministry bureau chief level
July 9	Vice-Minister for Administrative Affairs JDA visits ROK
Oct 12–16	MSDF flotilla visits ROK
Jan 6–8	Vice-Minister for Political Affairs JDA visits ROK

1999

Jan	Director-General JDA visits ROK
Aug	MSDF and ROK navy conduct joint search-and-rescue exercises in East China Sea

Sources: Ministry of National Defence Republic of Korea 1998; Bōeichōhen various years; Bōei Kenkyūjo various years.

Japan–ASEAN defence exchanges 1988–99

1988

Jun	Minister of Defence Indonesia visits Japan
Jun–Jul	Director-General JDA visits Indonesia and Singapore

1989

Jun	Minister of Defence Singapore visits Japan

1990

May	Director-General JDA visits Malaysia

1991

Apr	Minister of Defence Philippines visits Japan

1992

Oct	Director-General JDA visits Thailand and Cambodia
Nov	Minister of Defence Singapore visits Japan

1994

Nov	Minister of Defence Thailand visits Japan

1996

Jul	Minister of Defence Singapore visits Japan
Sep 24	Chief of Air Force Staff Indonesia visits Japan – talks with Vice-Minister for Administrative Affairs JDA, Chairman of Joint Chiefs of Staff SDF and Chief of Staff ASDF
Dec 2–10	Chairman of Joint Chiefs of Staff SDF visits Singapore, Malaysia and Indonesia

1997

Jan 21–30	Vice-Minister for Administrative Affairs JDA visits Indonesia, Vietnam, Thailand and Singapore
Feb 2–19	Chief of Staff MSDF visits Thailand, Malaysia
Mar	Vice-Minister of Defence Vietnam visits Japan
Jul 11–12	Vice-Minister for Political Affairs JDA visits Singapore
Jul 13–17	Commander of Special Forces Indonesia visits Japan – talks with Minister of Foreign Affairs and Chairman of Joint Chiefs of Staff SDF
Aug 27	Minister of Defence Singapore visits Japan

1998	
Jan 10	Director-General JDA visits Vietnam
May 26	1st Japan–Thailand Defence Authority Meeting (Bangkok)
Jul 6	Vice-Minister for Administrative Affairs JDA visits Singapore
Jul 8	Vice-Minister for Administrative Affairs JDA visits Indonesia
Sept	Vice-Minister of Defence Singapore visits Japan
Nov	Minister of Defence Vietnam visits Japan
Dec	Minister of Defence Singapore visits Japan
1999	
Feb	Supreme Commander of Thai Defence Forces visits Japan
May	MSDF training ship flotilla visits Vietnam

Sources*:* Bōeichōhen various years; Bōei Kenkyūjo various years.

Japan–PRC defence exchanges 1985–99

1985	
May	Vice-Minister for Political Affairs JDA visits ROK
1986	
May	Chief of Staff PLA visits Japan
1987	
May 29–Jun 4	Director-General JDA visits PRC
1994	
Mar 1	1st Japan–PRC Security Dialogue
1995	
	2nd Japan–PRC Security Dialogue
	Chairman of Joint Chiefs of Staff SDF visits PRC
1996	
Jan	3rd Japan–PRC Security Dialogue
Aug 20–23	Vice-Minister for Political Affairs JDA visits PRC
1997	
Mar 15	4th Japan–PRC Security Dialogue
Mar 24–29	Chief of Staff GSDF visits PRC

May 5–11	Chief of External Affairs Bureau Ministry of National Defence PRC visits Japan
Jun 19	Vice-Minister for Administrative Affairs JDA visits PRC
Nov 30–Dec 2	Vice-Chief of Combined General Staff PLA visits Japan – talks with Director-General JDA; Vice-Minister for Administrative Affairs JDA
1998	
Feb 3–8	Minister of National Defence PRC visits Japan – talks with Director-General JDA, agreement to promote military exchange with (1) visit of Director-General JDA to PRC; (2) exchange of visits of Chairman of Joint Chiefs of Staff SDF and Chief of Combined General Staff PLA; (3) Chief of Staff GSDF visit PRC in March 1998; (4) promote exchanges between Japan National Defence Institute and PRC National Defence University; (5) promote exchange in medical field, including acceptance in April 1998 of two Chinese students to National Defence Medical University; (6) investigate exchange of visits of warships
Mar 25–28	Chief of Staff GSDF visits PRC
May 1–5	Director-General JDA visits PRC – talks with Minister of National Defence

Sources*:* Bōeichōhen various years; Bōei Kenkyūjo various years.

Appendix 14.1

JOINT DECLARATION ON RELATIONS BETWEEN THE EC AND ITS MEMBER STATES AND JAPAN

On 18 July 1991 the following joint declaration was published in The Hague, Tokyo and Brussels at the end of the European Community–Japan summit meeting in The Hague:

Preamble

The European Community and its member states on the one part and Japan on the other part, conscious of their common attachment to freedom, democracy, the rule of law and human rights; affirming their common attachment to market principles, the promotion of free trade and the development of a prosperous and sound world economy; recalling their increasingly close ties and acknowledging growing worldwide interdependence and, consequently, the need for heightened international cooperation; affirming their common interest in security, peace and the stability of the world; aware of the importance of their deepening dialogue in order to make a joint contribution towards safeguarding peace in the world, setting up a just and stable international order in accordance with the principle and purposes of the United Nations Charter and taking up the global challenges that the international community has to face; mindful of the accelerated process whereby the European Community is acquiring its own identity in the economic and monetary sphere, in foreign policy and in the field of security; have decided to intensify their dialogue and strengthen their cooperation and partnership in order that the challenges of the future may be met.

General principles of the dialogue and cooperation

The European Community and its member states and Japan will firmly endeavour to inform and consult each other on major international issues, which are of common interest to both parties, be they political, economic, scientific, cultural or other. They will strive, whenever appropriate, to coordinate their positions. They will strengthen their cooperation and exchange of information both between the two parties and within international organizations.

Both parties will likewise consult together on the international situation and on regional matters with a view, in particular, to joining their efforts to bring about an easing of tensions and to ensure respect for human rights.

Objectives of the dialogue and cooperation

The two parties will set out to explore together areas of possible cooperation, including where appropriate common diplomatic action. They will endeavour to strengthen their cooperation in a fair and harmonious way in all areas of their relations taken as a whole, in particular with respect to the following:

- promoting negotiated solutions to international or regional tensions and the strengthening of the United Nations and other international organizations;
- supporting social systems based on freedom, democracy, the rule of law, human rights and market economy;
- enhancing policy consultation and, wherever possible, policy coordination on the international issues which might affect world peace and stability, including international security matters such as the non-proliferation of missile technology and international transfer of conventional weapons;
- pursuing cooperation aimed at achieving a sound development of the world economy and trade, particularly in further strengthening the open multilateral trading system, by rejecting protectionism and recourse to unilateral measures and by implementing GATT and OECD principles concerning trade and investment;
- pursuing their resolve for equitable access to their respective markets and removing obstacles, whether structural or other, impeding the expansion of trade and investment, on the basis of comparable opportunities;
- strengthening their dialogue and cooperation on various aspects of multifaceted relations between both parties in such areas as trade investment, industrial cooperation, advanced technology, energy, employment, social affairs and competition rules;
- supporting the efforts of developing countries, in particular the poorest among them, to achieve sustained development and political and economic progress, along with fostering the respect for human rights as a major factor in genuine development, with due regard for the objectives set by international organizations;
- joining their efforts in meeting transnational challenges, such as the issue of environment, the conservation of resources and energy, terrorism, international crime and drugs and related criminal activity, in particular the laundering of the proceeds of crime;
- strengthening cooperation and, where appropriate, promoting joint projects in the field of science and technology with a view to contribution to the promotion of scientific knowledge which is essential for the future prosperity of all mankind;
- developing academic, cultural and youth exchange programmes aiming to increase knowledge and improve understanding between their respective peoples;
- supporting, in cooperation with other States and organizations, Central and Eastern European countries engaged in political and economic reforms

aimed at stabilizing their economies and promoting their full integration into the world economy;

- cooperating, in relation with the countries of the Asia-Pacific region, for the promotion of peace, stability and prosperity of the region.

Framework for dialogue and consultations

Both parties are committed to engage in continuous dialogue to give substance to this declaration. To this end, in addition to the full use of all existing regular consultation mechanisms, both parties have decided to strengthen their mechanism for consultation and substantial cooperation on global and bilateral issues:

I especially they have decided to hold annual consultations in Europe or in Japan between, on the one hand, the President of the European Council and the President of the Commission and, on the other, the Japanese Prime Minister;

II an annual meeting continues to be held between the Commission and the Japanese government at ministerial level;

III six-monthly consultations continue to be held between the foreign ministers of the Community and the member of the Commission responsible for external relations (troika) and the Japanese Foreign Minister;

IV the representatives of Japan are briefed by the Presidency of the European political cooperation following ministerial political cooperation meetings, and Japan informs the representatives of the Community of the Japanese government's foreign policy.

In order to give substance to this declaration, both parties will make use of existing and above-mentioned forums with a view to regularly reviewing its implementation and to provide a permanent stimulus to the development of EC–Japan relations.

Appendix 21.1

MEETINGS OF HEADS OF STATE AND GOVERNMENT OF THE G7/8

15–17 November 1975	Rambouillet, France
27–28 June 1976	San Juan, Puerto Rico
7–8 May 1977	London, UK
16–17 July 1978	Bonn, West Germany
28–29 June 1979	Tokyo, Japan
22–23 June 1980	Venice, Italy
20–21 July 1981	Ottawa, Canada
4–6 June 1982	Versailles, France
28–30 May 1983	Williamsburg, US
7–9 June 1984	London, UK
2–4 May 1985	Bonn, West Germany
4–6 May 1986	Tokyo, Japan
8–10 June 1987	Venice, Italy
19–21 June 1988	Toronto, Canada
14–16 July 1989	Paris, France
9–11 July 1990	Houston, US
15–17 July 1991	London, UK
6–8 July 1992	Munich, Germany
7–9 July 1993	Tokyo, Japan
8–10 July 1994	Naples, Italy
15–17 June 1995	Halifax, Canada
27–29 June 1996	Lyon, France
20–22 June 1997	Denver, US
15–17 May 1998	Birmingham, UK
18–20 June 1999	Cologne, Germany
21–23 July 2000	Okinawa, Japan

For further details on such matters as the delegates who attended the meetings, see http://www.g8kyushu okinawa.go.jp/e/past_summit/table_e/index.html

Index

Note: Page references in *italics* are to illustrations